P9-BJS-215

Contents

Continued overleaf

Section V Evaluations of Thirty-two Boats

Preface

In 1979, an editor of a slick sailing magazine traded his place in the glossy four-color pages of *Sail* for the helm of a modest consumer magazine for sailors. At that time, *The Practical Sailor* was publishing 16 black-and-white pages monthly, and Jeff Spranger produced it singlehandedly for half a year.

Since then, the editorial staff has grown, and so has *The Practical Sailor.* Three editors joined the crew in 1980, and *The Practical Sailor* currently lists six names on the masthead. During that time, we began to perceive that a book was emerging from the pages of *The Practical Sailor.* The general outlines formed around a collection of sailboat evaluations written over a period of four years by Jeff and Associate Editors Nick Nicholson and Ed Adams. A natural introduction was provided by a nine-part series on choosing "The Right Boat" which Nick wrote in 1982. Ed's series on trailer boats and a handful of other articles on the general nature of boats complete that section.

Because the decision to buy a boat is so dependent on available finances, we added in Section Two discussions of the cost of boats and boat money, by Contributing Editors John Pazereskis and Antoinette Stockenberg. Boats can cost quite a bit of money; but there are ways to reduce costs. They usually involve trading money for time in one way or another: Jeff discusses time sharing yachts and amateur boatbuilding as possibilities, and Antoinette gives us some bittersweet advice about the romance of living aboard.

Getting down to the nuts and bolts of buying and owning a boat, Sections Three and Four are compiled from numerous *Practical Sailor* articles drawn from reader and personal experiences with those who sell boats and those who sail them. The chapters are not the stuff of which dreams are made. They are the most practical advice that we have had to offer on the everyday problems of real boatowners.

The hardest part of editing *Practical Boat Buying* has been deciding where to stop. The book developed a life of its own, growing beyond the original scope until we had to begin holding it back. Although the first part of it was written in 1979 (Pearson 30 evaluation), the analysis of selling a used Ericson 30 + rather rudely forced its way into the book at the last minute. Written to go with an article on the price of used boats in the December 15, 1983, issue of *The Practical Sailor,* it is so appropriate to our earlier analysis of the new boat cost that it could not be turned away. As this book achieved its final form, it caused us to wonder whether we may have another book on our hands before long.

Practical Boat Buying, then, is a continuing opportunity waiting to be taken. Like the wind, we need only to raise our sails and catch it.

— SW

PRACTICAL BOAT BUYING

PRACTICAL BOAT BUYING

By the Editors of *The Practical Sailor:* Jeff Spranger
Nick Nicholson
Ed Adams
Sue Weller

Edited by Sue Weller

International Standard Book Number: 0-9613139-0-0
Library of Congress Catalog Card Number: 83-83347
Englander Communications, Inc.
1111 East Putnam Avenue
Riverside, CT 06878

Designed by Jean Planka

I

In Quest of the 'Right' Boat

Nine Ways to Know it When You See it:

One

Decide What to Look For

Given the thousands of new and used boats available on the market, the prospective boat buyer faces a bewildering task. How, amid the hype and hoopla, conflicting claims, and relatively limited access to authoritative knowledge, can the average buyer come up with the right boat? A cynic might say that it doesn't really matter what boat you choose. They are all too expensive, they all break, and you're likely to use it so little anyway that it's not going to kill you, so just buy a boat and go sailing.

It is possible, however, to determine needs and abilities, weigh the options carefully, and with a little luck and a lot of perserverance come up with a boat that exactly fills the bill. Or at least, a boat that comes reasonably close to filling the bill, for few sailors, even if they build they boat of the their dreams, are capable of coming up with THE BOAT.

There are two big questions to be answered when buying a boat: how will it be used and what will it cost? Implicit in those two big questions is an almost endless array of other questions, some of which are easily answered; others will always remain unanswered.

How will it be used?
When choosing a boat, you must be ruthlessly realistic

about what you will do with it. Will you primarily daysail with the family, with occasional day racing? Is weekend cruising high on the list of things you want to do? Are you really going to take that trip to Hawaii or Bermuda, or is that a dream 10 years down the line?

Obviously, a heavy, underrigged ocean cruiser is out of place on a lake. Less obviously, it may be out of place in many coastal light-weather areas, too.

Choose a boat suitable for *most* of the sailing you do. You'll never find a boat that's perfect for all your sailing. If 90% of your sailing is daysailing on summer weekends in protected waters, buy a boat that is at its best in those conditions.

This may require considerable downscaling of your dreams. To some extent, almost all of us consider the boat to be some means of escape from the routine. Above and beyond the recreational aspects of the boat, it functions as a psychological cushion between the reality of the 40 hour work week and the dream of escape. Too often, perhaps, the dream dominates reality when the time comes to spend hard-earned dollars. This situation is hardly helped by much of the sailing industry's advertising, which touts every boat over 25 feet as a bluewater cruiser, and every boat under 25 feet as an easily handled trailer sailer with plenty of room for a family of five and two dogs. The industry also gets great mileage by playing on our dreams, so that we frequently end up with a boat more suitable for the type of sailing we'd like to do than the sailing we really do.

The cost of owning a boat

The price tag on any boat is only a percentage of the cost of owning a boat. In addition to the cost of equipping the boat, there is the cost of maintenance, insurance, dockage, storage. For a boat that is used infrequently, or a boat that is more boat than is really needed, the cost per sailing hour can be staggering. If you are really only going to use a boat for a few weekends a year, chances are that it makes far more sense to rent or charter than to own a boat.

A major cost of owning a boat that is not always apparent when you buy is what it's going to cost when you sell the boat. Boats are lousy investments. The temptation to consider a boat a good investment just because you can sell it now for more than you paid for it in 1975 is as misleading as it is to consider yourself better financially than you were in 1975 just because you make 50% more money now than you did then. While some boats may hold their own relative to inflation, few boats actually appreciate more rapidly than the rate of inflation.

As hard as it may seem, you must consider the boat's resale value before making the purchase. A boat is not a lifetime investment, no matter how well it seems to fill the bill now. Taste changes, your use of a boat changes, your expectations change. If you are a new sailor, the growth in your experience may lead to the desire for another type of boat very quickly.

There is no way to guarantee a high resale value for any boat, but there are simple rules to follow to protect yourself:

• buy a boat that is popular in your sailing area
• buy a boat that has a local dealer with a reputation of giving good advice
• buy a boat with a proven track record.

A boat that is popular where you sail is likely to be easier to sell when the time comes, and is likely to sell for a higher percentage of her original cost. The Whumpty Dump 25 may be a better boat than the Wham Bam 26, but if you have the only Whumpty Dump in an area where the Wham Bam is popular, you're likely to take a bath when you sell it.

One reason that a particular brand or model may be more popular than another comparable boat is the quality of the local dealer. Dealers, like boats, vary tremendously. Some dealers give excellent after-sale service, organize local racing or cruising, and give dockage or storage priority to the boats they sell. In this way, they develop customer loyalty that is translated into future sales. Another dealer may give great service before the sale, but give you the cold shoulder after he has your money in hand.

The only way to be sure about a dealer is to ask people who have bought boats from him. No one likes to get ripped off, and the boatbuyer who feels mistreated is usually more than happy to talk about it.

It pays to talk to more than one of the dealer's customers, however. The dealer is not always at fault in a transaction that goes sour. If he has a consistently poor reputation, though, there's likely to be more than a grain of truth to the complaints.

A boat that doesn't have a local dealer is unlikely to have a substantial local following no matter how good a boat it is. Having the only Bluewater 45 within 200 miles of your sailing area may garner you admiration at the local yacht club, but it's going to cost you big bucks when the time comes to sell it.

Unless you're willing to put up with some headaches, it's better not to buy a brand new model, even if it's built by the most reputable builder in the world. Every brand new boat has some teething problems, and if it's a brand new model as well, the problems are likely to be magnified. Every boat evolves during its production life, and this evolution is almost always for the better. Changes in engines, hardware, components of the interior layout, even rig changes are not uncommon. Independent of the actual condition of the boat or its age, where it falls in the production series is quite important. It may be nice to have the newest model, but that boat-show glow can quickly wear off in a series of warranty claims and factory retrofixes.

Sail the boat

It goes without saying that you should sail a boat before you buy it. If a boat is popular in your area, chances are good that you can without too much trouble get an owner to take you for a sail. If you are polite and show a serious interest, most owners are flattered enough to take the time to talk to you about their boat, even if they are not selling their own boat.

Sailing the boat is even more important if it is a relatively uncommon boat in your area. A short sail may quickly reveal why a boat is not particularly popular. A single sail is not guaranteed to show the boat's good and bad points, however, and unless it is obvious that the boat is totally unsuited for your needs—which you should be able to tell before you get to the point of sailing it—a single sail may cause more confusion than elucidation.

We once considered buying a rather tired 5.5 metre sloop. The owner was most eager to take us for a sail, for a very good reason. The boat was a sparkling performer under sail, fast and responsive. We were just about to write a check on the spot, but a more knowledgeable friend counseled us to think about it for a few days. We are constantly thankful that we followed his advice, for the only thing the boat had going for it was sailing performance. Other than that one admittedly important quality, it was about as suited for our needs as a Laser is for transoceanic sailing.

Finding the right boat is more than a matter of luck. It is more than a matter of visiting boat shows or dealer showrooms, although both of these are important. It is a matter of introspection and self-scrutiny, the patience to do your homework and to wait for the right boat, rather than jump at the first one that strikes your fancy.

Buy a boat for the type of sailing you want to do now, not the type that you might do in five or ten years. Your taste may change with the growth in your abilities. Unless you are a remarkably single-minded individual with a goal absolutely incapable of being altered by the vagaries of life, buy for today's needs, not tomorrow's.

Dreaming is an important part of sailing, one that cannot and should not be ignored. A dream tempered by a healthy dose of realism has a far greater chance of becoming realized. And the fulfilling of dreams, rather than the act of dreaming, is what being a practical sailor is all about.

Two

Know How it's Built: A Construction Primer

About 25 years ago the wonderful chemical technology of fiberglass made its serious debut on the production sailboat scene. Fiberglass was touted as "ending maintenance forever," and "indestructible, impervious to worm, rot, and corrosion." Fiberglass was the material that was going to free sailors from the slavery of maintenance that had been the bane of their existence—and the boon of the paint, sandpaper, fillers, and compound industries—since time immemorial.

Fiberglass has indeed revolutionized the boat-building industry, in ways both good and bad. The low cost of petroleum-derived polyester—at least until 10 years ago—and the relatively low level of skill involved in using it to build hulls, compared to the skill required to build a conventional wooden hull, made the mass production boatbuilding industry possible. Without fiberglass, it is safe to say that the phenomenal growth in the popularity of sailing in the last 20 years would have been significantly slower.

Unfortunately, as with any new technology, a whole new set of boatbuilding rules had to be created to take advantage of the wonder material. Seat of the pants engineering has been the rule rather than the exception in fiberglass boatbuilding, and with it has come a staggering array of ways to skin the cat.

Part of the problem has been the properties of the material itself. For a given weight and thickness, a fiberglass hull layup consisting of various layers of mat and roving has a remarkable combination of properties that are a boatbuilder's delight: it is both strong and light. However, coupled with these positive characteristics is a big negative one. Thin fiberglass panels, for all their strength, have all the rigidity of an inner tube.

A number of approaches to this problem have been taken over the years by the boatbuilding industry. Early fiberglass hulls were massively built, with hull skins almost as thick as the planking on a wooden boat of the same size. This achieved the required panel stiffness, but at the cost of inordinately heavy hulls, and consequently, relatively low ballast/displacement ratios. A good example of a modern boat built in this fashion is the CSY 44.

When oil cost $3 per barrel this was not an unreasonable way to build a boat, if you were willing to accept the tradeoff of a heavy hull with less ballast and slightly reduced interior volume. The interior volume of a heavy, solid hull layup was still far greater than a wooden boat with its complicated system of internal framing. With oil at $30 per barrel, however, this approach is a little extravagant.

The other approaches to achieving panel stiffness are: 1) coring, either with end-grain balsa (C&C Yachts, for example) or lightweight plastic foam (Airex, which is used by C.E. Ryder, or Klegecell); or 2) internal stiffening of a thin hull shell with stringers, bulkheads, or an internal molding attached to the hull (used by almost every builder of uncored boats). All of these methods are used in production sailboats, and all work to achieve panel rigidity. There are advantages and disadvantages to each method.

Coring provides an insulating barrier between the inner and outer fiberglass skins, greatly reducing the tendency of glass to transmit heat and cold (a cause of condensation inside the hull). For a boat which is used either in the tropics or in a cold climate, a cored hull is highly desirable for its insulating properties.

Cored hulls also deaden the notorious sound transmission of fiberglass, and are both stiff and light for their weight per square foot. They are not, however, without disadvantages. The hull layup is more painstaking and time consuming. Core materials are fairly expensive. In some cases vacuum bagging must be used to insure bonding between the core material and the surface skins.

Quality control in the hull layup is critical. Delamination of cored hulls is rare, but there have been lawsuits against builders alleging this type of failure.

The core material is usually cut out where skin fittings pierce the hull, where major bulkheads are to be bonded, and in the way of bonded-in chainplates. The hours for these jobs add up to increase hull costs.

A great deal of hoopla has gone on about whether or not end-grain balsa absorbs water if a hull skin is punctured. Lloyds for many years refused to class balsa cored hulls because of this fear.

From our observations, balsa core exposed due to puncture or abrasion of a hull will slowly absorb water, and that water can migrate through the core to some extent. This means that you must promptly repair damage to a balsa cored hull, whether the damage is above or below the waterline. It does not mean that balsa coring is unsuited for use below the waterline, as some advertising has indicated.

Plastic foam core materials, notably Airex and Klegecell, are also used in production boatbuilding, although far less frequently than balsa. The polyvinyl-chloride (PVC) foams have excellent structural properties, but are certainly more difficult to handle than a solid glass layup, and they are expensive. Difficulty and time in handling translate into increased cost, and increased cost is a killer in the highly competitve boat-building market. Foam cored hulls are exceptionally light and stiff, and the core will not absorb water in the event of a puncture of the hull skin.

More common in the US boatbuilding industry in "modern" times has been the use of a relatively thin fiberglass shell with stiffness provided by a molded hull pan or liner, or the bonding to the hull of internal components such as bulkheads and berth tops. The body pan or hull liner has been extremely popular. Major furniture components—cabin sole, settee fronts and tops, galley cabinets—can be molded outside the boat in one shot, greatly reducing labor costs. Good glass layup is still far easier to do than good interior joinerwork.

The body pan or hull liner is dropped into the hull, and is chemically bonded to the hull shell wherever the liner touches the skin. This is the kicker. The liner usually does not touch the hull in many places, and it is not possible to verify the degree of bonding of the liner to the hull. No matter how carefully done, attaching the liner to the hull is still a secondary bond, which develops less strength than a primary bond. (A secondary bond is any fiberglassing that is done to another surface after that first surface has cured. By definition, anything stuck to the hull after the original layup is a secondary bond.)

Bonding of a built-up interior of plywood panels to the hull has the same weaknesses as bonding a hull liner to the shell. Careful surface preparation—grinding and

PRACTICAL BOAT BUYING   11

Calling the way in which much interior joinerwork is attached to the hull "bonding" is a misnomer

degreasing—is required to get a good bond between a wood bulkhead, its tabbing, and the hull shell. Local distortions of the hull may occur wherever interior components are bonded to it. These are visible from the outside of the hull in the form of "hard spots," subtle ridges that form along the hull where bulkheads or furniture are glassed in. Hard spots are not necessarily indicative of an excessively thin hull shell, but they are aesthetically displeasing and do not inspire confidence in the builder. If he doesn't mind hard spots, what else doesn't he mind?

Many boatbuilders glass every internal component to the hull on the theory that the more you attach to the hull shell, the stiffer it will be. This is fine in theory, but in fact you rarely end up with reinforcement in areas that really need it, such as the broad, flat panels of the topsides aft of the bow.

In addition, calling the way in which much interior joinerwork is attached to the hull "bonding" is a misnomer. A plywood shelf that is attached to the hull with a single piece of fiberglass tape is no more bonded to the hull than the man in the moon. After the hull flexes for a few years, the "bond" often fails, increasing the unreinforced panel size, which increases flexing causing other secondary bonds to fail. It is not uncommon, on a five or ten year old boat with this type of construction, to find that half of these secondary "bonds" have failed, even on lightly used boats from builders with a good reputation.

This type of failure does not mean that the hull is necessarily too weak, but it does imply an undesirable degree of hull flexibility. The classic example is the famous production ocean racer of the late 60's which evoked the following catechism:

question: "how hard can you drive the boat?"

answer: "until the berths pop out of the forward cabin."

Since we have heard a number of boats used as the

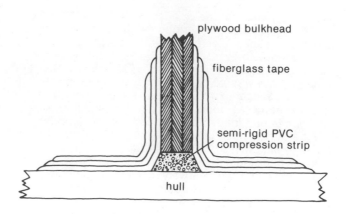

Proper attachment of bulkheads to hull: a compressible semi-rigid PVC foam strip helps reduce the likelihood of hard spots.

object of this criticism, we will delete the names of the accused, not for fear of insulting the innocent, but for fear of neglecting the guilty.

All of these approaches to hull stiffening can work. The most important input in all cases is the care that the builder puts into construction. This frequently comes down to the degree of experience and the level of supervision of the foreman on the production line. Almost nobody likes working with fiberglass, and it is not realistic to expect a $5 per hour glass man to take exquisite care that all surfaces are neat and clean, excess air and resin are rolled or squeegeed out, and the other steps are fully implemented that can produce a reasonably light, monolithic hull that is so easy to design on paper.

For maximum strength, the resin to glass ratio must

Lessons from the School of Hard Knocks

Sailboats, unlike blocks, shackles, and line, have neither a stated safe working load nor a rated breaking strength. Rather, your boat sits there looking benignly strong—or suspiciously weak—until the day when the sea may choose to test her mettle. The average boat is probably never truly taken to its limits. Like your automobile, it purrs merrily along with minimal hassle, safely carrying you to and fro.

Until the day when a Mack truck runs into you.

The nautical equivalent of a collision with a Mack truck might be the fate of a Southern Cross 31 we examined recently after a freak storm toppled four cradle-stored sailboats in a local boatyard. The Southern Cross was apparently struck by another boat which had broken its cradle, causing the 31 to fall heavily on its port side onto the asphalt parking lot. The mast of the Southern Cross broke as it struck the wall of an adjacent building, the mast tube collapsing halfway between spreaders and deck.

A quick glance at the outside of the boat showed what appeared to be superficial damage. A more careful look revealed more serious problems that should make owners—and builders—of lightly built cruiser/racers think long and hard about the way their boats are put together.

Hull Damage

The Airex-cored hull of the Southern Cross 31 survived relatively unscathed, other than the inevitable scratches and gouges. At the time this particular hull was built, Ryder boats were not gelcoated on the inside of the hull. Rather, they were finished with clear resin. While some might argue that this is esthetically unappetizing, it permits careful examination of the Southern Cross's cored construction. A hull interior not coated with pigmented gelcoat is translucent, almost transparent. Failures of the core-to-interior skin bond would show as almost opaque white sections, looking much like a void in the hull layup. Despite the tremendous impact of the fall, there was no apparent failure of the primary bond in the damaged Southern Cross.

Two things which did fail on impact were the hull-to-deck joint and a fair number of the boat's interior secondary bonds, including some major bulkhead and furniture tabbing.

In our August 1, 1981 evaluation of the Southern Cross 31, we expressed reservations about the vulnerability of the outward-turning flange joint used in the boat. Barring tremendous impact of the type suffered in this fall, it is doubtful that the joint would have failed in normal use. "Failed" is a relative word. The hull be carefully controlled. This means not only full saturation of the glass cloth, but removal of excess uncured resin while the hull is being laid up. It is not possible to tell by eyeballing a completed hull if the layup is resin rich or resin starved, neither of which achieves full strength. Ideally, the plugs cut from the hull where through hull fittings are installed should be saved for the surveyor, who can have them analyzed for resin and glass content by burning. Otherwise, you must take on faith the skill of the boatbuilder, or more specifically, the skill of the men in the molding room. One trip into the molding room of a boatbuilder is enough to convince most people that hull layup is just about the nastiest job in production line fiberglass boatbuilding.

Decks

Deck and cabin house surfaces are relatively flat. They are also fairly heavily loaded by being walked on, by the installation of gear for sail and ground tackle handling, and by lifeline stanchions and pulpits. We also intuitively dislike the feel of spongey decks underfoot. A large percentage of the boats built today therefore have balsa cored decks and cabin house tops, which result in light, rigid surfaces. Because decks are flat, construction of cored layup for decks and cockpits is far simpler than molding to the compound curves of the hull.

Balsa coring should be removed from the cabin top in the way of a deck-stepped mast to provide better compression resistance. It is also desirable to put more solid coring—either solid glass, or plywood—in other heavily loaded sections of the deck such as where cleats and winches are mounted.

It is common to see fairly sharp corners in some deck moldings, particularly in the cockpit. These areas should be well radiussed, or the hinge effect of repeated flexing of the deck can cause gelcoat cracking—not necessarily a structural problem, but very unsightly.

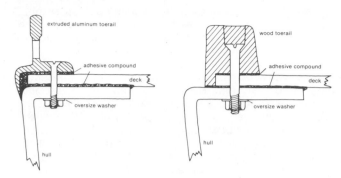

An internal flange, bedded with a flexible adhesive, through bolted with stainless steel hardware, and capped with a wood or aluminum toerail, is simple and reliable.

Joining Deck and Hull

Probably no single topic stirs up more partisan response and pigheaded stubbornness than how the deck molding is attached to the hull molding. In the early years of fiberglass boatbuilding, deck and hull were almost universally rigidly fiberglassed together. Although the exact technique varied widely, the general principle was to overlap the hull-to-deck joint on the inside of the hull—and sometimes on the outside, although this requires more cosmetic finishing—with several layers of fiberglass cloth, in effect making the hull and deck one piece. Once again, this is fine in theory, but in practice it is still a seconary bond, and therefore suspect. Thousands of hulls and decks have been joined in this manner, and the percentage of failures has probably been relatively small, but they do occur.

The subsequent variations on chemical bonding are almost infinite. There are inward turning flanges, outward turning flanges, coffee can lid flanges. Some are

and deck did not pull apart, and it is doubtful that enough water would have come through the crack to sink the boat even if she had been in a major gale at sea. What failed was the polyester putty used as a bonding agent between the two flanges. The tremendous impact of a six-foot fall, directly onto the exposed hull-to-deck flanges, simply exceed the elastic limit of the fairly rigid polyester putty.

Builders who believe in chemical bonding of the hull-to-deck joint without closely spaced through bolting could learn a lot by looking at this particular boat. The hull-to-deck joint of the Southern Cross 31 *is* through bolted at close intervals, and those bolts were the only thing holding the hull and deck together amidships after the impact. We shudder to think what would have happend if the joint were pop riveted or screwed with self-tappers, as it is on many production boats, and if the impact were the result of a fall off a wave rather than a fall off a cradle in the boatyard. Sailors rarely walk home from mid-ocean accidents resulting in separation of hull and deck.

Anyone who thinks that water cushions the impact of a fall off a wave, and that comparing such an impact to that of a boat falling over in a parking lot is comparing apples to oranges, simply ain't been there. One of the most sickening feelings you can get on a boat is the moment of near-zero gravity just after your boat has launched herself off a wave, and the subsequent

tremendous impact that sends you scrambling for the flooboards to see if the mast has gone through the bottom of the boat. Water hardly feels like a soft cushion in such conditions.

The real question is whether the hull-to-deck joint of the Southern Cross 31 would have remained watertight had the joints been filled with polyurethane caulk: 3M 5200, for example. While there's no way to prove or disprove that one, we feel that an elastic adhesive compound, with its inherent ability to flex on impact, is the only way to go in joining the hull and deck of an oceangoing sailboat.

By far the simplest and strongest hull-to-deck joint is an inward-turning hull flange with the deck laid over it and thoroughly bedded and through-bolted

---

glassed together with cloth, others use polyester putty between the flanges, some back up the chemical bond with fasteners such as self-tapping screws or through bolts.

Failure of a chemical bond in the hull-to-deck joint can be catastrophic, with complete failure of the secondary bond resulting. The classic story is of the boat which flexed so badly at sea during a delivery that the hull and deck began to separate. The skipper kept the two halves of the boat together by passing lines around the hull and tightening them with a Spanish windlass. Unfortunately, we've never seen one of those boats—the brand and model varies with the storyteller—that has experienced catastrophic failure in the course of normal use. We have seen serious hull-to-deck separation as the result of collision with other boats or impact with a dock. In most cases the break has been the result of a fracture of the secondary bond rather than the failure of either the hull or deck molding.

By far the simplest and strongest hull-to-deck joint is the inward-turning hull flange at deck level, with the deck laid over it and the two thoroughly bedded and through bolted at close intervals. This joint can be covered by a wooden toe rail, whose through fastenings form part of the mechanical hull-to-deck joint, or it can be covered by an aluminum extrusion specifically designed for the purpose.

The use of a powerful adhesive bedding compound such as 3M 5200 gives this joint much of the strength of a chemical bond without its brittleness, and through bolting at intervals of less than a foot—six inches is reasonable bolt spacing—effectively ties the two moldings together mechanically. Variations on this joining theme are becoming increasingly popular on every-

thing from the least expensive boats to the most expensive. Hunter uses it, and Swan does, too.

It is not reasonable to condemn rigid chemical joints out of hand. Few boats ever find themselves in the position where hull and deck are strained badly enough to cause separation. However, for a boat designed for serious offshore or coastal use, whether racing or cruising, we'll take a through bolted, flexibly bedded hull-to-deck joint every time.

Conclusion
Fiberglass hulls have revolutionized the boatbuilding industry in the last 20 years, eliminating many trouble spots, but they are not a complete panacea. Skill and quality control are essential to the production of strong, long-lasting fiberglass hulls. Unfortunately, it is not always possible to judge the quality of the hull simply by looking at it. Builders consider hull layup schedules to be proprietary, and even if he had the schedule in hand, it would mean little to the average boatbuyer.

It is not normally possible to have a boat surveyed while it is under construction. Usually, you buy the boat off the dealer's lot. Some builders refuse to have surveyors in their plant.

In the case of an expensive custom or semi-custom design, the owner would be foolish not to have a surveyor's opinion at various stages of construction.

Your best defense as a buyer of a production boat is to educate yourself as much as possible about construction, and ascertain the reputation of a boat or builder by talking to those who own the boats, not just to those who sell them. A survey of the boat at the dealer is always a good idea—before you accept delivery of the boat.

Interior Damage
The interior of the Southern Cross 31 fared less well than the lightly damaged hull and balsa-cored deck. There was no sign of failure of the bond between chainplate knees and hull—a secondary bond—but much of the joinerwork in the midsection of the boat had shifted enough—perhaps 1/2"—to tear bulkheads, shear tabbing, and shatter the teak mast compression post.

Ryder is not a sloppy boatbuilder. The tabbing of furniture and bulkheads is equal to or better than that of most boats we have looked at. The problem is not the execution of the work, but the whole theory of attachment of structural and non-structural components to the hull. Joining a relatively rigid structure such as a plywood bulkhead to a somewhat flexible fiberglass hull or deck is tricky business. It is nearly impossible to evaluate the strength of a secondary bond until it fails. Extra layers of tabbing don't help. What counts is the quality of bonding to the hull achieved by the intial tabbing layer.

In this hull, the major secondary bonds—chainplate knees to hull, main bulkheads to hull—did not fail; however, the inward squeezing of the hull on impact popped up the deck and deckhouse enough to break all the bonding of furniture and bulkheads to the deckhead and cabin trunk. Numerous less critical secondary bonds, such as shelves and settee tops to hull, failed.

And the fate of this particular boat? It is repairable to new condition, although the cost will probably be an eye opener. Fortunately, this boat can be returned to the

nearby builder for repair. The only way to undertake repairs that will guarantee the integrity of the boat is to remove the deck from the hull and replace the entire section of midships interior. This job is relatively easy for the builder, who has jigs and templates for all the components; it would be prohibitively expensive for the average boatyard, no matter how skilled the labor force.

Ryder's repair foreman feels that the integral fiberglass tanks should be pressure tested, the prop shaft removed and checked for bends, the seacocks checked, and gear such as electronics tested for damage. We agree, but will the insurance adjustor?

Conclusions
If this were a boat with a full hull liner, damage would be almost impossible to adequately evaluate. The secondary bonds of liner to hull would be suspect, and they would be almost impossible to survey.

We reiterate that storing boats on land with the mast in place is at best a dubious policy. The argument that only freak conditions could knock over a boat thus stored is comparable to arguing that you can go to sea in a poorly built boat because really bad weather constitutes only a small percentage of what you expect to encounter. While the cruising sailor need not necessarily go to sea in a Sherman tank, he might want something more suitable than a bicycle.

No boat, no matter how well built, is immune to damage either at sea or in storage. The prudent sailor minimizes his risk at all times by taking reasonable precautions and avoiding unnecessary risks.

Three
Understand the Ballast Keel

Your ballast keel keeps the boat upright under a press of sail, takes the boat's weight when she's hauled out, and is usually the first part of her anatomy to contact terra firma when you make a navigational error. This hard working appendage has in many ways been the bane of the boatbuilder's existence since N.G. Herreshoff and George Watson began hanging lead on the outside of their boats in the late 19th century. Attaching the ballast to the boat, and keeping it there, is one of the most basic of boatbuilding problems.

There are two basic approaches to ballasting a fiberglass boat. Ballast may be an external casting bolted to the hull, or it may be put inside a hollow keel that is part of the hull molding.

External Lead Keels

For a boat with a high aspect ratio fin keel, the simplest solution is the external ballast casting bolted directly to the hull molding. In the modern round-bottom light displacement boat,. unfortunately, attaching the keel directly to the hull completely eliminates the bilges. Any quantity of water inside the boat can make life miserable by migrating to and fro as the boat heels or rolls, always out of reach of the bilge pump.

Some builders of fin keel boats therefore construct a vestigial hollow keel stub, perhaps a foot deep or less, which serves as a sump. A shallow hollow stub, even a very narrow one, can be laid up without too much difficulty.

Traditionally, bronze keel bolts were used with lead keels. In recent years even Hinckley, the ultimate bastion of conservatism, has gone to the use of stainless steel keelbolts.

Stainless steel comes in as many varieties as Baskin-Robbins ice cream, and the stainless steels have widely varying properties of corrosion resistance. The fact that your boat has stainless steel keelbolts is no guarantee that your keel will stay attached forever.

Some stainless steels are very subject to certain types of corrosion, one of the worst being the result of the steel living in a salt saturated low-oxygen environment — for example the water-saturated underwater structure of a wooden boat. Theoretically this type of corrosion should not exist in a fiberglass boat, as long as the joint between the external ballast keel and the hull remains tight, and both the top of the keel and the keel landing on the hull are well bedded.

If the keel/hull joint is cracked open or rust stains weep from the top joint of a lead keel, the stainless steel keelbolts are suspect. For this reason, when purchasing a new boat it is a good idea to examine sisters that have seen several seasons of use to check the condition of the hull/keel joint. Corrosion of the stainless steel bolts is only likely to be a problem in salt water or in heavily polluted fresh water, or if there is an electrical problem aboard the boat.

Most keelbolts consist of cast-in-place threaded stainless steel rod. Theoretically, when the lead is poured it fills all the thread interstices of the rod, just as if the keelbolts had been tapped into a pre-cast keel. In fact, it is unlikely that all the threads will be perfectly filled. To compensate for this, it is best to cast the bolts in place with nuts and washers on the lower ends of the threaded rod, to take the keel load if the poured-in connection between keel and bolt proves to be inadequate.

We recently examined a 50 foot Grand Prix ocean racer less than two years old whose 18,000 pound lead keel was slowly pulling off the boat's massive cast-in-place all-thread bolts. The solution was to cut small windows in the keel — finding the end of the bolts isn't easy — install nuts and washers, and torque down on the bolts from inside the boat. Retorquing the keelbolts every few years isn't a bad idea. More than one boat has left the factory with its keelbolt nuts only hand tight.

The hull should be reinforced in the area of attachment of an external keel, due to the wracking forces exerted on the hull by a high aspect ratio fin keel. This means a thicker laminate, transverse framing members (floor timbers of wood, fiberglass, or metal), or an internal load-bearing structure such as the Pedrick designed Tri-axial Force grid in Ericson yachts. A fiberglass hull which shows no obvious internal reinforcement in the way of the ballast keel is a boat of which to be wary.

Lead keels are frequently delivered with finishes that are too smooth. A lead keel should be thoroughly sanded before the application of either fairing putty or bottom paint. This will remove surface oxidation and provide adequate tooth for the adhesion of paint and putty.

On a boat with a stub fiberglass keel with the lead attached below, the lead should be perfectly faired into the fiberglass stub. There is no excuse for a ridge or shoulder which will create unwanted drag at this point.

External Iron Keels

Iron keels have a set of problems all their own. Copper base bottom paints cannot be used on iron keels without extensive barrier coating, which can break down in a few years — or a few days, if the boat is run aground or grounds out at low tide in her slip — and leave you with a badly pitted, hydrodynamically inefficient surface. The lower density of iron also means that an iron-keeled boat must have a larger keel volume — and consequently more wetted surface — in order to provide the same stability as a smaller lead keel.

Galvanized steel keelbolts are usually used with iron keels, and these bolts are more susceptible to corrosion than more noble metals. Should the bedding compound between the top of an iron keel and a fiberglass hull fail to keep water out, heavy rust can build up on top of the keel, forcing it away from the hull and sometimes sheering the keelbolts or drawing them through the hull shell. We have seen this problem on several old Columbias which had iron keels. Any heavily rusted iron keel is going to be trouble as long as you own the boat.

New iron keels can be reasonably protected through the use of barrier coats such as epoxy bitumastic, and the use of non-copper anti-fouling paints, such as those containing TBTF. It will be very difficult even on a new boat to keep a perfectly smooth racing finish on an iron keel in salt water.

Internal Ballasting

Given the difficulty of fairing, attachment, and the prevention of leaking, it would appear to make some sense to put the ballast inside the hull shell, rather than outside. This is fairly common practice in boats of more traditional design — boats with relatively long, wide, shallow keels, as opposed to the deep, narrow keel of the modern cruiser/racer.

*An external lead keel can absorb a remarkable amount of punishment.
Repairs to the keel of an internally ballasted boat are another story*

The modern fin keeler would be extremely difficult to build with a molded fiberglass fin and internal ballast. Without wide, easily turning garboards, the molders simply couldn't reach down into the keel cavity to lay up the shell. Functionally, if the keel will be much less than a foot wide and extend much more than two feet below the canoe body of the hull, an external keel presents far fewer hull construction problems than an internal keel.

For boats of traditional design with hollow garboards, the use of ballast inside the hull shell is relatively straightforward. A molded keel cavity can be filled with lead shot, lead pigs, a single chunk of lead cast to fill the shell, random blocks of lead, or what have you. The "what have you" can cover a multitude of sins: boiler punchings in cement, steel reinforcing rod, scrap iron. None of these "what have yous" have anything like the density of lead, and can therefore offer only a fraction of the stability of a piece of lead of the same volume. It's fairly easy to tell if ferrous material has been used for ballast. A strong magnet passed over the outside of the keel will quickly answer the question.

Whatever material is used for inside ballast it must be thoroughly fixed in position in the keel shell. This is usually accomplished by filling the voids around the ballast with thickened polyester resin, which may need to be done in stages to prevent warping of the keel shell from the heat generated as the resin kicks off. If the keel shell yields at all when pressed on firmly, the ballast may not be firmly held in place.

With the ballast bonded in place, a frequent procedure is to heavily glass over the top of the ballast and the garboard area of the hull shell, in effect creating a double bottom. This should keep water out of the hull should the keel shell be damaged from grounding. Don't let this lure you into a false sense of security, however. Frequently a deep keel sump is left in the shell behind the ballast, and if this very vulnerable section of the keel molding is torn open by grounding, the fact that the top of the ballast is sealed in doesn't mean much in terms of keeping water out of the boat.

Damage from grounding is the real danger of internal ballasting. Keel damage is one of the most frequent problems with any sailboat. Usually, it is a simple matter of a boat drawing five feet being placed by her skipper in a depth of water of four feet, with the bottom in said location—be it sand, mud, rock, or coral—doing its best to reduce the offending boat's draft to the available depth of water. Needless to say, its efforts can wreak havoc.

An external lead keel can absorb a remarkable amount of this type of punishment. It will be abraded, bent, bashed, and gouged, but chances are that with a sledge hammer, a grinder, a plane, some putty, and some elbow grease, the keel can probably be restored to a semblance of its former self in short order. Plus, you don't really have to put it back in shape if you don't want to haul the boat at the time.

All you have to do to verify this is to visit a boatyard in Florida during the SORC. In some races the rule of thumb to stay out of the current may be to tack inshore until the boat bumps (only recommended in light air), then tack out until you can't see the bottom. After one of these races, there are frequent short hauls to repair the gouged-up lead fin keels.

Repairs to the keel of a damaged internally ballasted boat are another story. For all its strength, the abrasion resistance of fiberglass is extremely low, and even an inch thick fiberglass keel shell can be ground through after a few hours of pounding on rocks or beach. We have seen keel shells so abraded that the internal ballast has fallen through the bottom of the boat. It may take major damage to cause a single lead casting to fall out, but loose shot or lead pigs can fall through a pretty small hole in the bottom.

Repair of a badly damaged keel shell requires hauling the boat, cutting or grinding away both the damaged area and enough surrounding healthy surface for good bonding, thoroughly drying the ballast and the keel shell—and this isn't as easy as it sounds, for the water seems to just keep dripping out—reglassing, fairing, and painting. If you happen to be in an out of the way place when this happens, you may be out of luck. We examined a CSY 44 that had been on a reef in Honduras for a week, whose keel shell had almost been completely abraded away. Since no railway was available, the skipper glassed over the damage where she lay on the beach, dragged her off into deep water with a tug, and sailed the thousand-odd miles to Tampa and the factory to make proper repairs. We wouldn't have tried it with a lesser boat.

If all the water is not drained from the keel shell when it is repaired, the water may freeze and crack the fiberglass if the boat is stored out of water in a cold climate. If the internal ballast is iron, trapped water may cause a great deal of surface rust and consequent failure of adhesion of the ballast to the shell.

Despite the potential for problems there are advantages to inside ballast:
• barring serious grounding, the hull should be watertight with no keelbolts or ballast seam to leak;
• thickening the hull shell in the garboard area usually provides adequate support for the keel loads without additional reinforcement;
• a massive, hard to handle ballast casting is not necessary.

It is ironic that many boats touted as world cruisers carry the ballast inside a molded keel shell. The long distance cruiser may operate in poorly charted waters, under all conditions, and far from haulout facilities. The cruiser is the boat most likely to run aground, and more than any other boat should take advantage of the external lead keel. Nonetheless we would probably not turn down an otherwise suitable design that was internally ballasted. Good boats are hard to find. The perfect boat is rarer still.

A crunched lead keel: looks bad, but repair is relatively easy

Four
Good Deck Design and Construction

The one-piece molded deck, cockpit, and cabin trunk is one of the great revolutions of modern boatbuilding. Deck and cabin trunk leaks are the bane of existence of owners of wooden boats, who have learned to accommodate themselves to the inevitability of water coming through the bottom of their boats, but not through the top. With a molded deck, there is little or no excuse for leaks, and the dream of a dry berth should be a reality.

The decks of early fiberglass boats were solid layups, and the broad, flat deck expanses were frequently as bouncy as a trampoline. For a good example of this, take a walk on the foredeck of a 20 year old Triton sometime. The advantage of cored deck construction quickly became obvious, and today the majority of deck moldings of boats over 25 feet are cored, either with end grain balsa or with plywood.

There are advantages to balsa coring, notably good stiffness for a given panel weight, the ability of balsa to follow compound curves, and good sound and thermal insulating properties. The only disadvantage to balsa coring is that a balsa sandwich has slightly less flexural and compression strength than a fir plywood sandwich. At the same time, the balsa sandwich is significantly lighter.

Foam coring is rarely seen in decks except in custom boats. Airex, because of a tendency to soften at fairly low temperatures, is not normally used in deck construction even in custom boats.

Mounting of Hardware

Since balsa is inferior to plywood in compression strength, it is common practice in balsa cored decks to core the deck with plywood in areas where heavily loaded deck hardware—winches, for example—will be mounted. The only time this presents a problem is when you decide to mount new hardware in portions of the deck that are cored with balsa. In a finished boat, it is simply not practical to recore sections of the deck. If oversize, thick, load distributing plates are used, it is probably reasonably safe to mount hardware on balsa cored sections of decking. On boats with stainless steel hardware fastenings, these plates should be aluminum sheet. On boats with bronze hardware and bronze fastenings, the load distributing plates would ideally be bronze, although a plate of dense wood such as oak, used with oversize washers, is a reasonable substitute.

When mounting hardware on a deck cored with wood, it is a good practice to drill the bolt holes very slightly oversize, and dribble epoxy or polyester resin through the hole to coat the exposed core. If carefully done, this will keep water out of the core in the event of failure of the bedding compound under the hardware.

All deck hardware should be carefully bedded. Too much compound is better than too little. The ideal bedding compound would stay flexible indefinitely, but not be so tenacious that removal of the hardware is impossible. This requirement precludes the use of substances such as 3M 5200, which are such powerful adhesives that you can easily damage the deck trying to pry off hardware. We've seen cored decks on well-built custom racing boats delaminate from removing winches bedded with 3M 5200. Butyl, silicone, and polysulfide compounds are probably best for bedding deck hardware on fiberglass boats, although polysulfide is also a fairly powerful adhesive.

In production boatbuilding, it is common to mount as much hardware as possible on the deck molding before it is attached to the hull. This saves a lot of time on the production line, but it can create problems for the owner. Access must be provided to the back of every piece of through-fastened hardware on either the deck or the hull. If hardware is mounted after the deck, hull, and liner are joined, this is not usually the problem, but it does require foresight. A surprising number of boatbuilders overlook this seemingly obvious requirement.

When buying a boat, note the locations of deck hardware, then go below to see if you can get to the back of each piece. If the nuts are inaccessible, someday that's going to mean trouble. Murphy's law states that the less accessible a piece of hardware is, the more likely it is to leak or need replacement.

Hardware Quality

Most US production boats use hardware of good quality. There is probably little to choose between Nicro Fico, Schaefer, Merriman, or the other standard brands seen on production boats, although there are unquestionably specific pieces of gear made by each company that are superior to those of the competition.

While general quality may not vary greatly between brands, the way it is utilized by different boatbuilders can vary substantially. It is more common for stock boat hardware to be on the smaller and weaker side than it is for a builder to use oversize gear. A friend of ours who happens to be sales manager for a major marine hardware firm was sailing on a fast production racer/cruiser equipped with his hardware when a snatchblock disintegrated. To save a few dollars, the builder of the $100,000 boat had skimped a size on the blocks, and they simply weren't up to the demands placed on them.

The tendency to undersize gear is particularly pronounced in choosing winches. Almost invariably, if the builder offers a winch package with more powerful gear as an option, the standard winches will be barely adequate for the boat. It is ironic that the racing boat with its gorilla-sized winch grinders will have winches two or three times as powerful as those on the mom and pop cruising boat sailed by an out of shape middle-aged couple.

Deck hardware on imports is frequently inferior to that on US built boats. Far Eastern boats in particular have long had a reputation for using hardware of poor quality, and despite a great improvement in recent years, that criticism is still generally valid. It is becoming more common for Far Eastern boats to offer name brand hardware as an option, and it's usually worth paying the price.

On the typical production sailboat, the quality of the hardware is usually less a problem than where or how the item is installed. For example, properly mounted bow chocks have almost disappeared. The closer the chocks are to the stem of the boat, the better they are likely to function in terms of holding the bow of the boat into the wind at anchor. The basic purpose of bow chocks is to provide an unchafing, fair lead for anchor rodes and mooring lines. Without bow chocks—and a surprising number of boats lack them—a modern boat with high freeboard forward and relatively light displacement is almost guaranteed to sail around on her anchor.

Anchor wells should be self draining (not to the bilge), sealed off from the boat's interior, and have a lid with strong hinges and positive latch

Stern chocks are just as useful as bow chocks, particularly if a boat has wooden toe rails that could be abraded by dock lines. Midships chocks are extremely handy for spring lines.

Anchor Wells

The foredeck anchor well is one of the great innovations of the modern production boat. While carrying a lot of weight forward will increase a boat's pitching movement, most boats with moderate forward overhangs can carry a working anchor and rode in a foredeck well without seriously compromising bouyancy forward. Stored in a foredeck well, the working anchor is always close at hand, yet it out of the way. Spare anchors and rodes can be carried elsewhere, preferably low and toward the middle of the boat.

Large quantities of chain should not be carried in a foredeck well due to the heavy weight involved. While 200 feet of half inch nylon weights only 14 pounds, 100 feet of 5/16 inch chain—a reasonable substitute for 200 feet of nylon—weighs 115 pounds.

Foredeck wells should have provision for attachment of the bitter end of the anchor rode. Usually it's not too difficult to mount a heavy eyebolt in the well if the builder has overlooked this handy little item.

Anchor wells should be self-draining, with scuppers large enough not be clogged with mud from the anchor. The well should not drain to the bilge, and the well itself should be completely sealed off from the interior of the boat. The well's lid should have strong hinges and a positive provision for latching. Weak hinges and latches are common faults.

Any electrical wiring in the foredeck well—typically for running lights—should be secured under the deck with cable straps to prevent its being damaged when handling ground tackle. Splices and connections should be taped over and sealed with silicone. Be prepared to have a certain amount of trouble with wiring routed through an anchor well.

While foredeck wells have made ground tackle handling and storage easier, they have complicated the mounting of foredeck cleats. Rather than paired cleats mounted near the centerline, it is more common to see port and starboard bow cleats shifted outboard almost to the rail to clear the lid of the anchor well. This is a reasonable solution, although sometimes leads from the bow chocks will run afoul of the bow pulpit stanchions if cleat placement is not carefully considered.

Pulpits and Lifelines

Bow pulpits are a good place to mount running lights. The simplest running light arrangement is one of the new international style bicolor attached to the bow pulpit on the boat's centerline. This minimized alignment problems, avoiding overlapping port and starboard sectors or blind spots for oncoming vessels. Lights mounted on the pulpit will be vulnerable to collision damage, so you should forego the distressingly common practice of docking by braille.

Running lights mounted in the hull are a poor idea. They invariably leak and short out, and their position close to the water almost guarantees that they will be invisible to boats on your leeward side.

Bow and stern pulpits, like lifeline stanchions, should be through bolted and have substantial backing pads. Frequently, the underside of the deck molding is rough and irregular where stanchion and pulpit fastenings

pass through. This creates problems when installing backing plates, as it may not be possible to make the backing plate lie flat against the underside of the deck, particularly if the fastenings span the flanges of the hull-to-deck joint. Split plywood backing pads, distorted aluminum plates, and cracked fiberglass backers are frequently seen where an irregular interior surface exists under deck hardware. This can overstress fastenings or unevenly load decks, with gelcoat stress fractures a common result.

This particular problem can frequently be owner remedied. If the underside of the deck cannot be faired by sanding or grinding, remove nuts and backing plates and wax both the upper surface of the backing plate and the threads of the bolt where they stick through the deck. If the backing plate is cracked or distorted, replace it. Slip the waxed plate over the bolts, install the nuts loosely, and trowel the gap between the deckhead and the backing plate full of a dense mixture of epoxy and microballoons. Tighten the nuts evenly until the plate just touches the overhead. Stop there, and clean up the squeezed out microballoon mixture, which when dry will form a solid, even surface for the final tightening of the fastenings. This gives good load distribution on the deck and equally loads all the fastenings. The wax acts as a parting agent so that the backing plate and bolts can be removed if rebedding or replacement of hardware is ever necessary.

With boats getting wider, shrouds have moved inboard to keep headsail sheeting angles narrow enough for good upwind performance. This can either complicate or facilitate access to the foredeck. If the shrouds are moved far enough inboard, it is usually easiest to go forward by passing outboard of the shrouds. If, however, the shrouds are close to the lifelines, there may not be enough room outboard to get around that way, but the shrouds may be too far inboard to easily go between the shrouds and the cabin trunk. Easy foredeck access is necessary for headsail changing, docking, and the handling or ground tackle.

Handrails

The typical fiberglass sailboat has wood grabrails mounted along the outboard edge of the cabin trunk. These should be more than an attractive way to visually break up a bleak expanse of white fiberglass. Handrails should be through bolted to the top of the cabin. Merely screwing up into the rails through the deckhead is not adequate. Screws have relatively little holding power in tension, and the upward and outward pull you put on handrails—either by holding on yourself or by lashing your dinghy to them—is largely tension.

While handrails make a convenient lashdown point for anchors, boathooks, or even the dinghy, this is a poor practice. Things lashed to the rail may well interfere with its primary function: something to hang onto in heavy weather.

It's not a bad idea to have handrails running the full length of the cabin trunk. They can then be used as foot braces when working around the base of the mast as well as hand holds when moving along the deck.

Headsail Track

Many production boats use an L- or T-shaped aluminum extrusion to serve as both a bolting flange for the hull-to-deck joint, and a sheeting location for headsail snatch blocks. The disadvantage of this system is that

Headsail track can be added after construction, provided the deck is strong enough and good load distribution can be achieved with backing pads

in order to change headsail leads the snatch block must be unsnapped and shifted to the next hole in the toerail extrusion. With a sliding car on a T-track, headsail leads can be shifted when the block is under load, an important consideration for the racing boat.

A track that follows the sheerline results in a constantly changing sheeting angle relative to the boat's centerline, making optimum upwind trim difficult to attain. For a cruising boat whose shrouds are at the outboard edge of the deck, this problem is hardly serious. For the racing boat with shrouds set in from the edge of the deck, inboard track is a must for good upwind performance. Fortunately, track can frequently be added after construction, provided the deck is strong enough and good load distribution can be attained with oversize backing pads.

Whether you have toerail-mounted track or inboard track, be sure that it extends far enough fore and aft to allow effective sheeting of all overlapping headsails. Remember that the height of the jib's clew off the deck greatly affects the fore and aft sheeting position. By telling your sailmaker the length and location of your track, he can accommodate leech length to the length and position of the track for sails of different overlap.

Needless to say, headsail track must be through bolted and should have either backing plates or oversize washers. If gelcoat cracks develop around the track, the deck is not strong enough to take the load, and you'll either have to put still larger load distribution pads under the deck or actually reinforce the deck structure. Headsail track fastenings are a common source of deck

leak due to the heavy loads imposed on them. If you develop such a leak, remove the offending bolt and rebed under the head. If this doesn't work, the whole track will have to be removed and rebedded. Check the bolts periodically for tightness.

Deck Surface

Secure footing on deck is critical. Most boats have molded-in nonskid, which varies in type and quality. Good nonskid should:

- give secure footing when the decks are wet;
- be easy to clean;
- be reasonably non-abrasive.

These demands may be slightly mutually exclusive. The decks of C&C boats, for example, are just about as non skid as possible, but they are abrasive enough to wear through foul weather gear or water-softened skin in a short period of time.

Stark white is the worst possible color for decks and cabin tops. On sunny days, it's guaranteed to give the helmsman a headache from glaring reflection. Light tan, green, or blue are far more restful without absorbing inordinate amounts of heat that might make it uncomfortable below.

Probably more time is spent in the cockpit, both at the dock and under way, than anywhere else in the boat. A comfortable, functional cockpit whose design is consistent with the intended function of the boat is one of the true hallmarks of the carefully designed boat, and will be the subject of the next article in this series.

The deck of the S 2 8.6 Meter has several desirable characteristics: generally clean and unobstructed, it is equipped with adequate but not excessive hardware, inboard chainplates, sturdy double lifelines, and forward anchor well. We would add inboard genoa track for better sheeting angles. Visually, the contrasting non-skid areas break up large surfaces and reduce glare

Five

Take the Time to Study the Cockpit

The average sailor probably spends more hours in the cockpit of his boat than he does below. It is therefore ironic that belowdecks decor has become the main selling point of most production boats, while the cockpit is frequently considered an afterthought.

Like the interior, the design of the cockpit must meet demands that may be mutually exclusive. The cockpit should be roomy and comfortable in port for lounging and entertaining, yet it must be reasonably small if the boat is to do any offshore sailing. It should be laid out efficiently for the racing crew, yet with winches and sheets so arranged that the helmsman can run the boat when sailing shorthanded.

Given the fact that all these things may not be possible to attain in one boat, you must determine how the boat is to be used—basically what compromises you are willing to make—before deciding what arrangement works best for you. This may require some painful self-examination. The miniscule footwell with deck-level seating may be the right answer for singlehanding in the roaring forties, but if you're really going to be plugged into the dock most of the time and will do some serious entertaining, then a large, comfortable cockpit which accommodates six at the cockpit table for cocktails may be the answer. At the same time, if long-distance cruising is your bag, a cockpit that seats ten and is so wide that you can't brace against the leeward seat from the weather side isn't the right answer.

The offshore cockpit
For serious offshore sailing, the cockpit should meet the standards published in the Special Regulations of the Offshore Racing Council for Category 1 racing. Category 1 racing is defined as "races of long distance and well offshore, where yachts must be completely self-sufficient for extended periods of time, capable of withstanding heavy storms and prepared to meet serious emergencies without the expectation of outside assistance."

If you substitute the word "cruises" for "races," that sentence is as pure and simple a definition of offshore sailing as exists.

Seaworthiness is the prime consideration of the offshore cockpit. The concept is to minimize the amount of water that the cockpit could hold in heavy weather, keep that water from getting belowdecks, and facilitate its return to the sea.

The volume in cubic feet of the cockpit of the ocean-going yacht should be no more than .06L x B x FA according to the ORC. While "L", "B", and "FA" are hull dimensions measured under the IOR, a reasonable approximation for the cruising boat can be derived by substituting your boat's waterline length for L, her beam for B, and the freeboard at the corners of the transom for FA.

As an example, take a modern cruiser 36 feet on deck with a 29 foot waterline, a beam of 11.5 feet, and freeboard aft of three feet. The formula yields an allowable cockpit volume of 60 cubic feet. Note that this is the volume of the cockpit below the lowest coamings. A cockpit with side coamings but no coaming aft has considerably less volume than the same cockpit which is enclosed by a coaming across its after end.

For coastal or lakes sailing, ORC allowable cockpit volume is 50 percent greater. For a boat that is not to be used offshore, that number is the maximum allowable volume for a reasonably safe boat. If you buy a boat with a bigger cockpit than those rather generous allowances, you're on your own.

In all cases, the cockpit sole should be at least .02L above the waterline. This amounts to seven inches in our hypothetical 36 footer.

Cockpit drains
Proper cockpit drains are critical. As a minimum, a cockpit meeting the ORC volume requirements should have two drains no less than 1¼ inches in inside diameter each. Grates or screens over drains greatly decrease flow, and size of the drains must be increased accordingly if there is any restriction over the opening.

Cockpit scuppers should drain at any angle of heel. Surprisingly, many don't. A few years ago, we delivered a brand new C&C 36 from Newport to St. Thomas. For five days, the boat was heeled about 20° on port tack by strong easterly tradewinds. The starboard side of the cockpit had to be bailed hourly to protect the engine panel from submersion, as the cockpit simply refused to drain at that angle of heel. Drains at the aft end of the cockpit may actually siphon water into the cockpit if the stern squats or the boat pulls a large quarter wave at speed.

This problem is most acute where the cockpit extends aft almost to the transom—a typical arrangement in the modern cruiser/racer with little or no afterdeck. In such boats, the cockpit sole should pitch down toward its forward end, and the drains should be moved to the outboard forward corners of the cockpit. The Southern Cross 31 was modified in this way two years ago.

Since cockpit scuppers inevitably exist at or near the waterline, they should be fitted with seacocks. Double-clamped non-collapsing flexible hose is the best material for cockpit drain plumbing in a fiberglass boat. The flexing of hull and cockpit could fracture rigid plastic or fiberglass piping.

The Bridgedeck
In an attempt to maximize cockpit size and belowdecks accessibility, many boatbuilders have eliminated the bridgedeck. Frequently, the companionway sill is raised a few inches above the cockpit sole to keep water in the cockpit from getting below. This is a poor arrangement for any boat which contemplates serious cruising. A bridgedeck reduces cockpit volume, serves to increase belowdecks space (usually over galley counters), and is invaluable in keeping water out of the cabin. With a deep companionway, the temptation to leave lower drop boards out for the sake of convenience is simply too great, and is a thoroughly unseamanlike practice.

For all categories of racing—coastwise, as well as offshore—the Special Regulations require that companionways extending below the level of the main deck be blocked and secured to at least that level. In many production boats, this means leaving half the dropboards in place when sailing.

Another questionable practice is the use of wide companionways with sharply tapered sides. While tapering the sides of the companionway makes it easier to remove and insert drop boards and facilitates getting below, it also makes the boards more likely to fall out in a severe knockdown. In any case, drop boards must be fitted with latching devices such as barrel bolts or slide bolts to positively secure them.

A spare plywood drop board should always be carried for offshore cruising. We once lost a companionway drop board at the start of a race to Bermuda, and enough water got below during the course of the five day trip to make life miserable for all hands, despite a cockpit dodger and a jury-rigged drop board.

The use of hinged doors rather than drop boards is a poor practice in small boats. Doors require the companionway to be completely opened to get on deck or below, and they are easily torn from their hinges.

No bridgedeck and a sharply tapered companionway going almost to the cockpit sole limit this boat to coastal sailing.

Protecting the Companionway
For offshore sailing, a companionway storm hood—basically a box protecting the front of the companionway slide—is a must. Water driving under the forward edge of an unprotected slide can make belowdecks a rain forest in short order. A serious cruiser, whether sailing coastwise or offshore, will find the storm hood worth its weight in gold.

Storm hoods frequently incorporate a molded spray rail which may extend across the top of the deckhouse to form a dodger coaming. Without some form of coaming, a cockpit or companionway dodger's efficiency is severely limited. Even if it is pierced for sheets and halyards leading aft along the housetop, a properly designed coaming will go a long way toward keeping water from driving under the lower edge of the dodger.

Cockpit dodgers are rapidly becoming standard items on boats used in cooler climates. While a dodger limits visibility, adds windage, and can be an eyesore, the tradeoff in protection of the forward end of the cockpit may well be worth it. If a boat tends to be wet, has low coamings, and a low cabin trunk, a dodger can make the difference between comfort and misery in bad weather. In a boat whose aft cabin bulkhead slopes forward, the dodger also makes it possible to leave the companionway open for ventilation when it's raining.

Dodgers should be custom fitted to the boat to be sure that they do not interfere with winches, sheets, halyards, the main boom, and seating at the forward end of the cockpit. If properly designed, they need not make the boat look like a folding tent camping trailer.

Cockpit lockers
Improperly designed cockpit lockers are a recurrent theme in the modern boat. Cavernous, undivided space under the cockpit is practically useless. In boats with a quarterberth, there is frequently a shallow cockpit locker over that berth. This is handy for small items such as spare blocks and sail ties. Usually, the other side of the cockpit will have a huge locker, euphemistically dubbed a sail locker. Unless the locker lid is also huge, chances are that nothing larger than a carefully bricked storm jib will go through the opening. Chances are also good that screws, exposed bolt heads, and cables lurk inside the locker to rip holes in your new $1500 ¾-ounce triradial.

The cavernous locker may hold large quantities of junk, but whatever item you want is guaranteed to be at the bottom of the heap, under the barbecue and the storm anchor. You can make a big locker more useful by subdividing it with plywood or net partitions, installing hooks for spare sheets, generally organizing so that nothing must be piled in. If the cockpit locker provides access to the steering gear or stuffing box, make sure that your partitions are easily removable in an emergency.

An amazing amount of water can get below through leaking cockpit locker lids. The lids should be gasketed, have positive dogs, and have a scuppering system that will allow water to drain from the leeward cockpit seat with the boat heeled over 30°.

An excellent cockpit locker system, but one we've never seen on a stock boat, is to build the seats and lockers into the cockpit after it is molded, sort of like building enclosed benches on the inside of a bathtub. While this eliminates the possibility of really deep lockers, it makes it far simpler to keep water out of the interior of the boat. The lockers are then merely inserts into the self bailing cockpit. Admittedly, scuppering the leeward side will be more complex with this arrangement.

Seating
It is unfortunate that people do not increase and decrease in size depending on the size of their boats. If you want cockpit seats on which you can lie down, they must be six feet long whether your boat is a 25 footer or a 45 footer. The cockpit on a small boat invariably takes up a greater percentage of the boat's total volume than the cockpit of a larger boat. Seating simply doesn't scale down.

In order to have coamings high enough to offer any real back support, the cockpit seats must be sunk below the main deck level. The footwell must be lowered correspondingly. This, of course, increases cockpit volume.

Ideally, the cockpit seats should slope downward outboard, and the coamings likewise angle outward. This provides more comfortable seating, but it makes it more difficult to use the seats for sleeping, and renders it impossible to have the bridgedeck at the same level as the cockpit seats. Therefore, what is gained in comfort is lost in convenience. In any case, a gutter or scupper must be provided at the outboard edge of the seat, or those seated to leeward—although they shouldn't be there anyway—will suffer from wet seat syndrome.

The cavernous cockpit locker may hold large quantities of junk, but whatever item you want is guaranteed to be at the bottom of the heap

Steering

The pedestal-type wheel has become almost universal in boats over 30 feet. Although this steering system generally creates more room in the cockpit, it is more expensive, less rugged, and more prone to failure than a strong, simple tiller. While a tiller takes up cockpit space, it is generally preferred for its sensitivity by racing sailors graduating up from small boats.

Placement of a wheel steerer can be problematic. Some prefer the forward end of the cockpit for shelter under the dodger and accessibility to sail controls. Others prefer the aft location to free up the forward end of the cockpit for sail trimmers or casual sailing guests. For shorthanded cruising, the forward location is better. For racing, an aft position is probably preferable.

While you rarely sit directly behind the wheel when sailing, most boats with the wheel aft have a seat across the rear of the cockpit for the helmsman. This seat should be either concave or convex to provide a secure seat with the boat heeled 20°. If the boat has a high cabin trunk, a convex seat may help a short driver see forward. With a flat seat, the helmsman invariably slides to leeward.

If you like to steer from the windward or leeward rail, be sure that the wheel is large enough in diameter to be easily reached from the rail. This may require notching out the cockpit sole for the wheel on larger or exceptionally wide boats. Obviously these wheel wells must not extend below the waterline, and must be scuppered overboard.

Unless the cockpit coamings are wide and flat on top, the helmsman may have no place to sit outboard. The best solution to this problem is found on the Tillotson-Pearson Alden 44, which has a concavity in the top of each coaming for the helmsman's rear end.

Sheet leads and sail handling

Efficiency in sail handling must be a major consideration of cockpit design. Winches must be placed so that handles can be cranked through 360° without striking the dodger, lifelines, stanchions or pulpits. If the coamings contain molded-in winch islands, be sure they are large enough to accommodate bigger winches. We have never seen winches that were too large for the shorthanded sailor.

Placement of the mainsheet traveller can wreak havoc with cockpit layout. Nasty necessities such as the need to trim sails can interfere with cocktail-time seating for guests. Putting the traveller on the bridgedeck limits access below. Put it behind the helmsman, and the mainsheet loses efficiency by pulling aft as well as down, unless the boom is very long. An aft location for the traveller also tends to decapitate the helmsman, and requires putting the mainsheet trimmer in the end of the boat, where his weight does the least good.

Put the traveller on a bridge over the companionway, and you may render it impossible to fit the boat with a dodger. Move it forward of the companionway and the sheeting becomes inefficient unless the boom is very short. All things considered, that location on the bridgedeck starts to look pretty good.

Engine controls

With pedestal steering, engine controls should be mounted directly on the pedestal. With a tiller or worm gear wheel, mounting them on the side of the cockpit makes sense. Since most people are righthanded, the right side of the cockpit is usually the best location.

Throttle and clutch controls are notorious sheet catchers. Some boats therefore move these controls inside a cockpit locker. This can create problems operating under power in rain or heavy weather, compromising the watertight integrity of the cockpit if the locker must be kept open to operate the engine.

The instrument panel should be within sight of the helmsman when seated at the normal under-power driving position. An excellent idea is recessing the panel into the face of the bridgedeck. All panels, despite claims of watertightness, should have protection from heavy spray. The panel should not be so close to the cockpit sole that it can be shorted out by a few inches of water in the cockpit.

Sailing instruments

The aft cabin bulkhead makes a reasonable place to mount instruments, although it means that loungers at the forward end of the cockpit will probably block the instruments just when you need them most. Unless the steering position is very far aft, the ideal location for instruments is in a pod mounted atop the companionway storm hood. Then they will only be blocked by someone standing in the companionway, and that problem is easily remedied. The instruments will be just about at eye level, so that the helmsman can see them without having to glance down, and no unsightly holes will have to be cut in the main bulkhead.

Conclusions

No cockpit layout can solve all the problems of the racer, cruiser, and daysailor. Nonetheless, the basic tenets of safety, comfort, and function are reasonably universal. Next time you look at a boat, consciously resist the urge to plunge below into the world of teak and plush upholstery. Sit for a while in the cockpit. Imagine the boat rail down going to weather in a rip-snorting breeze. Imagine half a dozen friends gathered in the cockpit for a party. Imagine yourself and your wife or husband alone on a thousand mile passage. Forget the interior decor, until you find out if the cockpit works for your kind of sailing.

The cockpit of the Alden 44 has most of the desirable features of an offshore cockpit: a high bridgedeck, a good dodger breakwater, reasonable protection from the weather, and molded-in seats for the helmsman atop the coamings

Six

Look Below: Camping Out vs. Comfort

Probably few things have changed more in the last 20 years than the interior volume of the small cruising boat. When the Triton first appeared in the late 1950's, the fact that a 28-footer could have full headroom was seen as a major breakthrough. The Paul Coble designed Corsair of a few years later brought full headroom to 24 footers. Ever since, the interior battle has loomed larger in importance in boatbuilding and design.

Part of the gain in interior volume is due to the change from wooden construction to fiberglass. A wooden boat with a beam of 10 feet will sacrifice at least six inches of interior beam to the thickness of her planking, frames, and ceiling. A fiberglass boat of the same beam could lose less than an inch. Considering the small volume of the interior of a boat, those few inches add up to an amazing amount of space.

The same analogy applies to headroom. The wooden boat, with its deep floor timbers and deckbeams overhead, sacrifices a lot of headroom to accommodate the basic components of the boat's structure.

In addition, for a given overall length, sailboats have simply gotten wider and longer on the waterline. For example, take the Bristol 27, a popular small cruiser of the late 1960's. On a length overall of 27'2", the Bristol has a beam of eight feet and a waterline length of 19'9". Displacement is about 6,500 pounds.

While those dimensions were pretty reasonable 15 years ago, they look pretty skimpy today. Compare the Bristol 27 to the Tanzer 27, a typical small cruiser/racer of today. On a length overall of 26'7", the Tanzer has a beam of 9'6" and a waterline length of 22'6". Her displacement is about the same as that of the Bristol.

The Tanzer is a dramatically larger boat in interior volume, and typifies what's going on in the smaller cruiser market today. For a boat of the same length, today's buyer demands—and gets—more interior volume. Like it or not, interiors are the name of the game. Have you seen many boat ads recently that don't stress the interior?

Despite the gain in volume, general interior layout has changed relatively little. In boats from 25 to 40 feet, the most common interior arrangement still consists of a double cabin forward, head next aft with lockers opposite, a main cabin with settees parallel to the centerline and galley aft, and perhaps a quarterberth.

Obviously, the amount of headroom, elbow room, and leg room varies dramatically when you have the same general arrangement on boats ranging from 5,000 pounds to 20,000 pounds in displacement.

This interior arrangement emerged in the 1930's, when the galley forward manned by a paid hand who slept in the forepeak on a pipe berth began to vanish with the "democratization" of yachting. The arrangement has persisted mostly because it works.

Privacy

When there is more than one person aboard a boat, privacy rapidly becomes an issue. Whether it's dressing, using the head, or sleeping, most sailors in our privacy-oriented society have the occasional desire to separate themselves physically and psychologically from their fellow crew members.

The issue is not critical in a boat used for daysailing. Most of us are capable of putting up with almost anything for a few hours. Granted, a cedar bucket in the

A tremendous increase in interior volume is a primary feature of the modern fiberglass cruising boat. Wider beam, longer waterlines and the lack of interior structural components have combined to give the contemporary 35-footer the interior space of an older boat almost 25% larger

middle of an open boat has little to recommend it when sailing with a mixed crew, but generations have managed with little permanent loss of dignity.

However, when cruising for any period longer than overnight, some privacy is just about essential. When you look at a boat, think what it will be like aboard her for a long weekend, or a week's cruise in the rain. Then think about those six berths in a 30-footer, and see if you really want to cruise with them all filled. Then you may find the flaw in the question, "how many does she sleep?"

Down the Hatch

With that in mind, it's time to go below. Is there anything to grab onto when coming down the companionway ladder? Is the ladder so steep that you must go down facing the ladder, or can it safely be descended like a stairway? Steep ladders are not necessarily bad, but they must have provision for something to grab onto in a seaway, such as handholds cut into the sides of the ladder, or grab rails on the inside face of the companionway. Needless to say, the ladder should be positively attached to the boat. At the same time, if it is necessary to remove it in order to get to the engine for service, there must be a simple way to unlatch the ladder and move it out of the way without disassembling half the interior.

The forward cabin

Having negotiated the companionway, move all the way forward to the forward cabin.

"Vee berth in forward stateroom." Every boat from 22 feet up has it, and some of the worst travesties in design are foisted on boatbuyers in the name of that private forward cabin.

First of all, let it be said that a vee berth ain't a sea berth. If you intend to do sailing that requires sleeping aboard the boat while underway in anything more than a flat calm, pretend that the forward berth doesn't exist: it will be unusable. In fact, consider everything forward of the mast to be a bit of a twilight zone at sea, the part of the boat that you don't venture into unless you have to. The motion in the forward third of any boat much smaller than 50 feet when beating into a head sea has to be experienced to be believed. You quickly learn that only the toughest sleep forward except in port.

If cruising's your bag, and you consist of the typical husband and wife team, you may find it better to have storage forward than sleeping accommodations. This will run you right up against almost every production sailboat. That's why unusual interior arrangements, such as that of the Cape Dory 25D, really catch our eye. In a boat designed for two people, you just don't need to waste that space forward for sleeping. If you want a double berth, it is usually possible to modify a main cabin settee to serve the purpose.

If only occasional cruising with the kids or another couple is your thing, the forward cabin may be right up your alley. Most sleeping, after all, is done at anchor or at the dock, when the forward location is perfectly reasonable.

Given the reality of the forward vee berth, what should you look for? Inevitably, the berth is wide at the top and narrow at the bottom. Lie in it with someone else, and see if two of you can really be comfortable with your legs entwined.

Until a few years ago, there was inevitably a space at the forward end of the vee berth labeled an anchor locker. Unfortunately, in order to use any ground tackle stored there, you had to drag it out over the berth and up the forward hatch, knocking smelly mud over your cushions. Needless to say, the smell and mess of ground tackle stowed forward did little to make that cabin more comfortable.

Somewhere along the way, someone came up with the idea of the foredeck anchor well. Whoever put the first foredeck anchor well on a production sailboat will, if he can be discovered, be awarded Practical Sailor's Invention of the Last 20 Years award.

There is likely to be a large empty space under the vee berth. Since space on any boat is at a premium, something must be done to utilize it. One thing that is frequently done, but which really has little to recommend it, is to install a large water tank in the space. Unfortunately, under the vee berth forward is one of the least desirable locations for a water tank.

Begin with the mechanics of the installation. If a boat pounds in a seaway, much of that impact is going to be taken on the section of the hull directly under the vee berth. Any tank mounted there must be absolutely rigidly attached to the hull, and must be extraordinarily strong. Many forward water tanks have either split or come adrift when a boat pounds her way to weather. It's a most unpleasant sensation to discover that half or all of your fresh water supply has been transformed into bilgewater.

More serious than the installation difficulty is the effect on the trim and handling of the boat of a large weight far forward. A gallon of fresh water weighs about ten pounds. Put even a 20 gallon tank forward on a 30 footer, and the boat's trim will be noticeably altered. Worse yet, the boat's pitching moment is likely to be amplified, making her less comfortable in a seaway. To further confuse matters, as the fuel or water in the tank is used up, trim and balance will be continually changing.

Although it may be slightly inconvenient, the space under the vee berths is best given over to dry storage such as bedding and clothing. Although drawers waste space, they are more convenient to use, and may ameliorate the access problem of having to lift the cushions. Keep the tanks in the middle of the boat, where they belong. A tank that must be kept empty to keep from screwing up the boat's handling is worse than useless, as it keeps you from using the space for more appropriate things.

A forward cabin should have ventilation. This is most likely to consist of a hatch over the head of the berth in the deck or top of the cabin trunk. The aluminum framed, translucent hatch is another great modern invention. (Just remember that they are transparent at night, so that strollers at dockside can usually stare into your forward cabin if the lights are on.)

The aluminum framed hatch is one of the great developments in modern yacht construction. Strong, light, and far less likely to leak than their wooden and fiberglass predecessors, aluminum hatches come in just about every conceivable style, size, and shape.

In all but the smallest boat, there should be a light at the head of each side of the vee berth. This will make it easier for insomniac sailors to read without disturbing the person with whom they share the berth.

To improve privacy, some means of shutting off the forward cabin is desirable. In a small boat whose forward cabin merely consists of a vee berth, this could be something as simple as a curtain or a sliding panel. In a larger boat with real standing space in the forward cabin, a sliding or folding door will fit the bill.

Louvers in the door will aid ventilation, but at the sacrifice of some privacy. Again, compromise is a way of life in boats.

Storage can be augmented by shelves under the deckhead. These are most useful if they have high fiddles and are subdivided into smaller sections. If you mount too many things on the bulkhead at the head of the berth, there may be no comfortable place to lean while reading.

Few things are less attractive than the bare inside of

a fiberglass hull. We've never gotten over the insecure feeling of seeing the sun stream through translucent topsides. For both esthetics and function, some form of hull ceiling is desirable. More and more boats are sealing the interior of the hull with thin wood strips, the rebirth of a practice that makes the inside of a wooden yacht so enjoyable.

Teak is not the wood to use here, being heavy, dark and expensive. A wonderful alternative is eastern white cedar or western red cedar, both of which are highly aromatic and beautiful when varnished. We haven't found anyone who enjoys the smell of fiberglass so much that a little aromatic cedar can't warm his soul. Vinyl and carpet liners, while functional, make the boat look like an airplane or a house trailer. They may also be subject to mildew if they are not kept dry and clean.

Some form of hull liner will also help reduce the condensation that can make the interior of an uncored hull uncomfortable. Ceiling may not be necessary on a foam or balsa cored hull, but for pure esthetics, few things dress up a boat so quickly. Since forward cabins are inevitably cavelike, anything you do to brighten the decor is likely to be an improvement.

The head

Except in very small cruising boats, where the head may be located under the vee berths forward (which incidentally is a perfectly lousy arrangement) the head is usually located in a compartment immediately aft of the forward cabin. The degree of privacy attainable in the head is largely a function of the size of the boat.

In boats under 30 feet, it is usually desirable to have a head arrangement that can span the full width of the boat. While a cramped head compartment is hardly the end of the world, if it must be used for dressing and showering, a little elbow room is nice.

Two of the better small boat heads we've seen are in the Cape Dory 25D and the S2 8.5 Meter. The 25D gives up the forward cabin to create a large head. The S2 8.5 features a full width head that closes off from both the forward cabin and the main cabin with solid doors.

The primary fixture of any head is the water closet. The basic design of the marine toilet has not changed in this century. The toilet on our yawl *Hobnob* was installed when the boat was launched in 1923. Not only is it still possible to get parts for it, but the item is still in production.

Most stock boats come equipped with the cheapest toilets available, most frequently the Wilcox-Crittenden Head-Mate. While these toilets are perfectly serviceable, their small cylinders make them harder to pump and more likely to clog than a more expensive unit. Boatbuilders use cheap toilets simply to keep prices down. A Head-Mate or comparable Jabsco or Raritan toilet retails for about $125, while a top of the line head such as the Wilcox-Crittenden Skipper costs three or four times as much.

To clear the air once and for all, unless a boat operates in an enclosed body of fresh water, we don't believe in holding tanks. The well intentioned but poorly thought out head laws are no more than a bandaid on the gaping wound of water pollution. In tidal salt water areas, we have absolutely no guilt about pumping the toilet directly over the side. We seriously doubt if as many as 20% of the head-equipped boats in existence conscientiously abide by the head regulations.

Manufacturers, of course, must comply, so new boats are invariably equipped with holding tanks. Do yourself a favor. Install a diverter valve, and forget you even have a holding tank.

The head compartment must have grab rails which give you something to hold onto when using the head underway. There should also be ventilation in the form of opening ports for use in fair weather, and one or two large cowl vents for bad weather. An unventilated head compartment will be a misery forever.

While a sink may not strictly be necessary in the head, it is a useful addition if there is any room. The small, oval, round bottom sinks are less than useless. Water runs out of them if the boat is heeled more than a few degrees, and it's impossible to wash your face over one without soaking the counter. The head sink need not be as deep as the galley sink, but make sure it's more than a toy.

If the head has a shower—and this is another blessed modern development in small cruising boats—it should drain into a sump, not into the bilge. This is one of the most common faults in the production sailboat. Hair, soap, and grunge will clog your bilge pump and render the bilges as pleasant as a New York sewer. The only thing that belongs in the bilge is bilge water; not shower water, not icebox water, and certainly not engine oil.

The head should contain lockers for toiletries. Small cubbyholes or drawers which can be labelled with each crew member's name are ideal. Linen or hanging lockers, depending on the size of the boat, may be desirable.

If the boat lacks standing headroom in the head compartment, the head should be compact enough that everything can be reached when the toilet is used as a seat. This means that counters, grab rails, and mirrors will be a little lower than in the compartment with standing headroom.

Towel racks should be strong enough to double as grab rails. Nothing in a boat that looks like something to grab onto should come off in your hands when you do grab it.

The doors to the head should be large enough to accommodate the largest member of the crew. While this may seem an obvious requirement, you'd be surprised how often this simple thing is overlooked. The doors should also have a positive means of latching, so that if you're thrown against them you don't come piling out head first onto the cabin sole. We can attest from first hand experience that such an act does little to preserve dignity, and dignity is in precious short supply on the typical small cruising boat.

One head is perfectly adequate for almost any boat up to about 45 feet, unless the boat has a center cockpit layout. With a center cockpit, a separate head for the aft owner's cabin borders on the essential, even if it's nothing more than a toilet under a settee. No one wants to climb from the aft cabin to the forward end of the boat in the middle of the night.

Privacy, ventilation, security, and comfort are key words for the head. You won't necessarily be spending much time in the head while cruising, but a certain degree of comfort can help make the difference between cruising that's just camping out, and cruising in comfort.

Seven

The Main Cabin and the Galley

A cruising boat's main cabin must serve the multiple functions of living room, dining room, kitchen, and bedroom. And it must serve these functions heeled 25° bashing to weather as well as it does sitting tied to the dock or at anchor.

Because the main cabin is used for so many purposes, and because it's usually the first part of the boat you see when going below, probably more time is put into the layout of this small space than almost any other part of the boat. On the success or failure of the main cabin design hinges a significant percentage of boat sales. Builders are quite aware of this, and usually try to make the main cabin as attractive as possible. That first impression is critical. Unfortunately, attractive and functional are frequently two different things. What looks good may not work well, and what works well in port may be perfectly miserable at sea.

Settees and Berths

Main cabin settees must almost invariably double as berths. Unfortunately, a good settee usually makes a lousy berth. The most comfortable settee width is about 15″. There should be a back rest for the settee, and it should be angled slightly outboard for greatest comfort. The height of the backrest is not critical, but it should be high enough to offer some support. Figure on a minimum of two linear feet of settee space per person for seating. For reading, there should be a light at each end of the settee—preferably a light whose angle can be adjusted.

Now that we've created a comfortable 15″ wide settee, how do you change it into a comfortable 24″ wide berth? The simplest way is to have the back fold up and latch out of the way for sleeping. The space between the settee back and the side of the hull can usually be used to store bedding when the back rest is folded down for sitting. If the settee back latches up for sleeping, be sure that the latches are both positive in action and strong enough to retain the back when the settee is used for sleeping in rough weather. Having the back rest fall on you in the middle of the night is a rather unpleasant way to wake up.

On a boat equipped with pilot berths outboard of the settees, the settees frequently extend to form berths of the proper width. Positive latches should be provided to hold the settee in both sitting and sleeping positions.

Pilot berths make great sea berths, but they usually end up used more for storage than for sleeping. They are also frequently too narrow, poorly ventilated, and hard to get into. Unless a boat is used for extensive offshore cruising or racing with a big crew, the space given over to pilot berths might be better utilized for storage, which always seems to be in short supply.

Berths should be a minimum of 6′ 4″ long. A shorter berth may be fine for you, but what about that giant that wants to buy your boat five years from now? If a berth extends under a counter or into a footwell to get necessary length, be sure there is plenty of clearance over your feet, and enough room for you to roll over in the middle of the night.

While the space under the settees is usually given over to storage, this part of the modern bilge-less cruiser/racer is easily contaminated by bilgewater when the boat heels. The space under the settees is far better suited for tankage, keeping the heavy weights of water and fuel in the center of the boat where they will have the least effect on trim and pitching moment.

Deeply tufted settee cushions are popular items supposed to convey the idea that your settees are really expensive sofas fit for the living room of your house. Remember that if you have to use the settee for sleeping as well as seating, that elegant tufted upholstery is going to make an awfully lumpy mattress. Smooth cushions of dense polyfoam may not look as elegant but they're a lot more comfortable when the time comes to lay down your weary head.

Cabin Tables

On boats under about 35′, space is frequently so limited that the main cabin table must fold out of the way when not in use. Most foldup tables eliminate a good chunk of bulkhead space. Although many such tables have storage built in behind them on the bulkhead, this is relatively impractical storage, as the table must be folded down—usually no mean trick underway—to retrieve whatever is stowed behind.

The primary weaknesses of foldup cabin tables are poor latches for securing the table in the up position, and inadequate lateral support of the table in use. We have rarely seen a foldup cabin table that was strongly enough supported for use when sailing offshore. Offshore, having no table is frequently better than having a table that can't be leaned on and must be folded up after dinner.

Adequate securing is also a problem with fixed cabin tables. Any table which will be used underway should be capable of absorbing the force of a crewmember falling against it. The crewmember may break, but the table should survive.

Check the drop leaves of the cabin table—whether it's fixed or folding—to make sure they'll bear the weight of several crewmembers who forget their at-home table manners and put their elbows on the table. A minimum of two square feet of table area is required for each person at the table. This should include an absolute minimum of 15″ of table length per setting. Even this will be crowded if there isn't elbow room at each end of the table.

Dinette arrangements have been in vogue from time to time, and have their own advantages and disadvantages. A dinette moves people out of the traffic flow, so that if someone has to use the head in the middle of dinner, major maneuvers are not necessary. Frequently, a U-shaped dinette replaces the settee and pilot berth on one side of the boat. Make sure that the fore and aft portion of the dinette is long enough to convert to a comfortable berth, because you don't want to lose all the berths on one side of the main cabin.

One disadvantage of the dinette is that it usually eliminates symmetrical sleeping arrangements in the main cabin. For racing or cruising, a symmetrical sleeping setup allows optimum weight placement for performance or comfort.

In some boats, a dinette to one side is coupled with a galley opposite. This a poor arrangement in most cases. The cook is placed directly in the traffic flow. Usually,

Most iceboxes hardly need help in turning a 25 pound block of ice into 25 pounds of lukewarm water overnight

the most comfortable eating position offshore is bracing yourself in the leeward settee. If the galley replaces one settee in the cabin, half the time there won't be a leeward bunk to sit in.

The Galley

The basic components of the galley are the means of cooking food, a place to wash dishes, a box to keep things cold, storage areas for food and utensils, water, and counter space. Seemingly simple, but galley design may well be the most difficult part of designing the boat.

The galley frequently gets shortchanged. Berths and settees can't be scaled down, but galleys can, and frequently are in the small boat. Sometimes it seems that the requisite number of berths is put in the boat, and the leftover space, no matter how cramped, becomes the galley.

The modern cruising sailor is rarely content to live off canned stew heated on a single burner stove, and the modern offshore cook has every right to expect comfort, convenience, and function in the cruising boat's galley. Cruising doesn't have to mean camping out, and a great deal of the difference between cruising in comfort and camping out is in how you eat, and how difficult it is for the cook to perform the tasks of cooking and cleaning up.

The galley stove is probably one of the most consistently overpriced, poorly designed, and generally lousy pieces of equipment aboard the typical production boat. The typical two-burner tabletop or recessed alcohol stove makes cooking one of the least pleasant jobs aboard, since it will take two or three times as long to cook anything as your stove at home will.

Most small boat galleys simply do not have enough room for a proper stove. The installation of any gas stove requires so much plumbing and so many expensive components—bottles, bottle storage, solenoids—that they are rarely seen on boats under 35'. If your boat is equipped with one of these alcohol wonders, and there is no possibility for change, be sure that there is some bulkhead space available somewhere to mount a single burner, self-contained stove of the Sea Swing type if you plant to do any cooking underway.

Gas—either CNG or propane—is by far the best fuel for cooking. Propane is both more compact and more readily available, but the cost of installation of a permanent propane system can be staggering. On the few boats under 35' that offer gas stoves as options, the cost generally ranges from $750 to $1000 more than that of the stock two-burner alcohol stove. This assumes, of course, that the galley has room for the stove.

If the stove is to be gimballed, it must be mounted along the fore and aft axis of the boat. There are a few stoves designed for thwartships mounting, but they are custom made, outrageously expensive, and are to be resorted to only when all else fails.

Be sure that the stove is not recessed too far under the side deck of the boat, and be sure that there are not any curtains close enough to the stove to catch fire in the even of an alcohol flareup. A stove recessed under the side deck is likely to overheat the deck.

If at all possible, the stove should not be mounted next to the icebox. Most iceboxes are so poorly insulated that they hardly need help in turning a 25-pound block of ice into 25 pounds of lukewarm water overnight.

The proper design and construction of iceboxes has eluded boatbuilders since day one. An icebox placed under a counter beneath the companionway will heat up from the sun. An icebox that drains into the bilge will stink up the bilge. An icebox with no insulation in the top won't keep ice very well. An icebox with an ungasketed, poorly insulated lid won't, either. An excessively deep icebox is likely to become a swamp if the cook can't reach the bottom to keep it clean.

The lid of any icebox should be large enough to accept a 25-pound block of ice. There should be adjustable internal racks or shelves to keep food out of the bottom of the box.

If the box drains into the bilge, it may be possible to redirect the drain into the manual bilge pump with a Y-valve, allowing you to pump the box daily with little trouble, and keeping your bilges free of icebox grunge.

Sinks on small production boats are rarely deep enough to be really useful. The sink need not be large—a foot square will do—but it should be deep. Nine inches deep is a good round number for sink depth.

If a boat has a pressure water system, there must be a manual backup pump. We once raced to Bermuda on a boat without a manual pump. When the electricity failed, we drank our emergency water, which was stored in jerry jugs. If that had run out, the next step was to disassemble the berths to get at the top of the water tanks. Foot pumps are more efficient than hand pumps, since they allow you to use both hands when washing dishes. Be sure the foot pump isn't located in a position that will make it a hazard to cabin navigation.

Almost no boat has enough counter space or storage space in the galley. These are the first things to go in smaller boats. A miniature drop leaf table can be fitted to almost any galley counterfront to create additional work space.

Creating extra storage space may be more difficult. It may be possible to add bulkhead-mounted racks or storage compartments, or even build in shelves or bins in dead spaces, but making good, useful storage space in the galley is likely to be quite a task.

It is almost impossible to visualize how a galley will work until you try it out. The sink may be tucked so far under the bridgedeck that washing dishes is impossible. You may have to lean over a hot stove to get to the food storage. A short person may not be able to reach the bottom of bins or the back of cabinets. Drawers may not latch properly. There may be no kick space under the counters, making it difficult to get close enough to anything in the galley. The galley pump location may make it impossible for a lefthanded person to do the dishes.

When trying out a boat, the cook should walk through every stage of preparing a meal, from thinking out where things are to be stored, seeing if they can be reached, thinking about storage of pots and pans, cutting up and putting together food, to cooking and cleaning up. If the galley doesn't present obstacles to any of these activities, wonderful. If it does, how difficult will it be to modify, or how much inconvenience are you willing to live with?

A basic question to consider is how much the galley will really be used. For daysailing or weekending, inconvenience and lack of space may be minor considerations. If, however, you want to cruise for weeks at a time, a fully functional galley is a must.

If the nav station is located next to the companionway, make sure that it will be possible to rig a drip curtain

Ventilation

The interiors of many production boats are characterized by astonishingly poor ventilation. Opening ports are more expensive than fixed ports, but they can aid immensely to the livability of any boat.

Some form of opening hatch over the main cabin is highly desirable. A medium sized aluminum frame hatch is ideal for this. A hatch that is reversible—one that can be modified to open either fore or aft—is the best type for ventilation. In good weather the forward opening position is used. Any breeze at all will force a tremendous volume of air through the boat. In foul weather, the aft edge of the hatch can be lifted. If side curtains or a miniature dodger are fitted over the hatch, it can be left open in any weather at anchor, and almost any weather when sailing.

If the boat doesn't come with a ventilation hatch, is there room to install one forward of the companionway? Even a small hatch adds significantly to ventilation.

Dorade vents placed at the aft end of the main cabin will also be a great help. Be sure, however, that these do not preclude the installation of a companionway dodger. Dorades placed at the forward end of the main cabin do almost nothing for the ventilation of that cabin.

A main companionway dodger both protects those in the cockpit and is a real boon to belowdecks comfort. By sheltering the companionway, it allows the drop boards to be left out and the hatch left open in almost any weather. Galley smells and heat will be largely eliminated, the cook will not be isolated from cockpit activity, and the main cabin will be infinitely cooler and more comfortable.

The Navigation Station

For years, navigators on boats up to 50' struggled along using whatever surface was available for their tasks. The top of the icebox, the main cabin table, or a piece of plywood held in your lap comprised the nav station, and you were always being interrupted by crewmembers involved in the mundane tasks of cooking, eating, and sleeping.

With the proliferation of low-priced electronics, an incredible growth in interest in cruising, and the big boat feeling of having a separate office for the navigator, the nav station has emerged as an important part of the interior of any boat over 30'. However, a nav station that looks like a workplace for the navigator and one that really works are frequently two different items.

Unless a boat is to be used for serious cruising or racing, a nav station may be a luxury that wastes space. If your navigation equipment consists of a VHF radio, tide tables, and a couple of charts, and if your sailing consists of daysailing and weekending in familiar waters, chances are that you can get by with a piece of plywood which can mount out of the way over a berth, a shelf or drawer for hand bearing compass, dividers, parallel rules and pencils, and a few charts folded flat and stored under the berth cushions.

If, however, you plan on cruising for a few weeks at a time far from home, you plan on racing, and you have a loran, repeaters for instrumentation, a sextant, depthsounder, RDF, piles of charts, and tons of navigation books, you're going to need some place to put them.

A standard 13000 series chart folded in quarters is about 18" by 22". Any chart stowage space smaller than that is useless. Charts that have been rolled rather than folded are almost impossible to use, so chart stowage tubes or built-in tubular chart stowage is a waste of space.

To be of any real value, the chart table working surface should be about the size of half a chart. The quartered chart rarely has a compass rose in the right place for plotting, and you usually discover that where you are is in one quarter, and where you want to go is in another when the time comes to lay a course.

If the chart table has fiddles, they should be removable to allow you to drape that chart over the edge. Fiddles are useful for keeping pencils on the table, keeping your dividers out of the bilge, and providing a totally insecure handhold for crewmembers to break off when walking past the nav station.

Ideally, there should be a drawer for the two dozen pencils, five erasers, four sets of dividers, two sets of parallel rules, stopwatches, compasses, spare fuses for the electronics, and other assorted small stuff that ends up lost under the charts in the chart table. Ideally, the inside of the chart table would be used only for chart storage. Frankly, we haven't seen too many ideal nav stations.

Mounting of instruments also presents a problem. Usually, you end up sacrificing what little shelf space is available to mount radios and loran, then try to figure out where to put your books and sextant. We have never seen a production sailboat with proper sextant stowage, but being realistic about it, that's not really a consideration for 99 sailors out of 100.

Whether a chart table should be flat or angled is purely a matter of personal preference. If the chart table must serve multiple functions—serve as space for food preparation, or a typing table—it's going to have to be flat.

On boats under 40', the seat for the chart table is almost inevitably the head of a quarterberth. This is fine as long as the boat is upright, but the minute it starts to heel you're either sliding onto the cabin sole or sliding into your electronics—tough on your body, and tough on the instruments. As odd as it may sound, some sort of seat belt may be the answer.

Nav stations are usually located next to the companionway, opposite the galley. While this is good for communicating with the cockpit, it is also vulnerable to weather. In bad weather, off-watch crewmembers also have the habit of hanging around the nav station, dripping on your charts. If the nav station is located next to the companionway, make sure that it will be possible to rig a drip curtain—a triangular piece of dacron secured to the side of the hatch and the main bulkhead will usually do—to keep the nav station, instruments, switch panel, and navigator dry. Charts turn to pulp, electronics turn to green grunge, and navigators get cranky when they're wet. Rule number one is to keep the nav station dry.

Quarterberths

The quarterberth is frequently the best berth in the boat. If poorly designed, however, it can be cramped, claustrophobic, and wet.

It is becoming increasingly popular to install opening ports in the cockpit footwell to provide light and ventilation for quarterberths. Even if the builder doesn't provide them, they can usually be installed by the owner. They're an excellent idea.

A surprising number of quarterberths lack adequate

headroom and footroom. If you can't sit up in the berth, it's no good for reading. If there isn't enough clearance for your feet, you won't be able to turn over comfortably. Double quarterberths that extend under the cockpit are the worst offenders. The person stuck in the inboard berth position of a double berth frequently stares up up at the cockpit sole a few inches above his or her face. Double quarterberths are a great innovation, but be sure they have enough room for real comfort.

There should be a light at the head of each quarterberth for reading, and there should be a shelf for the stowage of small items. Make sure there is room to install nets, zip-up bulkhead bags, or shelves for the storage of clothes.

The quarterberth should be separated from the space under the cockpit. This can be done with a plywood bulkhead—provided it's removable to get at the engine for service—or by heavy canvas panels with zip-out panels for engine access.

Like the nav station, the quarterberth should be kept dry. Once again, a dacron curtain can be installed for real protection. Make sure it's easily removable to help air circulation in hot weather.

As obvious as it may sound, make sure that the positioning of the quarterberth gives some main cabin berths on both sides of the boat. While perfect symmetry—two berths to starboard and two to port, for example—is not necessary, a surprising number of boats have all the good sleeping places on one side of the boat, and nothing on the other. By definition, your boat will probably be on the wrong tack for sleeping comfortably half the time at sea. Having all the berths on one side also gives the boat an unseamanlike list at anchor.

Odds and Ends
Unvarnished solid teak makes the best of all possible cabin soles. The so-called teak and holly soles on most boats are ½" plywood with microscopically thin teak veneer. These must be kept varnished to keep the

veneer from disappearing, and a varnished cabin sole is an iceskating rink when it's wet. Putting non-skid compound in your varnish isn't really a good solution, since it makes the cabin sole hard to clean up. Non-skid fiberglass is equally hard to clean.

Carpet is fine when you're not sailing, but usually manages to slide around when you're walking on it with the boat heeled over.

Either overhead handrails or vertical posts should be provided to give you something to grab onto when moving around below underway. Getting thrown around the inside of the boat is no fun. Bruises will also be minimized if all corners are rounded off. Sharp corners have no place on a boat, on deck or below.

Decor is a matter of taste. We prefer light, airy main cabins to those resembling the inside of a teak box. A host of other woods—butternut, ash, and cedar, for example—cost less, weigh less, and are lighter in color than teak. They are likely to require more upkeep, and the initial cost of varnishing or sealing these woods is likely to bring the cost to the builder up to the cost of teak plywood. No wood other than teak is likely to maintain good appearance without fairly extensive finishing, although varnish on interior surfaces should last indefinitely.

A boat's main cabin should be comfortable, functional, and pleasing to the eye. Avoid oddball interior layouts or you may have a white elephant on your hands when the time comes to sell. Don't be afraid to personalize the interior, but realize the risks you run from over-customization. Will the next person really like your zebra-striped cushions and baby blue bulkheads?

Spend plenty of time in the main cabin of any boat you're considering buying. Think of how comfortable it will be with six people below on a hot, rainy day. Think of how functional it will be on a two-day beat to windward offshore. Think of how you'll cook, sleep, eat, navigate, and entertain. Thinking, and lots of it, is a major input into the boatbuying process.

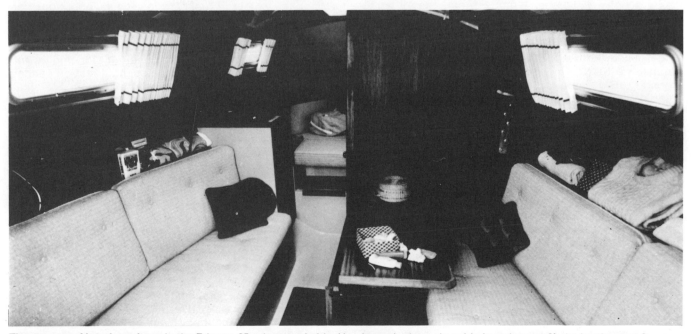

The amount of interior volume in the Ericson 25+ is remarkable. Headroom in the main cabin is an honest 6', the berths seat 6 in comfort, and the folding teak table is one of the sturdiest tables of this type that we have seen. It has enough teak to give a well finished appearance without turning the interior into a cave

Eight

The Powerplant

Whether inboard or outboard, the most expensive mechanical installation in any cruising boat is likely to be the engine. A few years ago, relatively few boats under 28' were equipped with inboard engines. In the first place, there were relatively few small inboards available. One and two cylinder gasoline engines had a terrible reputation. The workhorse Atomic Four was about as small and light as reliable engines came, and it was far more than enough power for almost any boat under 32'.

Since the mid 1970's, however, a flood of compact, lightweight diesels has appeared on the marine market. It is now feasible to equip even the smallest cruising boat with inboard power.

Outboards continue to be the primary mechanical power on boats under 25'. There have been relatively few innovations in outboard design in many years, although it is now possible to have outboard power equipped with electric starters and an alternator to provide electrical power for the small boat.

Inboard engines

The inboard gasoline engine has virtually disappeared from the new boat market. This is a startling change in the boatbuilding industry in the last ten years. In 1972, the overwhelming majority of inboard powered, American-built production boats under 40 feet had gasoline engines. The safety and efficiency of diesels, and the less stringent—hence less expensive—engine compartment ventilation requirements for diesel engines, have combined with the proliferation of small diesels to virtually eliminate the gas engine as auxiliary power in new boats. The real revolution has been the development of small diesels. There has been, unfortunately, no revolution in price. The modern small diesel may be compact in size and light in weight, but it is heavy in price. The Yanmar 1GM, at 6.5 horsepower and 154 pounds is about as small as inboards come, and costs a hefty $2,500. Its larger brother, the 19 horsepower, 3 cylinder 3GM, retails for about $3,850.

Small diesels are far more costly per horsepower than larger engines. In addition, the cost of a diesel engine in a 25-footer may be disproportionately high relative to the total cost of the boat. For example, the Yanmar 1GM installed in a 25-footer may represent almost ten percent of the total price of the boat. The Yanmar 3GM could be installed in a boat up to about 35 feet, and represent perhaps five to seven percent of the price of the larger boat.

The auxiliary components of an inboard engine installation are largely the same in cost whether the boat is a 25-footer or a 35-footer. Props, shafts, and tanks will be smaller in the small boat, but the cost—including both materials and installation—will not be significantly different. For example, an 11" Martec prop retails for about $300, while a 16" prop of the same style sells for just over $400.

Given that the new cruising boat you will buy will be equipped with a diesel inboard, what characterizes a good engine installation?

Fuel tank

The fuel tank is a major part of the power train. Diesel tanks may be made of aluminum, stainless steel, Monel, black iron, or fiberglass. Integral fiberglass tanks, which enjoyed brief popularity, are not a good idea, as they are sometimes slightly permeable to diesel oil. A fiberglass fuel tank should be a separate component, which can be removed from the hull without major disassembly—the same goes for other tanks—in the event of problems.

Black iron tanks are sometimes seen in Far Eastern boats, rarely on American boats. Their life span is likely to be less than stainless steel or aluminum.

Your new boat is most likely to have either stainless steel or aluminum fuel tanks. Monel is rare because of the cost, and it really has no advantage over stainless steel. Beware of an older boat that has been repowered with diesel while retaining the copper fuel tank that was used with the gasoline engine. Diesel oil and copper do not make a good long-term partnership.

The fuel capacity required depends on the size of the engine and the use to which the boat will be put. The small modern diesel is incredibly fuel efficient. One and two cylinder engines may burn from about a quarter gallon of fuel an hour to less than a half gallon. For coastal cruising, a range of about 125 miles under power is adequate. Assume that a 25-footer will cruise at 4½ knots, a 30-footer at five knots, and a 35-footer at 5½ knots. Cruising 125 miles should therefore take from 23 to 27 hours. A 30-footer powered by a two cylinder diesel of about 13 horsepower should therefore find a capacity of 15 gallons more than adequate for most purposes.

In the typical sailboat, the engine is mounted at the aft end of the main cabin, under the bridgedeck. The fuel tank is likely to be located under the cockpit, aft of the engine. If the tank is small—under 20 gallons—the location of the tank aft is unlikely to affect dramatically the boat's trim. Careful consideration must be given to the location of larger fuel tanks to minimize trim changes. Tanks located in the ends of the boat have much greater effect on trim than tanks mounted midships, and are thus to be avoided as much as possible. When the weight of fuel carried exceeds about one percent of the boat's displacement it's time to start thinking about the optimum placement of weight.

Fuel tanks must be securely mounted. They should be incapable of shifting in any conditions, including full knockdown or rollover. The tank should rest on padded chocks which are securely glassed to the hull. Stainless steel bands are often used to hold the tank down in its chocks. These bands should be padded—dense Neoprene does a good job—wherever they bear against the tank, to prevent damage.

There should be a fuel shutoff valve at or near the tank which is accessible without major disassembly of the boat's interior. There should be water and particle filters in the fuel delivery line near the engine. It is imperative that these filters be readily accessible for draining and element changing.

If some form of dipstick is to be used to check the fuel level, there must be a straight run from the fuel fill to the bottom of the fuel tank. If this isn't possible, a fuel gauge should be provided.

Most fuel tank installations use a non-metallic filler pipe and a metal deck plate. A copper jumper wire or strap should be clamped to both the metal nipple of the deck fitting and the metal neck of the filler pipe at the tank. American Boat and Yacht Council safety standards do not distinguish between gasoline and diesel fuel tank installation in requiring a metallic jumper in the fuel fill system. The fuel fill, incidentally, should be located on the main deck, rather than in the cockpit sole, to prevent spilled fuel from turning the cockpit into a skating rink. The cap should be marked "fuel" or "diesel."

Drip pans
There should be a drip pan under the engine. This may be integral with the engine bed moldings, or it may be a separate fabrication of stainless steel or fiberglass. The pan must be deep enough to contain a fair amount of oil with the boat heeled over. The deepest part of the pan must be accessible for cleaning. Leaving out a drip pan is an open invitation to dirty bilges. Even if the engine is absolutely tight—and few are—it is almost impossible to change oil and filters without spilling something.

Shaft installations
The modern lightweight diesel has caused some problems in shaft installation. The high compression of diesels usually means that the engines vibrate more than a comparable gasoline engine. To prevent transmitting this vibration to the hull, diesels are invariably equipped with flexible engine mounts. This is great for reducing hull resonance, but it can be tough on the drive shaft components if proper care is not taken.

If the boat is a modern fin keel type, the shaft system usually consists of prop, shaft, an external strut fitted with a cutless bearing, a shaft log/stuffing box, and the transmission/shaft coupling. The shaft is held fairly rigidly by the strut and cutless bearing. In most installations, the strut is far enough away from the engine that the shaft vibration inherent in a flex-mounted engine will only cause accelerated wear of the cutless bearing.

However, problems can develop if the boat is not equipped with a flexible shaft log. A flexible shaft log is easily recognized by the short piece of heavy rubber hose connecting the neck of the shaft log to the stuffing box just inside the hull. A flex-mounted diesel whose shaft exits the hull through a non-flexible shaft log is more likely to have stuffing box leaks, excessive shaft wear, leaking transmission seals, or a shaft that simply won't stay seated in the shaft coupling. This is particularly true where the distance from the stuffing box to the engine is short.

A traditional full keel auxiliary with the shaft exiting through the rudder post may be even more likely to have shaft problems with a flex-mounted engine. Part of the shaft vibration caused by the engine can be absorbed by the use of a flexible shaft coupling such as the Drivesaver (see PS, June 15, 1982).

The Engine
The proliferation of small diesels means that boatbuilders have a tremendous variety to choose from when deciding which powerplant to put in a particular boat. This can cause headaches for the owner.

When the Atomic Four was just about the only small boat engine, you could always count on any mechanic at any good yard being able to service your engine. If, however, you have a 13 to 18 horsepower diesel in your 32 footer, you may have a Yanmar, a Volvo, a Renault, or a Universal. Or you might have a Beacon-Sole, a Westerbeke, or a Sabb. In any case, the chances of a mechanic having the parts in stock are greatly reduced by the sheer variety of engines available. Check with a good local mechanic to see what engines he likes or

dislikes, services or doesn't service, and can get parts for before buying a boat. Remember that the engine manufacturer or importer—not the boatbuilder—is responsible for warranty service on the engine.

Aside from brand proliferation and model confusion, you must decide how much power you really need. Unlike the situation 10 years ago, when the Atomic Four was shoehorned into every small boat, today's production auxiliaries tend to be slightly underpowered. In the current competitive market, a builder may be able to save $500 or more by putting in a 13 horsepower engine rather than a 19 horsepower engine, leaving your $50,000 boat a little underpowered for punching into a head sea or a strong current.

Rules of thumb regarding necessary horsepower are risky at best, since they ignore differences in wetted surface, hull shape, and windage. Nevertheless, for the modern cruiser/racer, it is not completely out of line to say that for adequate power in anything other than a flat calm, about 1½ horsepower—at the engine's normal cruising rpm—per thousand pounds of displacement is necessary. Some purists may scream that this is far too much power, but we'd rather be overpowered that underpowered any day.

Instruments
Instrument panels vary dramatically in quality. No instrument panel is truly weatherproof, so some form of protection should be provided. A panel recessed into the bridgedeck with either a lifting clear plastic cover or a fixed shield with a cutout to accept the ignition key will do nicely. If a fixed cover is utilized, it should be scuppered to allow incidental spray to drain.

The panel should be located within view of the helmsman, and should not be so close to the bottom of the cockpit that it can be easily washed out.

At a minimum, the panel should include a tachometer plus oil pressure and water temperature warning lights and audible alarms. A proper panel will also include oil pressure and water temperature gauges, plus an ammeter to monitor alternator output. A engine hour meter is also handy for determining service intervals.

Engine Controls
Throttle and shift controls can be either of the single lever or dual lever type. There seems to be little difference in reliability or ease of use of either system.

In a wonderful step backwards, most controls are now made of die-cast zinc alloy, which invariably crumbles away after a few years of use in salt water. The aluminum housings used in some controls fare little better. So much for progress. Needless to say the engine controls should be so mounted that the helmsman can reach them without major contortions. This may be a problem in some boats that have optional wheel steering without an optional location for the engine controls.

The Engine Box
Access to the engine is a critical consideration. If you can't get to the engine to tighten belts, change oil and filters, and check the oil level, your engine's going to get neglected. If the engine box design lets water pour onto the engine when the main hatch is open, your engine will turn into an unsightly pile of rust.

If there's no soundproofing in the engine box, the boat will resonate like a drum. To be reasonably effec-

An exhaust system is hard to intuitively evaluate; if you have doubts about the exhaust installation, consult a good mechanic

---

tive the soundproofing should thoroughly line the engine compartment. The material used should be a fire resistant foil/foam sandwich.

Mechanical ventilation of the engine compartment is not required with diesel engines. Nevertheless, it must be possible for adequate fresh air to reach the engine for best performance. A cowl vent with a hose leading near the air intake of the engine is a reasonable ventilation arrangement, as long as there is a reasonable air flow through the vent.

Plumbing and Exhaust Systems
The raw water intake for engine cooling should be equipped with a seacock. The intake line should be double clamped at both the seacock and the water pump. An inline strainer—which must be readily accessible for cleaning—is far more efficient than an external strainer on the intake. An external strainer clogs easily with no simple means of cleaning, and creates unnecessary drag.

Exhaust systems are a wonderful bugaboo. Waterlift type exhausts are infinitely cheaper and easier to install than water jacketed exhausts. Care is required, however, to be sure that water cannot siphon back into the engine. The waterlift should be close to the engine. The top of the muffler should be well below manifold level. If the cooling water is injected into the exhaust near or below the waterline, the cooling water must be looped well above the waterline and must include a siphon break. The exhaust line itself must loop well above the waterline, but not so high as to exceed the lifting capacity of the engine.

Long exhaust runs should be avoided, as they can hold large amounts of water. Even if the exhaust discharge is well above the waterline when the boat is at rest, it may be underwater when the boat heels or squats underway. For this reason, a gate valve in the exhaust line is a good feature. It can be placed anywhere in the exhaust line that provides good access, but it requires a conscious act of will to remember to open and shut the valve. Failure to open a shut exhaust valve results in expensive lessons in memory enhancement.

An exhaust system is a hard component to intuitively evaluate. Its operation is subject to mechanical and fluid laws which may not be immediately obvious. If you doubt the exhaust system installation, consult a good mechanic.

A name brand boat is not necessarily protection against a lousy exhaust system. C&C Yachts, normally extremely thorough in its systems planning, produced what may be one of the worst exhaust systems ever in early hulls of the now-defunct Landfall 42. Our short-lived career as a charter captain nearly came to an ignominious conclusion when one of these boats proceeded to fill its engine with water after a night of pitching on the anchor. Removing the injectors and turning over the beast by hand enabled the engine to be freed of water. The deep scars on our hands from hand turning an engine not designed for hand cranking have left us with a permanent suspicion of all exhaust systems.

Props
If efficiency under power is the only consideration, a fixed-blade prop is the proper answer. Since we're talking about sailboats, however, other considerations come into play: specifically, how does the propeller installation affect the boat's performance under sail?

In a traditional long keel boat with the prop in an aperture in the rudder post, a two-bladed fixed prop is a reasonable answer. A three-bladed prop is more of a headache. A three-bladed prop is impossible to hide behind the boat's deadwood to reduce drag under sail. A three-bladed feathering prop—no production boat we're aware of comes with this—is the only answer to this problem.

If the boat has a two-bladed prop in aperture, is it possible to reach the shaft behind the engine to line up the blades behind the deadwood? For passagemaking or racing, this exercise is well worth the effort. An installation which doesn't allow you to line up the prop will always be a compromise.

With an exposed shaft, strut, and prop installation, the choices are more complex. Even a two-bladed prop mounted in an exposed location adds considerable drag under sail. According to PHRF, a two-bladed fixed prop in an exposed installation is six seconds a mile slower than a folding prop in the same installation. If you're cruising, this may not seem like much, but remember that the drag is probably even greater in light air.

A fixed prop in an exposed location is also much more susceptible to picking up floating objects, such as lobster pot lines. A folding prop in this type of installation has the advantage of being less prone to damage from debris, as well as reducing drag under sail.

Not that folding props have no disadvantages. Folding props are frequently recalcitrant when operating in reverse, and they may be less smooth under power, particularly as the pivot pins wear over time. They are also expensive to replace, although normally only the blades should require replacement rather than the entire prop.

A feathering prop may be used in an exposed installation, although it may be more expensive than a folding prop, and can still catch lines like a solid prop.

Reducing prop drag may seem like an unnecessary refinement for the cruising boat, but nothing could be further from the truth. The cruising boat will usually carry less canvas than the racer. She will also not be driven as hard, and probably won't have as good a bottom. Don't further handicap her with a slow prop installation.

Outboards
Outboard engines are mediocre auxiliaries at best for a cruising sailboat. They are fuel inefficient, noisy, awkward to stow, heavy, dirty, and have the bad habit of failing to start just when you need them. The worst experiences of our sailing life—bar none—have been associated with the use of outboards as auxiliaries.

A motor well may seem like the logical solution to using an outboard. However, an outboard mounted in a well is incredible drag under sail. Not only do you have the drag of the entire lower unit of the engine, you have the considerable drag of the well opening itself. The advantages of the well are that it provides permanent storage for the engine and tanks, and shifts the engine far enough forward to keep the prop in the water in most conditions.

A transom mounted engine bracket has its own set of problems. The engine leg must be long enough to reach the water even with the boat pitching. How many small outboards have you seen with the prop racing away in the air as someone went on the foredeck to drop a sail or pick up the mooring? How good do you think this is for the engine?

Unless the engine has an integral tank, you have to figure out where the tank will be carried when operating the boat under power. No outboard with an integral tank has enough capacity to be used as a serious cruising auxiliary, and few things are more dangerous than trying to refill an integral tank on a hot engine.

Admittedly, the equipping of outboards designed for use as auxiliaries with such features as electric starting and alternators for battery charging has removed some of the onus from the use of outboards, but they remain a serious compromise, to be used only in boats that are absolutely too small for inboards, or which simply weren't designed for the complexity of an inboard installation. Simple solution to the small boat auxiliary problem? Yes, but one that can come with big headaches. The decision of whether to use an outboard or dispense with auxiliary power altogether is not simple.

Conclusions
The biggest revolution in auxiliary power for the small

cruising sailboat in the last ten years has been the development of the small diesel engine. Inboard engine installations, however, are relatively complex and expensive, adding greatly to the cost of the small cruising sailboat. Used boat prices for inboard-equipped small cruisers indicate that much of the extra initial cost over an outboard-equipped boat is returned at the time of resale.

Our discussions with boat owners indicate that an amazing percentage of the problems they report with their boats have to do with engine installations. Sometimes it's the engine itself, but just as frequently it's a problem either with the components of the installation, or its actual mechanics.

An inboard is not something that can be neglected and then be expected to perform without hesitation at the push of a button. Perhaps more than any other component of the cruising sailboat, the engine needs loving attention, not only at the time of its installation, but through its life. That's the way you protect your investment, and that's the way the engine can protect you when you really need it.

A Simple Solution to an Exhausting Problem

Exhaust systems have always been the Achilles' heel of inboard engine installations in sailboats. Traditional copper waterjacketed exhaust systems are heavy, expensive to fabricate, must be designed to fit each engine installation, and are subject to hard-to-detect pinhole leaks that can reduce exhaust cooling efficiency and cause damage to your engine. In addition, most waterjacket systems have no exhaust muffling effect, so that your boat sounds like a tired tractor warming up.

The simple, efficient waterlift exhaust system has all but replaced copper jacketed systems in both custom and production boats, in much the same way that the diesel engine has replaced the gasoline engine. The modern waterlift system is just about everything the traditional exhaust system is not: lightweight, inexpensive, and flexible in installation. Unfortunately, tolerances in the design and installation of waterlift systems are small. There are rules that must be followed and common sense precautions that must be taken if a trouble-free exhaust system is to be the result. Failure to follow the rules can give you an expensive engine full of water.

The waterlift is simply an enclosed pot with inlet and discharge hoses. Engine cooling water is injected into the exhaust line near the manifold, gradually filling the pot. Exhaust pressure builds in the pot as it is filled with cooling water until the pressure in the pot is sufficient to blow water and exhaust gases out the discharge port. Since the exhaust gases do not travel straight from the manifold to the outside of the boat, much of the engine exhaust noise is absorbed in the waterlift, resulting in a quieter exhaust. The exhaust of boats with waterlift systems is usually easily recognized by the fact that the cooling water does not spurt out the exhaust in a continuous stream unless the engine is running at high speed. Rather, water is discharged in bursts, much like the flow through a diaphragm bilge pump.

A **waterlift muffler** is merely a pot to hold engine cooling water, equipped with exhaust inlets and outlet. The outlet pipe goes almost to the bottom of the muffler.

Waterlift mufflers are a bargain. A plastic waterlift costs about $30 for a unit suitable for a 25 hp engine. A good fiberglass muffler costs about $80, and a stainless steel muffler about the same. Reinforced rubber exhaust costs $3 to $5 per foot. The typical small cruising boat exhaust system, exclusive of the through-hull fitting, should cost only $50 to $125. A custom copper waterjacketed system, by comparison, would probably cost $300 or more, provided you can find someone capable of making it.

A waterlift system is a particularly practical system to use when an older boat is being repowered with a different type of engine. It would be pure luck if the manifold outlets of the old and new engines lined up properly, but removing the old waterjacket system and replacing it with a waterlift should be relatively easy.

Nine

Look up: The Right Rig

Most boatbuyers consider the boat's rig sometime after checking out the cabin sole, the toilet paper holder in the head, and the color of the upholstery in the main cabin. After all, the rig has only to stand up and hold up the sails, which most rigs manage to do with almost monotonous regularity. Fortunately, the typical modern production boat rig is overbuilt, to allow for the vagaries of inexperience, abuse, and just plain neglect that will be visited upon the rig by the typical boatowner.

To some extent most owners fiddle with their boat's rig, tuning, detuning, setting up, cranking down, whatever you want to call it. In any case, the rig is the one part of the boat that the owner "takes care of." You don't mess with your boat's hull-to-deck joint, you may rarely install hardware, but you're out there every year tuning the rig with wrenches and screwdrivers, tightening and loosening shrouds, banging on turnbuckles, kinking the rigging cable, and bending chainplates. Small wonder that most builders are conservative in rig scantlings.

This conservatism has negative as well as positive aspects, however. In the quest for a strong rig, the designer or builder may specify an excessively heavy spar, reducing the boat's stability. Or the rig may be too small or too inefficient to move the boat in less than a gale. Or the boat may be afflicted with unacceptable lee helm or weather helm.

There is no substitute for sailing a boat to evaluate the characteristics of the rig. At the same time, a careful visual examination of the components of the rig can serve the valuable function of eliminating boats with grossly inadequate or inappropriate rigs, as well as giving you clues to the general quality of the boat. Close your eyes to the four burner stove and the teak cabin sole for a while, and give some thought to the part of the boat that makes it go when the wind blows.

What rig is right?
The simplicity of the masthead single-spreader sloop rig makes it the overwhelming choice on production boats under 40' long. Under this size, the divided rig

adds excess windage and cost. The theoretical gains in handling ease from a divided rig are relatively insignificant until the boat exceeds 40'. A couple can easily handle a mainsail of 350 square feet, and headsails of even greater area.

It is ironic that low, inefficient split rigs are usually seen on "traditional" designs or "serious" cruising boats, which frequently have excess wetted surface, inordinately heavy displacement, and poorly faired underwater form—the very characteristics that demand a relatively high performance rig in order to have any performance at all. With modern sail handling equipment such as self-tailing winches there is no reason for a cruising boat to be saddled with an inefficient rig for the sake of ease of handling.

In general, the more performance-oriented the rig, the more suitable the boat is as a cruiser. Obviously, there are limits. It makes no sense to put a bendy triple-spreader rig in a cruising boat that will have one person on watch, but the other extreme—excessively heavy spar, long spreaders, wide shroud base—can compromise performance so severely that the pleasure of cruising can be greatly diminished.

Freestanding rigs have developed beyond the point of novelty, and are constantly being improved. Because the quality and performance of a freestanding rig are tied so closely to the experience of the builder and designer, we would be reluctant to choose a boat with a freestanding rig unless it was built by a company with a lot of experience. Even companies such as Tillotson-Pearson, which has probably built more modern freestanding rigs than anyone else, are constantly gaining experience and modifying their rigs to suit new spar materials and mast designs.

It may well be that freestanding rigs are the wave of the future. The road to the future is likely to be paved with failures as well as successes, however. If you want a freestanding rig, stick with a manufacturer with a long track record.

All current boats with freestanding rigs are cat-rigged, as the freestanding spars currently used could

A welded aluminum masthead fitting integral with the mast tube usually saves weight and reduces windage.

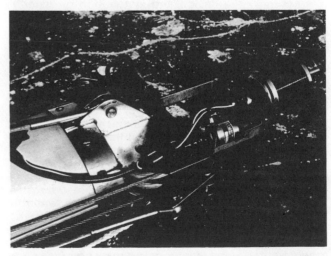

A stainless steel cap is typical of masthead fittings on production sailboats: strong, but often unnecessarily heavy.

It is often desirable, even on a cruising boat, to move the shrouds inboard from the edge of the deck

not support headsail loads. No cat-rigged boat will go upwind with an efficient sloop-rigged boat of the same size and type. The cat-rigged boat with freestanding spars is an off-wind boat, although the most efficient cat rigs will certainly go upwind as well as a lousy sloop rig on a poorly-designed hull.

The cutter or double headsail sloop rig offers advantages in larger single-masted vessels. Headsail area is broken into smaller units. Area forward can quickly be reduced by removing the jib topsail and leaving the staysail in place. There is little reason, however, to go to a double headsail rig on a boat much less than 35', as the headsails on the typical boat smaller than that are hardly big enough to cause a handling problem.

Some cruising boats are available with either a cutter rig or a ketch rig. Since the addition of a mizzen will substantially shift the center of effort of the sail plan, you should try if possible to sail the boat with both rigs before making a decision. At least talk with the owners of both rigs, which should reveal whether any balance problems have emerged from using either rig.

Mast steps and chainplates

The strongest mast won't stand up if the mast step and chainplates aren't strong enough. The majority of production boats under 35' that are available on the US market are equipped with deck-stepped masts (see sidebar below.) Basically, how the mast is supported is far more important than whether the mast is stepped on deck or through to the keel. The boat with a deck-stepped mast should have a support system that

A corroded mast bottom is the inevitable result of a mast step which sits in bilge water.

transfers the majority of the rig's compression load to the hull. This usually takes the form of a compression column under the mast. The column should be strongly tied to both hull and deck. If you can't see how the post is attached, ask for a drawing or a statement from the builder's engineering department. The number of compression columns that come adrift is astounding.

Bulkheads can serve to support a deck-stepped mast

Observations on the Deck-Stepped Mast

Is a deck-stepped mast a seaworthy arrangement for an offshore sailboat?

Like most of the big questions involved in sailing, there is no simple answer. There is little question that a deck-stepped mast complicates the design and function of the rig on a good-sized modern racing boat. However, there is enough empirical evidence in the unarguable form of cruising boats, some fairly large, that have completed hundreds of thousands of miles of trouble-free cruising to say that a properly engineered and assembled deck-stepped mast can go anywhere and do anything that any other rig installation can accomplish.

Support of a deck-stepped mast requires knowledgeable engineering and careful construction, just as a through-deck mast does. It is important that the under-deck compression column—whether it is a timber post, a bulkhead, or a metal pipe—be of adequate section to withstand the compression load on the entire rig. The compression load on a mast, whether it is deck-stepped or through-stepped, may under extreme conditions, roughly reach a force equal to the boat's displacement. In practice some of the compression load of a deck-stepped mast is absorbed by the deck or deckhouse structure. If the compression column is not rigidly attached to the hull at the bottom and the deck at the upper end of the column, or if the column bows or compresses under load, the deck may deflect enough to cause the distortion of interior joinerwork such as doors and drawers.

This type of distortion is not limited to boats with deck-stepped masts. Despite its strength, fiberglass is extremely flexible. Any hull which does not have adequate reinforcement such as longitudinal stringers and structural transverse bulkheads may change shape enough when sailing in a strong breeze to cause joiner-work to shift around on the inside.

If you don't believe that, just go below and listen to your boat talk to you sometime when she's hard pressed upwind in a seaway. Or better yet, look at a well-used ten year old production boat with an average hull layup and the interior furniture joined to the hull with simple fabric fillet bonds. You are likely to find some failure of the secondary bonds—anything bonded to the hull after the original layup—in even the best boats.

Although the ideal deck-stepped mast has its support column centered immediately below the mast, this arrangement is not absolutely essential. If there is much offset between the mast and its support column however, the deck structure in that area must be extremely rigid and strong. The more offset there is between the support column and the mast base the more likely you are to have deflection of the cabin top. With a deckhouse top that is plywood cored in the area of the mast step, such as that of the Southern Cross 31, slight offset between the mast and its support column is not likely to be a problem provided there is a solid connection at both the top and bottom of the compression column.

The step of either a deck-stepped or through-stepped mast must be properly supported and strongly tied to the hull

in small boats, but they, too, must be rigidly tied to the deckhead and the hull. It is rare for a bulkhead to fall at exactly the right place to properly support the mast.

The mast step of a through-stepped mast must also be properly supported and strongly tied to the hull. The hull must be reinforced in the area of the mast step for proper distribution of load, either through increased laminate thickness or a system of floor timbers.

The wide beam of most modern boats requires some serious decision-making about the placement of chainplates. In wooden boat construction, chainplates were either bolted to the outside or the inside of the hull, backed by a frame and sometimes by diagonal strapping attached to frames and floors.

Some fiberglass boats have similar installations, with the chainplates bolted to the inside or outside of a hull that has been locally reinforced. Unfortunately, mounting the chainplates at the edge of the deck in the typical beamy modern boat—whether it's a racing boat or a cruising boat—can measurably compromise the boat's windward ability.

It is therefore often desirable, even on a cruising boat, to move the shrouds inboard from the edge of the deck. The attachment of chainplates can then become a problem. With a boat heeled 35° hard on the wind, shroud loading can approach the displacement of the boat. To withstand this load, the shrouds must be firmly tied to the boat. The most frequent arrangement with inboard shrouds is to use flat bar chainplates which pierce the deck and bolt to a major structural member such as the main bulkhead. This bulkhead must be firmly tied to the

Inboard chainplates improve upwind performance on beamy modern cruiser/racers. The trick is providing a strong and leakproof connection with the hull structure.

hull, obviously, but not quite so obviously, it should be firmly tied to the deck. If it isn't, the deck is likely to shift as the boat works, and the chainplates are likely to leak. Chainplate leaks are just about the most annoying leaks a boat can have, and they are one of the most dif-

---

Because a deck-stepped mast functions as a column with two pin ends rather than the pin end and fixed end column of a keel-stepped mast wedged at deck level, a heavier spar section is required to achieve stiffness in a deck-stepped mast equal to that of the keel-stepped mast. The heavier mast section will to some extent reduce a boat's stability by putting more weight aloft. Although it would be unusual for righting moment to be substantially affected by the heavier mast, there is likely to be a measurable, if not noticeable, difference in the boat's stability.

Perhaps the greatest risk with a deck-stepped mast is that it may lift out of the step when pounding to weather in a seaway if the rig is set up too loosely, the deck has deflected excessively, or the hull has distorted. Shroud tension can be carried a little tighter than would be normal with a through-stepped mast to minimize this risk. If the mast step incorporates some method of securing the mast heel, such as a heavy through bolt, there is little danger of the mast jumping its step—provided the step itself is strongly attached to the deck.

While these complexities would seem to discourage the use of deck-stepped masts the fact is that the majority of American-built sailboats under 32' have their masts stepped on deck. Larger boats can also be rigged in this manner. The German Frers designed Beneteau R/C 42, which is basically a production version of a two tonner racing machine, has a deck-stepped mast. All Cheoy Lee boats—and these include designs by Bill Luders, Alden, Phil Rhodes, and Bob Perry, among others—have their masts stepped on deck.

Dave Pedrick, well-known yacht designer and engineer, designed the new Cheoy Lee 41 with a deck-stepped mast at the builder's request. Pedrick states that the mast design did not present any particular problems, although he did specify a stiffer mast section to compensate for the inherently greater flexibility of the deck-stepped rig, and used double spreaders on a boat where he might have used a single spreader rig with a through-stepped mast.

We have seen a lot of localized deck deflection on production boats with deck-stepped masts. In our experience this has been caused primarily by mediocre fitting or design of the compression column under the mast. We would be wary of any boat with a deck deflected so much as to allow water to puddle in the area of the mast step, a boat with gelcoat cracks radiating from the step, with obvious dislocation of joinerwork belowdecks in the area of the mast, or a boat whose compression strut has fractured its bond to the hull. If you imagine that the compression column is merely an extension of the mast, it becomes apparent that the attachment of the base of that strut to the hull, as well as the reinforcement of the hull in that area, are just as critical as the mast step area in a boat with a through-stepped mast.

While we would not go out of our way to choose a boat with a deck-stepped mast (except for a specialized installation such as a mast tabernacle for cruising the canals of Europe), we would also not turn down a boat just because it had a deck-stepped mast. We've seen it work too well on well-engineered boats.

ficult types of leak to fix, as they often result from a basic flaw in design that can't be remedied with a little bedding compound.

Another popular type of chainplate uses a deck padeye or U-bolt on deck which connects to a tie rod inside the boat. The tie rod must then be strongly connected to the boat's structure. This type of chainplate is generally more leak resistant than the normal flat bar chainplate, but it is more expensive and generally more difficult to install. Navtec pioneered this type of shroud anchorage on racing boats of all sizes.

Cape Dory, Camper and Nicholsons, Hunter, and some other builders use another variation, using a U-bolt or padeye which bolts through the hull-to-deck flange, which must be strongly reinforced to take the kind of loads to which it will be exposed. With this type of chainplate, not only should the hull-to-deck flange be extraordinarily strong, but the joint should be reinforced by bulkheads or hanging knees which are thoroughly tied to hull and deck immediately adjacent to the chainplates.

Backstay and forestay chainplates are relatively straightforward. They should be throughbolted and backed with either extra-large washers or a solid metal backing plate. The stem and transom should be strongly reinforced. This is not usually a problem with the stem, where the layup is likely to be quite thick. A large, flat transom, however, may need to be cored with plywood in order to be stiff enough not to distort badly under load.

Spars

The modern extruded aluminum spar is a wonderful thing: strong, relatively inexpensive, light, and capable of surviving almost complete neglect for long periods of time. It is not, however, immune to neglect, and should be cared for as part of the boat's regular maintenance program. The care of aluminum spars was detailed in the April 15, 1982 issue of PS.

The typical production boat has a mast which consists of an untapered aluminum tube capped with a welded stainless steel masthead fitting. Tangs are likely to be made of formed stainless steel bolted and machine screwed to the tube. While the untapered mast is by far the cheapest way to go, a considerable amount of weight and windage aloft can be saved by tapering the upper part of the mast tube and using a welded aluminum masthead fitting instead of a bolt-on stainless steel masthead fitting. While the few pounds of weight saved may seem insignificant, remember that the effect of weight aloft on the boat's stability is a function of the distance of that weight from the boat's vertical center of gravity. Five pounds saved fifty feet above the center of gravity has the same effect on stability as adding 50 pounds of lead on the bottom of the keel, if the keel is five feet below the vertical center of gravity.

While this may seem unimportant on the cruising boat, remember that most cruising boats have relatively low ballast/displacement ratios in the first place. Weight saved aloft makes a boat stiffer, and a stiffer boat can carry more sail in more wind. Not only does this mean a faster boat, it means a boat that goes longer before reefing or making a headsail change—important considerations for shorthanded cruising.

Saving weight in the mast tube may be even more important if you plan to clutter the masthead with anten-

nas, strobes, radar reflectors, and the like.

Windage aloft can further be reduced by the use of airfoil section spreaders instead of aluminum pipe spreaders or wooden spreaders.

Internal halyards are just about essential on racing boats. For a cruising boat, the savings in windage are offset by the difficulty in reeving new halyards should one of the internal halyards break. If internal halyards are used on a cruising boat, some form of external halyard is necessary as a backup. A properly rigged topping lift can serve as an emergency main halyard. A spare spinnaker halyard can serve as a jib halyard.

The exit boxes for internal halyards must be staggered both vertically and horizontally to prevent weakening of the mast. Even in a mast with properly staggered exit boxes the mast tube usually folds up at an exit box if it goes over the side. There should also be fair leads from the exit boxes to the halyard winches or turning blocks.

While internal running rigging may be a mixed blessing on a mast, it is a definite plus on a boom. The outside of the boom should be as uncluttered as possible. Internal reefing, internal outhaul, and internal topping lift are where it's at. The boom is perhaps the most dangerous piece of gear on any boat. If it hits you a good solid blow in the head when tacking or jibing, you may well be knocked overboard, in which case the question of whether the blow kills you or merely stuns you so that you drown is fairly academic. Nevertheless, a boom festooned with cheek blocks, cleats, and winches is likely to do more damage even in the event of a glancing blow. Keep the boom as clean as possible.

The rows of internal sheaves on this boom accommodate reefs, outhaul, and topping lift, while keeping the outside of the boom free of dangerous protrusions.

A mainsheet traveller is highly desirable whether a boat is used for racing or cruising. Be sure that its mounting does not preclude the use of a cockpit or companionway dodger if the boat is to be used for cruising offshore or in a cool climate.

Although the rig is usually the last thing you look at when buying a boat, you can't really afford to ignore it

---

Likewise, a boom vang is more than a convenience. Not only does it help in sail control, it can stabilize the main boom when reaching or running in a rolling sea. Make sure that there is somewhere at deck level that a vang can be attached. A slotted aluminum toerail is ideal. Welded bails on the bottom of the lifeline stanchions may not be strong enough to take boom vang loads on boats over 30 feet.

Note that no mention has been made of wooden spars. The reason is simple. Unless the boat is truly traditional—an older boat, or a modern boat of traditional design—there is absolutely no reason to have wooden spars. They require more maintenance, they are likely to be heavier, and they are likely to be generally inferior in quality to the typical aluminum spar. Wooden spars on new boats are usually seen on "character" cruising boats imported from the Far East. As a rule, the masts in these boats are unnecessarily heavy in both section and wall thickness, while the booms are inordinately light and flexible.

The wooden spars turned out by the best European and American yards before the advent of aluminum were things of beauty; tapered, streamlined, and no heavier than necessary. The typical modern wooden spar on a production boat is more likely to be a caricature of the sparmaker's art. If you want a spar that looks different from the typical uninspiring grey aluminum spar, paint it with buff-colored polyurethane paint. From a hundred feet away, few people will know the difference. Just don't let the halyards bang on it at the dock or on the mooring. That they'll notice.

Shrouds and stays, turnbuckles and toggles
Wire rope is one of the most reliable structural materials in existence. Weakness in standing rigging usually is the result of improperly applied end fittings or poor leads rather than defective material.

It is rare to see a production boat with undersize rigging. Most builders err in the opposite direction. As long as tangs, toggles, turnbuckles, and chainplates are

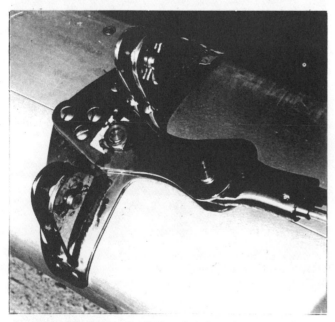

A well-designed spreader fitting and shroud tang on a production cruiser/racer. The welds are electropolished to inhibit corrosion, and the fitting is bedded with polysulfide.

heavy enough to accept the larger pin diameters of slightly oversize rigging, there is no particular disadvantage to an extra margin of safety. Oversize rigging in itself is useless unless it is combined with other overstrength components in the rigging system. It makes no sense to put a 5/8" clevis pin through a 1/8" thick chainplate.

Poor terminal swaging and improper shroud leads are probably the greatest cause of rigging failures. Most swaging in production boatbuilding shops is done with manual equipment in cable sizes up to 5/16". While it is possible to do a good job with this type of equipment, it is also possible to do a perfectly lousy job.

Swage terminal bodies should be perfectly straight. A fitting that has even a slight banana-shaped curve to it should be discarded. Likewise, if the swage fitting body is compressed to an oval shape where the cable exits the body, or if there are pronounced ridges along the body, the fitting is suspect. A properly rotary-swaged fitting has no ridges and is perfectly round in cross section. A rotary-swaged fitting is not necessarily stronger than one done with a revolving die, but the extra peace of mind makes it worthwhile.

Any crack in a swage fitting is totally unacceptable. Surprisingly, a fair amount of new rigging may have cracks in the fittings. You should carefully examine every swage fitting on a new boat for these cracks, which may be miniscule. They are a sign of over swaging: running the fitting through the dies more than once, fatiguing the metal of the fitting.

It is important that all clevis pins match the size of turnbuckles, tangs, toggles, and rigging. If all pins are not compatible, some part of the rig is not properly sized. This doesn't mean that every piece of standing rigging should be the same size. They may be the same size, but headstay, backstay, and lower shrouds may also be heavier than intermediate or upper shrouds to reflect the greater loads carried.

There must be a toggle at the lower end of every piece of standing rigging. This may be integral with the turnbuckle or it may be a separate component, but it must be there. In addition, it's a good idea to have a toggle at the upper end of the headstay to allow for the substantial amount of side loading applied to that piece of wire.

Turnbuckles should be of the open body type, so that the amount of travel left on the adjusting screws can be examined. The turnbuckles should be drilled for cotter pins rather than fitted with locknuts.

Conclusions
Although the rig is usually the last thing you look at when buying a boat, you can't really afford to ignore it. Fortunately, most defective rig components can be replaced if necessary. While there's not much you can do about a poorly designed hull-to-deck joint or a lousy hull layup, it would be possible to upgrade a rig if that were the only thing wrong with the boat.

As long as the basic components of the rig—chainplates and mast step—are adequate, you can change almost anything else. This can be an expensive proposition, however, and should only be considered in extreme cases. As a rule, a boat with a poorly designed or built rig is likely to have other problems as well. The best rig in the world won't turn an overweight slug into an upwind machine. A good rig can, however, improve performance, give you peace of mind, and turn a good boat into a better one.
—N.N.

An Overview of the Small Cruising Yacht

Small boat cruising can range from the rigors of camping out to the amenities of a large yacht. It all depends on the boat you choose.

For generations Europeans have routinely cruised small boats. Traditionally the boats have been spartan, often open craft without iceboxes or coolers, with rudimentary or no galley facilities, cramped berths, smelly oil lamps, oars or sweeps as auxiliary power (or, worse, a Seagull outboard), and primitive rigs. Such cruising demands a crew with a hardy constitution.

As smaller boats developed in the US, the trend was toward far more comfort, space, and convenience. Whereas the European small boat traces its lineage to open dory types, the US small boat is a literal descendant of larger yachts.

Although belied by the number of small boats on the market, the truth is that the "under 30" boat market has taken a fearsome beating for the last several years. First of all, as fuel prices (and car loan rates) have risen, cars have gotten smaller, too small for trailering anything but the smallest and lightest boats. It takes a most intrepid small boat sailor to own a heavy car or small truck so he can take his boat to distant cruising waters. And it is the trailerable boats that dictate the whole structure of small cruising boat design and construction.

Yet the major reasons for the decline of small boats parallel the economies of boatbuilding and marketing in general. Almost any boatbuilder would prefer to build, for instance, one 36' boat a month than four 22 footers. With one large boat he has to carry less inventory, do less advertising, move the boats around less during construction, maintain a smaller shop with fewer employees, and face a less competitive market. In the end he will make the same or (probably) more profit.

Similarly boat dealers would, for their investment and efforts, prefer to sell one bigger boat rather than four smaller ones. On one big boat they can make the same commission plus they make more on the markup they charge for selling and installing the greater amount of optional and add-on equipment demanded by the buyer of the larger boat. As one dealer put it, "The small boat buyer nickles and dimes me to death."

Finally, the buyer of the larger boat is likely to be financially better off than the small boat buyer. He can obtain better financing (most boat finance companies do not want to handle loans for less than $15,000, some don't want to touch loans for less than $25,000 and all are wary of the comparatively high repossession rate among new sailors buying smaller boats). The larger boat buyer also enjoys a considerably lower ratio of annual expenses to the overall value of the boat than does a small boat owner. Only when a boat is small enough and her owner experienced enough to take advantage of the boat's portability and non-professional maintenance does that ratio favor the smaller boat.

While oversimplified, these factors explain why the trend throughout the sailboat market in the last few years has been toward boats built at the more expensive end of the line, not the cheaper, smaller end. Moreover, it helps explain why a number of builders of small boats (eg, Ranger, AMF Paceship, Columbia) have gone out of business, chosen to discontinue one-time hot sellers (Pearson closed its Texas plant building Pearson 26s), or elected to stay in production with successful but outdesigned lines of small boats rather than bring out new models.

What is a small boat?

For practical purposes we define a small cruiser as virtually any boat less than 28' having built-in berths, onboard cooking facilities, a cooler or icebox, auxiliary power (either inboard or outboard), an enclosed cabin, and intended to sustain at least two crew members in a modicum of comfort for a weekend or longer.

We might also add that by our definition the small boat should be capable of handling with safety and reasonable comfort the most severe wind and sea conditions that would ordinarily be encountered in the waters in which she is sailed. This is not meant to imply such boats should be capable of sailing offshore; some are, of course, but most are not, nor would a prudent owner expect them to be able to.

We once heard from the owner of a Venture 22 who proposed telling the world how he had beefed up his craft and modified her to make passages on open water, his point being that anyone could adapt the same or similar boats for the same purpose. His proposal bordered on the downright stupid. The design and structure of the original boat was never intended to take a crew offshore (a point incidentally acknowledged fervently by Venture designer/builder Roger MacGregor when he heard of the idea).

The compromises

Any boat is a compromise; the amount of compromise is usually in an inverse proportion to the size of the boat. The most common compromises of smaller boats may be stated as a series of tradeoffs:

• Cockpit and deck space versus interior space
• Interior space versus well performing, attractive hull shapes
• Shoal draft versus sailing performance
• Size versus legal limitations for trailering
• Low cost versus high quality

The last on this list is, of course, the crux of the issue. All but the builders of the highest priced boats have to make compromises traceable directly to costs. The following is a partial list of the shortcuts builders typically make to keep the costs of small boats low enough to make that boat competitive in a highly competitive marketplace:

• Iron ballast rather than lead
• Minimum amounts of finish work (cabinetry, wood trim, hull lining, coated locker interiors, etc.)
• Simple undersized spars, rigging and sailplans
• Hardware of lesser quality or minimum capability for what it is called on to do (eg, undersized winches), and hardware not included in the price of a boat.

- Outboard auxiliary power
- Fresh water tankage and electrical power left as options
- Space wasted by not being enclosed as lockers or drawers
- Thin berth cushions and cheap fabrics
- Fragile cabin tables, drawers, joinerwork
- Easy-to-damage, difficult-to-repair rubrails and hull-to-deck joints
- Poorly faired keels, hulls, rudders
- Sails of minimum dimensions and mediocre quality

Then there are some more subtle tradeoffs:

- Long lists of optional equipment and features that are routinely standard on larger boats (eg, head, galley facilities, color choices, etc.)
- Mediocre quality design and engineering work
- Poor dealer/builder after-sale service
- Unresolved warranty claims
- High depreciation, low resale value

Obviously these tradeoffs are selective; some small boats on the market involve more compromises than others. More importantly, many boats and their owners are perfectly willing to accept many or even all of them in order to have a boat that fits within their pocketbook, usage, maintenance commitment, or sailing waters. That is why a closer look at the special features of small boats is worthwhile.

PERFORMANCE

Except for the small boat that can reach planing speeds and thus has to be light (all the compromises there would be against livability), small boats are limited to modest speeds. Potential boat speed is essentially a function of waterline length; short boats have a lower maximum speed than long boats. The small boat sailor thus has to accept that limitation on his craft. In addition, if the boat has shallow draft, windward performance will be severely hampered.

Typically many smaller production boats have short rigs and/or small sailplans. Proportionately the sail area of a small boat should be greater than a big boat. However, short rigs must be used when ease of raising and the lowering the mast is touted as a feature or when the boat is apt to be trailered with the mast on deck. Moreover, builders know that many novice sailors look for a stiff boat even at the expense of liveliness.

For these reasons many small production boats have advertised sailplans that show only a jib barely larger than the foretriangle or, if sails are supplied as standard, only a working jib. For performance, though, any small boat owner should consider adding a good sized overlapping genoa jib at the first opportunity. This is especially true if most of the sailing is to be done on a lake or bay where winds are apt to be light.

On the other hand, because it is smaller, the stability of a small boat is proportionately less than that of a larger boat. Small boats are quicker to heel in response to a puff. They are also more readily rolled down by wave action. Thus the nervousness that many inexperienced sailors may feel on smaller boats has some justification.

For these reasons, PS believes that any small boat to be used for cruising should be self-righting from a capsize, have a self-draining cockpit, and have some positive means of preventing water from getting below either during a capsize or from a cockpit that fills with water. These standards apply even to boats being sailed in usually benign waters.

The type of keel (ballast) in small boats is one of the more commonly treated subjects whenever anyone chooses to discuss small boats in writing.

While realizing that generalities can be misleading, we note that the most common instances of shabby engineering and construction among the small boats we have looked at seems to be in movable ballast and centerboards. Too many we looked at are poorly fitted, inefficiently shaped, unfaired, hard to maintain, composed of metals that are subject to corrosion, or just plain operate with more difficulty than they should. To a lesser extent, we find that pivoted swing-up rudders suffer from the same flaws, compounded by cheap pintles and gudgeons.

This observation simply reinforces the stand that the deep fixed keel is the best configuration for all but minimum size (and weight) small boats. If shoal draft is a high priority, we would rather see a centerboard housed in a stub keel than either a stub keel with no board or some form of retractable keel.

All small boats should have a bridgedeck at the companionway. Without reducing seating area, the bridgedeck reduces cockpit volume in the event of flooding and prevents flooding of the cabin. In reviewing many small boats for this article, PS staff members were appalled at the number of small boats with low sills at the companionway. Cockpit flooding from either a pooping wave or knockdown is a real threat in a small boat, which should have positive protection to prevent that water from going below.

While we are on the topic of performance, let's look at auxiliary power. Not many years ago the US-made outboard motor was designed exclusively for high-speed operation. The engine revolutions, gearing, and propeller design was simply too fast to develop the thrust needed to push a heavy boat at the typically slow speeds of a displacement sailboat hull. That is why the Seagull outboard, engineered for such duty, first became popular.

Within the last few years, US outboards have been adapted to the sailboat, turning more slowly, swinging props with more thrust at those speeds, and having longer shafts suited for transom mounting on sailboats, plus development of spring-loaded transom motor mounts that can raise the prop clear of the water. The result is an efficient, convenient, modestly priced auxiliary for boats up to about 26' and 4000 lbs.

Outboards do tend to drink fuel and, on the stern, they are vulnerable to theft, damage and weathering. But they can be easily unshipped for storage and servicing, perhaps their most practical advantage over inboard engines.

While outboard engines developed, so too did small inboard engines such as the 7 hp Vire and single-cylinder diesel engines. Such engines are expensive, not just for the engines themselves but for their installation. Operating costs are lower but not so cheap that you can expect to recover the initial investment in fuel savings.

In an attempt to marry the best features of both the inboard and outboard, Volvo Penta and OMC have both marketed the saildrive, essentially an outboard engine head and drive mounted through the hull. These installations have had a rough time. Their lower units have been subject to corrosion, they are as profligate with fuel as their outboard kinfolk, they offer more drag under sail than a folding prop on a shaft (and, of course, a retracted outboard), and they are expensive. From our observations, and from experiences related to us from readers, we think the saildrive is not yet an alternative worth considering. We wish it were. The concept seems perfect for small boats of the type we are talking about.

Otherwise, PS recommends outboard auxiliary power for any small boat under 24', especially one that is to be trailered. For the larger boat and/or the boat which will spend most of its time in a slip or at a mooring, we think the investment and convenience of an inboard is justified, especially since much of that investment can be recovered at resale.

LIVABILITY

The Cockpit

The interior accommodations of small boats is a superb example of yacht design/marketing schizophrenia — despite the fact that statistics show that small boats are daysailed 90% of the time, 90% of the design and marketing efforts seem directed to interior layout. From our experience with small boats we think the single most critical factor in the livability of such boats should be the cockpit layout. Interior layout should be secondary.

Most cruising sailors want a cockpit they can sit in. In the last couple of years a whole breed of high performance small boats such as the J/24, the Moore 24, the Santa Cruz 27, etc. have featured a cockpit that incorporates the sidedeck. The crew sits at deck level essentially unprotected from the weather. For racing this is definitely the way to go; for cruising it definitely is not.

In general, the cockpit should use the maximum space available, considering that the radius of the tiller swing reduces that area by a substantial amount. The seats should be close enough together to permit bracing the feet on the leeward seat to keep oneself on the windward one. Given the limited space of a cockpit in a small boat, the mainsheet should lead well aft. If the boom is short, it should have mid-boom sheeting over the house roof. Whatever the case, in the confines of such a cockpit, a traveler system in its midst can be at best an inconvenience; at worst, injurous.

The Interior

Although interior accommodations may be used but a fraction of the time, the success of the layout may well determine how often and for how long the boat is cruised. It is a well known axiom that no boat should have more berths than the number of crew members the boat can support with stowage, water capacity, head facilities, food, icebox space, and person to person proximity.

In short, if four persons strikes you as the maximum number with which you would cruise, then a fifth berth is a huge waste of space. Worse, five berths means that all of them may be cramped. Frankly, from our experience cruising on small boats, we'd like to see two first class berths, plus a couple of others in the forepeak where two kids could rest easy.

This means that we do not recommend "dinettes" that convert to a so-called double berth. In every small boat we have seen or sailed with one of these dinettes, the combination made for a poor place to eat and a worse place to sleep. The most practical layouts we have seen have either a pair of settee berths amidships or one or two quarterberths with galley facilities amidships.

Several years ago several small boat builders devised the so-called pop-top cabin roof. A section of the roof in the way of the companionway could be raised to give standing headroom in boats as small as 19'. It was an expensive option, adding as much as 10% to the basic price of the boat. The pop-top also added complexity. For these reasons the innovation has not been popular in the marketplace and most high volume builders discontinued the feature.

Present small boat design and construction seems to call for installing a 5 to 10 gallon fresh water tank, usually of polyethylene. Five gallons is barely adequate for a crew of four for one day unless one is sailing on a lake with water pure enough to use for at least cooking. Better to have tankage for at least one gallon per person per day for three days. Certainly the space is available without recourse to jerry cans. The rubberized fabric and shaped polyethylene tanks on the market seem ideal for small boat installation where space is at a premium and apt to be in odd configurations.

Do you, in a boat where space is critical, want the luxury of a structurally enclosed head? That is a fundamental question every prospective owner of a small boat must ask himself — and his family — before he chooses a boat. The alternative is a grandstand seat usually under a berth and nominally hidden by a curtain. Frankly, we want an enclosed head, but not because, as trimaran designer Jim Brown once noted, we are offended by the sounds from the sandbox. The real reason is because we have never been able to live with the seemingly inevitable odor that wafts up to our noses from under a berth where the head is too often located.

When those titans of industrial technology who make self-contained toilets can finally contrive to make a head that we can live with in the confines of a boat, this may cease to be problem.* Until they do, we'll build walls around the thing.

In addition to enclosing the head, we would install a conventional marine toilet and, if there was any chance we might be cruising in waters where any discharge is prohibited, a holding tank.

CONCLUSION

Small boat cruising can offer a charming pastime for a minimal investment in both money and maintenance. Moreover, with more than 60 production models between 18' and 26' on the market, we cannot imagine a buyer not being able to find a boat to suit his taste, planned use, and pocketbook. Many have been around for a long time (by marine industry standards), so used boats are as prolific as new boats.

Some are, however, better than others — some sail better, some look better, some are built better, some are better investments, and some are more comfortable. And price is not necessarily what marks the difference.

---

* But then we have always thought that the designers of Porta Potties and their variants should be required to install and use their products in their bedrooms until they recognize the fact that that is the way the damned things are typically used aboard boats.

The 'Trailerable' Sailboat: Diverse, Versatile, Hard to Define

While watching a 25 ton, 65' Twelve Meter America's Cup contender being loaded for a transcontinental haul, the thought occurred that even a boat of this size and weight can be "trailered," though it would hardly be thought of as "trailerable."

The project of trailering a smaller boat, say 26' or so, might seem equally formidable to some sailors, but to others it might be deemed almost routine. Many such boats are regularly taken by their owners to off-season backyard storage and on long trips to desirable cruising and racing waters. Some in this size range are even advertised as "trailerable" or "trailer-sailers," although the vast majority are treated just like larger yachts — moored at marinas or moorings, hauled and launched on railways or in Travelifts, and stored in boatyards.

What, then, is a "trailerable" boat? How can we set some reasonable limits defining boats that might be included in a discussion of "trailer-sailers"? The answer: only arbitrarily. And — arbitrarily — we arrived at three criteria:

- Weight: a maximum displacement of 2500 lbs or a "dry" weight of hull, rig, engine, sails, and normal sailing equipment of approximately 2000 lbs.
- Draft: inherent shallow draft or a mechanism for reducing draft to a shallow minimum (a centerboard, drop keel, or daggerboard).

The Weight of Small Boat Gear

Typically the specified weight of small boats includes only the hull, deck, ballast, spars and rigging. It is not likely to include optional equipment (even though factory installed), sails, or any of the gear typically needed to sail the boat. The following is a list of gear common to smaller boats and an approximate weight for each. This "extra" weight should be added to the weight of the boat and trailer to reach a more realistic figure for what a car will have to tow. Note that the list includes no personal gear, no food, and no bilge water.

Item	Weight in Pounds
Anchor (Danforth)	8
Anchor warp and chain	12
4 life jackets (dry)	6
Boarding ladder	7
Sails and bag	20
Distress signals	5
Fenders (2)	6
Stove and fuel	16
Head (portable, empty)	22
Battery (storage)	26
Outboard motor	30
Outboard fuel (6 gal) and tank	40
Water (5 gal) and tank	40
Docklines, spare rope	10
Tools and box	12
Pans, utensils	8
Icebox (portable, empty)	7
Misc. (flashlights, spare fittings, boat cleaning supplies, etc)	10

The 19' to 25' segment of the sailboat market is glutted with builders eager to hold off their competition

---

● Purpose: marketed to appeal to sailors who want a boat they can trailer but with enough amenities to make weekend cruising feasible, all at a modest cost of about $10,000.

Let's look at each of the three more closely. But, first, a look at the realities their builders must face.

Boatbuilding: A Matter of Economy
When you talk of a production boat over 20' and under 2000 lbs fitted with accommodations, you are talking about a light boat: lightly built, lightly ballasted, and lightly loaded. Boats built to a minimum weight usually cost a premium because the builder must use materials and techniques that are costly (see "Light Displacement: Weighing the Trade-offs).

Conversely, builders such as MacGregor, US Yachts, Santana, O'Day, and S 2 as well as a host of other builders of boats in the 20/2000 category have managed to market products at remarkably low costs.

It's not easy; builders of small boats work the hardest. They face the need for volume production and sales, they must appeal to a diversified (and to an extent, unsophisticated) market, and their dealers must work with smaller margins (ie, fewer options with high markups). Worse yet, the market is extremely price sensitive.

These restrictions have a number of ramifications. Shipping and marketing costs, as a percentage of the cost of each boat, are inversely proportional to the size of the boat. Small boat builders need plants near their market. Advertising, when it is done at all, is often in local publications in conjunction with dealers (eg, Mac-Gregor's national advertising in marine publications consists of classified ads; Catalina does not advertise in national publications).

Similarly the builders of smaller boats built to rigid cost limits must shop for hardware bargains (or make their own if volume warrants). The production line must be as "automated" as possible and they must use "prefabricated" fiberglass components such as hull liners, and drop-in cabinetry. The boats must be as uniform as possible: precise amounts of materials, efficient systems of jigging for installing components and mounting hardware, single color schemes and decors, and few if any factory-installed options. Typically joints are riveted, not bolted.

Then, to hold off the competition, builders must be forever ready to offer inducements or extras at little or no additional cost. For instance, many boats of this type are now routinely offered with a trailer as part of the "base price"; a few years ago all began to include sails.

The result has been an overcrowded marketplace filled with boats 19' to 25' with sails, trailers, and a variety of items such as galley units, heads, lifelines, electrical systems, and some required "sailaway" equipment, all offered as "standard." Dealers even throw in outboard motors at cost.

This segment of the market is glutted with builders. Many are small with but a couple of boats in their line. Builders come and builders go, and a few such as Mac-Gregor have done well for a long time. With this turnover it is no wonder that some of the tooling for boats of this size has seen a number of reincarnations by different builders under different names. Nor is it any wonder that some small boats have been around for generations with essentially no changes. Note the longevity (yea, seeming immortality) of such boats as the small Catalinas, the whole MacGregor/Venture line, the small Tan-

zers, and the Balboa line, to name a few.

What Does Weight Mean?
The weight of a boat is a factor common to all its equations, and it must be such that they can all balance.

Because a boat's weight — in materials, labor, and hardware — translates itself directly into costs and because weight is such a concern to buyers who plan to trailer, light weight is vital to both construction and marketing.

As a performance factor, the weight of a boat works in subtle, often contradictory ways. Ballast affects stability and hence safety and owner confidence. The mass market for small boats requires a boat that will not heel so much that it scares those who sail it, many of whom are new to sailing or who have moved up from capsizable small daysailers.

When estimating the weight of a boat, it is important that you define what is included in the figures you use. It is unlikely that the weight of the boat, loaded and ready to go, will be even close to published figures, even though builders will typically publish fairly accurate figures for boats of this size and type. They are conscious that a road accident resulting from trailering a heavier-than-advertised boat could result in a costly lawsuit against the builder who published those figures.

Be alert to the difference between the figures for "hull weight," "road weight," or "trailer weight," and the usually heavier "displacement." The two are not the same, although a number of builders use them almost interchangeably in their literature.

Displacement refers to the weight of the boat *in the water*. In addition to the weight of the boat, rigging and sails, displacement should include the weight of an outboard motor and fuel, some stores including fresh water, spare lines, fenders, safety equipment, ground tackle, plus at least a portion of the weight of the crew (typically two adults). Displacement is thus the weight of the boat when she is floating on her designed waterline.

Obviously if any of the weight normally aboard for sailing is left aboard for trailering, that weight has to be added to the road weight of the boat. So too must the weight of the trailer, typically 450 to 600 pounds. Incidentally, for determining the capacity of a vehicle to tow the weight, it does no good to take weight from the boat and repack it in the car. Weight is weight. Below we have made a representative list of such weights which can be used to estimate the weight of a boat for trailering with gear board.

Draft
Traditionally shallow draft has been characteristic of smaller boats, in part because of the matter of getting them in and out of the water. Because the effects of draft on launching, hauling and trailering are the topic of a separate article, this discussion is limited to the typical shallow draft boat.

As soon as a builder elects to provide a boat with shallow draft, he is presented with a set of choices.

He can keep draft to a minimum by making his keel retractable — a pivoting plate or casting or a daggerboard that lifts vertically through the deck; or by fitting his boat with a long stubby fixed keel; or by designing a combination: a stub keel that incorporates a centerboard.

The trade-offs are noteworthy. A shallow fixed keel must have more weight to achieve the same stability as

The dagger keel may weigh only enough to give the boat positive righting when capsized; stability comes from crew weight and beam

---

a deeper keel, fixed or retractable, because the weight is not as deep. Moreover, shallow keels do not perform as well to windward, offering too little lateral plane and too little "lift," deficiencies that are compounded as the boat heels.

In their favor, stub keels are simple; they have no hoisting cables to break or vibrate, pivot pins to leak, winches to jam, housings and boards that disappear in the hull to thwart maintenance, or openings that can pick up debris causing the keel to bind. And there is none of the annoying thumping to which drop keels and centerboards are prone when the boat is afloat.

Stub keels are fully exposed for fairing and painting. They offer a solid mass to absorb the impact of grounding, and they offer the same handy mass for supporting the weight of the boat when out of the water. They do not have housings and cables that intrude into the interior of the boat and clutter already limited space.

To a large extent the advantages of retractable ballast are the reverse. The ballast can hang farther below the boat where it is more effective and therefore it can weigh less. The keel can be an efficiently-shaped foil for windward performance and less drag off the wind.

Disadvantages? They are complicated. If housed in a trunk the slot creates drag, a drawback in pivoting keels made worse if the hoisting cable is exposed. Retracted they give minimal stability, perhaps barely enough to bring the boat upright if it were capsized.

Retracted they are a chore to paint; heeling the boat or lifting it to let the keel drop so it can be painted is a job and one half. Most are also rough iron castings that are tough to fair and to keep from rusting.

Add to these disadvantages the engineering problems: the hull in way of the drop keel must be capable of withstanding the loads that the heavy lever arm exerts with the boat sailing and the weight when the boat is out of the water.

Dagger keels have similar problems to pivoting keels.

With a shorter trunk they can get away with less hydrodynamic drag, but there are practical limits to their weight and movement. The trunk must divide the interior space in two parts, usually from sole to overhead. A grounding presents a worse threat, as such keels do not swing up when they hit an underwater obstruction as do pivoting keels. The shock of the impact must be absorbed by the keel and the hull.

For these reasons dagger keels are more commonly found on higher performance boats than the typical "trailer-sailer," where beam and crew weight provide stability, and interior comfort and space is subordinate to speed under sail. The dagger keel may weigh only enough to give the boat positive righting when capsized with the daggerboard extended in the down position (and locked in position).

An interesting novelty is the dagger keel with a bulb of ballast on the lower tip. Unlike the true daggerboard that can be fully retracted, even withdrawn from the trunk, these retract only until the bulb touches the bottom and usually only for trailering or storage. Since most of the drop keels of this type use a positive locking device to keep the keel extended, they can approach the efficiency of a fin keel in performance and the convenience of the shallow draft drop keel in handling out of the water. Nevertheless, engineering of the hull, the housing, and the hoisting system remain costly and complicated.

The hybrid keel-centerboard — a retractable, usually pivoted fin housed in a shallow keel — mixes the advantages and disadvantages of the purebred alternatives. Hoisted the boat has the shallow draft of a stub keel and may actually be capable of sailing to windward with the board up, albeit with considerable leeway. With the board down, lateral area and windward performance should be adequate. Housed in the exterior keel, the combination centerboard does not interfere with accommodations. Moreover, because the centerboard need have no more "ballast" than enough to "sink" it,

Four Variations for Shoal Draft

Stub keel

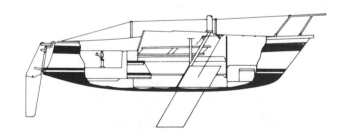

Dagger keel

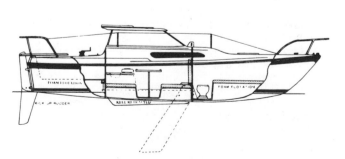

Drop or swing keel

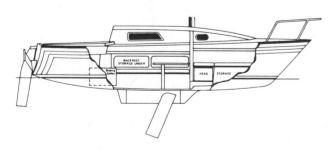

Stub keel with centerboard

the hoisting system can be simple, even a single line led to a cleat.

On the negative side, it is a chore to maintain, is liable to thunking, and tends to be costly compared to a stub keel without a board. For these reasons combination keel-centerboards are more popular on slightly larger boats, in locations where shoal water sailing is a higher priority than trailering, and in situations where cost per se is not a critical factor.

In general, small boats with stub keels (with or without integral centerboards) are heavier than boats of the same length with retractable ballast. However, economies realized from a simpler hull structure and a cast iron stub keel (the usual on boats built to a price) may allow the builder a bit more money to put into accommodations, decor or rig without pricing the boat out of the market.

It would be easy to lay too much emphasis on shallow draft for trailering. If *PS* Boatowner Questionnaires are any indication, owners of small shoal draft boats are as attracted by their ability to sail in shoal water (for gunkholing, beaching, etc) as they are by their trailerability. For this reason these boats are justifiably popular on inland and inshore waters. Under no circumstances would we consider boats of this size and type for use in exposed waters.

It's the Purpose That Makes the Difference

It is an axiom that anyone buying a boat should know what he plans to use her for before deciding what to buy. Apart from price alone the two major reasons for owning a small boat of the type we are talking about are ease of trailering and ability to sail in shoal water. Only if one or both of these are top priorities would you be happy with this type of boat, because performance, interior room, stability and even seaworthiness are all secondary considerations.

In almost all the boats we looked at for this article, the "cruisability" is subordinate. Livability is spartan at best. Headroom below is limited, amenities are scarce, berth comfort marginal, the galley incidental, and stowage at a premium.

Typically the V-berth is located so far forward that room at the foot disappears into a sharp point. Some have dinettes that convert to double berths without concern for the fact that two adults sleeping on one side of a 2000 pound boat will create 5° or more of list. Many boats cram four and five berths into space a couple might find claustrophobic, berths whose space might be far better used for stowage, a usable galley, sleeping-sized single berths, or even a decent head facility.

We suspect a lot of cooking aboard is of the one-pot kind, probably on a stove set on the cabin sole. The sink is too small to handle anything bigger than dentures and silverware. The icebox is typically the portable type with mediocre efficiency. There is room to stow neither utensils nor dishes, perhaps justifiable because there is too little stowage space for food as well.

Fresh water comes aboard in plastic bottles for which there is no built-in method to secure it. What stowage space there is under berths is often against the fiberglass of the hull, susceptible to dampness and dirt.

Because water getting below has no place to go, the bilges being shallow or non-existent, wetness in the accommodation space has to be a problem with too many boats of the type we have looked at.

The economies of their construction notwithstanding, many of these boats seem to have been designed more

Rigging the Mast

It sounds like the lead-in to an ethnic joke: How many sailors does it take to step a mast? But for owners of trailerable boats faced with the task of getting the mast up or down without dropping it overside or, worse, on the tops of their heads, it may not have the delight of a joke.

A rough guideline as to the maximum size — or more properly, the maximum *weight* — mast that two crew members can reasonably step or lower without a crane is a mast plus rigging that one person can lift with modest effort, perhaps 30 lbs complete.

Yet even with masts of this weight or less, the spar should be rigged for raising and the crew should have a plan for doing it. Start by making sure that the mast goes up or down close to the centerline of the boat. That is, with the butt in the step on deck (whether a hinged step or a tabernacle) and the shrouds attached, the mast can pivot but not fall off to one side or the other. The shrouds should be attached to chainplates slightly aft of the pivot at the step; otherwise, the shrouds must be loosened for raising or lowering the mast, a bother.

One person aft can then walk the mast up to an angle that permits a second person to pull it the rest of the way upright with a line, most conveniently the jib halyard. Lowering is the reverse.

It may help with masts that go up and down with regularity to use bolts with nuts rather than clevis pins and cotter pins to attach rigging. We do not recommend plunger-activated rigging pins, nor would we want to see nuts and bolts used on rigging for masts that are left standing (the nuts will eventually back off).

For heavier masts the only reasonable answer for on-board stepping is some form of A-frame or gin pole. However, this is a complicated system and should not be necessary for boats of the size we are talking about.

Finally, one strong word of caution. Before raising or lowering any mast, check that there is no chance the mast can come into contact with electrical wires. Electrocution from such accidents may well be the most common cause of small sailboat fatalities.

for the marketing department than for sailors. The effort seems to be to provide what buyers can be told they want (or need) rather than what might prove sensible in use.

Conclusions

Despite obvious drawbacks and some very tacky boats, there is no reason why many of the boats we looked at (even as small as 19') cannot be fun as pocket cruisers. For a modest investment a couple or small family can have a boat that can be trailered to wherever they might like to sail even using a compact tow car. The boats can be launched and hauled at a ramp or even a beach, rigged in minutes, sailed in knee-deep water, anchored with the bow one step from the shore, and swung into a campground en route to and from distant sailing waters.

We lament that too many of the boats we looked at were just plain schlocky. Flimsy hardware, chintzy decor, stowage space unfinished and cluttered with construction debris, bathtub-shiny white gelcoat surfaces topside and below, impractical burlap hull and overhead coverings, Nico-pressed standing rigging, and rough-cast keels all make boats look merely cheap.

Unfortunately it seems that buyers most attracted to the worst examples of such boats are new to sailing and boatowning. They are unaware of the equity their boats represent, that initial quality begets retained value at resale. There is not much to justify a boat that does not sail well, looks cheap, and makes living on board a chore.

If price is a top priority, think small but not cheap. Look at quality 20 footers rather than junk 23 footers. Spend less on the boat outright and then spend the difference in outfitting and making minor changes that she needs to make her a better boat for you. For $1000 you can, for example, add a genoa jib for performance, install larger genoa sheet winches for easier handling, add a good reefing system for safety, and buy a good stove.

There is no reason why, under these terms and with some careful shopping, a buyer with less than $10,000 to spend cannot have a little yacht with many of the amenities of boats at twice the price.

Selecting a Car

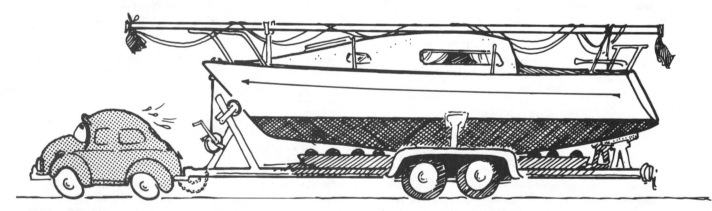

One of the more difficult questions facing the sailor considering a trailerable boat is how to pull it. Will his current automobile be sufficient as it is, or will it have to be modified? Will he need a new car? Ideally, the tow vehicle should be able to serve double duty as a family car. Yet, a gas guzzling family car can be as much of an economic burden as maintaining a separate vehicle solely to tow the boat. In either case, the car must have a trailering capacity that matches the trailering load.

The trailering "load" is not just the combined weight of the boat and trailer. The load is also dependent on the speed, altitude, temperature, and road conditions that the automobile will encounter. An automobile can pull a surprising amount of weight as long as it is driven slowly at low altitudes on smooth roads in cool weather. For example, a standard, unmodified Chevrolet Chevette, a subcompact car by anyone's standards, can pull 2200 lbs of trailer and boat at speeds under 25 mph without any risk of damage. Even more surprising is what a small car can pull given the proper additional equipment. A Chevette with a complete trailering package can pull a whopping 3300 lbs at 55 mph under normal highway conditions.

It's impossible to state the exact maximum that any car is capable of pulling. A car will not pull, say, 1000 lbs with ease, yet refuse to pull 1100 lbs. With any car the maximum load is a range without distinct boundaries. Determining a car's capacity is an exercise in balancing tradeoffs: the greater the load, the more wear and tear you put on the vehicle. Trailering with even a light load will wear out your car faster than if you don't trailer at all. You must decide how long you want your car to last, and treat it accordingly.

Manufacturer's Specifications

Despite the fact that, under the right conditions and/or with extra equipment, most cars can pull a surprising amount of weight, the manufacturer's specifications rarely reflect it. Instead, the manufacturer will often specify a surprisingly low trailering capacity for the standard, unmodified vehicle.

There is always a reason behind the capacity rating, and therefore it should not be ignored, according to Lorne Sherry, an engineer with Chevrolet and author of their trailering guidelines. Most often there is a good reason

Additional equipment can dramatically boost a car's towing capacity; the tough questions are what equipment to add, and when to add it

behind the manufacturer's rating. For instance, several years ago, the standard Chevrolet Camaro was rated for a capacity of only 1000 lbs, although the car's engine was powerful enough to pull a much greater load. What wasn't obvious was that the Camaro's suspension was too soft to carry the tongue weight required by a heavier trailer. Only with optional, heavy duty suspension was the Camaro able to tow more, according to Sherry.

Sometimes the rationale behind a low rating is less valid. It has been common with small Japanese-made cars for the manufacturers to advise against any trailering whatsoever. According to Sherry, this is not because these imports are lightly built and powered. Instead, it's because the manufacturer has not yet determined the car's towing capacity. Trailering is far less common in Japan than in the US, says Sherry, so there has been little demand for trailering specifications.

Manufacturers are predictably cautious about capacity ratings, not wanting to aggravate warranty claims. The car owner should be cautious, too. Don't exceed the manufacturer's specifications until you have determined the basis for those ratings. The automobile dealer may not be able to tell you what you need to know; it's better to call the manufacturer direct. Once you have determined the reason behind the rating, you will have a good idea where to start making the modifications — if any — to your car.

Modifications

The knowledge that a properly equipped car can usually pull a load equal to 1 to 1.5 times its own weight may be great news to the new car buyer. However, the knowledge is of less value to the owner of a used car, because it costs considerably more to retrofit trailering equipment. For example, a heavy duty cooling system that is a $50 option on a new car might cost as much as $200-$300 to retrofit on a used car.

While additional equipment can dramatically boost an automobile's trailering capacity the tough questions are what equipment to add and when to add it. Chevrolet has tackled this question in the *'83 Chevy Recreation and Trailering Guide*. Although the Chevy Guide is written specifically for Chevrolet vehicles, we think much of its information is applicable to other makes of automobiles, when considered with each manufacturer's individual specifications.

Before you can determine what equipment is needed, you first need to define the conditions under which you will be trailering. The severity of trailering conditions is determined by these factors:

1. The weight which you will be pulling. It is important to accurately total the trailering weight. Remember it is the combined weight of the boat, trailer and all of the boat's gear. Some boat manufacturers list boat displacement without taking into consideration spars, outboard engine, and optional equipment (stove, battery, head, etc). A fully loaded trailer-sailer may weigh 500-1000 lbs more than the published displacement. For sub-compact automobiles, the weight of third and fourth passengers should also be added to the trailering weight.

2. Cruising speed. The cruising speed of a car and trailer is governed by the weight of the load and the amount of windage created by the load. A powerboat with a large open cockpit has a great deal more wind resistance than a trailerable sailboat. Sailboats with a full keel present much more windage than shoal draft sailboats. Driving in-

to a 30-knot headwind can cut your trailering speed in half.

3. The temperature of the air. There is nothing tougher on a cooling system than pulling a trailer up a long hill on a hot day. If you avoid the heat, you can pull a lot more weight.

4. The altitude at which you must travel. An engine loses 4% of its sea level performance for every 1000' of altitude. When crossing a mountain 5000' high, your engine will have lost about 20% of its performance.

5. The road grades you will encounter. Long grades can be just as tough as steep grades. Interstate highways rarely have severe grades, but be sure to take into account any back roads you might take to reach your destination.

By considering these five factors, you can classify your trailering conditions as *light, medium or severe*. (see box). If usage falls into the light category, no additional towing equipment is needed; the standard automobile will suffice. As usage becomes more severe, it is necessary to modify your car to meet the additional load.

Here are the modifications you may need to consider:

Heavy Duty Cooling

Heavy duty cooling is essential for nearly all medium to severe trailering conditions. If any one of the five factors indicates more than light usage, a heavy duty radiator will probably be needed. If any one of the factors indicates severe usage, or any two factors indicate medium usage, a cooling modification will almost certainly be needed.

Unlike other modifications, which can be avoided at the expense of added wear and tear on the car, heavy duty cooling is critical. If your car overheats, your trailering trip comes to an abrupt halt.

Higher Axle Ratio or More Powerful Engine

These modifications are indicated when road grades, altitudes, and speed and weight factors exceed light conditions. However they are not needed for a medium to severe condition caused by air temperature; only a heavy duty cooling system is needed for this condition.

Most car owners know that available towing power depends on the size of the car's engine, as measured in cubic inches or cubic centimeters; what they may not know is that changing the car's axle ratio can also increase towing power. For a given engine size, a higher (numerically) axle ratio gives you better acceleration, and more power for passing other cars and climbing hills. A higher axle ratio also means the car's engine will go through more revolutions at a given speed. This means that the car will "wind out" at a lower speed, which effectively lowers the top speed of the vehicle. Changing to a smaller diameter tire has the same effect as increasing the axle ratio. However, with smaller tires, the car's handling will suffer, and could cause problems with a trailer.

Modifying the axle ratio on a used car is not a complicated job, assuming the car has rear wheel drive and the manufacturer has the necessary parts. On a car with front wheel drive, though, the cost and complicaton may be prohibitive.

In general, trucks and vans have a higher axle ratio than passenger cars, and therefore can pull a greater load in more severe conditions than a passenger car of equal weight. (The tables with this article are intended to define trailering conditions for passenger vehicles, not trucks.)

Power brakes are a particularly good idea because the weight of the trailer increases the effort required to brake the car

Suspension

Heavy duty suspension is usually a wise modification for more than light usage due to one factor — the weight which you will be pulling. Heavier suspension is not essential, though. If you choose to "make do" with standard suspension, the car may handle poorly and the car's frame may "bottom out" on the rear axle, but you can still drive.

A trailer should always have a "tongue weight" of 10%-12% of the combined weight of the trailer and boat. A lighter tongue weight will cause the trailer to "fishtail" excessively on the highway. The effect of tongue weight on the car's suspension is exaggerated by the distance of the trailer hitch behind the rear axle of the car. For example, 100 lbs of tongue weight on a hitch located 4' behind the axle has the same effect as 300-400 lbs of weight in the passenger car's trunk.

Another way to increase the vehicle's ability to carry tongue weight is to use a weight-distributing hitch. This type of hitch attaches the trailer tongue rigidly to the car's frame so the tongue can pivot on the hitch only in the horizontal plane.

Automatic Transmission

Many people think that a manual transmission offers more control of a car's power and therefore is better than an automatic transmission for trailering. Chevrolet's trailering engineer Sherry disagrees.

Sherry says an automatic transmission is better for two reasons. First, there is less wear and tear on the car's clutch. More importantly, automatic transmissions have "torque converters", which multiply engine torque when starting from a dead stop. This makes pulling a boat out of the water and up a launching ramp much easier.

Transmission Cooler

A transmission fluid cooler is another non-essential modification. According to Sherry, you have to trailer 20,000 miles under worse than light conditions before the extra cost of a transmission cooler becomes worthwhile. You can usually avoid the purchase by simply changing the transmission fluid more often. Sherry recommends changing it every 5000 miles.

Power Brakes and Steering

Power brakes are a particularly good idea for trailering, because the extra weight of the trailer increases the effort required by the driver to brake the car. It is not an essential modification, but common sense dictates power brakes for more than light trailering conditions caused by the weight of the load being pulled. You should also consider separate brakes for the trailer, which are required by most states for trailers above a certain weight. That weight varies from state to state.

Power steering is only necessary when using a weight-distributing hitch, because this type of hitch increases the effort required to steer the car.

Conclusion

Matching a car to a trailer is an inexact science. First you must decide how much you will be pulling, and under what conditions you will be traveling. Then you must balance the cost of the extra wear and tear of trailering with the cost of modifications to increase trailering capacity. By considering the guidelines presented in this article with each manufacturer's individual specifications, you should be able to determine your car's capabilities.

Determining the Severity of Trailering Conditions

This information, taken from the *'83 Chevy Recreation and Trailering Guide,* shows the system Chevrolet uses to match an automobile and equipment to the trailering conditions it will encounter. The severity of trailering conditions is dependent on the speed of the vehicles, the "weight factor" (weight of the trailer divided by the weight of the automobile), air temperature, altitude, and the steepness of the road grades. Although the system is designed for 1983 Chevrolets, it can apply, with certain qualifications, to other types of automobiles.

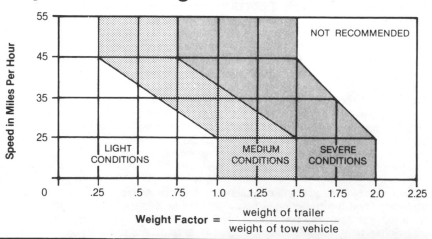

$$\text{Weight Factor} = \frac{\text{weight of trailer}}{\text{weight of tow vehicle}}$$

	LIGHT CONDITIONS	MEDIUM CONDITIONS	SEVERE CONDITIONS
Altitude	less than 2,000 feet above sea level	2,000 to 5,000 feet above sea level	over 5,000 feet above sea level
Temperature	less than 65°F	between 65°F and 85°F	more than 85°F
Road Grade	slight or no grades	medium grades	long (over 2 miles) or steep grades (steeper than those on interstate highways)

aunching the Boat

The trailer sailor's choice of a sailboat with deep draft or shoal draft will determine where he can sail. Deeper draft restricts the number of places he can sail, but provides better performance and more safety so he can sail farther and faster when he gets there. Reduced draft widens your choice of launching sites and makes launching easier, but the trade-offs are significant.

Is shoal draft worth the disadvantages?

How much *does* deep draft restrict the trailer sailor?

To help answer these questions, *The Practical Sailor* polled trailer yacht associations across the US as to cost, quality and availability of launching facilities in their sailing area. Fourteen questionnaires were returned from California (4), the Midwest (5), New York, Georgia, Florida, Texas and Arizona (1 each). What we learned from our study is that deep draft, while it has drawbacks, is not the great restriction that the manufacturers of shoal draft trailerable boats would have us believe. Proper trailering equipment can make a big difference.

What Are the Trade-offs?

When referring to *deep draft,* we mean a boat with a deep, fixed keel. *Shoal draft* denotes a boat with a shorter "stub" keel, or a centerboard or daggerboard which may retract into the hull. A ballasted centerboard that swings back against, but not into the hull is commonly called a *swing keel.*

The price of decreased draft can be threefold: you may pay for it in performance, safety, and sometimes in interior space.

Boats with a shallow keel are almost always slower, especially to windward, than boats with a deep keel. The shallow keel provides less lateral resistance, so the boat makes more leeway. It provides less stability for the same weight, so must be thicker to carry additional ballast, which increases drag.

A fully retractable daggerboard, centerboard, or swing keel can theoretically offer the performance of a deep, fixed keel. However, the cost of engineering this performance tends to be prohibitive. Holding down the cost means sacrificing other features, like a livable interior.

Safety is a consideration of prime importance to the sailor who plans to venture into open water. Swing keels and centerboards on trailerable sailboats rarely have provision to be locked in the "down" position. In a capsize, the centerboard can retract into its trunk, encouraging the boat to turn turtle (upside down). Similarly, should the centerboard's pivot pin shear off, the boat could be rendered very unstable.

Finally, interior space is lost to the centerboard or daggerboard trunk in boats with fully retracting boards. In addition, the cabin is awkwardly divided by the trunk.

These compromises make a boat with a full, deep keel look pretty inviting. The catch is in the difficulty of launching such a boat. The hull of a boat with a deep keel sits high above the trailer, so the trailer has to be pushed into deeper water before the boat will float off. On a steep, well paved launching ramp this might not pose a problem, but on a more gradual ramp of soft dirt, launching might be impossible. Of course, you can always launch a deep keel sailboat with a hoist, but there are fewer hoists in operation than there are launching ramps, and their use is much more expensive.

Hoists: How Many and How Much?

If hoists were as abundant and inexpensive as launching ramps, there would be a lot more deep draft sailboats on trailers. Unfortunately, hoists are neither abundant nor cheap. Our questionnaires report 604 hoists available "locally" for public launching, compared to 2155 launching ramps.

Hoists are more common in some areas than in others. Questionnaires from metropolitan areas of California list half as many hoists as ramps; areas on the Great Lakes list nearly equal numbers of hoists and ramps. By contrast, questionnaires from more rural areas indicate hoists are few and far between.

Hoist launching is not cheap. Reported charges range from $2 to $5 a foot per launching, which adds up to $40 to $100 to launch a 20' sailboat.

Annual fees at sailing clubs, which often include use of a hoist, are more reasonable; they range as low as $75 a year. Many sailing clubs and marinas offer "dry-sailing": space on land to store the boat between sails. A drawback to sailing out of clubs is that it effectively defeats the purpose of owning a trailerable sailboat: you are stuck in one sailing area.

If your boat must be launched by hoist, the same reasoning applies. One of the major reasons for owning a trailerable sailboat is to be able to travel to new sailing waters, but if you plan to travel to less populated areas, the choice will be limited by the dearth of hoists.

Condition of Launching Ramps

How many launching ramps are steep enough and well-paved enough to launch a deep keel boat, and how hard is it to use them?

As might be expected, launching a deep keel boat is deemd a lot harder than launching a boat of shoal draft. What sounds more discouraging is that, with a conventional trailer and hitch, and in best conditions, only 11% of the launching ramps reported on could accommodate a small boat with a deep keel. "Best conditions" means high tide or high water. If high tide occurs at noon and you go for an afternoon sail, you might not be able to get back on the trailer until well after dark. Likewise, sailing on a lake could be restricted to times of high water in the spring and early summer.

This problem, however, sounds worse than it is. About half of the ramps, 49%, will accommodate deep draft boats if the distance between the boat and the car at launching is increased to get the boat and trailer into deeper water.

There are two ways to increase that distance: use a trailer with an extendable tongue, or detach the tongue from the car. The second option requires using a chain between the trailer and the car, supporting the tongue of the trailer with a large diameter wheel, and pushing the trailer into the water.

Choosing a trailerable sailboat is a choice of compromises; you must make some decisions and choose the compromise best for you

While the number of ramps suitable for deep draft boats seems highly restrictive, the use of an extension on the trailer increases the number so much that, when combined with the available hoists, deep draft boats can be an acceptable option to many sailors.

An extension is useful to owners of shoal draft boats, as well. A swing keel or stub keel boat can be launched with no extension from about 51% of the ramps in our study. Using an extension makes 88% of the ramps usable.

A sailboat with a fully retractable centerboard or daggerboard can be launched at 84% of the ramps. Extending the trailer extends access to 95% of the ramps, a difference which probably would not justify the expense in time and money in most situations.

Some Common Launching Problems

We asked the trailer yacht associations to identify problems commonly encountered while launching a trailerable boat. Here is what they said:

● **Dockage:** Dockage at launching ramps is too often inadequate or non-existent. Often docks can only be found during the summer; during the spring and fall, when the water is coldest, you must get wet to get the boat on and off the trailer, and hang on to it while someone parks the car and climbs aboard.

● **Long waits:** On a busy summer day, respondents report, waits of up to 45 minutes are common at public launching ramps. Several complain that people waste ramp time by putting up the mast on the ramp instead of beforehand in the parking lot.

● **Power lines:** Despite a number of deaths in recent years, a surprising number of ramps still have power lines running nearby or overhead. One report notes that contact with power lines has caused six dismastings at one sailing club in the past eight years.

● **Bridges:** Bridges sometimes block access to open water, a problem most common in southern California. A mast which is hinged on deck can be tilted back to clear an overhead obstruction. With a keel-stepped mast, you are stuck.

● **Maneuvering onto the trailer:** Respondents were nearly unanimous in condemning "powerboat style" trailers where the boat is winched onto the trailer over a series of rollers. Superior for a sailboat is a "float-off" trailer with well padded keel guides, sideboards and bow stops. A float-off trailer with proper guides will allow sailing the boat onto the trailer even in a strong cross-wind or cross current, although extra caution is required in such conditions, especially if there is any wave action. A sailboat positioned improperly on its trailer supports is liable to serious damage.

● **Trailer jacks:** Trailer jacks are intended to be used to lift the trailer tongue off the car's hitch. If the jack has a wheel, it is usually too small to be used for anything but wheeling the boat around on level pavement. It should not be used as a third wheel to launch a boat because it will invariably get bogged down in the sand or muck at the bottom of a launching ramp. If you plan to use a third wheel and chain instead of an extendable tongue, get a separate wheel, preferably inflatable, at least 8" in diameter.

● **Parking lot security:** The best launching ramps have secure, well lit parking lots. Those located in parks with park wardens on all night duty are best.

Choosing a Trailer

We estimate that there are more than 100 trailer manufacturers in the United States. There are over 60 listed in *Sail* Magazine's Sailboat and Equipment Directory. Typical of prices and options offered are those from two manufacturers recommended by respondents to our questionnaire: *Triad* and *Trail-Rite.*

Triad (New Milford, CT (203) 354-1146) specializes in semi-custom trailers for sailboats. To get an idea of what a Triad trailer costs, we asked for a quote for a Cape Dory Typhoon, a 19', 1900 lb full-keel pocket cruiser. The basic trailer retails for $1245. With electric brakes the price is $1370, with surge brakes, $1470. The float-off option, which includes a bow stop, keel guides and an extendable tongue, adds $280 to the price tag. If you prefer not to use the extendable tongue, a retractable aircraft-type 10" inflatable third wheel is available for $160.

Trail-Rite (Santa Ana, CA (714) 556-4540) makes only float-off trailers for sailboats. A 10' tongue extension option adds $158 to $262 to the price of a trailer, depending on the trailer hitch size. Extensions up to 20' are available, at an extra $5.50 a foot for any length over 10'. For those who prefer not to use a tongue extension, a non-steerable, 8" diameter wheel can be welded onto the tongue for $85.

A trailer manufacturer renowned for its lightweight aluminum trailers is Trailex (Canfield, Ohio (216) 533-6814). Float-off models cost less than regular roller-type trailers from Trailex. A 12' extendable tongue costs an extra $117.

Conclusions

The sailor contemplating a trailerable sailboat has two problems special to trailer sailing. The weight of boat and trailer must be matched to an automobile capable of pulling it, and the boat and equipment must be matched to local launching conditions and to the owner's tolerance for launching hassles.

As with any sailboat, choosing a trailerable sailboat is a choice of compromises. Your choice depends on where and how you plan to use it. There is no answer right for everyone; you must make some decisions, and choose the compromise best for you.

The Results in Brief

A summary of statistics from 14 trailer yacht associations throughout the US:

Hoists identified available for public use — 604
Charge per foot per launching or hauling — $2-$5
Sailing club dues — $75/year
   (includes use of hoist) — and up

Public launching ramps identified — 2155

Ramps suitable for use with:	Retractable centerboard/ daggerboard	Swing or stub keel	Deep keel
Conventional trailer & hitch	84%	51%	11%
Trailer with tongue extender or detached from car	95%	88%	49%

The 'Transition Yacht': How Big Is Small?

At what point does a small boat cease being a "glorified daysailer" with minimal "accommodations" and become a cruising boat with genuine livability; a seakindly craft with small boat handling and large boat performance? We have wrestled in print with this question in evaluations of the Cape Dory 25 and 25 D, the Ericson 25, Freedom 25, and even the Flicka, J/24, and Olson 30. We wrestle in private with the same question every time we look over a small boat. The more boats we look at, the more clearly we perceive a transition point where a boat becomes, if you will, a yacht. For example, although the O'Day 25 is the same length as the MacGregor 25, the O'Day is clearly more of a boat; it weighs twice as much, it costs twice as much, and in our opinion, it offers the promise of twice the comfort, cruising range and value.

It's easy enough to identify boats on the ends of this continuum, but there's a range of small cruisers in the middle with a mix of these characteristics. We call them "transition yachts."

Historically, transition boats are a creation of the marketplace, developed with evolving technology to meet consumer demand. As the boom in production fiberglass boat building developed during the last 20 years or so, boat buyers indicated they wanted boats with more and more accommodations and better seaworthiness for a modest price. To answer that demand the waterline became longer, beam wider, and topsides higher. At the same time builders found that fiberglass reduced the amount of hull structure needed for strength. As a result interior volume increased without commensurate increases in either overall length or displacement. And hence, apart from inflation, neither did price.

By the mid 1970s the most popular boat in the marine marketplace became the smallest boat that had the space, amenities, and comfort of larger boats, or yachts. Today they are more popular than ever.

Essentially, these are small cruisers that try to offer the accommodations and performance of larger boats. They tend to have a minimum length of about 25' and a displacement of about 4500 pounds. Some are touted as trailerable, but questionnaires PS readers have sent us indicate that many, if not most, owners treat them like larger boats and seldom trailer them except perhaps home for offseason storage. Many come in shoal draft and deep draft versions, and offer inboard auxiliary power as an option to the standard outboard.

In general, their styling and proportions are those of larger boats. They have full accommodations below and an "offshore" type rig rather than a "one-design" type. For amenities they have a galley with a stove, sink, utensil storage, and built-in icebox; an enclosed head; fixed water tankage; and an electrical system — all routine features on larger boats.

In addition, an owner with the pocketbook and the inclination can add on goodies that larger boats boast as standard: spinnaker and gear, wheel steering, refrigeration, a shower, a stove with oven, even a pressure water system, as well as inboard power.

Intrigued with their promise, we set about to define the trade-offs, the compromises, between small size, full accommodations, price and performance inherent in transition cruisers.

The Performance Compromise

To a large degree maximizing livability and performance is an exercise in contradiction. This is the main reason why boxy, shoal draft boats with small rigs often sail slowly or, worse, handle poorly in a breeze or a seaway. The ultimate example of such clunkers is the Bayliner Buccaneer line produced in the mid-1970s. Conversely, it is the reason why high performance boats are often light and quick but have only spartan accommodations and cockpit comfort.

To complicate the competition between spacious accommodations and sparkling performance, designing for shoal draft works against both. A shallow keel configuration, with or without a centerboard to alter draft, is less efficient than a deep keel, particularly a high aspect fin. In addition, to provide comparable stability, the shoal draft keel must weigh more than a deep keel, increasing displacement and trailering weight.

Don't forget to consider the aspect of performance under auxiliary power. Clearly a boat 25' long and weighing over 3500 pounds is pushing the limit of capability of an outboard motor mounted on a transom bracket. A 9.9 hp outboard, barely adequate for smooth water powering, weighs almost 100 lbs, drinks fuel like a sot guzzling booze, does little to slow a boat of this weight in reverse (let alone permit her to back down), and pulls out of the water with any pitching (to which its weight on the stern contributes). Outboards do have advantages: namely, ease of servicing, and cost. The motor can be carried to a service center and it carries a price tag about 30% of that of an inboard installed.

By contrast, inboard engines, notably small diesels, are generally powerful, dependable and efficient. They typically are tucked away under the cockpit in space that is otherwise apt to be fairly inaccessible. Their fuel is safer and better stored. And they can produce what should be more than adequate electrical power.

For that convenience and effectiveness, the inboard engine is costly, $4000 or more. While it is hard to justify such a price tag, adding perhaps 20% to what might be an affordable base price, the inboard does prove to be a good investment. Boats with inboard power sell better as used boats than boats with outboard power, recovering much of the initial outlay. An outboard motor more than three or four years old puts a potential buyer of your boat in an excellent negotiating position.

One tempting alternative seemingly suited to boats of this size is the so-called sail drive — essentially an outboard motor mounted through the hull so that it acts like an inboard. However, we hear complaints about electrolysis in the lower units of these systems, so we think they should be considered only for fresh water installations.

When looking at a boat where there is a reasonable choice between outboard and inboard power, the buyer must face a compromise between cost and performance; it's not an easy choice to make.

Less a compromise but well worth mentioning is the

If there are berths for five, but space for only three or four, the additional berths waste space that is sorely needed

matter of the safety and seaworthiness of the transition cruiser. There is little question that for a given length, the transition yacht, as a junior version of a larger boat, will be a more seaworthy vessel than a "grown up" version of a daysailer. The latter may have lighter displacement, retractable ballast, an open cockpit, lower freeboard, and a less versatile rig, all of which makes it less suited to exposed waters than a transition boat of the same length.

In contrast, the transition yacht will have a self-draining cockpit, a seat-level bridgedeck to prevent water from going below, a companionway that can be secured, cockpit lockers with positive latches, a lifeline system. Fuel for the auxiliary is in a fixed tank if the engine is an inboard or there is a separate vented locker for a portable outboard tank.

In short, the proper transition yacht has adopted many of the characteristics of safety and seaworthiness that are typical of larger boats. This may not make them suitable for offshore passages per se, but the transition yacht should offer a much wider cruising range than its smaller, cheaper, lighter counterparts.

Less of a Compromise — Livability
It is truly remarkable how much in the way of accommodations and cockpit space the designers and builders of many of these boats have managed to provide. Routinely there are berths for at least four, often five. The head is fully enclosed. There is a small but fully serviceable galley, room to store plenty of sails, and abundant locker space for clothes, stores and utensils. Cockpit seats may exceed 6′ in length; headroom is 5′8″ or better. It is an impressive package.

At the same time, the packaging (as dictated by buyer demand in the marketplace) tends to be more impressive than the product. There may be five berths, but five persons trying to live aboard a 25-footer is more than fit the boat. The cabin table seats two better than four (let alone five). The water tankage — five to 10 gallons — is hardly enough for overnight with more than three drawing from it.

Similarly, head capacity is limited (unless the head is a flow-through system, seldom found on production models). So too is the capacity of clothes lockers, the icebox, and food storage space for a cruise of any duration. Perhaps worst of all, there is simply too little space aboard such a small boat for privacy. In short, the number of berths should not be the criterion for judging crew capacity; in fact, if cruising with more than three (four, if the crew includes young children) the additional berths are a waste of valuable space.

In that space designers and builders could make forward V-berths that don't disappear into a point where feet are supposed to fit; the galley could have some usable counterspace; the icebox could be large enough to hold a block of ice *and* a six-pack. There might be room for clothes lockers rather than the all-too-prevalent scuttles that open into bilge space under the berth.

A Few Things We'd Look For
It is, of course, difficult to delineate what boat will best suit any sailor, but there are guidelines worth keeping in mind when considering boats of this size and type.
● Define as well as possible her intended use. If primarily for daysailing, look at cockpit space and performance. If for trailering, consider weight and draft as well

as what will be needed to tow the boat and handle her at ramps. If for cruising, set realistic limits on the number of people who will be aboard and the duration of the cruise.
● Buy a boat that has a resale market in your area. For many buyers, this boat will be an interim step before "trading up" to a larger boat. With this a consideration, the boat they buy should have a resale value (and buyer demand) at least commensurate with the initial investment.
● Performance, construction, and seaworthiness are top priorities; decor, cosmetics, and styling are less important. Fold-up cabin tables look neat but are invariably flimsy. Fiberglass hull liners may look antiseptic compared to wood joinerwork and cabin sole but they are rugged and practical.
● Choose a boat you can abuse, not one you have to coddle. Boats are meant to be fun, not unrelenting work. This is one of the particular assets of smaller boats.
● Don't buy on impulse or shallow impressions. Try the berths for size and comfort. Measure icebox capacity. Feel scuttles for dryness. Open hatches and ports to check ventilation. If fitted with an inboard, take apart the engine box to see what is required to pull the dipstick. And on deck go through the routine of reefing to see how efficient the system is.
● Think carefully about options. Fancy electronics, extra sails, wheel steering, and the like take money and can be fitted at a later day.

The Bottom Line — Cost
Make no mistake about it: boats of this size are an investment. They can cost up to twice what other boats of the same length — the so-called trailer sailer — cost. In that respect they demand the same careful consideration any yacht deserves before purchase, new or used. And they require maintenance to protect the equity they represent.

Not long ago (it seems) $1000 per foot was a good eyeball estimate of the price of boats over 30′. Now that magic formula applies to the base price of 27–28-footers, or the "sailaway" price of a 25-footer of this type. This is lots of money; it should be spent as wisely as possible.

For a couple or small family the transition yacht offers a great deal for her price. For those on a modest budget and with normal amounts of leisure time, it can be a better *value* than a larger boat, both because of less initial outlay and because of lower annual upkeep costs.

In addition, many boats of this type are popular on the used boat market, appealing as they do to new, budget conscious sailors. They are, more than other boats larger and smaller, an asset that should be capable of being turned readily to capital if necessary.

Furthermore, these are the smallest and cheapest boats that interest marine finance companies. Their cost makes a worthwhile transaction, the boat herself represents a solid form of colateral, and ownership entails a firm commitment by their owners.

The bottom line is thus a form of encouragement. On the one hand these boats can give many sailors the type of sailing enjoyed by owners of much larger craft at economical rates. On the other hand, buyers of boats of this size should shop carefully and thoughtfully for the best boat for their purpose and the best value. There are plenty to choose from — about 60 models sold across a wide geographical area. Many are available in various configurations and with extensive options.

Heavy or Light?
Weighing the Trade-offs

Although the owners of many small boats are primarily concerned about having a boat light enough for trailering or for high performance, there are sailors who want small boats with relatively heavy displacement. Some but not all of these sailors want heavy boats for the right reasons.

Unfortunately heavy displacement is nowadays often equated with poor or sluggish performance. To an extent the relationship is justified. During the last 20 years, while performance of sailboats has improved as the boats became lighter, a number of production boats have been notable as heavy and slow. Most notable, of course, is the Westsail 32 but the sisterhood includes a host of designs adopted for chartering and others built in the Orient.

The common denominator of these heavy boats is their so-called traditional or "classic" character. They have "full-bodied" hull forms with "full" or long keels. They are rigged as cutters or, worse, ketches with low aspect sailplans that boast bowsprits to increase sail area yet seldom include overlapping headsails with their greater efficiency. Many further restrict performance by dragging solid propellers, often three-bladed, in big, unfaired apertures.

In fact, the disturbing factor about many of these boats, both large and small, is that they seem to flaunt their stodgy performance. As a result, many sailors seem to have grown up believing that heaviness and slowness in some mystical way guarantee seaworthiness. What a sad misconception.

Heavy Boats Misconceptions

There is no reason a heavy boat has to be slow. No where is this better exemplified than in the designs by Ted Hood: superbly performing cruising boats and racers that have remained competitive despite the trend toward lighter and lighter boats.

The key is, of course, that well performing boats have well designed sailplans with adequate sail area set on spars that are efficient over a hull that is stable and seakindly. The underwater surfaces are fair, windage kept to a minimum, and the boats not overbuilt or loaded down below their designed waterline. Note that there is nothing in these modest standards that in any way impinges on tradition. In this day and age there is no reason a sail must have the shape of a bag; a mast, the heft of a log; or a rudder, the bluntness of a plank.

In further contradiction to apparent popular belief, heavy displacement does not ensure a more comfortable motion than a light boat in a seaway. It can, however, help. Some displacement boats roll mercilessly in certain conditions, a discomfort compounded by tedium if the boat is slow or poorly balanced. But displacement boats are not generally subject to the snappy motion that afflicts light boats nor do the better designed ones require the concentration at the helm or to maintain sail trim.

Even better news is that weight does not automatically mean poor performance in lighter winds, an argument often lost amid the estatic outbursts from sailors on light boats as they plane by heavy boats in a strong breeze. Once having gained momentum a heavy boat properly designed with adequate sail area may leave its lighter and short-canvased cousins in its wake in light air.

Conceptions and misconceptions aside, the chief advantage of heavy displacement, especially in smaller boats, is that for the same overall length the heavy boat can be more roomy and carry a larger "payload"—crew, stores, spare parts, sails, etc—than a light boat without affecting performance.

To illustrate this point take, for example, the installation of an inboard auxiliary engine in a small boat. Install a 160-lb diesel engine (eg, a one-cylinder Yanmar or BMW) plus a fuel tank in a 26' boat with a modest displacement of 3600 pounds and her displacement increases by almost 8%, more than the weight of an additional crew member. The same engine, still adequate for propulsion, in a 8000-lb boat is a comparatively insignificant increase, less than 3%.

For this greater displacement there is a price. Displacement means a greater amount of materials plus the labor to assemble them. Coincidentally, heavy boats have more sail area which, in turn, means heavier rigging and fittings. They may also need bigger engines, more tankage, and more complicated sytems, all costly. Ironically, heavier displacement may not mean more ballast, but, then, ballast is relatively cheap compared to the rest of the structure of a boat.

Trend Toward Lighter Boats

In an era when modern materials and building techniques are producing lighter boats and cost is far and away the major factor in boat selection, it is no wonder that there are fewer and fewer comparatively heavy boats on the market. Builders of heavy boats have suffered: Westsail has disappeared, CSY folded, and so has Allied. Now the most common source for heavier boats is the Far East where low labor costs help keep heavy boats competitively priced.

Whereas livability—space, carrying capacity, seakindly motion, etc.—is the major advantage of a boat with heavy displacement, the top priority for the light boat is performance—speed, liveliness, etc. In general, these two priorities tend to conflict: heavy means room and light means fast. Neither relationship is guaranteed, but there is certainly no reason to pay the price in performance of a heavy boat and be cramped; nor to have a light boat and be slow.

A boat is considered heavy when her displacement-to-waterline length ratio is about 300 or more, and ultra light when it is under 100. Few modern yachts exceed 400 (a notable exception is the Westsail 32 with a ratio of 425); the trend has been away from exceedingly high ratios. At the other end of the scale, lower and lower ratios have been sought by several builders. The Santa Cruz 27, the boat that has attracted the most attention to the "fast is fun" light displacement concept, has a ratio of 95; the Olson 30 has a ratio of 77; and the skinny Fast 40, with a displacement of just 4160 pounds on a 36' waterline, has a ratio of 40.

Comfort and construction

While the popular notion is that heavy displacement means more comfort at sea and better overall construction, it is hardly axiomatic that light displacement results in the opposite. Comfort is a relative term and while it is true that the corkiness of a light boat may make for a bumpy ride, especially to windward, and squirrelly steering off the wind, it also means that with the wind from abeam aft the ride will be fast. Aficionados of lightness point out that on a passage of, say, 2000 miles the heavier boat may take 20 days and a light boat half that time, particularly when she can surf or plane. While the crew of the heavy boat spend the 10 added days in relative cruising comfort, the crew of the light boat enjoy complete dockside comfort after their exciting 10 days of sailing.

Construction quality is less subjective but no less controversial. One characteristic of the heavy boat is that she must be built strongly to carry the rig to move her weight. With greater rig size comes greater loads. Conversely, because a smaller sailplan and smaller rig is needed to move the light boat, construction can be lighter. In addition, the heavy boat tends to sail through seas while the lighter boat sails over them, a motion harder perhaps on the crew but easier on the hull and rig.

Nor in this day of technological developments does strength have to be equated with weight. The aircraft industry in particular has produced a whole line of exceptionally strong lightweight materials that can be applied to boat construction. F-Board, aluminum honeycomb faced with an epoxy-fiberglass laminate, is stronger, at a fraction of the weight, than the plywood normally used for bulkheads, cabin sole, and structural

Displacement: How Heavy is Heavy?

The displacement of a boat is equal to the weight of the water displaced by the boat as it floats upright in the water. Thus the displacement of a boat is the weight of the boat. Traditionally displacement is simply an application of Archimedes' Principle that a body immersed in water displaces a volume of water equal in volume and weight to the immersed body.

Traditionally displacement is the measure of the weight of a vessel because the volume of a hull below its designed waterline (DWL) can be calculated more easily than actually weighing the boat. The volume in cubic feet is multipled by the weight of water per cubic foot (usually sea water at 64 lbs) to give the displacement.

Another formula for the area of a boat hull at her waterline gives a figure for the additional displacement needed to "sink" (or raise) the boat per inch above her DWL. This permits the difference in displacement to be calculated if the boat does not float on her DWL.

The important factor in determining whether a boat is "heavy" or "light" displacement is the ratio of displacement to waterline length. The formula for the displacement-length ratio is the displacement in long tons (2240 lbs) divided by one hundredth of the waterline length cubed:

$$\frac{\text{Disp. tons}}{(.01 \text{ L})^3} = \text{Displacement-length ratio}$$

Example: the Ericson 30 has a stated displacement of 9000 pounds (4.02 long tons) and a waterline length of 25'4½".

$$\frac{4.02}{(.25375)^3} = 246$$

Smaller boats tend to have a higher displacement-length ratio than larger boats. The traditional average ratio for boats with a 20' DWL is about 300; for 25' DWL, 275; and for 30' DWL, 250. If the ratio of a boat is within 20% or so of the average on either the heavy or light side, her displacement is considered moderate. Higher than that range, displacement is heavy (the Westsail 32 is 425); lower, it is light (the Cal 9.2 is 190). Light planing boats have a ratio closer to 100 or even below (the Olson 30 is 77).

In recent years the average displacement-length ratio for sailboats has been getting lower and lower. Boats have been getting lighter and lighter. Three major factors are at work causing this trend. Waterlines have been getting longer in proportion to overall length. This combined with the use of modern building materials has permitted hulls and rigs to become lighter. Finally, the marketplace has been highly sensitive to price and price is a function of weight.

For the modern fiberglass production boat with a DWL of about 25' or less, the average ratio is now closer to 250. The Flicka with a displacement-length ratio of 334 is heavy even by traditional standards. For comparison, note the ratios for a number of other popular small (DWL 20' or less) production boats:

Stone Horse	325	Heavy
Cape Dory 25	307	
Nor'Sea 27	292	
Int. Folkboat	290	
Columbia 7.6	223	Moderate
Ericson 25	214	
O'Day 22	173	
Tanzer 22	168	
MacGregor 22	147	Light
J/24	139	
Moore 24	89	Ultralight

In calculating a displacement-length ratio there are two important factors to keep in mind:

• The figures supplied by builders for the displacement of their products are seldom precise. Some are little better than estimates. Few spell out under what conditions the boat will displace the stated amount, whether "ready to sail," on a trailer, as it leaves the factory, or something else.

• Displacement does not take into consideration the added weight of fuel (in some cases not even an engine), water, food, sails, clothing, or spare parts. Nor does it include crew members. Obviously the addition of this weight most affects the displacement of small boats. The addition of, say, 600 pounds of crew and stores to the light MacGregor 22 increases that boat's displacement more than 20%; the addition of the same modest amount increases the much heavier Flicka's displacement by less than 10%.

cabinetry. Similarly carbon fibers, vinylester resins, Kevlar fabrics, and balsa and foam coring materials are now regularly used to build lighter hull and deck structures with superb strength. Even present day plywoods, both shaped and sheet, are lighter as well as more attractive than the laminates used a few years ago.

For lightness, though, there may be a price. It is common knowledge that heavy boats generally cost more than boats of average displacement because there is more material and labor in their hulls as well as larger, more costly rigs, hardware and engines. Only in the largest and heaviest boats built of such materials as ferrocement and steel does the relationship between cost and weight begin to level off.

At the other end of the weight scale the labor and materials to produce lightness are also expensive (although the cost is coming down as exemplified by the modest price tag on many of the popular light production boats). If in the interest of saving weight the builder uses state-of-the-art materials, engineering, and workmanship, that effort pushes cost upward dramatically. One obvious example of this is the Stiletto catamaran.

Where the builder of the modern light boat can save on production cost is in the vestigial interior accommodations often provided in these boats. Joinerwork is the single most expensive component in the boatbuilding process. Keeping joinerwork, hence accommodations and amenities, to a minimum saves weight and cost. Untrimmed plywood cabinetry, extensive use of vinyl and other fabrics for overheads and ceilings, curtains rather than doors, scuttles rather than drawers and lockers, and bags against the hull for clothes are cost-cutting techniques which balance the expense of lighter, stiffer hull laminates, a stronger keel attachment, and beefier rudder assemblies. Only when the buyer insists on first class accommodations *and* the performance of ultra light weight does the cost rise precipitously.

The issue of stability

Contrary to popular belief there is no reason why a light boat should have appreciably less stability than a heavy boat. Stability (stiffness) is only partly a function of weight. Stability is also a function of ballast, hull form, and the height of the center of gravity (affected by a whole passel of factors including rig weight, hull construction, location of tankage and stores, the engine, and the crew).

Because crew weight makes up a larger proportion of

sailing displacement on a light boat than on a heavy boat, the location of that weight is more important to trim and stability. That is why, when the crew sits along the weather rail in a breeze upwind, the conditions when stability is most a factor, there is a greater effect on performance in a light boat than in a heavier displacement boat.

Then there are the questions of ultimate and inverted stability: how easily can a lighter boat be rolled over by seas and, once capsized, how readily it will roll back upright? The low freeboard, wide shallow hull, and low cabin house of the typical light boat do encourage rolling over. So too does her relative lack of weight and mass; the light boat may be better able to withstand the impact of a wave on hull, deck, and cabin structure but be less able to withstand the tendency of the wave to roll or to pitchpole the boat. Presently there are a number of studies underway to determine exactly what does happen to a boat when caught by a steep or breaking wave.

Although the amount (weight) of the ballast under a light boat may be less than or the same as that under a heavy boat of the same waterline length, the proportion of ballast to displacement is usually greater. The most popular modern heavy displacement boat, the Westsail 32, has a ballast-to-displacement ratio of 36% whereas the Olson 30 has a ratio of 50% as does Bill Lee's Santa Cruz 50.

Combined with a lighter rig and hull structure, the higher ratio means that the effectiveness of the ballast may be greater for the light boat than for the heavy. However, the light boat rapidly loses performance as the angle of heel increases. Light boats are meant to be sailed as nearly upright as possible. Whereas a heavy displacement boat may sail comfortably and even well with her rail close to the water, the light boat at even moderate heel angles becomes increasingly unmanageable, leeway increases, and speed drops.

Add to this drawback the fact the light boat seldom has a powerful enough rig to move it through sloppy seas and it is understandable why most of the lightest boats perform at their best in a relatively narrow range of conditions upwind. Moreover, in heavier winds and seas their motion is snappy and exhausting and they tend to be wet.

Downwind is the way to go

Downwind is a different story. Virtually any boat but the heaviest can surf down the face of a following sea given sufficient wave height and distance between crests. The lighter the boat the quicker and farther she will surf, and do so on smaller and shorter waves. Boats with displacement/length ratios below about 100 or so can also plane when their speed is no longer restricted by the wave formation of their hull. This ability to surf and plane in even moderate conditions is a big part of the great appeal of light boats and one of the major reasons for their fast downwind passages.

The concept of the very light boat offends many purists and traditionalists, while the boats' speed and rating characteristics often drive rating rule makers to distraction. However, the "fast is fun" phenomenon is clearly here to stay. The boats offer something many modern sailors crave. They are not for the distance cruising sailor nor perhaps are they for the coastal cruising family. Yet for the lowest price per foot and the lowest price per knot they cannot be ignored.

A Comparison of Light Boats

The single most reliable indicator of ultra light displacement is a displacement-to-waterline length ratio of about 100 or less.

	DWL	Disp. lbs	Displacement/ length
Moore 24	21'9''	2,050	89
Santa Cruz 27	24'	3,000	96
Olson 30	27'6''	3,600	77
Hobie 33	30'6''	3,800	60
Santa Cruz 40	36'	10,500	101
Fast 40	36'	4,160	40
Santa Cruz 50	46'5''	15,000	67
Hunter 54	43'6''	19,500	106

Custom vs. Production Racer: What's the Difference?

Despite the popularity of PHRF racing, it is generally acknowledged that, if you want to sail against the best competition, you have to sail under the IOR rule. The IOR rule earned a reputation in the late 1970's for being a rule only for custom, one-off racers, primarily for two reasons. First, the IOR rule has been, up to now, in a state of flux. Designers were finding loopholes in the rule faster than custom boats could be built to exploit them. Production designs were obsolete before the molds were finished.

Second, the builders of production boats were using technology that was, for the most part, light years behind that of custom builders.

With the advent of the eighties, the IOR rule stabilized enough so that 1980 designs were still winning in 1983. Production builders also caught on to some of the construction tricks that make a hull light and stiff. After avoiding the IOR market for several years, many production builders are now offering IOR racers again. These production IOR boats are offered in a variety of configurations, from "racer-cruiser" all the way to "semi-custom." However, despite the claims of production builders that their boats are as competitive as a custom boat, there are still some compromises that affect performance.

To get a feel for these compromises, the editors of *PS* spent several days sailing two boats — a stock production F-3 and a semi-custom 43' Tangent One. We compared them to two very successful flat-out custom racers: *Bright Finish,* a Peterson 42, and *Razzle Dazzle,* an Irwin 43. Here's what we noticed.

The compromises of the production racer begin, ironically enough, with the decision to build the boat. In order to be a financial success, a series-produced boat must appeal to more than one buyer. The owner of a one-off, however, can have whatever he wants. A 52' custom Frers built for a Japanese owner, for example, had no berths longer than 6', and maximum headroom in the owner's stateroom was about 5' 8". The owner was just over 5' tall, and his Japanese crew not much larger. The large Americans sailing the boat in the SORC had problems getting comfortable, however.

The person buying a production racer usually does so to save money relative to the one-off boat. In theory, the cost of tooling and design is amortized over a number of boats, and some economies of scale may exist when more than one boat is built.

The cost saving can be real, or illusory. A one-off aluminum 42-footer like *Bright Finish,* for example, probably costs about $300,000 by the time it gets to the starting line. A production racer like the Tangent One — a Peterson 43-footer — will set you back about $200,000 by the time of your first race.

However, one-off isn't all that expensive sometimes. Because she was built outside, by a small crew with relatively little overhead, total investment in *Razzle Dazzle* at the starting line was less than $175,000.

As a rule, however, the one-off racer costs more than the production racer. The reasons begin with construction.

Construction

The production racer is invariably built of fiberglass, and is usually of cored construction to achieve fairly high strength/weight ratios. Coring, either with balsa or foam, is a relatively effective way to produce a light, strong hull at a reasonable cost. A reasonable amount of exotic glass types may also be used in the production racer, adding to cost. The typical production racer has a hull lighter but stronger than the production cruiser/racer.

The one-off, however, can and usually does go to the extremes in construction. *Razzle Dazzle* may be a fiberglass boat, but the relationship of her construction to that of a production boat is not very direct. Kevlar, carbon fiber, and epoxy resin make up her "fiberglass" hull. These materials cost substantially more than those found in production racers, and they are lighter, stronger, and more difficult to handle during construction.

The results, however, can be astounding. Hull and deck of *Dazzle,* less fittings, engine, and ballast, weigh only about 1500 pounds. Despite the light weight, however, *Razzle Dazzle* is probably stronger than most production racers of the same size. Therefore she can be driven harder and carry heavier rig loads — a double dividend.

Weight savings in a good one-off aluminum boat like *Bright Finish* are equally impressive. The use of aircraft industry honeycomb cored panels for almost every flat vertical or horizontal surface — bulkheads, cabin sole — saves a remarkable amount of weight even over the lightweight cored materials used for the same surfaces in a good production racer like the F-3.

Needless to say, the savings in weight compared to the typical production racer/cruiser are staggering.

The weight saving fanaticism usually seen in the one-off racer's hull has a real purpose. Ironically, the one-off and the production racer may arrive at the starting line displacing almost the same amount. The difference will be in the proportioning and distribution of weight in the two boats.

A production racer like the F-3 or the Tangent One will have a ballast-displacement ratio of about 50%. *Razzle Dazzle,* on the other hand, has almost 70% of her total displacement in ballast, with a keel weighing about 8,000 pounds and about 6,000 pounds of inside ballast. The ballast/displacement ratio of *Bright Finish* is about the same.

The large amount of inside ballast in the typical one-off allows precise control of the boat's stability and flotation — two key inputs into the IOR rating. In addition, the concentration of weight amidships due to light hull construction reduces pitching moment, making the boat faster in a chop. At this time, no popular handicapping rule takes the effect of pitching moment into account in the calculation of rating, so a good custom racer usually enjoys a significant advantage over the production racer by careful control of weight distribution, even when the total displacement of the one-off racer and the production racer happen to be the same.

Interior
A quick look at the interior of a one-off racer and of a production racer makes the compromises of the production racer quite apparent. Most production racers are simply not stripped out in the way a one-off all-out racer is likely to be. Amenities most people take for granted frequently simply don't exist in the custom racing boat.

Enclosed heads are the exception rather than the rule on custom racers up to about 50′. Usually, the head is simply tucked ahead of the mast off to one side, perhaps partially hidden by a bulkhead. *Razzle Dazzle's* "legal head" is a porta potti, duct-taped shut so it won't ever be used. Her real head is a plastic bucket hanging from the mast.

Settees usually don't exist on the custom racer. Neither do drawers, fixed berths, a lot of lockers, a cabin table, a big icebox, or a lot of galley equipment.

Frequently, headroom is limited, and the belowdecks

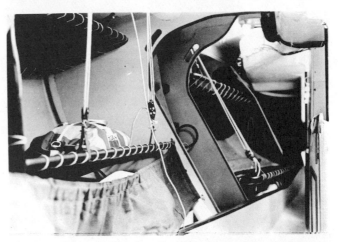

In place of luxurious settees and teak panelling, the custom racer has rows of lightweight adjustable pipe berths for effective distribution of the weight of the off watch when racing long distances.

is dark on the custom racer. Both *Bright Finish* and *Razzle Dazzle,* for example, are flush decked, with vestigial deckhouse bubbles. The Tangent One, however — a boat of the same length, with the same freeboard, and the same depth of hull — has a deckhouse 8″ or 9″ high and half the length of the boat.

The deckhouse gives greater headroom and allows ports to get light and air below, generally making the boat more livable. However, it also compromises deck layout and increases windage.

The fact is, most custom racers give minimal thought to creature comforts below, preferring to concentrate on sailing function. Open space belowdecks is more functional. Special attention is given to opening or eliminating the main bulkhead by the mast, relying instead on some more complex means of distributing rig loads. The cabin sole is wider and often there is nothing but empty space in front of the companionway. Open space makes it much easier to find and stow sails, essential with large IOR inventories. If the interior is cavelike, no one really cares, because the only time spent below is spent asleep.

Sleeping and navigating are the only two belowdecks human functions given much thought on most custom racers. The quarters of the custom racer will be jammed with pipe berths so that the weight of the offwatch crew can be used to the greatest advantage on long distance races. Likewise, the navigator is likely to be ensconced within close proximity to the helmsman, rather than in the middle of the boat.

The production racer, on the other hand, is likely to have a layout similar to that of a similar-sized racer/cruiser, with the exception that the forecabin is likely to be merely an empty space used for the storage of sails and spares when in port.

The bulkheads, permanent berths, galley fixtures, ports, hatches, and deckhouses of the production racer may make it more comfortable and more cruisable, but they are to some extent performance compromises.

Rating
Even in the midst of the process of getting measured for her IOR rating, the production racer is usually compromised. A custom racer which fails to reach her designed rating is likely to be modified to bring her down to

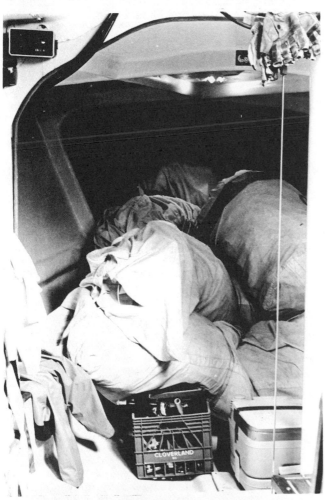

The forepeak of *Razzle Dazzle,* a custom racer. Milk crates are used to store spares such as winch handles and blocks. The head is a Porta Potti secured just forward of the mast. When racing, all sails are stored on the cabin sole, and the forepeak is completely empty.

The custom boat will likely benefit from better rating consultation and overseeing from the design office

that rating. This may include the addition or removal of inside ballast, or "bumping" measurement points such as the beam waterline or the depth stations.

All this is expensive. Even the measurement process is expensive, and the owner who has purchased a production racer in order to save costs may be reluctant to spend additional money to lower the boat's rating a tenth of a foot or so.

Reducing the rating may also involve minor or major adjustments to the sail plan, which again cost money for sail alterations and spar or rigging changes.

Other subtle but expensive differences in rating exist between the production boat and the custom boat. The propeller installation is a good example:

To some extent, the IOR gives rating credit for a prop that is deep below the surface. In practice, this is achieved by having the prop come out of the deepest section of the hull, which is the middle of the boat. Since the rule also gives some credit for engines located away from the center of the boat, the custom boat is likely to utilize an expensive hydraulic or V-drive installation in order to take full advantage of the rule. Since a good hydraulic drive can easily add $7,000 to the cost of a 45 footer, you see relatively few on production racers.

In addition, the custom boat will likely benefit from better rating consultation and overseeing from the design office. After all, the designer's next commission depends very much on the performance of his latest design, not a boat he produced two years before. Since everyone expects the one-off to perform better, the designer, sailmaker, builder, crew, and owner usually put out as much effort as possible to make sure that it does. It's a classic case of everyone wanting to back a winner.

Rig
Most stock production racers come equipped with a standard rig. Some semi-custom racers offer several choices of rig (as well as deck layout and interior). The rig of a stock production racer will invariably be "safer" (also slower) than that found on a custom boat. By safer we mean more forgiving of crew error.

A safe mast section will either be of larger diameter or of heavier wall thickness or both. Larger diameter is more common. A safe mast won't fall down if the crew is too slow with the running backstays in heavy air. A safe mast won't go out of column and crumple if the rig is mistuned. The stock mast on the F-3 is so stiff that its single running backstays are not needed until the wind blows over 20 knots. Safe masts are commonly recognized by double spreader rigs.

A custom boat will have a bendier mast that requires three or more sets of spreaders to stay in the boat. It will have upper running backstays, lower running backstays and sometimes even lower lower running backstays (count 'em, that's seven backstays to adjust). A custom racer will usually have a mast that can be bent as much and in any direction as desired, giving far more control over mainsail shape, and far less windage than the typical production racer mast.

Most production rigs are on a par with custom rigs in terms of the aerodynamic cleanliness of fittings, shrouds and running rigging.

Deck Layout
The deck layout can be one of the biggest compromises in a production racer. The crews of custom boats always seem to be hiking harder, tacking quicker, and making sail changes more efficiently. However, it's not always

because the crew is more proficient; often it's because their deck layouts make it easier for the crew to work.

The production racer's livable interior directly affects the deck layout. The companionway is likely to be farther aft to make the main cabin bigger. This means that cockpit space — space needed for the crew to work efficiently — is smaller. So as not to waste what precious little cockpit space they have, most production racers are equipped with a wheel. A wheel is less sensitive to changes in the helm than a tiller, no matter how large the wheel's diameter. While it may be less tiring to steer with a wheel, relief helmsmen are plentiful on a racing boat, and a tiller is feasible on boats as large as 44'. Any production racer smaller than 42' that has a wheel will be at a disadvantage, especially when sailing downwind in waves or when engaging in tight starting maneuvers.

Generally speaking, custom boats are better rigged. Mainsheet travelers work better because they are radiused to the swing of the boom. Winches are powerful enough for heavy air work; production racers almost always have winches one size too small. On a custom boat you can specify stoppers that won't slip, more expensive turning blocks (Harken or Penguin instead of the cheaper hardware lines usually found on production racers), and color-coded sheets and halyards. After

The cockpit of the custom racer is laid out for racing efficiency, with no compromises for cocktail comfort in the harbor. You never sit in the cockpit of a custom racer: there's no place to sit!

Another view of the cockpit of the custom racer shows the small companionway, oversize winches, and instrument repeaters. The angled hatch just forward of the tiller is over the nav station, allowing instant communication between navigator and helmsman.

you've bought a production racer, you'll find a lot of
rigging that could be done better — rigging that has
been done to a price. Often, the cost of doing it over
again right is prohibitive.

As mentioned earlier, the long cabin houses found on
production racers make more windage and more difficult crew movement than the flush or "bubble" decks of
custom boats. Cockpit seats and coamings, and raised
aluminum toerails also make life miserable for the crew.
The decks of most custom boats are flat from the edge of
the cockpit all the way out to the sheer. There is nothing
to trip over as the crew moves from one side to the other
during a tack. Once their legs are hung over the rail,
there is no toerail to bite into the backs of their thighs.

Aluminum custom boats have a welded hull-to-deck
joint, and use padeyes spaced at wide intervals to
attach snatch blocks to the rail. Fiberglass custom
boats often use sail track over the hull-to-deck joint, and
mount teak on the foredeck for the crew, but never aluminum toerail. Whereas the crew of a production boat

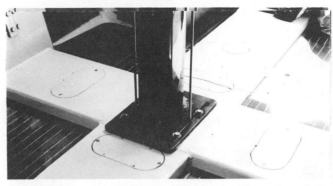

Since interior comfort is at best secondary aboard the
custom racer, structural elements which to some extent interfere with interior space, such as the massive aluminum beam
mast step and centerline stringer of Infinity, can be used.

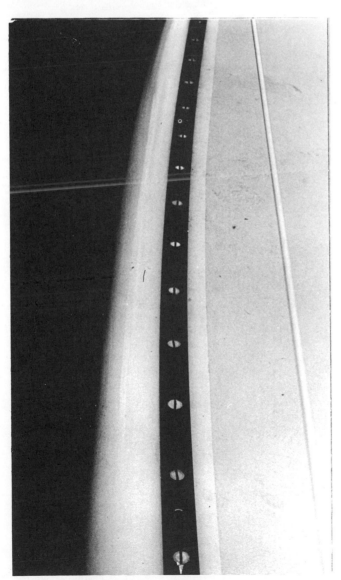

The rounded sheer of *Razzle Dazzle* allows the crew to hike
out for hours without having circulation cut off by a teak
toerail, or worse yet, by L-shaped aluminum toerail track.

will have to sit with their fannies 1½' inboard of the rail
to save the torture on the backs of their legs, the crew of
a custom boat can slide their rear ends a foot farther
outboard for significantly greater leverage. *Razzle Dazzle* has taken this technique to an extreme: her sheer is
rounded to about a 3" radius.

Conclusion

Given the disadvantages facing the owner of the production racer, why would anyone bother to spend the
money? There are a number of reasons, some obvious,
some less so.

Since the production racer is likely to be "safer" to
sail, that is, harder to break, the boat requires a lower
level of expertise. This means that a syndicate of doc-
tors or lawyers who want to race their boat every
weekend can do so without worrying about getting
together a high-powered crew every time they go out.

We know of custom boats, on the other hand, that are
owned by "amateur" owners who never touch the
wheel, whose crews consist of a helmsman from the sail
loft or design office, sail trimmers from the sail loft, and
friendly gorillas from other one-offs that don't happen to
be racing that weekend.

When the owner or his friends come aboard, they
simply sit on the rail or dispense beer and sandwiches.
That's not our idea of sailing.

Ironically, the poorly-sailed production racer may
have more value at resale time than the poorly-sailed or
non-competitive one-off. If the Hedgehopper 40 has a
good record, but yours simply won't go, the better record of her sisters will keep her value up. No one, however, wants a one-off that has always been a barker, even
if it's by a good designer. Good designers do, sometimes, come up with boats that never live up to their
advance billing.

A good production racer like the F-3 or the Tangent
One may be very competitive at the club level, and may
be reasonably competitive even at higher levels. To
some extent it depends on the degree of preparation of
the boat, the amount of attention paid to details such as
underwater fairing and smoothness, the quality of the
sails, and of course, the quality of the helmsman, crew,
and the original design.

It is true that the production racer often starts her
competitive life with two strikes against her. Remember,
however, that plenty of home runs have been hit with an
0-2 count.

II

The
Economics
of
Buying
a
Boat

How Much Does a New Boat Really Cost?

Boat prices, like most prices, simply will not stay still. However, this 1980 cost study of the price of a new boat can be applied to your own contemplated purchase, substituting the current cost of the boat and gear you want. The figures will change, but the method and message remain the same.

It's an all-too-common scene: a sailor steps into a yacht sales office shopping for a boat that he would earnestly like to have, and which is advertised at a "base" or "sailaway" price that he thinks he can handle.

An hour or two later he steps out of the office dazed and probably angry over what that boat, in the water and ready to sail, is actually going to cost. More than likely he is embarrassed; the talk about a new boat has been lunch time conversation with colleagues and supper time talk with his family for some time.

No one profits from this situation; not boatbuilders, nor boat sellers, nor boat buyers.

Some of the fault for the situation lies with the builders and their advertising agencies, which include an undefined price in the advertising and brochure material. The marine industry should adopt some uniform standards for the pricing of their products. For numerous and complex reasons, such standards are, in the words of one builder, something that will "never happen."

The difference between the base price and the actual price of boats delivered and ready to sail does, of course, vary, from boat to boat and builder to builder. One major builder, Hunter Marine, for instance, has had considerable marketing success reducing the gap to a minimum and attracting buyers, especially those with little confidence or experience in outfitting a boat as well as those who choose their boats largely on the basis of price.

Hunter's ploy is to include in the listed price an extensive assortment of equipment (including sails) in what that firm calls its CruisePac. This equipment is a package of items most other builders have as options

We think this is the type of information a sailor needs to make practical decisions in buying a boat

---

but which, with Hunter, is standard.

More typically, however, is that the average "base price" of production boats amounts to 75% to 80% of the final price of a boat as finally delivered to a boat buyer. Complete "from scratch" outfitting can run the final price to 30% greater than the base price. Add financing and the base price can nearly double, albeit over a span of several years.

Note that we have said nothing about two other widely separate alternatives. One alternative is partially completed boats with certain details, usually joiner-work and hardware installation, left for owner completion. At the other end of the spectrum are production boats which are "semi-custom" in that there are a number of options offered, especially in interior layout, engine installations, rig, and underwater configurations. Our concern here is with the vast majority of new stock boats purchased by conventional methods from dealers.

The only practical way to avoid disillusionment in pricing such a boat is to be armed in advance with a realistic idea of all the costs that buying a new boat entails. To this end *The Practical Sailor* set out to "buy" a boat.

We chose to price out a boat with wide appeal, the type that would meet the desires and needs of the widest possible market. Thirty feet seemed the right size; in unit sales it is the busiest part of the marine market for boats, because boats of this size have on-board livability and at least limited offshore sailing capabilities.

We selected a boat that is conventional and contemporary, neither an all-out racer nor an all-out cruiser. Finally , we wanted a boat manufactured by one of the larger boatbuilding firms for the simple reason that such a boat can more easily be compared with the products from other large firms.

The boat we chose is the Ericson 30+. However, before what we are doing be misconstrued as an advertisement for Ericson Yachts, let us state that this is not in any way an endorsement for a particular boat. Rather it is a cost study of a product; we could as easily have chosen to "buy" a C&C 30, Tartan 30, San Juan 30, Cal 31, or a host of other similar boats between 28' and 32'.

The Ericson 30+ is not cheap. It is a boat built and marketed to be competitive in both styling and price with the majority of other quality production boats in its size range. Market research indicates that the boat should enjoy a satisfactory volume of sales against other boats of her ilk.

Based on our experience, we made up an inventory for our "new boat." We tried to avoid idiosyncrasies (one practical sailor/writer hates electronics and electrics, and carries nothing on his 30-footer but running lights—backed up with oil lamps—but he also carries a sextant and three chronometers). Instead, we made the

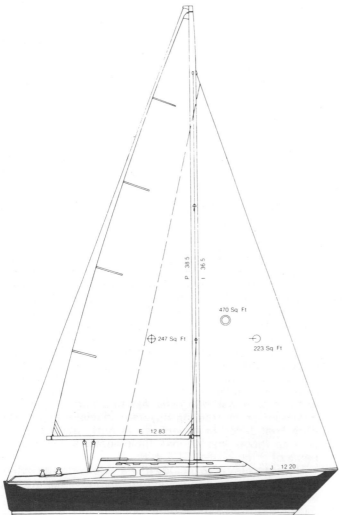

Ericson 30+

Main Standard Features

Running and steaming lights
Two Barient #10 halyard winches
Main, Jib, and Spinnaker halyards
Genoa tracks and fair leads
Two #21A Barient sheet winches
Slab reefing gear on boom
Topping lift
28″ SS wheel with brake and pedestal guard
Emergency tiller
Pulpits, stanchions, and double lifelines
Swimming ladder
16-HP Universal diesel with full instrumentation
25-gal. fuel tank
Two 12-volt, 90-amp batteries
Circuit breaker electrical panel
110 AC power, panel, outlets, and 50′ cord
25-gal. fresh water tank
6-gal. hot water tank
Hot and cold pressure water system
Galley foot pump
Whale Gusher manual bilge pump
Electric bilge and shower sump pump
6 cu. ft. ice box
2-burner, gimballed alcohol stove with oven
WC with 16-gal. holding tank and dockside discharge
Upholstered berth cushions and backs

How $44,800 Grows to $67,672.54 Without Even Trying

Base price of Ericson 30 + , Jan. 15, 1980	$44,800.00

Additions to base boat

Rig

Spinnaker gear

pole, Forespar XP-300 XP, double bridle	207.00
*jockey pole, Forespar, RSL 300 FF with mast sockets	200.00
*deck chocks for poles, four Forespar DC-2	98.00
*spinnaker pole track, 1'' w/ stops, cars, lines	128.00
*pole lift, tangs, block, line, snap shackle, and cleat	152.00
snatch blocks, two Merriman @$49.00	98.00
*spinnaker halyard winch, Lewmar 7A	94.00
*spinnaker winches, two Lewmar 16A	469.00
pole downhaul, ½'' dacron, 40 ft., with snap shackle and splice	60.40
*downhaul winch, Lewmar 7A	94.00
*Foredeck track for pole downhaul, 24''x1'' with UHMW car and C&W Block BL 41-BO1	157.45
spinnaker sheets, two ½''x50' dacron braid with Merriman 721-3 shackles	255.00
Boom vang, Merriman 271-3	90.15
*Windex wind indicator	47.45
Turnbuckle sleeves, six Davis Instruments, 20'' @$2.95	17.70

Deck

Boathook, 6' EZ-In	21.00
Anchors	
CQR, 25 lb. with 150' nylon line and 12' of ½'' chain	455.00
Danforth, 22 lb., standard with 150' nylon line and 12' of ½'' chain	385.00
Fenders, four PAR, 8''x22'' @$32.19	128.76
Cockpit cushions, fitted	175.00
Awning	100.00
Compass, Danforth Constellation, 5''	490.00
Screens for Main, midships and fore hatches, Velcro	80.00
Water trap vents, three Nicro PVC @$64.95	194.85
Installation	68.00
Docklines, four ½''x30' nylon with eye splice @$18.00	72.00
*Anchor Light, WC	85.00
Flag pole, bracket, and ensign	21.19
Deck brush, Lan O Sheen, 10'' with 4' handle	10.99

Electronic and Navigation Gear

*VHF radio, Motorola 440 with 3DB mast antenna	900.00
RDF, Vecta @$275.00 with Lake Michigan Crystal @$16.50	291.50
*Depth sounder, Datamarine S200DL	510.00
*Speedometer, Datamarine S100KL	510.00
*Log, Datamarine S100L II	295.00
Hand Bearing compass, Ritchie	75.00

Sails (Hood)

Main with 2 reef rows	956.00
#1, 150% jib	745.00
#2, 125% jib	646.00
#3, 105% jib	545.00
storm jib	249.00
spinnaker with turtle	922.00

Hull and Interior

Oil lamps, three WC 160200 with smoke bell @$46.50	139.50
Installation	24.50
Extra (2nd) manual bilge pump, Whale Gusher 10 with accessories	108.00
Installation	48.00
*Lever seacocks, six WC 1565 seacocks — $68	408.00
Clock, Seth Thomas Corsair	210.95
Barometer, Seth Thomas Corsair	145.95
Curtains with piping	200.00

Safety

Safety harnesses, four Forespar @$28.00	112.00
Fire extinguishers, three American La France F-200, 5BC @$15.95	47.85
Life preservers, six adult's @$7.65	45.90
Life preservers, three child's @$6.75	20.25
Horseshoe life ring and bracket, two	104.63
Man overboard pole, drogue, Forespar OP-120	95.80
First aid kit, J&J for six people	13.60
Fog horn, mouth operated	5.95
Bell	19.25
General signal kit	5.75
Olin 25mm pistol flare kit	103.70
Life raft, Avon Valise, six-man with canopy	2,205.00
Radar reflector and line	24.95
Overboard strobe, Honey	19.85

Miscellaneous

Cradle	495.00
Transportation to Waukegan, IL, 2,230 miles @$1.21	2,708.79
Dinghy and oars, Eli-Laminates, 8'	386.00
Commissioning by dealer	885.00
Total	63,598.61

Sales tax

State of Illinois @5.25%	3,338.93

Documentation and Insurance

Documentation, professional fee	115.00
Insurance, Fireman's Fund, 6 mo. dry, 300/300, 5,000 major medical, 1% ($620) deductible on $62,000 value	620.00
Total	**$67,672.54**

*Installed

equipment list representative of the way most buyers of such a sized boat will equip their yacht: not too spartan, not too exotic, and useful for most needs. We did not include some back-up gear such as lead line and patent log; these are items a sailor may already own or may opt not to buy, at least not as part of the original purchase.

The thinking that went into our inventory was based on certain basic premises. We feel, for instance, that sails are power and should not be subject to scrimping, even for a boat to be used exclusively for cruising. Therefore, we included a full sail inventory with the gear necessary to handle it. On the other hand, we did not include the specific sails and gear of the racer: spinnaker staysails, bloopers, drifters, multiple jib sheet tracks, barber haulers, and hydraulic adjusters. We also tried to avoid gear which is brand new to the market or is, to us, merely "in fashion."

Because one's life as well as the safety of the vessel can depend on them, we have specified a full complement of ground tackle and navigation and safety gear. A regular distress signal set and a special flare gun are listed, as is man overboard equipment. Full electronic navigation and communication facilities are also included. Also, we have added a second bilge pump and upgraded all through-hull fittings with lever seacocks.

On the other hand, because they require extraordinary maintenance and are not essential even for rac-ing, we have not put electronic wind instruments such as anemometers and apparent wind indicators on the list.

Above all, we want to stress that the list of gear we have compiled should not in any way be construed as items endorsed by *The Practical Sailor.* The criteria we used in their selection are that the items, for the most part, are widely recognized and available to sailor/consumers, and that they are the items a sailor is apt to consider in his shopping.

In common with most stock-built boats of her size and type currently on the market, the Ericson 30+ comes with a single standard layout and a standard package of basic equipment. We have spelled out what is standard; our list of supplemental items consists of other gear we think is needed for a reasonable use of the boat. Of course we omitted personal gear such as bedding, bikinis, pots, pans, and toilet paper; we want to talk about what it costs to buy a boat, not to support a lifestyle.

For a similar reason we did not include financing costs in our list. However, because in this day and age, financing is so often a consideration, we did work out separately a typical financing schedule for our total "purchase."

In shopping for our boat we went to Larsen Marine Service in Waukegan, Illinois, and yacht broker Don

Do We Really Want to Finance?

As soon as we determined what our boat was going to cost, we set about finding a way to pay for her. This process led us into the morass of high finance at a time when money was tight. And expensive. And scarce.

Our search for the best possible (or least objectionable) terms led us to do considerable shopping around, a project we earnestly advise anyone in our position to undertake. We asked a number of boat finance companies and banks. The finance companies seemed eager for our business; the banks were cooperative but unenthusiastic.

Throughout our investigation we talked in terms of a $62,000 value on the boat. The finance companies we approached wanted at least 25% down (although one hot-breathing spokesman indicated he might "shave" that figure a bit). That left a principal on our prospective loan of $46,500. These companies also preferred a 12-year term. A smaller principal and/or a shorter term raised the interest rate.

The banks, smiling indulgently, wanted shorter terms (five years), a smaller principal (60%), and higher interest. Their terms, hedging, and demeanor sent us to more promising pastures, notably the eager marine finance companies.

Terms for the loan we sought are by The Rule of 78, a repayment schedule that charges interest in proportion to remainder of principal and time on the repayment. Interest is thus highest at the outset, declining as principal is repaid, much in the manner of a home mortgage. With The Rule of 78 there is no penalty for prepayment of principal.

Incidentally, the amount we were discussing generated real interest (pun intended) with the lending com-panies. Had we been asking about financing a small boat with an amount under $20,000 or so, the enthusiasm would have been proportionately less. We did not pursue the matter, but for small loans the advice was to look to short term loans from banks at simple interest. Such loans are exorbitant, currently at an interest rate as much as 3% over prime, often requiring points (prepayment of non-tax deductible fees for borrowing) and carrying a charge for prepayment on the principal.

For our boat loan the 144 monthly payments on the $46,500 loan at 13% interest amount to approximately $635. The total of principal and interest over the term of the loan would thus be $91,440, a total interest charge of $44,940. On those terms the grand total on a boat valued at $62,000 would run to almost $107,000 if allowed to go full term. Of course, assuming the income tax laws remain as they are now over the life of the loan, we would recover a percentage of the interest as a tax deduction, a "saving" of perhaps $20,000.

All the lending firms we talked to require an insurance policy with coverage equal to the value of the boat (hence the $62,000 valuation listed in our table of costs) plus documentation, needed to obtain a first preferred ship's mortgage ("The only way we can put a lien on the boat," said one officer). The boat would be the collateral.

Finally we should include a word of warning. Unanimously the finance companies spoke to us on the presumption that we could afford a boat at the agreed valuation of $62,000, that our credit is acceptable, and that our annual income is approximately equal to the amount of the principal.

In the end we wound up with a $44,800 base-priced boat that cost us nearly $70,000, an almost 50% increase over the starting price

O'Keene. In our opinion, Larsen Marine is a fine yard and O'Keene a knowledgeable and honest broker. His first step in dealing with a client is to try to tell the client how much the yacht he wants is really going to cost, so he was quite willing to price out the Ericson 30 + and our choice of gear.

Note that in providing prices for the items we chose, O'Keene gave us only list prices. In negotiating the bottom line price of a boat such as the Ericson 30 + many dealers offer discounts, "packages," optional items as "standard," and so forth. Such price variations are so numerous that they make it impossible to discuss boat pricing as we have done here were we to take them into account. Instead, we chose to price our boat with no "deals" (which might reduce the total by 5%).

Larsen Marine is what might be termed a moderately expensive boatyard. Its labor rate is $23 per hour; all yard-installed gear on our list is installed at that rate. Larsen Marine also has a flat rate of $885 for commissioning an Ericson 30 +. Many owners would choose to do all or part of the commissioning themselves, but, again, the variations would make the alternatives impossible to explore here, so we give the flat rate. Note, though, that the Ericson 30 + comes from the factory with bottom paint.

Note, also, that we have included professional documentation costs and the insurance premium for the first year. Although we do not ordinarily consider these costs part of the price of a boat, we include them because many buyers do have to figure them in the purchase price, just as they may add the rental of marina space or a mooring (we did not include marina or mooring prices, however). Incidentally, usually insurance and sometimes documentation is required for financing.

In the end we wound up with a $44,800 base-priced boat that cost us nearly $70,000 by the time she was fully fitted, commissioned, documented, insured, and taxed, almost a 50% increase over the figure we started with. Realistically we then played with our long list of options, culling the more extravagant and less essential ones. Readers should do the same. In doing so we could have dropped the final price by almost 8% yet still a figure that can be disturbing and discouraging if we had hoped to buy the boat at close to the base or listed price.

We would like to emphasize that boats are not an "investment" in the sense that you make money on them. They are toys, expensive toys. Accepting the general rule of yacht value, the typical new boat depreciates at 10% the first year after purchase, 5% the second year, and does not depreciate the third year. Thereafter, you can expect about 5% per year appreciation on the "average" well-kept boat, assuming a continuing high inflation rate.

—J. Pazereskis

Used Ericson 30 + : For Sale Cheap

Three and one-half years after we "paid" $65,000 for our hypothetical Ericson 30 +, we became curious how much it would be "worth" were we to offer her for sale on the used boat market. We first deducted some figures: the additions to the base boat that we probably would not *actually* have bought (eg, life raft, clock); the one-time expenses of buying a boat (eg, shipping, dealer commissioning, sales tax, documentation expenses); and recurring annual costs (eg, insurance); none of which can rightfully be considered part of the *value* of our boat. We came up with a figure about $13,000 less than the original bottom line price. In short, the value of the boat we "bought" 3½ years ago was $54,500.

By fall, 1983, the "book value" of our Ericson 30 +, according to the BUC Used Boat Price Guide, is about $49,000 for the Great Lakes where we bought her and presumably would be trying to sell her. Frankly, the 10% depreciation in the value of our boat puzzled us a bit, exceeding as it does the typical appreciation/depreciation of boats in the high inflation that characterized most of the time we owned the boat.

Wondering how realistic our figures were, we looked up an ad for a used Ericson 30 + and phoned the owner. His Ericson 30 + is one season younger than the boat we priced out, having been bought in the fall of 1980. Otherwise the only differences that could account for any discrepancy in price are that this is a shoal draft version, is fitted with roller furling, and is located on the east coast. Reportedly she is in excellent shape.

The asking price on the advertised 30 + in September was $44,000 direct, $48,000 through a broker. The owner, seemingly a savvy fellow, regarded the price as realistic and apparently was not in much of a mood to negotiate. He did not, in fact, sell the boat, selling a share to a partner instead. As he had bought the boat used (after a few times sailing, the original buyer's wife insisted the boat be sold), the present owner does not know exactly what the first buyer paid for the boat but guesses it was close to our figure of $55,000.

In selling the boat at the going market price we would have to "eat" the approximately $7000 "new boat" costs we had paid three years before. With the exception of the sales tax, they are expenses the buyer of the used boat can save. After only four seasons of use we doubt if a buyer would have to replace any of the gear on the boat, at least not immediately. The working sails have reached about half life, the engine is not likely to need any overhaul (only, perhaps, tuning), and for the type of normal use we put on the boat, a new owner might need only do a thorough cleaning, replace some sheets and a halyard or two, and have the electronics checked.

Although the Ericson 30 + is no longer available as a new boat (regrettably since it was chosen for the article originally in hopes we could keep track of price changes year by year), a reasonable estimate of the value of the same boat bought new this fall and comparably equipped is $65,000, up about $9000 in the interim. Add to this another $7000 in new boat expenses. The finance charge (interest) is lower than it was 3½ years ago, but the amount of the loan is higher, assuming the same 25% down on the purchase price.

Without assessing the *quality* of the Ericson 30 +, only her dollar value as a used boat, our 30 + at less than $50,000 certainly makes a case for buying used rather than new. In the 3½ years we "lost" $15,000. Thankfully, it was only a paper exercise.

How Inflation Affected Boat Prices: 1975-1980

Early in 1981, after a period of high inflation, Antoinette Stockenberg analyzed the effects of inflation on boat prices over the preceeding five years. Some of the numbers are rather stunning, and their effects linger into today's market. Because boats vary so widely in type and condition, it is unlikely that any "typical" experience will apply directly to a particular boat. Nevertheless, the experience of the six boats in this sample and the resulting conclusions provide a useful tool for the boatowner who wants to know how his "investment" has fared over the past decade or so, and for anyone who wants to estimate the future return on a boat purchase.

Tain't necessarily so, that a boat's a hole in the water in which to throw your money. On the other hand, it's not exactly a money market fund. Certain boat owners who brood over the classified ads feel smug and rich as they watch boat values go up and up each year. Other boat owners may see their boats running in place or losing a little each year. And still others who plan to buy or move up are dismayed and depressed by the rocketing cost of their dreams. Inflation, in short, cuts all ways.

The Practical Sailor set about to explore the ramifications of galloping inflation on the new and used boat market. Specifically we wanted to compare the prices, five years ago and today, of a select sampling of production sailboats. How much has the cost of a 1980 boat gone up since its 1975 counterpart? And, of more interest to those who, like us, consider a boat an investment, how well has a sampling of boats maintained value or appreciated in the five years since they were built?

Our job was made easier by the fact that of the hundreds of production boats available today, only a handful were being built five years ago. For our analysis we selected the Hunter 30, the Endeavour 32, the Pearson 35, the Irwin 37, the Hinckley Bermuda 40, and the Morgan Out Island 41. These six boats seem a reasonably representative cross section of boats with a combination of popularity and long production runs. Note, however, that they do serve merely as a sampling in a study of how inflation has affected boat prices in general, not a definitive answer about these boats in particular.

One of the most telling features of our study has been the difficulty we encountered in obtaining basic data. We had no problem obtaining current brochure material, options list, and price sheet. Five-year-old material was another story. Clearly five years is a long time in this business: of the six manufacturers, only Hinckley and Irwin could locate the information completely and quickly.

Of the other manufacturers—almost all of whose representatives were courteous and apparently willing to cooperate—one found most, but not all of the information immediately; one produced the 1975 base price but had no extant literature; one (very obliging office) offered all kinds of extraneous information without quite having precisely what we needed; and one hadn't a clue. Pricing policies were treated as arcane knowledge; brochures and price sheets were "maybe in storage but probably not." Few of the marketing people held their positions five years ago—"I wasn't here then" was a favorite reply—so it was hard to get a general sense of a model's evolution.

Nonetheless, here's what we concluded from the data we did collect. First of all, the total inflation rate for the years 1975 to 1980 was 51.1%. Signficantly the construction of a fiberglass boat involves many of the factors that are used to determine the consumer price index: steel for rigging and fittings, a petro-chemical (polyester resin), rubber, fabrics, and a big chunk of labor. It therefore might be reasonable to consider sailboat construction and prices a microcosm of the economy and the economic behavior of boatbuilders to parallel that of the economy.

How Much Base Prices Increased
The base price of the Pearson 35 in 1975 (adjusted for our purposes to include a diesel engine which was not then standard), was $34,925. The base price of a Pearson 35 built in 1980 was $52,815 (diesel included). This represents an increase of 51.2%—virtually identical to the rate of inflation for the period.

Working from a 1975 options list we calculated that the "sailaway" price for a 1975 Morgan Out Island 41 similarly equipped to the OI 41 offered in 1980 would have been about $69,600. This price includes the ketch rig option, an overwhelming choice of buyers and a major factor in determining used boat appreciation. The low end of the 1980 sailaway range with a ketch rig is $107,200, an increase over the five years of 54%, just exceeding the inflation rate.

The Hunter 30 comes equipped with a sizable package of gear that on most other production boats is optional. This makes our task of arriving at a usable price for both the 1975 and the 1980 Hunter 30 relatively easy. The 1975 base price for a Hunter 30 was $21,500 (which included a 12 hp diesel). In 1980 the new Hunter 30 sold at $34,990. This represents a higher-than-inflation increase of 60.4%.

The Hinckley Bermuda 40 was as difficult to price as the Hunter 30 was easy. At the higher end of the price range for production yachts, the Bermuda 40 is available with an extensive range of optional gear and customized features. We estimate a buyer could readily add 20% to the base price of a Bermuda 40. However, we tried to stick with a base price in comparing new-boat price with the inflation rate for five years.

The base price of a Bermuda 40, a standard boat in commission, in 1975 was $89,500. In 1980 the cost was $145,000 an increase of 62.5%, well over inflation.

Irwin Yachts, like Hunter, produces "affordable" boats. The 1975 and 1980 versions of the popular Irwin 37 in 1975 was $38,950. By 1980 the base price had risen to $65,670, an increase of 68.6%. Granted, we think the newer 37 is a better quality product, but the increase is more than 17 percentage points above the inflation rate.

The sample boat with the biggest increase over the last five years is the Endeavour 32. Her base price went up a daunting 77%. Although Endeavor Yachts supplied us with the prices for the 32 for 1975 and 1980 ($22,500 and $40,700 with wheel steering becoming standard in the interim), the firm was unable to get some of the information that would have made our analysis easier.

New Boat Price Increases: 1975-1980

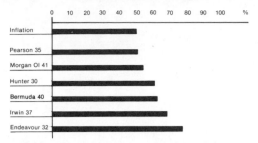

Graph 1: The price of all six sample boats has increased at more than the inflation rate during the last five years

Used Boat Appreciation: 1975-1980

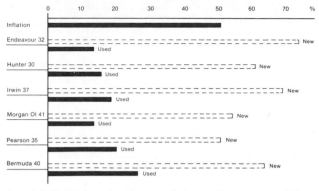

Graph 2: Based on the six sample boats there seems little correlation between the appreciation rate of a 1975 boat and the increase in new boat prices by 1980.

Because the builders who make these boats are, in our opinion, typical of the industry as a whole, we think further analysis would show a similar trend in other boat prices. We doubt if any major builder has been able to keep his prices *below* the inflation rate.

Used Boat Appreciation—1975-1980

Boats really have no right to appreciate at all in value. They are irrational, vulnerable, ephemeral purchases and we ought, we suppose, to be penalized for making them. Luckily that is not always so.

The typical modern production boat such as those included in our sample has appreciated. Now, five years after purchase, her dollar value should be greater than her owner's original outlay including the cost of additional gear an owner of a new boat puts aboard but whose cost is usually not considered part of the purchase price.

However, no one should expect the appreciation rate on any production boat to keep even approximate pace with the current inflation rate. In short, no one should consider a boat a hedge against the declining value of the dollar.

From our study we find the typical 1975 production boat has appreciated at 2-3% per year.

With all this in mind we set about to see how our six sample boats fared, how much each might have appreciated if bought in 1975 and well maintained. Again, to make purchase prices reflect reality we had to add a percentage to the 1975 quoted "base price" to bring the price more in line with what an owner actually invested in his boat. Note, though, that we are still talking about *averages* and a *sampling*. Anyone interested in a specific boat should compile his own sample.

In arriving at our figures we relied on the Used Boat Price Guide, an industry "bluebook" published by BUC International. For convenience we graphed the results.

Our study shows that, as might be expected, the Bermuda 40 with 20% added to the base or standard price ($89,500) for a typical array of options and put-aboard gear went from $107,400 in 1975 to about $145,000 for that same 1975 boat purchased used in 1980. This is an increase of 26%, an appreciation of about half the rate of inflation during that period. Matched against the 62.5% increase in the price of new Bermuda 40s from 1975 to 1980, this 26% appreciation has made the Bermuda 40 a good investment, perhaps as good an investment as any boat should be expected to be.

At the other end of the value scale the Hunter 30, even with a generous 10% added for gear to the 1975 base price ($21,500 which already included most gear othe boats have as optional) brought her price up to $23,650. In 1980 the going price for a Hunter 30 five years old was about $24,700, about 4% appreciation. Thus the Hunter 30 has been a disappointing investment from a strictly economic standpoint except in relation to the increase in cost of a new Hunter 30 between 1975 and 1980.

The Endeavour 32 has the poorest record in terms of used 1975 boats keeping pace with the increase in new boat prices. A 1975 Endeavour 32 with 15% added for options (as noted previously, we had difficulty in determining 1975 standard equipment), the all-up 32 went from $25,875 new in 1975 to about $29,100 used, only about 11% appreciation. Meanwhile, in 1980 the price of new 32s had gone up 77%.

The Morgan Out Island 41 on these same terms appreciated at 11% while the new boat prices rose 54% and the Irwin 37 increased about 19% matched against a 68.6% increase.

The Pearson 35 appreciated 22% figured on the same basic terms as the other five boats. When calculated against the lowest increase (51.2%) of the six in the price of a 1980 boat, the Pearson 35 comes across as having been, dollar for dollar, the best investment of any boat in our sampling. On the other hand, the 35 may not be the best when considered for purchase as a used boat. The gap between a five-year-old 35 and a new 35 is, in percentage, nowhere near as large. Incidentally, we understand that the brokerage market for Pearson 35s is definitely a sellers' market; the demand is high and the supply of available boats low. This fact has to reflect a degree of awareness of how the 35 has retained her value over the years.

What does all this mean? Well, it does show conclusively that there is a wide range in the amount boats appreciate. It also means that unless the money invested in a boat is unimportant, a buyer should take appreciation into account when he considers buying any boat. Boats may not give the return on investment that real estate, a mutual fund, or high yield paper might, but their appreciation cannot be ignored.

There are, of course, other factors to consider in determining the value of a boat. These include aesthetics, performance, durability, and versatility. There is also the matter of costs just to maintain their value. (Ironically the average 2-3% appreciation about equals the average cost of upkeep.)

Then there is the matter of financing. When you borrow money at 15% interest for 10 years to finance a boat that will appreciate from zero to 6% a year and costs 3% of her value to maintain, one has the makings of a wretched investment, from a purely economic standpoint.

That is, naturally, no reason not to buy a boat. However, it should make any prospective buyer sit down with a calculator, a collection of used boat prices, and some conservative projections about where the economy might go before making a commitment to buy any boat.

—A. Stockenberg

A Glimpse at the Six Sample Boats

The six boats selected for analysis represent a cross section of modern production yachts. All have been in production longer than is average for such yachts and all have proved popular. These were the only criteria for their selection.

Irwin 37

Irwin, like Hunter, produces "affordable" boats by operating a volume building facility with meticulous attention to production and marketing costs. The 37 is, in a variety of ways, typical of the cruising boats Irwin has produced over the last two decades. An extensive evaluation appears in this book.

The layout of the 1975 and 1980 models of the Irwin 37 is identical, as is the power plant (Perkins 4-108 diesel). Propane has replaced alcohol as the stove fuel, a stern pulpit is now standard, lifelines are double with gates on both sides, and teak has replaced shag carpeting on the main cabin sole. There has been an obvious trend to include more wood (teak) trim below. This added joinerwork marks the most evident difference between 1975 and later versions.

Endeavour 32

Endeavour Yachts came into being when John Brooks, a former employee of Irwin Yachts, bought the tooling for the Irwin 32. Renamed the Endeavour 32 when she was introduced in 1975, the boat was intended to be a more elegant version (spelled *Endeavour,* after all) of the popular but unadorned Irwin 32. She has a shoal draft, centerboard hull (by 1980 she was available with a deep keel as an option) and a masthead rig.

At her introduction, Endeavour touted the 32 as a "limited production quality sailboat at a realistic price." She is still described the same way five years later (although *realistic* has been changed to *competitive*). She has diesel power, more attention to details and finish than she enjoyed as an Irwin-built boat, and has attracted buyers looking for different ideas of interior decor inside a conventional and accepted hull shape.

Pearson 35

This Bill Shaw centerboard design, first launched in 1968, underwent only minor changes since 1975, understandable because the 35 has been one of the most popular and enduring boats in the extensive Pearson line.

Her builder, Pearson Yachts, a division of Grumman Allied Industries, has long enjoyed a reputation for dependability. The firm has what may be the best dealer network in the industry and has worked closely with those dealers in developing design ideas, warranty service, and promotion. Over the years Pearson's designs and construction have been, as a rule, quite cautious—cruisers and occasionally cruiser-racers appealing to a broad spectrum of buyers.

In keeping with its reputation for predictability, Pearson offered much the same options for the 35 in 1980 that it did in 1975. The most remarkable increase then was in the cost of having the name and hailing port painted on the transom — up 264% from $33 to $120.

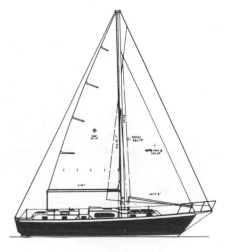

Irwin 37

Endeavour 32

Pearson 35

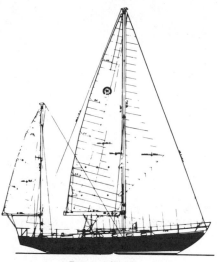

Bermuda 40

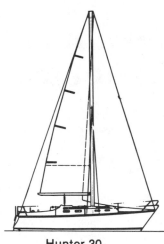

Hunter 30

Out Island 41

Hunter 30

When the Hunter 30 was introduced in 1974 it was the largest boat in the Hunter line. Her appeal since has been her price; the Hunter 30 is perhaps the cheapest boat for her length on the market. She is, as Hunter Marine likes to point out, "affordable."

In our evaluation of the smaller but otherwise similar Hunter 27 we note that Hunter has been able to keep costs to a minimum over a long period of time through rigidly standardized construction, volume purchase of materials and gear, and finish work of indifferent quality. More-over, Hunter Marine relocated from New Jersey to Florida where it could find a cheaper labor market and lower production overhead.

A buyer of a Hunter 30 has few options to choose from. The boat comes equipped with a long list of standard equipment in a package called the CruisePac that includes sails, safety gear, lines, and even a copy of Chapman's **Seamanship and Small Boat Handling.** Hunter standard-equipped boats are as close to "sailaway" as any major production boat on the market.

Bermuda 40

Ah, the Bermuda 40. Who hasn't sighed at the sight of one. And sighed at their unaffordability. Perhaps better than any other so-called stock boat, the Bill Tripp designed Bermuda 40 is a combination of traditional design, good construction, elegantly finished trim and joinerwork, and quality hardware. In production by the Henry R. Hinckley Co. since 1961, the Bermuda 40 is what many sailors consider the one true classic yacht in the history of fiberglass boatbuilding.

In the long production run of the 40 few changes have been made in her construction. Likewise, interior detail remains practically the same. A shower is now standard as are double lifelines. A few cowl vents have been eliminated and the winches have been upgraded.

Production of the Bermuda 40 is limited to 4 to 10 boats a year depending on orders and availability of space in the Hinckley facility—hardly assembly line volume. Nor is the 40 merely assembled. What separates the Bermuda 40 from the rest of the production boat fleet is extensive labor: teak grates, numerous crafted drawers and lockers, custom racks, detailing and fittings.

Hinckley makes no attempt to impress buyers with a short list of "standard" gear (a few life jackets and docklines tossed into her cockpit at commissioning). Instead, Hinckley offers a staggering list of options, factory-installed gear, and custom features from which a buyer may choose and all of which are costly. By the time a well-heeled owner sails his new 40 away, her price may be 25-30% over the so-called base price.

Morgan Out Island 41

First launched by Morgan Yacht in 1971, the Out Island 41 had evolved by 1975 (model 414) into essentially the same as today's OI 415. The beamy, center-cockpit, shoal-draft sloop was designed originally for the then-burgeoning bareboat charter trade, but the concept proved popular and total production now exceeds 700 units. Because the OI 41 has been the mainstay of the charter fleet, user feedback has been more extensive and better organized than for other production boats. As a result, by 1975 major changes had been made to the original OI 41. These included a walk-through passage to the aft cabin, a chart table and nav area, and improved ventilation.

In the last five years many items originally listed as options have been included in what is now called a "sailaway" price. Besides working sails, a larger power plant, and hydraulic steering, the standard equipment package now includes a teak cabin sole, forward shower, and most necessary deck gear (such as roller chock, anchor, stern pulpit, double lifelines and gate, a roller-furled genoa jib).

When the OI 41 first appeared, its space-age styling was startling by traditional standards—an accented raised deck, stubby profile, hefty rubrail, transom ports. The boat does have extraordinary interior volume albeit at the expense of performance, especially to windward under sail.

An estimated 100,000 sailors have cruised the OI 41 as charterers. This is exposure no amount of advertising can attract. Moreover, many 41s have been sold under a lease-back arrangement with such sizable charter firms as The Moorings.

Time Share Yachts: An Idea Whose Time Has Yet to Come

Is time sharing a reasonable alternative to purchase or charter of a sailboat? Well, yes and no: it may be appropriate in a very few circumstances. If the thought of time sharing a yacht has seemed tempting to you, examine it closely before you take the bait.

Time sharing is a recent innovation in yacht ownership, a spinoff from an idea that has gained popularity in real estate. Past attempts to sell time shares in yachts have not met with much success to date. However, none have been marketed as earnestly as are several at present and there is a chance that some of the present programs will succeed—at least for a while.

Even if the idea does catch on, it will not likely have all of the appeals as real estate time sharing such as swapping of time shares and a widespread market for brokering shares.

Basically time sharing consists of two variations on a theme. In one case the buyers of shares purchase a boat, and each shareholder owns a percentage equal to the amount of time he bought. The shareholders then manage the yacht (or pay to have the yacht managed), pay an annual fee for maintenance, and make decisions about where the boat will be based, when to make major repairs or replacements, and ultimately when to sell the boat and liquidate the partnership. It is this plan that we primarily address in this article.

In the other variation, ownership of the yacht is retained by a management company and shareholders buy a portion of time for a fixed duration. In this case the purchase price is in effect a pre-paid charter fee and the annual assessment helps cover the owner's expenses.

The appeal of time sharing

In both cases the chief selling point is that the cost of a week or more of sailing for several years will not increase as much as it would under a conventional chartering arrangement. How much the shareholder will save is contingent upon a number of factors, such as the quality of the yacht purchased, the conscientiousness and competence of the management of that yacht, the economic situation from year to year, the lifestyle of the shareholder and the opportunities it affords to take advantage of the time he has purchased.

What time sharing ownership does is let you have access as owner to a far larger and more luxurious yacht than you might otherwise be able to afford. Granted, ownership may only entitle you to sail aboard "your" boat for one week or so a year and does not give you much if any say in how that boat will be handled, but for that week you can be Onassis. You can invite your friends, have a paid crew sail your boat and serve you, set your own schedule and, within reasonable limits, choose your ports of call.

Indeed, if you normally sail only one or two weeks a year—too infrequently to warrant owning a boat and yet often enough to make you aware of the escalating costs of chartering—then time sharing might have appeal.

How time sharing is set up

The most common type of time share program starts with a management firm that sets up the structure, sells the shares, and then manages the boat for the shareholders. The programs we have looked at consist of 40 or more shares on boats ranging from 40' to 65'. To buy a share costs $6000 to $20,000 for one week per year.

An initial deposit assures a share and, on a first come, first served basis, a choice of the time. The money realized from selling these shares is used to purchase the boat. Until a stipulated minimum number of partners have signed on and the boat is ordered, the deposit money is put into escrow. If a minimum number of shareholders is never reached, that money plus interest is returned.

Thus far the management organizations that have gotten into trouble trying to set up time share yachts have been those that have invested money, usually borrowed, in a boat and *then* tried to sell shares. This sequence is more risky than the sequence of selling shares and then ordering the boat, but it does promise more money for the organizers if they can pull it off.

The organizers of the program realize the major return on their efforts when the boat is delivered. They get a standard dealer's commission, typically 15-18% of the purchase price. They also get the interest on escrow deposits if their selling of shares succeeds. If the organizers remain on the scene to manage the shareholders' yacht, they will continue to take a percentage of the annual maintenance and management fee which every partner is assessed. This percentage may be considerably less than the initial commission but it should still make management of the yacht a lucrative matter.

Anyone interested in the various investment possibilities in owning boats should realize that charter companies leasing boats and management firms managing them for owners make most of their money on commissions. They act as boat dealers. The fees derived from actual management or chartering are far less important and may only make possible sales of more boats and thus the opportunity to earn further commissions.

The success of any time share program, as with any yacht management operation, is directly related to how effectively the yacht is managed. In fact, the success may thus depend on factors over which the shareholders have the least control and get the least opportunity to evaluate prior to becoming involved. This is why time sharing plans have not developed rapidly and why they now have to be suspect.

Time sharing partners may sign an agreement which is open ended (have no expiration date) or be for a fixed period of several years (usually five or six). In open ended programs, the partnership ends when the shareholders so vote. At the end of the fixed period, the shareholders may vote to continue the program. In either case, when the boat is sold and/or the partnership terminated, the partners realize at least a partial return on their original investment in shares.

Since some parts of the year are better than others

for using the boat, time share plans may call for a sliding scale of prices. Those having a share during the "peak" season pay a higher price than those with a share in the "off" season. If the boat will move about, say from New England to the Caribbean, by the season, that difference will also be taken into account. The difficulty in selling the off-season shares has been one of the major reasons why time share programs with yachts have not thus far been popular or successful.

Although there may be a difference in price for the time reserved, there typically is no difference in the annual maintenance and management fee assessed the partners per share. In addition, while the time share cost is a one-time, up front charge, the maintenance fee varies depending on the needs of the vessel and the inflation rate. Major additional expenses such as for a new engine or new sails may be assessed as a flat charge or prorated over two or more years. The better management plans call for the gradual accumulation of a contingency fund that will help defray major costs. Whatever the case, shareholders must realize that no one can make any maintenance costs guarantees.

This annual maintenance fee is thus the primary question mark in any prospectus of the costs of time sharing. This fee covers insurance, wages of the professional hands, dockage, outfitting, management fees, etc. For most time sharing programs it also includes the separate expenses of each time share use such as fuel and food although these may be billed separately. In most plans, only liquor is left to the shareholder. The fee is billed to each shareholder annually along with an accounting of how the fee was spent the previous year.

In the programs we looked at we find the estimated maintenance and management fees at best optimistic; at worst, downright misleading. Assuming the ownership will be divided into 40 shares, a fee of .5% of the value of the boat per week of use or a total of about 20% of the value of the boat per year is not an unreasonable expectation, especially for the type of hard and continuous use such a boat will receive over a period of several years. This means that for a more realistic estimate of the average annual costs, prospective

Time Sharing: The Comparative Costs

A hypothetical but typical example of a time sharing program looks like this:

A 53' boat operating with a professional crew of two (plus delivery hands) on a 42-week year (42 shares) costs $433,000 delivered and ready for operation. Shares are sold on the following schedule:

- 20 weeks prime season
  in the Caribbean — $12,000 per share
- 4 weeks off season
  in the Caribbean — $ 9,000 per share
- 14 weeks prime season
  in New England — $ 9,500 per share
- 4 weeks off season in
  Chesapeake Bay — $ 7,000 per share
- 10 weeks maintenance and
  delivery passages

The total "take" on 42 shares sold is $437,000. Duration of the time share agreement is six years.

For shareholders the maintenance and management costs projected by promoters of the program are $1500 a year increasing by 10% per year after the second year. Thus, during the six year term of the agreement a shareholder should expect to pay $10,658 in annual maintenance.

The cost for a one week share for the first year breaks down as follows:

Investment (prime Caribbean)
$12,000 ÷ 6 (term of agreemnt)   = $2000
+ annual maintenance   = $1500
+ lost interest on $12,000
    investment at 10%   = $1200
                                          —————
                                          $4700

At current rates the charter of a similar size boat in season in the Caribbean would be about $4800.

At the outset the savings over chartering are a token amount. In future years, as charter rates rise, the savings presumably will be greater, since only the maintenance assessment increases to compensate for inflation. However, this conclusion depends on a realistic maintenance assessment. Any additional maintenance costs which might be levied will clearly change the picture.

How realistic is that maintenance estimate? Adding up the shareholders' contribution to management and maintenance for the first year, we get $63,000 (42 x $1500), or about $1212 per week. Those familiar with the long range maintenance of a 52' boat in essentially full time operation doubt if normal maintenance can be done for less than $2000 per week, and could easily run $2500 per week, including wages and meals of paid hands and delivery crew, dockage, outfittings, insurance, and provisioning for the shareholder's party. It is this type of optimism in the sales pitch of those selling time sharing that concerns us and should receive close scrutiny of anyone contemplating purchase of a share.

Not only is the annual maintenance fee likely to be higher than as promoted but shareholders should expect some major one-time assessments. Sails, rigging, and the engine are items most likely to occasion extraordinary expenses (although some of these costs may be recoverable upon sale of the boat).

Actual savings over chartering may not be realized until the boat is sold or the time sharing plan reorganized after a period of years. Then shareholders should get a portion of their initial investment back as proceeds from the sale of the boat or the shares. Resale value of a professionally maintained yacht used in a time sharing program for six years should approximate the original face value.

shareholders should *double* the figures cited by most of the salesmen whose plans we have seen.

What does a share buy you?

Those shopping for a time sharing plan should know exactly what they are buying. All yachts need turnaround time—a period of time for cleaning, reprovisioning, minor repairs, R and R for the crew, etc. in addition to several weeks free from sailing each year for refitting. Only if the program consists of six-day weeks of shared time (13 days for two-week shares) is there a reasonable opportunity for this turnaround. Thus, although it may be handy to consider the time each shareholder has aboard the yacht in week-long intervals, it is actually less. Beware of any program that advertises a turnaround of less than 24 hours between shareholders' use or more than 40 weeks of shared time each year.

Most time share programs wherein the shareholders own the boat have provision for trading time or chartering the boat when the shareholder is entitled to her. Thus shareholders do have some flexibility in their use of the boat and a way to recoup some of their costs if they do not use their time. Some management firms will arrange to trade the time or charter the boat for the shareholder at no cost or commission; others charge a charter broker's fee. Similarly the better organizations promise to arrange swaps between shareholders, and otherwise give the partners some options in the times they use the boat.

Shareholders can, in turn, sell, barter, bequeath, or give away their share. So far, we understand, the time share programs have not attracted speculators who invest in the better time periods and then sell them at a profit when the program is underway. When the speculators do get into the time share program, it will be evidence that the idea is catching on.

Unlike chartering, lease-back opportunities, and management programs, time sharing usually involves no tax benefits for the shareholder other than deduction of interest if the share is purchased with borrowed money or financed through the management firm. Two notable exceptions are corporate shareholders who purchase a share for business purposes (ie, business meetings, employee incentive programs, or legitimate business entertaining) and those who purchase shares for deriving an income from chartering rather than personal use. In general, though, we don't think anyone should consider time sharing for any reason other than personal pleasure (and even then, only under particular conditions).

The advantages of time sharing

• Use of a larger yacht than one might otherwise be able to afford
• Possible eventual savings of up to 25% over conventional chartering of a comparable boat
• Assured use of a boat for a predetermined period of time annually (assuming the share agreement provides for an alternative charter if the time shared yacht should be out of commission)
• A vacation package that may be exchange for another

Some disadvantages of time sharing

• Considerable money tied up and earning little, if any, return on investment. Time shares are not apt to appreciate in value in the foreseeable future until the concept proves viable.

• Any capital gain on the investment in the share upon sale of the boat is apt to be minimal, judging from the history of boat appreciation
• Anticipating the annual maintenance costs more than one to two years away is at best problematical. Most time share programs now being promoted seem to have underestimated future costs, some egregiously.
• Shareholder decisions will be made by majority (or two-thirds) vote and thus may not suit individual shareholders who will then have no choice but to go along or to try to sell their shares
• For time shares to be at all worthwhile, shareholders must make use of all their allotted time, either for themselves or for chartering
• Time shares on a boat that sleeps six or eight means that shareholders must be ready to invite friends or share their time with playing shipmates if they want full value for their investment
• Time sharing assumes continuation of a lifestyle and economic condition that originally made the arrangement attractive and feasible
• There seems to be no way to be sure that mangement of the yacht will be competent and in the best interests of the shareholders. Moreover, direct involvement in the mangement of the yacht by shareholders will be difficult if not impossible.

Conclusions

Time sharing is hardly for everyone; in fact, it should be appealing for only the limited few with some money to put into an untried venture that has little value if it fails. It offers, to an individual with disposable income and a yen to own a piece of a big yacht, a way to gratify that yen with a minimum of involvement or investment. If he is the type of sailor who would charter regularly, there may also be some savings over the years. However, those savings, if any, are not going to be on the order of what the promotors of a time sharing are promising.

One alternative to this shareholder profile is the group of couples who jointly purchase a share with the idea that they will use the boat together for the life of the plan. This assumes they will remain compatible and runs the risk of any collectively owned investment, but in cases where two or more couples charter together year in and year out, time sharing does seem a reasonable answer for them.

The most effective time shared yacht is large, new and built to charter specifications, the type of vessel that will withstand continuous use and deferred maintenance. Time share programs that offer bareboats do not strike us as worth considering. If time share yachts are to succeed, they will be yachts with well paid, competent professional crews.

Clearly time sharing in its embryonic present form represents a combination of high risk and splendid opportunity. In our investigation of the concept, perhaps what disturbs us the most is that those selling the programs have quick answers for all but the important questions. Slick and glib they sit in the cockpits of flashy new boats, in boat show booths, or in plush offices overlooking marinas where they have tables of figures at their finger tips along with a slick prospectus on a boat their clients could never think of owning, and a dream that they claim anyone can afford.

We suggest those who are qualified and interested wait until some others prove the idea works.

Should You—Could You—Live Aboard?

In the almost seven years I've lived aboard our boat, I've been approached by dozens of men, usually during spring haulout on one of my endless circuits of our 43' wood hull (scraping, sanding, priming, sanding, painting, sanding, painting) when, I admit, I must seem an inspiring phenomenon: a perfectly witless lackey who not only doesn't *mind* living aboard and working on a boat, but who seems to go at both with a vengeance. Perhaps because I look sincere, but more likely because I'm wearing a respirator and can't talk, these men to me pour out their hearts:

Boy, you've got your work cut out for you, haven't you. (Scrape, scrape.) Wish I had a wife like that. (Sand, sand.) My wife would never do that. (Sand, sand.) She hates boats. (Scrape, sand.) She begrudges every cent I spend on the boat. (Sigh.) And every minute I spend on it. (Sigh.) She really hates boats.

Invariably as the husband in question drifts wistfully away, dreaming his dream, I'm overwhelmed with sympathy for him. Why, I ask myself, won't the ogress live aboard a boat with him. What does she want, anyway. A house and two cars and a backyard with swings. Selfish old bat. Always take, take, take. Never asks him how *he'd* like to spend his money.

Hardly could the man have a more earnest advocate. At least, until recently. Call it age, call it feminism, but I'm becoming impatient with men who blame their women. Once I would have accepted the notion that nearly all women have an inviolable sense of nesting: that they require a rooted structure in a stable environment with predictable company in which to raise their young, and that a restless, heaving boat symbolizes for them the very opposite. That women are empire-builders: a washer, a dryer, and out of the next check, down payment on a deep freeze (a boat is finite, contained, essentially unexpandable). That women, last above all, are weaker, softer, and inclined or allocated to the frivolous (and nothing is stronger, less yielding and more purely functional than a boat).

Doubtless many women do share these characteristics. Yet I wonder whether some men don't use that stereotype of their women as an unassailable excuse for not realizing their dreams. For instance: it is assumed that a woman expects a high degree of comfort and it isn't wondered at when she says so. A man, on the other hand, cannot so easily confess that he hates being cold or wet, can't bear the thought of getting up in the night to check dock lines, won't give up his golf bag and table saw, needs someplace to hide from the family (what are garages *for?*) and can't watch television comfortably except from his lazyboy.

For such a man the answer is a little candid soul-searching, which at least should make him at ease with his obviously preferred life-style.

But assume the man really, truly wants to live aboard a boat with his wife. Has he said so to her (or am I the only one who knows)? Is his reluctance to say so because of misplaced altruism (too uprooting for her) or is he afraid she'll say yes? Obviously *some*one has to have the idea first. Run it up the flagpole; she may

salute. Give her a present of a book on living aboard. Or perhaps you know of a yard where people are living aboard a boat: make it a point to ask their advice; chances are they'll be quite flattered.

I have read that unless both partners are keen on the idea of moving aboard, it shouldn't be attempted. But I think naive enthusiasm is more dangerous than thoughtful hesitation. It *is* a different lifestyle, and your chances of succeeding at it are greater if you consider all the implications before jumping in with both feet. It's not easy to come up with a psychological profile of a typical liveaboard, but if both the woman and the man share at least some of the following traits, there's reason to hope. (Certain assumptions are made: that you enjoy being outside and on the water; that you have some sailing experience—we sailed for four years on a 22- and a 28-footer before moving aboard—and that whether cruising or in a 9-to-5 situation, you will spend at least some time moored, anchored, or at a minimum facility dock.)

(1) You should enjoy or at least not mind being alone, even isolate, for periods of time, especially in the Northeast where living aboard off season is not at all common. If you're the type who needs to hear the back door slamming all day from friendly neighbors going in and out, living aboard is not for you (except in southern marinas with large liveaboard populations). If you must dash—and remain—ashore every day of your annual two-week cruise, it suggests that you are someone who cannot, basically, sit put. Try staying on the boat for two or three straight days and see what happens. Can you amuse yourself within the confines of a small room? Are you fond of reading, knitting, drawing, writing, or (if all else fails) television? Although sailing is a reasonably active sport, to live on a boat you should be able to sit, sometimes, like a bump on a log.

(2) You should have a sense of moderation, more precisely defined as an acute awareness of waste. In the northern winter, running out of water means having to hook up eight or ten hoses to reach a water source because the dock supply has been shut off; so a sense of economy, if not instinctive, nonetheless quickly is developed. (My sister complains she no longer can enjoy a long shower since being exposed to boat living.) Similarly, having to lug propane bottles around for refilling means putting just enough water in the teapot. If you do not have access to dockside power, leaving an unnecessary light bulb burning falls somewhere between cardinal and mortal as an offense.

Yet there is profound pleasure to be derived in living a simple but comfortable life of moderation. If you are a person who is conscious of the limited resources of his environment, that pleasure is increased.

(3) You should not be a collector. There is no room. Aboard a boat, *Newsweek* must be read and tossed; if you haven't finished it by the end of the week—too bad. You own every single issue of *Woodenboat* and it'll be hard to give 'em up? Tough. This "can-overboard" syndrome—the feeling of utter relief every time you remove any object at all from the boat—is the very opposite of

the collector's instinct. It is the characteristic that separates boat people from dilettantes and dreamers. Acquisitiveness can, of course, be reversed. We were just getting into high gear collecting antiques when we suddenly decided to move aboard. We sold everything, including, on principle, a charming slant-top desk I still carp about. Heirlooms, I agree, are more problematic to dispose of. But look at it this way: once you move aboard, there isn't a furniture store in the world that will have meaning for you.

(4) You should not like to entertain on an inordinate scale. For us the main event is a turkey dinner for six. We have a four-burner gas stove with oven, so preparation of the bird and trimmings proceeds just as it would in a house. However: at carving and serving time, push generally comes to shove between my husband and me because there just isn't room enough in the galley. (Answer: carve the silly bird in an *au jus* board on the navigator's table.)

(5) You should either like adventure or bore easily. Although you may not avail yourself of the opportunity, you can change neighborhoods, states, countries at will. We moved from a small and friendly boatyard at one end of Narragansett Bay to a brand new marina in downtown Newport at the other end. No big deal, but just like land people one of us found the move rather painful and one of us—the Aquarian—did not. (Liveaboards sometimes forget that moving is doing what boats do best; they can travel all over the world without ever leaving home.)

(6) You should be able to live with a sense of insecurity. Your boat is constantly vulnerable, always a source of anxiety. Hurricane formations will make your blood run cold. Thieves are a consideration. Although many people live with a fear of their houses being burglarized, few could adjust to the possibility of those homes vanishing without a trace. One fellow I know sold his boat in part because he couldn't bear worrying about it whenever he was away, and rightly so: one stormy night he returned to the boat to find it had dragged its mooring to the edge of a rockpile.

If you are a secure person, this unstable situation will not bother you. If you are an insecure person, you may find the situation strangely stimulating; and in any case you will be necessary as the safety factor, the double-checker.

(7) You should like structure and routine. Despite the popular perception of liveaboards as unorthodox and even eccentric, living on a boat requires disciplined stowing methods and an utterly predictable pattern of movement between the parties. A warning: be prepared for some frustration while the two of you are developing and smoothing your traffic routes for daily chores (morning, bedtime, mealtime).

(8) You should have a sense of independence from peer opinion. The popular response to those living aboard ranges from envy (in season) to pity (off season). Expect also to run into hostility: while you may walk your decks well pleased with your sense of self-sufficiency, your landed neighbors justifiably may regard you with suspicion because you have chosen not to be bonded to their community by electric, gas, or sewer lines. While they are at a town meeting debating a proposed traffic light, you've taken your home to Maine for a month. Liveaboards live on the fringe of the public arena partly by design, and partly because they haven't any choice. It's difficult to register to vote when the civil servant in charge indignantly denies your request because "you can *leave* any time you want to." Throw off your tie, throw off your mooring, and you're gone. For the evening, the weekend, the rest of your life.

(9) Both partners should be reasonably handy. Neither need be a master anything, but it should be recognized that the mechanics of a vessel must operate in an ungracious environment and stand up to heavy daily use. Someone ought to be able to understand and repair such homely items as the myriad pumps aboard: fresh water, salt water, fuel, water pressure, sump, bilge. Someone has to tear apart and rebuild the head periodically. Someone has to keep the electronics humming. Someone has to compound and wax or sand and paint the hull; overhaul the running rigging; keep the varnish up, implement new ideas, and do hull repairs if necessary.

Theoretically a yard can do all of these jobs; actually, liveaboards do most of their own work. There is plenty of work for two, and it would be most unfair to assume that the relatively light housekeeping chores counterbalance other routine maintenance. Nor is experience as necessary as plain willingness and basic intelligence. We knew nothing about wood boats or Mechanical Things when we moved aboard, and I can honestly say it's been wonderfully satisfying to learn.

(10) Finally, and easily the most important: you must be very compatible with your mate. If you tend to try new things together—skiing, jogging, camping, antiquing, restoring a house, Scrabble (Scrabble is best)—you can live on a boat together. You should bear in mind, however, that arguments, as well as other simple pleasures, are far more intense aboard a boat. Differences and incompatibilities become enormously magnified. She likes to stay up late and read? He likes to play the stereo full throttle? There's no place to go to avoid such lapses in judgment of The Other, and compromise becomes essential for survival. (Answer: (a) focussed reading light; (b) earphones.) Alternatively, one person can do all the yielding for two.

As to sharing your space with pets and children: we have a cat aboard (a nuisance—must use a litter box); friends of ours have a dog aboard (bigger nuisance—won't use a litter box); and others I know are raising one or two children aboard. Obviously the rewards of having kids, dogs or cats aboard are directly proportional to the complexities involved in keeping them there.

Assuming that you are the correct mix of people and pets, the rest is up to your boat. There is the possibility that your boat may be too tiny, too uncomfortable, or simply too uninspiring for you to care to spend much time there, whether you be man or woman. A good liveaboard boat takes a lot of money or a lot of work.

Friends of mine were persuaded to move aboard a boat in part after experiencing a little epiphany aboard the beautiful *Stormsvala:* being invited by the owners on a raw and dreary day to share, in the sweet-smelling warmth of their cabin, a fresh-baked apple pie and a mug of hot coffee.

Think you can do it?   —A. Stockenberg

So You Think You Want to Build a Boat?

This is not an article on how to build a boat. Nor is it an article recounting our own lengthy boatbuilding experience. The former we are not qualified to write; the latter we are not inclined to write. In fact, we have yet to see a worthwhile book, or even a useful article on amateur boat construction, and question whether such exists.

Instead, this article is intended as a guideline to the host of sailors who might dream of building their own boat and as a practical guide for those just setting about that task.

Let's start with a couple of things amateur boat-builidng is *not*. It is not easy to build a boat, even less so for an amateur than for a professional. It is not cheap to build a boat, no cheaper than for professionals. Thus, while there are some legitimate reasons to build your own boat, it is a mistake if undertaken as an idle pastime to fill spare moments, or as a way to get an expensive boat for little money, or as a way to make money.

The legitimate reasons for building a boat include the following:

• You cannot find a design that fits your particular needs. This may seem hard to accept as a reason, what with the several thousand production, semi-custom and custom designs available, but the fact that so many designs exist tends to support the idea that many thousands of sailors look for different things.
• Given a fortuitous combination of circumstances, skills, resources, time, space and knowledge, building a boat is a feasible way to get a larger boat than one might otherwise afford, or to have a boat which represents more equity than cash investment.
• The project would fulfill some underlying urge to bring into being an enduring monument, to produce something of value, to meet a personal challenge, or perhaps to simply be able to say, "Yes, that's my boat and I built her."

Note that in these three reasons there is little that is rational and a great deal that is emotional. We have discovered, both from our own experience and from our discussions with others contemplating or in the midst of a similar project, that as carefully as the reasons may be couched in rationality, the real motivation is almost always irrational, perhaps inexplicable.

We find nothing inherently wrong with building one's own boat for emotional reasons; in fact, an amateur considering such a project should not analyze the personal reasons and simply accept them, even savor them. Don't try to justify them with practical reasons such as saving money, because the ultimate conclusion is that building your own boat is seldom a practical undertaking.

Let's define what we mean by *amateur boatbuilding*. We do not speak here of the project undertaken by the builder who may possess professional shipwright's skills, to create a boat for himself, and not for financial gain. We speak to the amateur who has not been actively and intimately involved with building a boat similar to the one he is planning to build. He may be an extra-ordinarily skilled craftsman, engineer, mechanic or draftsman. He may be a thoroughly experienced seaman. But he has only a layman's knowledge of boatbuilding.

What's Available?

The two most common types of boat built by amateurs are the kit boat and the boat built to purchased plans, from scratch.

Kit boats are most commonly built of fiberglass because fiberglass components are so readily producible, but they may be found in any boatbuilding material. Most kit boats are marketed in various stages of completion, from a simple hull shell to a nearly finished craft which may be sailed or powered away from the dock with a handful of details to finish or install. The price varies with the degree of completion, of course.

Generally, fiberglass kit boats have evolved from two sources. The majority are production boats, some still in production, others out of production but with tooling that is still usable. Most production builders, however, will not sell their products in kit form. They do not want to handle the seemingly endless questions from customers, and they don't want to be nickled and dimed to death filling orders for screws and bolts one at a time. Production builders are volume assembly line operations, not, in effect, retail outlets.

Moreover, most production builders want to retain control over their products. If an amateur builder decides, for instance, to add a two-story doghouse where none was meant to be, that boat remains a Wumty Dump 36. No amount of advertising can tell prospective buyers that the hideous doghouse version they saw was the product of an amateur builder. Conversely, an amateur product that exceeds the quality of the production version of the same boat is embarrassing to explain. For these reasons, the better production builders do not offer their products in any form short of fully finished. One notable exception is Westsail International.

Incidentally, contrary to some beliefs, there seems to be no validity in the notion that production builders do not sell kits because they cannot make the money they would make with completed boats. They can.

The builders who do sell kits as well as complete boats can have the same margin of profit as builders who sell only complete boats. One reason is the economy realized by the kit boat marketer in the amortization of the tooling over a greater number of boats, often a number well over the production or marketing capacity for finished boats. In short, a number of moldings sold from a tooling as kit parts will reduce the tooling costs per unit. It would be good business if a builder could get that return, but he may not wish to do so at the expense of the drawbacks listed above.

Increased productivity of tooling is also the reason for the marketing of a number of kit boats from discontinued production lines. When a boat is taken out of production, the tooling may be sold or turned over to a subsidiary of the builder, and components from the tooling marketed. This practice used to be more prevalent than it is now, with such firms as Morgan Yacht (Kit Kraft) and Islander Yachts selling kit versions of their boats.

Most recent on the kit boat scene is the builder specializing in kits of original designs for amateur construction. Luger Boats and Yacht Constructors are two of the better known firms producing kits exclusively. That this technique of catering to amateurs has not had more success is perhaps attributable to the rather prosaic designs available from many of these firms.

The second common type of amateur-built yacht is built to purchased plans, from scratch, which we will dub the plan/kit package. The two largest names in this business are Gen-L Marine Designs and Bruce Roberts International. These firms start by selling plans from an extraordinary collection of designs, then proceed to offer materials, hardware, fastenings, even sails. This form of boatbuilding is so extraordinarily complex that it deserves separate consideration. However, what we say here about amateur boat construction applies equally to the full range from kit boats and plan/kit packages to wholly custom designs.

There is a third alternative for the amateur: building a custom boat from plans sold by a naval architect in the same way a professional boatbuilder does. This is, of course, the most demanding way to build a boat, but it is also the way to have a boat truly customized to one's particular demands (and they may be particular!) Moreover, it is the way to have a genuine product entirely of one's own craftsmanship, and it need not be appreciably more expensive than other types of amateur construction, although the finished cost is more difficult to estimate.

Qualifications and Cost

Two principal factors should be carefully considered before beginning construction of a boat—even before making firm plans. In order of importance, they are qualifications and cost.

Anyone can build a boat. Anyone can build a house. Or an automobile. Or an atomic bomb. Or a chocolate mousse. How well you do and *whether you finish* depends on a lot of factors: time, patience, ingenuity, stamina, coordination, dexterity, and yes, intelligence and common sense. It also helps to have initiative and confidence. Some of these may be pretty esoteric qualities, and many human beings live a genuinely full life without them—and without building a boat.

Of these factors, the only one worth discussing here is time. A production boatbuilder can turn out a stock 30-footer in a week on an assembly line. The pieces are all on hand, there are plenty of specialized workers to put them together, and they have the tools, jigs, supervision, and incentive to do the job.

An amateur by way of contrast builds in his spare time, must dope out each step, has no jigs, must buy, rent, or borrow tools, and seldom can structure his time to make the most efficient use of it. The hourly cost of professional boatbuilding labor ranges from $18-40, a figure that includes wages, overhead, fringe benefits, insurance, workman's compensation, taxes, and profit. The amateur believes that if he can save this basic cost, he should have a boat for far less than the "list" price. However, the total labor cost on the average stock 30-footer is 20%-30% of the total cost (see graph). If he could save all of this by doing all his work himself and not value his time at all, the possible savings on a boat would still be only 30%-40% of the value of the stock equivalent.

Of course this percentage varies. The well-fitted pro-

duction boat with abundant handwork has a higher proportion of her cost in labor; the cheaper boat with little joinerwork, few finished details, etc , has a lower labor cost. The way for an amateur builder to "win," is to produce a boat with the fine details of an expensive custom-finished yacht. If he is just going to stick fiberglass components together, he will have saved nothing in cost and may have lost money.

This is one of the main reasons why the best boat for an amateur to build is the largest one he can afford and can find the time to build. The labor required to build a boat does not increase exponentially with length or weight. There is not twice the labor involved in building a 25,000 lb 40-footer than in building a 12,000 lb 30-footer. One engine needs installation, one maststep, one steering system, one keel, etc. It does not take twice the time to measure, cut, fit, fasten and finish an 8′ shelf fiddle as it does a 4′.

Material costs, which are related to weight, do rise exponentially. A 40-footer may have three to four times the amount of fiberglass and resin as a 30-footer.

Needed: Time and Help

There is, of course, no realistic way to estimate the time needed by any individual to build a boat. One man's 15 minute quickie is another's evening project. There is, however, something to be said for making a building schedule (and much to be said about not trying to follow it slavishly). Major interruptions during construction can threaten the whole effort. Initiative is hard to gain once lost. Ideas are forgotten, tools and parts become misplaced, and cost escalates with inflation.

Keep in mind that a boat is more than a spare-time project. It is simply inefficient to work on a boat in two-hour stints a few evenings a week, plus a day or two each weekend. There are few tasks that can be completed in a short time; after weeks of seemingly snail-like progress, you are bound to become discouraged. This discouragement, in turn, can become despair if your investment (in hopes and effort as well as money) never seems to have a return. Next to unrealistic ideas about costs, the seemingly interminable nature of boatbuilding is the most common cause for abandoning the project. Careful thought, planning and research before committing oneself to building a boat can save expensive heartache.

The most successful amateur builders we have talked with strongly recommend a schedule or life style that permits at least week-long bouts of boat work. Progress after a week or so is easily discernible and satisfying. But beware of interruptions and distractions; protect boatbuilding time zealously. Realize that building boats may have broken up more marriages than middle age.

In any case, know where the time is coming from before embarking on serious planning and certainly before spending any money.

Almost no one builds a boat by himself. Bouncing ideas back and forth, dividing the tedious jobs, sharing the sense of accomplishment, and just having someone help manhandle a sheet of plywood or support the end of a plank as it goes through the saw are enough reasons to want help. Be it with family, friend, or partner, boatbuilding should not be a reclusive activity. Beware, however, of becoming so dependent on help that the project would be threatened by its loss. Unless helpers have a vested interest—and maybe even if they do—they may become discouraged at slow progress, unexpected costs or mistakes, or may simply find something else they want to do. This peril is especially present when boatbuilding is conceived of as a family project. We can think of lots of ways to achieve family togetherness that are less risky than the protracted effort of building a boat. On the other hand, if it works for that purpose, it is unbeatable serendipity.

One source of help we strongly recommend is a part-time professional, perhaps someone who wants to moonlight from his work with a boatyard or builder. The right person with skills and initiative can be worth six to eight dollars an hour. One key is to get work, not merely advice and conversation out of him. Another is to give him the jobs that demand his professional expertise; do the routine jobs yourself.

One final piece of advice pertains to personality. Neither a boat nor a novel is something one puts together as one goes along. To do the most crafts-manlike, efficient and inexpensive job demands a discipline of, frankly, a rare type. You should have fairly extensive plans, not necessarily in fine detail but so complete that construction can proceed logically. One amateur we know decided to wait to install his engine (he wanted to delay the outlay of cash and to save wear and tear on the engine while constructing joinerwork around it). It was a mistake. Despite some reasonable thought on the matter, he had to remove most of the galley joinerwork in order to do a proper installation. By the time he had rebuilt his galley he figures he spent about 25 redundant hours.

The most common mistake made by the amateur builder is to deviate from his building plans, whether they are provided by the designer or his own schematic solution to a problem. Such deviations are what turn so many amateur-built boats into a graceless craft even if

it was a handsome design to start with. It also accounts for weaknesses and failures in such vital areas as hull-to-deck joints, chainplates, and keel attachments.

Moral: get proper plans and follow them carefully. If you consider a change, consult with a bona fide authority, preferably a naval architect. If we could give but one piece of hard advice to any amateur builder it would be to form a close working relationship with the firm that sold the kit or the architect who designed the boat. Then, don't make any structural changes without their okay.

Wood? Fiberglass? Steel?

We strongly recommend the amateur builder think in terms of fiberglass, whether he will work from scratch or from a kit. Fiberglass and polyester resin are messy, itchy, and smelly, but they lend themselves to amateur hull and deck construction for a variety of reasons. First, they are relatively easy substances to use. If you are going to build a boat, you want to work with a material that does not require a shop full of tools, a precisely controlled environment, and a long apprenticeship learning a skill for a one-time application. Above all, you want a building system that does not demand infinite patience. There will be enough tedious fitting of bits and pieces before the boat is launched; the hull and deck construction should be tailored to move as rapidly as feasible.

For the amateur, steel is a reasonable material and over the years the most widely used for larger boats. Yet we do not feel it compares favorably in any way with fiberglass as a construction material.

The same is true of ferro-cement. Boatyards and backyards are littered with partially built hulks of ferro-

What a Production Boat Costs

Shown is a typical breakdown of the costs of a 34' production boat. If the boat has a "sailaway" price, as commissioned by a dealer, of $60,000, approximately $24,000 of that price is in the construction materials, hardware, rig, and engine, all purchased at manufacturer's discount averaging 40% below retail list price. At one time most fiber-glass production boats relied heavily on a number of major molded fiberglass components, but in recent years, as polyester resin increased in cost and new products were developed, these components (such as hull and deck liners and hatches) have been replaced by vinyl, pressure laminates, molded plywoods and aluminum.

The labor cost of 20% may be a bit generous but takes into account all the salaries, wages and fringe benefits of the builder's work force. The typical 34-footer takes 600 to 900 hours of direct labor from molding to launching or shipping. As we have chosen a boat near the top of the price scale, it presumes a boat that may have detail work above average in quality, hence a high percentage of labor costs.

The cost of tooling and of marketing the typical production boat used in this example are percent-

Graph 1

ages that are almost universal throughout the production boat industry. The sales commission is likewise standard whether the boat is sold through a dealer or directly from the builder.

Overhead, like labor, is a variable cost as it depends on the builder's investment, efficiency, tax structure, and profit margin.

The costs for tools and site are approximately the same for any size boat, an example of why it "pays" to build the largest possible boat

---

cement, the jetsam of a sales campaign that once sold the notion of cheap, strong boats to countless earnest dreamers. We could wax long and eloquent about the reasons to stay away from ferro-cement, but we think our readers are basically practical and would not consider the stuff.

Wood is, of course, a delightful material to work with and even to dream of. However, the experience and skills needed to build a sturdy and handsome wooden yacht are not the type one wants to learn by trial and error on an investment the likes of a large boat.

To build your own boat, apart from basics in skills and temperament, we think you need the following: money, a site, time, tools, access to Original Equipment Manufacturer's (OEM) discounts, and some at least part-time help.

The key is, of course, money. From the heart—and the pocketbook—we can say that if you do not have adequate money to build a boat properly, do not start. Take into account inflation and contingencies.

Any kit-boat manufacturer or seller of plans who claims you can have a completed boat for less than 50% of the cost of a production *equivalent* is, in our opinion, blowing smoke. You can realize a 50% saving, but to do so would entail extraordinary discount opportunities (*minimum* 40%), a cost-free building site, an ex-

isting array of tools, sufficient available cash to avoid any interest rates and make cash purchases, plus a considerable amount of luck.

Note that in making the above statement we said *equivalent.* A number of firms that are in this business suggest that the way to bring costs down is to have your own fittings made (or even make them yourself). Yes, you can go this route, working with your local blacksmith on fittings, your nearby industrial rigger on rigging, and friendly plumbers and electricians on systems. For the moment this can represent a modest saving, perhaps as much as 10% on the total outlay for a boat, more likely on the order of 5%.

This sounds like a worthwhile saving until you reach the bottom line. Would *you* buy a boat with such fittings and systems? Everything you save on construction will be lost two to three times over as equity. The resale value, if indeed you can find a buyer at all, will be far less than for an equivalent-sized professionally built boat. This is a crucial factor to consider when pricing out an amateur boatbuilding project. If you build a boat that would cost $40,000 if purchased complete, but build it for, say, $25,000 in real dollar value when you resell, you saved nothing on construction and cost. To be able to claim you "saved" a percentage by building the boat yourself, the boat should be worth the full price

---

What an Amateur-Built Boat Costs

For the same $60,000 boat the cost of materials is about 15% higher for the amateur than for the production builder because few amateurs can realize the savings from discounts that the production builder can. Moreover, if the amateur is building a kit boat the price for the kit includes the costs to the molder including materials, labor, tooling, design fees, advertising, marketing, overhead and sales commission. In all, this amounts to $33,000 by the time the amateur has launched his boat.

At least incidental paid labor is hard to avoid for an amateur building a boat whether it is spent for direct physical help or more subtle forms such as designer's consultation. It is also the type of cost that may, at the bottom line, save money and/or time. For instance, most amateurs would do well to have professional help in engine installations.

Overhead includes a number of "hidden" and seldom considered costs, some of which may have little direct relation to actual building. As an example, one amateur builder we discussed this with estimated he drove about 3200 miles to and from his building site and in shopping for parts. A secondhand pick-up truck he bought to make that task easier was not included.

The 6% (or $3600) for tools includes everything from a 10″ table saw to disposable polyfoam brushes. Of course, much of this figure represents an investment with a partial return extending beyond completion of the boat, that cannot be included entirely in the cost of building the boat. But other tools already on hand may even things out.

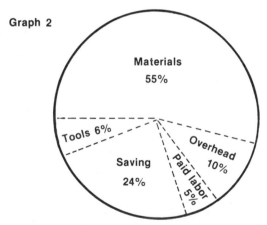

Graph 2

Materials 55%

Tools 6%

Saving 24%

Paid labor 5%

Overhead 10%

Bear in mind that tools are more difficult to acquire at discount than boat materials and equipment.

The final figure, a saving of 24% or $14,500, seems to us realistic and should be the percentage most amateurs use in planning costs of a boat building project. Ideally, of course, the skilled amateur may be capable of producing a finished boat that exceeds the $60,000 value of an "equivalent" production boat. In this case the saving in the construction and the equity in the finished product is proportionately greater. Note, though, that the average sale price of most amateur-built boats is fully 10% below that of professionally built boats of the same general size and type.

The amateur builder never knows until the boat is launched exactly how much money he will need. He may not know even then

when completed. There was a time when people bought boats with available disposable income; the equity in the boat meant little. Those times are gone, probably forever. Now equity is the key to owning any boat, production or home-built, for almost any boatowner.

How Much Should It Cost?

So how much should an amateur-built boat cost? The best rule of thumb we have yet come up with is that if you can save 30% over the "sailaway" price of a comparable production or custom-built boat, the project is worth considering, all other factors (ie, available time, initiative, skills, etc) being satisfactory.

The following is our estimate of fixed costs. Obviously, particular circumstances can change these costs, but they should give a working figure based on experience.

• **Tools:** The amount and quality of the tools needed to build any boat larger than a simple day sailer does not increase appreciably because of the size of the boat. Whether a 30-footer or a 50-footer you will need a table saw, assorted electric hand tools such as sanders, a grinder, drill, "Skil" saw, and saber saw. You will also need an array of manual tools such as saws, planes, chisels, and bits. In addition, a jointer, band saw, and drill press are almost mandatory. Add all of this up and if they have to be bought from scratch, the cost could be well over $2500. Granted this is a one-time investment, but keep in mind that many of the tools will have to be scrapped by the time of launching. This is particularly true of power tools used with fiberglass (we went through two $200 disc grinders in building our one-off). This figure also does not take into account items such as saw blades, sandpaper, drill bits, etc. that are consumed at an alarming and expensive rate during construction.

Tools are not a place to scrimp. Buy the best quality, industrial tools. A Sears Craftsman cut-rate 3/8" (3/4-amp) hand drill is attractive at its price but it is underpowered for many of the jobs you will ask it to do. Better to have a full 1/2" (3-4-amp) heavy duty hand drill that can do any job you ask of it without either wearing out or, worse, burning out.

• **Site:** It may sound simplistic but you do need a place in which you can build your boat. It needs to be secure, comfortable, well-lit, clean, accessible, and cheap. Boats cannot be built successfully exposed to the weather. And, let's face it, not everyone has a spacious backyard plus basement or garage space for a workshop. Nor in some places do zoning restrictions permit building a boat or erecting a shed in which to do it. The cost, whether by renting, leasing, or other arrangement, of a building site and a workshop/warehouse is an expense that must be figured into building costs. So too must electricity, heat, ventilation, taxes and insurance. Then there is the outlay (in labor and materials) for a shed, a largely unrecoverable expense because it may have to be a "temporary structure" so as not to be subject to local building codes. All of this may add up to $100 or more a month, an expense to be reckoned with.

Incidentally, make firm leasing arrangements. We know of several builders who found nearly ideal places in which to build their boats only to have the project prolonged (as should be expected) and then have to move their operations when their lease ran out, the building was sold or, as in one case, he fell out with a partner

who was providing the space to build the boat.

Remember, it is going to cost money to move a boat from the site to the water. At $25 an hour plus one dollar a mile, this is a "hidden" cost that should figure into choosing a site. So too is the commuter mileage to and from any site other than your backyard.

Note that the costs for tools and site are approximately the same for any size boat. This is a splendid example of why it "pays" to build the largest possible boat. Note also that we thus far have not spent any money actually building a boat. Let's see what you might reasonably expect to pay for the boat itself.

The Boat Itself

In the first part of this article we broke down graphically the typical costs of a production boat. For comparison, we do the same thing below for the typical amateur-built boat.

The costs of an amateur-built boat carry only one substantive saving over a professionally built boat: labor. If you start from scratch and build a custom boat using no paid labor (a virtual impossibility we might add), the saving is about 40%. A kit boat, by virtue of the fact that part of the cost of components includes labor, has less saving, more on the order of 30%.

The hull and deck of molded fiberglass in kit form should run about 10% of the cost of an equivalent completed boat. For instance, if the price of the same or similar boat professionally built is $65,000, the cost of the hull and deck moldings will be about $6500. Because the hull and deck should have attached the bulkheads, stringers, maybe engine beds, rudder and shaft tubes, maststep, chainplates, and other structural components before the boat is moved, the cost comes closer to 15%, or $9700 for a $65,000 boat. Then add to this figure the price of ballast (plus installation if encapsulated) and the realistic figure for the basic hull and deck kit is more than 20% of the price of a completed boat.

This is where many builders are, in effect, gulled when they are sold hull packages that boast "big savings." It is where others have been duped into building of ferro-cement for similar savings. Material costs are relatively fixed—about 50% of the final cost of the components. If you managed to build both hull and deck without any paid labor (again, unlikely), the saving on the finished cost of the boat is only about 5%. Many ferro-cement builders found to their chagrin that they took on the task of tediously wiring together a steel armature for months to save themselves a couple of thousand dollars. Other builders discover they spend weeks assembling a building jig on which to mold a fiberglass boat and save a similar amount. And all this assumes the builder can get materials at a price well below list.

Cash Outlay Has a Pattern

One factor in favor of building a boat as opposed to buying one "off the shelf" is that construction funds can be spread over a period of time. This schedule has its advantages and its disadvantages. The disadvantage is that the amateur builder never knows until the boat is launched exactly how much money he is going to need. He may not even know then.

Still, anyone who has built a boat can tell you that his outlay for his boat falls into a pattern. It begins with a high capital outlay for tools, construction materials, and possibly a building shed. If the boat is from a kit, he

One builder bought a whole hurricane wreck, a sistership of the boat he was building. Such windfalls are rare opportunities

---

shells out almost 30% of his ultimate investment at the outset. If he also purchases his engine, chainplates, rudder and shaft, and supply of wood for trim and joiner-work his investment rises to 40%. This means that for the $65,000 production-priced boat a builder is hoping to build for no more than $40,000, the initial cash outlay is about $12,000 and more likely closer to $16,000.

If such a cash investment is a hardship, beware of getting involved in a building project. This is not the time to borrow money or exhaust cash reserves. The next substantial outlay may look as if it is a ways down the line, but in reality the multitude of smaller purchases will continue relentlessly.

Until a boat is well along toward completion, the remaining investment is far more in time and labor than money. There are, of course, purchases—the engine, tanks, through hull fittings, perhaps a refrigeration unit and a pressure water system. However, the major expense is in the dollar-here, dollar-there variety—for boxes of fastenings, another five gallons of resin or glue, half a dozen tubes of sealant, a sheet of Formica. This is the time when organization is important; anticipate needs and maintain an inventory. Be ready to buy an item not immediately needed if the price is right. One builder bought a whole hurricane wreck, a sistership of the boat he was building, "as is" lying on a rocky beach for $3500 (included disposing of the carcass) and salvaged the rig, winches, some sails and most of her fittings worth over $12,000 if he had to purchase them under normal circumstances. He even thought he had an engine until he discovered it had been so abused it was not worth rebuilding. Such windfalls are rare opportunities, but this builder was prepared to move quickly and surely in the aftermath of the storm.

As the boat goes together, it increases in value (or at least as an investment), so the builder's-risk insurance should be increased proportionately. Keep in mind, though, that during this stage a boat has a cash value that is both difficult to determine and hard to realize if it has to be sold. If for whatever reason you want to bail out of the project with the boat half built, the chances are high that you will never recover more than a fraction of your cash outlay and most likely nothing on your labor. There is little that is attractive about acquiring someone else's partially executed ideas and mistakes. A half-built boat is defintely on a buyer's market.

A word about "scrounging." Bruce Roberts-Goodson, in his promotional booklet on amateur building (Illustrated Custom Boatbuilding) for Bruce Roberts International, suggests at the outset of his first chapter that "you can go around scrounging the items and searching the second hand and disposal stores..." Such scrounging sounds like fun. Imagine the goodies you'll find—old gimballed ship's lights, countless reel winches, boxes of mismatched turnbuckles, and all sorts of things that one does not need but will be tempted to pay good money for because they are cheap. To protect your investment, buy the best at the lowest prices you can find. Junk at any price is still junk.

The second massive outlay of cash comes with the boat 90% complete. This can be a staggering experience. Included is the purchase of the rig, sails, deck hardware, electronics, dinghy, lifeline system, and safety equipment.

The worst thing about this outlay is that these are the items most builders are unable to produce in any way themselves. For instance, the savings in assembling your own mast from purchased components is negligi-

ble. This is compounded by the fact that the average amateur builder is so deluged by the plethora of pieces that need to go on the boat and so justifiably anxious to get her afloat that straight purchase of gear seems wholly reasonable. It would be nice to think that buying such items can be spaced out over the construction time of the boat, but such planning seems to be rare.

This "final payment" can amount to 40% of the total investment. Most importantly it highlights the almost mandatory requirement that an amateur builder develop ways to get maximum discounts on what he buys. Realistically this should be 40% on hardware and gear, 25% on electronics, 20% on sails, and 20 to 30% on the spars and rigging. Remember that the installation of this gear is but a small fraction of its cost on a production boat even though the gear is priced out (either as standard or as options) at list price. If you buy it at list, your saving over a production boat is insignificant.

The bottom line should be clear. An amateur builder hopes to save money by doing his own labor, avoiding the $18 to $40 an hour a production builder charges when he prices out his boats. Yet, unless the amateur can also come close to matching the production builder in what he pays for his hardware and materials, the savings in labor costs alone barely warrant building one's own boat to save appreciable money.

Undoubtedly many readers at this point have reached the conclusion that whoever wrote this piece is an unmitigated pessimist when it comes to amateur boatbuilding. If we are it is because we have seen and heard countless fellow amateur builders face disappointment, strained family relationships, exhausting frugality and a host of other discomforts not because they should have foregone the task of building a boat, but because they could not foresee the toll it would exact from their lives or their pocketbooks.

Thus the conclusions we would pass on are:

• Build only after being positive that the boat you want is not available on the market (or one can be modified at reasonable cost).
• Work only with a reputable and qualified yacht designer and/or building firm who is willing to provide solutions to your problems.
• Choose a design that will not only make amateur construction feasible but also be attractive to future buyers so that the boat retains its equity; avoid startlingly unique designs or construction methods.
• Build the largest possible boat you can afford and can be able to handle.
•Carefully and realistically assess your capabilities and priorities before doing anything.
• Sort out as many details as possible (ie, building site, workshop, insurance, availability of tools, discount purchase arrangements, etc.) and thoroughly study the construction plans before taking delivery of a kit boat or starting construction of a boat from scratch. Develop a rough building schedule; make careful notations about the order in which certain items have to be installed so they don't get by-passed. Have a purchase schedule so that when items are needed, you already have them. In short, plan and organize.
• Have the money to do the project properly. The funds to half finish the boat should be considered risk capital; if you cannot afford to lose it, don't spend it
• If you have a notion to build a boat, indulge it. Send for plans, assess your chances, discuss it with the family, work out the details, and go to work.

III

Tricks of the Trade: Techniques for Shopping and Buying

Don't Let Your Dream Become a Nightmare

Buying a car is a major expenditure for most people, attended with due research, inspection, testing, legal affairs, and subsequent service and warranty.

Only the purchase of a house eclipses it in complexity, gravity, promise and expense. Or, for some, purchase of a boat.

A boat can combine the elements of both car and house: domicile; transportation; repository of much, if not all, of available capital; complex problems in evaluating its worth; complex maintenance; complex feelings about it.

When purchasing a boat, people logically invest commensurate amounts of research, inspection, testing, consultation — in a word, caution. Don't they? Well, sometimes.

Buying a boat is buying a lifestyle, be it a dinghy to use on weekends or a world cruiser to take you off into the sunset. On a boat you can go places, new places, inaccessible places — away places. The idea of buying a boat can be so glowing that it is difficult to see what is really there — or not there. Some buyers have such faith in their fantasies that they put their hard cash down for something which does not exist, with no guarantee that it ever will.

In one case, a Connecticut couple turned a $20,000 deposit over to a dealer who promised them their retirement in the form of a $175,000 Taiwan 54' ketch. Two agonizing years later, the boat had yet to materialize. Worse, the dealer and the $20,000, had evaporated. While this example is extreme, it illustrates the degree of naivete exercised in many boat purchases. "Understandings" about warranties, equipment and dates; verbal agreements; assumptions; and plain ignorance too frequently serve in place of written contracts, equipment lists, and schedules. Even conscientious consumers can be frustrated by the variation in the meaning of technical-sounding terms (base price, sailaway price) and the sheer inaccuracy of published specifications of boats and gear.

Dealing with dozens of consumer difficulties through *The Practical Sailor* has produced a fair base of experience in the business of purchasing boats, and we can make some fairly specific recommendations for insuring a satisfactory transaction. Perhaps the most basic and important, however, is also the most general: keep thorough written evidence of every phase of your purchase, from initial contacts and phone calls to legal documents. The common thread which runs through most of the unhappy experiences we encounter is the lack of records, and without written evidence it is often impossible to produce any remedy.

With that paramount precaution in mind, let's take a look at some specifics.

Dealing with the Dealer

As with many things in the marine industry, the choice of boat should be made partly for the reputation of the person who sells it. A dealer with a good reputation for handling warranty claims, for not foisting off unnecessary optional gear, for finding the fairest financing terms, and for being interested in his customers with an eye for getting them back for their next purchase — these are things to look for before you plunk down your money.

• **Accept the fact (cynically) that the marine industry, filled as it often seems with hale fellows well met, has its fair share of shysters and poor managers.** Fortunately, mismanagement is more commonly the cause of screw-ups than dishonesty — fortunately, because a fool's mismanagement is easier for most of us to foresee and avoid than a clever thief's fraud.

It may be more fun to search for the boat you want than for the dealer you like, but by the time the boat is — or isn't — delivered, you may consider the time spent checking the integrity of the builder and dealer and understanding your relationship to them to have been the better spent.

• **Know what committment you are making when you make a deposit, and under what conditions you are entitled to get it back.** Money passed over as a deposit, subject to certain specific and usually stated concitions, is binding for the purchase of a boat. If the buyer subsequently cancels his order, defaults on payment, fails to take delivery, or in any other way violates his side of that contract, then he stands to lose that deposit. In turn, if the dealer fails to deliver his boat (or delivers it after a contracted date) or conditions of the contract cannot be met (eg, the buyer cannot obtain financing), then the buyer is entitled to its return. In fact, legally he may be responsible for money in excess of his deposit if the dealer can show he has suffered additional loss.

Typically deposit money is placed in escrow pending the outcome of the transaction. It is not, contrary to what many boat buyers seem to believe, signed over to the builder as partial payment for the ordered boat. Also, it is not subject to interest rates although some boat dealers and builders have reputedly used deposit money as investment capital. Without ample documentation of the terms whereby the deposit was made, it can be very difficult for a buyer to get his money back. ("Possession is nine-tenths of the law" and all that). He should be prepared to show clear evidence that he did not break the sales contract and that the dealer did not incur expenses resulting from the original placing of the order.

Dealer policy commonly calls for returning most of the deposit as a gesture of good will or to avoid hassles. On the other hand, good will is not a promise to the buyer to return his money willy nilly of the circumstances. And there are variations on this theme.

The key, then, from a buyer's position, is to have a signed contract. Verbal statements by the dealer unconfirmed in writing are useless. Buyers should get a copy of a sales agreement, maintain a complete record of all written correspondence, cancelled checks, receipts, lists, etc. and keep a calendar of payment dates and the builder's schedule.

Deal with the Builder, too

Because you are taking a thorough approach, you will not rely on the dealer to be your exclusive source of information on your prospective boat and its builder. Do some research of your own.

• **Establish communications with the builder of the boat even before you place an order for his product.** Talk with a member of the builder's sales or customer service department. When you have signed an agreement to buy a boat, check with the builder to make sure the dealer passed that order on—in short, that he took your money and ordered a boat with it. The same with a warranty claim. Send a copy of your claim to the builder with a covering letter and ask the builder to acknowledge to you receipt of the claim from the dealer.

• **With either an order for a new boat or a claim, periodically check its progress.** Most builders regard customer visits to the plant as a nagging ache at the bottom of the back. But also most builders recognize that a boat is one hell of an investment that no sensible buyer is apt to take lightly. Again, builders may not have a legal responsibility to you as buyer, but they do have a moral one—which happily coincides with good business.

• **Contrary to widespread belief, a dealer is not a legal representative of the builder whose boats he sells.** Most dealers do not have any written contractual agreement with a builder. There are, however, certain terms they do agree on. For instance, the builder may agree to take orders for boats from that dealer and not take orders from other individuals within a geographical area. They may agree to share local advertising costs, to order and deliver boats on certain dates, to arrange methods of payment, to provide and install optional equipment, to commission boats in a particular way, and to settle warranty claims. Yet the sales contract for a boat is between a buyer and the dealer; the builder sells the boat to the dealer and the dealer adds his commission and sells the boat to the buyer. The boat buyer has no legal contract with the builder. (Exceptions: those major boat builders doing factory-direct sales, and occasional custom builders, discussed below.)

Variations in the buyer/dealer/builder relationship make it essential to keep records at each step of the way. The complexity of the web of responsibilities is illustrated by the following case, where the buyer ordered one thing at one price and received a slightly different thing at a higher price:

The boat, a Hunter 22, was ordered at a January, 1981, boat show. It was delivered later than the dealer had "suggested" it would be and, in addition, the price was $787 more than the agreed price because of a builder's price increase that went into effect between ordering and delivery. The buyer was further unhappy with a few

Ask if changes are slated to take place on a production line by the time your boat is built; this applies to standard as well as to optional equipment

cosmetic changes from the model he saw when he ordered and with some changes in specified equipment.

The fault in this instance lies with the dealer although not apparently to the extent that the buyer can expect recompense. According to Hunter Marine, the dealer (who is no longer a Hunter dealer, incidentally) knew of a scheduled price increase slated for February 1, but it is unlikely he could do more than guess about a delivery date. If the delivery date was after the date of the price increase, he would have to either pass part or all of it on to the buyer or reduce his own commission by that amount.

If the contract calls for the boat to be delivered before the date of the price increase and builder delay carries it beyond, then Hunter claims the price would remain as it was before the increase. This is standard (but by no means universal) policy in the industry; only a builder (like Hunter) with a firm production schedule can operate with such a policy. If there might be a doubt buyers should have the terms in writing when ordering the boat.

The implication is, of course, that in this instance the dealer, in the way of making a sale, kept talking the current price and did not see fit to clutter his pitch with mention of any kind of increase. His suggestion about delivery date similarly was optimistic; there was plenty of time to discuss realities after the buyer was sold.

As to the changes in styling and specifications, it is standard practice that these are subject to change by the builder. Again, the dealer probably knew of the changes and chose to forego spelling them out in the face of a hot prospect. Moral: ask if changes are slated to take place on a production line by the time your boat is built; this applies to what is standard and what is optional in the way of equipment as well.

Sorting Out Warranty Claims

A very common complaint on boat owner questionnaires in our files has been the handling of warranty claims by builders and dealers. Part of many problems stems from the fact that a boatowner may hold a builder at fault when it is in fact the dealer or another manufacturer who is at fault.

A typical example is the boatowner who attempted to get scratched spars repaired by the builder of his new boat. Coatings are typically not covered under builder warranties. Many will, however, repair (or have dealers repair) dings and scratches as a gesture of good will Spar coatings, where any warranty exists, are covered by the firm applying the coating.

In this particular case, the damage had plainly occurred during transit, which introduces another variable: the claim should more properly be lodged against the carrier's insurance policy covering damage during shipment.

• **On a warranty claim (and, incidentally on an insurance claim) do not take it upon yourself to authorize repair or replacement unless you are prepared to under-** take getting reimbursed yourself. Similarly, do not sign a release or cash a check acknowledging settlement of a claim until you are satisfied that the work has actually been done.

• **If you do find yourself in a situation where you must submit an invoice for reimbursement for warranty work already done and paid for, insist that the invoice you obtain itemize the warranty work and invoice it separately from any other work done.** It is not reasonable to ask for reimbursement with an invoice which does not clearly show the work done and the cost of that work, and only that work.

• **Know the terms of the warranty on your boat.** Go over those terms with the dealer before you take delivery of the boat. If the dealer adds, subtracts, or modifies any of the terms, write out the new terms and have him initial the change. If the dealer seems vague about warranty settlements or dismisses the possibility that you will have any, take your business elsewhere or be prepared for the hassle that could cost you money.

Federal Law on Damage Claims

The interstate Commerce Commission has clearly stated regulations that deal with loss and damage claims involving interstate transportation. A brief summation of the regulations that would apply to boat hauling follows:

• The claim(s) must be made in writing and are subject to specified time limits, terms of the bill of lading or other contract, and all applicable tarriff provisions.
• The written claim must include: (1) sufficient facts to identify the boat and gear, (2) a statement of the liability for the loss, damage, or delay, (3) a claim for payment of a specific amount of money.
• Notation of damage on a delivery receipt or other less formal notification is not adequate to fulfill the requirement for a written claim.
• The carrier must acknowledge receipt of a proper claim within 30 days and keep the claim in a separate file that must include all supporting documents. That file must be available for inspection.

• Investigation of a claim shall be prompt.
• The consignee is responsible for providing, as evidence to support a claim, correct copies of bills of lading, invoices, etc. If the value of a damaged or lost boat is not stated on the available documents, the consignee must verify the value of the boat and gear for which the claim is being made.
• The carrier is allowed 120 days from receipt of a written claim to pay, decline or make a compromise settlement. If the claim cannot be settled in that time, the carrier must contact the claimant at 60 day intervals with an explanation for the delay.

Note that the regulations are designed to protect both the carrier and the consignee. If you are interested in the exact wording of the regulations, ask a member of your Congressional member's staff to send you a copy of Title 49 — Transportation, Chapter 10 — Interstate Commerce Commission, Part 1005 (Pages 36-39).

Special Cases:
When There is no Middleman

When a Dallas, Texas, couple bought a Seafarer 37 FOB (Freight on Board) from the builder in Long Island, NY, it was shipped directly to them rather than to a local dealer. This method of boat buying, apt to become more common in the future, puts some responsibilities on the buyer which are ordinarily assumed by the dealer.

This transaction resembles the purchase of a custom-built boat in that it can be divided into two primary phases: construction and delivery. Like the custom boat client, the factory-direct buyer will likely have a contractual relationship with the boat manufacturer for the first phase, and with a hauling or delivery firm for the second (unless, of course, he shows up at the factory to take delivery in person.)

Before assuming these responsibilities, think through the following points:

• **Before the boat is shipped the buyer should have a clear understanding of written terms that state the responsibility that the builder and the buyer each assume.** The builder may assist the buyer in arranging for shipment, but the contract is apt to be between the carrier and the buyer. This means that the legal responsibilities for the shipment are shared by them, and not the builder.

• **Boats bought directly from a builder (not invoiced through a dealer) typically have a price that reflects a saving of the dealer's commission, maybe as much as 15%.** Moreover, the buyer may also be able to save some of what he otherwise would pay a dealer up front for shipping and commissioning. In turn, the buyer should probably accept the responsibility for small claims including token warranty claims which would routinely be handled by a dealer as part of the commissioning of a boat he sells.

• **A buyer should understand the terms set by a builder in fulfilling a warranty claim.** If the builder insists upon the return of purportedly defective equipment it seems unfair for a buyer to ignore those terms and then complain about the failure of a builder to satisfy the claim. Whereas return might not be required were a dealer involved (the dealer could be billed and given credit later when the defective equipment is returned), it is unlikely (and perhaps unreasonable) for a builder to send a replacement merely at the request of a buyer or a boatyard. This inconvenience is a price the buyer may have to pay when he buys a boat independently of a dealer.

• **Buyers should also realize that they can exhaust the good intentions of a builder.** Boats may be costly items. However, in the price paid for them there may not be enough "fat" built in to cover carte blanche work or gear ostensibly covered by warranty. We find that most boat builders work hard to satisfy their customers' claims even when not legally obligated to do so. We strongly feel buyers in turn should not take advantage of that good will.

Delivery of the boat involves its own set of problems, many of them common to both overland and water delivery. Delivery by water offers two primary advantages over other forms of shipping, but it is not always available. First, as the boat does not have to be removed from the water, it is not subject to strains of dry storage for which it was not really designed. Second, those loading a boat aboard a truck or onto a ship's deck are likely to view it as simply another piece of cargo. The sailors who deliver it by water may treat it more to its liking.

That said, let us examine some aspects of a common alternative, the overland hauling option. Interviews with several haulers produced unanimous agreement on one point: they want to be paid in cash (or the equivalent such as a certified check) on the spot by a consignee manning an already warmed up Travelift ready to off-load a boat as it arrives free from dent, scratch, or theft. A map marked with the quickest route out of town is also appreciated. They also evidence a remarkable inclination to cover their hindsides while remaining indifferent to what it means for a boat owner facing delivery of a proud new possession for which he has paid a small fortune (or put himself up to his ears in hock).

Make no mistake (we note cynically): when contracting to have a boat hauled, you will not be apt to be dealing as you would with that good-guy boat dealer with whom you closed the deal by sharing a drink at the yacht club bar. The big time boat haulers are truckers; they may be lugging your pride and joy, but to them they are simply hauling a large awkward and expensive piece of freight on a rig whose value probably exceeds the cost of the cargo and which earns them the most money when it is churning along at 10 miles over the speed limit on an interstate.

The good drivers are good because they own their own rigs, are hired by the boat transport firm for a lucrative set fee, and they appreciate and are fully aware of the responsibility they have for your boat. The bad drivers are bad because they don't care, because they get paid no more for civility and patience than they do for alternatives, and because once on the road they are their own bosses, answerable to no one unless a consignee sees fit to complain. Pray you get a good one for your boat.

Start by contracting for hauling wisely. Sign on only with an experienced boat hauler, one capable of handling your boat and boasting a reputation for care and fair settlement for damages. Use only a hauler with certified liability coverage. Compare contracts (even though most are nearly identical) so you know exactly what you are responsible for and what responsibility the trucker assumes. Know the terms for payment; it is almost always COD and not by personal check unless that check is cashed in time to be cleared before the delivery. Check to see how much time you are allowed after the boat's arrival before additional charges begin. By contract you should be entitled to a thorough examination of the boat while it is still on the truck to determine possible damage she may have suffered en route, but unwarranted delays to arrange for offloading

Sign nothing — notably the bill of lading — until you have clearly and completely itemized all the damage, if any

(which is the consignee's responsibility) can bring additional charges (which incidentally, also have to be paid in cash).

Preparing the boat for shipment is the responsibility of the consignee. If it is done by the builder, he assumes responsibility in the event of damage if it is done improperly. The hauler can, however, refuse to haul a boat he deems improperly "packaged" or insist it be repacked to his satisfaction. As with offloading, pragmatically most hauling firms build into their prices a reasonable amount of time for loading, but when it gets inordinate, it may appear on the final bill as a surcharge for which the consignee must pay. If charged, your only recourse is to go after the party in charge of preparing the boat.

Once loaded on the truck, the responsibility becomes the hauler's. He must see that the boat is—and remains—properly secured, that he does not submit it to excessive road hazards including potholes, thieves, errant drivers, low hanging limbs, fresh road tar, etc. He is not responsible for acts of God, the reason why boats should have their own insurance coverage for shipment over the road. Boat haulers typically carry one of, or a combination of, two types of insurance. Either they have a carrier who underwrites them, typically for $100,000 to $200,000, or they may be self-insured, holding in escrow a comparable amount to cover claims. In some cases the trucking firm may use a combination, carrying self-insurance to the amount of a high deductible in order to keep expensive premiums to a minimum.

In any case, the hauler will seek an estimate of the cost of repairing damage, often using an appraiser for major claims. Of the haulers we talked with, none undertake having the work done themselves. Instead, they may accept or negotiate on the basis of the estimate, and then pay the consignee directly. It is up to the owner to have the work done. The haulers may, however, do (or sub-contract) any shipping to and from the site where the work may be done or they may leave shipping up to the owner. If the latter, shipping costs should be included in the settlement.

As with any insurance claim, two factors thus become crucial. The first is that the owner realize that he is wholly responsible for examining the boat instant to its arrival to determine whether there has in fact been any damage. It is better that this be done on the truck bed before off-loading. The examination should be thorough, for hidden damage as well as cosmetic. For example, a boat that has traveled with too much load on the poppets may have fiberglass tabbing torn loose inside the hull behind the poppets. Such a claim may be against the hauler for too rough a ride or against the builder who provided the cradle, but it should be reported before the boat is off-loaded so possible blame cannot be passed off on the yard that off-loads the boat.

The second factor is that, although the owner is responsible for finding any damage, he must also handle the matter properly if he does find some. The recommended procedure is as follows:

• Point it out to the driver and, if possible, show him exactly what damage you have found. Don't try to assess blame, accusing him of anything; merely present him with information. Remember, unless he is an independent hauler working for himself, he can neither authorize any settlement nor make any binding recommendation.

• Phone the dispatcher or home office of the hauler and describe in detail the type and extent of the damage. If it is severe, the representative may authorize the driver to leave the boat on his rig until an appraiser can be sent to look at the problem. In such a situation you should not be charged for the idle time of the rig and driver; you may, however, be unable to recover for the delay if you contracted for a crane and labor to off-load the boat.

• Sign nothing—notably the bill of lading—until you have clearly and completely itemized all the damage. Your signature on the bill of lading transfers responsibility for damage from the trucker to you except for details you have spelled out on the bill above your signature. Note that after signing and off-loading you may find damage that could have been caused in transit. You can subsequently make a claim. However, the burden of proving that the damage was caused during the haul rests with you and settlement would most likely be for the damage itself, not any subsequent liability. (For example, unrealized by you, the rudder was wrenched during trucking and, as a result, the boat sinks six months later; only a lawsuit—not a damage claim—could recover for loss of the vessel).

• The builder (or those who prepared the boat for shipping) should be routinely notified and given the same information the hauling company receives. They too may want to send a representative to the site to establish whether the damage was the result of the preparation of the boat for which they are responsible (as the trucking firm may subsequently argue) or the fault of the trucker.

Note that this procedure puts you, the owner/consignee, square in the middle between two parties doing their level best to cut their losses. At the same time, you have a warm regard for your own investment, a regard you may share only with family and close friends.

Conclusions
The best attitude to take is a cynical one: something can go wrong so be prepared to handle it when it does. Read the contract terms on the back of the bill of lading before signing the contract to ship your boat. Know for what you are responsible (such as the manner of payment upon delivery) and live up to that responsibility scrupulously. Be prepared to inspect your boat meticulously (although there is no need to be paranoid about it). Accept the common hazards of over-the-road travel (eg, the bottom paint may well be pitted from small stones, and the once shiny topsides may drip with grime).

If there is damage, be prepared to negotiate a settlement. It is fair to get back the dollar value of what is damaged; it is unfair to even unconsciously try to get punitive dollars as well. And it is likely that there may be some expense—perhaps for damage so slight it is not worth filing a claim, or for surveyor and attorney fees that will never be reimbursed in a settlement.

Take the time to handle the situation calmly and sensibly. Leave the boat firmly in place on the truck until you are satisfied with the plans to make her whole again. Remember, until you sign the bill of lading, the driver and his firm remain responsible; he is not about to pull out the poppets and drop the boat in the parking lot. If the delay proves unwarranted, it may indeed cost you as much as $200 a day, but that is chicken feed against the possibility of a costly damage claim.

Know your rights, stick by them and to hell with a tired and dusty driver bewailing the fact that his wife and kiddies expected him home yesterday.

When Buying Foreign, The Dealer is Everything

Taiwan boats have traditionally been the butt of a lot of snide comments about overweight hulls, poor hardware, and masts that fall apart, all enhanced by a lot of varnished teak. Boatbuilding, much of it for US consumption, is a major industry in Taiwan. Boats built there vary just as much in quality as boats built in the US or anywhere else.

There is relatively little sailing in Taiwan, despite the huge boatbuilding industry. Most boatbuilders in the country have therefore had little sailing experience with the boats they sell. This has resulted in a variety of problems for the buyers of Taiwanese boats. Improper bedding of hatches and hardware, leaking hull-to-deck joints, and underengineered hardware have been common—and valid—complaints about Taiwan boats. Add the lack of seagoing experience to a substantial language barrier which may reduce the ability to explain improvements, and you have a most difficult situation.

While many boats built in Taiwan in the past have earned their reputations as overweight sluggards, that certainly doesn't apply to some of the current crop of Chinese boats, such as the Airex-cored Ted Hood design, Little Harbor 38.

One of the great weaknesses of Taiwan boats has been in the rig and hardware departments. Poorly finished bronze castings of unknown alloy, stainless steel that turns into a mass of rust, and heavy, poorly engineered rigs have been common complaints about the lower priced Taiwan products. It is becoming more common for Oriental builders to import winches and other hardware from the US, which greatly improves the general quality of the boats. Sometimes the rigs are built here and installed after the boats arrive. This, too, is a significant improvement.

Warranty problems have in the past created difficulty, since the builder is halfway around the world and may be more interested in building a new boat than fixing one they've already sold. We'd want to be very sure that our US dealer would immediately cover warranty claims rather than waiting for the builder to reimburse us.

Commissioning is another major factor. A thousand different things happen to a boat when she is shipped halfway round the world. Nuts come loose and fall off. Items disappear in transit. Rigging may not be labelled. Ask to see the dealer's commissioning list. If it's not at least three pages of single spaced notes, it may well not be thorough enough.

With the builder on the other side of the world, the relationship of the buyer and dealer must be perfectly spelled out. The buyer should assume nothing.

By all means ask your dealer to provide you with a list of owners of boats that he has sold. The importance of choosing the right dealer—one that will both help you with your choices before you buy the boat, and provide good service after you take delivery—cannot be overstressed. The builder is too far away to help you with your complaints: it's all up to the dealer.

Some Tips on Buying the Small Boat

Buying a smaller boat is basically no different than buying a larger boat. However, two factors are apt to be more critical. The first is that the lower costs mean that the builder and the dealer have less money with which to dicker, rectify minor flaws, settle warranty claims, etc. The second is that small boat buyers (and sellers of used boats) are apt to be less experienced and less certain of what they are looking for (and looking at) than those who are buying larger boats.

Both of these factors warrant some tips—some obvious, others more subtle—on buying a small boat either new or used. Be aware, though, that the following are generalities.

• **Shop around before buying.** Find out what others are sailing—and happiest with—in the waters where you plan to do most of your sailing.

• **Shop locally first.** The local dealer has a reputation and business to protect; he is likely to be more sympathetic to your desires than a dealer miles away.

• **Be cautious.** Small boats are seldom long-time purchases. Resale value is important. Boats from little-known builders (especially those some distance away), odd boats, high priced boats, character boats, etc. may pose problems if and when you want to sell them or trade them in.

• **Know the laws on trailering** if there is any chance you will trailer the boat any distance (or across state lines). These laws deal with maximum width (beam), length, lighting, and weight.

• **Sail the boat before buying.** A boat dealer may balk at giving you a trial sail, but there is nothing more worthwhile a buyer can do to avoid later unhappiness. Sail the boat in conditions typical of those in which you will normally sail.

• **Check fittings and hardware before delivery.** Replace inadequate fittings and add the ones you think you will need. Not only may the dealer give you an allowance on the original equipment but he may give you a break on installation costs.

• **Buy an outboard motor from the shop that will service it.** The major motors are generally uniform in quality and price; the servicing of those motors is not uniform, dependent as it is on local shops. Check these shops before buying.

• **The average dealer commission on a smaller boat is 17% on the "base price."** His markup on equipment he supplies and installs (not "factory installed") is about 40% (less on electronics). There's the same markup on trailers. His labor charges build in a 25% profit. These are the percentages with which you and he can bargain.

• **If you want to race, buy a racing boat; if to cruise, a cruising boat.** Dual-purpose boats at the low end of the size and price scale may do neither well.

• **Don't expect too much.** If you demand full headroom, you will get ungainly topside height and probably poor windward performance. If you want too many berths, you'll get a cramped interior. If you want a boat that does not heel, you'll get a boat that does not sail.

IV

The Morning After: Costs of Keeping a Boat

If You Have to Ask How Much, You Probably Don't Want to Know

How many boatowners actually sit down and total up the amount of money it costs to own their boat? Of course those in a position to write off boat expenses for taxes have every reason to. Those who can't are probably reluctant to even make a guess.

This latter conclusion is suggested by the

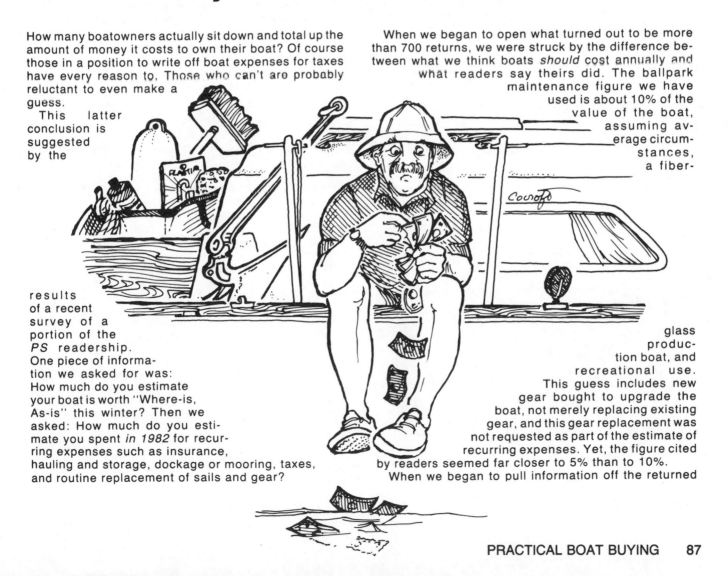

results of a recent survey of a portion of the PS readership. One piece of information we asked for was: How much do you estimate your boat is worth "Where-is, As-is" this winter? Then we asked: How much do you estimate you spent in 1982 for recurring expenses such as insurance, hauling and storage, dockage or mooring, taxes, and routine replacement of sails and gear?

When we began to open what turned out to be more than 700 returns, we were struck by the difference between what we think boats should cost annually and what readers say theirs did. The ballpark maintenance figure we have used is about 10% of the value of the boat, assuming average circumstances, a fiber-

glass production boat, and recreational use. This guess includes new gear bought to upgrade the boat, not merely replacing existing gear, and this gear replacement was not requested as part of the estimate of recurring expenses. Yet, the figure cited by readers seemed far closer to 5% than to 10%.

When we began to pull information off the returned

Compared to other endeavors and other forms of equity, there is nothing economical about owning a boat

surveys, two figures we worked with were the estimates of the value of the boats and the annual expenses. We realize that the questionnaire tends to "favor" larger boats, asking as it does for information on electronics and inflatable tenders. However, the figures we compiled from a sampling of almost half of the surveys returned surprise us. The estimated average value is over $40,000 and the estimated cost of annual expenses is less than $2500.* The percentage of expenses against boat value comes out at 5.5%.

This percentage strikes us as extraordinary. In fact, we did a double take. Two *PS* editors kept careful expense records for the last year (see sidebar): the one with a wooden boat didn't come close to that figure, running about 11-12% of value; the other felt that he had operated about as cheaply as was reasonable, yet ran up costs amounting to almost 8% of value.

The possible conclusions are:
1) that those responding to the survey generally underestimated recurring costs;
2) that they overestimated the value of their boats, or
3) they are so much more practical about how not to spend money than the editors of *Practical Sailor* that we have no business writing for them. For professional reasons, we shall discount the third possibility, and proceed to set some guidelines on how much is reasonable to spend on a boat.

Annual Costs: What Should Be Included
How much any boatowner spends on his boat is depen-

* A small percentage of the surveys returned were from owners of very small boats and one-design sailboat owners and were excluded from tabulation of annual costs. So too were the few returns from charter boat operators, boat dealers, and owners of boats having home ports abroad.

dent upon a lot of factors: type (and construction) of his boat, who does the work, the owner's degree of involvement, how the boat is used, the age and basic condition of the boat and her size and complexity.

Certain generalities apply. Fiberglass boats cost less than boats of other materials, especially wood. New boats are cheaper to maintain than older boats. Smaller boats are proportionately less expensive than larger boats. It takes more money to race than to cruise. Sailing experience saves money. The better built the boat, the lower the annual costs are relative to value.

To these simple generalities we might add another: compared to other endeavors and other forms of equity, there is nothing economical about owning a boat.

A couple of these generalities seem to beg for explanation. First of all, smaller sized boats owned by owners who are experienced and handy mean that maintenance can be of the do-it-yourself variety. Boatyard labor rates are now routinely in excess of $20 per hour and the help working on boats in those yards may be less qualified than the average boat owner. What these workers do have is time, equipment, and their choice of weather to work in. Many owners favor the argument that they can make more money doing their job than they can save by doing their own boat work. But invariably that choice runs up costs.

A second observation about the generalities is that they presuppose a boatowner maintains his boat in order to retain his equity. The more money he has invested in his boat, the more he is likely to be willing to spend to protect that investment. That is why better quality boats can take more money than lower quality craft. Yet quality does beget some savings; the stapled drawer sides of a Hunter are apt to need repair before

---

17 Ways to Keep Down Annual Costs

● **Choose a boat with annual costs in mind.** For instance, darker colored gelcoat topsides will deteriorate sooner than white or pastel.
● **Develop a habit of regular preventive maintenance.**
● **Do the routine boatwork yourself** rather than contracting it to a yard or marina.
● **Protect the boat during off-season storage.** Unstepping the mast and covering the boat will eventually save more than they cost.
● **Shop for price.** Take advantage of discounts, volume purchasing, group or co-op buying, used gear bargains, etc. Periodically compare boat yard and marina prices and insurance premiums.
● **Consider backyard storage.**
● **Give a work order to the boatyard as early as possible** so they can do the work before the crunch of outfitting (which should produce better, as well as possibly cheaper, results).
● **Make use of winter evenings** to maintain items that can be taken home.
● **Set limits on the cost of work** done by the boatyard and insist they notify you if they will exceed that limit.

● **Insure for the boat's fair market value** with as high a deductible as you can absorb.
● **Avoid impulse buying** especially at boat shows.
● **Keep the boat on a mooring** rather than at a marina slip.
● **Be on hand for mast unstepping and stepping.** Last year two *PS* editors halved the yard estimates by preparing the mast for unstepping and tuning it after stepping.
● **Protect sails** from sunlight, flogging, salt, and abuse.
● **Check engine periodically** for oil level, water intake, exhaust back siphoning, etc.
● **Plan major purchases** and yard work well ahead.
● **Know what your recurring costs are.** Set a budget and keep track of expenses; know what your boat realistically is worth, and keep it in mind when spending money on it.

Finally, remember that using your boat won't lower the cost of her annual upkeep, but it sure will do more toward justifying them.

the molded plastic drawers of a Sabre.

The variable that is impossible to predict is the intangible personal taste of the boatowner, which is a direct determinant of owner involvement. Some owners are fussier than others.

There are three costs of a boat: the initial purchase price (with or without financing charges), the annual cost of recurring maintenance that represent the basic price of owning and using a boat, and, finally, the more or less optional expense of upgrading a boat.

So what items should be included in estimating these costs? Those we include are the following:

• **Insurance:** premiums normally run from just over 1% of the agreed valuation of a boat to well over 2%. This includes property and personal liability, and damage to the boat. The premium rate will depend on the experience of the owner, the geographical range the policy covers, the amount of time the boat is in commission, the extent of coverage, the amount of the "deductible," the underwriters' evaluation of the degree of risk, and the probable cost of repairs. It usually does not pay to under-insure in order to reduce premium costs, but it may pay to increase the amount of the deductible, especially for an owner who does much of his own work or is savvy about contracting for work to be done.

• **Dockage or mooring:** usually this is a figure related to length, but it may include yacht club dues, launch service or dinghy storage, trailer registration and insurance, and a number of other items apart from the fee for the boat itself. In our harbor, for instance, it includes a city mooring tax that works out to 10¢ a pound for the mooring anchor.

• **Hauling, storage, and launching:** a figure that can vary widely. However, $15 per foot is a reasonable starting point. If the boat is handled by a boatyard, it can make the owner's job easier by simply checking off those jobs the yard does for decommissioning: winterizing the engine and head, spar storage, battery charging, frame erection, etc. However, while checking them off is easy, writing a check to pay for them is hard and can up the costs by 50%. Backyard storage can be cheaper than boatyard storage if trucking distance is reasonable.

• **Maintenance:** also a widely varying figure depending on where supplies are purchased, whether routine maintenance work is done by the owner or is contracted for, and other variables. It is also a cost that can be affected by efforts to protect the boat, thereby reducing the amount of maintenance she requires. When estimating the expense of routine maintenance, do not forget the bill from the sailmaker for washing, checking, and repairing sails, travel expenses to and from a boatyard, and the cost of an engine tune-up — items easily overlooked in any flight from fiscal reality.

• **Taxes and the like:** property taxes, mooring taxes, state boat registration fees, rating certificate renewal, documentation renewal fees, etc , all have to be figured into any total, as does membership in a yacht club.

• **Depreciation:** history tells us that boats tend to maintain their original dollar value over the years or even appreciate slightly in times of moderately high inflation. Therefore, for the average boat reasonably maintained there is no need to include depreciation on the basic boat (hull, rig, engine). Some gear does have a limited life, though, and will need replacement at regular intervals. Such gear as sails, electronics, running rigging, pumps, sailcovers, awnings and dodgers, outboard motors, and inflatable tenders probably should have a depreciation schedule based on 10 years or less. Few owners bother including this depreciation schedule in their thinking about annual boat costs, yet it may amount to 2-3% of the value of the boat each year.

Obviously many boatowners have found ways — real and imagined — to shave the total annual expense of their boats. One reader with a very low figure for the upkeep of his 40-footer notes he pays no dockage; it is included in his condominium. Another appended a line in the margin that he upped the figure after his wife read through the questionnaire.

Despite such ploys and self-deceptions, it still seems reasonable to believe that the recurring expenses of any boat over the size of a daysailer are likely to exceed 6% of the value of the boat. For owners who depend on boatyards to do their outfitting and who use commercial facilities for dockage, the realistic total has to be closer to 10%, especially if gear depreciation is included.

Then there are the more variable but inevitable costs of upgrading — the addition of gear and modification to the boat to increase her usefulness and, presumably, her value. Since this is not a recurring expense, detailed treatment is not appropriate to this article, but will be dealt with in an upcoming issue. Besides, any practical sailor who has read this far may have already decided he should dump his boat and get into less capital intensive activities such as gardening and golf.

Two Boats and What They Cost in '82

The following table represents the costs in 1982 of two boats, each owned by a *PS* editor. Both were essentially owner-maintained and kept on moorings. Their owners consistently shopped for supplies and gear at discount. Both are owned outright with no outstanding boat loans. The first is a home-built fiberglass sloop valued in 1982 at $25,000 (raised this year to $35,000) that has been backyard stored in the off season. The second is a 60-year-old, 47' wooden boat nearing completion of a partial restoration (the specific costs of which are not included in the record of 1982 expenses); it was wet-stored in the winter of 1981-1982 and backyard stored in the winter of 1982-1983. This boat is currently on the market for $42,000 and was insured in 1982 for $35,000. The expenses for 1982 are typical

Item	34' fiberglass sloop	47' wooden yawl
Insurance	$ 285	$ 817
Hauling/storage/launching	573	765
Mooring (inc. taxes)	465	624
Launch service	—	225
Maintenance-yard work	—	600
Maintenance-supplies	490	700
Sail repair/servicing	70	190
Documentation	15	15
Misc. (membership, rating certificate, etc.)	41	40
Total out-of-pocket expenses	**$1939**	**$3976**
Depreciation (sails, electronics, etc)	325	350
Total expenses	**$2264**	**$4326**

In addition, another $1260 was spent on purchases intended to upgrade the 34' sloop: folding prop, spinnaker pole, RDF, batteries, and winter cover frame.

About $2500 was spent on upgrading the 47' yawl, including a new headsail, wiring and electrical panels, and the seemingly endless supply of fastenings, wood, bronze, paint, varnish, and dozens of other items that go into a restoration project.

It Pays to Shop for Marine Insurance

Normally, when contemplating the purchase of any item costing more than, say, $100, a practical person —especially a practical sailor—will comb the stores, ads and discount houses for the best price.

Is that how you bought your boat insurance?

Or did you, like many of us, simply ask a reputable broker or agent for the required coverage and ante up the premium once a year?

If you did buy your insurance without shopping around, you may be out a few dollars that you didn't really have to part with. A sampling of insurance premiums conducted by *The Practical Sailor* indicates that shopping for insurance is worth the time in dollars, at least, and may be worth something more in finding the kind of policy that best suits your boat and your use of it.

We did our shopping by requesting quotes for a 30' fiberglass sailboat moored in Portsmouth, RI, with certain dollar amounts specified: $14,000 on the hull, $300,000 liability, and $3000 medical coverage. We then varied the deductibles to determine the effect on premiums. Out of curiosity, we took a sampling of West Coast quotes, hypothetically locating our sailboat in a slip at Marina Del Ray, California.

The figures are for 1981, but the lesson is in the comparison—not the actual cost of the coverage.

The result is at least interesting: the annual premium for the boat varied between $149 and $346, a difference of almost $200.

Much of the difference can be traced to the variation in the deductible ($500 versus $140), but even with the same deductible ($280), the premiums varied by nearly $150, from $170 to $319.

In general, insurance is cheaper in California than it is in New England, due, according to one agent, to greater exposure to violent storms and a less favorable claims history in the North Atlantic coastal areas. For the same reasons, the Florida and Gulf Coast rates tend to be even higher.

However, the difference in premiums within New England is significant, exceeding $100 for policies with the same deductible, and topping $150 when we increased the deductible from $140 to $280.

It is tempting to conclude that the cheaper policy must be inferior to the higher priced coverage, but that is not necessarily true. Nor is it safe to assume that the company that quoted us a low premium will necessarily produce a low quote for your boat. Different companies emphasize different factors in calculating premiums. For example, the high premium quoted by American

---

Help Your Agent Help You

Buying insurance immediately puts many people on the defensive: constantly wary of saying too little, or too much, one may never know what effect the information proferred has on premiums, how thoroughly the agent has scoured the market for the best policy or price, and, after the purchase, whether a claim against the policy will result in higher rates or (horror!) cancellation.

Despite the monolithic aspect of insurance companies, the fact is that you have a certain degree of control over the cost of your insurance and the recovery of losses which insurance is supposed to provide.

In fact, a marine underwriter has to develop a feel for a prospective policy holder as to how secure a risk he represents. You can help him with this task and help yourself in the process, by advising your agent of certain factors.

• **Experience.** Go out of your way to inform your agent of passages, local sailing experience, length of experience, professional or recreational qualifications you may have, education (such as US Power Squadron, US Coast Guard, or other courses you may have taken), types of boats with which you are familiar, and any other information you can think of to demonstrate your competence and familiarity with boats.

• **Seaworthiness of the boat.** Advise the agent of any unusual features of your boat which would contribute to its seaworthiness. If he is not familiar with your type of boat, make him familiar with it. Advise him of any equipment on board which makes the boat safer (fire control

systems, radiotelephones, depthsounders, Loran or other navigational equipment) or more secure (special mooring, burglar alarms, locks). If you acquire such equipment, advise your agent; you will want the new equipment covered, and you may influence your rate favorably. On the other hand, a company may refuse outright to insure a boat it deems unseaworthy.

• **Claims history.** Various techniques are used to build a good claims history into the policy premium. Some companies award a percent discount (10% the first year, less the second year, up to a maximum percent off the premium) for each loss-free year. Then, if a loss occurs, you pay the full premium the following year, and start building up your discount with the next loss-free year. Thus, before filing a claim, you might check with your agent to see if you will forfeit a discount that amounts to more than your loss. Other companies will let a single claim go, even a large one if you have a long loss-free history with the company, but will respond to a series of claims. You might be asked to buy a larger deductible, or your premium might be raised outright. A claim for a loss which involves poor seamanship on the part of the policyholder is more likely to elicit a response from the company than other types of claims.

• **Navigation limits.** Some companies offer lower premiums when a boat will be sailed within a small, specified geographical area, or if the boat is to be out of use for a substantial part of the year.

You must do your own shopping if you wish to find the best combination of price, expertise, service and coverage

International Marine can be expected, because the company's rate structure tends to penalize smaller boats. AIM would becme more competitive on hulls insured for $25,000 or more, said our agent.

Therefore, you must do your own shopping if you wish to find the best combination of price, expertise, service and coverage. Though we cannot recommend specific companies, we can offer advice on how to find your own best buy.

• Be sure to investigate group rates or special programs, such as the insurance offered through the Boat Owners' Association of the US (BOAT/US), or the Better Boating Association. The lowest premiums we found in New England were quoted under discount programs for members of the BBA or BOAT/US.

• Don't be modest; insurance companies are likely to quote their lower rates to sailors with extensive, documentable training and experience, well-equipped and well-maintained boats, and good claims histories.

• When you have collected your quotations, select the two or three you like best and carefully read through the sample policy you have requested. Compare coverage as well as premiums. Ask your agent to describe the advantages of one policy over another. Listen in the answers for the sound of familiarity with *marine* insurance, remembering that it is a specialized field, and that the agent you select will act as your advisor in dealings with the company.

When you are through, perhaps you will realize enough savings to buy a new winch.

A Sampler of Marine Insurance Premiums

Broker/Agent	Underwriter	Navigation limits		Deductible	Premium
		Months	Area		
Frank B. Hall of Massachusetts Boston, Mass.	Royal Globe Insurance Company	8	Eastport, Maine to Cedar Keys, Florida	$210 280	$257 239
John G. Alden Insurance Agency, Inc. Boston, Mass.	Marine Office of America (MOAC)	12	Eastport, Maine to Pensacola, Florida	140 280	228 202
John G. Alden Insurance Agency, Inc. Boston, Mass.	Insurance Company of North America (INA)	8	Eastport, Maine to Moorehead City, N. Carolina	140 280	271 239
John G. Alden Insurance Agency, Inc. Boston, Mass.	American International Marine (AIM)	8	Eastport, Maine to Cedar Keys, Florida	140 280	346 319
Kirby, Inc. Newport, Rhode Island	Aetna Insurance Company	8	Eastport, Maine to Brownsville Texas	140 280 560	342 280 238
Boat Owners Association of the United States (BOAT/US)	Omaha Indemnity Insurance Company	6	St. Johns, New Brunswick to Cedar Keys, Florida	140 280 500	194 185 166
Terheggen & Malone Inc. Long Beach, California	Marine Office of America (MOAC)	12	Pt. Concepcion California, to Pt. Rio San Tomas, Mexico	100 280	224 170
Harold A. Towle Company South Pasadena California	Safeco Insurance Company	12	North American Coast from 31°N to 40°N	100 250	187 171
Nationwide Insurance Company Sales Office Anaheim, California	Nationwide Insurance Company	12	US West Coast plus 50 miles north, south, and west	250 500	171 164
Ocean Marine Insurance Westminster, California	National American Insurance Company	12	Pt. Concepcion, California, to Pt. Rio San Tomas, Mexico	140 280	217 201

Premiums quoted on $14,000 hull, $300,000 P&I, $3000 medical.

How to Protect Yourself Against an Insurance Claim

Insurance coverage, like your life raft, medical kit, and umbrella, is one of those necessary, but annoying, things in life that we need to have but hope to never use. Recognizing the need, we go ahead and buy the coverage, and waste little time or energy mourning the money spent.

We even hope never to recover the money, for that would imply damage to something—or someone—and it's just fine to buy the peace of mind and let it go at that.

It's a different story, though, when your insurance premium is suddenly raised due to a spurious claim made against your policy, and you end up paying indirectly for a stranger's "windfall". In fairness, this kind of claim is not the rule, but it can, and does, happen.

In one occurrence, a wooden yawl anchoring in a crowded harbor came in contact with another boat, leaving a "smudge of white topside paint 2″ long" on the dark purple hull of a rather scruffy Triton. After an exchange of appropriate information, the boats went their own ways, and the owner of the yawl, George Carey, was neither surprised nor concerned when his insurance company informed him that a claim had been filed.

He was both surprised and concerned when notified that the claim had been settled to the tune of $612, and his insurance premium would increase by $131 per year. Subsequent checking revealed that the boatowner had apparently submitted an estimate for having his whole topsides painted as his claim, and the settlement had been made on that basis.

Indignant and puzzled, Carey called our office and told us his story, wondering what he should—or could—do about it. Not a cynic, Carey tested our cynicism. We had no answer except to suggest he check personally to see if the damage had been repaired, indeed whether there actually had been any damage. We also remarked that there is a moral to his misfortune that would be well worth passing on to other readers. He agreed and sent us his story in writing.

After reading his account, we realized that there should be ways to avoid or at least reduce the cost and indignation that Carey suffered. With that in mind we began poking around in the insurance industry to find out how the industry deals with claims of this type. Here are some of the things we found out.

• **You will almost invariably lose money on an insurance claim against you.** Some policies (such as Carey's) offer a premium discount of as much as 30% to reward accident-free policyholders; others have no actual discount but assign policyholders to a low risk category that effectively saves money on the annual premium just as a discount might. Any claim against that policy jeopardizes these lower rates. In fact, any "incident" that could have resulted in a claim (your boat drags and is hauled off rocks with superficial damage not warrant-ing a claim) can jeopardize either the merit discount or a low risk category.

If this practice strikes you as rather arbitrary, you probably understand it, nevertheless. Insurance officials claim it involves a decision based on specific circumstances, yet we understand that in a vast majority of cases the policyholder is the loser. Keep this in mind when you think of picking up a mooring under sail in a crowded harbor or, for that matter, when you think of passing on to your insurance company the bill for repairing scuffed topsides when you left your boat at a dock without proper fendering.

• **There is no requirement that damage be actually repaired before a claim is settled.** The amount of a settlement is usually negotiated between the insurance company (or its adjuster) and the complainant, and usually involves the boatyard(s) in a position to effect the repairs whether or not those repairs will eventually be done. The industry claims to have a handle on which yards are reputable and which ones are not. However, reputable or not, the yard is generally the choice of the complainant.

• **The better insurance companies investigate all but the most nominal claims (under, say, $150).** Usually they have an adjuster (their own or independent) assess the damage and establish a reasonable cost for its repair. Obviously some assessments are routine, others are complicated, including those that could entail writing off the loss as total.

It is unclear whether the adjuster checking the Carey claim for Chubb & Son Insurance Co. actually visited the boatyard and the Triton. However, the figure he suggested Chubb try to settle for apparently coincided with the estimate from the boatyard for the repair ($600) and was indeed the amount of the eventual settlement. There is some evidence that initially the claim was for both repairing the gelcoat and completely refinishing the topsides, a job that would exceed $3000. In his report the adjuster also seemed to have made note of the sorry state of the topside gelcoat. A representative of Chubb & Son would not tell us whether the adjuster described the damage that the Triton owner was claiming Carey inflicted.

• **Assume there will be a claim if you have an accident involving another boat.** We share Carey's feelings that heretofore the sea has seemed a place relatively free from the "louts and brigands" who have turned on-shore accidents into profitable enterprises. Yet we are seeing abundant evidence that those creatures have taken to the water. Moreover, on a more reasonable note, even the sweet charity of traditional sailors toward incidental damage to their boats has been tempered by the economic times in which we sail. Damage to the modern boat is complicated and costly

Remember that on a claim an insurance company's first responsibility is to itself, not to you

to repair and most of us quite legitimately would rather have someone else's insurance company pay the bill than our own if that someone else is indeed at fault. Under either circumstance, if you are involved in damage to another boat, you should be prepared to handle a claim.

• **Any offer to settle for cash on the spot is a mistake.** "It is," as one insurance official noted, "playing with your insurance company's money." By settling you are at least tacitly admitting fault for the incident and any damage, obvious and ancillary, that it might have caused. For example, superficial inspection might show merely cracked gelcoat and you offer $25 to cover the damage. For the $25 you get a release from the other party, ostensibly ending the matter and saving you from notifying your insurance company and hence risking any increase in your premium. Then, however, on closer examination the owner of the damaged boat detects a bulkhead that has become detached from the hull in the general vicinity of the bump, a condition that may or may not have been the result of the accident.

At that point you—or more properly your insurance company—are liable to a substantial claim. The cash you blithely passed over to avoid a claim becomes a statement of your liability and the release is not worth the paper it is written on.

Better advice is to examine the damage yourself, taking careful notes and even photographs, saying as little as possible about the cause or fault of the accident or extent of the damage to the other boatowner. Be amiable and cooperative but not agreeable. Most important, do not dismiss talk of costs of repair by mentioning your insurance coverage; to do so invites exorbitant claims on the philosophy that insurance companies are rich and ripe for the taking and ignores the fact that the cost of settlements they make will eventually be passed on to you. Thus, in dealing with the damage and the other party, act as an individual and state, if asked, only the name of your insurance agent. Give the impression the cost of repair will come out of your pocket and that you are vitally concerned about the nature and extent of the damage. Have the other boatowner send any claim to you directly and then you pass it on to your insurance company, specifically through your agent.

• **Work through your agent.** He is the chap who sold you the policy and its coverage, a service for which he received a commission. In dealings with your insurance company he represents you, his client. If there is a chance the other owner may send you a bill or claim for damage, make out an accident report as soon after the incident as possible—for credibility, before you see his claim. Include all details, especially your assessment of the damage as reflected in your notes. Send this form to your agent only when and if you receive a claim from the other owner. Append to it any disagreement you may have with the description of the damage and/or repairs in the claim.

Your agent should know your feelings and thoughts on the whole incident. Insist he act in your behalf in forwarding the paperwork. If the incident is such that you do not believe it should jeopardize your preferred premium, tell him so. This is why we suggest policyholders deal through a reputable agent, one who is familiar with boats and marine claims, even better, one who specializes in yacht insurance. Similarly, carry your insurance with a company that does extensive marine coverage and that has a claims department capable of properly handling the complicated claims typical of marine damage.

Incidentally, a good part of Carey's frustration seems to have stemmed from his agent's not having taken the time to explain to him the ramifications of the claim. The agent processed the papers but apparently took no active part in representing his client either with the claim or, later, with the loss of the merit premium discount.

• **Keep personal track of the progress of the claim against your policy.** It is clearly not enough to make out the forms, send them off to your agent or company and assume everything will be taken care of with your best interests in mind. Periodically check on what is being done to settle the matter, preferably through your agent but directly if need be. Remember that on a claim an insurance company's first responsibility is to itself, not to you. One way or another that claim is going to cost you money in the way of a higher premium. In the instance of the claim against Carey he could and should have insisted on seeing the adjuster's description of the damage and, if different from his assessment, demand an explanation.

• **In all dealings watch the words you use.** Terms like *fraud, collusion, padding,* etc. are loaded words. They take the matter out of a mere matter of insurance adjustment and put it in a civil or even criminal jurisdiction. It is one thing to be liable for a stove-in rail; it is quite another to have to answer to charges of slander or to have the matter deteriorate into irreconcilable recriminations. Similarly, reference to *court* (as "see you in court, buddy"), *suits,* and *lawyers* do little more than polarize the situation. Keep the threat of such action to yourself on the theory that the other party knows of such possibilities and has already taken them into consideration.

• **Finally, you have a last resort for insurance disputes: your state's insurance commission.** Insurance commissions are state agencies charged with regulating insurance companies operating in that state. If you have a complaint against a company, seek the assistance of that commission. Be prepared to thoroughly document your case and to show that you have exhausted all normal channels for settling the issue.

Perhaps we should make one last point. While it is true that the policyholder will sooner or later pay the price of the claim, it is also true that all of us who insure our boats will also be losers. Insurance underwriting being what it is, all our premiums will rise. A claim, any claim, diminishes us all.

We have fended off errant boats with inept helmsmen, cringed when they left our topsides dented, and waved them benevolently on their way albeit with gritted teeth and muttered imprecations. And we will continue to do so. It is our nature, not so cynical after all. But we will also be more wary of scruffy boats with purple topsides.

How to Collect for Damages

It is not safe to assume anything about insurance coverage, even if you think you have a straightforward situation, as we discovered when an insurance company offered to pay only half the damages from a port-starboard collision where the claimant, Fred Nichols, was clearly not at fault. Unfortunately, the other sailor's insurance agent, apparently unfamiliar with marine affairs, did not agree. The experience was a real eye-opener.

Nichols had not filed a claim with his own company, assuming that he would be fully reimbursed under the other boat's coverage. When he was offered only half reimbursement, he refused it and began to explore other alternatives. Utlimately, with the help of his own insurance agent, he received a full settlement.

What would have happened if he had not been insured? He would, in the words of one insurance spokesman, be "left to his own devices." A lawyer, a state insurance commission, or even consumer advocate organizations and publications are three possible "devices."

So What's the Best Protection?
How do you best assure yourself that you'll get settlement for damages when you cannot reasonably be held liable in an incident?

Quite simply, the best way is to have your own insurance, that is, unless in lieu of insurance you are prepared to turn efforts to settle over to a lawyer and pay him out of what you collect. Your own insurance company may ultimately be the source of your indemnity regardless of how much at fault the nimrod in the other, burdened boat was. Or how unjustified is the offer of settlement from his insurance company.

From the outset of your attempts to collect—indeed, from the time of the incident—you should work together with your marine insurance agent. This is not time to have a policy with a company that writes only incidental marine policies nor a time to have bought a policy from an agent unfamiliar with the difference between the pointy end and the blunt end of a sailboat. In this respect Nichols was on solid ground—he had a policy with a major marine underwriter, had an agent familiar with boats, and he was trying to deal with a company that has long been in the forefront of marine insurance.

Regardless of who was "at fault," submit the same information on extent of damages, a description of the incident and damages, and the whereabouts of the damaged boat to *both* your agent and the claims office of the "other guy's" insurance company. Ask your own agent to notify the claims office of your company of the possible need for an appraiser or surveyor to examine the boat and the cost of repair.

At the same time, if damage is severe, the circumstances of receiving the damage are in dispute or unclear, or if there was any personal injury, request a Coast Guard investigation. In the event that settlement must go to court, you may need to prove possible negligence in order to collect. Note that at this point the traditional warm camaraderie sailors feel for one another may be cooling fast.

The Constant Refrain: The Role of Your Agent
Although it is possible to approach your insurance company directly for information and advice on handling a claim, the proper ally is your agent. He is *your* representative with the insurance company whose policy he sold you. In return for the commission received when he sold that policy, you should expect his help when it comes time to make a claim—regardless of whether the fault for that claim is yours or not.

He should act in your behalf. He should immediately be able to notify the claims department so they can appraise the damage. He should be able to tell you how to submit a report of the incident and it is he who should, in turn, send that report through the proper channels for settlement. And he should be prepared to report to you the progress on your report/claim.

If your agent is unavailable (or unwilling, incapable, unknowledgable, etc.) to act in your behalf, call the regional claims office and ask for the claims representative handling your claim. If unhappy with his response, talk with the regional manager for marine claims (that representative's boss). If still not satisfied, conact that state's insurance commission (or equivalent). However, prior to this step, stop and ask yourself whether this is the most reasonable course of action at this time. Impatience, intransigence, threats, etc. may do more to hurt your cause which, after all, is a matter of negotiation, not demand. Remember, the voice of sweet reason wins more valid arguments than violence.

Limits of Liability

It seems commonly misunderstood, but there are limits to the liability an insurance policy covers.

What insurance companies usually do not pay are liability claims for damage that the company deems can be attributed to acts of God. If, for instance, your boat breaks loose from her mooring during a storm and damages another moored boat, the owner of that boat may not be able to collect on a liability claim against your insurance company. In such an instance, the insurance companies may have collectively agreed that the severity of the weather was such as to constitute an act of God. Then each claim is settled as a loss to the insured by his own insurance company.

On the other hand, the severity of the weather might not have been sufficient to justify the "act of God" clause, and the damage caused by your boat breaking loose would be covered by liability claims against your boat's policy.

Note that none of the above prevents you as owner of a boat from being sued for damages by another owner, a suit against which your insurance company may or may not aid you in defending yourself.

Boatyard Contracts are Meant to be Read

Boatyard storage contracts may sound boring—they are—but all people who utilize the haul out, storage, service, and repair facilities of boatyards must understand the basics of the contractual obligations involved if potential unhappiness or unexpected costs are to be avoided.

Over the past quarter century or so, we've stored our boats in five different yards, dealt with a number of others, and swapped boatyard tales with many fellow sailors. From all this we've concluded that most bad boatyard experiences are a result of the unexpected and that the unexpected can be avoided by choosing carefully the yard to which you give your patronage and by reading and understanding the contract.

There are many ways of choosing a boatyard which will not be detailed here, but we briefly suggest that fellow sailors are usually quite candid in their views regarding yards. Simply asking a number of experienced boatowners about Yard X will usually turn up a consensus. Beware of new owners, though; they may be either starry eyed or traumatized by the unexpected. Another good clue—though not an infallible one—is the state of cleanliness in the yard. Good yards—except perhaps at the end of a spring fitout weekend—usually look quite neat. We remember one exception: a brand new yard located in the grounds of an abandoned foundry which looked like the devil but which was well run and very cheap. The yard owner simply didn't have the personnel to start the yard *and* clear up the foundry detritus all at the same time. The clue which led us to store quite satisfactorily in that dump was the fact that the new owner-manager had been successfully managing a good, big yard for absentee owners.

Anyway, once you've located what seems to be a good yard, you need to *read and understand the particular contract*. We can't stress that too strongly. Read the contract—it is usually written in simple language—and if there's anything you don't understand, ask the yard for an explanation.

Most boatyard storage contracts are similar in general respects, but differ in details. Contracts discussed here were provided by Gerald and Kenneth Larsen of Larsen Marine Service, Inc, Waukegan, Illinois; Gene Herman of Palmer Johnson, Inc, of Racine, Wisconsin; and Grant Crowley of Crowley's Yacht Yard, Chicago, Illinois. In addition, we questioned several boatyards about specific provisions.

In reading a contract, you should realize several things. The operations of boatyards are regulated by maritime and state laws, and the primary purpose of the contract is to protect the boatyard. Boatyards are in the business of handling very expensive, privately owned possessions: boats. These boats are owned by both experienced and inexperienced sailors. Masses of people—young, old, bright, stupid, honest, and dishonest—have potential access to these possessions. Also, boatyards tend to be located on very valuable, very expensive waterfront property, and hence, have high overhead. Finally, boatyards are not philanthropic enterprises.

Because of these considerations, the following are fairly standard items on boatyard storage contracts. First of all, many yards have a catchall clause which requires an owner to comply with all posted regulations, both those in effect when the contract is executed and those later posted. These have mostly to do with hours of access, employee only areas, use of machinery, children, pets, etc.

Most yards specify in some detail what docking equipment—lines and fenders—are necessary when a boat is to be handled. Failure to provide this equipment can result in a bill to the owner for the purchase or rental of it.

Some yards have requirements regarding fuel and holding tanks. For instance, Palmer Johnson's reserves the right to fill fuel tanks and remove LP tanks, kerosene, oily rags, etc. to meet their insurance and fire law requirements; and Crowley's Yacht Yard requires that holding tanks be emptied before a boat is stored. Obviously, if an owner fails to perform these tasks, the yard may charge him to do so. Also having to do with fire laws are usually included provisions against cabin heaters, open flames, and electrical cords left plugged in overnight.

All storage contracts we've seen disclaim any responsibility regarding ladders, scaffolds, ramps, equipment, etc. The owner must accept responsibility for injuries to himself, his family, and his guests.

Who's responsible for damage?

Most contracts disclaim responsibility for damage to yachts except when that damage is a result of the yard's negligence. Owners do not always seem to realize that **boatyards to not normally carry insurance on the boats they store.** Some yards require proof of insuredness, but, in any case, it is the owner's responsibility to see that his or her insurance covers the storage period.

Here are some examples to further illustrate the idea of responsibility for damage: If a boat is damaged while being hauled, moved, or worked on, it's the yard's responsibility; if a boat is damaged by wind, storm, acts of God, etc., it's the responsibility of the owner. If a yard-supplied cradle collapses, it's the yard's responsibility; if the cradle belongs to the owner so, too, does the responsibility. Unless the yard contract specifically requires that the owner remove them before handling the boat over to the yard, yards are generally responsible for damage to masthead antennas, wind indicators, etc. when that damage is sustained while stepping or unstepping masts. If a boat suffers water damage due to leaking seams, the yard—while it should and usually will try very hard to prevent it—is not responsible. In most contracts this is spelled out in a separate clause.

Water damage due to improperly serviced through hull fittings brings us to another aspect of boatyard contracts. Any work which an owner authorizes in writing is a contract with the boatyard. So, if an owner has in writing instructed the yard to service the through-hull fittings, then water damage sustained through the leaking of those fittings is the responsibility of the yard; if the owner chooses to do this work himself, then the responsibility is his or her own. By the way, in a good yard, you'll always see a yard worker check the bilges of a newly launched yacht to see if it is leaking. That's one of the main reasons most yards require an owner to leave one set of keys to the boat with the yard.

If an owner contracts to have a yacht's engine or head winterized, the yard is responsible for freeze damage. This is one of the tricky areas of routine yacht servicing. If a yacht hauled early in the fall suffered freeze damage to its engine or head due to the fact that there was a freak freeze on September 15, then the yard could claim an act of God. If the yacht were hauled on November 1 and suffered freeze damage the next day, the yard is generally held responsible if the owner had contracted for winterization. Because of the fact that even good yards make mistakes—particularly during the rush haul out and launch periods—and because there are a very few engines the designs of which resist winterization, it is usual for boat yard winterization rates to include a small "insurance" factor.

How much does it cost?
That brings us to fees. Most boatyards today have set fees for routine service items like winterizing engines and heads, stepping, unstepping, and storing spars; removing batteries; erecting winter covers; supplying cradles; etc. Some of these fees—like removing batteries—are flat fees; others—like stepping and unstepping spars—are usually based on the size of the boat or length of the spar. So you won't be unpleasantly surprised, ask for a copy of the rate sheet or, in the case of a yard which performs this work on a time basis, get a quote beforehand. When the bill is in and all you can say is, "I didn't know it cost that much," it's too late to scream at the yard.

Most boatyard storage contracts specify payment dates and carrying charges for bills not paid on time. Every contract we've seen specifies that any unpaid bills constitute a lien upon the boat and reserve the right to refuse launching until all bills are paid. This latter provision appears to be increasingly enforced of recent years. Another usual contractual element is the stipulation of a non-refundable reservation fee. In fact, many yards will refund the fee if the change in plans is due to something unavoidable like the yacht being stuck for the winter in another port, but legally the yard may keep the fee.

Also related to costs is the fact that most boatyard storage contracts prohibit the use of paid labor other than that supplied by the yard unless the owner specifically arranges otherwise with the yard. Usually when an owner does make such an arrangement, the yard does the billing and adds a surcharge of ten to fifteen percent.

Regarding the permissible functions of professional crew, a few yards—mostly old, established ones—specify in the contract what work a paid crew may perform. Usually this is limited to above the rail and below decks. Should you employ a professional or two and should your contract not spell this out, you should make your arrangements with the yard in writing.

The usual contract has a stipulation about clean up fees. When such a stipulation is included the owner assumes responsibility for keeping the area surrounding his or her boat reasonably clean or paying for yard

clean up. This clause need not cause most of us much fear. It's there to protect us from real and inconsiderate slobs.

Prohibitions and limitations
More serious for some sailors is the sometimes encountered prohibition against spray painting. If you want to spray, make sure your chosen yard allows it before you sign a contract.

In the matter of selling boats, different yards have different policies spelled out in the contract. Some yards allow "For Sale" signs and some do not. Most yards will require that they be the listing agent in a brokerage sale but allow the option of making the listing available to other brokers for a participating fee in any sale so made. Although not usually spelled out in the storage contract, it is not a function of a yacht yard to show the boat to prospective buyers you might send over.

Time is often an included element in boatyard storage contracts. It is usual for a yard to specify a certain maximum time after launching that a yacht may be left at the yard before dockage fees are levied, and it's not unusual for the dockage fees to be specified in the contract; so too with time in the slings. Another time limitation usually defined in the contract is the duration of the storage period—typically in the North, October 1 through June 1. In addition, the "dead storage" fees which will be levied if the yacht is not launched and the continuation of the storage contract in the future for such yachts are often specified in the contract. Some contracts include summer storage charges for cradles left in the yard.

A last time element is the launch date. Many contracts specify a minimum time period between an owner's order and the launch—one or two weeks is usual. When so specified in the contract, the yard is legally bound to get the boat launched by the specified date if given the proper lead time. Boat yard managers wryly admit that this is the area where technical breaches of contract often arise during the spring rush. Happily for the yards a day or two delay is not important to most sailors and we know of no lawsuits ever levied on this point. Ken Larsen suggested that the one instance where a suit might be levied would be in a case where a sale was lost because of a failure to launch by a specified date.

The most usual contract includes haul out, bottom wash, storage, and launch (but no other services) as a part of the contract fee. This, however, is not universal and only by reading a particular contract can you know what is or is not included in the fee. Palmer Johnson's fees, for instance, include only storage. Haul out, bottom washing, and launching are each billed separately.

And finally, some yards require that they do certain work on the yacht like sanding and painting the bottom and/or covering the boat. Other yards require a certain percentage of the storage fee in contracted work. The only way the individual owner can determine what's what is to be familiar with a particular contract. And that, again, is what it all boils down to . . . read your contract and understand it.
                                                                —J. Pazereskis

V

Evaluations
of
Thirty-two
Boats

Catalina 22

O'Day 22

Tanzer 22

Flicka

J/24

Cape Dory 25 and 25 D

Ericson 25

Freedom 25

O'Day 25

Montego 25

Stiletto Catamaran

Hunter 27

Sabre 28

S2 8.5 Meter

Catalina 30

J/30

Nonsuch 30

Olson 30

Pearson 30

Cal 31

Southern Cross 31

Nicholson 31

Allied Seawind II

Freedom 33

Tartan Ten

Irwin 37

CSY 37

Tartan 37

Tayana 37

C&C Landfall 38

Whitby 42

Three 22 Footers

The large, varied and changing selection of small sailboats on the market prompted this study of three of the more popular small boats on the market, all 22-footers: the Catalina, O'Day and Tranzer 22s. In separate treatment of each boat, we arrive at some conclusions about these boats that would be applicable to many other boats of similar size, type and price.

The impression of size
The most lingering impression we have of these three boats is that the Tanzer seems to be a small boat enlarged for interior space whereas the Catalina and O'Day suggest larger boats scaled down. Generally, of course, they are the same—22' boats with approximately the same dimensions. The impression is subjective; others looking at the boats might get just the opposite impression.

We also looked at upwards of a dozen other boats of about the same size. We found that they create similar impressions about their size, utilizing a variety of subtle techniques including some that have nothing to do with actual dimensions. Scaling, proportions, and styling all contribute. Buyers should not pick one boat over another just because one *looks* bigger. Use a tape measure, check by lying on berths, sitting in the cockpit, walking forward on the deck and so forth. In the same way, do not try to judge speed or performance by looks; there are objective criteria (rating handicaps, for instance) that have more validity.

In any boat as small as these performance may not live up to expectations or hopes. It didn't for us. Of the three evaluated, the Tanzer 22 is a better sailing boat than the O'Day or the Catalina. As performance is important to us, that is where we would look first.

Related to performance is the question of drop or swing keels and centerboards. The swing keel is often a complex engineering problem. In the Catalina 22, the keel weighs more than 500 pounds and must be raised and lowered as well as supported during trailering, beaching, and sailing. Add to these drawbacks the reduced stability, lowered performance, more difficult maintenance, and where there is an option, the higher price, of either a swing keel or centerboard. In the end we think the fixed keel is the answer unless trailerability is a major priority.

Speaking of weight, a word of warning is in order about the weight or displacement figures in builder specifications, in particular where the boat is being marketed for her trailerability. There is no standard for what the term *displacement* represents. It can mean weight of the basic boat alone, it can mean the weight of the basic boat plus some optional equipment or it can even include food, water, and personal belongings of the crew. Of the three boats in our evaluation, only O'Day breaks down the published weights; hull and deck only, minimum trailering weight, and sailing weight with four persons aboard.

Whatever the case, prospective buyers should realize that the published weight is not likely to reflect the actual weight of the boat on a trailer. For such a figure, estimated at best, add about 10% to the specified weight. Then add the weight of the trailer itself. This is what the car will actually be pulling. We once trailered a 23-footer several hundred miles and back; the total weight of the boat fitted and stocked for cruising plus the weight of the trailer was more than 1000 lbs over the advertised weight of the boat alone, an increase of about 30%.

About Cockpits
All three of the boats in this evaluation have a generous beam carried well aft, an important feature. Beam at the cockpit helps stability and, of course, it affords cockpit roominess. Equally important is that the beam gives buoyancy to the after end. The weight of four adults in the cockpit of a boat the size of these could amount to 600 pounds, 25% of the displacement. Then there is the weight of an outboard on the transom and a gas tank. Unsupported this weight would make the stern squat in the water and reduce performance drastically. Beam gives this support. None of these three boats suffers excessively from cockpit loading.

Although cockpit roominess is a virtue, it can also be a fault. Despite the fact that all three cockpits are self-bailing and the boats self-righting from a knockdown, all three would be in real jeopardy if the cockpit filled with water as high as the seats. The three boats all have sills lower than seat level. They will keep incidental cockpit water out of the interior but not major flooding. Moreover, none has a lower hatchboard that can be fixed or locked in place. Owners of boats with low sills and no bridgedeck should make this provision and keep the lower hatchboard in place while sailing.

Worst in this respect is the Catalina. As is typical of most of the boats from Catalina, it has a wide companionway with substantial taper. A hatchboard needs to be raised only a couple of inches before it comes out of the channels on each side. Interestingly the sailing photos of the 22 in Catalina's brochure on the boat show all hatchboards in place and the companionway slide closed despite the relatively benign conditions in which it is being sailed.

Accommodations
While our standards call for performance first and comfort second, we did not ignore accommodations. After all, these three boats are *cruising* boats. In this respect, we think the O'Day 22 is the best. She has the two best berths, usable forward berths (for little folk), and best of all, an enclosed head that incorporates a semblance of privacy not only for the head but also between the two sleeping facilities.

Nevertheless, expectations for overnight comfort for more than two people aboard are unrealistic. A major part of the limitation is the stowage, a vital matter in boats of this size where anything lying about will be in the way. All three boats rely almost entirely on scuttles located under the berths. Not only is this space awkward to get to, but the space is dank, probably even wet. The bilges of these boats are shallow. Any water that gets below will tend to slosh under the liner/sole in-

The strong Tanzer and Catalina owners' associations help in maintaining the resale market for those boats

to the spaces below the berths. And even if water does not come in from outside, these are places where condensation will occur, encouraging dampness, mustiness, and mildew.

Although we like the O'Day's berths, the Catalina gets high grades for her decor, which has to be the envy of builders trying to compete with that firm. For sheer space (or at least the illusion of spaciousness) the choice is the Tanzer; there's nothing like carrying the cabin house out to the sheer to create roominess and the maximum amount of headroom even if it is just sitting headroom.

What about auxiliary power?
Most owners of these three boats will, sooner or later, want some form of auxiliary power. All three are designed to take an outboard motor mounted on an optional lift-up bracket on the transom. A long-shaft 4.5 hp motor is adequate for owners who would sail in anything but a flat calm. However, for powering against any kind of wind or chop the minimum of a 7.5 hp motor is needed and then don't expect powerboat speed or handling. In purchasing an outboard, select one serviced locally and suited for installation on a sailboat.

Inboard engines including the suspect saildrive make a hefty investment for a boat the size and price of these. Such an engine with its capacity for generating electricity, dependability, power, and convenience does make it appealing. However, you should consider installing one only if the boat is a long time purchase and powering an important consideration. And plan for a cost including installation to run three times that of an outboard.

Rigs, sails, and rudders
In any boat of this size and type the mast should be capable of being raised and lowered without recourse to a crane. All three of these boats have hinged mast steps on deck for this purpose. Success in hoisting or lowering a mast with these systems depends on smooth water, a gentle breeze, and an experienced crew of at least two. The masts weigh at least 40 pounds and range from 25' to 30' in length, so getting them up and down requires some care and planning.

All three boats come equipped with a mainsail and working jib (or lapper) as standard. The standard sails are all of routine quality, made to a price commensurate with the price of the boat. Unfortunately it is doubtful if buyers can negotiate enough of a rebate on these sails to justify getting better quality on a custom order with a sailmaker. Again, this is a matter of how high a priority an owner places on performance and how long he expects to keep his boat.

Of the three boats only Catalina lists a pivoting or kick-up rudder as available. The pivoting rudder lets the draft of the rudder match the draft of the boat with the keel retracted. Such rudders are expensive ($125 from Catalina), subject to wear and corrosion, and of dubious value for anyone but the sailor most interested in ramp hauling and beaching.

The bottom line
Price is important. The Catalina and O'Day 22s clearly are built with a low price in mind. Sales of the Tanzer 22

are hurt by her higher price. Base price of the Catalina 22 is about $6500; of the Tanzer, over $10,000. With add-ons to make the Catalina a "sailaway" the price runs to over $10,000. Outfitted comparably the O'Day goes for $11,000 and the Tanzer for $12,500.

Wistfully we wish most buyers had some criteria other than price even in this rather modest price range. An additional $1500 or so would make all three of these boats better boats; not necessarily bigger but better appointed, outfitted and built. But they would not sell as well (if at all). In our opinion the higher priced Tanzer is a better product than either the O'Day or the Catalina. In looking at a number of other small boats similar to these the same premise seems to hold true for most of them: the more you pay, the more you get. Or for about the same price a buyer can trade off specific features. For instance, the same $10,000 will buy sparkling performance and whopping cockpit for daysailing in the 22' S2 Grand Slam 6.7 but at the expense of accommodations and interior space. The same is true of the snappy 23' Sonar for fleet racing.

As initial cost is important, so is resale value. It is especially important because most owners of the 22 footers in our evaluation are not likely to keep their boats for more than a few years. Then sale of the 22 is apt to represent a down payment on a larger, more expensive boat and return of at least most of the dollar value of the original investment.

The value of such a boat for resale is based on many of the same factors that appealed to the owner when the boat was new—price, cosmetics, decor, suitability for the expected use, etc. Maintaining the boat, repairing damage, and adding amenities all serve to protect the investment.

In investigating used boat prices for the earliest boats built we find the Tanzer 22 has appreciated in value the most; 10-year old boats in good condition are selling for twice what they sold for new, appreciation more than offsetting the inflation rate.

Clearly the strong owners' associations for the Tanzer and Catalina help in maintaining the resale market. They are strong marketing allies not only of the builders but of boat owners. Suggestion: if you buy a boat with such an organization, join it and stay in touch with their activities even if you do not take part in them.

Dealers for the three boats are a mixed bag; there are good, cooperative ones and lousy ones. PS had a favorable experience with one, unfavorable with another; neither was indicative of the how anyone else might be treated nor would we let the experiences form any judgment about the dealer network of any of the three builders. Certainly Catalina dealers are far more numerous and geographically widespread than are O'Day and Tanzer dealers, a reflection of the vastly greater number of boats sold. One does not have to look very hard around water to find Catalinas; one might have to call Tanzer to find the nearest dealer or, away from the East Coast, call O'Day for its local dealer.

Owners of boats in this size and price range making warranty claims, seeking answers to questions, or asking for special service on orders or service should realize that the relatively low markup on small boats such as these does not make dealers stand at attention. Trial sails, financing, trades up from smaller boats, special options, and so forth are similarly treated. In general, however, the owners of these three boats report satisfactory treatment by dealers and builders.

Catalina 22

THE BOAT AND THE BUILDER

In its 10th anniversary issue in 1980, *Sail* magazine named the Catalina 22 the boat that had represented the "breakthrough" in "trailer/cruisers" (sic) in those 10 years. We might quibble with its selection over more out and out trailerable boats such as the Ventures but there is no denying the popularity of the Catalina: more than 10,000 have been built and sales continue to be strong.

For many buyers the Catalina 22 is their first "big" boat and an introduction to the Catalina line. Many remain with Catalina and buy up within that line.

Catalina is the largest boatbuilder in the world in dollar volume and the firm is one of the lasting success stories in the industry. It foregoes national advertising in favor of local dealer-sponsored ads, and has remained a privately owned (in fact, one man—Frank Butler) company while the trend has been toward conglomerate-owned boatbuilding.

Simply stated, Catalina builds boats to a price—a low price—making the most of volume buying of materials and hardware, long-lived models, a high degree of standardization, and all the cost savings of high volume production. The Catalina 22 was the first boat built by Catalina.

The 22 is a dated boat. A lot has happened in boat design and construction since she was introduced. Not all that has happened has been good, but many of the boats on the market with which the Catalina 22 competes for sales perform better and have accommodations more comfortable than the venerable Catalina. Yet it is to Catalina's credit that the 22 continues to sell and continues to be many sailors' first boat.

CONSTRUCTION

It's hard to argue with the construction of a boat after 10,000 have been built, but we do. The PS evaluation of the Catalina 30 notes that the hull-to-deck joint—a plywood reinforced hull flange joined to the deck with a rigid polyester "slurry" and self-tapping fasteners—is not our idea of acceptable construction. The same type of joint is used on the 22 although we are less concerned because obviously the structure is for a much smaller boat which, unlike the 30, is not marketed for offshore sailing.

Catalina Yachts is proud of the contention that the Catalina 22 has remained essentially unchanged from the day it was introduced in 1969. Only the pivot for the swing keel version was changed about boat #250 and then, according to a Catalina statement, it was done for production purposes. Later a pop-top option was added and now 90% of the boats sold have this feature.

Catalina takes credit for pioneering the one-piece hull liner that has become standard in most high volume small boats. However, it should be noted that the liner is basically a cosmetic component, not a structural member, and the hull must get its strength from the hull laminate and bulkhead reinforcement.

The swing keel, also chosen by 90% of the buyers, is cast iron and, in its retracted position, remains substantially exposed (accounting for more than half of the 2' draft of the shoal draft model). It is a rough 550 lb iron casting of indifferent hydrodynamic efficiency. Oddly its configuration hoisted encourages ropes and weeds hanging up on its forward edge.

Specifications

LOA	21'6"
LWL	19'4"
Beam	7'8"
Sail area	212 sq ft

Retractable keel model
Draft, board up	2'
board down	5'
Ballast	550 lbs
Displacement approx.	2250 lbs

Fixed keel model
Draft	3'6"
Ballast	800 lbs
Displacement approx.	2490 lbs

Catalina Yachts
21200 Victory Blvd.
Woodland Hills, Calif. 91367

The swing keel is hoisted with a simple reel winch located under a vestigal bridgedeck with its handle protruding through a plywood facing. We'd guess that Catalina owners soon become conditioned to its presence, though it can trip those stepping up or down through the companionway.

The drop keel of the Catalina evoked a number of observations from owners in the PS boat owners' questionnaire. Several note that the keel mounting bolts loosen and leak in time. Another reports he had to replace his wire pennant twice. Replacing the pennant requires hoisting the boat high enough to have access to the top of the keel.

As with all Catalina-built boats, decor is a major selling point. The line, including the 22, is attractively appointed. They create a highly favorable impression

By any objective standard the Catalina 22 is hardly a spritely performing small boat. There have been too many compromises

which has to encourage sales, especially for first time boat buyers.

In fact, the Catalina 22 outside and inside is one of the most visually appealing small boats we have seen. It has enough trim and finish to look pretty. Similarly, her hull and rig, although dated, are well proportioned. It is about her performance and livability that we have the most serious qualms.

PERFORMANCE

By any objective standard the Catalina 22 is hardly a spritely performing small boat. There have been too many compromises to performance: trailerability, shoal draft, cockpit space, low cost, and interior accommodations, as well as giving her a placid disposition for novice sailors. The boat needs a genoa jib, a smoother, and more efficient swing or fin keel shape and some hardware of even the most modest go-fast variety. Even then the prognosis is that she will remain a rather tubby boat in an age when much of the fun of boats is in their responsiveness, if not speed.

With almost all the Catalinas having been built with the swing keel, the appeal has been her shallow draft for trailering. Yet even with 2' of draft with the keel hoisted, the boat has too much draft for beaching. Given the tradeoff in performance, the difficulty of maintenance, and loss of stability, one hopes that indeed buyers of the swing keel 22 have made good use of it for trailering.

The deck of the Catalina 22 is a decidely unhandy working platform. The sidedecks are narrow and obstructed by jib sheets and blocks. The three shrouds per side effectively block access to the foredeck, and complicate headsail trim and passage of the jib across in tacking. In fact, so difficult is it to go forward on the 22 we recommend getting rid of the lifelines. They are already too low to offer anything but token protection and they anchor near the base of the bow pulpit where they give no protection. Instead, handrails should be installed on the cabin top.

LIVABILITY

Ironically for a boat as popular as the Catalina, the boat incorporates the most incredible amount of wasted space we have ever seen in a sailboat large or small. In a size where stowage is at such a premium, there is a cavernous unusable space. The entire area under the cockpit and most of the area under the port cockpit seat (except where the gas tank sits) is all but inaccessible. The loss of this space limits stowage to scuttles under the berth bases.

The convertible dinette which seats only two with elbow room is a vestige of the 22's design era and the vee berths forward form that singularly noisome combination of bathroom and bedroom away from which human beings evolved about the time they moved out of caves.

The result is that the Catalina 22 has but one berth suitable for sleeping, the settee on the starboard side, and even that berth is shared with the optional galley facility that in use takes up about half the berth area.

The Catalina 22s now have a pop-top as standard; most of the cabin top lifts 10" on four pipe supports. Most owners we have heard from seem to like the system, particularly those in warmer areas. Headroom

at anchor is pleasant but we'd rather see room for stowage, sleeping, etc. as well.

One definitely unappealing and even unsafe item is the stowage for the remote gas tank for a transom-mounted outboard auxiliary. The tank sits on a molded shelf (part of the hull liner) in a seat locker at the after end of the cockpit. This puts the gasoline inside the boat including the cabin. The locker is vented but it should also be isolated. Spilled fuel can make its way unimpeded to the inaccessible low point under the cockpit. Moreover, there is no way to strap the tank securely nor a way to route the hose without pinching.

There's a strange and stubborn attitude at Catalina yachts in reaction to criticism of its boats, a righteousness that is exemplified by the notion that if one has sold several thousand of them, then nothing is wrong with them. Well, there are things wrong, and the gasoline stowage in the cockpit locker of the 22 footer is one egregious example.

One of the Catalina's better features is her cockpit. It is long (7') and comfortable, a place where the crew can sit with support for their backs, a place to brace their feet, and with room to avoid the tiller. It is unobstructed by the mainsheet that trims to a rod traveler on the stern.

CONCLUSIONS

Many boat buyers shop for a boat of this type with price foremost in mind. They probably will get no farther than their local Catalina dealer. At $10,500 they can get a boat that is the same size and similarly equipped as boats costing $2000 more. It's apt to be a boat identical to many of those sailing on the same waters. Better still, they are more than likely to have sailing friends who not only have (or had) a Catalina but belong to one of the most widespread and active owners' class associations in the sport. The whole package has a powerful appeal superbly orchestrated by the Catalina organization.

For performance, accommodations and even construction they might do better at a higher price, but the prospective buyer of the Catalina is likely to be unsure of what to look for. Understandably they turn to the 22.

At a weight of about 2500 lbs. loaded for the road plus a trailer, the Catalina 22 has marginal trailerability behind the modern small car. For this reason PS urges buyers to consider carefully before purchasing a trailer with the boat. Unless and until they are convinced they will trailer the boat enough to make a trailer's purchase worthwhile, it could be a waste of money. One Catalina salesman we overheard talking with a client gave this advice and spelled out the reasons. High marks to that chap. Later he ruefully admitted to us that many buyers ignore his suggestion.

For the $10,500 "sailaway package" price (East Coast), the buyer gets some features he might not opt for if he had a choice (e.g. the pop-top, Mercury outboard, and lifelines and stanchions). However, Catalina Yachts, like Hunter Marine, has learned the advantages of packaged boats with bottom line pricing that is still lower than competitors' so called base boat prices. And boat buyers get what they need (and probably want) without having to know what they need or want.

Other than price, PS sees little to recommend the Catalina 22 over many other boats of the same size on the market.

O'Day 22

THE BOAT AND THE BUILDER

O'Day Boats has been around a long time by fiberglass boatbuilding standards—more than 20 years. Originally the firm was a leader in small boats typified by the Uffa Fox-designed Day Sailer that is still in production.

By the early 70s O'Day had moved into the trailerable cruising boat market where they have been the leader on the East Coast. In the meantime the firm was acquired by Bangor Punta along with such other major boat builders as Cal and the now virtually defunct Ranger Yachts. In recent years, with the decline in volume sales of small boats, O'Day has had problems. To help alleviate these, O'Day has been producing larger and a larger boats, first a 30, then a 32, and most recently a 34 and a 37.

All the cruising size boats in the O'Day line have been designed by C. Raymond Hunt Associates in one of the most enduring designer-builder relationships in the industry (rivaled, in fact, only by Bill Lapworth's tenure—just ended—as Cal's house designer and Bruce King's with Ericson Yachts). The result of the relationship is a family resemblance in the O'Day line that is more than superficial. What proves popular in one boat is apt to be adopted in subsequent kin. Therefore, any study of the O'Day offerings over the years reflects a process of evolution.

When it was introduced, the O'Day 22 was touted as a competetive contender on the race course, a contrasting companion to the rather boxy 23-footer which it would soon phase out. The 22 had a masthead rig, a stylish rake to the transom, shallow (23") draft with a short stub keel and no centerboard, light weight (advertised 1800 lbs) for trailering, and a price under $3000.

Since then the 22 has acquired a fractional rig, a centerboard, 300 advertised pounds and a price tag almost $7000 higher.

CONSTRUCTION

O'Day once set a standard for small boat construction and stying. That was before on and off labor problems in its plant, management changes under Bangor Punta, the decline in sales of boats in its size range, and increasingly fierce competition for buyers who became more cost than quality conscious. The most recent O'Day 22s we have looked at have been, frankly, a mixed bag of quality and shabbiness.

The spars, rigging, and hardware are as high quality as we have seen in comparable boats. Our only reservation is with the stamped stainless steel hinged maststep that we know from personal experience requires a steady hand and boat when raising or lowering a mast. We also think that a mainsheet which terminates in a cam action cleat 16" up the single backstay may be economical and simple but it is neither efficient nor handy, again a reflection of scrimping to keep price low.

The quality of O'Day fiberglass laminates has always been high but there have been reader reports of gelcoat voids and there is consistent evidence of printthrough (pattern of laminate in gelcoat).

Exterior styling and proportions are superb, an opinion iterated by owners who have returned the PS Boat Owners' Questionnaires. The O'Day 22, despite her age, is still not outdated.

On a boat of this size and price, a minimum of exterior trim is understandable. What is less understand-

Specifications

LOA	21'8"
LWL	18'11"
Beam	7'2"
Sail Area	198 sq ft
Draft, board up	1'3"
board down	4'3"
Ballast	800 lbs
Displacement	approx. 2183 lbs

O'Day Boats
Bangor Punta Marine
Box 991
Fall River, Mass. 02722

able is the poor quality of the interior finish and decor. Belowdecks the O'Day 22 epitomizes the pejorative label *Clorox bottle,* used to describe fiberglass boats. Sloppily fitted bits of teak trim are matched against teak-printed Formica, at best a tacky combination. Cabinetry, such as there is, is flimsy, and in general the whole impression is of lackluster attention to details.

PERFORMANCE

Without a centerboard the O'Day 22 simply did not have the performance to go with her racy image. Even with the centerboard she is hardly a ball of fire under sail. She does not point well; tacking through 100° is not uncommon and she is tender, with a disconcerting desire to round up when a puff hits. In light air, with her 3/4 fore triangle and working jib she is under canvased and slug-

O'Day literature boasts berths for two couples in 'absolute privacy,' but privacy in a 22 footer has to be one of the more relative features

gish. In such conditions a genoa with substantial over-lap is essential.

Since changing jibs is at best a dicey exercise on a 22 footer, the first step in reducing sail is to reef the main-sail. Jiffy reefing is standard and owners of the O'Day should have a system in good working order and know how to use it. Owners of the boat in waters where squalls are a threat may also want to consider roller furling for the larger jib, trading off the loss of perfor-mance and added cost for such a rig for the conve-nience and, in the case of this boat, the safety.

The O'Day is most hurt in light air downwind and most owners will want either an 8'-or-so whisker pole for winging the jib, or a spinnaker. It is a fun boat on which to learn spinnaker handling. With her fractional rig the spinnaker is realtively small and yet the boat is big enough to provide a foredeck platform for setting the sail.

The trouble is that the O'Day 22 scrimps on the hard-ware needed for ease of handling with or without a spin-naker. The two #10 Barient sheet winches are, in our opinion, inadequate for anything larger than a working jib and we suggest replacing them with optional #16s. Similarly, the working jib sheets lead to fixed blocks whereas the optional lengths of track with adjustable blocks is far preferable for optimizing sail trim.

The O'Day does not come with halyard winches as standard. It is a large boat for setting and reefing sails with hand tension alone. Most owners will want at least one small winch (#10) on the cabin roof, with the jib and main halyards led aft through jam cleats or stoppers to the winch.

The fairing of the O'Day 22 under water is better than average, helped by the fact that the lead ballast is encapsulated in the fiberglass hull molding. The center-board will, however, be difficult to maintain.

LIVABILITY

Like many other boats of her size on the market, the O'Day 22 is baslcally a daysailer with incidental over-night accommodations, notwithstanding that her builder (or its ad agency) heralds its comfort, privacy, and space.

The cockpit of the O'Day is almost perfect: a spacious 6½' long, the seats are spaced to allow brac-ing of feet on the one opposite, and the coaming pro-vides a feeling of security and serves as a comfortable arm rest. It is also self-bailing although the low sill at the companionway means that the lower hatchboard must be in place to prevent water going below in the event of a knockdown.

Seat locker space is excellent for a boat of this size with quarterberth below and we like the separate sealed well for the outboard remote gas tank (but not the fact that the hose can be pinched in use).

O'Day literature boasts berths for two couples in "ab-solute privacy." Privacy in a 22 footer has to be one of the more relative features. A sliding door encloses the forward cabin and another door, the head.

The layout of the O'Day 22 is a noteworthy example of the tradeoff between an enclosed head and berth space. It does indeed have a head area that can be enclosed, a rare feature indeed on a boat of this size. With a conven-tional marine toilet and through-hull discharge where permitted, this would be a most serviceable facility.

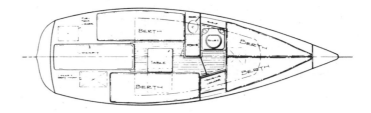

The tradeoff is a pair of terrible vee berths forward. Coming to a point at the forward end, there is simply not enough room for two adults on even the most intimate terms. They are thus suitable only for a pair of small children who do not suffer from sibling rivalry.

By contrast the two settee berths in the main cabin are a bit narrow but a fit place for two adults to sleep. In contrast to the dinette layout of other boats, we think the more traditional layout of the O'Day would be the choice for most owners, especially those cruising with children. However, the settees are not comfortable to sit on, lacking as they do backrests.

The initial version of the O'Day had the then fashion-able dinette arrangement but was quickly replaced with the present version of a pair of opposing settees. We doubt if many owners would bother setting up the port-able cabin table between the berths, as it prevents the fore and aft passage through the cabin.

The galley with its small sink and space for a two-burner stove is rudimentary but adequate for a boat of this size. Inadequate is the bin/hanging locker opposite the head. Its usefulness escapes us. Enclosed it could have been better used space. But then the O'Day 22 desperately needs stowage space.

CONCLUSIONS

At a minimum trailering weight of 2200 lbs. (more realistically 2500 plus the trailer), the O'Day 22 is above the maximum for trailering without a heavy car and special gear. If she isn't going to be trailered and launched off a ramp, the 2' minimum draft is an unwar-ranted sacrifice of performance and stability. We would look for a fin keel boat unless shoal draft is the highest priority.

On the other hand, with some additional sails and hardware the O'Day 22 should appeal to the sailor who wants a minimum size (and therfore price) boat primari-ly for daysailing and occasional weekend cruising (maximum one couple plus two young children).

Clearly the O'Day 22 is a minumum boat built tightly to a price. She is attractively styled. As she is apt to be a first boat, resale is important. O'Day boats have enjoyed good value on the used boat market; whether the pre-sent diminished quality of the 22 will enjoy a similar success in the future remains to be seen.

Yet the price of the O'Day 22 is not all that cheap—about $10,500 (O'Day does not quote prices, leaving that for its dealers). To that base price, add about $1200 for the extras (genoa and gear, stove, big-ger winches, etc.). Thus, for almost $12,000 you get a sleek looking small boat with a good cockpit, a modicum of privacy and two good berths. You also get a schlocky decor and a slow boat.

Tanzer 22

THE BOAT AND THE BUILDER

Like the O'Day 22 and the Catalina 22, the Tanzer 22 is a longtime member in her builder's line of boats. Designed by Johann Tanzer, the Tanzer 22 was originally built exclusively in Canada but now the line is built also in North Carolina and Washington, giving the boat widespread geographical distribution as well as saving on duty for US buyers.

Dating from 1970, the 22 has been a staple in the Tanzer line as the number of 22s approaches 2000 boats. Helping that growth has been a strong Tanzer 22 Class Association that boasts 700 members in the US and Canada. The association sponsors both racing and cruising and is purportedly independent of the builder. Such an organization has much to recommend it, both to the builder in his marketing efforts and to owners for the comaraderie and the ready resale market it affords. Best of all, for both sides there is a source of feedback on weaknesses, changes, and policies. Especially in areas where the organization is strong, Tanzer 22s have appreciated in value.

One drawback to promotion as a one-design boat is that the design has to remain essentially static to protect older boats. Even desirable changes may not be possible. This means that the initial design has to be successful. It is to Tanzer's credit that despite the age of the 22's design, the boat remains a popular product, albeit a bit out of date for today's styling.

CONSTRUCTION

The Tanzer 22 seems to be basically well built, perhaps better than the average small boat. There is no evidence of flexing or gelcoat crazing, two common symptoms of the under-built or poorly engineered hull and deck structure. The hull-to-deck joint is now a combination of semi-rigid adhesive and 3/16" machine screws on 6" centers holding together an exterior flange, a construction method PS approves in a boat of this size. The resulting flange is one which would be difficult to repair in event of damage. However, it is covered with a vinyl molding that does afford better than average protection.

As is typical of boats of this size, the interior is a molded fiberglass head liner and hull liner. The hull liner incorporates all the basic components of the layout—berths, cabinets, cabin, sole, etc. In a small boat it is a most practical interior. The disadvantage of such a liner is the difficulty of attaching add-on deck hardware and repairing damage to the hull laminate behind it.

Certain details of the Tanzer 22 are bothersome. For instance, the rudder is a two-part molded piece with a flange around the edge. While strong, it is needlessly crude in this day of well faired rudders. For another instance, a foredeck well which is now standard (and a good feature on a small boat) carries a solid, heavy fiberglass cover, loose and held in place only by flimsy wood toggles. However, these are correctable details.

PERFORMANCE

The Tanzer 22, particularly the full keel version, is a peppy little boat, among the best performing boats of her size, weight, price and purpose. She rates and sails with boats 2' longer, years more modern, and touted for their performance. What she might do to windward with an

Specifications

LOA	22'6"
LWL	19'9"
Beam	7'10"
Sail Area	227 sq ft

Keel-centerboard version
Draft, board up	2'
board down	4'
Ballast	1500 lbs
Displacement	3100 lbs

Fixed keel version
Draft	3'5"
Ballast	1250 lbs
Displacement	2900 lbs

Tanzer Yachts
Box 67
Dorion, Quebec, Canada J7V 5V8

up-to-date keel shape rather than the less efficient swept back fin makes for interesting conjecture. The same goes for her rudder blade shape.

Fairing of the cast iron keel is only adequte and of the flanged rudder, poor. If performance in light air is a priority, owners will want to work at getting smoother surfaces.

Performance upwind with the keel-centerboard combination shoal draft version is less snappy, but with the board raised, downwind speed—already the envy of sailors on other boats up to about 26'—should be even better. This point may be a moot one, though, as only a small fraction of the Tanzers sold are the shoal draft model. Apparently the Tanzer appeals to more performance-oriented buyers.

As with most boats of her size on the market, the mainsail and working jib are standard. A larger jib is a highly desirable option at a cost from the builder of about $450. With that sail should be included a genoa track and blocks. As sheet winches are all optional, buyers should order the larger two-speed ones when selecting options. Similarly with the spinnaker and gear: opt for pairs of coaming-mounted winches. We also recommend taking the option for cockpit-led halyards. Tanzer 22 owners responding to the PS owners' questionnaire also mention jiffy reefing, traveler, cunningham and vang as highly desirable options, again a reflection of their interest in sail handling and performance.

However, while the Tanzer 22 is a relatively smart performer and with add-on gear can be made more so, do not mistake her potential for that of the hot light-displacement dinghy types such as the J/24 and its ilk.

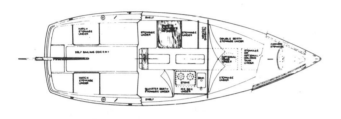

LIVABILITY

In keeping with our belief that the cockpit is the most critical area for comfort in a boat of this size, we have reservations about the cockpit of the Tanzer 22. It is large, wider than average, which is a virtue and a fault. On the one hand, there is plenty of space to stretch out; six adults can sit down inside the coamings that offer both protection and support. The distance between the seats allows for bracing with the feet and the short tiller leaves most of the cockpit free of its swing.

On the negative side, though, this width coupled with the 22's low freeboard invites water aboard in the event of a severe knockdown. And it is a big cockpit which can hold much water. Those sitting on the leeward side in a breeze are going to be on intimate terms with the water, although the raised deck does afford protection not found on boats with trunk cabin configurations. There is no bridgedeck, merely a low (too low) sill in the companionway.

Unfortunately the cockpit is complicated by the mainsheet that is fixed to the center of the cockpit floor just forward of the tiller. It is handy to the helmsman and safer than a sheet with traveler mounted on a bridgedeck at the forward end of the cockpit, but it does effectively divide the cockpit and reduce its spaciousness. A traveler is optional equipment but does nothing to alleviate the fault with location.

Do not be put off by the fact that the cabin house extends to the sheer, a rather old fashioned feature. While it does make going forward a bit more awkward, the deck space it provides is welcome. Best of all is the interior space that is obtained in a boat that, with her low sheer, would otherwise be hopelessly cramped below.

The Tanzer 22, like the Catalina 22, is a victim of the time when she was designed. In the late 1960s the boat-buying public became infatuated with dinettes. Boat builders obliged. The fad expired when owners tried to eat at the table and sleep on the so-called double berth converted from the dinette. In the five-year interval a lot of boats were built with that feature, including the Tanzer 22.

The dinette leaves the Tanzer 22 with but one proper berth, a good quarterberth, plus a pair of vee berths forward. The vee berths suffer from vee-berth syndrome—stacked feet. This, coupled with the head (optional Potpourri) located under them makes the Tanzer 22, like so many boats of this size with similar arrangements, one of the less appealing accommodations we have seen.

As if this were not enough, the icebox (standard) more properly belongs on a powerboat than a sailboat. It is one of those infernal built-in front-opening types: open the door with the boat heeled on starboard tack and be buried by the contents. Moreover, front-opening boxes such as this lose their cold with every opening (or what is left of the cold; insulation is only 1" of styrofoam).

In an attempt to provide some sunny weather headroom, Tanzer now offers a "convertible hatch" whereby the sliding companionway hatch assembly is hinged and can be raised to boom height. It is a $400 option that can also be retrofitted by owners on older 22s. According to a spokesman for the builder, 90% of the 22s now being sold come fitted with the device. As with the pop-top option on other boats, we'd plan to stay stooped and spend the money on more practical options.

CONCLUSIONS

In sum, the Tanzer 22 is a moderately well built boat with mediocre accommodations and better than average performance. Buyers into fleets of Tanzer 22s will benefit from an active family racing and cruising program. As with almost all boats of this size, we think the deep keel version is better than the shoal draft version as the boat is apt to be too much for most sailors to trailer.

The deck and the cockpit of the Tanzer should appeal to a family sailor looking for daysailing room. The interior will have much less appeal and we recommend any prospective buyers do some shopping around to see what layouts are most suitable for the type of sailing they plan to do before settling on this boat.

At the bottom line the Tanzer 22 is a moderately expensive boat with a list base price for the fin keel version at $10,550. Add to that most of the amenities for both comfort and performance and a well outfitted Tanzer 22 will run at least $12,500. Properly maintained, the Tanzer 22 should at least retain her value for resale, especially in those areas where the boat is known.

One final note: Tanzer owners we have heard from give high marks to the builder and Tanzer dealers. By contrast, in doing this evaluation, we anonymously discussed the boat with a Tanzer dealer. We could have been serious buyers. That dealer could tell us nothing about the boat he was selling; he had never sailed one, nor had he apparently ever looked to see how the boat is built. The questions we asked were neither formidable nor esoteric, yet given the competitiveness of the market for this size and price boat, his diffidence is hard to fathom.

The Flicka: Owner's Delight

THE BOAT AND THE BUILDER

The Pacific Seacraft Flicka has perhaps received more "press" in the last few years than any other sailboat, certainly more than any production boat her "size." Publicity does not necessarily make a boat good but it sure does create interest. A PS evaluation of the Flicka is one that readers have requested most often.

The Flicka is unique. There are no other production boats like her and only a few, such as the Falmouth Cutter and the Stone Horse, that offer the Flicka's combination of traditional (or quasi-traditional) styling and heavy displacement in a small cruising yacht.

As the number of Flickas built by Pacific Seacraft approaches 300 plus an indeterminate number built by amateurs early in its history, the boat seems to have become almost a cult object. High priced, distinctive, relatively rare but with wide geographical distribution and easily recognized, the Flicka invariably attracts attention and seems to stimulate extraordinary pride of ownership. The owners we talked to in preparing this evaluation all seem to be articulate, savvy, and involved. Moreover, they all show an uncommon fondness for their boats.

The Flicka was designed by Bruce Bingham, who is now known as an illustrator, especially for his popular Sailor's Sketchbook in *Sail*. Originally Flicka was intended for amateur construction, the plans available from Bingham. She was designed to be a cruising boat within both the means and the level of skill of the builder who would start from scratch. Later the plans were picked up by a builder who produced the boat in kit form, a short lived operation, as was another attempt to produce the boat in ferro-cement.

Pacific Seacraft acquired the molds in 1978 and, with only minor changes, the boat as built by Seacraft remained the same until 1983. A number of modifications made early in 1983 are described at the end of this evaluation.

Seacraft is a modest sized builder which has specialized in heavier displacement boats. The first boat in the Seacraft line was a 25-footer, followed by the 31' Mariah, the Flicka, the Orion 27, and most recently the Crealock 37.

Seacraft has 22 dealers nationwide but concentrated on the coasts. Apparently the firm was able to survive the hard times that have befallen some if its brethren, giving credence to the axiom that to succeed a boatbuilder should produce an expensive boat to quality standards that appeals to a limited number of enthusiastic buyers.

The hull of the Flicka is "traditional" with slack bilges, a full keel, a sweeping shear accented with cove stripe and scrollwork, and bowsprit over a bobbed stem profile. In all, the Flicka is not an actual replica, but she does fulfill most sailors' idea of what a pocket-sized

Specifications

LOA	23'7''*
LOD	20'
LWL	18'2''
Beam	8'
Draft	3'3''
Sail area sloop	250 sq ft
gaff	288 sq ft
Displacement (cruising)	5500 lbs
Ballast	1750 lbs

* Includes bowsprit and rudder

Pacific Seacraft
3301 S. Susan Street
Santa Ana, California 92704

classic boat *should* look like whether or not they are turned on to that idea.

The price of the Flicka ranges from about $13,000 for a basic kit for amateur completion to $35,000 for a "deluxe" version, with $25,000 a realistic figure for a well-appointed standard model. This is a high tab for a boat barely 18' long on the waterline, 20' on deck (LOD), and less than 24' overall with appendages. With that high priced package you get a roomy, heavy and well built boat that appeals to many sailors' dreams if not to their pocketbooks.

One of the more serious questions we have about the engineering of the Flicka is the under-deck mast support

CONSTRUCTION

The Flicka *looks* well built even to an untrained eye. And to the trained eye that impression is not deceiving. This is a boat that should be fully capable of making off-shore passages. The basic question any buyer must ask is whether he is willing to *pay* (in money and performance) for this capability for the far less rigorous cruising on Lake Mead or Chesapeake Bay, to Catalina Island, or up and down the New England coast.

The hull of the Flicka is a solid fiberglass laminate to a layup schedule adequate for most 30-footers of moderate displacement. The deck has a plywood core rather than the balsa core common in production boats. In a boat of this displacement-length ratio the heavier plywood reduces stability but probably only marginally. Its virtue is that installation of add-on deck hardware is easier.

The hull-to-deck joint is done in a manner PS strongly advocates: the hull has an inward flange on which the deck molding fits, bonded with a semi-rigid polyurethane adhesive/sealant and through bolted with 1/4" ss bolts on 4" centers. These bolts also secure the standard aluminum rail extrusion; on boats with the optional teak caprail in lieu of the aluminum, the bolts pass through the fiberglass, and the caprail is then fastened with self-tapping screws. As the rail sits atop a 1/2" riser, water cannot puddle at the joint. We have heard no reports of any hull-to-deck joint failure in a production Flicka.

The interior of the boat uses a molded hull liner that is tab bonded to the hull. Given the ruggedness of the hull laminate, we doubt if this stiffening adds much to the hull itself, but it does make the relatively thin laminate of the liner feel solid under foot.

One of the more serious questions we have about the engineering of the Flicka is the under-deck mast support. Reflecting the quest for a completely open interior, the design incorporates a fiberglass/wood composite beam under the cabin house roof which transfers the mast stresses through the house sides to the underdeck bulkheads. Apparently these bulkheads are not bonded to the hull, only to the liner.

The builder defends this construction, claiming that it will support over 8000 lbs (more than the Flicka's displacement). In addition, beginning in 1983, a turned oak handhold post was added between the mast support beam and cabin sole, which further increases the strength of the mast support system.

Cabinetry, detailing, and finish are top quality for a production boat. However, keep in mind that the basic interior component is a fiberglass molding. Functionally the ease of keeping a molded liner clean has much to recommend it; aesthetically the sterility of the gelcoat may offend some tastes.

If it does yours, consider the fact that at least for the time being the Flicka is sold as a kit for amateur construction in various states of completion. The builder does not push the kit versions for many of the reasons discussed in the article on amateur boatbuilding, "So You Think You Want to Build a Boat?," in Section II, The Economics of Buying a Boat.

A clever amateur might realize a 30% cash saving over the price of a builder-completed boat by carefully choosing the state of completion he can handle. The most popular version is the "sailaway" package that lets the owner install some deck hardware and commis-

In 1983, a turned post was added to the Flicka's interior to provide a handhold in the otherwise open cabin

sion the boat while he finishes the interior. He can also delay installing an inboard engine.

This would be a more attractive project if the owner wants an interior substantially different from the standard or an all-wood interior rather than the fiberglass liner. However, a 20' boat is too small to make drastic modifications.

Instead, buyers should consider the experience of almost every Flica owner with whom we talked (including some who have the kit). All recount changes that have been made—additional stowage space, galley modifications, shelving, etc. These owners strike us as a resourceful group. They all seem inventive, handy, and above all, willing to go at their boats with saber saw, pre-fab teak components, and a list of the designer's suggestions to make the boat they love a better boat for their purposes.

A few other specific construction details deserve note:

• The hardware on the Flicka is generally excellent, whether it is the standard or the optional cast bronze package, provided your taste allows for a mixture of traditional and modern. Since weight has not been a factor, most of the fittings are rugged, even massive. All through hull fittings are fitted with seacocks. Particularly impressive is the tabernacle maststep, a contrast with the flimsy sheet steel versions on cheaper boats. A notable exception to this endorsement are a pair of inadequate forward chocks.

• The scribed "planking seams" in the fiberglass topsides as well as the scrollwork are especially well done. However, any owner of a wood boat who has spent untold hours fairing topsides to get rid of real seams has to wonder at anyone's purposely delineating phony seams in fiberglass.

• There is a removable section of cockpit sole over the engine compartment that gives superb access for servicing the engine and permits its installation or removal without tearing up the interior. It is a feature many boats with under-cockpit engines should envy given the chronic inaccessibility of such installations. Access to the Flicka's engine from the cabin is no better than that

on most boats even for routinely checking the oil level.
• External chainplates eliminate a common source of through-deck leaks but at the expense of exposing the chainplates to damage.
• There is good access to the underside of the deck and coaming for installation of deck hardware. The headliner in the cabin is zippered vinyl.
• Anyone with a modern boat with its vestigal bilge sump has to appreciate the Flicka's deep sump in the after end of the keel.
• The ballast (1750 lbs of lead) is encapsulated in the molded hull, risking more structural damage in a hard grounding than exposed ballast but eliminating possible leaking around keel bolts.

PERFORMANCE

Handling under sail

In an era that has brought sailors such hot little boats as the Moore 24, the Santa Cruz 27, and the J-24, any talk about the performance of a boat with three times their displacement-length ratio has to be in purely relative terms. In drifting conditions the Flicka simply has too much weight and too much wetted surface area to accelerate. Add some choppiness to the sea and she seems to take forever to gain way.

When the wind gets up to 10 knots or so, the Flicka begins to perk up, but then only if sea conditions remain moderate. With the wind rising above 10 or 12 knots the Flicka becomes an increasingly able sailer. However, she is initially a very tender boat and is quick to assume 15° angle of heel, in contrast to lighter, shallower, flatter boats that carry less sail but accelerate out from under a puff before they heel.

In winds over 15 knots the Flicka feels like much more boat than her short length would suggest. As she heels her stability increases reassuringly. Her movement through the water is firmer and she tracks remarkably well, a long lost virtue in an age of boats with fin keels and spade rudders. Owners unanimously applaud her ability to sail herself for long stretches even when they change her trim by going forward or below.

PS suggests those looking at—and reading about—the Flicka discount tales of fast passages. While it is certainly true that the boat is capable of good speed under optimum conditions, she is not a boat that should generate unduly optimistic expectations. In short, there may be a lot of reasons to own a Flicka but speed is not one of them.

One mitigating factor is that performance consists not only of speed but also ease of handling, stability, steadiness, and even comfort. In this respect, the Flicka may not go fast but she should be pleasant enough to sail that getting there fast may not be important.

The Flicka comes with two alternative rigs, the standard masthead marconi sloop and the optional (about $1,500) gaff-rigged cutter. Most of the boats have been sold as sloops. The gaff cutter is a more "shippy" looking rig, but for good reasons most modern sailors will forego a gaff mainsail.

If you regularly sail in windy or squally conditions, you might want to consider a staysail for the sloop rig. However, for a 20' boat an inventory of mainsail fitted with slab reefing, a working jib, and a genoa with 130% to 150% overlap should be adequate. For added performance the next sail to consider is a spinnaker and, if offshore passages are contemplated, a storm jib.

Handling under power

Any observations about handling under power raise the question of inboard versus outboard power. In fact, this may be the most crucial issue a potential Flicka owner faces. In making the decision, start with an observation: at a cruising displacement of over 5000 lbs, the Flicka is at the upper limit for outboard auxiliary power. Then move to a second observation: small one-cylinder diesel engines such as the Yanmar and BMW fit readily into the Flicka, albeit at the expense of some valuable space under the cockpit sole.

Without going into all the pros and cons of one type of power versus another, we suggest installation of a diesel inboard either as original equipment or as soon after purchase as feasible. The Flicka is a boat that seems to beg for inboard power (most small boats do not); she has the space, and weight is not critical. Moreover, cost should not be critical either. Inboard power adds about 10% to the cost of the boat with outboard power, a small percentage of an expensive package. Much of the additional cost is apt to be recoverable at resale whereas the depreciation on an outboard in five years virtually amounts to its original value.

LIVABILITY

Any discussion of the livability of the Flicka should be prefaced by a reminder that above decks this is a crowded, cluttered 20 footer and below decks this is a boat with the space of a 26 footer. The Flicka is a boat with a enough space below for one couple to live aboard and yet small enough topside for them to handle easily.

The Flicka should have at least semi-permanent means of keeping water in a flooded cockpit from going below

Deck Layout

Nowhere is the small size of the Flicka more apparent than on deck and in her cockpit. The short cockpit (a seat length of barely over 5', too short to stretch out for a nap), a high cabin house, sidedecks too narrow to walk on to windward with the boat heeled and always obstructed by shrouds, the awkwardness of a bowsprit, and lifelines that interfere with jib sheet winching are all indicative of the crowded deck plan.

The stern pulpit is an attractive option. However, it makes manual control of a transom-mounted outboard difficult. The pulpit incorporates the mainsheet traveler although the lead for close sheeting is poor.

For outboard powered Flickas there is a lidded box that permits stowage of the fuel tank at the after end of the cockpit, a sensible and safe feature. For those owners who want propane and have inboard power, this same space fitted with a sealed box and through-transom vents would make a suitable place for gas bottles. (The builder supplies alcohol or kerosene stoves.)

At the other end of the cockpit, the lack of a bridge-deck or high sill is, in our opinion, decidedly unseaman-like. The Flicka should have at least semi-permanent means of keeping water in a flooded cockpit from going below. The builder is aware of this shortcoming and plans a lower hatchboard fitted with barrel bolts. PS strongly recommends that existing Flickas be retrofitted with this or a similar device.

If we owned a Flicka we would run all halyards (plus a jib downhaul) aft to the cockpit on the cabin top. We would not rig a fixed staysail stay, and we would certainly not use a clubfooted staysail. The boom should have a permanent vang. If we were finishing a kit boat, we would extend the bulkheads to the cabin top in way of the mast and move the chainplates inboard to the house sides for closer headsail sheeting and better access to the foredeck.

Below decks

The builder has made every effort to keep the interior of the Flicka open and unobstructed from the companion-way to the chain locker, a noble endeavour that gives an impression of spaciousness rivaling that of 30 footers. Headroom is 5'11" for the length of the cabin (find that in another boat-shaped 20 footer!). Better yet, height is retained over the galley counter, the settee berth, and the after section of the vee berths. Flicka's high topsides permit outboard bookshelves and galley lockers, stowage under the deck over the vee berths, and headroom over the quarterberth.

Two notable features of the interior are conspicuous as soon as the initial impression wears off. There is no enclosed head and there is no sleeping privacy. How important these factors are is purely a matter of individual taste and priorities. For a cruising couple a four-berth layout is a waste of space. Imagine the space that eliminating just one berth could provide—an enclosed head, a double width berth, and/or a second cockpit seat locker, to mention a few alteratives. If the deck layout could take one less berth into consideration, the cockpit could be of adult proportions, an item high on our list of priorities given the amount of time most sailors (plus guests) spend in the cockpit both sailing and at anchor.

Incidentally, this observation about berths is not meant to imply any special deficiency in the Flicka. It is true of too many boats on the market. They are built for a boat buying public that seems to think the number of berths in a boat is almost as important as whether the boat will float.

The absence of an enclosed head in a small yacht of the proportions of a Flicka requires a conscious decision from any potential owner. The small space between the vee berths is designed to hold a self-contained head such as Portapottie. A "privacy curtain" that slides across the cabin gives a modicum of respectability. Of course, its use is discouraged when anyone is sleeping forward. One owner solves this by lugging the head to the after end of the cockpit at night and encloses the cockpit with a tent, thus creating a privy or outhouse that boasts perfect ventilation. We hesitate to suggest his lugging it another few inches aft.

Less enterprising owners could consider installing a conventional marine toilet plus a holding tank under the vee berths. If sailing is done in waters where a through-hull fitting and diverter valve are permitted, then such a system is far more worthwhile than any self-contained system. Such a unit should make sharing your bed with the head as palatable as it will ever be.

Frankly, the lack of an enclosed head in a boat that

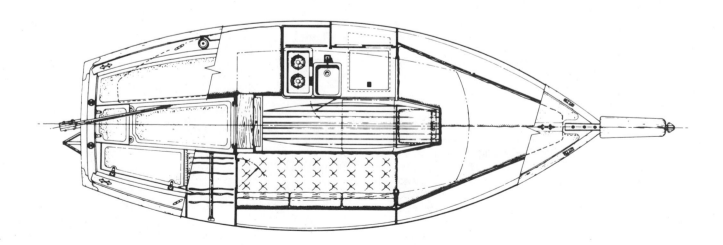

otherwise can boast of being a miniature yacht is the most serious drawback to her interior, surplus berths notwithstanding. An alternative interior with an enclosed head is now available.

Virtually every owner we talked with has added stowage space one way or another. Some have done it by removing the fiberglass bins that fit into the scuttles under the berths, others enlarge the shelves behind the settee berth and over the forward berths and others cut openings through the liner to give access to unused space.

Other modifications owners report having done include fitting the boat with a gimballed stove, adding fresh water tankage (20 gals standard), installing a third battery and/or moving them forward to help overcome a tendency for the Flicka to trim down by her stern, and fitting the cockpit with a companionway dodger.

One feature that does not seem to need any improvement is ventilation. The Flicka has an uncommonly airy interior, although we would add an opening port in the cockpit seat riser for the quarterberth. Her vertical after bulkhead means that a hatchboard can be left out for air without rain getting into the cabin.

Anyone considering the Flicka should ask Pacific Seacraft for a copy of the articles written by Bruce Bingham and Katy Burke on the changes they made to their *Sabrina* while living aboard and cruising extensively for more than two years.

CONCLUSIONS

Buyers put off by the price of the Flicka should consider the fact that this is a 20' boat with the weight and space of a 26- to 28-footer of more modern proportions. That still may not put her all-up price tag for the "deluxe" model of $35,000 in crystal clear perspective. It shouldn't. The Flicka is still a damned expensive boat. She still has a waterline length of merely 18', true accommodations for two, a too cozy cockpit, and a lot of sail area and rigging not found on more conventional contemporary boats. Nor does she have the performance to rival more modern designs. (One owner reports a PHRF rating for his Flicka of about 300 seconds per mile, a figure that drops her off the handicap scale of most base rating lists we have seen.)

At the same time the Flicka is a quality package that should take a singlehander or couple anywhere they might wish to sail her. There are not many production boats anywhere near her size and price that can make that claim.

The faults with the Flicka have to be weighed against her virtues as is the case with choosing any boat. Fortunately, though, her faults are the type that can be readily seen; they are not the invisible ones of structure, handling, or engineering so typical of other production boats. Similarly her virtues are traditional and time tested. She is built by a firm to whom the owners give high marks for interest and cooperation and the few Flickas that have come on the used boat market have maintained their value better than the average production boat. At the bottom line is a boat with much to recommend her.

What's New in New Flickas?

Early in 1983, the need for building a new deck mold for the Flicka to replace the worn-out original occasioned a number of "major and minor improvements" to the boat's design, both inside and out. Rather than delete descriptions of earlier boats, we decided to describe the changes along with the earlier evaluation, allowing the reader to make comparisons between versions of the boat. Here, in the words of the builder, are the changes:

In the *PS* evaluation of the Flicka, there were two criticisms that we were able to remedy in the retooling process. First, we incorporated a bridgedeck into the cockpit layout. This provides a fixed barrier to water between cockpit and companionway.

Second, because of the bridgedeck, we are now able to offer an optional roller bearing traveler arrangement which spans the bridge and provides a much better lead for close sheeting than the standard traveler mounted on the stern pulpit. Some people may still prefer the standard arrangement, as it is somewhat less likely to interfere with living space in the cockpit.

Other changes incorporated in the new tooling include a superior non-skid pattern, a larger and better sealed engine access hatch and provisions for an optional seahood.

Not directly related to the new deck is the addition of an interior arrangement with an enclosed head compartment. To make room for the enclosed head the starboard settee berth has been shortened from 6' 5" to 4' 2". About half of the Flickas now being produced have this feature.

H. A. Mohrschladt
President
Pacific Seacraft Corp.

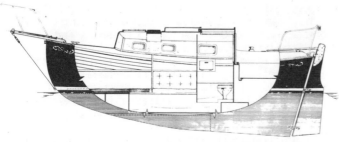

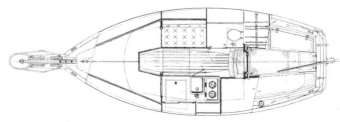

The J/24:
Class Counts

THE BOAT AND THE BUILDER

The J/24 is one of those boats that happened along at just the right time, with the right marketing to a ready market. Some may wonder whether the tale of her success would make a better textbook or a better story-book. Either way, much of the marine industry has studied her story, and then flattered her with the praise of emulation. However, no imitation or variation of the J/24 has yet to achieve her popularity.

Since her humble beginnings in 1976 in the garage of an amateur designer, over 3600 boats have been sold from factories in Rhode Island, California, Australia, Japan, Italy, England, France, Brazil and Argentina. All of the builders are licensed by a company called J-Boats to build the J/24 to strict one-design tolerances.

J-Boats is owned and run by two brothers—Bob and Rod Johnstone (the J in J-Boats). Bob is the marketing whiz and Rod is the designer. Conservative estimates put their total revenue from the J/24, after buying the boats from the builders and selling them to the dealers, at upwards of $4-$5 million. Not bad considering how it all began . . .

Ragtime was a 24' inspiration evolved by Rod Johnstone and his family in their garage as a two-year weekend project. Rod was a salesman for a marine publication, and an avid racer with a successful background in high-performance one designs. He had undertaken, but never completed, the Westlawn home-study course in naval architecture (although he has since been awarded an honorary degree so the school could use his name in its advertisements). *Ragtime* was launched in 1976, and was an instant winner, taking 17 firsts in 19 starts in eastern Connecticut. People began asking for their own *Ragtimes.*

At this time, brother Bob, also a respected racer, was working in the marketing department of AMF Alcort (Sunfish, Paceship, etc.). When Alcort declined to produce the J/24, Bob quit and formed J-Boats. Tillotson-Pearson, builder of the Etchells 22 and the Freedom line of boats, was more receptive and production began in 1977. The first J/24s were as fast as *Ragtime,* and dominated regattas like the 1977 MORC Internationals. Bob made sure that the favorable results were well publicized; more than 200 boats were sold that year, and nearly 1000 the next.

It was a big hit for a number of reasons. She moved into a void, appealing to two groups of sailors who were ripe for her type of racing: those who had outgrown athletic small boats, yet still yearned for the competition of one-design racing, and those who wished to compete without the expense, hassels and uncertainties of handicap racing.

The J/24 is a one design's one design. Like the Laser, Windsurfer, and Hobie Cat, she is proprietary—built under the supervision of one company. Unlike most proprietary one designs, sails are not provided by the J/24's builder. This was a particularly astute move by the Johnstones as it involved sailmakers in the class. Sailmakers comprise many of the big names in racing;

Specifications

LOA	24'
LWL	19'5"
Beam	8'11"
Draft	4'
Displacement	3100 lbs
Ballast	950 lbs
Sail Area	261 sq ft

J-Boats
24 Mill Street
Newport, RI 02840

by getting them in the regatta results, the Johnstones added instant credibility to the J/24's budding status as a "hot" class. By the midwinter championship in 1979, almost every boat in the top 15 finishers had a sail-maker on board.

The big advantage that proprietary one designs have over "independent" one designs (classes with competing builders) is the power of centralized, big-bucks promotion. J-Boats has organized and promoted regattas, and had a heavy hand in running the class association. J/24s got a lot of press, thanks to J-Boats. Full color, multi-page advertisements appeared monthly in the

J-Boats has organized and promoted regattas, and had a heavy hand in the class association. Promotion has been primary; money is no object

slick sailing magazines. Promotion has been primary; money is no object. J/24s have been donated for several high visibility USYRU championships. Big discounts have been given for fleet purchases (sometimes to effectively crush interest in competing one designs). With the help of British enthusiasts, the Johnsones were able to make the J/24 an IYRU (International Yacht Racing Union) recognized class. More international lobbying got the J/24 into the Pan American Games.

There are some disadvantages to proprietary one designs. First, the class is in a real bind if the builder goes bankrupt. Likewise if the builder should ever abuse his power by ignoring class administration or changing construction of the boat to suit economic demands. Although a proprietary builder faces competition from other types of boats, there is no competition building *his* boat. This can inflate the price, especially when there are three substantial markups in the pricing structure (builder, J-Boats, and the dealer).

The J/24 is not cheap. Base price is $15,900; when you include sails, an outboard, lights, battery, and halyard winches, the price is over $20,000. If you want to go to distant regattas, a trailer runs about $1800. Used boats appear to hold their original value. Even the oldest J/24s, which originally sold for $9800, are now selling for $14,000 or more. In areas where the J/24 has been popular for years, used boats are readily available. Production in the US dropped from 10 boats per week in 1981 to 5 boats per week in 1982.

CONSTRUCTION

The J/24 has the distinct advantage of having been produced in great numbers and been subjected to the rigors of hard racing. It's safe to say that nearly everything that could have broken, has broken, and that the J/24 is now almost bulletproof. J-Boats has done a commendable job in correcting nearly all of the "bugs" in the J/24. However, if you are planning to purchase a boat several years old you should be watchful for some of the old bugs.

Boats built during the first two years of production had particular problems with leaking along the hull-to-deck joint, delamination of the main bulkhead, and the attachment of the keel to the hull.

The hull-to-deck leak was due to failure of the silicone sealant in the joint. The inward-turning hull flange is overlapped by the deck, which is bedded in sealant and through-bolted at close intervals through a teak toerail. Now the joint is bedded with 3M 5200, a pliable strong adhesive, and leaks are infrequent. Fortunately, the internal side of the joint is exposed throughout the J/24's interior, so recaulking is not difficult.

Harder to rectify is the problem of delamination of the main bulkhead. J/24s are raced hard, often with substantial rig tension. The chainplates pierce the deck and are bolted to the main bulkhead. The plywood bulkhead is tabbed with fiberglass to the hull and deck. The mast is stepped through the deck and sits on an aluminum beam, which is also tabbed to the main bulkhead. Rig tension pulls upward on the bulkhead while mast compression pushes downward on the beam, resulting in tremendous shearing forces on the bulkhead and its tabbing.

On some of the older J/24s, the plywood has delaminated, letting the mast "sink" 1/4 inch or more.

Owners of these boats have either returned them to the factory for replacement of the bulkhead, or ground off the delamination and reglassed the bulkhead themselves. The builder now uses a better grade of plywood and installs screws to reinforce the bulkhead tabbing. As an added precaution, the boat owner may wish to bolt the mast-bearing beam to the bulkhead with an angle-iron.

The third problem with some of the older J/24s is the keel-to-hull attachment. The builder used to fill the keel sump with a vermiculite mixture of resin and plant fiber. The keel bolts were fastened through the vermiculite which, when saturated with water, is less rigid than solid laminations of fiberglass. After several years of sailing, or a hard grounding, the keel bolts would begin to work, and the keel would loosen enough to be able to be wobbled by hand with the boat suspended from a hoist. The first sign of this problem is the appearance of a crack along the keel stub. Tightening of the keel bolts, which are quality stainless steel, is a simple but temporary fix. What is needed is a backing plate for the bolts, bedded on top of the vermiculite.

There was a variety of other problems with early J/24s: The mast has three internal halyards; two jib halyards exit below the headstay with the spinnaker halyard above. On the older boats, a large square hole was cut in the mast to accommodate the sheaves, leaving an open, poorly supported space adjacent to the spinnaker sheave. This space is sometimes the source of mast cracks; the fix is to weld a plate over it.

In January of 1980, the J/24 got much-improved companionway and forward hatches. The hatches on older boats were molded of thin fiberglass, and had a tendency to leak and fracture under the weight of heavy crewmembers. The new forward hatches are lexan, and the companionway hatch is now much heavier with a lower profile.

The J/24's rudder is heavy and strong. The builder claims you can hang a 900 pound keel from the rudder tip without breaking it. Although the J/24's rudder pintles appear more than adequate, after several years of use they have been known to develop corrosion cracks where the pintle is welded to its strap. In 1981, the builder began equipping J/24s with weldless pintles; the builder also offers the new system as a replacement for old boats.

The starboard chainplate bolts through both the

bulkhead and the hull liner. The port chainplate bolts through only the bulkhead. After the first two years of production, the port bulkhead was reinforced with fiberglass in the chainplate area. On earlier boats, a backing plate should be added to prevent the chainplate bolts from elongating their holes.

The hull and deck of the J/24 are cored with balsa, which makes them stiff, light, quiet and relatively condensation-free. We have heard of occasional delaminations resulting from trailering with improperly adjusted poppets.

The Kenyon mast section is the same as that used on the Etchells 22, a bigger boat. It is more than adequate for any strength of wind.

The J/24 does not have positive flotation, and she has been known to capsize in severe conditions. This is usually not a problem as she floats on her side with the companionway well out of the water. However, should the leeward cockpit locker fall open, water can rush below, filling the cabin and causing her sink. While fastening the lockers in heavy weather prevents the problem, the manufacturer began to seal off the lockers from the cabin with an additional bulkhead several years ago, as an added safety measure.

Of the 2500 J/24s sold in the US, nearly 2000 of them have been built by Tillotson-Pearson in Rhode Island. The others were built by Performance Sailcraft in San Francisco, which is now defunct. New boats are now shipped cross country. Top west coast sailors tell us they favor the east coast built boats, claiming the keels and rudders on the west coast built boats are too thick to be competitive. The west coast keels are thick because they are covered with injection-molded gelcoat. Tillotson-Pearson fairs the keels with autobody putty.

PERFORMANCE

Handling Under Sail

The J/24's PHRF rating ranges from 165 to 174, depending on the handicapper. She rates as fast as or faster than a C&C 30, Santana 30, or Pearson 30. One must remember that, because the J/24 has attracted competent owners, her PHRF rating is probably somewhat inflated. While the J/24 is an excellent training boat because she is so responsive, a beginning racer may have an especially hard time making her perform to her PHRF rating.

Aside from her speed, the J/24's greatest asset is her maneuverability. With her stern hung rudder she can be turned in her own length, sculled out to a mooring in light air, and brought to a screeching halt by jamming the rudder over 90 degrees.

The J/24 has a narrow "groove"; it takes a lot of concentration to keep her going at top speed. She is sensitive to backstay trim, sheet tension, weight placement and lower shroud tension. The lower shrouds act like running backstays, because they are anchored aft of the mast. They must be loosened in light air to create some headstay sag, and then tightened in heavy air to straighten the mast, making backstay tension more effective in removing headstay sag.

Sheet tension is also critical. Top crews rarely cleat the genoa sheets, having one crewmember hold the tail while hiking from the rail. Some of the best sailors even lead the jib to the weather winch so the sail can be trimmed without sending crew weight to leeward.

The class rules allow you to race with a mainsail, a 150% genoa, a working jib and a single spinnaker. This makes sail selection simple and the inventory affordable (about $2600 total). However, the one genoa must carry the boat all the way from a flat calm up to 20 knots or more. To be competitive in light air, the genoa must be full; yet to hold the boat level with this full genoa in a strong breeze, you need a lot of crew weight. Most of the top crews are now sailing with five people on board for a total crew weight of 800 to 900 pounds. The J/24 is a small boat, and the additional fifth crew really makes the boat cramped. Add to this the increasing trend of some skippers making the crew sit in the cabin on the leeward bunk in light air, and you have a boat which can be less than fun to crew on.

There are two worthwhile improvements that can help a J/24's performance. To decrease the boat's slight tendency toward a lee helm in light air, the mast should be cut to minimum length allowed in the class rules, and the headstay should be lengthened to the maximum allowed to give the mast more rake. The other improvement is fairing the keel to minimum dimensions. The keel is much thicker than is necessary for optimum performance. It comes relatively fair from the builder, but most owners will want to grind off the builder's autobody filler and sharpen the trailing edge. On some of the older boats, the trailing edge is twice the minimum thickness. Some racers go so far as to spend $500-$1000 to have the keel professionally faired.

While all indications are that the builder has excellent quality control, there have been complaints that some of the spars provided by Kenyon in the last two years have come with the wrong length shrouds, or widely differing bend characteristics. One top sailor said he would never buy a used J/24 without first making sure that he could make the mast to stand straight sideways with substantial shroud tension.

The J/24 is best suited for racing; there are many boats in her size range that are far more comfortable and practical for daysailing. However, the J/24 is a joy to sail under mainsail alone. Unlike most boats, she balances and sails upwind at a respectable speed, and her maneuverability gives her tremendous freedom in crowded harbors.

If you want to seriously race a J/24, trailering is a necessity. Make no mistake, however; trailering is expensive

Handling Under Power
The J/24 is powered by an outboard engine; an inboard is not feasible or available. Class rules require that an outboard with a minimum of 3.5 hp be carried while racing. Most owners opt for a 3.5-4 hp outboard. It provides adequate power and is as much weight as you want to be hefting over a transom. Although the cockpit locker is plenty big enough, most owners stow the outboard under a berth in the cabin to keep the weight out of the stern. This makes using the outboard inconvenient. The factory-supplied optional outboard bracket has a spring-loaded hinge to lift the engine for easy mounting; we recommend it. Because the outboard is likely to be stored in the cabin, a remote gas tank will keep fuel spillage and odor to a minimum.

LIVABILITY

Above Decks
The J/24 is very well laid out, yet she is still not a comfortable or easy boat to crew on. When she was first launched, sailors said her layout could be no better, and she was copied by manufacturers of competing boats. However, after years of racing, sailors have discovered several things that could be improved.

Cockpit winches are located just forward of the mainsheet traveller, which spans the middle of the cockpit. Many sailors have moved the winches forward, so the crewmember tacking the genoa can face forward instead of aft during a tack.

The standard mainsheet cleat is attached to the traveler car so that, when you trim the sheet, you inadvertently pull the car to weather. Many sailors have solved this by mounting a fixed cleat with a swivel base at the center of the traveler bar.

On older boats the backstay was single-ended at the transom. Boats now come with a double-ended backstay led forward to the helmsman on each side of the cockpit. Foot blocks need to be mounted on the traveller to keep helmsmen from falling to leeward as the boat heels (you must steer from forward and well outboard of the traveler).

For those who plan to try cross-sheeting to the weather winch, leading the jib sheets through Harken ratchet blocks is advised. Most sailors will also want to mount barber haulers to pull the genoa sheet outboard

J/24: How Trailerable?

The J/24 is not launchable from a boat ramp, unless the ramp is steep, paved or of hard sand, and you use a long extender between the tongue of the trailer and your trailer hitch. Her 3100 pounds (fully loaded) require a big, 8-cylinder vehicle to tow her. She is easily launched from a 2-ton hoist which can attach to a strap on her keel bolts. However, the main hatch slides just far enough forward to allow the hoisting cable to clear it, so the hatch tends to get chewed by the cable.

The J/24 was originally designed to sail at a displacement of 2800 pounds. The class minimum was later increased to 3100. The original single axle trailer provided as a factory option was barely adequate for the intended, 2800 pound boat, and totally inadequate for a fully loaded boat. Tales abound of blown tires and broken trailer welds. The factory now offers both a single and double axle trailer; we recommend the double axle.

If you want to seriously race a J/24, trailering is a necessity. Local fleets grow and shrink each year with the whims of their members, but national and regional regattas continue to attract many participants. Make no mistake, however; trailering is expensive. The owning and maintenance of a big car, the gas and tolls of trailering, and the housing of crew are not cheap.

in strong winds. Cam cleats for the barber haulers should be mounted on the companionway so they "self-cleat" when led to the weather winch.

Cabin-top winches for the halyards and spinnaker guys are optional and essential. Because the J/24 has single spinnaker sheets, most sailors mount "twings," which pull the guy down to the deck outboard of the shrouds when reaching.

In the search for a cleaner deck, it is now common to mount the spinnaker halyard cleat on the mast. Most sailors use only one jib halyard. Although a second jib halyard is optional, it is necessary only for long-distance handicap racing. On short one design courses, it is better to struggle along overpowered than to place crew weight on the bow to change headsails. Instru-

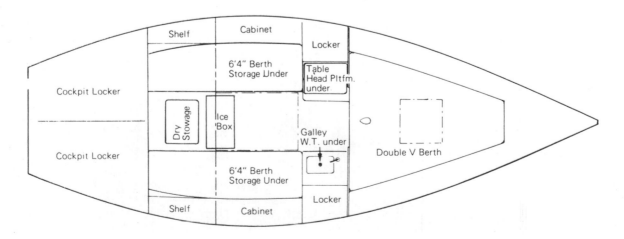

ments are also unnecessary in one design racing. There are more than enough boats on a one design race course to judge your speed without the help of a speedometer.

The J/24 comes equipped with a Headfoil II grooved headstay system, which works very smoothly. Early boats came with Stern Twinstays, which have occasionally failed when the bearings freeze up with age. Some sailors have exchanged the grooved headstay system for cloth snaps on their headsails (you seldom change sails anyway). We applaud this idea, as it makes the sails all the more manageable in severe weather.

Although the flat decks are well suited for racing, the cockpit is less than comfortable for daysailing. There are no seat backs and the boom is dangerously low. Visibility with the deck-sweeping 150% genoa is terrible, and is often the cause of nightmarish collisions on crowded race courses. Lower life lines are optional and recommended for those who sail with children, but they interfere with fast tacks when racing.

The boom is rigged with a 4-to-1 vang, which is swiveled on the more recent J/24s to be adjustable from either rail on a windy spinnaker reach. The boom is also rigged with reef lines which exit through stoppers at the gooseneck. Top sailors have discovered that the boat always sails better without a reef, which is a good thing, because the stoppers are both difficult to operate and have a history of slipping.

Belowdecks

The interior is simple and functional. On most boats it is used for little more than sail storage. However, for a couple who enjoys roughing it, it could make for occasional weekend cruising. The first thing you notice when you go below is the lack of headroom. You can sit in comfort, but to move about you must crawl.

The interior is finished off in bare white gelcoat. Early boats had coarse, non-skid gelcoat on the overhead. While this may have been more attractive than smooth gelcoat, it really did a number on elbows and bald heads. It also tended to collect dirt and mildew. The through-bolted deck fittings until last year were capped with acorn nuts. Now the nuts lie flush with the overhead and induce far less pain when bumped.

A molded hull liner is used to form the two quarter berths, the cabin sole, and two lockers and a galley just aft of the main bulkhead. One locker is deep enough to serve as a wet locker for foul weather gear; the other is best used to store the rudiments of a meal. The galley consists of a sink with a hand pump. A small, two burner stove could be mounted in the small, removable "table" forward of the port quarter berth. The icebox, a large portable cooler made by Igloo, has a piece of teak glued to it and doubles as a companionway step. After a season or two of jumping on the ice chest, tack after tack, the lid disintegrates.

The forward V-berth, although divided by the mast, is still large and comfortable enough for a couple. The boat does not come equipped with a head. To avoid the extra drag of a through-hull fitting, "porta-pottis" are often used. We would rather use a cedar bucket—there simply isn't enough space in the cabin of a J/24 to cohabitate with a portable head. If you plan to seriously race, you won't want to load the boat's lockers with cruising equipment. If you do cruise, it will probably be out of a dufflebag.

CONCLUSIONS

The appeal of the J/24 is as a racer. If you plan to do anything else, she is not for you. Although the J/24 is relatively easy to sail, she is very difficult to sail well. To many people, she represents a chance to compete in the big leagues; by traveling to major regattas you can sail against some of the best sailors in the country. However, the big leagues are tough—if you like to race with a pick-up crew and a hangover you'd also better be satisfied with finishing at the back of the pack.

One appeal of the J/24 is that, unlike many big league boats, you can always come home and sail because the boat has so big a following. There are enough boats to race it one-design almost anywhere; and in a pinch, there is always handicap racing. As long as you don't want to travel, the boat is inexpensive to maintain.

Despite our effort to highlight every flaw that has appeared throughout the J/24's evolution, we'd like to emphasize that she is more hardy than most boats of her type. Few boats can take the punishment that a J/24 gets during a season of hard racing and come through with so few scars. No racing boat is ever a good investment—that is, it won't appreciate; but the J/24 has shown that she can at least keep her value.

The dream boat with the fairy tale success story has turned out, after all, to be a rugged winner in the real world.

Cape Dory 25 and 25D: Sisters but not Twins

THE BOATS AND THE BUILDER

Cape Dory Yachts is one of the more conservative firms in the boatbuilding industry. With the exception of a brief fling with modern cruiser-racers—the Intrepid series—the company's stock in trade since the late 1960's has been traditional, full keel auxiliaries and sailboats, most from the design board of Carl Alberg, the octogenarian dean of American designers. It is ironic that a man who began his designing career drawing schooners and Universal Rule racing sloops in the office of John Alden should find his greatest popularity designing production fiberglass boats 60 years later.

The Cape Dory line currently includes 10 boats from 18' to 36' long, each a larger or smaller development of her sisters. The company will leap into the bigger boat market later this year with a 45-footer, another traditional Alberg Design.

Since he picked up the tooling for the well known 18' 6" Typhoon in 1969, Cape Dory owner Andrew Vavolotis has shown an almost unswerving loyalty to the long keel with attached rudder, and to designs by Alberg. Only two non-Alberg designs have been part of the Cape Dory line of larger boats: the Ted Hood designed Cape 30 (the company's first big boat, and totally different from the current 30), and the Cape Dory 25.

Credit for the basic design of the Cape Dory goes to George Stadel. The boat was originally built by Allied as the Greenwich 24. Vavolotis purchased the tooling during one of Allied's frequent business disasters, redesigned the boat to suit his own ideas, and put the Cape Dory 25 into production in 1973. In the next nine years, almost 850 25s were built, and the boat has rightly been termed a modern classic.

In the fall of 1981, Cape Dory introduced a new 25 footer, the 25D. "D" is for diesel, but there's much more difference between the two boats than just the power plant. Although a certain amount of confusion has existed about the two boats, the only thing that the 25 and the 25D have in common is overall length. The 25D is an entirely different boat: wider, heavier, deeper, with inboard engine, a dramatically different interior, and a price tag 50% higher than that of the 25.

In a time when retrenchment was the watchword in the boatbuilding industry, Vavolotis had a cheshire cat grin on his face when he said, "We've found our niche in the industry."

For a number of years, that niche was narrow indeed. While racer-cruisers proliferated in the 1970's, while the fat fin-keeler with the high aspect ratio rig became the industry vogue, Cape Dory continued to espouse long keels with attached rudders, relatively narrow beam, attractive sheerlines, moderate freeboard, and substantial overhangs—"old fashioned" boats.

While there are a number of companies that offer a few traditional, heavy displacement boats, no other builder can claim a full line of ultraconservative designs. It might seem that Cape Dory has created so many models that their prime competition is between boats in their own line, but apparently there is enough product differentiation to support five different models between 25' and 30'.

CAPE DORY 25D

Specifications

LOA	25'
DWL	19'
Beam	8'
Draft	3'6"
Displacement	5,120 lbs
Ballast	2,050 lbs
Sail Area	304 sq ft

Cape Dory Yachts
160 Middleboro Avenue
East Taunton, MA 02718

Cape Dory customer loyalty is tremendous. Probably more owners trade up through the line than change builders when the time comes to upgrade. The cynic might say that it's because no other builder caters exclusively to buyers of "traditional" boats. In fact, a large percentage of the product loyalty is generated by consistently good quality, high resale value, and excellent builder support on warranty work.

While Cape Dory offers a fairly industry-standard one-year warranty, owners report that the company has consistently made good on problems well after any legal liability to do so. We think this policy is a key to customer satisfaction and long term loyalty, and one that other builders should emulate.

CAPE DORY 25

Drawing depicts old style ports; the large fixed main cabin ports have been replaced with smaller opening ports on newer models.

Specifications

LOA	24'10"
DWL	18'
Beam	7'3"
Draft	3'
Displacement	4,000 lbs
Ballast	1,700 lbs
Sail Area	264 sq ft

Cape Dory boats are not for everyone. By any standard, both the 25 and the 25D are heavy displacement boats.

Interior volume of both boats is substantially less than that of "modern" 25-footers due to their relatively narrow beam and short waterline. By way of comparison, the Ericson 25 is almost three feet longer on the waterline and over a foot wider than the Cape Dory 25D, with almost identical displacement, ballast, sail area, and price.

The Cape Dory 25 is really a daysailing and weekending boat. Although the boat has berths for 4, accommodations are cramped and creature comforts minimal.

The 25D is a very different concept. She is a miniature cruising yacht. Inevitably she will be compared to that star of an earlier generation of pocket cruisers, the Laurent Giles designed Vertue.

The 25 and 25D are as different in price as in concept. Typical equipped price of the 25 is $19,000 to $21,000 in May, 1982. The 25D sells for $32,000 to $35,000.

CONSTRUCTION

Construction of all boats in the Cape Dory line is similar. Hulls are moderately heavy solid glass layups of mat and roving. Ballast in all cases is a lead casting. The casting is carried in a hollow keel molding, with voids between the casting and the molded shell filled with polyester slurry. The casting is heavily glassed over on the inside of the hull. While the workmanship and materials used in these ballast installations are excellent, we prefer an external, bolted-on lead casting for its shock absorbing qualities.

Decks and cabin tops are cored with end grain balsa. This results in a firm, stiff surface with good sound-absorbing and insulation properties.

Gelcoat quality of the 25 and 25D is excellent. Light roving printthrough is evident, but there are neither external hard spots nor evidence of distortion of the hull from the attachment of the deck.

Cape Dory uses a wide internal flange for attachment of the deck molding. The deck is joined to the hull using a semi-rigid polyester compound. This joint is incidentally reinforced by the screws which attach the toe rail, by the through bolts of the pulpits and lifeline stanchions, by the chainplate bolts, and by deck hardware bolts. Our belt and suspenders approach to construction would prefer through bolting of the joint at close intervals in addition to the chemical bond and random fastening.

Cape Dory's chainplate installations merit special comment. On the 25D, shrouds are attached to cast bronze lugs which rest on the deck over the hull/deck flange. Each of these lugs is bolted through the flange with two 3/8" diameter stainless steel machine screws. On the underside of the hull flange, a heavy aluminum plate is glassed in place using unidirectional roving, which also extends down the inside of the hull.

This is an immensely strong installation for a boat of 5,000 pounds displacement. The chainplates are less prone to leakage than conventional flat bar stock plates bolted to bulkheads.

The only disadvantage of this system is that it locates the chainplates at the outboard edge of the deck. This gives the shrouds a wide base for supporting the mast, but interferes with close sheeting of overlapping headsails.

All Cape Dory rudders are hung from the back of the keel. The primary advantages of this type of rudder are strength—a fairly important consideration for the cruising yacht—and relative invulnerability to damage.

The only real drawback to Cape Dory's rudder installation is that dropping the rudder for repair is fairly complex. The cast bronze gudgeon/heel fitting must be removed by grinding off the heads of its fastenings at the base of the keel. Then the rudder and stock are pulled out from below, necessitating either a deep hole under the boat or lifting the boat with a crane or Travelift while the rudder is being removed.

All deck hardware is through bolted using stainless steel bolts and aluminum backing plates. The forestay fittings on both the 25 and 25D are heavy bronze castings, as are cleats, winch islands, and portlights.

We have one reservation about Cape Dory's hardware installations. The mixture of bronze castings, stainless bolts, and aluminum backing plates strikes us as less than ideal. While the deck hardware is not immersed in an electrolyte, there is a difference in voltage potential between the aluminum backing plate and the manganese bronze casting. The type 304 austenitic stainless fastenings are relatively inert, but they do join very dissimilar metals. Below the waterline, Cape Dory uses silicon bronze fastenings in their bronze castings.

Cape Dory has its own hardware division—Spartan Marine Products—which produces a broad range of deck and hull hardware, as well as assembling all spars for Cape Dory. Spartan was founded in 1975 when it became increasingly difficult to get cast bronze hardware to complement Cape Dory's traditional designs.

We have previously been critical of Spartan for the poor finish quality of their products. While their castings were excellent, the hardware was only available in what is traditionally known as "burnished" finish—ground and tumble polished to remove roughness from the casting process, but not mirror finished. Now Spartan offers most of their hardware in burnished, polished, or chrome finish. Polished hardware truly accents the classic yacht. In acknowledgement of that fact, Cape Dory has made polished hardware standard on their flagship 36-footer.

Spartan seacocks are used on all through hull fittings below the water on the 25D, including head intake and discharge, cockpit scuppers, engine cooling water intake, and galley sink drain. Engine exhaust and bilge pump discharge exit through the transom, and have no provision for shutoff. On the 25, bronze ball valves are used in place of seacocks.

The 25D uses a full molded hull liner which incorporates all the major furniture components. Interior trim and systems are installed in the liner before it is fiberglassed into the hull. The liner itself is a heavy solid layup almost as thick as the hull. The only disadvantage to the full hull liner is limited access to the inner surface of the hull in the event of catastrophic damage. Bilge access in the 25D, for example, is only through a small trap in the main cabin sole. Repairs requiring access to the inside of the hull skin will require major surgery.

The general standard of workmanship in Cape Dory boats is very good, and both the 25 and 25D sustain this standard. The 25D, with its emphasis on fairly serious cruising, is a far more complex boat than the 25 in both systems and construction. The 25D is probably one of the strongest boats of her size on the market.

PERFORMANCE

Handling under sail

While both the 25 and 25D are cruising boats, neither should be a dog under sail. Owners of the 25 report average speed compared to other boats that size.

Thanks to a ballast/displacement ratio of almost 43%, the 25 is a reasonably stiff boat despite her narrow beam and slack bilges. Stability is enhanced by a short, low aspect ratio rig. Owners report that a 150% genoa is a must to keep the 25 moving in light air.

The 25D may actually have better performance potential than the 25. The 25D's rig is substantially more modern in design, with a mast 4 1/2' taller than that of the 25, a J measurement over a foot longer, and a higher aspect ratio mainsail. The extra 6" of draft, 9" of beam, hard bilges, and 350 pounds of additional ballast should make her quite stiff.

The 25D comes with recessed inboard jib track as well as the rail-mounted genoa track common to both boats. Both have full width mainsheet travelers mounted at the aft end of the cockpit.

Cape Dory boats 30' and under come with factory-supplied sails built by several different lofts. OEM sails rarely come up to the quality of sails custom built for a particular boat sailed in a specific locale. Though the stock sails may be adequate while you're learning to sail the boat, they probably won't be when you become interested enough in good performance to appreciate the difference between a mediocre suit of sails and a really good suit. With either the 25 or 25D, the first sail you'll want to add to the boat is a 150% genoa, no matter where you sail. A lot of sail area can compensate for a lot of wetted surface when sailing in light air.

Both the 25 and 25D have deck-stepped masts. In the 25, most of the mast compression is carried by the main cabin bulkhead. In the 25D, an aluminum compression column directly under the mast transfers the rig compression to the keel. Cape Dory's support systems for deck-stepped masts are among the best we've seen.

The mast on the 25D was originally designed to step through to the keel. The sales department feared that a large mast tube in the main cabin might turn off potential buyers, so the mast tubes were shortened, and a complex, more expensive deck stepping arrangement was incorporated. This isn't the first time in the industry the sales department has overridden the engineering department, and it won't be the last.

The main boom of the 25 is equipped with roller reefing, a method of sail reduction that has, thankfully, just about vanished. It is almost impossible to get good sail shape going to weather with a roller reefed main, and you really haven't lived until you've tried to crank in half a dozen rolls in a rising gale offshore while the reefing gear binds and the sail luff grinds itself to shreds in the reefing gear. Jiffy reefing, which is standard on the 25D, is preferable to roller reefing in almost every way.

In performance, neither the 25 nor the 25D will be

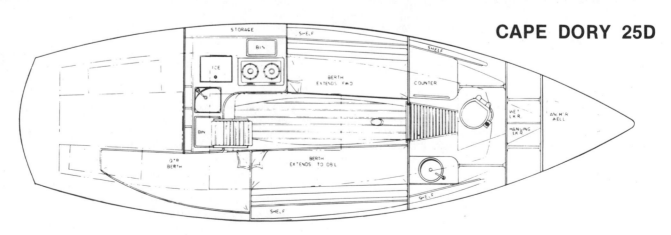

CAPE DORY 25D

mistaken for a racer-cruiser. Nevertheless, the owner concerned about improving performance can make real improvements by fairing in through hull fittings, wet sanding the factory-applied KL-990 bottom paint, and buying higher-performance sails.

Handling under power

A major difference between the 25 and 25D is their mechanical propulsion systems. The Cape Dory 25 has an outboard well at the aft end of the cockpit, while the 25D has inboard diesel power.

The outboard engine installation of the 25 is less than 100% successful, according to owners responding to our survey. The cover to the engine compartment must be kept open to provide adequate air for the outboard engine when running under power. The engine well resonates loudly, making the 25 noisy under power.

The 25 will accommodate engines up to 15 horsepower, but the most commonly used engines are the Johnson and Evinrude 9.9 horsepower units, which provide more than adequate power for the boat.

The engine's location aft of the rudder means that there is no prop wash effect on the rudder to aid low speed maneuvering. Coupled with the 25's long keel, this means that the boat will be slower to respond under power than a modern fin keeler of similar displacement.

Handling the 25 in reverse is a problem, according to owners. A large percentage report in our survey that the boat "doesn't maneuver in reverse worth a damn."

The 25D has a conventional inboard engine installation, using a raw-water-cooled Yanmar 1QM 7 1/2 horsepower diesel. At 154 pounds, this is one of the lightest small diesels available. The 13 gallon fuel tank, mounted under the cockpit, should give the 25D over 50 hours of operating time under power, or a range of about 250 miles.

A two-bladed solid bronze prop is standard, tucked in an aperture at the aft end of the keel. The aperture extends into the rudder, which will cause some cross ventilation and slight loss of rudder efficiency under sail. The 2.62:1 reduction gear should allow the little engine to achieve full power in driving the 25D.

The engine installation is excellent, and meets ABYC standards for the installation of gasoline engines, as well as the far simpler standards for diesels. A lift-out plastic storage bin in the top of the engine box removes for routine service of belts and filters, as well as for checking oil. The compartment is not soundproofed.

More thorough access to the engine can be gained by removing the companionway ladder and unscrewing the plywood front panel of the engine box.

LIVABILITY

Deck layout

The 25 and 25D share a simple, uncluttered deck layout, although the 25D has some features lacking in the 25. The 25D has a large foredeck anchor well capable of holding the normal working ground tackle for the boat. The 25D's stemhead casting incorporates an anchor roller. We would add a large eyebolt to the anchor well to secure the bitter end of the anchor rode.

While the 25 has a single centerline foredeck cleat, the 25D has twin cleats outboard of the well. Bowlines should be secured to the cleat on the opposite side from the bow chock to avoid blocking access to the well.

You can have any hull and deck color from Cape Dory as long as it's Cape Dory offwhite and tan. The white of the cabin house is a warm brownish white, and will not unduly reflect light on bright days. Tan nonskid areas avoid the desolate appearance of white on white found on some boats.

The 25 and 25D both have teak toerails and rubbing strake, teak cabintop handrails, and teak cockpit coamings. We strongly recommend that these be kept in good shape by the application of a teak dressing. Despite the fact that teak is reasonably forgiving of neglect, it does require some maintenance to avoid warping and checking.

Bow pulpit, stern pulpit, and single lifelines are standard on the 25D. A bow pulpit is standard on the 25, but lifelines and stern rail are optional. The 25D incorporates Aqua Signal international style running lights in the pulpits.

Cockpits of both boats are large and reasonably comfortable, although the coaming sides are vertical rather than being slanted at a good angle for really comfortable seating. Older models of the 25 had a low cockpit sill, with the lowest companionway drop board six inches above the cockpit sole. New models have a substantial bridgedeck.

Both the 25 and 25D have large cockpit scuppers leading to through hull fittings with shutoff valves. The scuppers are properly located at the forward end of the cockpit, which prevents flooding by the quarter wave.

There are large lockers under both cockpit seats on the 25. The 25D has a shallow locker to starboard over the quarterberth and a deep locker to port. Access to the stuffing box on the 25D is through the port locker.

The tiller on both boats takes up a lot of the cockpit whether sailing or at anchor. A few 25Ds have been delivered with pedestal steering, which seems a little presumptuous on a boat this size, but does free up the

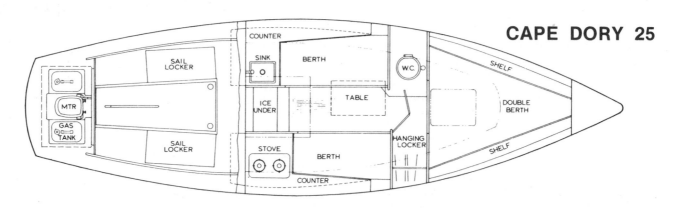

CAPE DORY 25

Without substantially raising either freeboard or cabin trunk, the 25D has been provided with honest headroom of about 5'11"

---

cockpit for seating.

With a good solid bridgedeck, big scuppers, and a companionway that is almost parallel sided, the 25D has a cockpit suited for offshore use, although its volume is at the upper limit for a small boat. The use of plywood drop boards is rather disappointing on a boat of this quality. A properly made solid board is as warp-free as plywood, and certainly looks better.

Belowdecks
The most obvious difference in the two boats is belowdecks. The 25 is a minimal short term cruiser for two adults and two children, while the 25D has a genuine cruising interior for a couple.

The 25 has what could best be described as stooping headroom. The forward cabin has a sharply tapered vee-berth that is too small for two normal size adults. Immediately aft is a cramped toilet compartment, divided from the vee-berths by a curtain and from the main cabin by folding doors.

The main cabin settees double as berths. Actually, they are berths doubling as settees, as there are no backrests for comfortable sitting. Because the galley sink hangs over the foot of the port settee, owners report that as a berth it is only comfortable for a fairly short person.

The galley consists of platforms port and starboard at the foot of the settees. The starboard platform can hold a two burner stove, which is optional, or can be used for navigating. The port counter contains the aforementioned sink. There is a small icebox under the companionway step.

Stepping from the 25 to the 25D is a confusing experience. On a marginally larger hull, Cape Dory has produced a boat with an interior that a couple could find comfortable for fairly extended cruising. Without substantially raising either freeboard or cabin trunk, the 25D has been provided honest headroom of about 5'11".

One way this has been accomplished has been by dropping the cabin sole well into the bilge. Headroom is gained at the cost of cabin sole space. In this case, it's a fair tradeoff. The only real impingement into the headroom is the teak finishing piece for the overhead companionway hatch, which extends down a full two inches. Many people will find this a real headcracker.

The interior of the 25D is unusual in that a forward cabin has been eliminated, and a huge head, which can be fitted with a shower, installed in the space that would otherwise be a cramped berth.

The head compartment has headroom of 5'9", two hanging lockers, a small sink, and two solid towel rack/grab rails. Anyone who has spent any time in the head in rough weather will appreciate the grab rails.

Although there is little storage space in the head for sheets, towels, medicine, or other small items, there are two large blank bulkheads crying out for the handy boatowner to install cabinets or shelves.

The shower, if installed, drains directly into the bilge, an arrangement that leaves something to be desired. A Bomar hatch over the head provides good ventilation, as do the two opening ports in the head compartment.

Attractive is an overused word, but it is truly descriptive of the main cabin. The hull outboard of the settees is lined with ash ceiling, a welcome change from the teak used by most builders.

Main cabin settees extend through the head bulkhead into alcoves that form the dresser surfaces in the head.

These alcoves are handy for storing bedding or other loose items under sail.

Cape Dory gets an A+ for main cabin settee comfort in the 25D. The settee backs are nicely padded, properly angled, and the settee tops have been reduced to the proper width for comfortable seating. Thank God someone has discovered that most people don't sit bolt upright when they can avoid it. For sleeping, the backs fold up on hinges and latch out of the way.

The starboard settee extends, with a little maneuvering, to form a double, giving the 25D nominal accommodations for four adults. We doubt if two couples would really want to share one cabin on a 25 footer for any period of time.

A 20 gallon polyethylene water tank is mounted under the starboard quarterberth—undeniably the best berth in the boat, but one that is likely to be used more for storage than for sleeping if the boat is cruised by a couple. Ironically, this water capacity is four gallons less than that of the Cape Dory 25.

With a little imagination, the galley of the 25D could probably be made far more serviceable for the serious cruiser. There is little storage space for any quantity of food, although there is enough room under the bridgedeck and outboard of the stove to create much more. The sink is tucked away under the bridgedeck, and truly is almost impossible to use. To reach the fresh water pump, being a contortionist would be a virtue. Washing dishes would be an acrobatic exercise.

The galley stove is a two burner recessed Kenyon alcohol model with integral tank, a type of stove about which we have grave reservations. Alcohol is a poor cooking fuel for a serious cruising boat, being expensive, bulky, and inefficient.

Cross ventilation of the main cabin is excellent, with four opening bronze ports. Cowl vents in dorade boxes should be fitted at the aft end of the main cabin for foul weather and offshore ventilation.

With the exception of the galley, the interior of the Cape Dory 25D is one of the most functional we have seen for a small cruising boat. Putting the head in the forepeak and eliminating the cramped vee-berth are excellent ideas in a boat of this size. The lack of privacy in the head, a major complaint in small cruising boats, is a problem Cape Dory has solved in one bold stroke.

CONCLUSIONS

For two boats of similar size and type, the Cape Dory 25 and 25D are radically different from each other. The 25 is a daysailer and weekender, with cramped accommodations. The 25D has the potential to be a comfortable long-term cruiser for a couple, with a roomy interior whose only real flaw is a mediocre galley arrangement.

Construction of both boats is solid, and they are well finished, although not perfectly so. Finish detail is substantially better than on Cape Dory boats of 5 years ago.

The 25D is tough enough to be a serious cruising boat. We won't be surprised to hear that someone sails one across the Atlantic, although ocean voyaging in so small a boat is not our personal cup of tea.

Cape Dory boats are for traditionalists. In a time when traditionalism and conservatism seem to be growing in popularity, the popularity of boats such as those produced by Cape Dory is bound to grow. Yes, Cape Dory has found its niche in the market, and that niche isn't nearly as small as it was ten years ago.

The Ericson 25: Small Family Cruiser

THE BOAT AND THE BUILDER

Just a few years ago, the prospective buyer of a 25' sailboat knew that serious compromises awaited him. His 25-footer would probably have little more than sitting headroom, might have four shelves that could reasonably be called berths, and probably had a head stowed under the forward berth. The galley? With luck, a two-burner alcohol stove, maybe a sink, and a water tank holding ten gallons.

Auxiliary power? Usually a 6 hp outboard hanging off the stern or in a well in the lazarette.

With today's phenomenal interest rates, more and more people who a few years ago might have considered a 30-footer are downscaling their size expectations to something more realistic, perhaps a 25- or 27-footer. While they may downgrade their expectations in terms of the length of their boats, they have not downgraded their expectations in terms of the size boat they want. This is not the contradiction it may seem. The fact is that there are a number of boats less than 27' in overall length that offer room and features akin to those offered in the 30' boat of just 10 or 15 years ago.

For better or worse, economic reality has forced many of us to downsize our boat expectations in much the way we downsized our automobile expectations.

Enter the new generation of small cruising auxiliaries. The state of the art in the modern 25' "family" sailboat has 6' headroom, berths for a family of five—if privacy isn't a high priority—enclosed head, and perhaps an inboard diesel engine. A regular miniature yacht.

The Ericson 25+ is as good an example of the trend toward more boat in less length as any boat built today. The proof of the popularity of this concept shows in the numbers. Over 660 units were built in the first three years after the Ericson 25+ was introduced in late 1978.

Designer Bruce King has had a long and successful relationship with Ericson Yachts, starting with the Ericson 23, 30, 32, and 41 of the late 1960's, and continuing today. He has not been exclusively an Ericson "house" designer—witness the magnificent Herreshoff-inspired 90' ketch *Whitehawk* to his design—but the vast majority of Ericson boats have come from his board.

Bruce King and Ericson have found a formula not unlike that of Bill Shaw and Pearson: build a wide range of boats of similar type in two to three foot increments, develop customer loyalty, and watch the customers move up through the ranks. Keep the really popular models, such as the Pearson 35 or the Ericson 35, and bring out other models every few years to catch the latest trend. That formula works whether you're on the East Coast or the West, and like Pearson, Ericson has the formula down pat.

With the exception of a few forays into the cruising market with the clipper-bowed Cruising 31 and the Cruising 36 (later to be called Independence), the Ericson formula has been to produce a well-finished cruiser-racer with good sailing characteristics. The Ericson 25+ is the continuation of this successful formula.

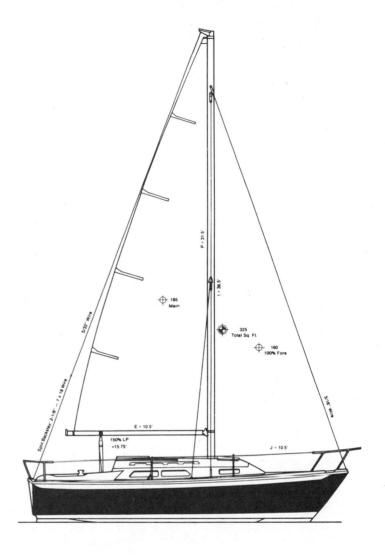

Specifications

LOA	25'5"
LWL	21'10"
Beam	9'3"
Draft	
standard	4'11"
shoal	3'11"
Displacement	5,000 lbs.
Ballast	2,000 lbs.

Ericson Yachts, Inc.
1931 Deere Avenue
Irvine, CA 92714

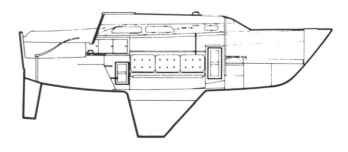

We prefer a mechanically fastened hull-to-deck joint, because the strength of secondary chemical bonds is hard to evaluate.

CONSTRUCTION

The hull of the Ericson 25+ is a solid hand layup. A molded fiberglass body pan is glassed to the inside of the hull, functioning as the base for much of the interior furniture and adding a certain amount of rigidity to the hull. The deck, cockpit, and cabin trunk molding is balsa cored, with plywood replacing the balsa in high stress areas such as under the deck-stepped mast and where deck hardware is mounted.

Exterior glasswork is of good quality, with little roving printthrough. Gelcoat work is good.

The hull-to-deck joint depends on a secondary chemical bond. Both the hull and deck have an external molded flange. Glass-reinforced polyester resin is used as a bedding compound between these flanges. The inside of this joint is then lapped with four layers of fiberglass mat and cloth. This joint is covered on the outside by a plastic extrusion with a soft plastic insert which functions as a rub rail. We prefer a mechanically fastened hull-to-deck joint, because the strength of secondary chemical bonds is very difficult to evaluate.

The deck of the 25+ has a remarkably solid feel thanks to its cored construction. Neither the deck, cockpit, nor cabin top had any of the sponginess frequently associated with small boats.

Deck hardware of the 25+ is well mounted. Stanchins, pulpits, cleats, and winches have adequate aluminum bearing plates. The tiller head is a substantial chrome-plated bronze casting. The transom is plywood cored, greatly adding to its rigidity.

The mast of the 25+ is a black, deck-stepped extrusion. The stainless steel mast step looks surprisingly fragile. Because the mast is designed to be owner-stepped if desired, the forward lower half of the base of the mast is cut away to allow the mast to pivot forward for lowering. We doubt if there are many owners who will step their own masts. The design of the mast step to facilitate raising and lowering has greatly reduced the bearing surface of the heel of the mast.

In contrast to the mast step, the shroud chainplates are of surprisingly heavy construction. The 25+ utilizes Navtec chainplates, shroud terminals, and turnbuckles. Chainplates are strongly tied to the hull.

All through hull fittings below the waterline have Zytel valves, a reinforced plastic. Most have double-clamped hoses, but the icebox drain hose has a single clamp. Although modern plastics are strong, we suggest that you carefully inventory through hull fittings, as they are a major culprit in many sinkings of otherwise undamaged boats. Plastic valves may be immune to electrolysis, but they cannot be forgotten any more than bronze seacocks can be ignored.

PERFORMANCE

Handling Under Sail

Despite the chubbiness of the 25+, owners report that she is a fast boat under sail. There are a number of features that contribute to this speed. She has minimum wetted surface, despite a displacement that is average for her overall length, though fairly light for a waterline length of almost 22'.

The Ericson 25+, 28+, and 30+ all feature Bruce King's trademark, the "delta" fin keel. King states that this keel form has very low induced drag, and the 25's

performance reinforces his belief. The optional shoal draft keel reduces draft a foot, reduces lateral plane, and no doubt reduces windward ability. Unless you are bound and determined to have a boat drawing under four feet, by all means get the deeper draft version.

The rig of the 25+ is a high aspect ratio 7/8 sloop rig. The mainsail hoist of 31.5' is unusual for a 25' boat. In light air, tall rigs are usually faster, and we would expect the boat's best point of sail to be upwind in light air. Since a great deal of the sailing in the world seems to be upwind in light air, this approach to the rig is a rational one.

With the addition of a backstay adjuster—easy because of the split backstay — it is possible to induce a reasonable amount of mast bend to control sail shape. A full width mainsheet traveler mounted on the cockpit bridgedeck greatly enhances mainsail control.

Shroud chainplates are set well inboard, allowing narrow headsail sheeting angles. The genoa track is also located inboard, almost against the cabin side.

There is no main boom topping lift. We think this is pretty indefensible on a cruising boat, and despite the additional windage, a topping lift is greatly to be desired on a racing boat. Without a topping lift, reefing becomes a real exercise in agility. Dropping the mainsail is greatly complicated, especially when cruising shorthanded. Should the main halyard break when sailing closehauled, the main boom could brain anyone sitting on the leeward side of the cockpit.

Two-speed Barient headsail sheet winches are now standard. There is room on the cockpit coamings both for the addition of secondary winches for spinnaker handling and the replacement of the standard winches with larger ones. A single halyard winch is mounted on the mast. There is no main halyard winch. We would choose the optional aft-leading halyards to facilitate shorthanded cruising.

The 25+ should sail with almost any other production cruiser-racer of her size. Her wide beam and deep draft should offset the additional heeling moment of the tall rig. Like all wide modern boats she should be sailed on her feet. Get the crew weight out on the weather rail in a breeze, and she should carry sail well.

Ericson wisely no longer supplies the boats with sails. Go to a local sailmaker for your sails. He is more likely to understand both your sailing conditions and your sail needs than someone a thousand miles away.

Handling Under Power

There are probably more power options for the 25+ than any similar-sized boat on the market. They include: outboard power, OMC gas saildrive, Volvo diesel saildrive, and Yanmar diesel inboard.

The 25+ is small enough to be driven fairly well by a 10-hp outboard. There is about a $3500 difference in equipping the boat with an outboard engine versus the diesel inboard. The choice depends largely on how the boat is to be used. Few boats of this size are used for long-distance cruising. For daysailing and racing, an outboard engine is more than adequate.

If extended coastal cruising is to be the boat's primary activity, then one of the inboard options should be considered. Frankly, we have little love for saildrive installations. If you really want an inboard engine, the new Yanmar single cylinder inboard diesel is the real choice. At resale time the Ericson 25+ with diesel inboard in good condition is likely to be worth about

The single 1½" diameter scupper has more cross sectional area than two 1" drains, and is less likely to clog

---

$2000 more than the same boat with an outboard. Opting for the diesel will therefore cost money both when you buy and sell the boat. There is not likely to be a great deal of difference in cost to operate the gas outboard or diesel inboard. The gas outboard will burn more fuel. There is now little difference in the cost of diesel fuel versus the cost of gasoline.

As a pure investment, choosing the diesel would appear to be an irrational decision. At the same time, the boat equipped with an inboard diesel is a very desirable package, one that will definitely be more salable in the future.

No matter which engine is ordered, the boat is equipped with a 20-gallon aluminum fuel tank. With a one-cylinder diesel engine, given a four-knot cruising speed and fuel consumption of about ¼ gallon per hour, the range under power is almost 350 miles—a truly astounding range for a 25' boat. That's probably more range under power than the average boat is likely to need for an entire season.

The problem with the diesel inboard is that it pushes the price of the boat up to about $35,000 for the well-equipped 25-footer, a not inconsiderable sum.

LIVABILITY

Deck Layout
With shroud chainplates set well inboard, and a reasonably narrow cabin trunk, working on the deck of the 25+ is fairly easy. There is adequate room between the shrouds and the lifelines to walk outboard of the shrouds with ease.

There is a small foredeck anchor well, adequate for the stowage of a single Danforth and rode. There are no bow chocks, but there are two cleats located forward at the outboard edge of the deck.

Molded-in nonskid of color contrasting to the primary deck color is standard. This relieves eyestrain in bright sunlight and reduces the basically austere external appearance of the boat.

The cockpit of the 25+ is comfortable. Coamings are angled outward rather than being vertical, allowing a more natural sitting posture. As in most tiller-steered boats, the sweep of the tiller occupies a large percentage of the cockpit volume. In port, the tiller swings up and out of the way, providing uncrowded seating for up to six adults.

A single cockpit scupper 1½" in diameter is recessed in a well at the back of the cockpit. The well allows water to drain on either tack. A stainless steel strainer over the scupper reduces its effective area by over 50%. Since the drain size is large enough to pass on through almost any debris that is likely to be found in the cockpit, we would remove the strainer for sailing. A single 1½" diameter scupper has more cross sectional area than two 1" drains, and is less likely to clog.

There are two cockpit lockers. The starboard cockpit locker is a shallow pan suitable for storing small items such as winch handles and sail ties. At its after corner is a deeper bin which will make a handy icebox for cold drinks. The port locker is a large, deep affair which suffers from the common failing of not being adequately separated from the under-cockpit area. A snap-in Dacron bag would convert this locker to reasonable sail stowage.

The companionway uses thick, well-made solid teak dropboards with proper step joints to prevent spray from working below. Unfortunately, the very strong taper to the companionway slides allows them to be removed by lifting less than an inch. For sailing in rough water, a positive means of securing these slides—a sliding bolt, for example—must be installed.

It is gratifying to see a real bridgedeck in a boat this size. Except for the strong taper to the companionway sides, this is one of the best designed cockpits we have seen in a small boat.

Belowdecks
The amount of interior volume in the 25+ is truly remarkable. The boat easily has the headroom and elbow room of most 30-footers of 10 or 15 years ago.

The forepeak contains the usual vee berth with filler to form a nominal double. We truly mean nominal. Two normal-sized people do not fit in the forward berth of the Ericson 25+. Consider it a large single, or a double for two children. Water and holding tanks occupy the space under the berth.

The 25+ has a genuine enclosed, standup head, an almost unheard of luxury in a boat this size. The head has an opening port for ventilation. There are two small lockers in the head, but both are largely occupied by plumbing hoses.

Opposite the head is a small hanging locker. This locker is fully lined with teak plywood, a nice finishing touch.

It is in the main cabin that the 25+ really shines. Headroom is an honest 6'. Two comfortable settee berths seat 6 in comfort. A fold-down drop-leaf table is big enough to serve 4, and is one of the sturdier tables of this type that we have seen.

The main cabin of the 25+ is well finished with a combination of off-white fiberglass and teak. This is a

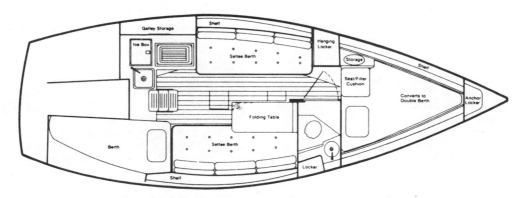

very successful decorating job, without so much teak as to turn the interior into a cave but with enough to give a well finished appearance. Hull ceiling of teak strips is now standard, and the cabin trunk sides are veneered in teak. A teak and holly cabin sole is standard, with two access hatches to the bilge.

There is a real bilge, unusual in a boat of this size. The strainer for the cockpit-mounted Whale Gusher pump is accessible through one of the cabin sole hatches.

Under the settee on each side of the cabin there are storage bins. These utilize molded polyethylene drop-in liners, a most practical solution which recognizes the reality that under-seat storage is rarely completely dry. An optional extension to the starboard settee converts it to a double berth, but at the expense of easy access to the storage bins underneath.

The galley is surprisingly complete for a 25' boat. There is a well-insulated icebox of five cubic foot capacity. The insulation is exposed in the port cockpit locker, and will be vulnerable to damage from items stowed there. It could easily be sealed off with either plywood or fiberglass to protect it. The icebox lid is an uninsulated molding advertised as a removable serving tray. If it is used as a serving tray, then the icebox is uncovered, allowing the ice to melt. Whoever thought up that bright idea should go back to the drawing board or look around for some common sense.

For some reason, icebox lids are one of the poorest design features of most sailboats. It's quite remarkable on boats with otherwise thoughtful design and construction to see poor icebox design. Perhaps there is collusion between the Union of Icebox Designers and the Association of Manufacturers of Ice to maximize the consumption of ice aboard sailboats.

There are storage lockers both above and below the icebox-stove counter. The stove is a recessed Kenyon two-burner alcohol unit with a cutting block cover. These stoves have the fuel fill located between the two burners, and we feel they are a poor choice for use aboard a boat. The burners must be absolutely cool before the fuel tank is filled to eliminate the possibility of explosion or fire.

It is not necessary to step on the galley counter when coming down the companionway. This is a real plus. Footprints on the counters have never appealed to us.

A human-sized quarterberth is a welcome feature. With adequate headroom over, it eliminates the coffin-like aura of so many small-boat quarterberths, and is without a doubt the roomiest, most comfortable berth on the boat.

With an outboard engine, the room under the cockpit that would normally house an inboard is given over to storage. The tiny one-cylinder Yanmar diesel would easily shoehorn into the same space.

Without a doubt, the interior of the Ericson 25 + is a real accomplishment. It is well finished, generally well designed, and remarkably roomy for a boat of this overall length. There is some miniaturization of components, such as the galley sink, head sink, and hanging locker. Nonetheless, she's a big little boat, and would be truly comfortable for extended coastal cruising for a couple. That is something that can rarely be said for a 25' boat.

CONSLUSIONS

Ericson has come very close to achieving their goals in the 25 +. She is about as much boat as can be crammed into this overall length.

An interesting option is an E-Z Loader trailer. With a beam of over 9' and a weight of 5,000 pounds, the 25 + is no trailer sailer. It takes a large, powerful car or truck to tow a boat of this size, and the beam could present legal problems in some states. The trailer would be most useful for taking the boat home for winter storage, rather than frequent over-the-road transport.

Workmanship and finish detail are generally of good stock boat quality. Exposed joiner work is good. Fillet bonding varies from good to only fair, with glasswork generally good.

The Ericson 25 + is probably a good example of something to be seen more and more often as slip prices, fuel prices, and boatyard prices increase. She is a good small cruiser for a young family, and offers enough sailing performance to be a reasonable choice for club racing.

Unlike many small cruiser-racers which concentrate on interior volume and forsake sailing ability, the 25 + really will sail. This means that the new sailor will not quickly outgrow her as he or she learns what makes a boat go fast.

With good hardware such as Barient and Navtec and a fairly high degree of finish detail, it is easy to see why the boat goes at nearly $30,000 sailaway with outboard power, and considerably higher with inboard. For those used to the $20,000 25-footer, the cost will be a shock. It helps a little to think of her as a 28-footer with the stern cut off.

With an inboard diesel, a good light air rig, and lots of interior volume, she's a good little cruising boat for a couple. A maximum boat for minimum length, she's a modern solution to skyrocketing costs of sailing. At maximum price for her length, she's not an example of "more for less" but as Ericson points out, there's no free lunch in the sailboat market. That's for sure.

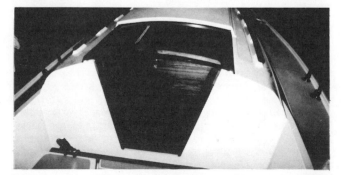
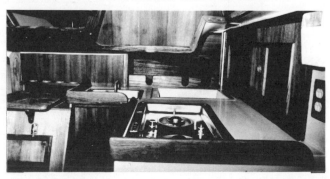

Redesigned in 1982 models of the Ericson 25: smoked lucite hatch cover and galley

The Freedom 25: Wave of the Future

THE BOAT AND THE BUILDER

"Why evaluate the freedom 25?" you might ask. There are so many other 25-footers, like the Catalina 25 and the O'Day 25, that are far more popular. However, none of them scream for attention like the Freedom 25. She is a radical departure from the run-of-the-mill cruising daysailer. The unstayed mast that is the trademark of the Freedom line has spawned several, less sophisticated imitations. The Freedom 25 takes this trademark a step further—such a big step that we suspect it will take imitators a good part of the next decade to catch up. Because she may represent sailboats of the future, we think she deserves attention.

Garry Hoyt is the moving force behind Freedom Yachts, and Tillotson-Pearson is the builder. (See the Freedom 33 evaluation for more on Hoyt and Tillotson-Pearson.) Hoyt's unusual story began when he retired from his advertising executive career and champion one-design sailing exploits to look for a cruising boat that both performed well and handled easily. He couldn't find one. The typical racer-cruiser didn't satisfy him: racing rules dictate stayed masts and multiple headsails, which are difficult for a shorthanded cruising crew to handle.

"Uncompromised" cruising boats err in the other direction, tending to be undercanvassed and overweight, which make them slow and sluggish, especially upwind. Hoyt's solution is the unstayed mast with wrap-around sails and wishbone booms. The unstayed mast offers strength and simplicity—no maintenance, no worry about losing the rig to a cracked turnbuckle, etc. "Airplanes did away with stayed wings 40 years ago," argues Hoyt. The wrap-around sails helped overcome the aerodynamic drag of the larger section of the unstayed mast (albeit at doubling the cost of a sail and causing chafe problems).

A line of Freedoms, beginning with the Freedom 40, were designed by Hoyt (with help by professional naval architects like Halsey Herreshoff) with his unstayed, wrap-around rig. Except for the Freedom 44, none had fin keels; hence, upwind performance, especially in light air, was less than sparkling. They did perform well off the wind, however, and true to Hoyt's predictions they were easier to handle than boats with conventional sloop rigs.

When Hoyt got the high-performance bug, his ever creative mind wandered off in a different direction. After years of co-designing Freedoms, he drew the lines for a 25-footer by himself. In the time since the first Freedom 25 was built, the boat has undergone a radical metamorphosis. She started with a foot less freeboard, a ketch rig with wrap-around sails set on two stubby unstayed masts, a bulb-ballasted daggerboard, hiking wings hinged outboard of the gunwale, and the earliest version of the Gun Mount

Specifications

LOA	25'8''
LWL	20'
Beam	8'6''
Draft	4'5''
Displacement	2500 lbs
Ballast	1025 lbs
Sail Area	260 sq ft

Freedom Yachts
49 America's Cup Avenue
Newport, RI 02840

spinnaker pole system. Hoyt finagled a MORC rating and entered his creation in the 1980 Block Island Race Week. However, upon screaming into the harbor on a planing reach, Hoyt aroused enough consternation among his competitors to get his rating revoked (hiking wings and wrap-around sails did not fit "the rule").

Hoyt also found out at Block Island that, although his 25 was a flyer on a windy reach, she was just as lacking as the larger Freedoms upwind. So the ketch rig was discarded in favor a single, wing-shaped rotating mast made of wood by the Gougeon brothers. This wooden mast was so heavy that it nearly capsized the little 25-footer. It was removed from the boat and used as a plug to mold a lighter spar out of carbon fiber. These spars were too light; Hoyt broke the first seven prototypes before finding an optimum section.

The builder says the mast has a safety margin which allows it to withstand an accidental casting off of a running backstay in winds up to 25 knots

Somewhere during this lengthy story, Hoyt decided that his racy 25-footer would never collect in the numbers required for one-design racing, nor would the evil arbiters of "the rule" ever allow her to compete in handicap races. So he raised the freeboard, added a keel and an interior and made her the little cruising boat with the funny rig that she is today.

Hoyt made a wise choice in Tillotson-Pearson as the builder of the Freedom line. Not only is Tillotson-Pearson a leader in the development of balsa core sandwich construction (they build J/Boats as well as Freedoms), but they also have extensive experience with carbon fiber, having made tennis rackets and oars of that material. This experience enabled Hoyt to replace the aluminum masts standard on the early Freedoms with a lighter and stiffer spar of carbon fiber.

Coincidental with the development of the Freedom 25, Tillotson-Pearson was also tooling up for the production of large fiberglass windmill blades. This defrayed the R&D needed to fabricate the Freedom 25's wing mast. There are very few, if any, production boat builders who have the technology to laminate unstayed masts of carbon fiber. Tillotson-Pearson and Hoyt appear to have cornered the market.

CONSTRUCTION

Construction of the Freedom 25 is comparable to that described in the evaluation of the Freedom 33. Tillotson-Pearson's construction is among the best in the production boatbuilding industry. The boat's hull and deck are cored with balsa, which offers the advantages of a lighter, more rigid hull that is less prone to condensation and deadens sound better than an uncored hull. The hull-to-deck joint is the standard Tillotson-Pearson inward turned flange, sealed with semi-rigid 3M 5200 adhesive and bolted through the teak toerail—a strong, seaworthy system.

The external, 1025 pound fin keel is bolted into a small but adequately deep sump. In their years of building J/24s and J/30s, Tillotson-Pearson has learned to build rudders and rudder fittings strong enough to withstand heavy air. The Freedom 25's outboard rudder has pintles and gudgeons beefy enough for a 30-footer.

Tillotson-Pearson does not part easily with details of the construction of their carbon fiber spars. From what we understand, the spars, which are hollow, are not molded in two separate halves and joined together because the resulting seam would be a weak point. Unidirectional carbon fiber is laid onto an inflatable bladder, and then a mold is clamped around it. When the bladder is inflated, it "vacuum bags" the mast into the shape of a wing. The mast is sanded smooth before being painted with polyurethane. A plastic sail track is then riveted to the trailing edge of the wing.

While the idea of a mast without stays might be unsettling to some sailors there is no need to worry as long as the mast step, partner and mast section are properly engineered. This engineering is realtively simple with a round, non-rotating mast such as the ones used on the Freedom 25's larger sisters; but it's not so simple with a rotating wing mast. The 25's wing section begins above deck—below deck it is round to enable it to bear evenly on the step and partner. A wing section is inherently strong in the fore and aft plane, but it is susceptible to side bend because it is so thin in the athwartships plane. There are two ways to break an unstayed wing mast: either sail upwind in a strong breeze with an unreefed main and the mast rotated in the wrong direction (right angles to the boom), or set a large staysail from the masthead without the support of running backstays. Both of these mistakes put extreme side load on the mast. Running backstays are part of the optional spinnaker package; the builder says the 135 pound mast has a safety margin which allows it to withstand an accidental casting off of a backstay in winds up to 25 knots.

To allow free rotation and prevent excessive wear and tear on the step and partner, the Freedom 25's mast is stepped in a stainless steel bearing race and sleeved at the deck with Delrin. Maintaining those two pressure points should be infinitely easier than the upkeep on all of the standing rigging on a conventional spar. The mast fittings are fastened with aluminum rivets and bedded with 3M 5200. Bedding is essential, as Tillotson-Pearson claims the corrosion of aluminum in contact with carbon fiber is even more severe than aluminum in contact with stainless steel. The gooseneck lever that controls rotation was bolted to the early masts, creating a weak point that caused several to fail. The lever is now glued on.

PERFORMANCE

Upwind

We doubt that there is any cruising boat with a more efficient rig than the Freedom 25. Wing masts have been used for years on catamarans and iceboats because the drag of a wing is so much less than a conventionally shaped mast. A typical cruising boat mast usually creates enough turbulence to render the forward quarter of the mainsail useless, reducing effective sail area. A round unstayed mast, as is used on the larger Freedoms, is larger in diameter than a stayed mast, so drag can be even worse.

A wing mast, however, causes virtually no turbulence because it is so thin in the athwartships dimension. When a wing is rotated so it is aligned in the plane of the leading edge of the mainsail, it acts as an extension of the sail and effectively increases sail area. This is how the Freedom 25 can be powered by a 260 sq. ft. mainsail alone, while comparably-sized conventionally-rigged boats usually have more area in their main and working jib combined.

A wing spar must be able to rotate independently of the boom. To align with the mainsail's leading edge it must be rotated about 20° beyond the boom's angle off centerline. Sail trim fanatics might want to adjust the rotation slightly as they adjust the draft of the mainsail, or to affect the side bend of the mast. The Freedom 25's rotational control line has no purchase, so it is difficult to adjust.

The independent rotation of the Freedom 25's wing mast, although necessary for good performance, does create some minor problems. While sailing, mainsheet tension keeps the mast in place. However, when the mainsheet is lightly trimmed in light air the mast has a tendency to swing as a powerboat wake or big sea passes under the boat. Whenever the boat is not sailing, the mast must be lashed to keep it from rotating back and forth.

When tacking in a strong breeze the mainsheet must be eased to allow the mast to rotate. If it doesn't rotate, the leech puts extreme side load, instead of fore-and-aft

Despite the efficiency of her wing spar, the Freedom 25 still lacks the windward ability of racing sloops in her size range

load, on the tip of the mast if the main is not reefed. This shouldn't be a problem with the Freedom 25 as she begs for a reef in winds over 15 knots.

As is common on boats with wing spars, the Freedom 25 has a fully-battened main. Full-length battens make the mainsail an almost rigid airfoil—the sail never luffs. Luffing is murder on a sail; because the Freedom's sail won't luff, it should last 2-3 times as long as a conventional sail (and at nearly half the price of a wrap-around sail). The sail is also easier to furl—as Hoyt says, it folds like a venetian blind between the lazy jacks rigged to both sides of the boom.

The problem with full-length battens is that, because the main won't luff, the boat doesn't slow easily when docking, mooring or anchoring under sail. Owners tell us that they have to drop the main before they make a landing, and sail the rest of the way on the power of the wing spar. (Owners also tell us that the wing spar makes the boat sail back and forth on the mooring.) This difficulty in landing is offset by the Freedom 25's maneuverability (like a J/24, she turns in her length). However, most sailors will want the security of the optional inboard engine.

The Freedom 25's main is trimmed differently than the mainsail on a conventionally rigged sloop. If you center the boom, trim the mainsheet hard and pinch her like a jib-headed boat you will go nowhere. Like any catboat, you have to let the boom out over the quarter, twist the leech and foot the boat. Since the full-length battens don't allow the sail to luff as you feather into the wind, you have to sail by telltales placed on both sides of the sail a few inches back from the luff, just as you would with genoa telltales on a sloop-rigged boat.

When Hoyt designed the Freedom 25's rig, he envisioned a boat that would go to windward like a J/24, yet handle with the ease of a catboat. Despite the efficiency of her wing spar, the Freedom 25 still lacks the windward ability of racing sloops in her size range. This is most noticeable in light air. However, she is the equal of any cruising boat and she does handle with virtually no effort. We have heard that Hoyt is experimenting with "spoiler" foils attached to the wing to accelerate the wind flow on the leeward side of the mainsail, as would a jib.

The Freedom 25's reefing system, although not a new idea, is nonetheless ingenious. We wish all boats had it. Instead of using a hook or a separate line for securing the tack, there is one continuous line to secure both the tack and the clew. It runs from the clew, through the boom, then out a sheave at the gooseneck, up through the luff grommet, then back to the base of the mast and aft to a stopper. Ease the halyard and pull this one line and the sail is reefed in seconds without sending any crew out of the cockpit.

Offwind

On a broad reach the Freedom 25 is at least the equal of most racing boats in her size range; she blows the cruisers out of the water. Her speed can be attributed to her relatively light (3500 lb.) displacement, and the positioning of most of her sail area well forward in the boat. The patented Gun Mount puts most of the spinnaker forward of the bow. The result is a boat that has virtually no tendency to round up on a heavy air reach. Even in a strong puff the rudder does not load up as it would on a sloop-rigged boat with a normal length pole. With the Freedom's unstayed mast, you also don't have to worry

about wrapping the spinnaker around the headstay.

We were skeptical of the Gun Mount at first; it's hard to believe that anything that looks so awkward and complicated can possibly live up to its billing. The Gun Mount, which consists of an oversize spinnaker pole run through a sleeve on the bow pulpit, rests on the lifelines when not in use. You can't store it on deck, so visibility is always obstructed. The spinnaker is hoisted out of and retrieved into a long sock tied to the deck. The spinnaker feeds into the sock via a wide-mouth plastic scoop hung on the bow pulpit. This adds to visibility obstruction, but the scoop and sock can be removed for storage below deck.

There are 16 lines leading back to the Freedom 25's cockpit—nearly twice as many as you might find on another 25' daysailer (the builder specs over 500' of line for the Freedom 25). Ten of those lines are needed for the optional Gun Mount package. However, if you can overlook the cluttered bow and keep the rat's nest of lines coiled, the Gun Mount works like a charm.

To set, jibe and douse the spinnaker, you never have to leave the cockpit. You adjust two lines to center the pole in the Gun Mount, then pull two more lines to haul the clews of the spinnaker out to the ends of the pole, and then set one of the running backstays if it is windy. To ease the task of hoisting, it helps to put the boat on a reach so the spinnaker will luff. Once up, the spinnaker is fixed to both ends of the pole; you adjust the pole with two "reins." Because the pole is balanced, there is absolutely no pressure on either rein—there is no need for winches to trim the sail. You can jibe at will, and adjust the pole at your leisure as there is no tendency to round up.

The Gun Mount makes the spinnaker too easy to fly. You are tempted to set the sail in 20-30 knot winds because the boat is so easy to control

We took the Freedom 25 for a long sail on a tight reach in a shifty breeze. When the wind shifted aft we hoisted the chute; when it shifted forward we took it down. We must have done this every five minutes for nearly an hour without leaving the cockpit or raising a sweat.

Although few in number, there are some drawbacks to the Gun Mount. Aside from its windage and obstruction of visibility, the Gun Mount works poorly on a beam reach, because as one end of the pole is let forward for tight reaching, the other end of the pole pulls the clew almost into the mainsail. This so closes the slot that the sail tends to stall. If you sail without the spinnaker, the boat is just as slow. A separate staysail is needed for tight reaching.

The other problem with the Gun Mount is that *it makes spinnaker flying too easy.* Sailors without much heavy air downwind experience are tempted to set the spinnaker in winds of 20-30 knots because the boat is so easy to control. However, if you should accidentally jibe and slam the boom against the running backstays, or accidentally let off one of the backstays, you stand a fair chance of breaking the mast. If the spinnaker hoists were ¾ of the way up the rig instead of at the masthead, or if there were diamond shrouds to control side bend, the mast would be far less likely to fail. (In fact, on the Freedom 21 currently under development, there are plans to use a wing mast with a ¾ spinnaker hoist.)

If you are thinking that you might want a Gun Mount on your current boat you might as well forget it. Hoyt is not selling Gun Mount kits, although he is planning to license certain builders to offer the Gun Mount as an option on their own boats. The Gun Mount wouldn't work well on sloop-rigged boats, because the headstay would interfere with the launching sock. Hoyt admits that the Gun Mount was "an afterthought" on the Freedom 25 and says he might recess the sock and funnel into the hull on future models in the Freedom line. If this were done, we don't see why he couldn't also remove the lifelines forward (you never leave the cockpit anyway), and lower the pole and Gun Mount to deck level to improve visibility.

Under Power
Inboard power is a $4600 option. The Freedom 25 is probably as large a boat as can be powered with an outboard. We don't think anyone, especially if there is any tendency toward back problems, should be hefting an outboard that is heavier than 45 pounds over a transom.

This effectively limits outboard power to 4-5 hp.

Despite the cost, we recommend the inboard option for most sailors. Most of the extra cost should be recovered when you sell the boat. The Yanmar 7½ hp auxiliary offered with the Freedom 25 has a Martec folding propeller, weighs only 154 lbs, and it will push the boat at more than six knots—much faster than an outboard. The inboard also makes docking or mooring in a tight spot easier, a task that can be a problem with a fully-battened mainsail.

The inboard is mounted under the companionway, the top step of which lifts for supposed access to the oil dipstick. However, try as we did, we could not reinsert the dipstick without removing the whole engine box. This difficulty will tempt owners not to check the oil as frequently as they should. The engine box removes easily, but is heavy and awkward to reset on its mounts. Access to the engine is relatively good with the box removed.

Even though the propeller shaft is mounted slightly off center to compensate for the pull of its rotation, the boat still pulls hard to one side when the engine is opened up. You cannot let your eyes off the compass for even a few seconds without wandering off course; if you let the tiller go the boat will do a screaming 360° spin before you can bat an eye. In short, it's a lot more work to power in a Freedom 25 than it is to sail. Like most Yanmars, engine vibration is excessive at low rpms. Fuel capacity is 10 gallons; range is 100 miles.

LIVABILITY

Deck Layout
The center of all activity on the Freedom 25 is the cockpit. Those 16 lines that are the running rigging lead into the cockpit through Easylock stoppers to Barient #10 winches mounted on either side of the companionway. The Easylock stopper has a clutch action that enables you to cast off a line without taking up the tension on a winch, a feature that helps the Gun Mount work so handily. We recommend installing several cloth bags on both sides of the companionway to separate and store all of the control lines.

It's a good thing that you never have to leave the cockpit to sail the Freedom 25: with the mast stepped on the foredeck, the Gun Mount and spinnaker sock occupy the little remaining space. There is no anchor well, although there is plenty of space to set one into the huge forward locker. However, unless the funnel for the

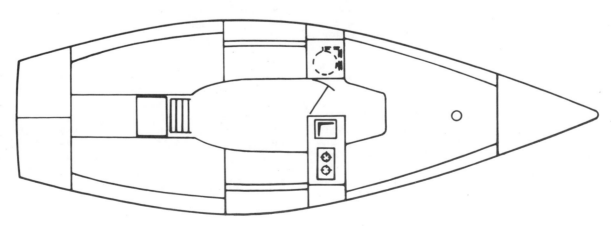

spinnaker sock is unhooked from the bow, access to the hypothetical anchor well or the bow chocks is difficult. You cannot store the anchor on a bow roller either, for the exposed prongs of the anchor could tear the spinnaker. Luckily, the ground tackle needed for a 25-footer is light enough to be easily carried from a cockpit locker to the bow.

The cockpit of the Freedom 25 has deep seats with a substantial coaming for dryness and security and angled seat backs for comfort. There is no traveler or backstay to obstruct the cockpit. The cabin table is portable and can be used in the cockpit, fitting easily and securely onto brackets with Faspins attached to the transom. The tiller lifts out of the way to let 4-6 people eat in comfort.

The mainsheet traveler is mounted over the companionway hatch. To minimize visibility obstruction, the builder has used a low-profile traveler made by Harken. Although the traveler is bent to the camber of the deck, it is not radiussed to follow the swing of the boom. If it were radiussed, the mainsheet might not have to be eased during a tack to allow the mast to rotate. The traveler is easily adjusted by the helmsman, but the mainsheet is just out of reach. We would recommend that owners install a boom knocker cam cleat on the end of the boom, and lead the dead-ended part of the mainsheet to it.

The running backstays were led to cam cleats in the cockpit in early Freedom 25s, but after losing several masts the builder now installs Barient #8 winches for extra safety. There are two low-profile Beckson ventilators mounted on the cabin house, and a lexan hatch made by Gray.

Interior

The Freedom 25 has what we feel is an attractive and sensible interior. She does not have standing headroom. For a 25-footer to have standing headroom, it must have either a high cabin house, which is ugly, has excessive windage and severely limits visibility from the cockpit, or it must have deep bilges, which often means poorer performance. A 6' person can move freely about the cabin of the Freedom 25 in relative comfort, though stooping is required.

There is an enclosed head, which we feel is essential for comfortable cruising. Too many small cruisers have Porta Potties under the forward V-berth. You wouldn't put one of those under your bed at home, so why should you on a boat? The Freedom 25 has a Groco head, which the builder claims has better seals than the Wilcox-Crittenden. It is equipped with a Y-valve for overboard or holding tank discharge.

The interior is trimmed in blond-colored ash, which lends a more open and warm appearance than teak. In general, we feel that teak should only be used on parts of the interior that are likely to get wet. The Freedom 25's cabin sole is teak and holly, and the companionway steps are also teak. However, the ash veneer on the settee berths extends to the floor, so it is easily blackened with scuff marks from shoes, and any salt water that may penetrate the finish will discolor the wood.

The settees in the main cabin have straight seat backs, which make for comfortable eating posture but are less comfortable for lounging about. The portable cabin table is fastened to the companionway steps with Faspins. When the table is set up you have to climb on it to get out of the cabin. Stepping on it is no cause for

worry, though, as it is one of the most sturdy tables we have ever seen on a boat this small.

The settees extend aft under the cockpit and widen into quarter berths that could be used as double berths in a pinch. The forward cabin is enclosed by the door to the head, and contains a V-berth divided in half by the mast. There is a bulkhead separating the head and the main cabin from the V-berth; to make it easier to climb through the opening in the bulkhead the front of the V-berth is cut back. This not only completes the separation of the V-berth's occupants, but it also makes each side of the berth uncomfortably narrow. One owner we talked to has put a piece of plywood and added a cushion across the front of the berth so he can sleep with his mate.

The galley consists of a small sink with a hand pump, and a two-burner pressurized alcohol stove made by Seaward. It can be a chore to use a galley in a boat without standing headroom. To solve this problem, the Freedom 25's galley is laid across the main bulkhead, so you can work at the galley while sitting on the settee. There is space under the sink for a medium-sized cooler. Food and knicknack storage space is ample, but the absence of a good clothes locker means you will be living out of a duffle bag. If you forego the inboard option, you gain storage space under the companionway.

There is no headliner on the Freedom 25; the overhead is sanded and finished with white gelcoat. All the deck fastenings are exposed for easy service. Bolts are capped with barrel nuts. On the boat we sailed, the finish was smooth in the main cabin, but unusually sloppy for Tillotson-Pearson around the companionway and cockpit.

CONCLUSIONS

We think the Freedom 25 is a pretty neat little boat. She's well built. Her interior is pleasing to the eye and comfortable for weekend cruising. The interior joinerwork is well above average. She gives you reasonable performance upwind and a real thrill downwind—all for much less effort from the crew than required by a conventionally-rigged boat. While she is a great coastal cruiser and singlehanded daysailer, the Freedom 25 is not a trailer-sailer. With her fin keel and heavy, keel-stepped mast, she is not easily launched from a trailer without a crane. There are also few cars on the road today that can pull her 3500 pounds of weight.

The Freedom 25 is not cheap, but she is less expensive than many 26' pocket cruisers. The base price is $21,900; the inboard is a $4600 option; and the Gun Mount a $1200 option; sails run about $1400 for the main, $750 for the spinnaker, and $100 for the spinnaker sock. This means that the sailaway price is still under $30,000.

The Freedom 25's rotating unstayed wing mast, fully-battened mainsail and Gun Mount spinnaker may be a bit too radical for the boat to be widely accepted in this decade. After all, it has taken Garry Hoyt nearly 10 years to convince the public of the merit of the simple unstayed mast with a wrap-around sail found on the older Freedom models. Hoyt is not waiting for acceptance, though; he plans to build a 21' (trailerable) and a 28' version of the Freedom 25. We expect that as her rig evolves, the mast will be made unbreakable and the clutter of the Gun Mount will be cleaned up. If so, it may truly be the wave of the future.

The O'Day 25 and The Montego 25: A Tale of Two Cruisers

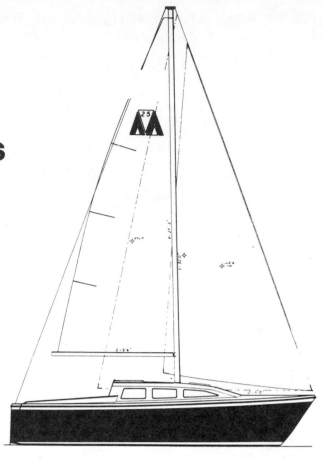

THE BOATS AND THE BUILDERS

The O'Day 25 is really two boats: a fairly fast, stiff, deep keel boat, and a slower, tippier, keel-centerboarder which has made performance compromises in order to create a maximum size trailer sailer.

The Montego 25, on the other hand, despite its shoal and deep draft versions, is too deep, wide, and heavy for ordinary trailering. It is a transition yacht,* by virtue of its size and accommodations.

The O'Day 25 is one of the most successful of all 25 footers. Almost 3,000 have been built in the eight years since its introduction, and they continue to be cranked out at a steady pace by Bangor Punta's Fall River, Massachusetts plant. The O'Day 25 tries to be the all-purpose 25-footer, with short or tall rig, deep or shallow draft, outboard or inboard power.

In trying to be the 25-footer for everyone, the O'Day 25 has made a number of compromises:

- beam is limited to 8' for uncomplicated trailering;
- the shoal draft version lacks the stability to carry the tall rig the boat needs for really good performance;
- the boat is heavy enough to require a size of outboard for auxiliary power that is a big handful.

At the same time, the sheer volume of production of the O'Day 25 means it is a boat whose cost is kept to a minimum, a boat with an established market value and good resale potential almost everywhere, and a thoroughly debugged boat. All of these are important considerations for the buyer of a 25-footer, who may already be looking forward to owning a 27- or 28-footer a few years down the line.

In addition, the keel-centerboard version of the O'Day 25 does provide a maximum-size trailerable cruiser with adequate accommodations for normal vacation-length coastal cruising. This assumes, of course, that you have a vehicle capable of towing 4,000+ lbs, and a heavy trailer — owners suggest a trailer with a capacity of 6,000 lbs. The O'Day 25 adds up to a big package for trailering.

By all indications it's a popular package. Almost 90% of the O'Day 25's sold have been the trailerable keel-centerboard version.

Surprisingly, fewer than half the respondents to our owners' survey considered shoal draft or trailerability of primary importance in their decision to buy an O'Day 25. This may be a reflection of a common phenomenon:

---

* A 'transition yacht' is a small cruiser, often "trailerable," that tries to offer the accommodations and performance of a larger boat. (See, "The 'Transition Yacht': How Big is Small?"

MONTEGO 25
Specifications

LOA	25'3"
LWL	20'6"
Beam	9'1"
Draft	standard 3'6"
	deep 4'6"
Displacement	4,550 lbs
Ballast	1,800 lbs
Sail Area	306 sq ft
	(100% foretriangle)

Universal Marine Corporation
1421 Bay Street SE
St. Petersburg, FL 33701

owners of maximum sized trailerables often find the hassle of trailering, launching, and rigging more than they care to go through for a day or weekend of sailing. After a year or two of this the boat ends up in a slip or on a mooring.

With the Montego 25, the decision has already been made to move from a trailerable to a non-trailerable boat. Despite characteristics such as a shoal draft option and outboard power, the Montego 25 buyer has made the choice to move into a boat whose home for the sailing season is a marina, rather than the driveway at home. The choice of shoal draft and outboard power for the Montego 25 are determined by the waters sailed and the depth of the buyer's pocket, rather than the need to keep weight and draft to a minimum for trailering.

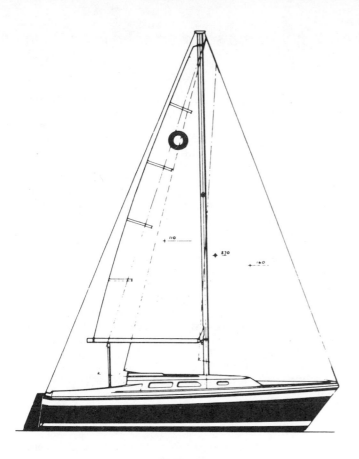

O'DAY 25
Specifications

LOA	24'10"
LWL	21'
Beam	8'
Draft	cb 2'3"
	keel 4'6"
Displacement	cb 4,007 lbs
	keel 3,962 lbs
Ballast	cb 1,825 lbs
	keel 1,775 lbs
Sail Area	cb 270 sq ft
	(100% foretriangle)
	keel 290 sq ft
	(100% foretriangle)

Bangor Punta Marine
Box 991
Fall River, MA 02722

CONSTRUCTION

The O'Day 25 and Montego 25 are generally similar in construction. Both are solid uncored hull layups with wood cored deck moldings. The Montego 25 uses plywood coring, the O'Day 25 uses balsa.

Both boats use what we consider to be "small boat" hull-to-deck joints. The O'Day 25 uses a simple coffee can or shoebox joint, fastened with self-tappers and adhesive compound. The Montego 25 uses an outward-turning flange which is riveted and glassed over on the inside. Vinyl rubrails cover the hull-to-deck joints on both boats.

This is the maximum size boat suitable for external hull-to-deck joining. External joints are subject to dam-

age in collisions or even in hard docking. Covering the external joint with a rubrail may give the impression that it's okay to use the joint as a bumper. It isn't.

Neither boat uses faired-in through hulls. A handy owner can resolve this lack in a couple of hours using epoxy and microballoons and a little elbow grease. Gelcoat quality of both boats is good.

Although both the Montego 25 and O'Day 25 come in shoal and deep draft versions, their approaches to the problem are quite different. Both the shoal and deep draft versions of the Montego 25 use external cast iron keels, bolted to a shallow keel stub. On the deep draft boat we examined, the keel had been faired to the stub using fiberglass cloth, which had begun to separate from the iron keel in several places after a season of use.

Any dings in an iron keel such as that of the Montego 25 should be ground to bright metal and coated with coal tar epoxy before applying bottom paint. Direct application of copper or tin bottom paint to an iron keel will create severe surface erosion if the boat is used in salt water.

The differing draft versions of the O'Day 25 are very different in character. To make the boat trailerable, the shoal draft O'Day 25 uses a long, shallow keel stub with inside lead ballast. A centerboard gives additional lateral plane for going to windward, but adds little to stability. Over the years, O'Day has gradually added several hundred pounds of inside ballast to the shoal draft 25 in order to improve stability, which has of course increased the weight for trailering.

In the deep draft O'Day 25, a deep glass stub keel replaces the long, shoal keel box of the centerboard boat. A high-aspect ratio fin keel is bolted to this stub keel, giving a substantial draft of 4'6". The external keel casting is lead, but it took a little work to figure that out. Some at O'Day said the keel was iron, others insisted it was lead. The argument was settled by drilling into the keel casting. It is, we can report with confidence, lead.

It's a good thing that the keel is lead, because it needs a bit of fairing to improve efficiency. The trailing edge is blunt, and the keel casting is poorly faired to the fiberglass stub keel. Lead planes almost as easily as hard wood, so refairing the keel of the deep draft O'Day 25 is a simple task. Of the dozen or so deep draft O'Day 25's we looked at, about half the owners had taken the time to fair the keels. It should be worth the effort in improved performance.

Some owners report trouble with the rudder of their O'Day 25. In the centerboard version, the rudder is five inches deeper than the keel stub. This means that the first part of the boat to contact the bottom when you run aground is the rudder. If you're moving along at a fair clip, a grounding can tear the rudder off the stern of the boat.

Construction of both boats is perfectly adequate for usage up to and including coastal cruising. We would not particularly want to take any boat of this size offshore, independent of the quality of construction.

PERFORMANCE

Handling under sail

The fin keel, tall rig O'Day 25 and the deep draft Montego 25 have identical PHRF ratings of 219. The rating of the O'Day 25 changes significantly with different rig, keel, and engine combinations.

The outboard powered keel-centerboarder, for example, has a rating of 234 — 15 seconds per mile slower than the deep keel, tall rig boat. This difference reflects the vastly different character of the two versions of the same boat. The deep keel boat has a more efficient lateral plane and a lower center of gravity, giving much better performance than the keel-centerboard model. Owners report the keel-centerboard boat to be tippy, and the fin keel boat to be stiff.

In addition, the tall rig of the deep keel boat gives slightly greater sail area — enough to make the boat a competitive family racer. Unless very shoal draft and trailerability are essential, the deep keel, tall rig version of the O'Day 25 is the obvious choice. The extra stability, extra sail area, and underbody efficiency add up to a boat that behaves more like a big boat than a small boat.

Both the deep keel and shallow keel versions of the Montego 25 are good performers. If the depth of your sailing waters allows, we would choose the deep keel version for the greater stability and extra lateral plane.

The rigs of the O'Day 25 and the Montego 25 are almost identical Kenyon rigs, but halyards of the Montego 25 lead aft to winches, while O'Day's winches are mast mounted.

These are big boat rigs, with substantial mast sections, airfoil spreaders, and good-sized standing rigging. Booms are set up for jiffy reefing. Mast fittings, tangs, and chainplates are substantially heavier than would be found on boats only marginally smaller.

In other words, these boats have transcended the "toy boat" syndrome so often seen on boats in the 20' to 25' range, and have rigs strong enough for more than fair-weather sailing.

Handling under power

The 4,000 lb O'Day 25 and 4,500 lb Montego 25 are at the real outside limit for using outboard power. With high freeboard and no remote controls, starting and throttle operation are a bit of a nuisance, since the outboard must be mounted far down the transom to keep the prop in the water. Remote outboard controls are a must.

Most owners will use a 10 hp outboard on either boat. In a flat calm, it should easily be able to push the boat. However, once there is any wind or sea, the weight and windage of these boats mean that a 10 hp outboard is close to minimum power. Unfortunately, a larger outboard is heavier, more expensive, and stretches the capacity of most outboard brackets. In addition, the propellor of any outboard will have trouble staying in the water as the boat pitches.

The O'Day 25 has a molded-in outboard fuel tank holder in the port side of the cockpit. The Montego 25 has none, so right away you must figure out where you'll keep the gas tank.

There is a growing tendency to put small diesels in boats of this size. Both the Montego and the O'Day offer the Yanmar 1GM as optional auxiliary power. O'Day charges $3900 for this option, Montego $4500.

Inboard power adds over 100 lbs to the weight of the O'Day 25 compared to the outboard version of the boat.

For a boat that's already pushing the upper limit of easily trailerable weight, every pound hurts.

However, inboard power greatly adds to either boat's function as a cruiser. If all your sailing is done on a lake — where strong winds and seas are not likely to be a problem — inboard power is probably an unnecessary expense. On the other hand, if you plan to do a considerable amount of cruising along the seacoast or in the Great Lakes, the convenience, range, and power of an inboard engine begins to make sense.

If we trailer-sailed on Lake Lanier, Georgia, for example, we might choose the centerboard O'Day 25 with outboard power. If we kept our O'Day 25 on a mooring in Newport, Rhode Island, and cruised to Block Island, Nantucket, and the Elizabeth Islands, we'd be more likely to choose the tall rig, deep keel O'Day 25 or the deep keel Montego 25 with inboard power.

These boats are really at the break-even point for the inboard power option. Most of the cost of the inboard installation will come back at resale time, unless you sail in a small inland lake. A five year old outboard, on the other hand, adds little or nothing to the value of the boat.

LIVABILITY

Deck layout

Neither boat has a particularly complicated deck layout. Both have an anchor well forward, single lifelines, and a fairly large cockpit.

Because its shrouds are set well inboard, it's far easier to get to the foredeck of the Montego 25. The inboard shrouds should also produce narrower sheeting angles and give better upwind performance.

Both boats have cockpit seats long enough to double as fair-weather berths. Both boats also have substantial bridgedecks, fitted with a mainsheet traveler. The mainsheet traveler on the O'Day 25, however, is merely a flat piece of track with a slider. Several O'Day 25 owners said they'd prefer a ball bearing traveler, such as that on the Montego 25. We would, too.

The tiller on both boats takes up a lot of the cockpit. In addition, the tiller fitting of the Montego 25 we examined had a fair amount of play in it. O'Day 25 owners report the same problem. This can frequently be remedied by the owner.

Belowdecks

The trade-off between a trailerable 25 footer and one not constrained in beam by the highway laws is immediately apparent when comparing accommodations of the Montego 25 and the O'Day 25. The extra foot of beam of the Montego 25 gives the boat much greater interior volume than the O'Day 25.

Much of the $4000 difference in price can also be explained by the interior of the two boats.

MONTEGO 25

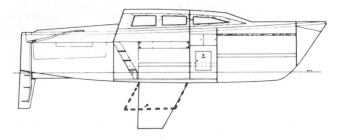
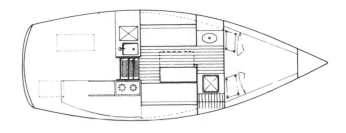

Unfortunately, the "How many does she sleep?" syndrome is alive and well in both boats, at the expense of storage space and galley space

O'Day has the fine art of mass production boatbuilding down pat. Nowhere is this better seen than in the interior of the O'Day 25. Much of the interior furniture is incorporated in the body pan. A fiberglass headliner finishes off the overhead. This saves a lot of time in building the boat, and keeps the cost down.

On the other hand, the Montego 25 also uses a molded body pan, but does not use a deck liner. Instead, the inside of the cabin trunk is faced with teak veneer, and the overhead is finished with a vinyl liner. The cabin sole of the Montego 25 is teak ply, and the boat uses a solid teak companionway ladder and solid teak companionway drop boards.

By contrast, the O'Day 25 has a fiberglass cabin sole, and uses a molded box step and the top of the galley counter as a companionway ladder. In other words, finish detail of the Montego 25 is better than that of the O'Day 25, and you pay a price for the difference.

Interior accommodations of the two boats are remarkably similar, but the extra beam of the Montego 25 gives greater elbow room. Headroom of the Montego 25 is almost 6' under the main hatch. The O'Day 25 has 5'6" headroom.

With V-berths forward, two main cabin settees, and a quarterberth, each boat sleeps five, although a slide-out settee in each brings nominal sleeping capacity to six. Do you really want to sleep six on a 25 footer? The zoo that the interior of either boat would be on a rainy morning when everyone was trying to get up and get dressed would probably be enough to turn the most sociable of sailors into a singlehander. Unfortunately, the "How many does she sleep?" syndrome is alive and well in both boats, at the expense of storage space and galley space.

Both boats are big enough to have a separate head compartment. Separate from the main cabin, that is. The head is really part of the forward cabin on both boats, a not unreasonable compromise in a five-berth 25 footer.

Small boat galleys rarely offer much except headache for the cook, and neither of these boats is an exception. The O'Day 25's icebox is tiny — the auxiliary box in the cockpit is really a daytime beer cooler — and is almost cut in half by the centerboard pennant trunk. While the O'Day 25 has a deep sink, it is almost directly underneath the companionway. Coming below with the boat heeled on port tack you're likely to put your foot in the sink.

The Montego 25 has a larger icebox with an insulated lid. The insulation for the lid is styrofoam, however, and is exposed on the underside of the lid. It is likely to take a lot of abuse.

The Montego 25 has a slide-away two burner alcohol galley stove which stores over the quarterberth. It is slightly easier to use than the same stove on the O'Day

25, which must be removed from a storage compartment and set on the galley counter for use. Since cooking under way is barely practical on a boat of this size, the lack of gimballing for the stoves is not a serious shortcoming.

Both boats have a reasonable amount of storage, as long as you don't want to unpack your seabag. Undersettee storage bins, found on both boats, would be far more useful with drop-in molded plastic trays, which are better for keeping things dry. O'Day offers the plastic trays as an option in the 25.

CONCLUSIONS

Both the Montego 25 and the O'Day 25 are good examples of the transition yacht — boats for owners wishing to move up from trailer sailers to small cruisers. Both retain some small boat features — outboard power, shoal draft options — while having many of the basic components of larger boats. These big boat features include deep draft options, sturdy cruising-type rigs, inboard power options, enclosed heads, and permanent galleys.

The shoal draft version of the O'Day 25 is still trailerable, but it is at the outside limit of size and displacement. The compromises in performance to make the O'Day 25 trailerable — short rig, less stability, keel-centerboard configuration — make the trailerable version of the boat more of a "small boat" than a "big boat."

Adding factory options to the O'Day 25 to make the boat comparable in equipment and features to the standard Montego 25 brings the price up to $19,400 from the base price of $18,600. The Montego 25 costs $23,900 with the same equipment.

Part of the difference in price is explained by the 500 lb difference in displacement of the boats. Boatbuilding materials cost money, and until you get into exotic lightweight construction, a heavier boat will always cost more than a light boat.

Much of the rest of the difference in the cost of the two boats is the result of O'Day's use of modular components, the large number of 25s they have built, and Montego's greater attention to finishing detail.

Equipped with an inboard engine and a deep keel, either boat will make a good coastal cruiser for a couple with two small children. Putting more people on the boat for anything but daysailing will be more like camping out than cruising.

At about $23,500, fully equipped and with inboard engine, the deep keel, tall rig O'Day 25 represents just about the minimum investment you can make in a new inboard-powered pocket cruiser. For the couple or small family moving up from a trailer sailer such as the O'Day 22, Catalina 22, or MacGregor 22, either the Montego 25 or the O'Day 25 provides a true transition from the weekender to the true pocket cruiser, at a minimum investment.

O'DAY 25

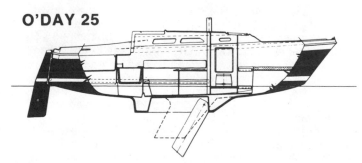
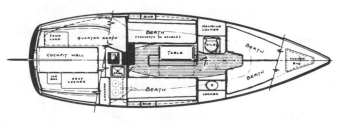

The Stiletto Catamaran: Performance at a Price

THE BOAT AND THE BUILDER

Many sailors consider multihull sailing to be on the fringe of our sport. If that is true, then the Stiletto catamaran is dangling one hull off the edge. It's hard to mistake her appearance, with blazing topside graphics and aircraft-style, pop-top companionway hatches. It's also hard for the average sailor to appreciate the sophistication of the Stiletto's construction—epoxy-saturated fiberglass over a Nomex honeycomb core.

The 26'10" Stiletto is anything but conventional. Multihulls larger than 20' can usually be classified into one of two genre. The largest group is that of the "cruising" multihull, characterized by beamy hulls, with a cabin house across the bridgedeck, stubby under-canvassed rigs, and monohull-like displacements. They often have mediocre performance, and are sometimes regarded with embarassment by multihull enthusiasts.

The other genre of large multihulls is characterized by light displacement, powerful rigs and lean interiors. Custom ocean racing trimarans fall into this category, as do a very few production catamarans like the Stiletto.

The Stiletto's builder touts her trailerability, "scorching performance" and "cruising comforts." She is supposed to be the next step for the sailor weaned on small high-performance catamarans. In fact, three of the five owners we spoke to were former Hobie 16 sailors.

Almost anyone can understand why catamarans like the Hobie 16 are so popular—they offer breathtaking performance without making great demands on a sailor's expertise or pocketbook. To step up to a Stiletto is expensive, however. She is offered in three versions. For $17,950 in 1982, the Standard Stiletto had a mainsail and a jib, but stripped interior and no options. The racing version, called the Championship Edition, came with a few options like deck hatches, rubrails and removable berths, plus extra racing sails, winches and a knotmeter; it cost $22,900. The cruising version, called the Special Edition, cost $24,900. That healthy chunk of cash bought the boat equipped with the options needed for pocket cruising, such as galley, head, berths, carpeted interior and running lights. The builder reports that 75% of Stilettos sold are Special Editions, 20% are Standard and 5% are Championship.

Force Engineering, a small, high-tech outfit in Sarasota, Florida, formed to build the Stiletto in 1978. Since that time, they have produced more than 300 of them. Before he joined Force Engineering, co-owner/marketing director Larry Tibbe was an aircraft account salesman for Ciba-Geigy, a manufacturer of Nomex. Nomex coring is used in a variety of aircraft parts (for example, helicopter blades). Force makes several non-marine products out of Nomex, which helped them survive the recession of 1981. Force employed 35 people when business was booming, but most were laid off in 1981, according to Tibbe. When we visited the plant in March, 1982, Force had only 17 employees. Tibbe said orders were beginning to roll in

Specifications

LOA	26'10"
LWL	24'
Beam	13'10"
Draft—board up	9"
board down	4'
Sail Area:	
Main	230 sq ft
Jib	106 sq ft
Reacher/Drifter	265 sq ft
Displacement	1100-1570 lbs

Force Engineering
Sarasota, Florida

and he was planning to hire more help, but he admitted that Force could not have survived a spring as bad as the winter. Tibbe says they also have plans to build a 50' IOR racer and a 60' OSTAR trimaran, both out of Nomex.

The boat owners we talked to had no negative comments about dealer/builder service. One Stiletto sailor from New Jersey's Barnegat Bay reported that his dealer serviced a broken chainplate eye, even though his boat was out of warranty. The dealer shipped the boat to Florida, where it was repaired and shipped back, all free of charge.

The deck is only epoxied to the hull without screws or bolts, inviting separation in the event of a catastrophic collision

The Stiletto class organization holds a national championship each year. Class organizations help owner/builder relations, and maintain interest which enhances resale value. Owners report that their boats have appreciated. Probably due to shipping costs, most of the boats are sold to east coast sailors; the biggest fleet, 44 boats, is in Annapolis, Maryland. Freight, which costs 85¢/mile, is significant on a $20,000 boat (roughly $2500 for west coast delivery).

CONSTRUCTION

Very few boats are cored with Nomex honeycomb as are the Stiletto's hulls and bridgedeck. Sandwiching a core material between two layers of fiberglass laminate is not a new technique; many boatbuilders use cores of balsa wood, Airex foam or Klegecell foam. Core construction offers several advantages over single-skin construction. It is stiffer for a given weight, lighter for a given stiffness, makes the boat quieter and reduces condensation.

Honeycomb is rarely used for boatbuilding because the molding procedure is far more sophisticated (and expensive) than with balsa or foam cores. Honeycomb can be made of several materials. We question the use of paper or aluminum honeycomb in boats, because of their susceptibility to water damage should the outer laminate of the core be ruptured. The Stiletto's Nomex honeycomb core is made of nylon.

Force Engineering claims that a Nomex honeycomb-cored panel, for a given weight, is stronger, stiffer, less brittle and more puncture resistant than foam or wood cores. Nomex is also said to be impervious to water, so there would be no water migration between the honeycomb cells should the outer skin be ruptured.

These grandiose claims depend on a sophisticated and expensive molding procedure. Getting the honeycomb to bond to the fiberglass skins isn't easy. First, Force Engineering buys its fiberglass cloth *preimpregnated* with epoxy resin. Most boat builders use polyester resin, which is an inferior adhesive, and saturate the fiberglass after it has been laid into the mold—a messy and inexact procedure. Preimpregnated cloth, or "prepreg," has an exact resin-to-cloth ratio, which means that the builder always has the optimum strength-to-weight ratio. Most boat builders must err on the resin-rich side when saturating cloth, which increases weight but not strength.

To keep the prepreg cloth from curing before it is laid into the Stiletto mold, it must be shipped and stored in a refrigerator. To completely cure the prepreg after layup, the mold is placed in a long, modular oven and baked at 250° for 90 minutes. At the same time, the fiberglass skins are vacuum-bagged to the honeycomb to ensure proper adhesion. Vacuum-bagging cored hulls is not a new technique, but for many builders it simply means laying a sheet of plastic into the mold and sucking the air out with a single pump (polypropylene line is often placed under the plastic to help distribute the vacuum). Force Engineering uses a blotter to absorb any excess resin and 15 spigots to distribute the vacuum, a more effective technique. When finished, each of the Stiletto's hulls weighs only 220 lbs. and is impressively strong and stiff.

The Stiletto's hull and bridgedeck may be state-of-the-art, but the rest of her rig, like her aluminum mast and crossbeams, is built with conventional (and relatively heavy) technology. All-up, the Stiletto weighs 1100 to 1570 lbs, depending on optional equipment. By comparison, an Australian-made, single skin imitation of the Stiletto has hulls that weigh more than double the Stiletto's, but the all-up weight of the boat is only 2000 lbs.

All of Force Engineering's business revolves around the molding of Nomex products. They are the leading proponent (and salesman) of honeycomb to the marine industry. They fervently believe that it is the material of the future for tomorrow's weight conscious boat owner. We wonder whether building the Stiletto of Nomex is worth the extra trouble and expense, or if she is being used as a platform to prove the material's viability.

Gelcoat cannot be used in the Stiletto's molding process. Instead, each boat must be faired with putty and painted with polyurethane. Paint has the advantage that it will not chalk like gelcoat, but it is more susceptible to nicks, scrapes and peeling, especially if improperly applied. The Stiletto's optional hull graphics are sticky-backed vinyl. Both the paint and the graphics were chipping on one five-year-old Stiletto we looked at.

The spars and the crossbeams are also painted with polyurethane. Although Force says it carefully sands and primes the spars, several of the masts we looked at had adhesion problems. The fittings were unbedded. The crossbeams were not anodized, and were only painted on the outside. Water can get inside the beams and accelerate corrosion.

The deck rests on an inward-turned hull flange, a common, safe design. But the deck is only epoxied to the hull without screws or bolts, inviting separation in the event of a catastrophic collision. Epoxy is undoubtedly stronger than polyester. However, we prefer mechanical fastenings in addition to a flexible adhesive like 3M 5200.

The Stiletto has a single daggerboard that is mounted on centerline through a slot in the bridgedeck. It is held snugly in place by a latticework of stainless steel tubes extending downward from the underside of the bridgedeck. This daggerboard frame is designed to collapse in the event of a hard grounding; a new frame costs under $200. There is no chance of the hull rupturing, as there would be with a daggerboard trunk built into the hull itself. The Stiletto's single board is not as efficient as the dual boards found on other catamarans, and the board's support frame does tend to drag in the water while sailing. To keep water from squirting through the bridgedeck slot, the slot is covered by cloth gaskets. The gaskets occasionally jam.

Full length battens dampen luffing, so the sail will last much longer. However, this inability to luff can present a real safety problem in a sudden squall

The Stiletto has an airfoil daggerboard. Older models were made of wood, and chipped trailing edges were a common problem. The board now is molded of fiberglass and more resistant to minor damage.

The Stiletto gets high marks for her rudders. They have strong aluminum heads and double lower pintles. To be beachable, a catamaran must have kick-up rudders; these kick-up systems often refuse to work when you need them most. However, the Stiletto's rudders worked smoothly and positively.

PERFORMANCE

Trailerability

Force Engineering emphasizes the Stiletto's trailerability. True, she is light enough to be pulled by a modern automobile of modest power. But all of the owners we talked to said they rarely, if ever, trail their boats. Force says 80% of the boats are sold with trailers, but it appears that most are used only for winter storage.

Rigging and launching the Stiletto is not a simple chore, despite the fact that the builder claims a man and woman can do it in only 45 minutes. Owners say it takes at least several men well over an hour to do the job. The Stiletto has a beam of 13' 10"; legal highway trailering width in most states is 8'. To solve this problem, both the Stiletto's crossbeams and the trailer collapse to legal width. The compression tube that spans the bows must be removed for trailering, as must the dolphin striker beneath the mast step, and the 125 lb. bridgedeck.

To raise and lower the mast, the headstay is shackled to a short, pivoting gin pole mounted just aft of the trailer winch. The winch is used to pull the gin pole, which in turn provides leverage to hoist the heavy mast. Owners say that lifting the bridgedeck and manhandling the spar is next to impossible with just a man and woman. The Stiletto assembly manual points out, *". . . she never fails to draw a crowd, so help is usually available if you are shorthanded."* As long as you have the muscle, this clever system does work.

Sailing

The Stiletto is a performance catamaran. In a breeze, owners report, she is as fast or faster than a Hobie 16, but a bit undercanvassed in light air, especially with her 106 square foot working jib. This is preferable to overcanvassing; a catamaran of the Stiletto's size cannot afford, for safety's sake, to be a bear in heavy air.

According to owners, the Stiletto does not have some of the bad heavy air habits of smaller catamarans. They say she is relatively dry to sail, does not hike up and "fly a hull" too easily, has no tendency to pitchpole, and does not get "light" as she comes off a big wave sailing upwind. Like most catamarans, the Stiletto has a fully-battened mainsail. The advantage of these sails is that they can have a much larger roach, and because the battens dampen luffing, the sail will last much longer. However, this inability to luff can present a real safety problem in a sudden squall. The builder says it is prudent to reef when the wind reaches 20 knots. A smaller roached, short-battened cruising mainsail is available as an option for offshore cruising. The sails that come as standard equipment seem to be of better than average OEM quality.

Stiletto sailors told us that they sail very cautiously in a strong breeze, knowing the dangers of capsizing so large a multihull. Once capsized, a catamaran turns turtle (completely upside down) very quickly. A turtled multihull with a mast full of water is nearly impossible to right. The Stiletto's builder offers a self-righting kit as an option, but they have sold very few. The kit consists of a bulky foam float permanently mounted to the masthead, and a 17' righting pole stowed under the bridgedeck. The float is supposed to prevent the boat from turning turtle while the righting pole is extended outward and its three stays are rigged to the underside of the boat. Then two crew swim out to a ladder dangling from the end of the pole, climb up to right the boat, then quickly swim free before the ladder drags them 17' toward Davy Jones Locker. It's no small wonder that the self-righting kit is not a popular option.

Force Engineering points out that the air cells of her honeycomb construction make her unsinkable in the event of a holing or capsize. However, they do not point out that once the hull is flooded, the boat cannot be sailed or motored home without inviting the flooded hull to submerge and pitchpole the boat.

The Price of Performance

Multihulls are separated from the monohull mainstream by several things (in addition to the number of hulls). The first is performance. Multihulls, particularly catamarans, are lighter, more easily driven and hence far more exhilarating to sail than most monohulls. Yet even a novice can enjoy catamaran performance in most wind conditions because of the tremendous initial stability that a catamaran's beam offers.

The flip side of this hot performance is safety. Catamarans also have tremendous stability after they have capsized and turned turtle. All but the smallest catamarans are nearly impossible to right after they have gone completely upside down, especially if the mast is not airtight.

When reaching in strong winds, many catamarans have a nasty tendency to bury the leeward hull and pitchpole. Some cats can even be blown over backwards if a very strong puff catches the underside of the trampoline. Nearly all trimarans that are raced offshore have watertight hatches on the *bottom* of the main hull to allow the crew to escape if the boat flips over.

Another price of performance is comfort. Multihulls tend to be wet. When you're flying along at 20 knots, even a light spray can feel like a firehose. It's harder to find a comfortable spot to relax in when you're sailing. The trampoline/bridgedeck separating the two hulls of a catamaran is usually flat—you sit *on* it, not *in* it. Moreover, the hulls of a thoroughbred multihull are narrow, so there is little space in which to put creature comforts. The wide-hulled, cabin-housed "cruising" catamarans are no more spritely than a monohull of similar displacement.

Multihulls are also less maneuverable than monohulls. They can be difficult to tack without getting into irons, and they have a much wider turning radius. Sailing in a crowded harbor takes greater care.

The bridgedeck, which is where you spend most of your time, has no seats and is said by several owners to be uncomfortable

The Stiletto, like most high-performance catamarans, has a rotating mast. Owners say they have not had problems with the mast popping out of rotation while sailing upwind. The older masts have only athwartships diamond shrouds; the newer masts have an added third diamond extended forward to control fore-and-aft bend in a strong breeze. This three-diamond system is strongly welded together and a real plus for heavy weather sailing.

LIVABILITY

Deck Layout

The Stiletto has a solid bridgedeck stretched between the two hulls aft of the mast, and a polypropylene cloth trampoline forward of the mast. Those few sailors planning to venture offshore might want to remove the trampoline, lest it collect water in heavy seas. On Stilettos older than two years, the trampoline is laced with a series of hooks. On the newer boats the trampoline has bolt rope edges, and slides into tracks on the hull and crossbeams, a simpler and cleaner system.

The bridgedeck, which is where you spend most of your time, has no seats and is said by several owners to be uncomfortable. Because of this, the temptation when sailing is to sit on top of the flimsy companionway hatches. We feel that a "cruising" catamaran should have proper seats with angled seatbacks.

A wire stretched between the bows forward of the headstay acts as a traveler for the optional reacher/drifter. Most sailors opt for this sail before they buy a cruising spinnaker. Poleless cruising spinnakers are more effective on a catamaran than on a monohull because they can be tacked on the weather hull, away from the blanketing effect of the mainsail. A roller furling headsail with a Hood Seafurl system is a $777 option. Headsail winches are standard on the Championship Edition, otherwise they're a $160 option. A main halyard winch, which owners recommend, is a $133 option.

The Stiletto has a ball-bearing mainsheet traveler, a worthy item rarely found on catamarans. But the mainsheet has only a 6-to-1 purchase, which owners say is insufficient in a breeze. The tiller extension passes behind the mainsheet and the tiller crossbar is adjustable so you can align the two rudders. The jibsheets are led to Harken ratchets to make trimming easier. The outboard engine bracket is hung off the aft compression beam.

Interior

Those of you who have peeked below on the Stiletto might ask, "What interior?" It's a valid question. The Standard Stiletto version is nothing but an empty shell below. Depending on the care that was taken during the vacuum-bagging process, the interior hull surface can be smooth or quite rippled. Either way, the Nomex gives the boat a long-lasting smell similar to mouse droppings (we could still smell it on a five year old boat).

The popular Special Edition is described by the builder as a "luxury coastal cruiser"; though it costs nearly $25,000, we would be more comfortable on a $10,000 Catalina 22. The Special Edition's interior is completely covered — ceilings, overhead and sole — with Aqua Tuft marine carpeting. Owners say it is durable and does not mildew, but we feel carpet belongs in a house, not a boat.

The Stiletto has the narrow hulls of a fast catamaran, which means that her berths are only 31" wide. The Special Edition has 14' of built-in berth forward of the companionway in each hull. For two people to sleep easily in a berth, they have to lie end-to-end. Crawling toward the bow to get to the forward berth is like crawling down a narrowing tunnel—it gave us claustrophobia. If a normal-sized couple really wanted a good night's sleep, they woud have to bed down in separate hulls. There is stowage area under the berths, but access to it is just plain difficult.

The Special Edition has a self-contained head under one berth. Porta Potties and their ilk usually begin to reek before a weekend cruise is over. A pump-out head is not an option. The Special Edition also has a small galley built of "marble finish" plastic laminate over plywood; we think that even the most "with it" cat sailor would consider it gaudy. The galley has a sink with a hand pump and a 2-gallon water tank. There is no permanently mounted stove; a portable stove is more practical for the weekend crusier.

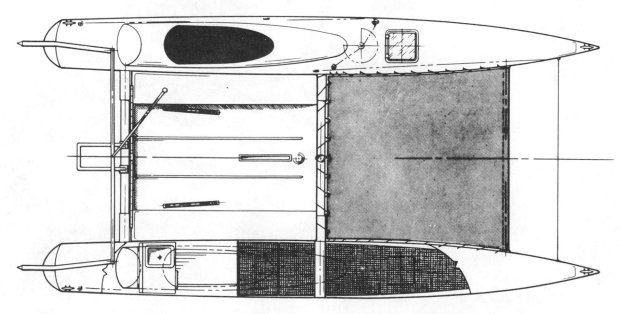

An option that we recommend is the $695 mosquito-tight bridgedeck tent. The bridgedeck cushions that are standard on the Special Edition should make the tent, and hence the whole boat, somewhat livable. The Special Edition is also the only version of the Stiletto that has running and interior lights.

Perhaps the most distinctive feature of the Stiletto is her conical companionway hatches (canopies is what the builder calls them). It's hard to be impartial about their appearance—you either like 'em or you don't. We don't. The canopies are formed of dark, bendy plastic. They open vertically like a pop-top hatch, and swing on flimsy aluminum tubes that are not well secured to their mounts.

Owners say the canopies are watertight, but the rubber gaskets in which they sit were rotting badly on the older boats we saw. For that matter, the rubber gaskets on the bridgedeck were rotting, too. Trying to sleep in the Stiletto's hulls could be very stuffy on a rainy night. Because the canopies rock forward as they "pop-up," it's hard to leave them open a crack like a conventional hatch, and there are no companionway boards.

CONCLUSIONS

There is probably no production hull built in the US with a better strength-to-weight ratio than the Stiletto catamaran. Her Nomex honeycomb fabrication is truly impressive. But is it necessary? Just as some builders "overkill" with heavy solid laminates, we feel that Force Engineering has overkilled in the other direction. Conventional coring probably could have created an adequately strong and light boat that would have provided just as much sailing fun for less money.

The next question is, "What do you do with her?" The Stiletto seems to appeal to the catamaran sailor hooked on high performance, but who wants a boat in which he can "go someplace." The Stiletto is quick, but she won't get someplace any faster than a small catamaran. She may be dryer, but she still lacks comfortable seating and sleeping. When you get to where you are going you have very little comfort for $25,000 worth of boat. And when you get home, you have a considerable chore ahead of you if you plan to load her onto a trailer.

All the owners we talked to said they love the way the boat sails and have no complaints about her construction or about dealer service. Yet we still don't feel the Stiletto is practical. There are other, less expensive options for the multihull sailor who wants to weekend cruise. Any catamaran can be rigged with a tent on the trampoline/bridgedeck. Inflatable air mattresses stow easily and make fine temporary berths. And some catamarans, like the $5000 P-Cat 2/18, have the dry stowage in their hulls to carry camping supplies. Small catamarans are ultimately safer, because they can be righted from a capsize, and they are infinitely easier to trailer.

The Hunter 27: Popular Basic Boat

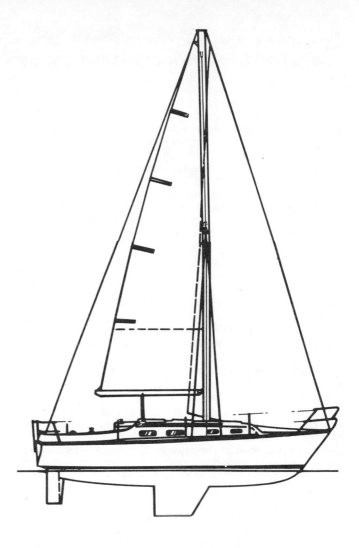

THE BOAT AND THE BUILDER

The Hunter 27 is the third smallest boat in the Hunter line, which presently includes boats from 22' to 37' in length. The Hunter 27 is a popular boat with first-time sailboat buyers, and with small-boat sailors purchasing their first auxiliary cruising boat. Since the boat was introduced in 1975, more than 2,000 have been built.

Like other boats with a reasonably long production run, the Hunter 27 has gone through minor changes since its introduction. Wheel steering is now standard. The boat utilizes a split backstay to allow a stern boarding ladder and to prevent the helmsman from hitting his head on a centerline backstay. All the ports open for ventilation. There is now only a diesel inboard version, rather than both inboard and outboard-powered models. The mainsheet lead has been altered, and there have been other minor modifications, such as a switch to European-style pulpits and running lights.

Judging from the response of Hunter owners we've talked to, all Hunters, including the 27, are purchased for one reason: price. The Hunter 27 is just about the cheapest diesel-powered 27' cruising boat money can buy. The average price of the typical used Hunter 27 of any vintage is, for example, about $5,000 to $6,500 less than that of the typical Catalina 27 of the same vintage.

In their advertising literature, Hunter stresses that efficiency in construction, standardization of components, and low overhead keep their prices low. To some extent, this is true, and it is neither new, nor is it anything to be ashamed of. The Herreshoff Manufacturing Company, known neither for cheap boats nor low quality, pioneered in component standardization and assembly-line construction.

By eliminating factory-installed options, every Hunter 27 can be built the same. No going to the stockroom for an optional item. No time-consuming reading of each boat's specifications as it moves down the assembly line.

There are trade-offs, however. An inability to custom-tailor a boat. A lack of flexibility in deck layout. The Hunter 27 owner must customize his boat at the dealer level, or do it himself. This appeals to dealers, who often make as much on the installation of options as they do on commissions.

The Hunter 27 is a bit high-sided and sterile looking. High freeboard and a high cabin trunk are almost necessary in a 27' boat that claims over 6' of headroom. The sterility comes from the Hunter bone white on bone white color scheme, and paucity of external teak trim. Exterior teak is to the fiberglass boatbuilding industry what chrome is to Detroit. There are no hull and deck color options.

Specifications

LOA	27'2"
LWL	22'
Beam	9'3"
Draft: Shoal keel	3'3"
Deep keel	4'3"
Displacement	7000 lbs
Ballast: Shoal keel	3200 lbs
Deep keel	3000 lbs
Sail area	360.2 sq ft

Hunter Marine
Route 441
Alachua, Florida 32615

CONSTRUCTION

Construction of the Hunter 27 is solid glass layup, with plywood reinforcement in high-stress areas such as winch mountings and locker tops. Gelcoat and finish quality of the hull molding are good. No roving print-through is evident, and the hull is quite fair—more than can be said for many more expensive boats.

The hull-to-deck joint of the Hunter 27 is simple and strong. The hull molding has an internal flange molded at right angles to the hull at deck level. This flange is heavily coated with adhesive bedding, the deck molding is laid over the flange, and the joint covered with a slotted aluminum toerail which is through-bolted with stainless steel bolts at 6" intervals. This is an obvious and very satisfactory answer to the hull-to-deck joint problem. The faying surfaces of the joint appear to match well, and the adhesive compound has squeezed out along the joint where it can be inspected.

Across the transom, the joint is less satisfactory. The gelcoat and putty with which the joint is faired at the stern was sloppy on every boat we examined.

The keel of the Hunter 27 is a narrow, high aspect lead fin weighing 3,000 lbs. The shoal draft version has a much shallower lead fin weighing 3,200 lbs. The additional weight of the shoal keel is to make up for the shift in the vertical center of gravity of the boat that would occur if a shoal keel of the same weight as the deep fin were to be used.

The keel-to-hull joint has caused problems in some Hunter 27s. The narrowness of the lead keel at the point of attachment to the hull results in considerable leverage on the hull when the boat heels. Several Hunter 27 owners who returned *The Practical Sailor* boatowner evaluations report oilcanning of the hull, leaking keelbolts, or vertical misalignment of the hull and keel. We have observed this vertical misalignment in the Hunter 25, but we have not seen it specifically in the 27.

The chainplates of the Hunter 27 consist of stainless steel U-bolts fastened through the anodized aluminum toerail. No backing plates are used with these. The chainplates are likely to carry any load to which they will normally be subjected. However, a simple U-bolt, no matter how heavy, is a poor choice for a primary chainplate unless the arc of the U-bolt is radiussed to the diameter of the clevis pin which goes through it, and unless the strain on the bolt lines up with its vertical axis. U-bolt chainplates of the correct configuration are used in some European boats, notably the Nicholson and Bowman lines. Both of these lines of boats carry Lloyd's Bureau of Shipping classification certificates. We strongly suggest that Hunter 27 owners consider installing aluminum or stainless steel backing plates under their U-bolt chainplates, and check them periodically to be sure that the nuts are tight. With only two nuts on each shroud anchorage, this check is extremely important.

The rig is a modern, high aspect ratio masthead sloop. The mast is a deck-stepped, white Kenyon spar, supported by a wood compression column attached to the main bulkhead. We have seen no sign of compression stress in the Hunter 27 mast step.

Hunter uses gate valves on underwater skin fittings. We prefer seacocks. We also prefer some kind of shutoff valve on any skin fitting remotely near the waterline. Few builders provide them. Hunter is no exception.

PERFORMANCE

Handling Under Sail

The Hunter 27 comes with a mainsail and 110% genoa. The total sail area with this configuration is 360 square feet, an average amount for a modern 7,000 lb boat. A larger genoa will be required for sailing in light-air areas.

Despite a ballast/displacement ratio of almost 43%, owners do not consider the Hunter 27 a stiff boat under sail. They also consider the boat's performance under sail only fair to good. There are several reasons for the boat's mediocre sailing qualities.

The boat comes factory-equipped with sails. This means cheaper sails, for they are bought in quantity by the builder. It also, almost inevitably, means sails that are not designed for specific local conditions. Average sails make for average performance.

There is no provision for headsail sheeting angle adjustment. Without genoa track, all headsails must sheet to the slotted toerail. On a wide 27-footer with this arrangement, the headsail slot will rarely be the proper width for good windward performance. With a small headsail, the lead will almost always be too far outboard.

There is also no traveler for the mainsheet. This limits the creation of the proper angle of attack of the mainsail, and complicates draft control.

A relatively fat boat such as the Hunter 27 rapidly acquires weather helm as the boat heels. This is due in part to the asymmetry of the boat's submerged sections. The judicious use of sail controls such as travelers, vangs, and flattening reefs greatly enhances

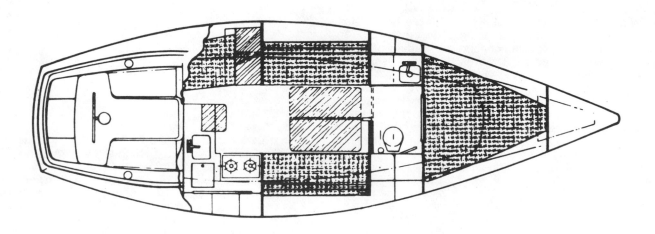

Windward performance is one of the trade-offs made for low price. The buyer must decide how much it is worth to him

the ability to keep the boat sailing on her feet, which will help reduce weather helm. Hunter 27 owners complain that the boat suffers from extreme weather helm.

Chainplates set at the outboard edge of the deck also compromise windward performance. This arrangement makes it almost impossible to close the slot effectively with a large headsail.

If the Hunter 27 were equipped with well-made sails, inboat chainplates, inboard and outboard headsail tracks, a good vang, and a mainsheet traveler, we suspect that there would be a substantial improvement in the boat's windward ability. There would also be a marked difference in price. Should you desire to make these changes, the parts would probably cost about $1500. Then the problems begin. How do you attach the chainplates? Will the deck take the vertical loading that will be on the track? Can the boom handle heavy vang loads? We are not talking about turning the Hunter 27 into a hot racer. We are only talking about improving the performance of the boat to a reasonable level for cruising.

Windward performance, then, is one of the trade-offs made for low price. Only the prospective purchaser, after considering how the boat is to be used, can decide how much that is worth.

Since the shoal-draft Hunter 27 is more heavily-ballasted than the deep-draft version, its stability is likely to be similar. However, the deep, high aspect ratio fin is likely to be more efficient.

Handling Under Power

With only eight horsepower to push around a 7,000 lb, high-sided boat, do not expect a Hunter 27 to be a sprightly performer under power. In 1979, the power plant of the Hunter 27 was changed from the eight horsepower Renault diesel. The Renault diesels are relatively untried in the US marine market. The Yanmar engines, though noisy and noted for their vibration, are also known for their reliability.

At least one owner we talked to was, to put it mildly, disappointed with the Renault installation. Although the engine runs well, the attachment of the shifting mechanism to the transmission lever has the disconcerting habit of vibrating itself loose. When docking, the results of this shortcoming could be less than amusing to both the boatowner and his insurance company.

Owners of Renault-powered Hunter 27s should definitely be aware of this potential problem.

Another owner reported leaking strut bolts and shaft wear due to improper shaft alignment. All engine installations should be realigned after the boat is launched for the first time. This should be a routine part of commissioning, but it rarely is.

Engine access is good, behind the removable companionway ladder. There is partial soundproofing in the engine enclosure, but not enough to shield the interior from a substantial amount of noise.

Fuel capacity is 12.5 gallons, in an aluminum tank located in the starboard cockpit locker. The tank is held in place by a stainless steel strap. There is no grounding jumper between the fuel fill and the tank. This is in violation of the standards for fuel tank installation of the American Boat and Yacht Council, which sets minimum standards used in the industry.

Owners consider the boat underpowered with either the Renault or Yanmar engines. They consider the boat's performance under power only fair to good.

LIVABILITY

Deck Layout

Because the Hunter 27's decks are relatively free of sail control hardware, there are relatively few toe stubbers. Even the grayest cloud has a silver lining.

New Hunter 27s have international style running lights mounted on the bow and stern pulpits. These are far superior to the inhull running lights on older Hunters, and better than those used on many more expensive boats. New boats also have a good-sized foredeck anchor well, incorporating a well-designed latch and a heavy stainless steel eye for the attachment of the bitter end of the anchor rode. The well has a large scupper which drains through the stem.

Although owners consider the cockpit of the Hunter 27 small, we find it comfortable for five, and certainly large enough for a 27' boat. Wheel steering has definitely made the cockpit seem bigger. With five people in the cockpit, the stern of the boat begins to squat. A bigger cockpit would only encourage sailing with more people, causing the boat to squat even more.

Current models have Yacht Specialties pedestal steering. There is good provision for an emergency tiller, which is supplied with the boat.

Because the decks are relatively free of sail control hardware, there are few toe stubbers. The boat would perform better, though, with a few modifications such as inboard chainplates, outboard headsail tracks, and a mainsheet traveler

Access to the steering gear is excellent, through the lazarette locker. Unfortunately, because the steering gear, scupper hoses, and exhaust hose go through this locker, it cannot be used for storage. To do so would be to risk damage to vital parts of the ship's systems.

There is a large locker under the starboard cockpit seat. Unfortunately, because the fuel tank is located in this locker, nothing can really be stowed there without risking damage to the fuel system. Wet lines or sails stored in the locker would drip on the aluminum tank, inviting corrosion. Shelves installed in both these lockers would make them more useful. The shelves should not limit access to systems, however.

To raise the cockpit sill above the level of the lowest cockpit coaming, the lower dropboard must be left in place. This complicates access below when underway, but having the companionway blocked up to deck level is essential for sailing in unsheltered waters or heavy weather.

The cockpit bulkhead slopes forward. This means that a dodger must be installed if one wishes to ventilate the cabin in rain or heavy weather.

The high cockpit coamings provide good backrests for those sitting in the cockpit. They should also help keep the cockpit dry. These coamings have molded-in

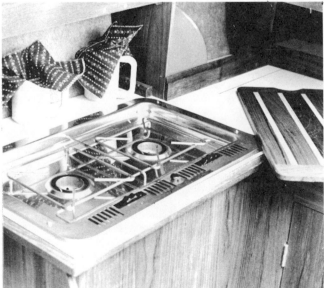

sheet winch islands. The owner wishing to upgrade to winches larger than the standard Lewmar 7s will discover that the islands are too small for a much larger winch. For the owner who wishes to use a large genoa, this could be a real problem. Despite these shortcomings, the T-shaped cockpit is reasonably comfortable, and is one of the boat's better design features.

Interior

The Hunter 27 is a roomy boat. Headroom is just over 6' under the main hatch, and almost 5'10" at the forward end of the main cabin.

The forepeak contains a double berth. Aft of that cabin is a full-width head. Newer Hunter 27s have a holding tank system. Older boats are likely to have Porta Potties.

The main cabin has settee berths port and starboard. These settees extend under the forward bulkhead. While this arrangement reduces seating area, it also allows more room for the galley and quarterberth. It's a reasonable trade-off.

To port, at the aft end of the cabin, there is a quarterberth. A folding chart table is located over the forward end of the quarterberth. To starboard is the galley, with sink, two-burner alcohol stove, and icebox.

With eight opening ports, two opening hatches, and the companionway, ventilation in new Hunter 27s is excellent at anchor in good weather. Older models have fewer opening ports. As with many boats, there is no provision for ventilation in heavy weather.

With a molded glass headliner, teak-finished bulkheads, solid teak trim, and teak cabin sole, the cabin has a finished appearance. There is good storage for a boat of this size for short-term cruising. Joinerwork is of fair stock boat quality. It is greatly improved over earlier Hunters, however.

CONCLUSIONS

At a sailaway price of $29,500, commissioned in southern New England, the Hunter 27 is about the least expensive boat in its class—$4,000 to $7,000 cheaper than many other boats of this size. The boat also comes standard with items that are optional on other boats, such as wheel steering, life jackets, anchor, and fire extinguishers.

However, it is not realistic to expect a boat that is 15% cheaper than another boat of the same size and type to be equivalent in quality. There is just so much that efficiency, standardization, and bulk buying can do toward reducing the price of a boat. Inevitably, the price of a boat is a function the time, materials, and incidental costs that go into it. There is no magic way to reduce the cost of building a boat.

The Hunter 27 graphically demonstrates how costs can be reduced. A great deal of time is saved in construction by hurrying finish work, by using staples instead of screws, by eliminating the necessity to customize each boat.

Hunter owners are the first to admit the influence that the low price of the boat had on their boatbuying decision. Many are happy with their boats. Some are defensive about them, and others are really unhappy with them. For the relatively unsophisticated sailboat buyer—the new sailor, the powerboat convert—the Hunter 27 may represent a good value. As his experience grows, we expect he will be willing to pay more, in order to get more.

The Sabre 28: A Quality Cruiser-Racer

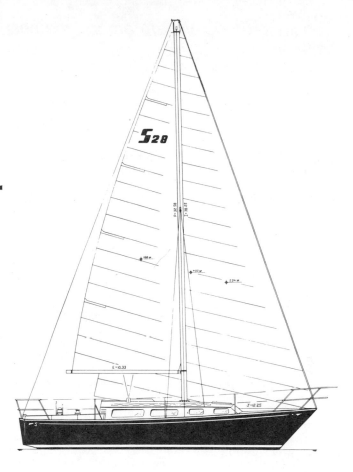

THE BOAT AND THE BUILDER

The Sabre 28 is the smallest boat in the line produced by Sabre Yachts of South Casco, Maine. Over 900 boats were built in the 10 years since the introduction of the Sabre 28 in 1972.

The Sabre 28 was the only model produced by the company until 1977, when the Sabre 34 entered production. In 1979 the gap between the Sabre 28 and the 34 was filled with a 30-footer of a design very similar to that of her two sisters. In 1982, the Sabre 38 was introduced, and features both a standard and an aft-cabin layout.

All boats in the Sabre line are of the modern cruiser-racer type, with fin keel and skeg-hung spade rudder.

With a 1981 base price of about $37,000, and an average delivered price in southern New England of about $40,000 without sails or electronics, the Sabre 28 is a relatively expensive 28' boat.

Despite a fairly high initial cost, the Sabre 28 has proved to be a good investment for her owners. One owner responding to *The Practical Sailor's* boatowners' survey reported that he paid $14,900 for his boat in 1973. That same boat in 1981 was worth about $24,000. A Sabre 28 purchased in 1976 cost $22,000, and was worth about $29,000 in 1981.

Owners report that the primary motivation for purchasing the boat can be summed up in one word: quality. Sabre is quite conscious of their image as producing a high-quality boat. The boat attracts buyers willing to pay a little more than average for a boat that is better than average.

As with all boats that have been in production for a number of years, the design of the Sabre 28 has evolved and improved over the years. In particular, a number of minor changes were made in August, 1982, some of which are noted below. Therefore, the price of a used Sabre 28 may be a function of whether it has some of the more desirable features. For example, an older diesel-powered Sabre 28 brings about $2300 more than a comparable Atomic Four equipped boat.

The Sabre 28 is conventionally modern in appearance. She has a modest concave sheer, straight raked stem, and short after overhang.

CONSTRUCTION

The hull of the Sabre 28 is a slightly heavier-than-average hand layup of mat and roving. Some roving printthrough is evident, but there are no visible hard spots in the hull. Gelcoat quality is excellent.

There are optional hull and deck colors besides the stock white on white. On an early Sabre 28 we exam-

Specifications

LOA	28'5"
LWL	22'10"
Beam	9'2"
Draft: Standard model	4'8"
Shoal model	3'10"
Displacement	7900 lbs
Ballast	3100 lbs
Sail area: cruiser	393 sq ft
standard	403 sq ft

Sabre Yachts
Hawthorne Road
South Casco, Maine 04077

ined, the red gelcoat had faded to a dull pink, and the boat was past due for painting. In general red hulls are more susceptible to fading.

The deck of the Sabre 28 is balsa-cored for stiffness, with plywood inserts at stress areas such as winch mountings. The hull-to-deck joint uses a fairly standard internal hull flange, butyl bedded, and through bolted on 6" centers with stainless steel bolts. These bolts also serve to attach a vinyl rubrail and the teak toerail: The hull-to-deck joint is through bolted across the transom.

All deck hardware, including stanchions, pulpits, and cleats, is through bolted and backed with thick aluminum plates which serve to distribute load. The stem fitting is a well-finished aluminum casting.

Construction details are among the best that we've seen on a production sailboat

Skin fittings are recessed flush with the hull surface. All underwater through hull openings are fitted with bronze Spartan seacocks. Spartan seacocks have a short, lipped hose tailpiece rather than the more typical long straight tailpiece of other seacocks. This short tailpiece precludes double clamping of hoses. This single hose clamp on below water fittings is fine as long as the hose clamps are kept tight. We recommend that they be checked at regular intervals.

In general, construction details are among the best that we've seen on a production sailboat. All fillet bonding is absolutely neat. There are no rough fiberglass areas anywhere. All exposed interior fiberglass surfaces, such as bilges and the inside of lockers, are gelcoated or painted.

Although tiller steering is standard, about 90% of the boats are delivered with Edson pedestal wheel steerers equipped with Ritchie compasses. The wheel steering option has proven so popular that in 1976 the cockpit of the Sabre 28 was redesigned to accommodate the wheel without interfering with the seating arrangement. Access to the rudder stock for emergency steering is via a plastic plate in the cockpit sole. An emergency tiller is provided with wheel-steered boats.

The mast of the Sabre 28 is a straight section Awlgripped aluminum extrusion built by Rig-Rite. Internal halyards, internal clew outhaul, topping lift, and two-point jiffy reefing are standard, as is a transom-mounted ball-bearing mainsheet traveler. The mast is deck-stepped in an aluminum casting. In new boats, this mast step has been redesigned to incorporate attachment points for blocks, facilitating the leading of halyards aft to the cockpit. Halyard winches mounted on the cabin top are another popular option.

Mast compression is transferred to the hull structure by a teak compression column incorporated in the main bulkhead. Shroud chainplates are heavily through-bolted to the main bulkhead, which is solidly glassed to the hull.

Originally, the Sabre 28 was rigged with single upper and lower shrouds. In 1975 forward lower shrouds were added to reduce mast pumping under sail and vibration at the mooring. Mast vibration in high winds, even at anchor is a common problem with deck-stepped masts. Not all older Sabre 28's have been retrofitted with the additional set of lower shrouds. If purchase of a pre-1975 model is contemplated, either ascertain that the forward lower shrouds have been installed or contact Sabre for templates and parts to do the job yourself. It is a straightforward job, with the new chainplates bolting onto the cabin sides forward of the mast.

The ballast keel is an external lead casting, well faired to the hull. Keelboats are accessible in the bilge for periodic tightening. Thorough wet sanding of the bottom should be done before applying bottom paint on a new boat, as the boats are shipped with the bottoms unprepped.

Construction of the Sabre 28 is strong without being overly heavy. There is no evidence of hurrying to finish the job anywhere in the boat.

PERFORMANCE

Handling Under Sail
With optional wheel steering, optional cockpit-led halyards, and optional self-tailing headsail sheet winches, the Sabre 28 can easily be handled by one or two people. The mainsheet is within easy reach of the helmsman. Unfortunately, his head is also within easy reach of the mainsheet when jibing, except on newer boats; the mainsheet was relocated to the cabin top in 1982.

With main chainplates set well inboard, the headsail sheeting base of the boat is quite narrow, particularly if the boat is equipped with the optional inboard genoa track in addition to the standard toerail-mounted genoa track. The sheeting base is, for example, almost a foot narrower than that of the Hunter 27. This allows the Sabre 28 to be reasonably closewinded. With her relatively small wetted surface and a big genoa, she will be fast in light air.

Unless the water in your cruising area is spread very thin, we suggest the standard keel version rather than the shoal keel. We suspect that the shoal keel presents a less efficient lateral plane for windward work.

Some attention will have to be paid to the size of headsail used. Owners report that, although the Sabre 28 more than holds her own with other boats of her size and type, she is not a particularly stiff boat. Owners consider her performance well above average, although her PHRF rating suggests only average performance compared to similar cruiser-racers. Due to the off-center solid prop, the boat may be faster on one tack than the other, and owners who intend to race the Sabre 28 should experiment to see if this is the case.

Handling Under Power
Several different engines have been used in the Sabre 28. Until 1975 all were equipped with the Atomic Four gasoline engine. In 1975 a 10 horsepower Volvo diesel was offered as an option. In 1978, both these engines were dropped, and the Volvo MD7A diesel became standard. The MD7A is a two cylinder engine rated at 13

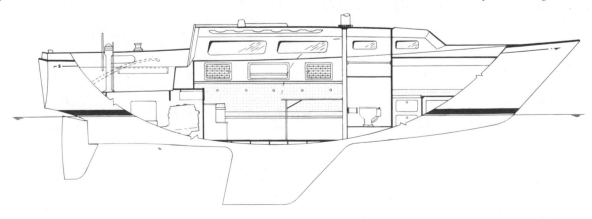

horsepower. In 1981 it was replaced by the Westerbeke 13.

The propeller shaft on the right hand turning Atomic Four is offset to port. On the left hand turning Volvos, it is offset to starboard. On the earliest Sabre 28 s the shaft was on centerline. This change in engines from right hand to left hand rotation means that replacement of engines in off-center located Atomic Four powered boats will be limited to either the Atomic Four gas engine or some other right hand turning engine. Otherwise there will be considerable compromise in handling characteristics under power.

Owners report that engine access on early Atomic Four equipped models is poor. In current Volvo-powered models, access for routine service is good. Some joiner-work disassembly—planned in, fortunately—is required for engine removal. Routine service is via doors and panels.

There is no oil sump under the engine. Access to the stuffing box, needed annually for repacking and adjustment, is poor.

Engine instruments—a full bank, with no idiot lights—are mounted in the bridgedeck, with engine starting and stopping controls under the helmsman's seat. While this may seem awkward at first, it does protect the always-vulnerable ignition switch from water. This is an unusual, but reasonable arrangement.

Owners consider the boat's handling under power to be good. With her fin keel and spade rudder, she will turn in a tight circle. Owners report that any of the engines will drive the boat at or near "hull speed" under most conditions.

LIVABILITY

Deck Layout

In 1976, a foredeck anchor well was added to the Sabre 28. The well is large enough to hold adequate primary ground tackle for the boat. It has provision for securing the bitter end of the anchor rode in boats built since 1982. We would add an eyebolt or a U-bolt to the well for this purpose if it is not already there.

The water tank vent is located in the anchor well. This is a rational location for an item whose position is commonly an afterthought. Frequently, tank vents are located in the topsides, just below the sheer. This can cause backsiphoning of salt water into fuel or freshwater tanks. We saw this occur on several boats—not Sabres—in the 1979 Marion-Bermuda race, which featured four days of slogging to windward in heavy air.

The Sabre 28 is one of the few boats we have seen that uses Skene bow chocks. Skene chocks effectively hold the anchor rode or mooring lines in the chocks, even if the boat sails around on her anchor. This is an important consideration in many modern boats, for the Sabre 28, like many modern sloops of moderate displacement, probably sails almost as many miles while anchored or moored as when underway.

Heavy teak handrails and a very effective molded-in nonskid surface facilitate movement on deck in a seaway. The side decks are of necessity narrow due to the wide cabin trunk.

The cockpit of the Sabre 28 is large and comfortable. It is as large a cockpit as we would consider safe for off-shore sailing on a 28' boat. With wheel steering the cockpit easily seats five.

Cockpit lockers deserve special comment. There are two molded-in recesses in the winch islands, handy for winch handles, sail stops, and other small items. There is a shallow lift-top locker under the port cockpit seat, a deeper locker under the helmsman's seat, and a deep locker under the starboard seat.

The deep starboard locker is bulkheaded off from the bowels of the boat so that sails, fenders, and lines will not migrate to the depths of the bilge. This locker contains built-in holders for the companionway drop boards and emergency tiller, as well as a shelf arranged for line stowage. Although the lid to this locker is a little small for the easy removal of sails, it is one of the best designed cockpit lockers we have seen.

By comparison, the companionway is a bit of a disappointment. Although it is suitably narrow and has a good bridgedeck, the opening is sharply tapered, allowing removal of the drop boards by lifting them only about an inch.

The drop boards themselves are ½" teak-faced plywood in early boats, solid teak in post-1982 models. The exposed edge grain of the plywood core will soon turn grey unless the boards are well varnished. Eventually they may delaminate. We believe that plywood should not be used where it will be subject to weathering. Frankly, the boards look a little cheap on a boat of this quality.

New boats have a translucent smoked plexiglass companionway hatch top. Older boats have fiberglass hatches. The plexiglass hatch allows a good deal of light below. At night, when tied to the dock, it also allows people on the dock to stare into the main cabin. An often forgotten corollary to transparent hatches is that if they allow light below during the day, they allow it out at night. The glare of a white light belowdecks can

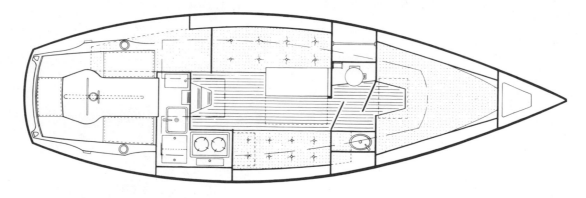

wipe out the helmsman's night vision. Not a common problem, admittedly, but a real one nonetheless.

Belowdecks
The first impression of the Sabre 28 belowdecks is that she is roomy, neat, and well-finished. Headroom is 6' under the main hatch, and an honest 5'11" in the main cabin.

The forward cabin contains V-berths with a filler to form a double. The 30-gallon molded polyethylene water tank is located under the forward berths. There is a drawer and a bin under each berth. With the forward hatch open, it is possible to stand and dress comfortably with the berth filler removed.

The head is full width and closes off from both the forward cabin and main cabin by doors. The Sabre 28 comes standard with a 22-gallon holding tank. A Y-valve diverter is optional. If we were purchasing a new boat, we would plumb the holding tank as a freshwater tank to double water capacity. Then we would install either an overboard discharge sewage treatment system, or, if our conscience allowed, a direct discharge system.

Despite a lot of teak bulkheads and trim, the main cabin is bright and attractive. There are substantial grab rails overhead. The port settee extends to form a double berth. With all berths filled, the Sabre 28 sleeps six. Frankly, six people on a 28' boat is too many, even for a weekend. We would prefer an alternate four-berth interior arrangement that provides a larger galley. Some older Sabre 28's are equipped with such a layout.

A bulkhead-mounted fold-down cabin table seats four comfortably. It is secured in the folded position by a screw-type hatch dog, a good idea, since a rattling table can drive you to distraction.

At the after end of the main cabin, the galley is located to starboard, with a quarterberth to port. Galley storage is good, with four drawers and several lockers. The galley sink is located just off centerline, almost under the companionway. While this location is good for ensuring that the sink will drain on either tack, care must be taken going below when well heeled on the port tack to avoid stepping into the sink.

The galley stove is a recessed two-burner Kenyon alcohol stove. Stoves of this type, which have integral fuel tanks with the fuel fill located between the burners, present a potential fire hazard if the fuel tank is refilled before the burners have cooled adequately.

On pre-1982 boats, the icebox is well insulated with the exception of the top. Given the fact that Sabre has gone so far as to install an icebox pump to keep ice melt from smelling up the bilge, we were pleased to see them complete the otherwise good icebox in 1982 by insulating the top and lids.

Wiring, plumbing—in general, all finishing details—are well designed and neatly finished. The location of the main electrical panel next to the companionway, where it is vulnerable to spray, is an exception to the generally well thought out installations.

Four opening ports are standard; an additional hatch over the main cabin is optional. We recommend this additional ventilation if the boat is to be used in a warm climate. The dorade box over the head is the only provision for foul-weather ventilation.

CONCLUSIONS

The Sabre 28 is an attractive, well-built, well-finished boat. Although her price is above average, construction and finish details are also well above average for a stock boat.

Despite her modern underbody, she is a conservative design, conservatively built. The fact that, after a decade of production, she continues to be built at a steady rate, means that the boat should never be an orphan.

Sabre Yachts has an excellent reputation for service and personal attention. Owners repeatedly cite their personal dealings with Roger Hewson, chief designer, chief inspector, and founder of the company, for their personal service to owners. Dealers report excellent warranty response by the builder.

The Sabre 28 is neither an all-out racer, nor an all-out cruiser. She is a good compromise boat, strong enough to cruise with confidence and fast enough not to embarrass.

She is good-looking in a modern way, without being so modern as to be trendy. She will probably not appeal to the hard-core traditionalist, nor to the flat-out modernist. She appeals mostly as a well turned out coastal cruiser for the couple or a small family. The Sabre 28 may be no Swan, but she's a long way from an ugly duckling.

The S2 8.5 Meter: Conventionally Modern

THE BOAT AND THE BUILDER

When Leon Slikkers founded S2 Yachts in 1973, much of the attention to detail that had characterized Slickcraft powerboats—Slikkers' earlier boatbuilding venture—traveled with him to the new boatbuilding company. In the last nine years, S2 has produced a variety of modern cruising designs from the board of Arthur Edmunds, all characterized by longish fin keels, freestanding spade rudders, straight sheerlines, and a staggering variety of draft options and cockpit locations.

In the last year, S2 has reached more for the performance market with the Grand Slam series of small boats, and the new 10.3 "offshore racer-cruiser." These higher performance boats are designed by Scott Graham and Eric Schlageter, well known for their MORC and smaller IOR designs.

In addition, the company produces a line of powerboats from 20 to 32 feet long. S2's nomenclature has always been confusing. Referring to the boats by their metric lengths (8.0, 8.5, 9.2, 11.0) has probably caused a number of people to underestimate the size of the boats. The 11.0, for example, is a 36-footer—not the 33-footer that may spring to mind to those of us incapable of instant metric conversion.

The S2 8.5 is a 28-footer cast in the company's traditional mold. Her hull dimensions, sail area, displacement, and general design characteristics put her square in the middle of the modern 28-footers such as the Tanzer 8.5, Newport 28, O'Day 28, and the Pearson 28.

The boat's styling is conventionally modern. She has a fairly straight sheer, fairly high freeboard, and low, raked cabin trunk with dark tinted flush ports.

S2 owners show considerable loyalty to their boats. The builder has the reputation of providing good warranty service. Surprisingly, owners report mixed results in their relationships with dealers. The two dealers that owners complained about—one on the West Coast and one in Florida—have since lost their S2 franchises. Both dealers have left some owners holding the bag. As one owner reports, "If you want service, call S2 direct." We agree.

CONSTRUCTION

The hull of the S2 8.5 is a solid hand layup. Glass work is excellent, and is noted by owners as one of the main considerations in buying the boat. Gelcoat quality is excellent.

Slight roving printthrough is evident, but it is not objectionable. Minor hardspots are visible in the topsides, probably caused by the attachment of interior furniture and bulkheads.

The deck molding is cored with end grain balsa, giving a solid feel underfoot as well as providing reasonable insulating properties.

Specifications

LOA	28'
DWL	22'6"
Beam	9'6"
Draft:	
deep keel	4'6"
shoal keel	3'11'
Displacement	7,600 lbs
Ballast	3,000 lbs
Sail Area	400 sq ft

S2 Yachts Inc.
725 East 40th Street
Holland, Michigan 49423
(616) 392-7163

S2's hull-to-deck joint is the basic type that we would like to see adopted throughout the industry. The hull molding has an inward-turning flange, onto which the deck molding is dropped. The joint is bedded in flexible sealant, and through bolted on six inch intervals by bolts passing through the full length slotted aluminum toerail. The joint is also through bolted across the stern.

All deck hardware is properly through bolted, although pulpits, cleats, and winches merely use nuts and washers on the underside of the deck, rather than the aluminum or stainless steel backing plates we prefer.

Because of the high freeboard and considerable windage of the 8.5, the standard engine is the absolute minimum power plant for the boat

---

Another feature of the hull-to-deck joint is a heavy, semi-rigid vinyl rubrail at the sheerline, quite aptly termed a "crash rubrail" by S2. This will go a long way toward absorbing the shock of the inevitable encounters with docks and the other hard objects that seem to be attracted to the topsides of the typical sailboat. Although this rail is black when the boat is new, it had dulled to a chalky grey on older S2's we examined.

The builder advertises "bronze seacocks on all through hull fittings." These are not traditional tapered plug seacocks, but are ball valves mounted directly to through hull fittings. A proper seacock—whether it uses a ball valve or a tapered plug—has a heavy flange to allow through bolting to the hull. This is an important safety feature. Should a valve seize, it may become necessary to apply a great deal of leverage to the handle in order to open or close the valve. The deeply threaded through hull stem can easily break under these conditions, and more than one boat has been lost in this manner.

We also suggest that seacocks be installed on the cockpit drain scuppers and the bilge pump outlet, both of which may be under water while the boat is sailing. Light air performance would benefit by the fairing in of the through hull fittings, particularly the head intake and discharge, both of which are far enough forward to have a significant effect on water flow past the hull.

Ballast is a 3,000 pound lead casting, epoxied inside a hollow keel shell. We prefer an external lead casting bolted to the hull for its shock-absorbing qualities and ease of repair. This preference was reinforced recently when we examined an old Bristol 27 just sold by a friend. The surveyor noticed dampness near the bottom of the leading edge of the keel, which showed slight external damage. Probing the loose putty revealed some abrasion of the glass keel molding. In order to sell the boat, it was necessary to grind away a large portion of the glass at the front of the keel, dry out the ballast, and reglass the lead—a job that took several days of work and cost our friend a fair chunk of money.

Much of the boat's interior structure is plywood, glassed to the hull. Fillet bonding is neat and workmanlike with no rough edges to be found.

Chainplates are conventional stainless steel flat bar, bolted to bulkheads and plywood gussets in the main cabin. These are properly backed with stainless steel pads. Due to the fact that the hull is lined throughout with a carpet-like synthetic material, it is not possible to examine the bonding of the chainplate knees to the hull. The stemhead fitting is a stainless steel weldment, through bolted to the deck and hull and reinforced inside the hull with a formed stainless steel gusset to prevent deflection of the deck from the pull aft of the headstay. We'd like to see a metal backup pad behind this fitting rather than the washers which are used.

General construction is thoughtful and well executed, with excellent glasswork, a strong and simple hull-to-deck joint, and reasonably installed hardware and fittings.

PERFORMANCE

Handling Under Power
Although some early models of the 8.5 used a seven horsepower BMW diesel, the 1982 version employs an eight horsepower Yanmar. The new generation of small Yanmars are quite impressive, light in weight and far smoother than the company's rockcrushers of a few years ago.

Because of the high freeboard and considerable windage of the 8.5, the standard engine is the absolute minimum power plant for the boat. Recognizing this fact, the company offers a 15 horsepower, two-cylinder Yanmar as an option. For another 75 pounds and $1150, we would want this option on the boat if the ability to get places under power is a real consideration.

The extra fuel consumption of the larger engine will scarcely be noticed. The 18 gallon aluminum fuel tank will probably give a range under power of over 250 miles—more than adequate for a 28 foot cruising boat.

The fuel tank is located under the cockpit and is securely mounted and properly grounded. There is an easily-reached fuel shut off between the engine and tank. Unfortunately, the fuel fill is located in the cockpit sole. Spilled diesel oil turns even the best fiberglass nonskid into an ice skating rink. Fuel fills should be located on deck, where spills can be efficiently washed away.

Engine access is via a large removable panel on the inboard face of the quarterberth. This panel lacks any kind of handhold to make it easily removable, which will discourage regular checking of the engine oil. The top companionway step also removes for access, but it's a long reach to the dipstick.

There is no oil pan under the engine. It will be necessary to be very careful when changing oil to keep the bilge clean. We have yet to see anyone change oil and filters without spilling something.

With the quarterberth panel removed, access for routine service is excellent. The quarterberth has remarkable headroom over, so that the mechanic will not feel like a trapped spelunker after a half hour of work. Engine removal will require some joinerwork disassembly.

Handling Under Sail
The S2 8.5 is no slug under sail. Her PHRF rating of 174 to 180 compares very favorably to other boats of her size and type. The Sabre 28, for example, has a rating of 198, the Pearson 28 about 195, and the O'Day 28 about 198.

Part of this is no doubt due to the fact that the standard sails on the boat come from the North loft. While North's OEM sails may not be the vertical cut Mylar-Kevlar wonders that adorn custom boats, they're a damn sight better than most.

S2 now uses Hall spars. The simple masthead rig is extremely clean, with airfoil spreaders and internal tangs. The boom features an internal outhaul and provision for two internally-led reefing lines, with cam cleats at the forward end of the boom.

The deck-stepped mast is mounted in a stainless steel deck plate incorporating plenty of holes for the attachment of blocks. Halyards and cunningham lead aft along the cabin house top to a pair of Lewmar #8 winches. Lewmar #16's are optional, but hardly necessary.

The main is controlled by a six-part Harken rig mounted on the end of the boom, and a Kenyon traveller mounted on the aft cockpit coaming. This will work fine with the tiller-steered version of the boat. With wheel steering, the mainsheet is likely to be a nuisance to the helmsman.

The high-quality rig and sails add to the price of the S2, but they are additions well worth the cost

Because of the end-of-boom sheeting, a boom vang will be essential for full mainsail control. Ironically, the boat's drawings show almost midboom sheeting, with the traveller mounted on the bridgedeck at the forward end of the cockpit. This is probably a better arrangement, although it heavily loads the center of the boom and requires more sheeting force.

Despite the fact that the shrouds are set well in from the rail, the boat lacks inboard headsail tracks. Rather, you are limited to snatch blocks shackled to the toerail track. A six-foot piece of track set inboard of the rail would be a useful addition.

Standard headsail sheet winches are two-speed Lewmar #30's. Options include both larger winches and self-tailers, both of which are worth considering for either racing or cruising. The cockpit coamings are wide enough for mounting larger primaries and secondaries.

The high-quality rig and sails add to the price of the S2, but they are additions well worth the cost.

LIVABILITY

Deck Layout

The deck layout of the 8.5 is clean and functional, with no toe stubbers to catch you unawares. There are two foredeck mooring cleats, but no bow chocks. The necessity to lead an anchor line well off the boat's centerline, coupled with high freeboard forward, is likely to result in a boat which sails around on her anchor or mooring. The 8.5 has a pair of wide stainless steel chafing strips at the bow which will greatly protect the deck from the chafe of the anchor line.

The 8.5's foredeck anchor well is one of the best we've seen. It is shallow—just deep enough to hold an anchor and adequate rode. There are double scuppers, which offer less likelihood of clogging. The lid is held on by full-length piano hinge, and there is a positive latch.

The shallow locker well above the waterline means that water is less likely to enter through the scuppers, which can be a real problem with a deep anchor well. When the bow pitches into waves, a deep anchor well can fill with water, and if the scuppers clog with debris, you can find yourself sailing around with several hundred pounds of extra weight in the worst possible location. There is no provision for securing the bitter end of the anchor rode, but a big galvanized eyebolt installed in the well by the owner will solve that one.

The running lights leave something to be desired. Their location at deck level just aft of the stem makes them vulnerable to damage when handling ground tackle. We much prefer an international style bicolor mounted on the pulpit, another two feet off the water: easier to see, and out of the way. Wiring for the running lights is exposed in the anchor well, and should be secured out of the way.

A recessed teak handrail runs the full length of the cabin trunk, serving the dual function of heavy weather handhold and cabin trim piece. Its shape makes it far easier to oil or varnish than the conventional round handrail, although the wide, flat section seems somewhat awkward after years of grabbing round rails.

The 8.5's cockpit is the maximum size we'd want to see on a boat of this size. The T-shape is designed to accommodate the optional wheel steerer, yielding a somewhat odd layout for the tiller-steered version. A bench seat spans the aft end of the cockpit. Although this makes good seating in port, we doubt that you'd want anyone sitting there under sail: too much weight in the end of the boat. It does make a natural helmsman's seat for wheel steering. Engine controls and instrument panel are also located at the aft end of the cockpit, basically inaccessible to the tiller-steering helmsman.

There are two lifting lids in the aft cockpit bench, giving access to a cavernous space under the cockpit. To be useful, dacron bags should be fitted to the inside of these lockers. Then, they'll be handy stowage for spare sheets and blocks.

There are comfortable contoured seats along each side of the cockpit, with a huge locker under the port seat. Although plywood pen boards somewhat separate this locker from the engine space under the cockpit, it would be far too easy for deeply piled junk to get knocked over the board and into the engine. This locker should be partitioned into smaller spaces unless it is to be used exclusively as a sail locker. The battery boxes, fitted at the forward end of the locker, could benefit from plywood or fiberglass lids to keep battery acid off gear which might find its way onto the batteries. The box is designed to take two batteries—one battery is standard—stored in plastic containers. A single lid covering the whole box would be more efficient.

The huge cockpit will accommodate up to six for sailing, and eight for in-port partying. Cockpit seats are contoured, and the cockpit coamings slope outboard for more comfortable seating. The seats are both too narrow and too short for sleeping.

The forward end of the cockpit is protected by a narrow bridgedeck. However, the cockpit coamings extend a full foot above the level of the bridgedeck. To block

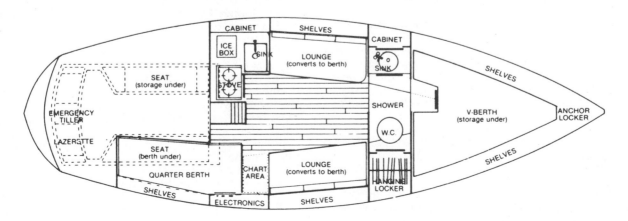

the companionway to the level of the top of the coamings will require leaving two of the three drop boards in place when sailing.

Although there is moderate taper to the sides of the companionway, making it easier to remove the drop boards, it is still necessary to lift each board about five inches before it can be removed. This is far safer than many tapered companionways, where boards practically fall out if you look at them wrong.

The companionway slide is one of the best we've seen. It's a contoured piece of Acrylic fitted with a convenient grabrail. It slides easily in extruded aluminum channels, and is fitted with a fiberglass storm hood.

As on many boats, the aft cabin bulkhead slopes forward, rendering it impossible to leave the drop boards out for ventilation when it rains.

Belowdecks

Owners consistently praise the interior design and finishing of S2 sailboats. From looking at the 8.5, it's pretty easy to see why.

There are no exposed interior fiberglass surfaces except the head floor pan molding. The hull and cabin overhead are lined with a carpet-like synthetic fabric. While this will undoubtedly cut down on condensation, we wonder how this fabric will hold up over time. Inevitably, the hull liner and even the overhead will get wet. In freshwater areas, this is no problem. The water will eventually evaporate. In salt water, however, wet fabric never seems to dry. Salt draws moisture like a magnet draws steel. Although the fabric-covered interior is attractive, formica, wood, or even gelcoat surfaces are probably better in the long run on boats used in salt water.

Interior layout is fairly conventional, with V-berths forward, and immediately aft, a full width head. The head can be closed off from both the forward cabin and the main cabin with solid doors—a real luxury. There is a large hanging locker in the head, and reasonable storage space for toilet articles.

The word for the main cabin is "wide," with the settees pushed as far outboard as they can go. Decor is a little heavy on the teak for our taste, but it is one of the better coordinated interiors we have seen. S2 has a good interior decorator.

A fold-down dining table seats four. When folded against the bulkhead, it is held in place by a single latch, which makes us nervous.

Neither settee is full length. The foot of the port settee runs under the galley counter, making it long enough for sleeping, although your feet may feel a little claustrophobic in the tiny footwell.

The starboard settee is an unusual configuration. The aftermost 12" of the settee folds up to form an arm rest, leaving a gap between the end of the settee and the head of the quarterberth. Inexplicably, this gap is referred to on the accommodation plan as a "charting area," although there is neither a standard nor an optional chart table. It's sort of like the designer ran out of energy before completing the interior design.

Over the non-existent "charting area" is the best electrical panel we've seen on a 28 foot boat. The panel has a locking battery switch, battery test meter, and a panel with room for 14 circuit breakers, although only half are installed on the standard boat.

Most quarterberths tend to induce claustrophobia. That of the 8.5 is more likely to exacerbate any tenden-

cies you might have to agoraphobia. At last, a quarterberth which will not give you a concussion when you sit bolt upright in the middle of the night after your neighbor drags down on you in a wind shift.

The standard main cabin sole is carpet-covered fiberglass. For another $325, teak and holly is available for the traditionalist. We'd want it.

Unfortunately there is no access to the bilge in the main cabin. None. This is inexcusable, and could be dangerous. A few hours with a sabre saw should solve this rather basic problem.

The galley is workable and accessible, with no awkward posturing required to do the dishes. The sink gets an A+. It is a full nine inches deep, is large enough to take a frying pan, and mounted close to the centerline.

In contrast, the icebox gets a C−. It is larger than normal on a boat of this size, but it drains to the bilge, has a poorly insulated top, and a tiny, uninsulated hatch without a trace of a gasket. Boo.

Because of limited counter space, the two burner Kenyon alcohol stove is mounted athwartships, rather than fore and aft. This means that the stove cannot be gimballed, and that it is necessary to reach across the inboard burner to reach the outboard one. Given the fact that countertop gimballed stoves are usually dangerous, the lack of gimballing doesn't bother us much. What does bother us is that if you want to upgrade the stove to something more functional, the limited space allocated will stretch your ingenuity.

A fold down table at the end of the galley counter gives additional counter space, but it must be left up in order to use the port settee for sleeping.

Roominess, excellent execution, and good color coordination are trademarks of the interiors of all S2's, and the 8.5 fits well into this enviable tradition.

CONCLUSIONS

With a base price of $37,200, and a typical sailaway price of about $40,000, the S2 8.5 Meter is not a cheap boat. With a full-blown list of options, including such items as hot water, larger engine, spinnaker and genoa, and wheel steering, the price could easily exceed $45,000.

The options list for the boat is the most extensive we've seen on a 28-footer, including a wide range of both performance and comfort packages. For the person who wants to personalize a 28-footer, and doesn't mind spending the money, the options list is intriguing. We quickly ran the price of an 8.5 over $50,000 by drooling over the options list.

With money becoming tighter, dockspace tougher to find, and boatowners generally downscaling their size expectations, we're likely to see more lavishly equipped, well finished small boats. The cost of these smaller boats can be a little staggering.

The S2 8.5 is a good boat for cruising the Great Lakes or any coast in comfort and a certain amount of style. Her appearance may be a little modern for traditionalists, with her straight sheer and European-style cabin windows.

Pricey? yes, but when you look at the things that go into the boat—the rig, good sails, and a comfortable, well finished interior—the price may seem a little less painful. You still pay for what you get.

The Catalina 30: Most Boat for Least Money

THE BOAT AND THE BUILDER

Catalina Yachts is one of the world's largest manufacturers of fiberglass cruising and racing sailboats over 21' long. The company has two plants, one in Florida, one in southern California. Between the two, they turn out several thousand sailboats every year. The Catalina 22 is probably the most popular small trailerable cruiser ever built. Over 10,000 of the pop-top weekend cruisers had been built by November, 1980.

The Catalina 30 may well be the most successful 30' cruiser-racer ever built. By November 1980, over 2200 Catalina 30's had been produced. At the current base price of $30,000, over $66,000,000 worth of 30-footers have been manufactured.

Since the Catalina 30 went into production in 1975, output has been at a steady pace of about 470 units per year. Dealers report that they could easily sell more, if they could only get their hands on them. Offshore Sailing Yachts, the Catalina dealer in Rhode Island, reported that they requested 18 Catalina 30 s in 1980, but because of demand for the boat from other dealers, they were able to get only 9. Almost all were sold before they were even delivered to the dealer.

The success of Catalina is even more remarkable when you consider that the company does no advertising. You will not find a single ad for Catalina in any national magazine. The company depends on its extensive dealer network—about 150 dealers nationwide—and on word of mouth promotion from satisfied owners.

The average boat manufacturer spends between 5% and 10% of gross revenues on advertising. By eliminating national advertising, Catalina may well be saving as much as $1,000 to $2,000 per Catalina 30. Any way you look at it, that translates into a lower price in the marketplace.

The entire Catalina line is extremely popular with new boat dealers, who are required by Catalina to represent other lines as well. Usually, the Catalina line is priced about 5% lower than a comparably equipped boat of the same size and type from other manufacturers. For example, the typical out-the-door price for a Newport 30 from a Rhode Island dealer is about $39,000. The price for a comparably-equipped Catalina 30 is about $37,000. The two boats are almost identical in layout, design, and appearance. The customer who resists the higher price of the Newport 30 could quite easily be redirected to the Catalina 30.

Catalina owners frequently trade up through the line. Some dealers make a policy of offering the customer full trade-in value for a smaller Catalina traded up for a larger one within the first two years after purchase. A remarkable number of owners do.

Specifications

LOA	29'11"
LWL	25'
Beam	10'10"
Draft: standard	5'3"
shoal	4'4"
Displacement	10,200 lbs
Ballast	4200 lbs
Sail area	444 sq ft

Catalina Yachts
PO Box 989
21200 Victory Boulevard
Woodland Hills, Calif. 91367

In 1981, Catalina filled the gap in their product line between the 30- and 38-footers with a 36-footer of the same general type.

The Catalina 30 is a typical, fairly light displacement modern design. The boat has a swept-back fairly high aspect ratio fin keel of the type made popular by IOR racing boats in the early 1970's. The high aspect ratio spade rudder is faired into the underbody with a small skeg.

On a waterline length of 25', the Catalina 30's displacement of 10,200 lbs is slightly above average for modern cruiser-racers. By way of comparison, the

When considering the purchase of a used Catalina 30, be sure that the chainplates have the new reinforcements

---

Newport 30 displaces 8,000 lbs, the Cal 31 9,200 lbs, the O'Day 30 11,000 lbs.

The boat is conventionally modern in appearance. She is moderately high-sided, with a fairly straight sheer and short ends. The cabin trunk tapers slightly in profile, and is slightly sheered to complement the sheer of the hull. When coupled with the tapered cabin windows—a Catalina trademark—this yields a reasonably attractive appearance compared to many modern boats.

CONSTRUCTION

The hull of the Catalina 30 is hand layed up of solid fiberglass. In areas of high stress, such as the tops of the cockpit coamings, where winches are mounted, the laminate has been reinforced with plywood inserts.

The external lead keel is bolted to the hull with stainless steel bolts. On most Catalina 30s we examined, there was slight cracking at the joint between the hull and ballast, which is typical of boats with narrow external ballast keels. The surface of the keel is roughly faired with polyester putty at the factory. This must be sanded properly fair by the owner or commissioning yard before the boat is launched, or light air performance will suffer. The bottom of the hull must also be heavily sanded before paint is applied, or there is likely to be paint adhesion failure.

The hull-to-deck joint is simple. The deck molding is wider than the hull molding. At the outboard edge of the deck, the molding forms a downward-facing right-angle flange. This is slipped over the hull molding, and the joint filled with what appears to be fiberglass slurry. The joint is finished with a soft plastic rubrail held by an aluminum extrusion. The aluminum extrusion is held in place by stainless steel self-tapping screws, which reinforce the chemical bond. An integral solid wood sheerstrake, laminated into the hull, further strengthens the joint. This joint is suitable for use in a boat which is used for daysailing and coastal cruising. We would not choose it for an offshore boat. Any projection beyond

the side of a boat's hull can be subject to tremendous strains from bashing into a head sea. Despite the fact that the joint and rubrail project only about ½" beyond the hull, there is some inherent weakness in this mode of hull-to-deck attachment.

There was some play in the rudder stocks of every Catalina 30 we examined. This is similar to the problem found in the Pearson 30. It is more likely to be a minor annoyance than a serious problem.

Lifeline stanchions are more closely placed than on almost any production boat we have seen. Double lifelines are standard, as are double bow and stern rails. Stanchions are through bolted, but with washers rather than the backing plates we prefer. Some owners report problems with leaking stanchions. This is easily corrected, as the stanchion fastenings are readily accessible from inside the boat.

The rig is a simple masthead sloop, with a straight section aluminum spar, double lower shrouds, and, at least on older models, wooden spreaders. The mast is stepped on deck, supported by a wooden compression column belowdecks. All the boats we examined showed local deflection of the top of the cabin trunk in the way of the mast step. This varied from as little as 1/16" to over ¼". There was no evidence of stress in the form of cracks around any of the steps, however.

It is difficult to assess the method of attachment of the chainplates and bulkheads to the hull. The interior of the hull is completely lined, showing no raw fiberglass, nice to look at but preventing examination of the internal structure of the hull. Lower shroud chainplate attachments have been beefed up since the first hulls were produced. Owners warn that when considering the purchase of a used Catalina 30, be sure that the chainplates have the new reinforcements installed.

A shoal draft model, drawing 11" less than the standard model, is popular in some areas where the water is spread thin, such as Florida and the Chesapeake. A taller rig is also offered, and might be recommended in traditionally light air areas, such as Long Island Sound.

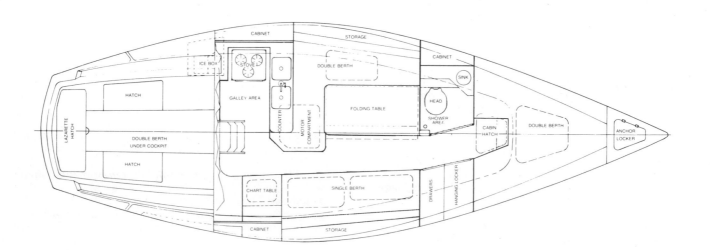

The Catalina 30 is a very stiff boat, due to extraordinary beam, deep fin keel, high ballast/displacement ratio, and small sail plan

PERFORMANCE

Handling Under Sail

With the standard rig, the Catalina 30 will be slightly undercanvassed in areas with predominantly light weather conditions. In areas with normally heavier conditions, such as San Francisco, the standard rig should yield good performance. The working sail area with the standard rig is 446 square feet. For comparison, the Pearson 30, with the same sail area, weighs 1,900 lbs less than the Catalina 30. To get good performance in light air, the boat will either have to be ordered with the taller rig, or very large headsails must be carried. If headsails larger than a 150% genoa are carried with the normal rig, turning blocks will have to be added aft in order to get a proper lead to the headsail sheet winches.

The Catalina 30 is a very stiff boat. The combination of a high ballast/displacement ratio, extraordinary beam, a deep fin keel, and a fairly small sail plan produce a boat that stands on her feet very well. Owners consider the boat to be just about as fast as other boats of the same size and type. PHRF ratings suggest that the tall rig boat is substantially faster than the boat with normal rig. With the tall rig, and well-cut racing sails, the boat should be competitive with other cruiser-racers that are actively raced, such as the Pearson 30, the O'Day 30, and the Ericson 30-2.

Sails are available from the factory. At a total of about $1,700 for a main, 110% lapper, and 150% genoa, they are cheaper than one is likely to find either from a local racing sailmaker or one of the big national names. If the boat is to be used only for daysailing and cruising, the factory-supplied sails are likely to be adequate. If, however, you are concerned with performance, it is always advisable to have sails made either by a national sailmaker with a local loft, or by a local racing sailmaker. The sailmaker who is familiar with local weather conditions, and who probably races himself, is most likely to provide a faster suit of sails for any boat than those provided as a factory option.

The Catalina 30 does not have any particularly disturbing or exciting characteristics under sail. Like many wide modern boats, it rapidly develops weather helm when heeled. The boat should be sailed on her feet. Because she is quite stiff, headsail changes will not be as frequent as with a boat such as the Pearson 30.

Handling Under Power

The standard engine for the Catalina 30 is the workhorse, 65 cubic inch Atomic-4 gasoline engine. For an additional $785, the boat can be delivered with a 31 cubic inch, 11 horsepower Atomic-Diesel. The Atomic-4 is the much more powerful engine. We have seen it used in 40', 20,000 lb sailboats. The small diesel is barely adequate power for a 10,200 lb boat. The 16 horsepower Atomic-Diesel might have been a better choice.

In a flat calm, the small diesel will push the boat at about 5 knots. With the Atomic-4, the boat should easily reach hull speed under power.

Although the engine has flexible mountings and a flexible shaft coupling, there is substantial vibration under power with the small engine. This is felt most acutely in the cabin, because of the midships location of the engine. The engine box has no soundproofing. The main cabin is very noisy under power. Long periods of powering would be uncomfortable for the people belowdecks.

With a fin keel and spade rudder, the boat is quite maneuverable under power, both ahead and astern. With the wheel steerer—one of the most popular options—very little steering effort is required.

LIVABILITY

Deck Layout

The deck layout of the Catalina 30 is typical of small cruiser-racers. There is a small foredeck anchor well. Access to the hull-mounted running lights is via this well. The running lights are protected from damage inside the well by molded fiberglass covers. We are not fond of running lights mounted in the topsides, which almost invariably short out. Other manufacturers who mount the lights in the hull could take a lesson from Catalina, however. Neither C&C nor Cal protects their running lights on the inside of the anchor well.

There are double bow cleats, but no bow chocks. There are also double stern cleats, but no stern chocks.

Despite the wide cabin trunk, it is reasonably easy to maneuver on deck. The shrouds are placed far enough inboard to allow going outside them on the way to the foredeck. There are well-mounted teak grabrails on the cabin top.

*The company's goal is to provide 'as much boat for the money as we can.'
The Catalina 30 is definitely among the lowest-priced 30-footers*

The cockpit is large and comfortable. With wheel steering, it easily accommodates the helmsman and four companions. There is a large sail locker under the port cockpit seat, and a smaller locker under the starboard seat. There is also a fair-sized lazarette locker. The sail locker is properly separated from the under-cockpit area.

The cockpit is too large for offshore use. There are only two fairly small cockpit drains, whose size is greatly reduced by strainers. Despite the fact that the companionway has a fairly high raised sill, at least two of the three companionway drop boards would have to be in place to raise the sill to the level of the main deck.

The strong vertical taper of the companionway allows the drop boards to be removed by lifting them only about 1.5". In a bad knockdown in really severe weather, the boards could fly out or float out much easier than if the companionway were more parallel-sided.

The sliding companionway hatch is unnecessarily large. This is useful when sitting in a marina in a hot climate, such as southern California, but it is a disadvantage at sea.

Because the main cabin bulkhead slopes forward, the drop boards cannot be left out of the companionway for ventilation when it rains. For this reason, boats used in rainy climates frequently have cockpit dodgers. Otherwise, they become stifling below in wet weather. There is no provision for ventilation below in rain or heavy weather.

There is a permanently mounted manual bilge pump operable from the cockpit. Other manufacturers would do well to include such a pump as standard equipment. Not many do.

Interior
The interior of the Catalina 30 is roomy, and quite well laid out. The forward cabin has large, tapered V-berths which form a large double when used with a filler. A molded hatch which forms part of the front of the cabin trunk, will provide good ventilation in port, but is likely to be a leaker in heavy weather.

The head is quite comfortable. The optional shower drains directly to the bilge. Marine toilet installations are all optional. There is good storage space for clothes in a hanging locker and drawers opposite the head.

Interior bulkheads are teak-faced plywood. The hull is completely lined with fiberglass hull liners, yielding a very finished appearance.

The main cabin is large and comfortable for a 30' boat. There is an L-shaped settee to port, and a straight settee to starboard. The cabin table folds up against the forward bulkhead when not in use.

The engine is mounted under the settee and part of the galley counter. It's a tight fit. Access for service is excellent through traps in the settee. The location of the engine in the lowest part of the bilge does make it vulnerable to bilgewater, however.

Under the cockpit to starboard, there is a large double quarterberth. Unfortunately, the occupant of the inboard half of the berth had better be pretty thin and non-claustrophobic, for headroom over that portion is only a little over one foot.

A large, U-shaped galley is to port. A gimballed alcohol stove with oven is standard, as are double sinks. The icebox is uninsulated except for the side facing the stove, and it drains directly to the bilge. Storage space in the galley is plentiful, although not as much as it might first appear, for the lockers under the sinks are filled by hoses for the engine and water tanks. Batteries are well-mounted under the small chart table opposite the galley.

The general appearance of the interior is one of spaciousness and good design. This initial impression breaks down somewhat on careful examination of details. Interior finish is of average stock boat quality.

CONCLUSIONS

According to Frank Butler, president and chief designer of Catalina, the company's goal is to provide "as much boat for the money as we can." The Catalina 30 is definitely among the lowest-priced of the 30' cruiser-racers. This boat is similar in price to the Hunter 30, which has an average sailaway price of about $35,000 to $36,000. For their displacements, these are two of the least expensive 30' cruiser-racers on the market. It is not reasonable to compare these boats with more expensive 30-footers such as the Ericson 30+ or the Cal 31. There are definitely trade-offs to be made when one purchases a cheaper boat. In boats, as in most other things, you may not always get what you pay for, but you always pay at least for what you get.

The J/30: Stepping Stone to the Big Time

THE BOAT AND THE BUILDER

The J/30 is the second boat produced by the combination of Rod and Bob Johnstone and Tillotson-Pearson. It comes on the heels of the incredibly popular J/24, and has great promise of becoming another industry success on the scale of the Triton or Pearson 30.

The appeal of the J/30 is high performance at a moderate price. When a sailor with a $35,000 boat can beat a sailor with a $70,000 boat, he has reason to feel he's getting his money's worth. With the J/30, he's getting his money's worth.

What he's not getting is a pretty boat in any traditional sense. The J/30 is slab-sided, with little sheer, short overhangs, and little grace. Fortunately, it goes like hell under sail. This contrasts with another "offshore one-design," the Mega, which is slab-sided, has little grace, and doesn't go like hell under sail. The J/30 can also be compared with another of the offshore one-design concepts, the Tartan Ten, which is pretty and fast, but which gets a D-minus for livability.

For about the same money, you get to stand up in the J/30, which you can't do in the Tartan Ten. You also get to sail faster under many conditions. You also have some privacy, and some comfortable berths. This is a reasonable expectation in a boat that sold in 1981 at a base price of about $35,000 less sails.

A J/30 survived the Fastnet, and another sailed solo across the Atlantic to compete in this year's OSTAR. She is a boat that inspires confidence. She is a young sailor's boat, a stepping stone to the big time. The J/30 should make the Johnstones a lot of money, and it will make a lot of long-term J-Boat customers. Many will move up from the J/24 to the J/30, and on to the J/36, which entered production in 1980.

CONSTRUCTION

The J/30 is built by Tillotson-Pearson in Fall River, Massachusetts. The Pearson in Tillotson-Pearson is Everett Pearson, one of the pioneers in fiberglass boat construction. The hull of the J/30 is cored with Baltek Counterkore end-grain balsa. After the balsa core is glassed to the outer hull skin, the two-part mold is bolted together, and the centerline joint heavily glassed over. The layup is then finished the same as any one-piece molded hull.

Specifications

LOA	29'10"
LWL	25'
Beam	11'2"
Draft	5'3"
Sail area	450 sq ft
Displacement	7000 lbs
Ballast	2100 lbs
Ratings:	
IOR	25.7-25.9
PHRF	Base 134-145

J-Boats
24 Mill Street
Newport, RI 02840

Exterior finish quality of the molding is good, with little evidence of gelcoat blistering or roving print-through. The hull-to-deck joint is made by laying the deck molding over the internal flange of the hull molding. This joint is heavily bedded in 3M 5200 and through-bolted on 8" centers with ¼" stainless steel bolts. The joint is covered on the outside by the teak toerail, which is cut away around the lifeline stanchion bases to provide deck scuppers. The toe rail is through-bolted, further backing up the hull-to-deck joint. The deck molding and the hull flange are not always a perfect fit on the inside, and in some areas there is no evidence of the bedding compound squeezing out on the inside. This joint can be visually inspected on the inside of the boat throughout most of its length.

If the hull and deck flanges matched better, this

would increase the faying surface and thereby increase the strength of the bond.

All deck hardware is through-bolted, with either washers or backing plates. Stanchion bases and chainplates utilize what appear to be acrylic plastic backing pads. Aluminum backing plates might allow higher torque on the fastenings without the risk of cracking the plates. There is no backing plate behind the stem fitting.

Through-bolts which intrude into the cabin overhead space utilize acorn nuts, which yields a finished appearance. Unfortunately, acorn nuts are notorious head-crackers. In Bob Johnstone's J/30, they have been replaced in high-traffic areas with a new type of recessed tubular nut which yields an even more finished appearance without encroaching on headroom. *The Practical Sailor* would like to see these nearly flush nuts used not only on the J/30, but in all boats. Acorn nuts or exposed bolts can be a serious hazard in rough conditions.

The outboard high-aspect ratio rudder is very strongly attached to the boat with stainless steel pintles and gudgeons. The bolts which attach these to the rudder should be periodically tightened.

The tiller head is also a strong stainless steel fabrication. A stainless steel tiller extension on the ash tiller allows the helmsman to sit on the weather rail with the rest of the crew. The steering system is simple, strong, and cheap. It should give little or no trouble if the fastenings are checked periodically.

Many J/24s had a disconcerting structural shortcoming: the main bulkhead tended to come adrift. Since the main bulkhead provides almost all of the transverse rigidity of the J/30, quite a bit more thought has gone into it. The main bulkhead of the J/30 is a fairly sophisticated combination of cored and solid construction—solid where the chainplates attach, cored elsewhere.

This bulkhead is glassed to the hull along its outer perimeter, and butt-joined with 3M 5200 to the deck molding. A recess in the deck molding to receive the

bulkhead would be better than a simple butt joint. There is no evidence of this bulkhead's moving—panting or creaking, for example—as the boat works to windward. In fact, the inside of the boat is remarkably quiet going to weather.

Two large fiberglass moldings form the floor pans and the basic furniture structure. In our test boat, the forward floor pan was cracked in the area of the maststep, and had separated from the main bulkhead. It had obviously buckled upward when glassed into the boat, and had been cracked by the compression load of the mast.

Water tanks are cast polyethylene. Although these have glassed-in retainers, we would want to reinforce them before going offshore for any period of time. Large storage bins under the berths and settees have polyethylene liners, a practical solution to keeping anything dry in these areas. The boat also has a good-sized bilge sump, an absolute necessity in a boat with flat bilges.

The J/30 has a bendy, fractional Kenyon Spars rig with swept-back spreaders and single swept-back lowers. Both uppers and lowers share a single stainless steel chainplate. Playing with the rig adjustments is an integral part of making the J/30 go fast. Despite the apparent fragility of the rig, it has shown little tendency to crumple. It is obviously stronger than it at first appears.

A remarkable variety of hull colors and graphics is available from the factory. You can have the J/30 in any one of 17 hull colors at no extra charge. The multiplicity of hull and deck color and graphic combinations is the ideal way both to add individuality to the boat, and to disguise the fact that, with its short ends and wedge-shaped profile, the J/30 is really a somewhat homely boat. Anyone who orders an all-white J/30 must like homely boats.

PERFORMANCE

Handling Under Sail
"Performance under sail" is the hallmark of the J/30, just as it is for the J/24, and promises to be for the J/36. The J/30 was not designed to rate well under any rating rule, and she doesn't. What she does is sail fast with a minimum of hard work.

The J/30 is a delight for the sailor who loves to tweak rig and sails for maximum performance without spending a fortune. The boat is the ideal choice for the racing sailor with two-ton aspirations and a mini-ton pocketbook. The J/30 one-design class specifications limit sails to mainsail, three jibs, and one spinnaker when racing. There are minimum specified cloth weights for all sails.

Wisely, the Johnstones have not insisted on a single sailmaker for one-design racing. Sailmakers have become the gurus of the modern racing sailor, and like charismatic religious or political leaders, each racing sailmaker has his own band of faithful followers. Specifying a single sailmaker, as C&C originally did with the Mega, is the sure kiss of death for a boat which is intended to be mass-marketed in all parts of the country.

Despite a maximum beam of just over 11', the J/30 has a relatively narrow waterline beam. This produces a boat which has fairly low initial stability—good for light air—but which rapidly acquires form stability when heeled. Note that the J/30 has a ballast/displacement ratio of only .30, less than that of the CSY 37.

With the 18-22 knots of wind over the deck, the J/30

One J/30 owner commented, "Having sailed the C&C Mega 30, this boat is fantastic!"

---

will do about 5.5 to 6 knots to windward in a slight chop using the 105% genoa and a single-reefed mainsail. In puffy conditions, the mainsheet traveler should be played constantly to keep the boat on her feet. This is typical of fractionally-rigged boats with their relatively large mainsails. As with all modern, low-wetted-surface boats, the J/30 goes fastest when sailed almost upright, and a great deal of sailing effort should be directed to keeping her in that upright trim.

With light displacement for her waterline, the J/30 should be sailed around waves rather than into them. It is important to keep the boat from bobbling in a chop, which can stop her dead in her tracks.

Spinnaker reaching, the boat is far more stable than the typical IOR boat, which has a pronounced rounding-up tendency when overpowered by the spinnaker. This lack of broaching tendency is the characteristic that makes the J/30 sail well above her rating off the wind in heavy air. Under these conditions, the typical IOR boat spends a substantial part of her sailing time dragging her rudder through the water sideways in an attempt to keep the boat on her feet and pointed in the right direction. The J/30 has a straight, relatively flat run aft, with the rudder well aft of the normal waterline. This produces a boat which surfs easily and quickly while maintaining fairly straightforward steering characteristics.

There are no hydraulics on the J/30, but there are still plenty of ways to play with the rig. The powerful block and tackle backstay adjuster is easily capable of putting all the bend in the rig that you could ever want without loading the backstay heavily. Since both upper and lower shrouds lead aft of the mast, backstay tension increases forestay tension without the need for either jumpers or running backstays. For offshore work, however, it would be a good idea to equip the boat with running backstays to minimize pumping. Because the shrouds lead aft and to some extent double as backstays, shroud tension should be much tighter than you would normally expect to use in a boat of this size. If there is any slack in the leeward shrouds when going to windward even in heavy air, there is not enough tension on the shrouds.

Sailing any fractional rig is substantially different from sailing the masthead rig. The mainsail is far more important in the fractional rig, both because of its size and the fact that the leading edge of the main is the highest sail on the boat. For this reason, J-Boats recommends that the full main be carried whenever possible, to keep the upper part of the sail in clear air.

Fortunately, the J/30 class newsletter is full of suggestions on how to sail the fractional rig. Given the fact that the boat is a 30-footer that rates the same under the IOR as many as 34- to 36-footers, many sailors will have to learn a new set of sail trim rules to be competitive. There is no doubt that with good sails and the ability to use them, the J/30 can sail up to and even above her IOR rating.

The J/30 is one of the first boats that will receive a standard MHS rating. This will allow owners to participate in high-level open racing while minimizing measurement costs. The J/30 is treated quite fairly under MHS. Average speed predictions are 4.24 knots in eight knots of wind, 5.35 knots in 12 knots of wind, and 5.92 knots in 16 knots of breeze.

Despite her comfortable interior, it is sailing performance that is selling the J/30. She has sailing performance to sell, too. One J/30 owner commented, "Having sailed the Mega 30, this boat is *fantastic!*"

Handling Under Power

The J/30 comes with a two-cylinder 15 horsepower Yanmar diesel, raw water cooled. Fresh water cooling is a $420 option. This is more than adequate power for a 7,000 lb boat. Owners report excellent handling under power.

The Yanmar engines have a reputation for a fairly high level of vibration and noise. The one in the J/30 is no exception. We have never cared for Yanmar instrument panels, which are long on idiot lights and short on instruments.

The engine of the J/30 is unlikely to accumulate many hours. The boat sails so well that there is little excuse to use the engine except to charge batteries, and for motoring in a truly flat calm. With the optional shower, the engine may acquire a few more hours heating water for a little post-race cleanup—a luxury on a 30' racing boat.

LIVABILITY

Deck Layout

Under the strict one-design class rules, the deck layout of the J/30 is tightly controlled. Since the deck layout is the product of much careful thought by the Johnstones, it is unlikely that anyone would want to alter it substantially.

As with most modern boats, less thought goes into

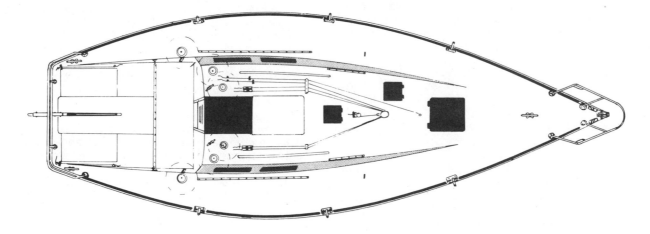

The J/30 is a high-performance racer with surprisingly good accommodations: no luxury cruiser, but quite habitable

the arrangement for mooring and anchoring than in the arrangement for sailing. The J/30 does have two bow chocks, but their location well back from the stem accentuates the boat's tendency to sail around on the mooring or anchor. The class rules allow for the changing of the mooring cleats and chocks. Sailors who plan to cruise the boat much are likely to take advantage of this allowance.

There is an excellent self-draining anchor well in the starboard deck abreast the mast. This is designed to hold a Danforth 22-S or 20-H, either of which is more than adequate for the boat. Anchor warp is carried in the forepeak locker, feeding onto the deck via a hawsepipe. A second anchor can easily be carried in one of the cockpit lockers, which are too small for sails anyway.

Location and length of jib tracks have been pretty well refined, and leave little room for modification under the class rules. The boat comes equipped with six Barient winches. The only winch option is the substitution of Barient 27 self-tailers in the place of the standard Barient 25 primaries.

Cam stoppers are used for halyards and guys. Care is required when releasing these stoppers under load, for they are either on or off.

It is easy to move around the deck of the J/30, even when the boat is well-heeled. The deck features excellent molded-in nonskid. The decks are likely to be slippery when the boat is new due to traces of mold release, which can be removed by scrubbing with a stiff brush and some detergent.

The cockpit of the J/30 is not particularly comfortable. There are no cockpit coamings. The tiller sweeps most of the cockpit. It is difficult to brace well while grinding winches. We found that the best way to trim headsails was from the windward side, taking a wrap around the leeward sheet winch, leading the sheet across the cockpit to the windward winch. This allows the crew weight to be kept on the windward rail.

It is fairly convenient for the helmsman to control the mainsail. The mainsheet traveler is recessed in the bridgedeck, and is close to the hand of the helmsman. The helmsman also has convenient teak foot braces on either side of the deck. These do complicate sitting in the cockpit when at anchor.

The cockpit scuppers drain directly through the transom, a simple and seamanlike solution. There is unfortunately no real provision for the storage of a man-overboard pole, required equipment for long-distance racing.

The companionway bulkhead slopes forward. This means that the dropboards cannot be left out when it is raining. Since there is no other means of ventilation during rain, it could be quite stuffy below in a prolonged period of bad weather.

Generally, the deck layout of the J/30 is clean and efficient for racing, but less than comfortable for cruising. This not so subtle difference puts the J/30 more in the class of the "racer-cruiser" rather than the "cruiser-racer," however those two ambiguous terms are defined.

Interior
The interior of the J/30 is light, roomy, and well thought out. The general appearance is high-tech traditional, with varnished white cedar ceiling, laminated ash trim, and the optional, but highly-recommended solid teak and holly cabin sole.

Headroom is a good 6' at the after end of the main cabin, tapering to about 5'6" at the forward end of the cabin.

The forward cabin features a large V-berth, with molded storage alcoves over and watertight bins under. A privacy curtain can separate the forward cabin from the head.

The head compartment is surprisingly comfortable. Both the mast and an ash grabrail offer good handholds and bracing points. It is most comfortable to use the sink while sitting on the toilet seat, a practical solution in a small boat.

Ventilation is provided in all three interior areas by three plastic-framed opening hatches. There is no provision for ventilation in heavy weather.

The main cabin of the J/30 is quite remarkable for a 30' racing boat. It is wide, comfortable, and attractive. There is no hull liner. The interior of the deck molding is finished with gelcoat. There is good storage both behind and under the settees. The standard layout features lockers with sliding doors behind the settees. Bob Johnstone's own boat has three deep, cedar-lined bins behind the settee, one for each member of the racing crew. This is a good solution to the problem of housekeeping during the race.

The icebox/chart table deserves special comment. As in many smaller boats, the top of the icebox is the chart table. In the J/30, however, the chart table surface is not the top of the icebox. Rather, it slides away to expose the icebox trap. This provides a "real" chart table, which will not allow charts to become soggy from dripping water every time someone dives into the icebox.

Quarterberths are very large. This allows them to be used for sail storage at the same time they are slept in—a common practice in offshore racing.

The galley is'nt particularly imaginative, but it rarely is on a 30' boat. The cook must reach over the sink to get to the stove, a gimbaled two-burner alcohol unit. There are wood shelves directly over the stove, a possible fire hazard. Galley locker space is limited by the size of the boat.

While the J/30 is no luxury cruiser, the interior is quite habitable, intelligently finished. Joinerwork and finish are of good stock boat quality. We would strongly recommend the optional cabin table, a well-mounted and fiddled dropleaf unit with storage bins under traps in the center section. The table will seat six for dinner in reasonable comfort.

CONCLUSIONS

The J/30 is a high-performance racer with surprisingly good accommodations. It is in general intelligently laid out, strongly built, and well finished.

The J/30 offers the opportunity to get into "big-boat" style racing and high performance at a reasonable cost. It is therefore a reasonable alternative for those who might otherwise consider a "stock" one-tonner but feel they can't afford it.

The J/30 will not be out-designed under any rule, because it was not built to any rule. Because of this, it is likely to enjoy a long production run, and should be a logical step up for the several thousand owners of the J/24. The Johnstones know their market—the young, performance oriented sailor. They are tuned in to him, and they are cashing in when others are bailing out.

The Nonsuch 30: An Odd Eye-Opener

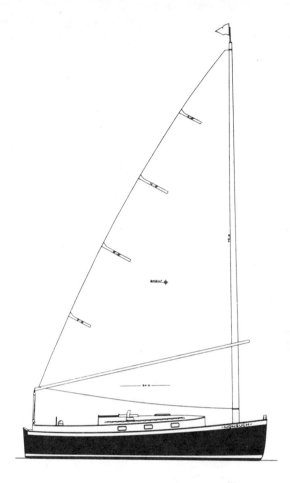

THE BOAT AND THE BUILDER

The Nonsuch 30 is an oddity. She is a fin keeled, spade ruddered boat with an unstayed wishbone cat rig. Weird.

She is built in Canada, whose main boatbuilding export has been C&C sailboats. Come to think of it, all her construction details look very much like those of C&C boats. This isn't unusual, since George Hinterhoeller, the builder, was formerly the president of C&C, and one of the founders of the three-company merger that created C&C Yachts.

When Hinterhoeller left C&C to recreate Hinterhoeller Yachts Ltd., he took with him those characteristics that have given C&C a reputation for quality: good attention to finish detail and high-quality balsa-cored hull construction.

The Nonsuch 30 is the concept of retired ocean racer Gordon Fisher, the design of Mark Ellis, and the created child of Hinterhoeller, who is one of the few production boatbuilders with the legitimate title Master Boatbuilder, earned the hard way through apprenticeship in Europe.

The Nonsuch 30 was originally a Great Lakes phenomenon, which is to be expected considering her origins. She is now becoming established on the US East Coast, however, and the boat shows every sign of increasing in popularity. This is not surprising considering the amount of boat that has somehow been slipped into an LOA of less than 31'

CONSTRUCTION

George Hinterhoeller's reputation as a builder is not unearned. His balsa-cored hulls are known for being light and strong. It is probably not an exaggeration to say that he knows as much about cored construction as any boatbuilder around.

Both hull and deck of the Nonsuch 30 are balsa cored. The hull and deck are joined by a through-bolted, butyl-bedded joint capped with an aluminum toerail. The butyl tape used for this purpose has no real structural properties, but does create a good watertight seal. A sealant such as 3M 5200 provides equivalent sealant properties with greater structural properties, and we prefer its use in hull-to-deck joints. It is hard to quibble with the Nonsuch's strongly through-bolted joint, however.

The external lead keel is bolted on with stainless steel bolts. These pass through floor timbers of unidirectional roving, transferring keel loading from the garboard section to a greater area of the hull.

The cockpit seats and coamings contain a surprisingly large number of sharply-radiused turns. Gelcoat cracks are likely to develop here earlier than anywhere else in the hull.

Specifications

LOA	30'4"
DWL	28'9"
Beam	11'10"
Draft	5'0"
Displacement	10,500 lbs
Ballast	4,500 lbs
Sail Area	540 sq ft

Hinterhoeller Yachts Ltd.
8 Keefer Road
St. Catherines, Ontario
Canada L2M 7N9

The freestanding mast requires modification of normal construction methods. While no chainplates are required, substantial bulkheading is required in the area of the mast to absorb the considerable forces generated by the unstayed mast. The forward six feet of the hull is strongly bulkheaded for this purpose, and no sign of undue strain could be detected.

Because there is no rigging to hold the mast in the boat should she capsize, alternative means must be found. This is accomplished by lagging a cast aluminum, hexagonally-shaped female mast step to the hull. The butt of the mast is fitted with a hexagonal male counterpart which is strongly joined to the mast step by stainless steel hexhead set screws. The mast is further connected to the hull by a deck-level pin which passes through the mast and the cast aluminum deck collar.

Deck hardware is properly backed for load distribution.

The Nonsuch does not suffer from "catboat disease"—the tendency to develop monstrous weather helm as the breeze pipes up

There are a few surprising shortcomings. The aluminum rudder quadrant stops have sharp edges which could easily cut into the exhaust line inside the cockpit lockers. This could happen—it had happened on the boat we sailed—if the upper rudder retaining nut is loose, allowing the rudder to drop down slightly. Gate valves are used on most through hull fittings below the waterline, rather than seacocks or ball valves, and no valves at all are fitted on drains and exhaust lines at the bottom of the transom, despite the fact that they could be submerged in a heavily loaded boat.

Despite these deficiencies, construction is generally to very high standards, well above average for the industry.

PERFORMANCE

Handling under sail

The Nonsuch 30 is one of the most boring boats we have ever sailed. Tacking requires no yelling, releasing of sheets, cranking, tailing, or trimming. The helmsman simply says "I think we'll tack" and gives the wheel a quarter turn, being careful not to upset his Mt. Gay and tonic. Nonsuch quietly slides through about 85° and settles on the other tack with a minimum of fuss. Beating up a narrow channel simply requires repeating the above process.

The person who learns to sail on a Nonsuch 30 will receive a rude awakening when switching to a more athletic boat—which means almost any other 30 foot sailboat. The Nonsuch 30 is simply one of the easiest boats to sail we've seen.

This doesn't mean that it's necessarily easy to sail well. Getting the most out of the boat upwind definitely requires some practice. The aluminum mast is quite flexible, allowing the top of the mast to fall off as the wind increases. The sail's draft will shift, changing its efficiency. In about 10 knots of breeze, the top of the mast falls to leeward about a foot. This can be a little disconcerting to those used to a fairly rigid stayed mast.

Sail shape is controlled by the "choker," a line which controls the fore and aft trim of the wishbone and functions as a clew outhaul. Tensioning the choker pulls the wishbone aft, flattening the sail. The sail is slab reefed pretty much the same as a conventional mainsail.

The Nonsuch mainsail is 540 square feet, with a hoist of 45 feet and a foot of 24 feet. By way of comparison the mainsail of the Irwin 52 is 525 square feet, and that of the Cal 31 210 square feet. The sail does not handle like a sail of 540 square feet, fortunately. The wishbone is rigged with permanent lazy jacks which hold the sail as it is dropped. Furling merely involves tying ties around the neatly cradled sail for the sake of aesthetics. Dousing the main or reefing is easily accomplished by one person, as all sail controls lead back to the cockpit.

The Nonsuch does not suffer from "catboat disease"—the tendency to develop monstrous weather helm as the breeze pipes up. She is, rather, remarkably well mannered, with a surprisingly light helm in the light to moderate winds in which we sailed her. Downwind she held course with the wheel brake off and hands off the wheel. Performance was almost as good upwind at moderate angles of heel.

She is a stiff boat. The flexible mast allows a substantial amount of air to be spilled from the main as the wind pipes up, removing much heeling force. We found that the boat went better upwind with a reef in the main even at moderate angles of heel once the upper mast began to fall off. Getting sail off the more flexible upper part of the mast allows better draft control as the wind increases.

Having only one sail can be a real nail-chewer to the uncured racer. Whether it blows five knots or 25, the maximum amount of sail you can have is already up. Some unreconstructed racers have equipped the Nonsuch 30 with a blooper for light air downwind performance, and gear for handling this sail is now a factory option at $450.

The Nonsuch 30 is no Cape Cod catboat under the water. She has a moderate aspect ratio fin keel, low wetted surface, and a freestanding semi-balanced spade rudder. These characteristics greatly add to her performance.

With all sail controls led back to the cockpit, she is a natural candidate for singlehanding. We strongly recommend the optional self-tailing winches for all functions if shorthanded sailing is contemplated. An option is being developed which would replace the cumbersome six-part mainsheet—over 100 feet of it—with a less-powerful tackle and a self-tailing winch. This will definitely be a desirable option, for otherwise the mainsheet trimmer is up to his knees in dacron line when the boat is trimmed from broad off to hard on the wind.

The Nonsuch 30 is not the boat for the hardcore grand prix racer. Her entire sail inventory consists of that one big sail, with perhaps, but not necessarily, a single downwind sail. You will not become the bosom buddy of any racing sailmaker by owning a Nonsuch. Then again, no sailmaker will ever have a second mortgage on your boat, either.

Handling Under Power

The Nonsuch 30 was originally equipped with a 23 horsepower Volvo MD 11C diesel with saildrive. This basically eliminated engine installation and alignment problems for the builder, saving both time and money. These units have an integral cast zinc to protect the vulnerable aluminum lower unit from galvanic corrosion. A special Volvo-supplied zinc is required—not an item that you can pick up in any boatyard. About hull number 125, this installation was changed to a more conventional engine and shaft arrangement, utilizing a new 27 horsepower Westerbeke diesel.

Either engine will drive the boat to hull speed. We greatly prefer the conventional engine installation, which is understood and can be worked on by most boatyards. It is less vulnerable to corrosion, and runs quietly and smoothly. The saildrive installation is still available, but we recommend that its use be confined to fresh water.

Because of her high freeboard the Nonsuch 30 will be susceptible to crosswinds when docking. With most of her windage forward she will have a tendency to blow bow downwind. A good hand on the throttle and gearshift will be a real plus in tight docking situations. Without the complication of wind we found her easy to back down into a slip, once a sharp burst of throttle was given to activate the folding prop with which our test boat was equipped.

If this boat is to be called an offshore sailboat, we think there should be an optional cockpit arrangement

LIVABILITY

Deck Layout

Because the Nonsuch 30 has no standing rigging, her side decks are devoid of obstacles. Because she has no headsails there are no sheeting angles to be concerned with.

For cruising the optional bowsprit/anchor roller with hawsepipe to the otherwise unusable forepeak is highly desirable. Otherwise, anchor and rode must be stored in one of the cockpit lockers and dragged forward every time you wish to anchor. We also recommend the installation of a bow pulpit. With no shrouds to hold when forward there is a great feeling of vulnerability on the bow. These things may make the Nonsuch 30 uncatboatlike in appearance, but they will greatly add to the safety and convenience of both sailing and anchoring.

The cockpit of the Nonsuch 30 is large and deep. It is not particularly comfortable, and without four inch or thicker cockpit cushions it is impossible for a person of average height to see forward over the cabin. The helmsman's position is elevated above that of the other seats, but visibility even from that position is only fair.

With the standard white-on-white gelcoat scheme the cockpit of the Nonsuch 30 is sterile and generates a lot of glare on sunny days. The optional contrasting nonskid and teak cockpit grate would alleviate part of this problem.

The large cockpit creates other problems. First, you should never raft up with other boats at anchor. A friendly crowd of eight could easily fit in the cockpit.

There are more serious problems associated with the cockpit design. The Nonsuch 30 is promoted as a "new offshore concept." We think this is an unfortunate choice of words, because the standard cockpit is not suited to offshore use. There is no bridgedeck. The companionway goes almost to the level of the cockpit sole—about three feet below the level of the lowest point in the cockpit coamings. Coupled with the huge cockpit volume, this creates a situation that cannot in any good conscience be called an offshore configuration. If this boat is to be called an offshore sailboat, we think there should be an optional cockpit arrangement—a large bridgedeck which could incorporate life raft storage, two more large cockpit drains, and perhaps a raised cockpit sole to further reduce the cockpit's volume.

There are three cockpit lockers: deep port and starboard lockers, and a lazarette propane locker set up to hold two ten-pound gas bottles. The large side locker should incorporate some form of easily-removed retainer system to prevent items there from rolling under the cockpit.

On the boat we sailed the drain line from the propane locker overboard was too long. At the low point in the loop water had collected in the hose, which exits through the transom and is under water in many sailing conditions. This water prevents any propane leakage from draining overboard as designed. The hose should be shortened to remedy a potentially hazardous situation.

When tacking or jibing it is easy for the helmsman to get caught by the mainsheet as the boom comes over. A better lead would be welcome here, perhaps having the mainsheet system incorporated into the stern rail.

Interior

The interior volume of the Nonsuch 30 is an eye opener, even to those used to the modern trend toward maximum interior volume on minimum overall length. To anyone used only to the interior space of an older boat, the interior of the Nonsuch 30 is absolutely stunning.

The waterline and beam of the Nonsuch 30 are about the same as that of a modern 36 foot cruiser-racer, and that beam is carried quite a bit further forward. Coupled with high topsides and a highly-crowned deck house, this yields a boat with tremendous interior volume for her overall length.

The interior layout is unusual but practical. There is no forward cabin in the conventional sense. This isn't a real drawback. The forward cabin on the typical 30 footer is only useful for sleeping or sail stowage, and frequently has berths which narrow so much forward that an all-night game of footsie for the occupants of those berths is a necessity rather than a pleasure.

The forwardmost six feet of the boat is given over to two huge hanging lockers and a great deal of storage space which has been created by the three transverse and two fore and aft bulkheads that stiffen the hull in the way of the mast. This storage space is not readily accessible, and will probably end up as the boat's attic, collecting little-used piles of gear until the day when it must be all removed to get at the mast step to remove the mast.

The rest of the boat is basically one large cabin. What would be considered the main cabin occupies the forward third of the interior. At the forward end are the

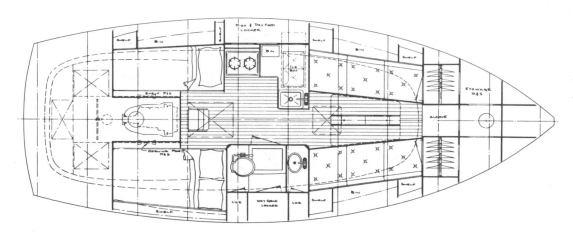

aforementioned hanging lockers and a bureau. There are shelves and bins outboard of the two long settees that face each other at a comfortable distance across the cabin, with a dropleaf table on centerline. Varnished pine ceiling behind the settees is a welcome note in an otherwise dark teak interior.

The galley is to port midships. The cook is out of the traffic flow yet located in the center of activity if there are people both below and topsides. The galley has a gimballed propane stove with oven, a well-insulated icebox with (hurrah!) an insulated, gasketed lid, and a deep sink nearly on centerline which will easily drain on either tack. The icebox melt water is pumped into the galley sink. For the sake of aesthetics the icebox drain should tee into the sink drain below the sink, relieving the cook of the dubious pleasure of watching the things which dribble to the bottom of the icebox flow through the sink.

The head is opposite the galley. Because of the pronounced deckhouse camber, headroom there decreases rapidly as you move outboard.

An unusual option is a demand propane-fired hot water heater. This compact unit mounts on a head bulkhead, and has electric ignition. When a hot water faucet is turned on the heater fires, and will heat steaming hot water as fast as the water pressure system will deliver it. This is considerably less complicated than the normal engine water heat exchanger/110 volt powered storage water heaters found on most boats. Since the boat is already plumbed for propane, installation of this compact heater is straightforward. We would expect to see more utilization of this type of heater on boats in the future.

There are quarterberths port and starboard aft of the galley and head. The standard berth starboard is a double, with a single to port. An option provides doubles on both sides, although filling all the berths on the boat requires an open mind and no highly-developed sense of privacy.

Despite the open interior of the boat, privacy can be attained through another unusual interior option. For another $695 a hidden slide-up partition is installed between the galley and the forward/main cabin, and a bifold louvered teak door which folds up against the head bulkhead. When closed, the door and partition divide the boat into two large compartments for sleeping, with reasonable separation between them. The occupants of the thus-created forward cabin must enter the aft cabin either to go on deck or to use the head, an inconvenience.

Like the cockpit, the huge interior invites company. In the event of a sudden rainstorm, the eight people who previously occupied your cockpit could easily move below to continue their revelry. If there were already eight below—a not unlikely circumstance—you may be in trouble. Sixteen people is too many belowdecks even in the Nonsuch 30.

Ventilation of the interior is excellent, with seven opening ports, two hatches, and two dorade boxes. The propane heater vents overboard through its own exhaust stack.

CONCLUSIONS

The Nonsuch 30 is an unusual boat by any standards. The unstayed wishbone cat rig is becoming increasingly popular. It does greatly reduce the cost of sails, spars, and rigging.

The general appearance of the boat is similar to a traditional catboat, although she will never be taken to be a product of the Crosby yard. Her generally catboatlike hull dimensions produce the maximum hull volume on a minimum overall length.

Her average delivered price of $67,000 seems high for a 30 foot boat. What must be remembered, however is that she is more the size of a 36 footer with the ends cut off. The price is a little less painful when viewed in this manner.

Despite her billing we do not consider her an offshore cruiser with her standard cockpit arrangement. She will make an excellent coastal cruiser for a couple or a family with up to three small children or two older children.

Because she is easy to sail and rig, has a big cockpit and a roomy, well-ventilated interior, she should make a good Caribbean charter boat for two couples, although head access is a minor problem from the forward cabin. Surprisingly, none have entered the southern charter business.

The Nonsuch 30 is not a traditionalist's catboat. She lacks the sweeping sheer, low freeboard, gaff rig, and barndoor rudder of the Cape Cod catboat. She also lacks that boat's infamous sailing characteristics—ferocious weather helm, inability to go to windward, and a man-killing mainsail.

She is a relatively simple, easily sailed boat for the convivial sailor who doesn't mind being seen in what many might consider an oddball boat with an oddball interior and an oddball rig. The more you look at it, the less oddball it seems.

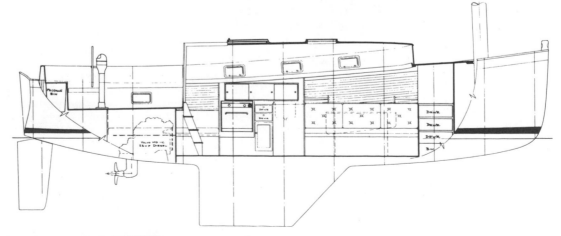

The Olson 30:
Ultra Light, Ultra Fast

THE BOAT AND THE BUILDER

The Olson 30 is of a breed of sailboats born in Santa Cruz, California called the *ULDB,* an acronym for *ultra light displacement boat.* ULDBs are big dinghies—long on the waterline, short on the interior, narrow on the beam, and very light on both the displacement and the pricetag. ULDBs attract a different kind of sailor—the type for whom performance means everything.

For some yachting traditionalists, the arrival of ULDB has been a hard pill to swallow. Part of this is simple resentment of a ULDB's ability to sail boat-for-boat with a racer-cruiser up to 15' longer (and a whole lot more expensive). Part of it is the realization that, to sail a ULDB might mean having to learn a whole new set of sailing skills. Part of it is a reaction to the near-manic enthusiasts of Santa Cruz, where nearly 100 ULDBs race for pure fun—without the help of race committees, protest committees, or handicaps (in Santa Cruz, IOR is a dirty word). And part of the traditionalists' resentment is their gut feeling that ULDBs aren't real yachts.

In 1970, Californian George Olson tried an experiment and created the first ULDB. He thought if he took a boat with the same displacement and sail area as a Cal 20, but made it longer and narrower, it might go faster. The boat he built was called *Grendel* and it did go faster than a Cal 20, much faster than anyone had expected. The plug for *Grendel* was later widened by Santa Cruz boatbuilder Ron Moore, and used to make the mold for the Moore 24, a now popular ULDB one-design.

In the meantime, George Olson had joined up with another Santa Cruz builder by the name of Bill Lee, and together they designed and built the Santa Cruz 27. Olson also helped Lee build his 1977 Transpac winner *Merlin,* a 67', 20,000 pound monster of a ULDB (she has subsequently been legislated out of the Transpac race). Then Olson and several other of Lee's employees started their own boatbuilding firm (in Santa Cruz, of course) called Pacific Boats.

The first project for Pacific Boats was the Olson 30, which was put into production in 1978. Two hundred and ten of these 3600 pound ULDBs have been sold since then, and the builder claims they have gathered in great enough numbers for one-design racing in Seattle, the Great Lakes, Annapolis, Texas and Long Island Sound, as well as several spots in California. Pacific Boats is a small firm (23 employees) that builds only the Olson 30 and the Olson 40, both to quality standards.

CONSTRUCTION

Some people wonder how ULDBs can be built so light, yet still be seaworthy offshore. The answer is three-fold: first, a light boat is subjected to lighter loads, when pounding through a heavy sea, than a boat of greater displacement. Second, there is a tremendous saving in

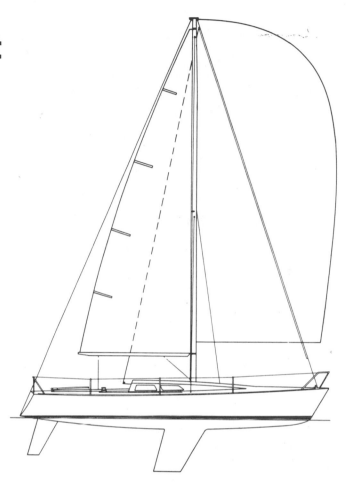

Specifications

LOA	30'
LWL	27.5'
Beam	9.3'
Draft	5.1'
Displacement	3600 lbs
Ballast	1800 lbs
Sail Area (RSAT)	380 sq ft

Pacific Boats
1041 17th Avenue
Santa Cruz, CA 95062

weight with a stripped-out interior. Third, as a whole, ULDB builders have construction standards that are well above average for production sailboats. The ULDB builders say that their close proximity to each other in Santa Cruz combined with an open sharing of technology has enabled them to achieve these standards.

The Olson 30 is no exception. The hull and deck are fiberglass vacuum-bagged over a balsa core. The process of vacuum-bagging insures maximum saturation of the laminate and core with a minimum of resin, making the hull light and stiff. The builder claims that they have so refined the construction of the Olson 30 that each finished hull weighs within 10 pounds of the standard. The deck of the Olson does not have plywood inserts in place of the balsa where winches are mounted, instead relying on external backing plates for strength.

The hull-to-deck joint is an inward turned overlapping flange, glued with a rigid compound called Reid's adhesive, and mechanically fastened with closely spaced bolts through a slotted aluminum toerail. This provides a strong, protected joint, seaworthy enough for sailing offshore. We would prefer a semi-rigid adhesive, however, because it is less likely to fracture and cause a leak in the event of a hard collision. The aluminum toerail provides a convenient location for outboard sheet leads, but is painful to those sitting on the rail.

The Olson 30's 1800 pound keel is deep (5.1' draft) and less than 5" thick. Narrow, bolted-on keels need extra athwartships support. The Olson 30 accomplishes this with nine 5/8" bolts and one 1" bolt (to which the lifting eye is attached). The lead keel is faired with autobody putty and then completely wrapped with fiberglass to seal the putty from the marine environment. Too many builders neglect sealing autobody putty-faired keels, and too many boat owners then find the putty peeling off at a later date. The Olson's finished keel is painted, and, on the boats we have seen, remarkably fair.

The keel-stepped, single-spreader, tapered mast is cleanly rigged with 5/32" Navtec rod rigging and internal tangs. The mast section is big enough for peace of mind in heavy air. The halyards exit the mast at well-spaced intervals, so as not to create a weak spot. The shroud chainplates are securely attached to half-bulkheads of 1" plywood. In addition, a tierod attaches the deck to the mast, tensioned by a turnbuckle. While this arrangement should provide adequate strength, we would prefer both a tierod and a full bulkhead that spans the width of the cabin so as to absorb the compressive loads that the tension of the rig puts on the deck.

The rudder's construction is labor intensive, but strong. Urethane foam is hand shaped to templates, then glued to a 2" thick solid fiberglass rudder post. The builder prefers fiberglass because it has more "memory" than aluminum or steel. Stainless steel straps are wrapped around the rudder and mechanically fastened to the post. Then the whole assembly is faired, fiberglassed, and painted.

PERFORMANCE

Handling Under Sail

For those of you who agonize over whether your PHRF rating is fair, consider the ratings of ULDBs. The Santa Cruz 50 rates 0; *that's right—zero.* The 67' *Merlin* has rated as low as minus 60. The Olson 30 rates anywhere from 90 to 114, depending on the local handicapper. Olson 30 owners tell us that the boat will sail to a PHRF rating of 96, but she will almost never sail to her astronomical IOR rating of 32' (the IOR heavily penalizes ULDBs).

ULDBs are fast. They are apt to be on the tender side, and sail with a quick, "jerky" motion through waves. Instead of punching through a wave, they ride over it. You may get to where you are going fast, but with the motion of the boat and the Spartan interior you won't get there in comfort. Olson 30 owners tell us that they do far less cruising and far more racing that they had expected to do when they bought the boat. They say it's more fun to race because the boat is so lively.

Like most ULDBs the Olson 30 races best at the extremes of wind conditions—under 10 knots and over 20 knots. Although her masthead rig may appear short, it is more than powerful enough for her displacement. Owners tell us that she accelerates so quickly you can almost tack at will—a real tactical advantage in light air. In winds under 10 knots they say she sails above her PHRF rating both upwind and downwind.

In moderate breezes it's a different story. Once the wind gets much above 10 knots, it's time to change down to the #2 genoa. In 15 knots, especially if the seas are choppy, it's very difficult for the Olson 30 to save her time on boats of conventional displacement, according to three-time national champ Kevin Connally. The Olson 30 is always faster downwind, but even with a crew of 5 or 6, she just cannot hang in there upwind.

In winds above 20 knots, the Olson 30 still has her problems upwind, but when she turns the weather mark the magic begins. As soon as she has enough wind to either surf or plane, the Olson 30 can make up for all she looses upwind, and more. The builder claims that she has pegged speedometers at 25 knots in the big swells and strong westerlies off the coast of California. That is, if the crew can keep her 1800 pound keel under her 761 sq. ft. spinnaker.

The key to competitiveness in a strong breeze is the

ability of the crew. Top crews say that, because she is so quick to respond, they have fewer problems handling her in heavy air than a heavier, conventional boat. However, an inexperienced crew which cannot react fast enough can have big problems. "The handicappers say she can fly downwind, so they give us a low rating (PHRF), but they don't understand that we *have to sail slow* just to stay in control," complained the crew of one new owner.

Like any higher performance class of sailboat, the Olson 30 attracts competent sailors. Hence, the boat is pushed to a higher level of overall performance, and the PHRF rating reflects this. An inexperienced sailor must realize that he may have a tougher time making her sail to this inflated rating than a boat that is less "hot."

The two most common mistakes that new Olson 30 owners make are pinching upwind and allowing the boat to heel excessively. ULDBs cannot be sailed at the 30 degrees of heel to which many sailors of conventional boats are accustomed. To keep her flat you must be quick to shorten sail, move the sheet leads outboard, and get more crew weight on the rail. You can't afford to have a person sitting to leeward trimming the genoa in a 12-knot breeze. To keep her thin keel from stalling upwind, owners tell us it's important to keep the sheets eased and the boat footing.

Being masthead-rigged, the Olson 30 needs a larger sail inventory than a fractionally rigged boat. Class rules allow one mainsail, six headsails (jibs and spinnakers) and a 75% storm jib. Owners who do mostly handicap racing tell us they often carry more than six headsails.

Handling Under Power

Only 3% of the Olson 30s sold to date have been equipped with inboard power. This is because the extra weight of the inboard and the drag of the propeller, strut and shaft are a real disadvantage when racing against the majority of Olson 30s, which are equipped with outboard engines.

The Olson 30 is just barely light enough to be pushed by a 4-5 hp. outboard, which is the largest outboard that even the most healthy sailor should be hefting over a transom. It takes a 7.5 hp. outboard to push the Olson 30 at 6.5 knots in a flat calm. The Olson's raked transom requires an extra long outboard bracket, which puts the engine throttle and shift out of reach for anyone much less than 6' tall: "A real pain in the ass," said one owner. Storage is a problem, too. Even if you could get the outboard through the stern lazarette's small hatch, you wouldn't want to race with the extra weight so far aft. So most owners end up storing the outboard on the cabin sole.

The inboard, a 154 pound, 7 hp. BMW diesel, is a $4500 option. Unlike most boats, the Olson 30 will probably not return the investment in an inboard when you sell the boat, because it detracts from the boat's primary purpose—racing.

Without an inboard you have a problem charging the battery. Owners who race with extensive electronics have to take the battery ashore after every race for recharging. If the Olson 30 weren't such a joy to sail in light air, and so maneuverable in tight places, the lack of inboard power would be a serious enough drawback to turn away more sailors than it does.

LIVABILITY

Deck Layout

In most respects, the Olson 30 is a good sea boat. Although the cockpit is 6½' long, the wide seats and narrow floor result in a relatively small cockpit volume, so that little sea water can collect in the cockpit if the boat is pooped or knocked down. However, foot room is restricted, while the width of the seats makes it awkward to brace your legs on the leeward seat. The seats themselves are comfortable because they are angled up and the seatbacks are angled back. There are gutters to drain water off the leeward seat. The long mainsheet traveller is mounted across the cockpit—good for racing but not so good for cruising.

The Olson 30's single companionway dropboard is latchable from inside the cabin, a real necessity in a storm offshore. A man overboard pole tube in the stern is standard equipment. Teak toerails on the cockpit coaming and on the forward part of the cabin house provide good footing, and there are handholds on the aft part of the cabin house.

The tapered aluminum stanchions are set into sockets molded into the deck and glassed to the inside of the hull, a strong, clean, leak-proof system. However, the stanchions are not glued or mechanically fastened into the sockets. If pulled upwards with great force they can be pulled out. We feel this is a safety hazard. Tight lifelines would help prevent this from happening, but most racing crews tend to leave them slightly loose so as to be able to lean farther outboard when hanging over the rail upwind. If the stanchions were fastened into the sockets with bolts or screws they would undoubtedly leak. A leakproof solution to this problem should be devised and made available to Olson 30 owners.

The cockpit has two drains of adequate diameter. The bilge pump, a Guzzler 500, is mounted in the cockpit. The Guzzler is an easily operated, high capacity pump. However, its seeming fragility worries us (see PS,

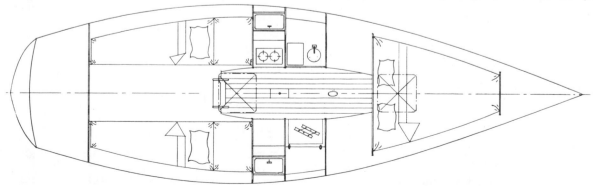

August 1, 1981). As is common on most boats, the stern lazarette is not sealed off from the rest of the interior. If the boat were pooped or knocked down with the lazarette open, water could rush below through the lazarette relatively unrestricted. As the Olson 30 has a shallow sump, there is little place for water to go except above the cabin sole.

A "paint-roller" type non-skid is molded into the Olson 30's deck. It provides excellent traction, but it is more difficult to keep clean than conventional patterned non-skid.

The Olson 30 is well laid out with hardware of reasonable, but not exceptional, quality. All halyards and pole controls lead to the cockpit though Easylock I clutch stoppers (see PS September 15, 1982). The Easylocks are barely big enough to hold the halyards; they slip an inch under heavy loads. Older Olsons were equipped with Howard Rope Clutches. The Howards had a history of breaking (although the manufacturer has now corrected the problem).

The primary winches, Barient 22s, are also barely adequate. Some owners we talked to had replaced them with more powerful models. Schaefer headsail track cars are standard equipment. One owner complained that he had to replace them with Merrimans because the Schaefers kept slipping. Leading the vang to either rail and leading the reefs aft is also recommended.

The mast partner is snug, leaving no space for mast blocks. The mast step is movable to adjust the prebend of the spar. The partner has a lip, over which a neoprene collar fits. The collar is hose-clamped to the mast. This should make a watertight mast boot. However, on the boat we sailed, the bail to which the boom vang attached obstructed the collar, causing water to collect and pour into the cabin.

The yoked backstay is adjustable from either quarter of the stern, one side being a 2-to-1 gross adjustment and the other side being an 8-to-1 fine tune. A Headfoil II is standard equipment. There is a babystay led to a ballbearing track with a 6-to-1 purchase for easy adjustment. The track is tied to the thin plywood of the forward V-berth with a wire and turnbuckle. On the boat we sailed, the padeye to which the babystay tierod is attached was tearing out of the V-berth.

There is a port in the deck directly over the lifting eye in the bilge. This makes for quick and easy drysailing. The Olson 30, however, is not easily trailered; her 3600 pounds is too much for all but the largest cars, and her 9.3' beam requires a special trailering permit.

Belowdecks

The Olson 30 is cramped belowdecks. Her low freeboard, short cabin house and substantial sheer may make her the sexiest-looking production boat on the water, but the price is headroom of only 4'5". There is not even enough headroom for comfortable stooping; moving about below is a real chore.

To offset the confinement of the interior, the builder has done all that is possible to make it light and airy. In addition to the lexan forward hatch and cabin house windows, the companionway hatch also has a lexan insert. The inside of the hull is smoothly sanded and finished with white gelcoat. There are no full height bulkheads dividing up the cabin. All of the furniture is built of lightweight, light-colored 3/8" thick, Scandinavian plywood of seven veneers.

The joinerwork is above average and all of the bulkhead and furniture tabbing is extremely neat. There isn't much to the Olson 30's interior, but what there is has been done with commendable craftsmanship. The interior wood is fragile, though. There are several unsupported panels of the 3/8" plywood; if someone were to fall against them with much force it's likely they would fracture. The cabin sole is narrow, and with the lack of headroom the woodwork is especially susceptible to being dinged and scratched from equipment like outboard engines. Once the finish on the wood is broken, it quickly absorbs water, which collects in the shallow bilge.

The Olson 30 is not a comfortable cruiser. Even after you've taken all the racing sails ashore, the belowdecks is barely habitable. To save weight the quarterberths are made of thin cushions sewn to vinyl and hung from pipes. These pipe berths are comfortable, but the cushions are not easily removed. Should they get wet it's likely they would stay wet for quite a while. Two seabags are hung on sail tracks above the quarter berths, which should help to insure that some clothes always stay dry.

Just forward of each quarterberth is a small uncushioned seat locker. Behind each seat is a small portable ice cooler. In one seat locker is the stove, an Origo 3000 which slides up and out of the locker on tracks. The Origo is a top-of-the-line unpressurized alcohol stove (see PS June 1, 1982), but to operate it the cook must kneel on the cabin sole. To work at the navigation station, which is in front of the starboard seat, you must sit sideways. In front of the port seat is the lavette, with a hand water pump and a removable, shallow drainless sink. Drainless sinks eliminate the need for a through-hull fitting, a good idea; but they should be deep, not shallow.

The head is a Porta Potti mounted under the forward V-berth, which we think is totally unsuitable for a sailboat. Who wants a smelly toilet under his pillow? Although there are curtains which can be drawn across the V-berth, we think human dignity deserves an enclosed head, especially on a 30' boat. The V-berth is large and easy to climb into, but there are no shelves above it nor a storage locker in the empty bow. In short, if you plan to cruise for more than a weekend you had better like roughing it.

CONCLUSIONS

The base price of the Olson 30 is $25,495. With a one-design class inventory of seven sails (about $6400), an outboard and minimal electronics, the cost approaches $35,000. For 30-footers, that's cheap; but for boats of similar displacement, it's damned expensive.

What do you get for $35,000? You get a boat that is well-built, seaworthy, and reasonably well laid out. You get a boat that, in light air, will sail as fast as boats costing nearly twice as much. Downwind in heavy air, you have a creature that will blow your mind and leave everything shy of a bigger ULDB in your wake. If you spend all of your sailing time racing in a PHRF fleet in an area where light or heavy air dominates, the Olson 30 will probably give you more pleasure for your dollar than almost anything afloat.

However if you race often in moderate air or enjoy more than a very occasional short cruise, you are likely to be very disappointed. Before you consider the Olson 30, you must realistically evaluate your abilities as a sailor. There's nothing worse than, after finding out that you can't race a boat to her potential, knowing that she is of little use for the other aspects of our sport.

The Pearson 30: Moderation in All Matters

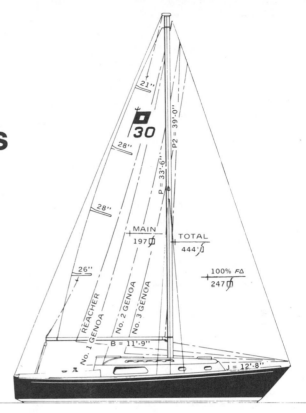

THE BOAT AND THE BUILDER

The Bill Shaw-designed Pearson 30 entered production in late 1971. By January 1, 1980, 1,185 of the fin-keel, spade-rudder sloops had been built in the company's Portsmouth, Rhode Island plant. Peak production years were 1973 and 1974, with about 200 boats produced in each of those years. Production tapered off to about 70 boats per year in the last three years of production, and the P30 was discontinued with the 1981 models, to be replaced in the Pearson line by the Pearson 303.

The Pearson 30 was designed as a family cruiser and daysailer with a good turn of speed. The boat is actively raced throughout the country, however, with about 20 holding IOR certificates, and many more racing in PHRF, MORC, and one-design fleets.

The P30's swept-back fin keel and scimitar-shaped spade rudder are fairly typical of racing boat design from the late 1960s and early 1970s but look somewhat dated next to today's high aspect ratio fin keels and rudders.

The boat's underwater shape is somewhat unusual. The hull is basically dinghy-shaped. The sections aft of the keel are deeply veed, however, so that deadrise in the forward and after sections of the boat is similar. Coupled with a fairly narrow beam by today's standards, this provides a hull form which is easily balanced when the boat is heeled—an important consideration in this relatively tender 30-footer.

Above the water the Pearson 30 carries out the standard Pearson credo—moderation in all matters. The hull has a moderate amount of conventional sheer curvature with modest overhangs at bow and stern. The cabin trunk is well proportioned but is of necessity somewhat high to achieve headroom in a small boat without excessive freeboard. Styling is clean and modern with—thankfully—no attempt to incorporate "traditional" detailing. The boat's appearance may not stir the soul, but neither will it offend the eye.

The Pearson 30 has a well-proportioned masthead rig. The mainsail comprises 44% of the working sail area, more than is found on many modern "racer-cruisers," but a reasonable proportion for a true multi-purpose boat.

Base price in 1971 was $11,750. By November 1979, base price had jumped to $28,300. The builder's option list included about $8,000 worth of goodies for the gadget addict, including wheel steering, a LectraSan toilet system, and a $500 stereo system. Average 1979 sailaway price was about $35,000.

The Pearson 30 has proved a good investment for its owners. Even the earliest models commanded an

Specifications

LOA	29'9"
DWL	25'0"
Beam	9'6"
Draft	5'0"
Displacement	8,320 lbs
Ballast	3,560 lbs
Sail Area	444 sq ft

Pearson Yachts, Division of
   Grumman Allied Industries
West Shore Road
Portsmouth, RI 02871

average of $21,000 on the East Coast used-boat market in 1980.

After years of using the Palmer 22 horsepower and 30 horsepower Atomic Four gasoline engines, the Pearson line is now entirely diesel powered. Late model Pearson 30s come with a two-cylinder Universal diesel, which weighs about the same as the Atomic Four.

CONSTRUCTION

Pearson is one of the oldest fiberglass boatbuilders in the country. Their Triton and Alberg 35 are two of the classic "modern" boats. With over 20 years of fiberglass boatbuilding experience, Pearson has solved most of the construction problems that seem to plague some builders.

The layup schedule of the Pearson 30 did not change during the production life of the boat. The hull structure

The error in using aluminum rudder stocks was far outweighed by Pearson's willingness to correct the problem

is a hand layup in a one-piece mold of alternating plies of 1½-ounce mat and 18-ounce woven roving. Two layers of omnidirectional mat are used beneath the gelcoat to prevent "printthrough" of the first roving layer, an unsightly and unfortunately common problem with some builders.

Below the waterline, the Pearson 30 hull is a solid seven-ply layup, yielding an average bottom thickness of .29". Along the keel, the plies from each side are overlapped, doubling the thickness in this critical area. The topside skin is five plies of mat and roving, with an average thickness of .21". The deck is a fiberglass-balsa sandwich. The hull-to-deck joint is made by glassing together the external flanges of the hull and deck. This chemical bond is backed up by stainless steel self-tapping screws at intervals of approximately 4". The flanges are covered by an extruded plastic rubrail holder, covered by the familiar Pearson soft vinyl rubrail. One Pearson 30 owner who races his boat reported that the hull-to-deck joint had opened slightly at the bow from excessive headstay tension. No other owner reported this problem, and examination of a large number of Pearson 30s failed to reveal another hull with this problem. Excessive headstay and backstay loading is often found in racing boats and can damage any boat not designed for this type of loading.

The Pearson 30's spade rudder has provided the only recurrent problem with the boat. The rudder stock consists of a thick-walled stainless steel pipe. The stock enters the hull through a slightly larger diameter fiberglass rudder tube, which projects above the waterline to the cockpit sole, eliminating the need for a stuffing box. The rudder stock rides in two Delrin bushings, one at the top and one at the bottom of the fiberglass rudder tube. Wear in these Delrin bushings causes play to develop in the rudder stock. This wear can be accelerated by failing to tie off the tiller when the boat is at rest, thus letting the stock turn from the natural motion of the boat. The bushings are owner-replaceable when the boat is hauled out, requiring removal of the tiller fitting and dropping the rudder through the bottom of the boat. The bushings can then be pried out and replaced.

The frequency with which rudder bushings must be replaced varies with the amount of use the boat receives. Pearson considers the bushings an item of routine maintenance. We would recommend that they be replaced whenever any slop develops. About 30% of the boats we examined showed significant bushing wear.

We also found annoying and excessive play in the tiller fitting which might sometimes be confused with bushing wear. Correcting this requires shimming or bushing the cast aluminum tiller socket.

The first Pearson 30s had an aluminum pipe rudder stock rather than stainless. Several rudders broke off as a result of corrosion at the narrow gap between rudder and hull. To Pearson's credit, the firm recalled and replaced the rudders on the approximately 200 boats built with aluminum stocks. The error in using aluminum stocks was far outweighed by the company's willingness to correct a potentially serious problem.

The Pearson 30's 3,560 lbs of lead ballast is encapsulated in the fiberglass keel molding. This avoids the necessity of keel bolts but makes the keel more vulnerable to grounding damage.

The deck-stepped, polyurethane-painted aluminum mast is supported by the main cabin bulkhead and an oak compression column. This column is glassed into the top of the keel.

If coaming-mounted genoa turning blocks are installed—and they are necessary for genoas larger than 150%—it is essential that large backing plates be used. Some of these blocks which were improperly installed by owners have pulled through the coamings, which are a relatively thin solid fiberglass molding.

Through hull fittings appear to be bedded with silicone, a less than ideal choice for underwater fittings. Proper seacocks or gate valves are installed in all underwater openings, although none are installed with backing blocks, which is highly recommended. Chainplates, where visible, are properly bolted to primary structural bulkheads.

Much of the interior construction is bonded to the hull, including the molded fiberglass floor pan and molded headliner. Molded hull liners are relatively expensive, and are seen less and less frequently in modern stockboat construction. Interior surfaces are teak- or Formica-covered plywood. Exposed plywood edges are covered by glued-on plastic trim, which, we noted, has often pulled off, even on new boats.

Seat-back lockers have friction catches, which unless properly aligned can let the seatback/locker doors come open when the boat is heeled. The cabin sole is non-skid fiberglass. Exposed interior fiberglass surfaces are now covered by foam-backed tan basket weave vinyl which enhances appearance.

Pearson hull strength has never been questioned. Their boats tend to have slightly heavier scantlings than average, which is hardly a shortcoming. The construction of all their boats, including the Pearson 30, is of above average stockboat quality.

PERFORMANCE

Handling under sail
The Pearson 30 is an active sailor's boat. We find it responsive, and a pleasure to sail. It is also tender, and very sensitive to the proper sail combination. All owners responding consider the boat to be somewhat "tippy." The P30 does, in fact, put the rail under quite easily. In 15 knots apparent wind, we find that the boat is almost overpowered with the full main and 150% genoa. Gusts of 12-14 knots bury the rail, slowing the boat. The P30 does not, however, carry any substantial weather helm even when overpowered. Any tendency to round up or spin out can usually be controlled by a strong hand on the tiller and easing the mainsail.

As you would expect in a dinghy-hulled, spade-rudder fin-keeler, the boat is quick in tacks. It is so quick, in fact, that the jib-sheet winch grinder is likely to be growled at by the skipper for being too slow. The winch grinder is also handicapped by the difficulty of his bracing himself properly to exert full power on the winches, a common problem on production boats of almost any size. *We strongly recommend the optional Lewmar #40 jib-sheet winches, whether the boat is used for racing or cruising.* The standard halyard winches are perfectly adequate. The optional roller-bearing mainsheet traveler is practically a must for effective trim of the mainsail although it does reduce cockpit room.

Although the Pearson 30 was not specifically designed for racing, some of the boats have had very successful racing careers. Pete Lawson's *Syrinx* won the Three-quarter Ton North American Championship in 1972. Under IOR Mk IIIA, the boat's average rating has

Owners report they typically spend 80% of sailing time daysailing the Pearson 30, with the remainder divided evenly between racing and cruising

dropped nearly two feet, making the boat rate just over Half Ton. The boat is still a successful club racer and is hotly raced as a one-design class in some areas, including Chesapeake Bay. Pearson 30s also race in MORC classes, and the boat has been measured for USYRU-Measurement Handicap System (MHS) for hull standardization.

Owners report that typically only about 10% of their sailing time is devoted to racing. Another 10% is spent cruising, while fully 80% of sailing time is spent daysailing.

The boat will be sailed quite differently by racers and cruisers. Experienced Pearson 30 racers keep the boat moving by reefing the main and carrying on with larger headsails as the breeze pipes up.

Cruisers will find it more comfortable to sail with smaller headsails and more mainsail even though there will be some sacrifice in performance on the wind. A good selection of headsails—at least a 150% genoa, a #3 genoa, and a working jib—is necessary. A small heavy-weather jib would be a good idea for boats that cruise in exposed waters.

Handling under power
The Pearson 30's underwater configuration creates a boat that maneuvers remarkably well under power. The P30 easily turns in a circle its own length in diameter. The standard two-cylinder Universal diesel pushes the boat well, albeit with some vibration, although it lacks the power of the old Atomic Four when punching through a chop.

A strong arm on the tiller is required when backing down under power. "It's a tough boat to handle in reverse. It can tear your arm off," said one experienced Pearson 30 sailor. The aft-raking unbalanced rudder will easily go hard over if too much helm is applied while backing down, and an unprepared or off-balance helmsman could be thrown off his feet by the sweeping tiller under these conditions. Applying minimum rudder corrections reduces this tendency, but a rudder of this type, which is free to rotate through 360°, can pose a real threat to the unwary.

LIVABILITY

Deck layout
Certain compromises in deck layout are inherent in almost any 30-footer; the Pearson 30 is no exception. The shrouds hamper access to the foredeck, so that it is easier to walk on the cabin top to go forward than along the sidedecks. This is almost a universal shortcoming in boats of this size, as the requirements of interior living space necessitate a large cabin trunk and relatively narrow sidedecks.

The bow cleat is located well forward and is adequate for the size of lines likely to be used on the boat. However, we would prefer two bow cleats, nearly side by side, in the same location. This is particularly useful in boats which spend a major amount of their lives tied to a dock, as the rule of thumb is that the dockline which needs adjusting is always the bottom line on any cleat.

The vinyl rubrail around the hull-to-deck joint presents a problem when anchoring the Pearson 30. It will undoubtedly be chafed by the anchor line. Redesign or relocation of the bow chocks would be necessary to correct this potential chafe problem.

The large starboard cockpit locker is designated as the boat's sail locker. We recommend that the locker be put to its intended use. The locker is so deep that small items would end up in a heap in the bottom almost out of reach if they were stored here. Space in the lazarette locker—a natural place for fenders, docklines, and sheets—is limited by the engine exhaust hose. Rerouting this hose would increase the usefulness of this space.

The large cockpit seats four adults comfortably for daysailing and six if they are active enough to stay out of the way of the tiller and the mainsheet. The 4' long tiller definitely encroaches on the cockpit living space. We would normally be reluctant to recommend wheel steering for a high-performance 30-footer: it would, however, increase cockpit space and might reduce the idiosyncrasies created by the spade rudder when handling the boat under power.

Interior
The Pearson 30 has a light, roomy interior for a boat of its size. In the 1980 model, all four ports in the head and forward cabin are of the opening type, greatly improving ventilation, particularly when coupled with the optional, but recommended foredeck-mounted cowl ventilator.

The overhead hatch in the forward cabin is basically a ventilation hatch and is too small for either sails or emergency exit. Anchor storage is awkward without a foredeck anchor well, a welcome addition to many more recently designed boats the size of the Pearson 30.

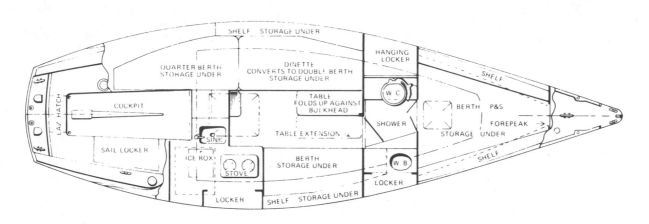

PRACTICAL BOAT BUYING 169

The 22-gallon water tank and the standard holding tank occupy much of the space under the forward double berth. This double berth is actually the entire forward cabin, and can be closed off from the full-width head by double doors. The standard marine toilet is equipped with a proper vented loop. The discharge line incorporates a Y-valve for overboard discharge of sewage when pump-out facilities for the holding tank are unavailable. This is a practical solution to the MSD boondoggle. The head wash basin is tucked under the deck and is difficult to use for anyone with less agility than a contortionist. The location of this wash basin is the only serious flaw in the otherwise functional head compartment.

The P30's main cabin is large and comfortable, with capacious storage above, behind, and below the settees. Owners may find these storage spaces more useful if they are subdivided by partitions to prevent gear stored in one locker from ending up in another. The under-settee and under-galley lockers cannot be considered dry storage unless the bilge is kept bone dry. Although the lockers are sealed to the bilge at the bottom, owners report that, with their boat heeled, bilge water finds its way into the lockers by running up the inside of the hull behind locker partitions, then down into storage spaces. Most dinghy-hulled boats lack real bilge space or a sump, and as little as a gallon of water in a boat of this type can be annoying.

It is unfortunate that a large number of berths has become a criterion for livability in modern boats. In the past, a 40-footer was likely to have four or five berths. Now six berths are standard on a 30-footer, including the Pearson 30, seven on a 35-footer, and eight on a 40-footer. Cruising longer than overnight with six on a boat the size of the Pearson 30 is a sure way to terminate friendships and wreck marriages. No responding Pearson 30 owner reported cruising with more than four people on a regular basis.

The standard fold-down cabin table is a practical solution on a boat of this size. The optional slide-out chart table limits room over the quarterberth and lacks the fiddles which are necessary because of its slanted surface.

The Pearson 30 galley is typical of 30-footers. As much as possible is jammed into a necessarily small space. The deep lockers behind the stove and icebox will probably be partitioned into several smaller compartments by the moderately handy owner. Annoyingly, a short person has a hard time reaching the depths of the icebox, particularly if the stove is in use.

We cannot recommend the self-contained alcohol stoves almost always installed on the Pearson 30 and other boats of this size. There is a very real and well-documented risk of explosion if the stove must be refueled while hot. Liquid-fuel stoves should have a separate fuel tank with the fill located far enough away that there is no possibility of overflow onto a hot stovetop or burner surface. *It is the fault of the marine stove industry—and an uninformed consuming public —that these potentially dangerous stoves are still used on many boats.*

The galley sink and spigot partially block the companionway. The top companionway step is actually the lid of a nifty storage box, handy for winch handles, spare blocks, and tools.

Engine access is via the companionway steps, which lift out to expose the front of the engine. Two slatted doors in the quarterberth provide additional if awkward access to the engine and fuel tank under the cockpit. There is no soundproofing in the engine compartment. The new, smaller diesel engine is more accessible for service than the old Atomic Four. It has molded fiberglass engine beds and drip pan, an excellent idea, although some engine vibration is transferred to the hull despite the flexible engine mounts and shaft coupling. It is rare for a 30-footer to have good engine access. The Pearson 30 is no better than average in this respect.

Despite the above shortcomings, the P30 is highly livable. The advertised 6'1" headroom is really an honest 5'11" in the main cabin. Achieving good headroom in a 30-footer without serious compromises in appearance is nearly impossible. The Pearson 30 comes as close to achieving this as any boat we have seen in its class.

CONCLUSIONS

The Pearson 30 is an industry success story. The boat is fast and responsive. Finish quality is above average. The interior is comfortable and reasonably roomy within the limitations inherent in a 30-footer. Many of the minor design problems can be corrected by the imaginative and handy owner who enjoys tinkering.

Pearson has a reputation for building solid, middle-of-the-road boats: a deserved reputation well in evidence in the P30. Though out of production, the Pearson 30 would be an excellent choice of boat for the aggressive and self-confident beginning sailor who desires high performance for daysailing or club-level racing as well as for reasonably comfortable short-term cruising. It is not the boat for the timid sailor, male or female. The family with two children will find it a comfortable cruiser. Sailors with friends who enjoy spirited sailing and who don't mind frequent sail changes will also find it a good choice for daysailing and local racing.

The long production run and continued popularity have created a boat with few inherent major problems and high resale value. The Pearson 30 is a good investment.

The Cal 31: Pricey Racer-Cruiser

THE BOAT AND THE BUILDER

The Cal 31 is the thirteenth Bill Lapworth-designed Cal boat between 27' and 34' built by the Costa Mesa, California firm. Cal, a pioneer in fiberglass sailboat construction, is now a division of Bangor Punta Marine, whose boatbuilding group also includes O'Day and Ranger. Cal and Bill Lapworth are best known for the breakthrough Cal 40, which 20 years ago began the trend toward moderately light displacement, fin-keel spade-rudder ocean racers.

The hull configuration of the Cal 31 is typical of Lapworth designs: shallow-bodied and round-bilged, with a fairly short fin keel, a shallow skeg, and a well faired high aspect ratio spade rudder. The Cal 31 is the middle boat in the current Cal production line, which includes boats from 25' to 39'. Production of Cal 31 began in the fall of 1978; 130 boats were built in the first three years.

Cal is heavily promoting the entire line as dual-purpose boats, the ubiquitous "cruiser-racer" which now seems to dominate the sailboat market. The company's colorful, catchy ads are prominent in current sailing magazines and are geared toward the affluent 30- to 40-year old consumer with a lot of experience.

Surprisingly, many Cal 31 purchasers are buying their first sailboat larger than small one-design daysailers. One Cal 31 owner reported that the 31 was his fourth Cal boat. Cal 31 owners typically spend 70% of their sailing time daysailing, 20% short-term cruising, and 10% club racing.

Owners report relatively few defects requiring warranty claims, but the ones they do report are recurrent, and almost exclusively associated with water getting where it's not supposed to be—inside the boat. The most common problems with the Cal 31 are leaking stanchion bases, leaking chainplates, and leaking hatches. These are probably the most common warranty claims throughout the industry and are generally the result of the fact that adequate bedding to prevent leaks requires fairly careful work, can be messy, and takes time to clean up. Owners do report that their dealers have been prompt in settling any warranty claims.

CONSTRUCTION

The hull of the Cal 31 is a solid hand layup. Cal hull weight, less ballast, is about average for performance cruisers of comparable length and beam, although total displacement tends to be lighter than average.

Exterior cosmetic finish is good. There is slight print-through of the first layer of roving, and some pinholes appear in the gelcoat where surface blemishes have been patched.

Specifications

LOA	31'6"
LWL	25'8"
Beam	10'
Draft	5'
Sail area	490 sq ft
Displacement	9,170 lbs
Ballast	3,600 lbs

Cal Boats Division of
 Bangor Punta Marine
PO Box 991
Fall River, MA 02722

The deck molding is plywood-cored in areas where heavy hardware is mounted. The cabin top is sandwich construction: Klegecell foam, cored with plywood inserts in the mast partner area. The cabin top under the deck-stepped mast is solid ¾" fiberglass.

The companionway of the Cal 31 is about its weakest design point. It is too wide and has a strong taper which allows drop boards to be removed by lifting a little more than an inch. The mating surface between the two solid teak drop boards is a simple square butt. In every Cal 31 we examined, daylight was visible between the two boards—in one case, almost ¼". Simple reverse

The Cal 31 is one of the few current production boats with a real bilge sump; unfortunately, both icebox and shower drain into it

bevels, or preferably, a stepped joint, would take about two minutes more to make and would be infinitely better in terms of water-tightness.

The companionway slide design is not waterproof. The optional sea hood is essential on any boat going offshore or sailing in areas with boisterous conditions.

The split backstay arrangement allows use of an integral centerline swimming ladder incorporated in the stern rail. Backstay chainplates are through-bolted, but fiberglass backing plates are used where we would prefer aluminum or stainless steel. The welded combination bow fitting and chainplate is through-bolted but lacks a backup plate. In fact, the only deck fittings, including winches and cleats, which utilize backup plates are the lifeline stanchions and bow pulpit.

Dick Cumiskey, Research and Development Director of Bangor Punta Marine, states that backup plates are unnecessary since the deck is plywood cored in areas where hardware is likely to be mounted. As a rule, *The Practical Sailor* prefers to see metal backup plates on through-bolted fittings, even cleats and winches which are normally only subjected to shear loads. Overkill in the mounting of hardware is cheap insurance.

The hull-to-deck joint is made by chemically bonding the two moldings together. An extruded rigid plastic rubrail holder and soft vinyl rubrail insert cover the hull-to-deck joint on the outside of the hull.

The ballast keel is an encapsulated lead casting. The fiberglass-covered, high-density foam-cored rudder utilizes a stainless steel rudder stock.

The main structural bulkhead is a teak-faced plywood, bonded to the hull with fiberglass fillets. To avoid hard spots, the bulkhead itself does not touch the hull. The mast is supported by a teak compression column which rests on a deep molded fiberglass floor timber, part of the molded floor pan, which is bonded to the hull.

Chainplates for the inboard shrouds are heavy stainless steel flat bar, properly bolted to the main bulkhead and other plywood webs. Inside the head locker, the chainplates are bolted through a web which is covered with the carpet-like hull liner before installation of the chainplates. We would prefer to have the chainplate and backup pads bear directly on the wood or fiberglass web, rather than on the hull liner.

The rig is a basic masthead sloop with single airfoil spreaders and double lower shrouds. Lower shroud terminations are inboard and about a foot from the molded fiberglass toerail. The Cal 31 utilizes a polyurethane-coated Kenyon aluminum mast and boom. Although rope-to-wire tailspliced halyards are listed as standard, the boat we sailed had eye-spliced halyards. The wire portion of the main halyard was too short to allow an adequate number of wire wraps around the winch. Other boats we examined had properly spliced halyards.

Water tanks are cast polyethylene, with flexible plastic hose piping. A definite plastic taste is imparted to the water by this system. The fuel tank is welded aluminum. Tanks and batteries are mounted under the cabin settees, below the waterline with the weight concentrated in the middle of the boat. This location utilizes a space often given over to lockers which in many boats tend to be wet from bilge water. The battery boxes are well secured, but it is difficult to remove the box covers to inspect the battery electrolyte level.

The Cal 31 is one of the few current production boats with a real bilge sump. Unfortunately, both the icebox and the shower drain through the bilge to this sump. Organic matter and food particles in icebox water quickly lead to smelly bilges. Soap residue from showers can gradually clog impeller-type bilge pumps, which could be a problem in the event of a serious hull leak.

Through-hull fittings below the waterline are bronze, recessed flush with the hull surface and well bedded but without backing blocks. Shutoff valves are glass-filled nylon ball valves originally developed for the chemical industry. Above-water through-hulls are nylon, with no provision for emergency shutoff. One owner we contacted had bronze seacocks installed on underwater openings, as he was leery of the standard nylon valves.

PERFORMANCE

Handling under sail

Sailing performance of the Cal 31 is consistent with her performance-cruiser image. Most owners consider the boat somewhat tender. The boat does tend to bury the rail quickly in gusts about five knots above mean wind speed. On the wind, with 14 knots of breeze over the deck, the boat is on the verge of needing a short reef when sailed with a 145% genoa and full main.

The Cal 31 is not particularly wide, but her beam is carried well forward and aft. She therefore develops less weather helm when overpowered than a comparably-sized racing boat and will be a bit more forgiving of improper sail combination than a wider boat whose ends are more pinched.

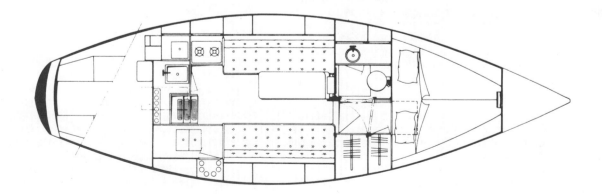

The Cal 31 handles well under power, but the engine transmits substantial vibration to the hull

The Cal 31 is a comfortable boat for a couple to handle. The boat we sailed had Barient 23 self-tailers instead of the standard Barient 21s. We would recommend the larger self-tailers instead of the standard winches on a boat that will be used for shorthanded cruising.

The Cal 31 will hold her own with other performance cruisers of comparable size. She is closer-winded and faster than the Cal 29 in light air. Most owners consider the boat faster than similar boats, but few Cal 31s have raced enough to make a comparison meaningful. Tentative PHRF rating is 150 in southern California, 156 in San Francisco. This implies a boat that is at her best in light air.

The Cal 31 has generally good handling characteristics under sail. She balances well and can be made to sail herself on the wind with judicious use of sail trim. The boat has a good, solid feel under sail, more like a 35-footer than a 31-footer.

Handling under power

The standard engine in the Cal 31 is a two-cylinder 16 horsepower Universal diesel. Earlier models were equipped with two-cylinder Volvo diesels. Owners consider the engine adequate power for the boat.

The instrument panel is mounted on the forward end of the cockpit, and includes gauges for alternator output, water temperature, and fuel level. There is an oil pressure warning light. An oil pressure gauge and a tachometer would be welcome.

The boat handles well under power, but the engine transmits substantial vibration to the hull. This vibration could be tiring if long periods of motoring are required.

Handling in forward gear is uncomplicated. Like most fin-keel boats, the Cal 31 turns in a very tight circle. Handling in reverse is more complicated. With the Volvo engine, owners report that the stern of the boat pulls sharply to starboard. Some owners of Universal-powered boats also report uncertain steering behavior in reverse. We find the steering reasonably predictable, but she does require a firm hand on the tiller or wheel to keep the rudder from going hard over once sternway is made. Gradual application of rudder in reverse prevents rudder stall, which could cause unpredictable steering.

LIVABILITY

Deck layout

The initial reaction of most owners to the cockpit of the Cal 31 is that it is too small. Their response after living with it is that it is just about the right size. With either the wheel or the tiller, it is comfortable for a maximum of four when sailing.

There is a wide bridgedeck at the forward end of the cockpit. The roller-bearing mainsheet traveler, with its essential athwartships control lines, is located on the bridgedeck.

There are two huge cockpit lockers. These would be more useful if divided into smaller spaces and if partitions were inserted to prevent gear from slipping under the cockpit, where it might fetch up against the engine.

The cockpit lockers have an excellent molded-in scupper arrangement which allows the leeward seats to drain at all angles of heel. Unfortunately, the boat has an inexplicable method of securing the locker lids. A line is attached to the underside of the starboard lid. This leads under the cockpit to a jam cleat which is reached through the port cockpit locker. The port locker has a similar arrangement which can only be released from belowdecks, in the galley. If the lockers are secured, one must go below, release the port locker hold-down, go back on deck, open the port cockpit locker, and release the starboard hold-down to get into the starboard cockpit locker. The logic of this system escapes us.

Access to the rudder stock head in wheel-steered boats is via a deckplate in the cockpit sole. If this were removed to rig emergency steering, a substantial amount of water could find its way below in rain or heavy weather.

The inboard shrouds provide a narrow sheeting base for jib leads but make it almost mandatory to go over the cabin top to go forward of the mast.

There is an anchor well at the forward end of the deck. This well contains a strong eyebolt for securing the bitter end of the anchor rode, an excellent idea. Connections for the pulpit-mounted running lights are under the deck immediately forward of the lid to the anchor well and will be subject to rapid corrosion from water finding its way below as well as to mechanical damage

Newer Cal 31s have mainsheet traveler over the main companionway, moving it out of the cockpit

The interior of the Cal 31 is one of the most livable and attractive we have seen in a boat of this size

when stowing the anchor rode.

The stemhead fitting incorporates a roller, handy for stowing an anchor. There are no bow chocks. The anchor roller can be used as a starboard chock, although the lack of a fair lead to a bow cleat is a serious shortcoming. Anchoring with two anchors would be problematic without good bow chocks.

The long inboard track for jib lead blocks provides for flexible sheet leads but should be augmented by a toerail-mounted track for greater variety. If genoas larger than 150% are used, the stock track will prove too short for optimal leads.

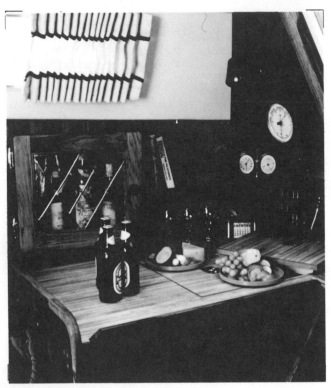

Typical of the attention to detail in the Cal 31's interior are the lead glass liquor cabinet, well insulated icebox lids, and plenty of room for books and instrumentation in the nav station

Interior

The Cal 31 has perhaps the most spacious and attractive interior in its class. It is the boat's most outstanding feature. Belowdecks, it is hard to believe you are aboard a boat only 31' long. "The interior sold us on the boat" was the most common owner response.

The forward cabin has large V-berths with an insert to form a huge double. There is a good sail bin under the port berth, and shelves at the foot of the berth. Most owners find the short hanging locker in the forward cabin useless. Most would prefer more drawers instead.

The foredeck-mounted hatch provides good ventilation and is big enough for sail bags, but its location requires that it be tightly secured when sailing to prevent water from getting below. Close attention will have to be paid to the water-tightness of the hatch if the berth below is to be kept dry.

The large head is comfortable and incorporates a shower. An overhead deadlight augments the light provided by the opening port. The door to the head also serves as the door to the forward cabin. When this door is used to shut off the forward cabin, the door to the large starboard hanging locker can be used to separate the head from the main cabin.

The main cabin interior is rather dark due to the abundance of teak. This is somewhat offset by a bright carpet. The cabin would be much brighter if a lighter wood, such as butternut or ash, had been used below.

The main cabin is huge. There is good storage in bins and alcoves behind the settees. A large magazine and book rack on the bulkhead behind the foldup table is inaccessible without folding down the table.

There is no means of positively securing the table's fold-down leg to the cabin sole. The leg could be accidentally kicked out of place when the table is in use, allowing it to fall down. The table is too small to accommodate even four with real comfort. The cabin is wide enough to utilize a permanently fitted table.

The main cabin sleeps three in a large single berth and an extension double. The deeply-tufted settee cushions look rich and are comfortable for sitting but are miserable to sleep on.

Cooks will appreciate the galley, which is excellent for a boat of this size. There is a large gimballed stove with oven, well secured and capable of being latched in place in port. It is available in both alcohol and gas models.

The icebox top is one of the few we have seen which can reasonably double as a chart table. The icebox lids are insulated, but are poorly fitted, allowing a large gap—over 3/8"—between the two trap-type lids. The lids are also usually not flush with the icebox top, a complication for doing smooth chart work.

There is a large-diameter tube for rolled charts which extends under the cockpit. With a good surface available for chart work, folded charts make much more sense.

The engine is reached for service by lifting out the companionway steps. The steps should have a positive latch to prevent their bouncing out of place in rough conditions. Engine access for maintenance is excellent.

Selection valves for the water tanks are located under the deep galley sink. This is typical of the well-thought out plumbing and wiring systems, which are generally well-bundled and usually protected from chafe when passing through bulkhead cutouts.

Basically, the interior of the Cal 31 is one of the most livable and attactive we have seen in a boat of this size. Interior finish work is of very good stock boat quality.

CONCLUSIONS

The Cal 31 is one of the best designed and better executed 31-footers we have seen. Her interior is remarkable. She has a wide range of buyer appeal, selling to first-time sailboat buyers as well as to the more experienced. She is a reasonably good club-level racer, yet a comfortable cruiser for up to four adults. Realistically, the boat will be used more for cruising and daysailing than for racing.

To those not familiar with what inflation has done to boat prices, the price of the Cal 31 will come as a rude shock. With a 1980 base price around $43,000, delivered price ran close to $50,000. A well-equipped Cal 31 could easily top $55,000, making the Cal 31 almost the "priciest" 31' stock boat on the market. Ultimately, consumers will judge whether the Cal 31 merits that risky high rung on the price ladder.

The Southern Cross 31: Ocean-going Dream Machine

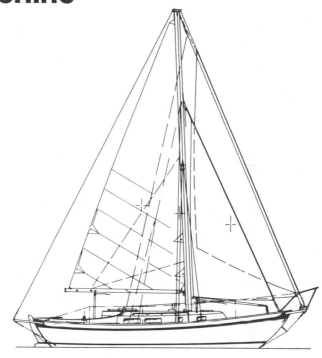

THE BOAT AND THE BUILDER

The Southern Cross 31 might best be described as a double-ended ocean cruising cutter of moderate beam, moderate draft, moderate-to-heavy displacement, and moderate sail area. She has a pronounced concave sheer, moderately cut away forefoot, and outboard rudder. To many she would embody the ideal ocean cruising hull form.

The Southern Cross 31 might also be termed a dream-machine. She is a boat pitched to those sailors whose idea of sailing—whether they achieve it or not—is palm-fringed islands, the aquamarine of the sea off-soundings, and long tradewind passages. She is the type of boat to make accountants from Iowa run away to the South Seas.

In the early 1970's an effective promotional campaign by Westsail rekindled a relatively dormant interest in the wide, heavy, double-ended hull form of the Norwegian rescue boat for long-distance cruising. Since then that hull form has proliferated to the point of faddish absurdity. Arguing whether the double ended hull form—whether the stern be of the "cruiser," "canoe," or "Baltic" variety—was better than all others for seakeeping ability dominated conversation among would-be long distance cruisers in much the way that the cutter cranks and the sloop supporters duked it out in the late 19th century. A generation of cruising boats, many over-heavy, under-canvassed, poorly designed, poorly built, and with all the windward ability of a sand barge flooded the market. If it wasn't pointed at both ends, or at least rounded, it wasn't a world cruiser.

In 1976, in the midst of the double-ended doubletalk, Clarke Ryder, who had set up a fiberglass molding company for industrial parts, began building the Southern Cross 31. In the next five years over 130 hulls were built, many finished off by their owners.

At first glance the Southern Cross 31 might appear to be another boat designed to leap upon the Colin Archer bandwagon, because of the double-ended hull, long keel, and outboard rudder. With those characteristics the resemblance of the Southern Cross 31 to most of the "modern" offshore cruising double-enders ceases.

The Tom Gillmer designed Southern Cross 31 is very similar to another of his designs, the Allied Seawind—now reincarnated, modified, and called the Seawind II. The original Seawind was the first fiberglass sailboat to circle the world. The Southern Cross 31 is basically the same hull as the original Seawind with the stern redrawn from transom-type to a canoe-type stern, the beam increased by 3", and the displacement increased by 1500 lbs.

Specifications

LOA	31'
LWL	25'
Beam	9'6"
Draft	4'7"
Displacement	13,600 lbs
Ballast	4,400 lbs

The C.E. Ryder Corporation
47 Gooding Avenue
Bristol. RI 02809

For the single-handed or double-handed world cruiser who tends toward the conservative the Southern Cross 31 may appear to be the ideal combination: a proven cruising hull design combined with a pointed stern.

By producing a boat of this type Ryder has put himself in a position of dubious enviability. The builder of a boat touted as a world cruiser is guaranteed to be deluged by calls from dreamers, schemers, and would-be conquerors of Cape Horn as well as knowledgeable cruising sailors looking for the ideal boat. Combine the

Airex and balsa coring relieve the Southern Cross 31 of some of the least desirable characteristics of fiberglass construction

design and marketing approach with the fact that the Southern Cross 31 is available in several stages of completion as well as a finished boat and you have a situation ready-made to drive a builder to the brink.

Remarkably enough, Ryder shows few signs of being driven to distraction. This is even more remarkable given the diversity of activity of the plant. In addition to the Southern Cross 28, 31, and 39, Ryder builds the Sea Sprite 23, 27, and 34, has recently taken over construction of the Kirby-designed Sonar, and molds hulls for a number of other builders. Boredom with constant production of the same boat would never seem to be a problem at Ryder.

CONSTRUCTION

The Southern Cross 31 is one of the few Airex-cored production boats built. The hull is molded in one piece, with solid laminate along the centerline, Airex-cored from the turn of the bilge nearly to the sheer line. The glass laminate is solid abreast the mast where the main chainplates are attached.

The deck is a one-piece molding, balsa cored for rigidity. The cabin top is also balsa cored, although the area around the mast step is cored with plywood rather than balsa for greater strength in compression.

Airex and balsa coring relieve the Southern Cross 31 of some of the least desirable characteristics of fiberglass construction. Coring greatly reduces the pronounced tendency of fiberglass to sweat in cold weather, deadens the notorious sound transmission of glass construction, and provides strength and rigidity without either a heavy solid layup or a complicated system of internal framing. Coring also functions as an insulator, making a glass hull cooler in the summer and easier to heat in the winter.

We have some reservations about the Southern Cross hull-to-deck joint. There is no doubt that it is simple and strong. At the sheer the hull molding turns outward 90°. The deck molding drops down into the hull, with an external flange overlapping the hull flange. The hull and deck are bolted together, the joint filled with a polyester compound. Our reservation is that the flange sticks outboard of the hull more than an inch, almost at right angles to the hull. Not only is this hard to finish off neatly, but it is somewhat vulnerable.

Consider the boat tied alongside the government dock in St. John, U S Virgin Islands. The ferry from St. Thomas comes in, dragging a large wake. If your boat rolls this flange into the dock from the wake of the ferry, it could easily be damaged, and repair would not necessarily be simple. An inward-turning flange might be more complicated to engineer or lay up, but it would be far less vulnerable to damage of this kind. We also suspect that the exposed stainless steel nuts on the underside of the flange will discolor and begin to bleed on long passages.

Ballast of the Southern Cross 31 is an internal lead casting, glassed into the keel cavity. This obviates the need for keelbolts, and the attendant possibility for leaking. It has the disadvantage that should the vessel run aground—a not infrequent event for the long distance cruiser, who frequently enters unfamiliar ports, the hull rather than the lead keel takes the brunt. We have seen other internally-ballasted fiberglass hulls so abraded by a few hours on rocks or coral that the ballast literally fell out of the hull. For our world cruiser, we'd prefer an externally bolted-on lead keel, which should be capable of surviving a severe grounding without damaging the fiberglass hull.

The rudder of the Southern Cross 31 is set well up from the bottom of the rudder post, protected from grounding damage. Rudder design has been changed from a traditionally-shaped rudder to a more modern design with greater area near the bottom of the rudder blade.

Pintles and gudgeons are heavy stainless steel weldments. We prefer castings to weldments for use under water, particularly if the metal chosen is stainless steel. Bronze is usually considered superior to stainless for underwater fittings due to the greater susceptibility of stainless steel to some types of corrosion.

Bulkheads are glassed directly to the hull using Airex fillets. Tanks are of molded fiberglass, set deep into the bilge. There are bronze seacocks on all through-hull fittings.

In 1981, for another $1275 above the base price of $62,500 for the finished boat, the standard anodized aluminum or epoxy-coated deck hardware could be replaced with all bronze hardware. For the person simply seeking a boat to get away in this may be an extravagance. For the person seeking to keep a very traditional looking boat completely in character, the bronze option may be worthwhile.

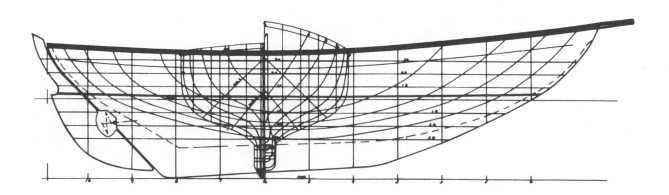

There is nothing in the hull form of the Southern Cross 31 that implies poor sailing characteristics

The Southern Cross 31 is neither a cheaply constructed, nor cheaply priced, imitation of an ocean-going sailboat. In general, her construction characteristics are up to her billing as a real offshore cruiser.

PERFORMANCE

Handling under sail

A boat designed for offshore passagemaking is not likely to have the windward performance of a modern fin keel racing boat. At the same time, she should be able to claw off a lee shore in a gale—something that many of the so-called "world cruisers" would be hard pressed to do.

In many ways the all around performance of the long-distance cruiser must be better than that of the coastal cruiser or daysailer. She must be able to sail in light winds, for few small offshore cruisers can carry enough fuel to motor to distant ports. She must have a motion that doesn't tire her crew. Her rig must be easy to handle, and must offer sailing versatility without the huge sail inventory of the racing boat.

The Southern Cross 31 can be expected to meet most of these requirements. A huge masthead genoa can be carried in light air, but a staysail and double reefed main should carry her to windward in heavy going. The hard turn of her bilge implies good initial stability.

There is nothing in the hull form of the Southern Cross 31 that implies poor sailing characteristics. This is borne out by the record of the prototype, which finished third in class in the 1977 Marion-Bermuda Race. Owners report that the boat sails well, and there is nothing to indicate otherwise. Her displacement of 13,600 lbs on a 25′ waterline is a little heavy by modern standards, but is certainly not excessive by any traditional standard.

Standard rig of the Southern Cross 31 is modern masthead cutter. The anodized aluminum mast is stepped on the cabin top. Compression is transferred to the keel via a wood compression column securely glassed to the hull structure. At least one owner who had a taller than standard rig reported a depressed cabin top in the area of the mast step. Ryder repaired that with an oversize load-distributing steel plate attached to the cabin top. If the boat is to be owner-finished, care must be taken to be sure that the wood compression column adequately bears the load of the mast.

The standard boat shows intermediate shrouds led slightly aft of the after lower shroud. Both the main boom and the mainsail will bear on this intermediate shroud when running before the wind. Care must be taken to protect the main from chafe. We would prefer running backstays, which would lead further aft, giving a better angle for tensioning the forestay. With the runners set up, mast pumping in a seaway—a problem not uncommon with deck-stepped rigs—could probably be pretty much eliminated.

Originally, the boat was drawn with a short boomkin to accommodate the standing backstay. This complicated the mounting of a vane steerer. The backstay is now split, carried to chainplates at either side of the back of the cockpit. The mainsail should be cut with little or no roach to avoid fouling on the backstay with this arrangement.

While a cutter rig may seem unnecessarily complicated on a boat this small, it does allow strength and versatility. These are definitely desirable characteristics in the shorthanded cruiser.

Handling under power

With a 22 horsepower diesel to push just short of seven tons, the Southern Cross 31 is very adequately powered. The fuel capacity of 34 gallons will probably give about 65 hours of powering at five knots, for a range of about 325 miles under power. This provides very adequate cruising range under power without the need to carry extra fuel in cans in the cockpit, which is always a nuisance, and can be dangerous.

LIVABILITY

Deck layout

Deck layout of the boat is clean and functional. Side decks are fairly wide and unobstructed. The low bulwarks provide a feeling of security when working on deck. We would prefer all halyards led aft to the cockpit for shorthanded sailing, and we would make all winches self-tailing.

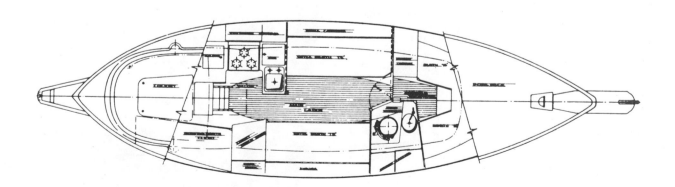

The Southern Cross 31 has what is really the minimal amount of interior volume for one or two people for long-distance cruising

A molded seahood is standard, and is an absolute must for any offshore cruiser. A molded-in spray rail will accommodate a cockpit dodger, another very useful piece of gear for the offshore sailor.

The cockpit is small and fairly deep, with a good bridgedeck. The deck mold was retooled beginning with hull 85. The crown of the deck was changed slightly, provision was made for a hatch over the main cabin, and the cockpit was lengthened about 6″ aft. Cockpit scuppers were moved from the aft end of the cockpit to the forward end, and the pitch of the cockpit sole changed slightly to facilitate draining.

Deck layout is clean and functional. A life raft can be carried on top of the main cabin—a little high for such a substantial weight, but perhaps the best solution on a boat this small. We would prefer that the winch islands be big enough for a set of secondary headsail sheet winches.

The small cockpit gives a great feeling of security. This is a very important characteristic in a boat designed to carry her crew to distant places. Big cockpits may be nice in port, but at sea all you can think of is the amount of water they could hold if the boat were to be pooped. We'll take a small cockpit for offshore use.

Belowdecks

The Southern Cross 31 has what is really the minimal amount of interior volume for one or two people for long distance cruising. There are two standard layouts—one with fixed chart table over storage space, the other with a folding chart table over a quarterberth. Although as a rule we are partial to quarterberths, the space in this case is best given over to storage space, and the larger fixed chart table is more useful.

With this arrangement, the main cabin settees must be used as berths at sea. This is not really an inconvenience for the shorthanded sailor. The windward settee, fitted with a lee cloth, would keep the sleeper's weight high and on the proper side of the boat for going upwind, while the leeward settee will provide secure sleeping if upwind performance is not a consideration. The forward cabin would be used for sails and other storage when passagemaking.

The galley is small, as it pretty much must be on a boat of this size. Double sinks are now standard, rather than the single sink of early models. The standard stove is a two-burner Shipmate with oven, alcohol fueled. We feel that only a masochist will cook for long periods of time on an alcohol stove (or perhaps a hermit trying to learn the ultimate lessons of patience).

With eight opening ports and two hatches plus the main companionway, ventilation is not a problem. At sea the main cabin overhead hatch could be left open if fitted with a small dodger.

Those who finish off kit boats frequently have weird ideas of what the interior of a boat should look like. If you are contemplating finishing a Southern Cross 31 from one of the unfinished versions, think long and hard before making major alterations to the standard layout. A boat which you think is ideally suited to your needs in terms of interior layout frequently proves to be a genuine white elephant if you ever decide to get rid of it. The standard interior of the Southern Cross 31 is a good, if prosaic interior. We think this may well be better than a highly-personalized but perhaps offbeat interior when the time comes to sell the boat.

CONCLUSION

Is the Southern Cross 31 a good boat for offshore cruising? Most definitely so. We would, however, change some of the details of her construction, as outlined above.

We have carefully avoided a discussion of whether or not you should consider buying such a boat in unfinished form for owner completion. Our opinions on this subject are expressed in the article in Section II, "So You Think You Want to Build a Boat?" About half of the Southern Cross 31s sold have been "stage" boats, rather than factory completed. No one really knows how many of those have actually been completed, and how many rest in driveways and back yards. We suspect that a fair number are still in the unfinished stage. We looked at one such boat that the owner had been "working" on for two years. We're sure it looked worse than when he started.

For this reason, there is no real established market value for owner finished boats. With the base price of a factory-completed boat at $62,500, the "stage two" (sailaway, less engine) starts to look pretty good at $27,500. You would think that such a boat could easily be finished off for the $35,000 difference in price. Perhaps so. But in boatbuilding, as in most other ventures, there is rarely—if ever—a free lunch.

She is no doubt a very expensive 31′ boat when finished off by the factory. In cruising trim, you could easily have $75,000 invested without being extravagant. How much is your dream worth to you, and how soon do you want it?

The Nicholson 31: A Go-Anywhere Boat

THE BOAT AND THE BUILDER

Few British sailboats have been a success in the US market. The traditional strength of the British pound against the dollar has meant that British boats have been inordinately expensive compared to American boats of similar quality. Coupled with the design eccentricity of some imports—eg, the smaller Westerly boats with their bilge keels and bulbous deckhouses—the high price has been a formidable obstacle to a successful invasion.

With the pound hovering around $1.70, however, British boats become more interesting. And quality British boats, out of sight in price when the pound was worth $2 or more, begin to look like relative bargains.

Nicholson yachts are well known for quality construction. The firm was a pioneer in British fiberglass boatbuilding. If experience counts, then Nicholson must be somewhere near the top of the list: the firm of Camper & Nicholsons, Ltd, has been building yachts since the days of Lord Nelson.

The Nicholson 32 was an archetypical boat of the British boatbuilding industry, much like the Triton in this country. Despite a long and successful production run, the Nicholson 32 was starting to look dated: narrow, low freeboard, with longish ends. In 1976, the venerable 32 was replaced by the Nicholson 31, maintaining the concept of a real cruising boat on a small scale, with more modern styling, more volume, and more displacement. About 120 Nicholson 31s have been built; perhaps 20 have been imported into the US.

In appearance, the Nicholson 31 is not unlike many of the current generation of production cruiser-racers. She has a straightish sheer, moderate forward overhang, and a low profile cabin trunk.

Below the waterline, however, there are substantial differences. She has a deep, powerful hull, and a moderately long keel with attached outboard rudder. Her displacement of almost 15,000 pounds is fully 50% more than that of the typical cruiser-racer, and equal to the heaviest of the pure cruisers currently in production.

Even with the pound at $1.70, the Nicholson 31 costs a heavyweight $67,000, duty-paid and delivered in the US. With the pound at $2, the same boat would go for almost $80,000. A big chunk of that cost is tied up in shipping. Unfortunately, a 31' boat costs almost the same to ship across as a 40-footer. More than 10% of the final cost of the Nicholson 31, $7,500, is simply the cost of cradling and shipping the boat from Gosport to New York. Another $4,500 is eaten up in duty and local shipping in this country.

Before the price scares you away, you must recognize that the boat comes unusually well equipped, including such items as sails, dodger, anchor, chain, docklines and fenders, pressure water, even the dishes in the galley. Oh yes, and the name and hailing port painted on the stern.

This is a go-anywhere boat. She is not a teak-veneered Colin Archer copy, and she is not a fast coastal cruiser or racer.

She is austere to the point of plainness. External wood consists of a teak toerail, teak grab rails, a

Specifications

LOA	30'7"
LWL	24'2"
Beam	10'3½"
Draft	5'
Displacement	14,750 lbs
Ballast	5,300 lbs
Sail Area	497 sq ft

Camper & Nicholsons
(Yachts) Ltd.
Gosport, Hants P012 1AH
UK

cockpit grate, the companionway drop boards, and the tiller. On the positive side, this austerity means low maintenance for the cruiser.

At the same time, she is no Clorox bottle. Detailing and workmanship are excellent. The boat looks functional and businesslike, and she is.

CONSTRUCTION

Like many European boatbuilders, Camper & Nicholsons do not mold their own hulls. Rather, the hulls are subcontracted to another firm which specializes in hull molding.

The hull of the Nicholson 31 is a solid glass layup, reinforced with foam-filled longitudinal stringers. Isothalic resin is used in the gelcoat layer to reduce porosity and the subsequent possibility of osmotic deterioration. Deck and cabin trunk are balsa cored. Molding and gelcoat quality are very good.

When through hull fittings are installed in the boat, the cut out hull pieces are burned to determine the resin to glass ratio.

Construction of the Nicholson 31 is strong and heavy, perhaps too heavy for coastal cruising in light air

The Nicholson 31 is available in a wide range of hull and deck colors at no extra cost. Because the deck molding is a large, unrelieved area of fiberglass, we would recommend ordering the deck nonskid in a color contrasting to the base deck color. For those concerned with improving the aesthetic qualities of a boat that is admittedly a little austere, teak decks are available as an option.

Hulls are molded to Lloyd's specifications, and Lloyd's hull certificates are available. Full Lloyd's classification of the finished boat requires slight modification to the standard boat, notably the addition of more ground tackle, some alterations to the electrical system, and more ventilation for the battery box. The Lloyd's modifications, additional equipment, and surveys would add about $1500 to the price of the boat.

Hull and deck are joined with a wide internal flange, bedded with polysulfide and through-bolted at close intervals with stainless steel bolts. Fit of the hull and deck flanges is excellent, with no gaps or irregularities. A through-bolted teak toe rail covers the hull-to-deck joint.

All deck hardware is properly through-bolted. Removable panels in the interior give access to every part of the underside of the deck.

Ballast is an internal lead casting weighing 5,300 pounds, giving a ballast/displacement ratio of 36%. It is ironic that the Nicholson 31, a true cruising boat, has internal ballast rather than an external lead keel. An external keel is far less vulnerable to damage in either an intentional or inadvertent grounding.

Nicholson chainplates deserve comment. They consist of stainless steel rod formed into an inverted V-bolt. The top of the V is properly radiussed for the appropriate size clevis pin. The legs of the V-bolt pass through the deck and hull flanges and a heavy backup plate. The hull flange is about ½" thick. Two major structural bulkheads and a hanging knee reinforce the hull and deck immediately adjacent to the chainplates.

The same chainplate arrangement is used on larger boats in the Nicholson line. The obvious advantage is that the chainplates are just about leakproof.

A few years ago we would have been skeptical of the strength of this installation. However, we have examined a Nicholson 40—equipped with the same chainplates—which was rolled over and dismasted during a winter passage south. The chainplate had bent about 45°, but there were neither deck leaks nor stress cracks in the deck or hull. They work, and you can't argue with that.

The reasons that the chainplates work are an exceptionally thick hull flange and local reinforcement with knees and structural bulkheads.

The outboard rudder is attached to the transom by massive nylon-bushed stainless steel pintle and gudgeon castings. Polished stainless castings are infinitely preferable to weldments in a fitting exposed to salt water, since they are less vulnerable to corrosion.

A large molded fiberglass water tank fills most of the bilge space. The tank is gelcoated inside, and is equipped with two large manholes for easy cleaning. The manholes are also used to fill the tank, as there is no deck fill pipe. While this is a slight nuisance, it pretty much insures that salt water will not get in the tank. The water tank is properly vented inside the boat, rather than outside. Again, the risk of contamination by salt water is eliminated.

Unlike many modern boats, there is a deep bilge sump aft of the water tank. The bilge slopes sharply aft to the sump, so that any water getting into the bilge will quickly drain to the sump. Bilge water lapping about the cabin sole should not be a problem.

Construction of the Nicholson 31 is strong and heavy, perhaps too heavy for coastal cruising in light air. The boat's displacement of almost 15,000 pounds yields a staggering displacement/length ratio of 468, one of the highest we've ever seen. That heavy construction and Lloyd's hull certificate will be comforting, however, hove to in a 60 knot nor'easter in the Gulf Stream or a typhoon in the South Pacific.

PERFORMANCE

Handling Under Sail
With her displacement/length ratio of 468, the Nicholson 31 is no racer-cruiser. She's not even a cruiser-racer. Just a pure cruiser, and one close to being underpowered at that.

Fully loaded for cruising, she will displace 18,000 pounds or more. At that point the boat will need all the sail that can be piled on in light air.

Shrouds mounted at the outboard edge of the deck will limit the boat's ability to point. She is most definitely at her best off the wind.

There is a great deal of inherent stability in the hull form of the Nicholson 31. With her relatively hard bilges, wide beam, and reasonable ballast/displacement ratio, the boat is quite stiff, particularly when these hull characteristics are coupled with a fairly short rig.

Spars are by Proctor. The mast is a heavy, untapered section with airfoil spreaders. The boom is equipped for slab reefing. A short mainsheet traveler mounted on top of the transom will help mainsail control. A boom vang is supplied as standard equipment.

Lewmar winches are used for sheets and halyards. They are of adequate size for the job, although we would consider slightly larger self-tailing winches than the standard single-speed Lewmar 34 ST's. All sheets are within easy reach of the helmsman.

The boat comes with mainsail and #1 jib. These are made by Horizon, and are of mediocre quality. We would rather take delivery of the boat with no sails, then purchase a full inventory from a local sailmaker who understood how we were going to use the boat. On a boat which lacks inherent speed, fast, high-quality sails are critical.

A Hydrovane VDA2 self-steering gear is a factory option. Since we'd plan to do a lot of off-wind sailing on our cruise, we'd like to have an autopilot such as the Autohelm 2000 in addition to or in place of the vane steerer. Modern autopilots draw very little power and will steer the boat in a light following breeze or under power in a flat calm—something that no vane can do.

The characteristics of the Nicholson 31 that make her such a good offshore cruiser—stability, heavy displacement, and good motion in a seaway—will make her a poor choice for daysailing or even coastal cruising in areas of light air. On a long offshore passage, however, the boat should shine—provided you've got big headsails, including a spinnaker, for light air.

Handling Under Power
Standard engine is a three cylinder, 22.5 horsepower,

Hidden carpentry inside the engine box is as well executed as any finish work in the boat

---

raw water cooled Yanmar. If you want pressure hot water on the boat, it is necessary to order the fresh water cooled version of the engine. Independent of the hot water system, we'd prefer the fresh water cooling.

The engine is just about the right size for the boat. She should putt along at about five knots using less than a half gallon of fuel per hour. That's when the autopilot comes in handy. Steering under power is the most boring job on any sailboat.

The fuel tank is of molded fiberglass mounted under the cockpit sole. The top of the tank, in fact, forms part of the cockpit sole. This means that the teak cockpit grate must be kept in place to keep from walking on top of the tank.

We have always been leery of fiberglass diesel fuel tanks. Unless the proper type of resin is used, the tank may be slightly permeable to diesel oil. Fortunately, the fuel tank of the Nicholson 31 is a separate molding and is not integral to the hull. Even if trouble were to develop over time, removal and replacement of the tank would be relatively easy.

The fuel tank is equipped with a small sump on the bottom which is fitted with a drain to remove accumulated water. While this is a good idea, ABYC standards specifically preclude a drain on the bottom of the fuel tank. Lloyd's is not quite so finicky in that respect.

Capacity of the tank is 25 gallons. This should give the boat a range of 250 to 300 miles under power, perfectly adequate for a 31' cruising boat. The location of the fuel fill on the cockpit sole makes it easy to check the fuel level, but a fuel spill could turn the cockpit into a skating rink if the grate were not in place.

For long passages, it is desirable to be able to line up the prop in the aperture behind the deadwood. Unfortunately, access to the stuffing box and shaft requires climbing into the port cockpit locker after removing the access hatch, an exercise most people will find not worth the effort.

The engine installation is a good one. There is a deep molded drip pan under the engine. The shaft is fitted with a flexible shaft log and a flexible shaft coupling, as well as flexible engine mounts. This combination of flexible components is essential with a vibration-prone diesel engine.

Access to the engine for service is excellent. The companionway steps remove for access to the front of the engine, and a side panel in the quarterberth removes for access to the rest of the engine. The engine is easily removed through the companionway with no disassembly of joinerwork. However, there is no easy access to the oil dipstick.

The entire engine compartment is equipped with excellent soundproofing. All wiring and plumbing in the engine compartment is neat and workmanlike. Hidden carpentry inside the engine box is as well executed as any finish work in the boat.

Power to Weight Ratio: How Does it Affect Performance?

One factor that can be used to predict the performance of almost any boat is the relationship between sail area and displacement. If displacement represents what must be moved, then sail area represents the power to move it.

The ratio of sail area to displacement is best indicative of relative performance in moderate winds —how quickly the speed of the boat can be expected to increase as wind strength increases. The same ratio gives a fair indication of how quickly the boat may accelerate after tacking or after being slowed by waves.

The commonly used formula for determining the sail area to displacement ratio is the nominal (or rated) sail area in square feet divided by the displacement in cubic feet to the two thirds power:

$$\text{Sail area to displacement} = \frac{\text{Sail area}}{(\text{Disp. in cu. ft.})^{2/3}}$$

To determine the displacement in cubic feet, divide the displacement in pounds by 64, the weight per cubic foot of sea water.

Since the headsail overlap or the setting of multiple headsails (ie, a staysail and jib topsail) are not taken into account, the ratio is not a direct indicator. However, as a general parameter for predicting for performance that the average sailor can compute from available specifications, sail area to displacement should be added to such equally calculable parameters as displacement to length, ballast to displacement, and speed to waterline length.

A sail area to displacement ratio of about 15 or less is likely to indicate a boat that is underpowered for her weight. The average is between 15 and 17. Some ultra light boats have comparatively high ratings that may be misleading until one realizes that the usual figure for displacement does not take into consideration the crew weight and stores that increase the actual sailing displacement of a light boat by a much greater proportion than the same additional weight on a heavier boat.

Using published figures (which are subject to some suspicion), we calculated the sail area to displacement ratios for a number of familiar boats. For further comparison the table includes the displacement-length ratios to show the correlation.

Boat	DWL	Dspl.	Sail Area	Dspl. Length	Sail Area Dspl.
Southern Cross 31	25'	13,600	447	389	12.5
Nicholson 31	24'2"	14,750	497	468	13.2
Westsail 32	27'6"	19,500	631	419	13.9
CSY 33	25'	15,200	538	434	14.0
Endeavour 32	25'6"	11,700	470	315	14.6
Seawind II	25'6"	14,900	555	401	14.7
Catalina 30	25'	10,200	444	291	15.1
Hunter 30	25'9"	9,700	473	253	16.6
Sabre 30	24'	8,400	432	271	16.7
Ericson 30	25'4½"	9,000	470	244	17.4
Cal 31	25'8"	9,170	490	242	17.5
J/30	25'	7,000	453	200	19.8
Santa Cruz 27	24'	3,000	396	97	30.4

LIVABILITY

Deck Layout

Deck layout of the Nicholson 31 is that of a pure cruiser. The recessed stemhead fitting is a massive stainless steel weldment equipped with two heavy cast bronze rollers. If the rollers are used with rope anchor rode they will have to be polished out, as the roller castings are rough enough to damage line. The rollers are designed to stow CQR anchors. Standard equipment includes a 35-pound CQR and a 15-fathom shot of 5/16" chain.

The anchor well is unusual. The lid has a strong, positive latch, and the well contains a large mooring bitt, lashing eyes for anchors and the bitter end of the anchor rode, and a pipe to the chain locker. The chain locker pipe should have been extended higher above the bottom of the anchor well to keep water out of the boat's interior when she takes solid water over the bow.

Because the stemhead fitting and anchor rollers are recessed below deck level, the 35-pound CQR actually stows inside the anchor well, so that sheets and sails cannot snag on it. There is also enough space inside the well to install a windlass, and two different models are listed as factory options. This is perhaps the best anchor well and anchor stowage arrangement we've seen on a small cruising boat.

There are full length hand rails on either side of the deckhouse. Bow and stern rails, double lifelines, and tapered stainless steel stanchions are standard, and are properly mounted.

The cockpit is a good compromise for a cruising boat. Seats are narrow, but are over six feet long for comfortable lounging. A high bridgedeck protects the companionway.

The companionway is fairly narrow and almost parallel-sided, with two drop boards. Because the companionway sill is well below coaming level, the lower drop board should be left in place for offshore sailing. In accordance with ORC requirements for offshore racing, drop boards and companionway slide have permanent positive inside latches to prevent accidental opening in a rollover.

Cockpit scuppers consist of two large holes through the transom, fitted with external flaps to keep following seas from crawling through the scuppers into the cockpit.

The cockpit sole, a removable teak grate, lacks a positive means of securing in place, so that it could fall out in a severe knockdown or rollover.

There is a shallow locker under the starboard cockpit seat for lines and other small items. At the aft end of this locker is a molded recess for a single propane bottle. The bottle locker is designed for a European bottle, which may prove difficult to replace if it rusts out.

The scupper for this locker drains into the cockpit. Inevitably, the steel gas bottle will turn into a pile of rust, staining the cockpit where the drain discharges. An aluminum gas bottle or a thoroughly epoxied steel bottle is called for here.

No provision is made for the storage of a spare gas bottle. We'd like to see the bottle locker modified to take two aluminum cylinders of at least 10 pounds capacity.

Under the port cockpit seat is a deep locker which can rightfully be called a sail locker. The lid is large enough for the largest headsail on the boat. The locker should accommodate most if not all of the boat's inventory. It is sealed off from the bilge and the underside of

Enclosed storage for a valise life raft is built into the cockpit of the Nicholson 31, as it should be in every serious cruising boat.

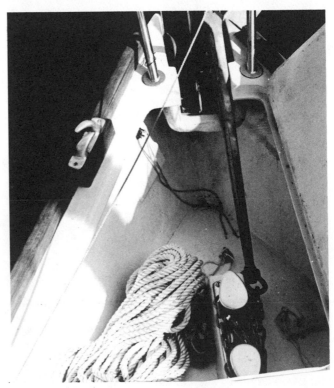

The anchor well is the best we've seen on a small cruiser. The standard 35 pound CQR fits completely below deck level, but can be dropped almost instantly.

The main cabin has a number of excellent features, not the least of which is a strongly mounted dropleaf cabin table

the cockpit, and the lid is deeply scuppered.

A full width cockpit dodger is standard. It fits neatly into a plastic extrusion attached to a wrap-around breakwater. The forward end of the cockpit will be dry, dry, dry, even in heavy weather, allowing the upper drop board to be left out until it gets really nasty. The only disadvantage of the molded breakwater and low dodger is that the halyards cannot be led aft without fairly complex modifications to the breakwater.

The cockpit is deep and well protected. It is so deep that a short person will have a hard time seeing over the deckhouse.

We'd like to see a molded-in transom tube for a man overboard pole, since this is a serious cruising boat.

All in all, deck layout and cockpit are well suited for serious cruising: simple, clean, and devoid of toe bashers. It is a layout designed not for high performance, but rather for a long haul.

Belowdecks

The interior layout of the Nicholson 31 approaches the ideal for a minimum long distance cruiser for two, but falls short in a few important details. There is a total of six berths, equally divided between the port and starboard sides. Each berth is equipped with a lee cloth.

The forward cabin contains the standard V-berths with an insert to form a double. Shelves along the side of the hull and a small linen locker over the foot of the berth are standard.

There are large bin-type lockers under the V-berths with molded drop-in liners. These should provide good dry storage in any conditions.

A Camper & Nicholsons (Canpa) aluminum framed hatch over the berth provides ventilation and can be used as an exit. Teak steps mounted on the bulkhead serve as a ladder for climbing out the hatch.

Aft of the forward cabin is a full width head. A full width head makes a lot of sense on a small boat. In the attempt to avoid a full width head in a small boat, builders invariably end up with a cramped compartment barely big enough to turn around in, much less shower or dress in comfort.

The water closet is the unique Lavac design, which uses a separate diaphragm pump in place of a built-in pump. This is an incredibly efficient toilet which absolutely will not splash when pumped.

Outboard of the toilet is a good-sized hanging locker. It is, unfortunately, the only hanging space on the boat. The lack of a wet hanging locker will be sorely felt by the serious cruiser.

A pressure cold water shower is standard. The shower sump is fitted with a separate electric pump, and does not drain to the bilge.

Opposite the toilet is a huge sink, the largest we've seen in the head of any boat. The sink is fitted with both manual and pressure water taps. The head sink has the only manual fresh water pump on the boat. We would also install one in the galley. A heavy stainless steel grab rail is mounted horizontally in front of the sink. Above the sink, tucked under the side deck, is a mirror-fronted medicine chest. The mirrors are angled upward so that it isn't necessary to duck to see your face in the mirror when shaving—a small touch, but typical of the thought which has gone into the interior.

The head compartment has solid, heavy sliding doors which have positive latches to hold them open. They are held shut only by magnets, which could prove inadequate offshore. Ventilation is provided by a small cowl vent in a molded dorade box. We would replace the cowl with a larger one.

The main cabin has a number of excellent features, not the least of which is a strongly mounted dropleaf cabin table. Bolted to an aluminum plate under the cabin sole, the table is as sturdy as any we've ever encountered. The folding leaves should be fitted with fiddles, however, for use in a rolly anchorage. (At sea, a lap is more often used than a table. We can recall very few sit-down dinners at sea.)

Settees port and starboard are fitted with lee cloths, as are the pilot berth and quarterberth. There is good dry, compartmented storage below, behind, and above the settees. Footwells under the chart table and galley counter make the settees long enough for sleeping. Both settees pull out to increase width for sleeping.

While the pilot berth and quarterberth afford permanent sea berths on both sides of the main cabin without using the settees, this configuration wastes storage space that the cruising couple would find handy. We doubt if four berths in the main cabin are really necessary. Instead, we'd like to see the pilot berth replaced by lockers and bookshelves similar to those above the settee on the starboard side. The port settee could then be shifted outboard almost a foot, allowing two or three more galley drawers to be added under the existing single drawer. Galley counter space would be increased by eliminating the pilot berth extension into the galley, and the main cabin table could be shifted slightly to port to give a wider passageway to the head and forward cabin.

While we normally refrain from redesigning boats for builders, these changes would be so much better for the cruising couple that we can't resist.

The galley is the weakest part of the interior, as it is on most small boats. Current Nicholson 31s are fitted with a single small oval sink. The sink has a flush lid which reverses to act as a cutting board. Unfortunately,

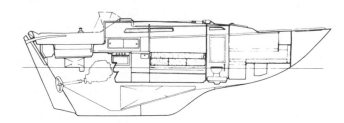

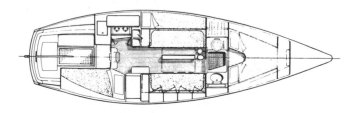

on the boat we examined the sink lid is asymmetrical, and doesn't quite fit into the sink when reversed.

There is one small drawer in the galley. It's the only drawer in the whole boat. Admittedly, drawers are expensive and waste a certain amount of space, but the one place they do make sense is the galley, and one is barely adequate.

A two burner, gimballed, strongly mounted propane stove with oven and broiler is standard. The stove is a simple enameled steel model, and will probably last for only a few years of hard service before it rusts out. At the same time, it probably only cost a couple of hundred dollars rather than the $600 or more you would pay for a good stainless steel model.

The gas system lacks a shutoff valve belowdecks, a violation of ABYC standards for propane installations. We suggest you fit a Marinetics or Bass electro-magnetic propane solenoid, or a good manual valve somewhere in the galley.

As is typical in many European boats, the icebox is a bit of an afterthought. In much of the world, ice isn't the readily available commodity that it is here, and people simply learn to do without. When cruising offshore, ice only lasts a few days anyway, so unless you have a refrigeration system, why bother with an icebox? So the logic goes, anyway. In this country, most cruising is well within range of sources of ice, and we'd damned well want a good box to keep it in.

While the icebox of the Nicholson 31 is well insulated, including the lid, the lid lacks a sealing gasket. The lid is so small that a 25 pound block of ice must be broken in half to pass through, and a gallon jug of wine would be a close fit. In addition, the rounded cabin trunk liner protrudes so much into the space over the icebox that access is difficult. This inconvenience is totally unnecessary, as there is plenty of dead space behind the liner that could be eliminated to make the galley more workable. The icebox also lacks shelves to keep food off the ice, and it drains into the bilge sump.

There is fairly good storage outboard of the stove in well-fiddled shelves behind plexiglass sliding doors. Crockery and glasses are provided as standard items.

Treadmaster is used on the cabin sole in the galley and at the aft end of the main cabin. This is an excellent nonskid surface which is, unfortunately, very difficult to clean. The rest of the main cabin sole is varnished teak and holly plywood.

On the starboard side opposite the galley is an excellent nav station, with a huge chart table and plenty of bulkhead space for radios, instruments, book cases, and other goodies. The electrical panel—again typical of European boats—lacks adequate circuits for the addition of many extras. The electrical system does have a built-in ground system utilizing an external ground plate, which greatly improves the functioning of SSB radios, shortwave receivers, and Loran.

The navigator sits at the head of a large, comfortable quarterberth. Batteries mount under the quarterberth in the best battery box we've seen, with a positively latched lid. Two heavy-duty 95 amp-hour batteries are standard, and should be adequate for the electrical needs of a 31' cruising boat. The battery box does lack adequate ventilation to disperse charging gases, a fairly easily remedied problem.

Ventilation of the main cabin is provided by a large aluminum framed hatch in the middle of the cabin, and two small cowl vents in molded dorade boxes at the aft end of the cabin. These tiny, low, 3" diameter cowls should be replaced by taller 4" vents, which have almost twice the cross-sectional area—hence twice the air flow—of 3" vents.

The ventilation hatches in both the main and forward cabins open aft. When fitted with side curtains, they can be left open at sea for additional ventilation. Forward facing hatches are fine in port, but cannot normally be left open at sea.

The interior of the Nicholson 31 is clearly that of a seagoing boat. There are full length hand rails along each cabin side, and vertical posts in the galley and nav station.

With the changes mentioned above, this interior would be just about ideal for a cruising couple. Interior workmanship is excellent, with a good blend of very light teak and off-white molded components. The interior is cheery and homelike. It's easy to imagine a long cruise aboard.

CONCLUSIONS

The Nicholson 31 is a well designed, well built serious cruising boat. Her somewhat modern appearance above the water may confuse those who connect serious cruising boats with lots of teak, bowsprits, sweeping sheers, and "traditional" appearance.

The Nicholson 31 is not a copy of any "ideal" cruising hull form. She is, rather, a well thought out answer to the problem of putting a lot of carrying capacity, volume, and comfort in a minimum size boat for extended cruising.

If the British pound were valued at much above $2, the Nicholson 31 would be prohibitively expensive, as almost all Nicholson boats have been in the past. At current exchange rates, however, she represents an excellent value for someone willing to go through the logistics of importing a boat.

There are only two US agents for the boat: Camper & Nicholsons of North America (Box 3296, Annapolis MD 21403) and Dunbar Yachts (Bowen's Landing, Newport RI 02840). There is no such thing as a stocking dealer for the boat, either in England or the US. In England, the boat is sold directly by the builder.

The prohibitive transatlantic shipping cost of a boat as small as the Nicholson 31—about $7,500—tempts us to offer an alternative. Arrange to purchase a boat through one of the US agents, or through the builder: the price is the same either way. Take delivery in England in the spring. Spend the summer cruising England and perhaps some of northern Europe.

In the fall, begin the migration south with other European boats, arriving in the Canaries in late fall. When the northeast trades fill in and hurricane season is past, depart the Canaries for the long, downwind passage to Barbados. Spend the winter working north through the Caribbean. In late May, depart north toward Bermuda and the east coast of the US or west toward the Panama Canal.

The money you've saved on transatlantic shipping will have gone a long way toward paying for your year of cruising. And you'll have a good, solid boat under your feet, a few thousand miles of cruising under your belt, and some memories you'll never forget. Just hope that your boss understands when you ask for a year's leave of absence. And hope you can make the right decision when the time comes to go home, or move on.

The Allied Seawind II: Staying Power

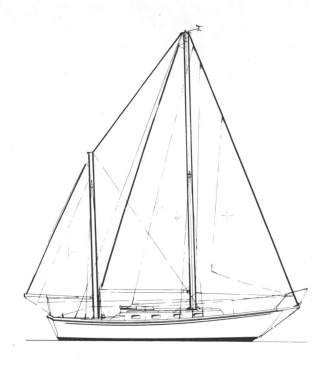

THE BOAT AND THE BUILDER

When Allied Yachts went out of business for the fifth — and last — time at the end of 1981, they did so in a rather messy fshion. At least two potential owners were left holding the bag, having made down payments of about $20,000 each for boats that were never built. Brax Freeman, who managed Allied, seemed to disappear, along with the dreams of the would-be owners of the unbuilt Seawind IIs.

Sailboat dealer Freeman took over management of Allied Yachts in the spring of 1980, when the venerable boatbuilding firm in the unlikely town of Catskill, New York, was on the verge of financial disaster for the fourth time in less than 20 years. Over the years Allied had suffered from mediocre management, severe under-exposure, and the vagaries of the boatbuying public — a not unusual story in the boatbuilding industry.

Allied had the reputation of fashioning solidly built (if uninspiringly finished) boats, unabashedly oriented toward cruising, with the exception of a single foray into the world of racing yachts with a Britton Chance 30-footer.

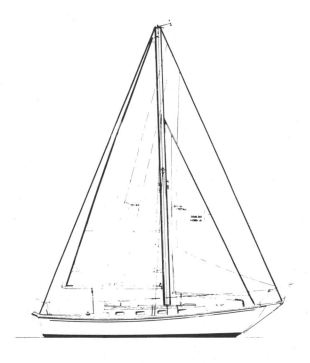

Allied had already secured its place in the boatbuilding pantheon with the original Seawind ketch, which became the first fiberglass boat to circumnavigate, and the Luders 33, recognized as a classic design of the era preceding the introduction of the fin keel racer-cruiser. Unfortunately, while its products were heading for glory on the high seas, the company was repeatedly headed for the boneyard.

In 1975, Allied began building the foot-longer, foot-wider, Gillmer-designed Seawind II as a replacement for the original 30'6" Seawind. The extra foot of length and beam, 1½ feet of waterline length, and 2,700 lbs of displacement add up to make the Seawind II a significantly larger boat than her predecessor.

Like its cousin the Southern Cross 31, the Seawind II is a dream machine. Walter Mitty's escape hatch. The dream comes with a hefty price tag. Base price for a new Seawind II with its extensive standard inventory was $75,000. For this you got a well-equipped, well-built, proven world cruiser with standard features such as hot and cold pressure water, shower in the cockpit and below, shore power, and wheel steering.

Freeman tried hard to overcome Allied's dowdy image. Older Allied boats were heavy on woodgrain Formica, bland expanses of fiberglass, and mediocre woodwork. He actively sought to overcome that hard-to-shake reputation by using large quantities of interior wood (which hide most of the interiot glass), good hardware, and the imagination of a builder who has spent a good deal of time living on boats.

Specifications

LOA	31'7"
DLW	25'6"
Beam	10'5"
Draft	4'6"
Displacement	14,900 lbs
Ballast	5,800 lbs
Sail Area:	
ketch	555 sq ft
cutter	512 sq ft

CONSTRUCTION

The hull of the Seawind II is a solid hand layup. Deck and cabin trunk are balsa cored. The top of the cabin trunk in the way of the deck-stepped mast is cored with solid filled epoxy for greater compression strength.

The hull-to-deck joint is complex, expensive, time-consuming to make, and extremely strong. In this day of simple through-bolted inside flanges it is an anachronism. Both hull and deck have outward-turning flanges at the sheer line. These flanges are coated with 3M 5200 and a teak batten is placed between them, laid on the flat. Hull, deck, and batten are through-bolted vertically with stainless steel bolts. After the sealant cures, which takes several days, the joint is ground off on the inside of the boat and heavily glassed over.

On the outside a heavy aluminum extrusion is filled with bedding, slipped over the flange, and fastened horizontally with screws into the teak batten. (Now you know what the teak batten is for.)

This is an incredibly labor intensive joint, substantially improved over the old Seawind joint which was the same basic design but had a reputation for developing small leaks. The aluminum extrusion makes an excellent rubbing strake, but damage to it would require getting a replacement piece from the builder, rather than a patch job with resin, putty, and a little teak. The rubbing strake may look a little massive for a boat of this size, but it is an excellent idea for a serious cruising boat.

Though rather primitive, this hull-to-deck joint has been retained because it was cheaper to beef up and modify the old design than to modify the Seawind tooling, given Allied's low production volume.

The ballast keel is lead, molded to shape and glassed into the keel. While this technique eliminates keel bolts, it also makes the fiberglass hull more vulnerable to grounding damage.

The mast is stepped on deck, and uses a massive oak compression frame under the cabin trunk for support. This frame forms the head door framing, and is solidly, though a little crudely, attached to the top of the ballast.

Seacocks are used on all through hull fittings. These are through-bolted to the hull and have double clamped hoses—cheap insurance for any boat.

All deck hardware is through-bolted and reinforced with fiberglass backing plates. We prefer aluminum backing plates to fiberglass for their greater strength and rigidity for a given thickness and area.

There is very little exterior wood on the Seawind II. The molded toerail is capped with teak; there are teak hand rails on the cabin top, and teak trim around the edge of the cabin. That's all. Even the dorade boxes are molded in. This results in low maintenance, a highly desirable characteristic on a serious cruising boat, but one that leads to an appearance of austerity that can border on plainness. The austere appearance of the Seawind II is greatly relieved by contrasting cockpit, deck, and deckhouse molded-in non-skid surfaces. The Seawind II will never look as flashy as a Taiwan-built teak plantation, but neither will her owners have to make the decision between endless wood maintenance or the drabness of unfinished "natural" teak—ie, mildewed gray.

PERFORMANCE

Handling Under Sail
The standard rig of the Seawind II is a masthead ketch. The ketch rig is not particularly desirable for a boat of this size. The mizzen adds considerable weight and windage and almost no drive upwind, since the mizzen sail acts almost completely in the backwind of the mainsail. The real purpose of a mizzen upwind is to balance the boat, and for this purpose the smaller, more out-of-the-way mizzen of the yawl is equally useful.

Off the wind, the area of the mizzen plus the added bonus of a mizzen staysail do provide considerable drive.

The mizzenmast clutters up the cockpit, although it does provide a good handhold. Its position five feet forward of the helmsman is guaranteed to make him cross-eyed if he has the habit of sitting directly behind the wheel.

Sail area of the Seawind II is small enough that the oft-cited advantage of the ketch rig—smaller individual sails—is rather unimportant. A mizzen is useful for heaving to, for anchoring and weighing anchor, and to enable the boat to weather-cock in a rolly anchorage. It is, however, a most inefficient rig upwind.

An optional cutter rig is available. It uses the same mainmast as the ketch rig, but shifts it aft about a foot. The mainsail is longer on the foot and the base of the foretriangle is a little longer than that of the ketch rig. The total sail area of the cutter rig works out to slightly less than that of the ketch rig, but the reduced windage and slightly increased stability probably make up for the loss of sail area. For tradewind passages, the double headstays on either rig allow the use of twin downwind jibs. With a working sail area of just over 500 square feet for a displacement of 14,900 pounds, the Seawind II is not underrigged as are many cruising boats.

The Seawind II's rudder is a rather large, old fashioned design of the barn door variety. It would be interesting and not at all difficult to change it to a more modern Constellation style rudder, which could slightly reduce wetted surface and perhaps give a little better performance with no loss of control.

With the cutter rig that we prefer, twin running headsails, and sails built for speed as well as durability, the Seawind II should have good performance for a pure cruising boat. Without a large genoa she will not be at her best in light air, although owners report that she is surprisingly spritely in those conditions. Unfortunately, she will not be able to use a genoa to its full efficiency upwind due to the wide shroud base and wide spreaders.

Handling Under Power
The Seawind II is powered by a lightweight four-cylinder Westerbeke 27 horsepower diesel. This is plenty of power for the Seawind II's displacement. A welded aluminum fuel tank is located in the bilge.

The standard propeller is a three-bladed fixed bronze in-aperture installation. Rather than be burdened by the considerable drag of such a propeller, we would install a two-bladed model that could be lined up behind the deadwood to reduce drag when under sail. Alternatively, a two- or three-bladed feathering propeller could be installed. On a boat with the considerable wetted surface of the Seawind II, reducing drag becomes critical to performance in light air, and no matter what

The narrow companionway, coupled with a good bridgedeck and a molded seahood, provides thoroughly well-designed access for people, but not water

the builders of ocean-going dreadnoughts may tell you, much of the sailing in the world—even on the ocean—is in light air.

Do not expect the Seawind II to maneuver like a modern fin keeler under power. Despite her cutaway forefoot, there is enough lateral plane here to require a little planning ahead in a tight situation under power; but then you should plan ahead no matter how well your boat handles.

LIVABILITY

Deck Layout

An unusual feature of the Seawind II is lifeline stanchions and pulpits that stand 30" off the deck rather than the more usual 24". Coupled with a fairly high toerail, they give the foredeck hand a real feeling of security. Unfortunately, they also require that a long tack pennant be installed if you want to get the foot of the jib above the lifelines. The cutter rig is an advantage here, for a high-cut yankee jibtopsail will easily clear the lifelines.

The bowsprit is a massive teak platform with attached rail. There are double bow rollers at the end of the bowsprit, but these are so far outboard that the anchor chain or warp chafes against the forward pulpit stanchion when the rollers are used. This defect also prevents secure storage of an anchor in the roller, as the stock would bear against the pulpit. The pulpit is a comfortable and secure place to handle sails or ground tackle.

The Seawind II is one of the few boats we've seen with properly sized bow cleats. There are two 12" foredeck cleats, with hawsepipes to the divided anchor rode locker outside of each cleat. An anchor windlass is optional, and will fit nicely between the cleats.

Because of the width of the cabin trunk, it is easier to get to the foredeck by walking over the cabin top than by squeezing inside the shrouds. Good nonskid on the cabin top makes this fairly easy.

Unfortunately, it's not particularly easy to hoist the sails on the cutter rig, because the two dorade boxes fall exactly abreast the mast, making it necessary to straddle them awkwardly. This is less a problem with the ketch rig, whose mast is stepped further forward. For shorthanded cruising, it makes more sense anyway to lead the halyards aft on the cabin top to the forward end of the cockpit.

A variety of mainsheet leads have been used on the

Seawind II. One version uses a Fico traveler mounted over the companionway sea hood. In this version, the blocks are located far apart on the boom, giving poor mechanical advantage. The best of the Seawind II mainsheet arrangements consists of a traveler mounted on the bridgedeck, which reduces seating but gives much better sail control. This should be used on either the ketch or the cutter, as the old end-of-boom arrangement was only necessary with a roller furling mainsail, which should appropriately be considered a thing of the past.

The standard steerer on the boat is an Edson rack and pinion model, mounted directly on the head of the rudder stock. This is the only steering placement possible with the ketch rig.

There are more possibilities with the cutter rig. The most appealing would be to mount an Edson pedestal steerer at the forward end of the cockpit. Then the helmsman could reach the mainsheet on the bridgedeck, the headsail sheets, and even the halyards if they were led aft. If a cockpit dodger were also installed, the helmsman would be protected from all that nasty spray when going upwind. Since each Seawind II is custom built, we suspect that these modifications could be arranged—at a price, of course.

The cockpit is large and reasonably comfortable. It was probably made so large to accommodate the mizzen mast, which also serves as a handy foot brace. Without the mizzen, the cockpit looks rather large and empty. It is too wide, in fact, to adequately brace your feet on the opposite cockpit seat when the boat is heeled over.

There is a deep gutter at the back of the cockpit seats on either side. This is a good feature, for it means that water will not collect in a puddle against the leeward coaming on a long, wet beat to weather.

Be sure to check the fit of the emergency tiller. The rudder stock of the new boat we examined had been improperly machined, and the emergency tiller was overly sloppy in its fit.

A large underseat locker on either side of the cockpit will hold a lot of gear, and is equipped with drop-in dividers to keep items from the depths of the bilge. Another unique feature of the cockpit is a fresh water shower, whose spray head and hose are recessed into the side of the footwell. This means that it isn't necessary to track either sand or salt water belowdecks after a swim.

The companionway is narrow with almost parallel sides. While this may make it a little less convenient to get below, it is far more seamanlike than most compan-

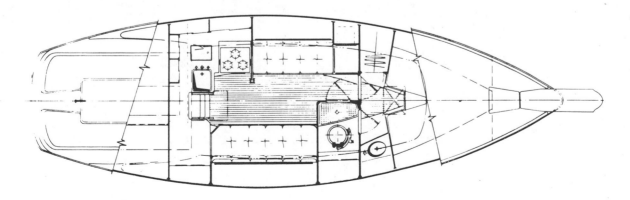

ionways, which seem to be more concerned with letting overweight sailors get below than with keeping water out of the interior. Coupled with a molded seahood, and a good bridgedeck, it provides thoroughly well-designed access for people, but not water.

Belowdecks

The days when it was necessary to ignore the mediocre detailing on the inside of Allied boats happily appear to be behind us. The new Seawind II we examined had the best finished interior of any Allied boat we've seen.

The layout was conventional. As befits a cruising boat, there is tremendous storage throughout. There are also a number of storage options, such as a bureau, extra drawers, and extra cabinets, which allow the owner to tailor the boat to his or her individual needs.

A forward cabin contains vee berths, a hanging locker, and a wash basin. There are drawers and bins under the berths, and a large stainless steel holding tank. We would replumb the holding tank as a fresh water tank — before it's used, of course — to greatly increase the standard water capacity.

A door from the forward cabin gives access to the head without entering the main cabin. The primary door between the main cabin and the forward cabin does double duty as a door which shuts the head off from the main cabin.

The head is small, containing only the water closet and the shower. Having the head wash basin in the forward cabin is unusual, but does make that cabin much less cramped.

Despite the spacious interior, the Seawind II is not a fat person's boat. The head doors are extremely narrow, since their heavy framing also carries the compression load of the rig.

Because the settees in the main cabin are asymmetrical, it is not possible to accommodate more than four people at the fold-down dining table. Since, quite rationally, there are only four berths in the boat, this should rarely be a problem. The space behind the settees is given over to storage, rather than attempting to cram more berths into the boat.

A number of galley stove options were available, including surface burner kerosene and alcohol stoves, gimballed kerosene or alcohol stoves with oven—which sacrifices galley storage space—or a three burner, gimballed LPG stove with oven. Alcohol should not be considered as a cooking fuel for a serious cruising boat, and kerosene, while hot, soon turns the galley overhead to a dingy greyish-brown.

The icebox is insulated with four inches of urethane foam, and has a tight fitting, well-gasketed top. It is second only to the icebox of the CSY 37.

Although there is no navigation station—which would be a little much to expect on a boat of this size—there is a large dresser surface on the starboard side aft of the settee. Like most boats, there really isn't enough room at the table for navigation electronics, a sextant, and the navigator's pile of books.

The large, deep sink is equipped with both pressure fresh water taps and a manual pump—absolutely essential as a backup or to save electrical power at sea.

Engine access is poor. The engine is tucked away under the cockpit, and it is necessary to remove both the companionway ladder and the bulkhead panel behind in order to check the oil. Needless to say, this is not conducive to good engine maintenance. There is an oil pan under the engine, so that spilled oil will not drain into the bilge sump. Neither the shower nor the icebox drain to the bilge either, a welcome feature.

With its wide cabin trunk, good headroom, and no attempt to sleep an army in tiny, uncomfortable berths, the Seawind II provides excellent accommodations for a couple either living aboard or for extended cruising. That is what the Seawind II is all about.

CONCLUSIONS

The Seawind II is truly a boat that can call herself a world cruiser without apology or explanation. Her construction is strong without being inordinately heavy. She makes no attempt to be all things to all people. It would be a shame to see her tied up to the dock in a marina, for she deserves better.

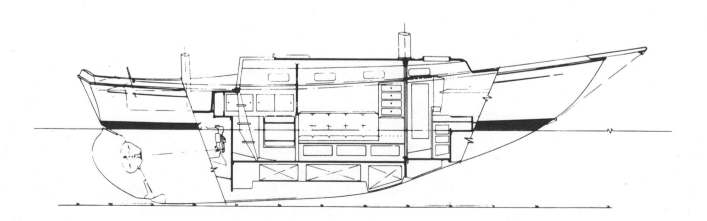

The Freedom 33:
Selling a Concept

THE BOAT AND THE BUILDER

When a restless 40-year-old advertising executive with a background in one-design sailing (1970 World's Sunfish Champion) went shopping for a cruising boat some years ago, he could not find one that made him happy. Conventional cruisers he found poor performers, needlessly difficult to sail shorthanded with their big headsails and complicated rigs, and with hull forms that demand auxiliary power any time the wind is forward of abeam.

It was in 1972 that this sailor, Garry Hoyt, set about developing an alternative. His alternative was the original Freedom 40. Discarding conventions one by one, he came up with a long-waterline, quasi-traditional hull form and a wishbone cat-ketch rig. Then, to prove he had something, he took his prototype to Antigua Race Week and decisively out-performed the cruising boats with which he had been so unhappy. Granted, his talents as a sailor were considerably better than those of his competition and granted, his prototype without an engine had no propeller or aperture drag; nevertheless his concept gained a qualified validity.

In the intervening years Hoyt refined his rig and developed a whole line of boats: a 21, 25, 28, 39 (express and pilothouse models), and the 44. The Freedom 33 is no longer in production, having been replaced in the line by the 32, which is a single masted "cat sloop" with a self tacking jib and gun mount spinnaker. More rig innovation.

Hoyt's natural ingenuity produced the innovative boats, basic good luck led him to Ev Pearson of Tillotson-Pearson when he went looking for a builder, and his background in advertising let him create attention-getting explanations of his concept. His one notable weakness has been in marketing; until recently he tried with little success to bring potential buyers to the boat rather than putting together a dealer network that takes the boat to the public. Freedom Yachts is now signing on dealers from coast to coast.

The US builder, Tillotson-Pearson, has been one of the most successful low-profile boatbuilders over the last 10 years, putting together such popular boats as the J-Boat line and the Etchells 22 one-design. The firm has been a leader in the development of balsa coring for hull structure and carbon fiber for light, stiff laminates.

Unlike the situation with more conventional craft, selling the sailing public on the concept behind the Freedoms is a stiff challenge. The rig in particulr is un-

Specifications

LOA	33'
LWL	30'
Beam	11'
Draft (Board up)	3'6"
(Board down)	6'
Displacement	12,000 lbs
Sail area	516 sq ft

Freedom Yachts
Bend Boat Basin
Melville, RI 02840

familiar to most cruising sailors and for the concept to gain acceptance they need to be educated. Not only must they be convinced that the stayless masts, wishbone booms, and wrap-around sails are durable, they must be literally taught how to use them advantageously. For this reason reception to the idea has been mixed, and thus far the appeal of the Freedom has been to sailors outside of the mainstream.

CONSTRUCTION

Basic construction of the Freedom 33 hull and deck is, in our opinion, among the best in the production boat building industry. From our observation as a result of examining boats both finished and under construction, we can detect no serious cost cutting or scrimping in the way of materials or techniques.

The Freedom 33 (as with other boats in the Freedom line) has a balsa-cored hull and deck. There are advantages to this type of construction—hull rigidity, thermal and acoustical insulation, reduction in hull weight—that we believe recommends it for hull structure *provided it is properly engineered.* In the case of the Freedom 33, we believe it is.

Lead ballast, 3800 lbs, is cast in wedge-shaped pieces and fiberglassed into the bilge. The aluminum fuel tank (25 gallons) is also deep in the bilge. The centerboard, a combination of lead and fiberglass, is a hefty 1200 lbs, also contributing to stability. The centerboard is the product of perhaps the most thoughtful design and engineering on the boat. It is pivoted in a channel, eliminating the need for a pin that breaches the hull. Hoyt, with his eye firmly on performance, adopted an idea of designer Jay Parris for a centerboard configuration having a triangular profile and a constant chord. The design permits a centerboard with a shape that gives lift at any angle and, more importantly in reducing drag, a centerboard that fits its slot closely.

If the centerboard is not the most extensively engineered feature of the Freedom 33, then the spars are. Initially the Freedom 33 had two-part aluminum tubular masts that were heavy, reducing stability and increasing pitching moment. To help cure this weakness, Tillotson-Pearson undertook a research program into building one-piece spars using a carbon-fiber laminate. The result is an approximately 30% saving in weight and considerably stiffer spars. The saving translated itself into markedly better performance, so much so that we suggest any buyer considering one of the increasing number of boats available with stayless spars should look into spar weight and stiffness. And, incidentally, we also think stayless spars are the next most significant development in sailboat design.

Additional construction details of note on the Freedom 33 include a hull-to-deck joint through-fastened with 5/16″ stainless steel bolts and bonded with 3M #5200 adhesive sealant, a technique we recommend. Bulkheads are tabbed to the inside fiberglass skin, leaving the core intact to prevent hard spots from showing up on the topsqdes. The interior joinerwork, fetchingly of oak, ash, and spruce, is done to a high quality; our only serious reservation is discussed below.

PERFORMANCE

Our evaluation of the performance of the Freedom 33 is in part the product of having spent a week sailing aboard the boat during Antigua Race Week. For comparison with that experience on the prototype, we recently sailed a production version, as well.

For those sailors used to masthead headsails and conventional mainsails with their sheeting, reefing, and halyard systems, the rig of the Freedom 33 does require some re-education. Initially one has the impression that the boat is under-rigged and that the sailplan is inefficient. That impression is, however, deceptive. The boat does have speed and liveliness that exceeds that of most out-and-out cruising boats of her size and in many conditions can rival the performance of the many so-called racer-cruisers or "performance cruisers."

The mainsail and mizzen are efficient in that almost all their area forms an effective airfoil. The wishbone boom permits a longer luff than a conventional boom and does not interfere with the draft at the foot. The wishbone does create windage, though. Draft control is easier with a wishbone boom through either outhaul tension (the Freedom 33 mizzen) or adjustment of the effective length of the wishbone (the mainsail). Similarly the wrap-around sails are more efficient aerodynamically than sails set on a mast track or groove which are in part blanketed by the spar section. Given the greater diameter of stayless spars versus conventional spars, the wrap-around system is important in this type of rig.

For performance, proper sail shape, adjustment, and trim are as vital for this rig as for more conventional rigs. There are still some aspects of the Freedom rig about which we have reservations but from our experience we believe the Freedom line has come closer to perfecting the system than any of its rivals boasting similar rigs. Incidentally, Ulmer Sails (in particular Ulmer sailmaker Bob Adams), has worked hard to develop Freedom sail shape plus reefing and trimming systems and we therefore urge buyers to order the sails offered as "factory installed options" rather than trying to find another sailmaker who will have to go through the extensive design exercise needed to provide suitable sails.

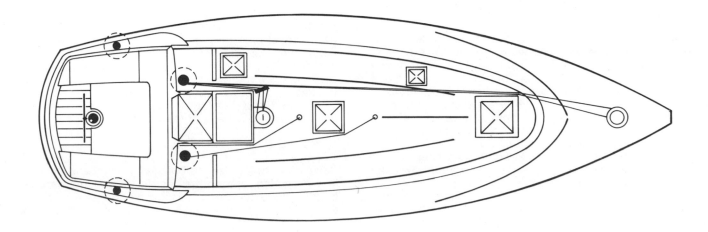

The Freedom 33 is stiffer (and, we think, foot-for-foot, faster) than her sisters in the Freedom line. Her sailplan gives optimum performance in a mid-range of wind strengths, say 10 to 15 knots. In winds below 10 knots, especially to windward in any chop, the stubby hull, with a centerboard and plenty of wetted surface, is sluggish. In fact, no Freedom is as lively as we would wish in lighter winds, a factor to consider in such areas as Chesapeake Bay and Puget Sound. For such conditions we strongly recommend at least one mizzen staysail. Moreover, although we are not sold on poleless spinnakers (ie, Flashers) for conventionally rigged cruising boats, we think they are superb as a mizzen spinnaker on a boat like a Freedom 33.

The wishbone booms and stayless masts combine to make the Freedom a delightful boat to sail with the wind from astern. The absence of shrouds lets the mainsail (and boom) swing forward of thwartships, encouraging her to sail wing and wing with the wind as much as 25° or so off the quarter. Moreover, the sail stays out to windward in light winds without a preventer. Nor does it need a vang; the angle of the wishbone boom off the mast eliminates any tendency for the boom to lift. On a run almost any sailor accustomed to wrestling with blanketed or poled out headsails, cringing as his mainsail chafes on shrouds, and paranoid over the threat of accidentally jibing, will have to appreciate the Freedom rig.

Closewindedness is a relative term but a major attraction of the better modern designs. The Freedom 33 is not closewinded, as much as a result of her hull shape as her rig. However, she does not give away anything upwind to boats with shallow hull forms and long keels. Boat for boat she will sail by Morgan 41s, Irwin 44s, CSY 44s, Westsails, and their ilk.

The Freedom rig uses a slab or jiffy reefing system. Moreover, instead of the reefed portion gathering above the boom as with conventional sailplans the excess material gathers at the wishbone in aerodynamically messy folds. It is just not a rig that lends itself to simple, uncluttered reefing and we think finding combinations of reduced sail using staysails would be a better solution than trying to reef main and mizzen. Yet the present rig seems to have proven itself in offshore sailing. Several boats have made long passages without difficulty and weathered severe storms at sea with no breakdowns or crises. In fact, we sailed a Freedom 33 that a few days before had beat her way up Long Island sound in an easterly gale with gusts as high as 60 knots.

The sails are two-ply loosely connected at the leech. Furling is easy; the sail gathers into a basket formed of shockcord stretched across the wishbone. More shockcord across the top keeps the sail secured. The convenience of this system, obvious as it may be, is one of the major recommendations of the rig, doing away with the onerous chores of conventional mainsail furling and headsail folding and bagging.

In all, we have been favorably impressed with the performance of a boat that experience and instinct tells us should be poor. The wrap-around sails take getting used to, but the more we played with them, the more effective they seemed to be.

LIVABILITY
Deck layout
Other than to handle ground tackle or docking lines, there is no reason why anyone has to leave the cockpit of a Freedom 33 under sail. All halyards, sheets, outhauls, reefing pennants, and the centerboard pennant lead aft to the cockpit where they are handled by a pair of self-tailing winches (Barient 23s) and an array of sheet stoppers. Moreover, the cockpit is short enough so that anyone handling these lines can also keep one hand close to the steering wheel, a boon for shorthanded or singlehanded sailing.

The cockpit seating is deep and the coamings are unobstructed perches on the Freedom 33. Best of all, the cockpit space is entirely usable. In fact, because the mizzen traveler is mounted aft, the Freedom 33 is a distinct rarity among production boats—a boat in which the traveler does not threaten to squash one's legs or the mainsheet garrot the crew. The feature alone makes the cockpit of the Freedom noteworthy.

The steering wheel on a pedestal is mounted well aft, the helmsman standing (or sitting on a fold-up seat) on a teak grate under which, uncommonly accessible, is the steering cable and quadrant for the outboard rudder. The grate also serves as the cockpit drain with scuppers through the transom, a most effective arrangement for quickly draining a flooded cockpit. A sliding door at the after end of the cockpit houses propane fuel bottles.

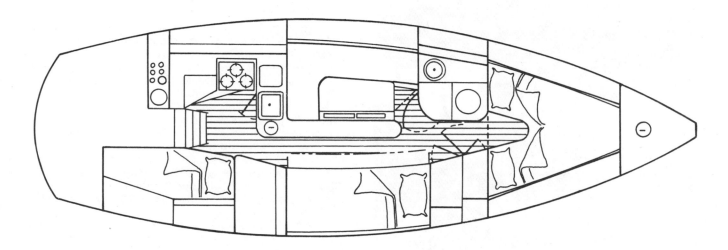

The aesthetic impression created by the interior joinerwork is among the best we have had about any production boat

The decks and house top are uncluttered sundecks and lounging platforms. Sailors used to gingerly stepping around a conventional deck may feel disoriented—missing are chainplates and shrouds, headsail sheets and blocks, and a spinnaker pole. The anchor cats in an optional fiberglass bowsprit. Man-sized chocks on either side of the bow and amidships are integrally fitted into the teak toerail.

Interior

Garry Hoyt's forte as a designer is clearly in his ability to develop performance. It has not been in his ability to design an interior. The Freedom 40 originally appeared with amidships cockpit and an interior so broken into segments as to be a disaster. The public understandably could not accept an accommodation plan in a 40-footer that was best suited for a chummy young couple (that to go with a rig that already took a vivid imagination to comprehend). Marketplace pressure dictated an alternative version with an aft cockpit and more versatile layout and the present Freedom 40 is a more successful product.

Similarly the Freedom 33 was first designed with an aft cabin that reduced cockpit space and a main cabin that succumbed to, rather than accommodated itself to, the centerboard trunk dividing it. The present production version does away with the aft cabin, locates the galley conventionally at the base of the companionway, tucks a dinette (convertible to a double berth) to port of the trunk, and has a settee berth to starboard. The result is a main cabin laid out much like other production boats of comparable proportions.

By having her waterline stretched out to virtually the overall length of the boat, the 33 has exceptional roominess for her modest length on deck. Moreover, with her mast stepped close to the stem, her hull fullness has to be carried well forward to support the weight. The forward cabin with its V-berth is the beneficiary. Farther aft the roominess is deceptive, however, because the main cabin is broken up by a 5' long, waist high centerboard trunk running down the middle and the mizzen mast rising at the after end of it.

Had Hoyt not had his eye so fixed on performance, he might have opted for a longer, narrower centerboard

Usable space is a plus in the cockpit

permitting a lower trunk that could be located where it would intrude little if at all into the main cabin. As it is, the centerboard does offer minimum drag, does not "thunk" annoyingly in the trunk, and is rugged. It also needs a trunk that makes casual conversation awkward and it makes the dinette a cul-de-sac, leaving the person on the inside no convenient way to get out.

The aesthetic impression created by the interior joinerwork is among the best we have had about any production boat. All the wood below—and there is plenty—is a combination of oak, ash, and spruce (plus the teak and holly cabin sole). We have long been critical of interior decor relying on dark woods such as teak and mahogany. The mellow warmth and the illusion of spaciousness imparted by these blond woods will appeal to many sailors. It certainly does to us.

There is a place for teak below. Grab rails, companionway treads, the framing around hatches, and the trim in the head—all areas liable to wear and getting wet—would be better in teak than in woods like ash and oak which are subject to staining. Moreover, oak is less dimensionally stable than teak, so moisture may eventually affect the structure as well as the finish.

We have some further observations about the interior. The comfortably wide quarterberth to starboard has little overhead foot room. The pilot berth to starboard is accessible only to a person shorter than 4' and weighing less than 40 lbs; it is either a luxuriously cushioned shelf or a berth for an agile ship's cat. Both the chart table and the clever dinette table need removable fiddles, and the hinges on the chart table lid would be better recessed.

And we have some incidental compliments. The stowage capacity of the Freedom 33 is by far the best we have seen in a boat of this size. In particular, the huge galley drywell, incorporating a sliding section for seldom used items, is nonpareil. The engine (Yanmar 3GM diesel) under the companionway is well above average in accessibility. The forward cabin can be completely closed off from the rest of the boat, including the head, by its own door.

The Freedom 33 thus offers an intriguing dichotomy —impressive and innovative decor and layout offset to a disturbing extent by drawbacks that may justifiably turn off many buyers and give owners things they will "have to live with."

CONCLUSIONS

The Freedom 33 is an interesting boat. She is, however, not a conventional boat and the concept behind her rig takes getting used to, especially for someone born and raised in the tradition of headsails, standing rigging, mainsails that ride on tracks, hulls with overhangs and aesthetic proportions, and other quaint qualities.

The base price ($69,900 in 1980) is steep for a 33' boat. With sails plus reasonable other options and amenities the bottom line would not be less than $75,000. However, when measured against other boats of comparable waterline length and displacement, the tab is more proportionate (but still high). Comparably equipped a better quality conventional production boat such as the Sabre 34 would run about $64,000 and a Cal 35, about $70,000.

Whether the boats in the Freedom line retain their value as equity remains to be seen. If the concept continues to gain followers, the Freedom 33 should be at the forefront of boats of her type.

The Tartan Ten: Performance One-Design

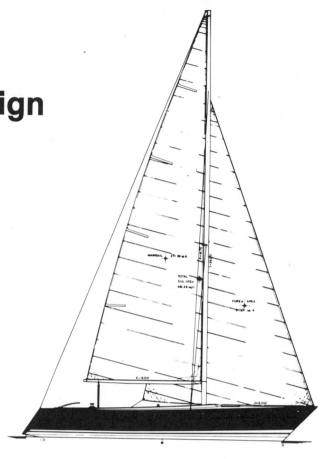

THE BOAT AND THE BUILDER

The Tartan Ten was born out of a popular rebellion against the International Offshore Rule (IOR) in the mid-1970's. This was the worst period in the IOR's history, when production sailboats were outdesigned even before their molds were finished. Although the IOR has since then gotten its act together, a great many of its early proponents had been lost for good by 1979. The disenchanted went in two directions — PHRF and offshore one-design.

The Tartan Ten is the child of Charlie Britton of Tartan Marine. Britton was one of the first to recognize the market for offshore one-designs. While he was conceptualizing the Tartan Ten, the J/24 — soon to become the most successful offshore one-design — was being tooled up for production, although Britton didn't know it was on the horizon. He was impressed by the Danish-built Aphrodite 101. It's no coincidence that the Tartan Ten bears a resemblence to some of her features. Sparkman and Stevens designed the boat for Tartan in 1977; production began in early 1978.

Nearly 350 boats were built in the next five years, most of which went to sailors on the Great Lakes, and most of which spend most of their time racing one-design. There are 200 boats in the national class association, and 80% of those members race in one-design fleets on Lake Erie and Lake Michigan. According to class secretary David Hamister, there is one-design racing every weekend on Lake Erie, and small fleets in Long Island Sound, Chesapeake Bay, Houston and Jacksonville. Unlike a great many boats that tout themselves as offshore one-designs, the Tartan Ten is one of the few boats that has accumulated in enough numbers to *actually* race as a one-design.

When the Tartan Ten was introduced in 1978 at a base price of $21,500, she sold easily. Several boats a week were produced in the years immediately following. Then a steady series of price increases, the recession of 1981 and the first signs of a saturated market began to take their toll on sales. For Charlie Britton, a boatbuilder first and a businessman second, the problems of running so large a business was more than he wished to handle. So in the spring of 1982, production of the Tartan Ten ceased and Britton put his company up for sale. By the spring of 1983 he found a buyer in John Richards and production began again at the rate of two Tartan Tens a month. However, only a few dealers are actually stocking the boat. Most boats are built only to order.

Company involvement in the Tartan Ten is, for the most part, exemplary. The only complaints we received were from sailors outside the Midwest who complained

Specifications

LOA	33'2"
LWL	27'0"
Beam	9'3"
Draft	5'10"
Displacement	6,700 lbs
Ballast	3,340 lbs
Sail Area	486 sq ft

Tartan Marine
320 River Street
Grand River, OH 44045

that the company's promotional efforts were biased toward the Great Lakes. Both Britton, who has stayed on with Tartan as a consultant, and new owner Richards, own and race Tartan Tens. Marketing manager Pat Black also sails a Tartan Ten. Owners report that Tartan is quick to settle warranty problems, and to rectify construction flaws so as to prevent future warranty claims. Typical of comments from owners are, "I've called for advice on a number of occasions, and was always given courteous and useful information," and "I can't praise the people at Tartan Marine enough."

The 1983 base price of the Tartan Ten is $33,800. With a one-design sail inventory (main, jib and spinnaker), spinnaker gear, cradle, genoa tracks, compasses, and double lifelines the price climbs to $39,110. Most owners report that their used Tartan Tens have appreciated. The exception was an owner in Chicago who said a glut of used boats was keeping the price down.

There have been a number of problems with the Tartan Ten, the worst in the first 100 boats. Tartan has generally been responsible in correcting them

CONSTRUCTION

While we wouldn't consider the Tartan Ten to be one of the better built racers, she doesn't have to be. Since she is primarily intended to race against her sisters, consistency between boats is perhaps more important than superior (and hence, more expensive) construction. The major construction criterion she must meet is to be sufficiently seaworthy to endure an occasional short offshore race. She meets this criterion, although, like too many production boats, she barely meets it.

There have been a number of problems with the Tartan Ten over the years. Tartan Marine has generally acted responsibly in correcting them. The worst problems occurred in the first 100 boats. For example, the original hollow stainless steel rudder posts were too light and bent too easily. According to Tartan, every boat with that type of rudder post was located and repaired by inserting a second post inside the original one.

A second problem was with the reinforcement of the hull around the keel sump and under the mast step. From 5′ forward of the transom, the Tartan Ten's hull is cored with ½″ balsa, except in the bilge area, which is stiffened by a grid of hollow, hat-shaped fiberglass floors and stringers. Because the Tartan Ten has a relatively flat underbody and fin keel, she is more susceptible to flexing of the bilges than a boat with deeper, more rounded bilges.

In the first 90 boats, the grid was neither stiff enough nor attached to the hull securely enough to prevent flexing. As a result the fiberglass tabbing which holds the grid to the hull began peeling off. On a few boats, small cracks developed in the grid and in the bilges. Tartan claims that it sent repairmen all around the country to track down and fix every boat earlier than hull #84. In most cases the repair consisted of removing the old tabbing and re-tabbing with a heavier laminate. In cases where the grid or hull actually showed damage, more

substantial repairs were made. According to Britton, "We got every one of them."

The mast step has been strengthened several times during the Tartan Ten's history. The Tartan Ten has a deck-stepped mast, rare in non-trailerable racers, because they offer less control of mast bend. They are no less seaworthy than a keel-stepped mast, provided there is adequate support underneath the mast, such as a compression post or bulkhead in the cabin.

The Tartan Ten's compression post sits on top of the floor grid. After the initial problems with the first 83 boats, a 5″x4″x¼″ aluminum plate was used under the compression post to distribute the load. The thickness of the aluminum plate was later increased to ½″. Mast step problems still existed to some degree after the first 83 boats. On a hull numbered in the 150's, we observed that the compression post had been moved off the floor grid (presumably because it was crushing it) and lengthened with a threaded extension so it rested directly on the hull.

Unlike most boats, which have shroud chainplates which extend above deck, the Tartan Ten's shrouds pass through the deck to chainplates in the cabin. Although this may reduce windage and genoa chafe, the hole in the deck is difficult to seal. Many owners report chronic deck leaks around the shrouds.

The chainplates are anchored on a heavy fiberglass "tab" which extends up from the topsides inside the main cabin. According to the manufacturer, there were two chainplate tab delaminations in the first 100 boats. Tartan attributes this to the hull being cored under the tab. Tartan didn't take steps to correct the potential problem until nearly 100 boats later. One owner of a 150-series boat reported that he had reglassed one chainplate tab after he noticed the telltale signs of delamination — the color of the tab changing from dark green to white where it is anchored to the hull.

By hull #200 Tartan had eliminated the core under the tab and began anchoring it directly to the outer skin of

the hull. This didn't completely solve the problem, according to Britton. Because the section of the topsides around the chainplates was uncored, that section could dimple inward slightly under heavy rig loads, causing isolated incidences of gelcoat blistering and delamination. Tartan corrected this problem shortly afterward — "about hull #270," according to Britton — by widening the chainplate tab from 12″ to 18″.

Although the Tartan Ten is cored through 80% of her hull, she exhibits a fair amount of structural flexing. As one successful Tartan dealer pointed out, "she's not overbuilt like the rest of the Tartan line." We had several reports of the cockpit flexing noticeably while sailing in rough weather. Part of the reason is that the bulkheads under each side of the cockpit are glassed firmly to the hull, but very poorly attached to the cockpit seats. Also the main bulkhead is well forward of the mast and divided by the forward berth. A bulkhead in two halves located away from the chainplates is not very effective in absorbing rig loads. Instead the hull will flex.

The Tartan Ten's hull-to-deck joint consists of an inward turned hull flange overlapped by the deck and topped by an aluminum toerail. The hull-to-deck joint is bedded with butyl tape, which stays soft and rubber-like for the life of the boat. It has no adhesive properties, but is a good watertight sealant. We have seen it melt and "bleed" out of hull-to-deck joints on occasion.

A strip of aluminum is glassed under the hull flange. This allows Tartan to fasten the hull and deck with bolts, but without nuts, by tapping the bolts through the aluminium insert — a real time saver. The bolts must be bedded, though, or corrosion would compromise the integrity of the joint, especially important since there is no chemical bond to fall back on. Tartan beds the bolts with silicone, which is probably adequate, but a chromate paste would be a better (although more expensive) bedding material.

The hull laminate was strengthened when production was into hulls numbered in the early 100's. A heavier mat was added to improve the bond between the balsa core and the laminate. An extra layer of fiberglass was added to the hull laminate as well.

Rig

The mast of the Tartan Ten is a "safe" section. It bends easily with the backstay, but is sufficiently strong to sail without running backstays in a strong breeze. The shrouds are swept back.

The mast is not anodized. Until last year, it was finished with clear lacquer; now it is painted black. According to Frank Colaneri, of Bay Sailing Equipment, who rigged all Tarten Ten masts until this year, finishing with lacquer or paint is cheaper than anodizing.

On the first 150 or so boats the jib and spinnaker halyards are both wire and exit the mast above the hounds. They then lead through "bullseye" fairleads which have a tendency to chew the wire. (Colaneri called them "wire eaters.") This system was redesigned so that now the wire jib halyard exits below the mast without a fairlead, and the spinnaker halyard, still exiting above the hounds, was changed to rope.

Schaefer booms were used on the first 70 boats, and bent reefing hooks were a problem. Since then Tartan has used Kenyon booms. The Kenyon booms have no outhaul car, instead relying on clew slugs to support leech tension. According to Colaneri, many booms had to be retrofitted with stainless plates over the sail slot because the clew slugs had pulled through the slot.

The mast of the Tartan Ten is currently rigged with a gate to accommodate luff slides. Before boat #175 the gate was positioned to accommodate a bolt rope.

PERFORMANCE

Handling Under Power
Since hull #309, the Tartan Ten has been equipped with an 11 hp Universal diesel. Before then a Farymann 7.5 hp diesel was standard. On boats prior to hull #200,

The shrouds of the Tartan Ten pass through the deck to chainplates below. Owners report that the deck is hard to seal from leaks

The Tartan Ten's mast is deck-stepped into an aluminum casting. The step has integral sheaves through which the running riging exits. With this system the mast's integrity is not compromised by exit holes

excessive vibration and shaft coupling failures were a problem. According to Britton, the cause was poor shaft alignment. Britton says flexible shaft couplings were used on the first 200 boats, because Tartan was afraid the boat would bend under rig tension. The use of flexible couplings meant less attention was paid to alignment — hence occasional coupling failure and excessive vibration. Solid couplings were used on subsequent boats. "We thought we were bending the boat (by tensioning the rig), but we were wrong. Now we know it's better to concentrate on alignment and use solid shaft couplings," says Britton.

Because vibration could be a problem, when considering a used Tartan Ten you should check both the engine mounts and the electrical harness on the back of the engine. The covering of any wires attached to the engine should be checked for wear.

Tartan Ten owners report that the Farymann is relatively trouble free, runs well and is easy to hand start should the battery run down. Owners also say it tends to be underpowered. "Doesn't do well into the wind," reported one owner. A folding prop is standard equipment.

Access to the engine is excellent. The fiberglass engine box is light and lifts off easily and, because it also doubles as the companionway step, slides forward without obstruction. The box is easy to refit and latch in place. With the box off, all engine parts are accessible.

Handling Under Sail

Tartan Ten owners rave about her performance. She may not be a ULDB, but she's fast for a 33-footer. Typical comments are "Offwind we pass 36' masthead rigs," "rides waves well; good control downwind," and "recorded 15.2 knots, sustained 10.5 knots."

However, owners do not rave about her handicap ratings. The Tartan Ten was not designed to fit any handicapping rule. She carries an astronomical IOR rating of about 28.5. Under PHRF she rates from 123 to 132, depending on the handicapper. Most PHRF fleets assume that you have a 155% genoa, and the most common rating is 126. Some fleets, such as Detriot, allow the Tartan Ten to sail with its one-design inventory (100% jib) at a rating several seconds slower.

Owners report that she will sail to a rating of 126 in light air with a 155% genoa. However, with her narrow beam, she is tender and becomes overpowered quickly. In winds over 12 knots, she has difficulty winning with a rating of 126. Using a one-design inventory, the Tartan Ten will sail to a rating of 132 in medium winds. Although she is always fast downwind, owners say she has a difficult time making up what she loses upwind in a strong breeze.

Those who want to race both one design and PHRF have several problems. Until 1982 headfoils were illegal for class racing. The class has dropped this rule to encourage Tartan Ten owners to race PHRF. Running backstays are still illegal for class racing. Although they're not necessary to keep the spar in the boat, backstays nonetheless will improve performance slightly without rating penalty. Another, more subtle problem, is that a sailmaker will design the working sails of a class inventory differently than he would for a larger inventory. For example, a 100% jib that must be used for both light and heavy air in one-design racing will be a lot more powerful than a 100% jib for a larger PHRF inventory.

Despite its drawbacks the Tartan Ten still makes for enjoyable PHRF racing because its sailplan is so manageable, the boat is so maneuverable, and its cockpit is so easy to work in. It's hard to believe you're on a 33' when you're racing one; the boat feels much smaller.

As good as PHRF racing can be, one-design racing is even better. Owners report that all boats are extremely well-matched. In this year's 40' national championship, the second and third place teams sailed borrowed boats — boats that had not done well in previous regattas. Tartan Ten sailors may push their boats hard, but as a whole they don't push them hard enough to cause major gear failures. We have no doubt that a hot SORC team

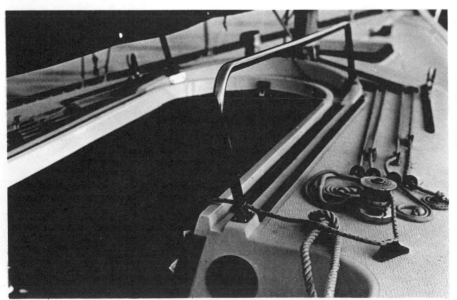

The Tartan Ten's large companionway is covered by a three-piece removable hatch, and protected from errant feet by full length handrails. When opened the companionway provides the cabin with a minimal amount of standing headroom

The stanchion bases are rigidly bolted to both the toerail and deck, but several owners reported weld failures where the socket is fastened to the base

As with any light displacement boat, you must be quick on sail trim to keep her level and driving

---

could rip a Tartan Ten apart, but for its purpose the boat is well suited.

Before each boat leaves the factory, it is placed in an outdoor pool, and 50-100 lbs of lead is glassed to the hull 5' forward of the mast to make her float on her lines. Flotation marks are molded into the hull to insure that the lead is not subsequently moved to change the boat's trim. This helps make the boats equal in performance.

The keels are relatively fair from the factory, although most racers will want to spend a weekend making them smoother. The class is planning to publish keel offsets for those who want to make templates.

Most Tartan Tens race with a crew of 5-8. Although she is a light boat, her narrow beam limits the effectiveness of crew weight. Unlike beamier counterparts, such as the J/30, packing on more crew in a strong breeze is not essential. For best performance, the backstay and traveler must be constantly adjusted. Some of the more successful racers routinely barber-haul the jib outboard in strong puffs. As with any light displacement boat, you must be quick on sail trim to keep her level and driving.

LIVABILITY

Deck Layout

The Tartan Ten is equipped with a tiller, as any boat this small and light should be. With a tiller, though, you need a larger cockpit. The cockpit of the Tartan Ten is 9½' long, which gives the crew plenty of room for racing. The companionway, though, is obstructed by long stainless steel handrails. When tacking, the crew must all pass through the cockpit.

The cockpit seats have short, outward-angled seatbacks with a small coaming. This provides a modicum of daysailing comfort without sacrificing much racing efficiency. The slotted aluminum toerail does, however, compromise racing comfort. The crew could slide farther outboard for more hiking leverage if it weren't for the toerail painfully biting into the backs of their thighs.

Owners report that the cockpit drains quickly when pooped by a large wave. It nevertheless is worrisome, because its large volume would hold a lot of water, and its 6" companionway sill would do little to keep that water from rushing below. We wouldn't race it in rough weather without all companionway drop boards locked in place.

The rudder post exits the deck through a cockpit coaming that wraps around the stern. A tiller is attached to the post; when lifted and lashed to the backstay it leaves the cockpit unobstructed for an extraordinary amount of cockpit space at the mooring.

The mast is stepped into a cast aluminum collar on deck. The collar is not hinged. The running rigging exits through the bottom of the mast, then runs through sheaves built into the collar and aft through sheet stoppers to Lewmar 16s on each side of the cabin house. Several owners said they had moved or replaced the stoppers made by Delta. Tartan has plans to begin rigging boats with Easylock clutch stoppers, a far superior choice.

The primary winches are Lewmar 30s. Secondary winches are permitted under class rules, but are not offered as a factory option. Some owners report that larger primary winches are helpful to trim the genoas used for handicap racing. On the boat we sailed, the sheet tracks were backed with strips of aluminum, but the backing plates for the winches were ⅛" plywood.

The deck gelcoat provides good traction, but this also makes it more difficult to clean. Stanchion bases, made for Tartan by High Seas, bolt through the deck and through the toerail. On the boat we examined there were no backing plates on the thru-deck stanchion bolts, but bolting through the toerail gives the installation adequate rigidity. Several owners reported that the welded sockets for the stanchions have failed.

The boom vang runs in a single part up from the mast step to the boom, then forward to the gooseneck, down to the deck via a 6:1 purchase, and aft to a winch. At the gooseneck, it attaches to a small welded eye, which could be of heavier gauge.

The backstay is split with a 4:1 purchase dead-ended on the stern. A crewmember would have to sit aft of the helmsman to play the backstay. The ball bearing traveler spans the cockpit and is easily adjusted with its 3:1 purchase. The 5:1 mainsheet dead-ends on the traveler car.

Belowdecks

For a 33-footer, there isn't much to the Tartan Ten's interior. Headroom is only 5'2". However, the companionway hatch is in three pieces and lifts off for stowage below, opening a 5" long "skylight" in the cabin. This feature provides some amount of standing headroom below, without having to sacrifice the clean lines of the deck to a high cabin trunk. Erecting a dodger over the companionway encloses the standing headroom. The hatch cover could be stronger: we nearly cracked it by stepping on it.

There is no icebox in the cabin. A portable cooler stores in one of the two cockpit lazarettes. The standard head is a Porta Potti, stowed under the forward V-berth. Nearly every owner we talked to complained of its smell

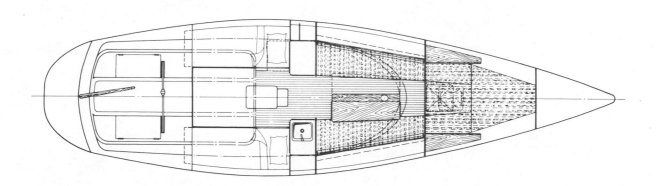

and that it is difficult to empty. Most had either discarded it for a cedar bucket or installed a full marine head. There is no built-in stove and the chart table is small.

There is a small sink with a hand pump on the port side. On boats prior to hull #200, the water tank was installed under the starboard quarterberth, with the fuel tank under the port quarterberth. With the water tank and sink on opposite sides, all the water in the tank would drain out through the sink on port tack. Tartan's retrofit was a rubber plug for the sink nozzle. By hulls numbered in the early 200's, they had switched the position of the fuel and water tanks, solving the problem.

The interior of the Tartan Ten is dark. The bulkheads, cabinetry and cabin sole are teak-veneered plywood. We would paint the settees white. The forward V-berth is a comfortable 6' long. The "filler," or section of the berth that covers the Porta Potti is removable for access to the head. However, the filler sits on very narrow cleats, so when you climb over it to get out of the berth, the filler frequently falls off its cleats and you tumble onto the head (Ugh!).

Vertical posts from the overhead to both the sink and the nav station make good handrails for moving about below in a seaway. Under both the sink and nav station are small lockers with zippered cloth coverings instead of doors. There is further stowage under the main berths and quarter berths. These stowage bins are not insulated from the hull, but because the boat is cored, condensation should be minimal. The bins are sealed from the shallow sump; if they weren't sealed, any water in the bilge would predictably soak their contents. One owner commented, "There should have been no attempt to create six berths at the expense of adequate storage."

On the boat we sailed the joinerwork and furniture tabbing were mediocre. The overhead panels were sloppily fitted. The ceiling is covered with a padded vinyl liner. A strip of wood covers the hull-to-deck joint.

There were several major changes to the interior after hull #160. In earlier boats, both the main berths and quarterberths were "root" berths. Root berths are somewhat like pipe berths. They consist of cloth anchored to the side of the hull and slung to a pipe running the length of the berth. The pipe fits into notches so that the angle of the berth can be adjusted to suit the boat's angle of heel. Another piece of cloth attaches with Velcro to the pipe to form a seat back. While the root berth makes for comfortable sleeping under way, it is far less comfortable than a fixed berth to sit in while the boat is anchored.

After hull #160, the root berths in the main cabin were abandoned for fixed berths, with a dual purpose design backrest/leeboard. Additional stowage bins were added over the main berths. A drop leaf table was also added between the main berths. It is doubtful whether it would survive the rough and tumble of hard racing. We suspect most owners remove it for racing.

CONCLUSIONS

Like any boat, the Tartan Ten is built to a price for a particular purpose. She is not built as well, nor laid out as lavishly as, say a J/30; but she is also $10,000 less expensive. People don't buy Tartan Tens to make long offshore passages, nor do they buy them for extended cruising. People buy them to day race, either as a one-design or under a handicap rule. Maybe they throw in an

occasional weekend cruise.

The Tartan Ten is a joy to day race. It is easy to manuever and crew on, offers lively performance, and is affordable. We think that one-design racing would be far more fun than handicap racing. At least under one-design you are competitive in all wind velocities. The Tartan Ten class association appears to be well organized, which should help keep the resale value of the boat high. If you live near a Tartan Ten fleet, you should give offshore one-design racing a try. But beware: you'll probably get hooked.   —EA

The CSY 37: Ersatz Traditional Charter Boat

THE BOAT AND THE BUILDER

The CSY 37, designed by Peter Schmitt, is the mid-sized boat in the CSY line. Primarily designed for the Caribbean bareboat charter trade, 87 of the raised-deck cutters have been built.

Schmitt has combined some features most often found in "traditional" boats—the oval stern, raised deck, and semi-clipper bow—with a relatively modern underbody featuring a fairly long fin keel and a skeg-mounted rudder. On paper, the boat looks pretty good. In person, she is rather tubby and high-sided.

The CSY 37 most closely resembles the Ericson Cruising 36. The styling of both these boats can best be termed "ersatz traditional."

With the short standard rig and shoal keel, she is no performance cruiser. With her huge cockpit she is not really a seaboat. Rather, she is a boat designed for a specific purpose, bareboat chartering, a purpose which she serves admirably. To expand her appeal to the general sailing public would be difficult, as CSY discovered. The company went out of business in 1981.

Most CSY 37's go into charter service, usually on lease-back arrangements. The boats have to be strong and reliable, for a week out of service for repairs means $1,300 in lost revenue to the charter operator. That the boats can stand up to this constant use and abuse is a credit to both designer and builder. Few other boats could, as CSY's charter experience has shown.

CONSTRUCTION

There are really only two words to describe the construction of the CSY 37: *massive overkill.* This is a mixed blessing. It means you have a strong, heavy hull. It often also means that you end up with a boat that is undercanvassed in light air. Very often it means a boat that has a fairly low ballast-to-displacement ratio.

Forty percent of the CSY 37's advertised displacement is in the ballast keel. With a 29' waterline, the displacement of about 20,000 lbs is about average by traditional standards, heavy by modern standards.

The hull is an extraordinarily heavy solid glass layup as is the deck. No core materials are used anywhere. Without coring such as balsa or Airex, a glass hull can

Specifications

LOA	37'3"
LWL	29'2"
Beam	12'
Draft (deep draft)	6'
(shoal draft)	4'8"
Displacement	21,000 lbs
	(approx.)
Sail area	610 sq ft

sweat in a cold climate and can be excessively warm in a hot, humid climate.

The hull-to-deck joint is simple and effective. The hull and deck flanges, which overlap to form a molded rail, are bedded in 3M 5200 and through-bolted with stainless steel machine screws on 4" centers. 3M 5200 is about the most effective and tenacious adhesive sealant on the market.

Keel construction is unusual. The cast lead keel is glassed into the hollow keel molding, any voids being filled with fiberglass slurry. This is then glassed over to form a double bottom and to keep the ballast in place. This ballast arrangement is identical in both the shoal and deep draft versions. The deep draft boat, however, has a 16" deep keel extension filled with about 600 lbs of cast concrete. If a shoal draft boat is desired, this extension can simply be cut off. The shoal draft boat, therefore, with less lateral plane will make more leeway.

The hull is molded in two pieces, then joined in the

middle with heavy overlapping layers of mat and roving. This allows some flexibility in hull design allowing such features as a molded-in rubbing strake and a stern with substantial tumblehome.

Installation of hardware is excellent. This is one of the few boats we have ever seen with through-bolted bronze seacocks. Backing plates are used on deck hardware such as cleats and winches.

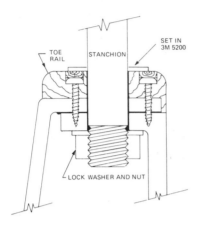

Lifeline Stanchion Installation: CSY uses a unique and very strong method for mounting lifeline stanchions

The rudder stock is a solid 2" round bronze bar. The cast bronze rudder heel fitting would look more at home on a 60' boat than on a 37-footer.

The bow fitting is a massive stainless steel weldment, incorporating an anchor roller, a welded chock, and the headstay chainplate. The edges of the bow chock are not rounded, and could easily chafe an unprotected anchor rode. This bow fitting could double as an effective battering ram. We suspect that the dock boys in the West Indies are pretty wary every time an inexperienced charterer brings one of the CSY charter boats into the slip.

Chainplates are heavy stainless steel flat bars with load-distributing welded webs through-bolted to the hull. The hull layup is reinforced in the way of the chainplates, an almost extraneous precaution, given the heaviness of the regular hull layup.

Interior bulkheads are heavy waterproof plywood, attached to the hull with solid and neatly made fillets. Airex pads along the outboard edges of the bulkheads distribute the bulkhead stresses on the inside of the hull, preventing hard spots.

Cabin sole supports are clear fir. The teak-faced cabin sole is screwed to these bearers, with only limited access openings to the bilge. *The Practical Sailor* would prefer that most of the cabin sole be removable, providing access to the bilge spaces in an emergency. CSY appears to be counting on the massiveness of the hull construction to prevent holing. This conceit could backfire. Remember the Titanic?

Hatches are molded fiberglass with translucent panels. They have good gasketing and good holddowns, but a short person will have trouble reaching overhead to open the hatches due to the tremendous headroom.

Exterior finish is of good stock boat quality. Joinerwork is clean with the exception of an awkward transition from the railcap on top of the raised deck to the sheer-level railcap in the foredeck well.

The molded fiberglass trailboards are now shielded below the bow by a somewhat awkward molded glass panel. This was installed after a number of CSY boats blew off their trailboards in heavy seas. We would have preferred it if they had just left the trailboards off entirely.

Construction of the CSY 37 is heavy and strong. It is doubtful if there is a stronger hull of this size in production anywhere. Unfortunately, this greatly increases the price of the boat.

With oil price increases, and the concomitant increase in the price of resins and fiberglass, it is very difficult to see how CSY can continue to use such a massive layup. A little engineering—reducing the shell thickness and incorporating a stringer system—would probably produce a hull that is just as strong and use substantially less material.

PERFORMANCE

Handling under sail
The CSY 37 is available in two keel configurations, and with two rigs. The four possible combinations offer very different performance characteristics.

Most boats are delivered with the standard short rig. In areas of normally heavy air, such as the West Indies in winter, the normal rig is adequate. In light air with the short rig, the boat is a slug. The engine will come in handy under these circumstances.

Performance is greatly enhanced by the tall rig, which is about 8' taller than the standard rig and incoroporates two sets of spreaders.

With the chainplates set at the outboard edge of the hull, the sheeting base is excessively wide. Sheeting a genoa in tight enough to go to windward effectively would be difficult.

To avoid the necessity for running backstays, the intermediate and after lower shrouds are attached to the deck several feet aft of the mast and the upper shrouds. Unfortunately, when broad reaching, the boom and main fetch up on these shrouds far too soon. This is ironic in a boat whose best point of sail is off the wind.

Our test boat had the tall rig and the shoal-draft keel. This is not the combination we would choose to own. Performance with the tall rig is greatly enhanced. However, the higher sail plan does make the boat more tender, and with the cutdown keel combines to produce a boat that makes excessive leeway when heeled more than about 20°. We would prefer to combine the tall rig with the deep keel.

Our test boat was overpowered with full main, staysail and large jib topsail by gusts of a little over 15 knots over the deck, sailing hard on the wind. She also made substantial leeway. With a reef in, the helm eased, the boat stood up better, and leeway was less.

Off the wind, the CSY 37 comes into her own. She is stable as a church and visions of long tradewind passages instantly come to mind. Under those conditions she would shine if you had plenty of chafe protection on those aft-leading shrouds.

Halyard winches are mounted on the keel-stepped painted aluminum mast. The boom does not overhang the cockpit, and has a well-made boom gallows which provides a good handhold on deck as well as being an excellent place to store the boom when at rest, or when sailing under the storm jib alone in heavy weather.

Performance under sail is not sparkling, but with the tall rig—now available on both the 37 and the cutter-rigged 44—the CSY boats are gradually outgrowing their "Tampa tub" reputation.

Handling under power
With such high topsides, the Perkins 4-108 is the smallest engine we would want in the boat. As it is, handling at slow speeds in a crosswind can be tricky. A great deal of practice is required to handle such a high-sided boat under power in a breeze.

The turning radius of the CSY 37 is substantially larger than with a shorter-keeled boat. With her heavy displacement, acceleration is not exactly neck-snapping. She should have enough power to get her out of tight spots, however.

Handling in reverse is tricky. The boat does not go where you aim it until you learn to use a combination of rudder and bursts of throttle. Designer Peter Schmitt easily handles the boat going astern, but like tightrope walking and figure skating, the expert always makes it look easy.

Engine access through the large cockpit hatch is good, but the heavy hatch should have a more positive means of holding it in the upright position. If it fell on your head, you'd remember it, if you were lucky enough to then remember anything.

To those who have been spoiled by the handling under power of some modern boats, the CSY 37 may be a disappointment. It handles like a boat, rather than a compact car, requiring some patience and planning ahead.

LIVABILITY

Deck layout
With her raised deck amidships, the CSY 37 has an amazing amount of deck space, giving the on-deck impression of a small ship. There is plenty of space on deck to carry a rigid dinghy. Schmitt's own CSY 37 carries a beautiful little dory with a varnished transom as a tender; she fits neatly on the starboard side and serves as a catchall for fenders and lines.

Deck space is important in boats used extensively in the charter trade. Lounging on deck is the primary charter boat activity. In this category, the CSY 37 gets five stars.

Anchor handling is fairly easy with the stub bowsprit. There is, however, only a single bow cleat. This is a pet peeve of *The Practical Sailor,* for it greatly complicates anchoring with two anchors, a common practice for cruising boats. The optional "anchoring package" includes a good length of stainless steel chain, which is miserable stuff to handle by hand. Use galvanized instead.

We do not recommend the $380 optional electric anchor windlass. If you plan on using a windlass, get the optional S/L 555 manual unit. At $990, it is hardly a bargain. This includes a $220 charge for installation; for that price, we'd do it ourselves, particularly if we could get the windlass at a discount.

Heavy travelers for both the main and the staysail are located on the main deck. Thwartships control lines should really be used with these to get optimum performance from the sails—essential on a boat which must be tweaked to get a reasonable level of performance on the wind.

The cockpit of the CSY 37 is huge—too big for an offshore boat but good for the charter trade. The large cockpit lockers are well divided and are partitioned from the engine space under the cockpit.

The starboard cockpit locker contains the best battery box installation we have seen on a stock boat. The port locker contains the optional 110-v AC refrigeration compressor. Unfortunately, its wiring is exposed to the weather when the locker lid is opened. The sound-insulated engine room hatch occupies much of the cockpit sole.

There are four large cockpit scuppers, which are imperative to have with the huge cockpit. The companionway sill should be higher if the boat is to be used offshore. A fiberglass seahood, protecting the forward end of the companionway slide, is standard equipment.

Interior

Two interior arrangements are available, a two-stateroom, two-head plan, and a single-stateroom, single-head plan. The two-stateroom plan is used primarily in the charter trade. It is really too much interior to try to cram in a 29' waterline and designer Schmitt is not particularly proud of it.

The single-stateroom layout is also unconventional. It gives over the forward 40% of the interior space to a large cabin with built-in double berth and a huge head compartment in the forepeak. The problem with this arrangement is that should you have guests aboard, they must troop through the owner's cabin in order to use the head—a major inconvenience.

The space given over to the head in the single-stateroom model is almost exactly the same space occupied by the forward cabin in the two-stateroom model. With a single-stateroom layout, interior space might have been better utilized with a "conventional" layout of sleeping quarters forward with the head and hanging lockers

dividing the forward cabin from the main cabin. Unfortunately, the "conventional" layout is not an option.

The interior volume of the CSY 37 is huge, thanks to the raised deck. There are many well-thought-out interior details, too many, unfortunately, to catalog here. The ice box, for example, is divided into two compartments with separate opening traps. The icebox has a minimum of 4" of urethane foam insulation, probably more than any other stock boat on the market. It also has a good kickspace underneath, greatly facilitating reaching into depths of the box for a cold beer.

There are, however, lapses in this good design. Galley counter tops in our test boat were covered with a slate-like laminate, difficult to clean and too bumpy for a good work surface. Head counters and some shelves were covered with marble-grained plastic, looking more like a slice out of a multi-colored bowling ball than real marble.

The mixture of excellent design details, strange lapses in taste, and execution which ranges from fair to excellent is difficult to evaluate reasonably. It was pleasing to see, that after years of using teak-grained mica-covered bulkheads, CSY switched to real oak-faced bulkheads in new production boats.

Ventilation of the interior can only be described as excellent. There are six opening hatches or skylights in addition to the companionway. Some dorade boxes, however, might be welcome in steamy climates with frequent rain.

One could spend a great deal of time analyzing the interior details, primarily because a lot of thought has gone into them. Both of the interior layouts are unusual, and each will have adherents and detractors.

CONCLUSIONS

CSY was an unusual company, and the CSY 37 is certainly an unconventional boat. The boat is strongly built—overly built, in fact. The 1980 base price of $91,670 seems high until you consider that this is a 20,000-lb boat, and very well equipped. Hot and cold pressure water, Edson pedestal steering, and gimballed propane stove are all standard, for example.

CSY boats were probably the strongest production boats ever marketed. They may be ungainly in appearance, and not the hottest performers under sail, but they are tough. That should be an important consideration if you're trying to get the most for your money.

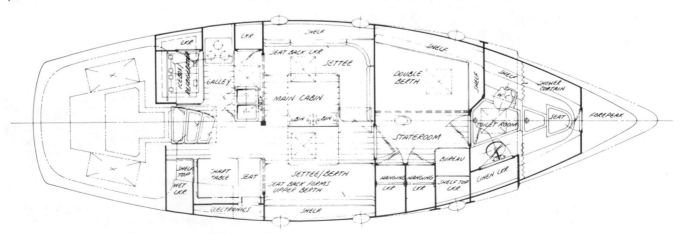

The Irwin 37:
A Production Cruising Boat

THE BOAT AND THE BUILDER

An evaluation of the Irwin 37 threatens to expose all our prejudices about boat builders and cruising boats. In general we like sturdily built, finely finished, well performing boats that reflect traditional standards (if not design) and lasting value.

Irwin Yachts, one of the two or three largest production builders, builds boats of mediocre quality and finish and markets them to buyers looking for as much boat as possible for the price. In every sense of the word, Irwin boats, of which the Irwin 37 is archetypal, are *production* boats. They are mass produced, carefully priced, simply advertised, and widely sold to a broad spectrum of customers.

More than 600 Irwin 37s have been sold since the boat went into production in 1971. The current version is designated the Mark V, representing the popular strategy of numbering the steps in the evolution of a design even though the changes may be minor.

From the outset the Irwin 37 has been a roomy, appealing cruising boat that was once described as the Chevrolet Belair of the boat market. Her greatest appeal has been to the sailor/owner who is not into tradition, sailing performance, elegance, construction details, or investment.

Designer/owner/president Ted Irwin is Irwin Yachts. He is involved in all aspects of his independent firm (in contrast to the subsidiaries of parent corporations that many other major boat builders have become). From all reports he is one tough fellow to work for. He delegates little responsibility or authority, and turnover (at least at the executive level) is considerable. In this respect Ted Irwin is a Florida counterpart of an equally powerful and successful independent builder, Frank Butler of Catalina Yachts in California.

Irwin has sailed all the boats he has designed from his stock cruising boats such as the 37 to state-of-the-art SORC racers. The Irwin line has always been a blend of out-and-out cruising boats and almost out-and-out racing boats.

Ted Irwin has his eyes firmly fixed on his business. One eye he keeps glued on production costs. Irwin Yachts has perhaps the most meticulously priced out boats in the industry. Virtually everything except hardware and sails are produced in house. This includes the tooling for the boats, spars, rigging, and woodwork. That way Ted Irwin can control design and price. Unfortunately he has never seemed to be able to match quality control with price control.

Specifications

LOA		37'
LWL		30'
Beam		11'6"
Draft	Full keel	5'6
	Shoal keel	4'
Displacement		20,000 lbs
Ballast		7800 lbs
Sail area (sloop)		625 sq ft

Irwin Yacht & Marine Corp.
13055 49th Street North
Clearwater, FL 33520

Irwin Yachts is considered to have the most notoriously slipshod quality control among the larger boat builders. No other boats have as poor a reputation for warranty claims, delays in commissioning, missing or incorrect parts, and mislocated hardware as Irwin. Similarly an examination of virtually any Irwin-built boat reveals details that reflect cost savings, some, in our opinion, serious (gate valves on all through hull fittings) and some trivial (through hull fittings not installed flush with the hull).

Irwin's other eye is perhaps the keenest in the industry in seeing what the buying public wants, what it will buy (not always the same as it seems to want), and what it is willing to pay. Irwin Yachts makes what it heralds ambiguously as the "value yacht." It is a boat

The Irwin 37 is a classic example of the all-too-common cruising boat that does everything better than handle as a sailboat

that rather openly and obviously makes compromises that keep the price under those of the major competiton.

And make no mistake: say what you will about an Irwin-built boat, the firm has for 15 years been a remarkable success story. There has never been any question that it has been profitable for Ted Irwin, a rare exception in an industry rife with tales of economic brinksmanship.

CONSTRUCTION

There are no basic industry standards for fiberglass construction; the primary criterion for adequate hull laminate strength seems largely a matter of in-use durability. Some builders, in the absence of such standards, overbuild their products (CSY, for example). Irwin Yachts, on the other hand, molds hulls and decks to specifications that are, by industry comparison, light. As with everything else, Irwin maintains a tight control over tooling costs and the amounts of resins, glass fiber, and labor that goes into each hull. By our standards the Irwin fiberglass layup is minimal; that is one reason the boats have a low price. Yet basic laminate is not where cost savings are most apparent.

More conspicuous are cosmetic flaws. In two of the new 37s we looked at, there are obvious deep (up to ½") hollows in the bottom. These are evidently the result of pulling a still "green" hull from the mold and setting it in a four-point building cradle. The supports dished the laminate, probably permanently.

For years Irwin Yachts have suffered from print-through whereby the pattern of the underlying roving in the laminate was visible in the topside gelcoat. Recently this has been considerably reduced with the use of Cormat between the roving and the gelcoat; in the new 37s we examined, printthrough was negligible. This printthrough remains an unsightly feature of older 37s, especially in the dark paint of the sheerstrake.

In our examination of the 37s we also noted sloppy underwater fairing around the rudder gudgeon and where the "Adapt-A-Draft" keel is attached. These types of flaws, coupled as they are with such details as protruding through hull fittings and squared off trailing edges, produce a needless drag for a boat whose performance under sail is already suspect.

The earliest Irwin 37s did not have bowsprits. The result was a boxy gracelessness that was accentuated by obvious unevenness in the sheerline, unrelieved topside expanse, and Clorox-bottle styling, not to mention dimples and gelcoat blemishes. To improve performance with more sail area Irwin added a molded fiberglass bowsprit. Serendipitously the extension did wonders for the aesthetics. Less fortuitously the glass sprit also became a source of warranty claims when, if tightening the rigging caused it to flex, the gelcoat crazed.

The present bowsprit is of welded aluminum. In a year old boat we examined, the bobstay is a threaded stainless steel rod with jaw terminals at each end. The new boats have the rod welded between two plates on each end, a less costly fitting. As the lower end will be continually awash and thus vulnerable to corrosion, we think the welded construction is a mistake. Similarly we are concerned about the stainless steel rudder gudgeon; in the year old boat we already found evidence of stress corrosion.

The Irwin 37 has a history of warranty claims against defective gelcoat—too thin (or missing), too thick, discolored, crazed, or covering voids. Where this happened in the diamond pattern non-skid deck surfaces that Irwin produced until this year, inconspicuous repair was well nigh impossible. The problem drove Irwin dealers and new owners to distraction and fueled much of the scuttlebutt about Irwin's poor handling of warranty claims. Now Irwin is putting on a random non-skid pattern, easier to repair. We also understand that Irwin has gone to a better quality gelcoat.

Another common question about Irwin Yachts has been its hull-to-deck joint. Contrary to common industry practice, the joint in the Irwin 37 consists of overlapping flanges joined with a polyester slurry and fastened on about 6" centers with stainless steel self-tapping screws. Most builders now use a semi-rigid adhesive and bolts, a technique we favor. We believe this more positive attachment is called for on boats going to sea.

The chainplates of the 37 are stainless steel webs laminated into the topsides during the hull layup. This technique was developed by Irwin and is imitated by a number of builders whose chainplates are at the outer edge of the deck. It seems to be a satisfactory installation and indeed preferable to early Irwin 37s which had the chainplates through-bolted to the topsides.

PERFORMANCE

Handling Under Power
Virtually everyone from whom we elicited information on the Irwin 37 either dismissed as unimportant or derided her performance under sail. She seems a classic example of the all-too-common cruising boat that does everything better than handle as a sailboat. A number of owners we talked to do not seem bothered by this shortcoming. We, again with our prejudice, would be.

The Irwin 37 comes standard with a sloop rig; the roller furling genoa is an almost unanimously specified option at a cost of $2150. A cutter rig (with a club jib package at $1835) and a ketch rig ($2695 additional) are two other options. In any configuration she is a boat that seems ideally suited for a couple to sail. The sail area is modest with the ketch carrying about 60 square feet more sail than the sloop, just about enough to compensate for the windage of the mizzen mast. Personally we think the cutter rig is the best answer of the three, the staysail providing a handy headsail in hefty conditions and doing away with the clutter, expense and windage of the mizzen.

Plainly the standard shoal draft keel without a centerboard is inadequate for sailing to windward. If a buyer wants shoal draft, he should consider the centerboard option ($1300). The board does thunk in its trunk when down, a harmless if annoying distraction. Fully raised it remains quiet; what a relief in the middle of the night at anchor.

For optimum performance we recommend the deep keel. What bothers us is that the tab runs to $1500 for the 18" add-on. Still, do not hope too earnestly for scintillating windward work; for such joy you should consider a host of boats other than the Irwin 37.

Owners have indicated to us their willingness to accept indifferent performance under sail. However, we have heard complaints about the amount of attention the helm needs and some difficulty in steering the boat both under sail and under power ("Steering is stiff and my wife (98 lbs) has difficulty at times"). We suspect some of this chore is the result of an unbalanced semi-spade rudder being driven by a relatively small diameter steering wheel through an aft-cabin layout that requires considerable routing of the steering linkage.

Handling under power

The Irwin 37 has a 40 hp Perkins 4-108 diesel engine driving a three-bladed propeller with 2:1 reduction through the after edge of the keel. That is a combination that bespeaks of performance under auxiliary power. In fact, with the standard shoal keel and that combination for power, the Irwin 37 might reasonably be labeled a motorsailer if that term had not fallen into such disfavor in recent years.

The combination also suggests that the Irwin 37 should appeal to the powerboat owner looking to sail as a way to reduce his fuel consumption without sacrificing the room and amenities of the moderate sized powerboat. Certainly we think it is a worthwhile alternative to the ad hoc conversions of sailboat hulls and rigs to sailing powerboats with their high deckhouses, awkward sail handling systems, and sundry other hermaphroditic compromises.

LIVABILITY

Interior

If performance is not a priority in the design of the Irwin 37, livability is. The Irwin 37 is a coastal cruiser for two couples or a family of four. She has the most practical aft cabin layout we have seen on a stock boat under 40 feet. The layout has remained essentially unchanged since the 37 was introduced and features a spacious aft cabin, a step-down galley, a more-than-adequate walk-through passageway, and a forward cabin that should not make its occupants feel like they are in steerage.

Fundamental to the Irwin Yachts design and marketing philosophy is that the interior should instantly appeal to women. The decor is Production Boat Contemporary: tufted velour cushions, plenty of teak, and "color coordinated" carpeting. We are not impressed with the so-so craftsmanship and unsanded finish of the joinerwork nor with the antiseptic molded hull liner, but these are details that do not immediately affect the illusion of quality, comfort, and spaciousness.

Thus the interior of the 37 minimizes seagoing machismo: there are no handrails, sea berths, navigation sanctum, or sailbag stowage. Below, with the possible exception of the gimballed stove, one can easily forget that under certain circumstances a sailboat may not always be upright or free from motion.

It would be hard to imagine being aboard an Irwin 37 at sea. There is no berth one could sleep in comfortably. The settee berth to port is too narrow and the settee to starboard is too short. One owner remarked that even when the settee berth is to leeward, a nap-taker is rolled out of it during a gentle afternoon sail.

But what the 37 may lack at sea she more than makes up for at bedtime at anchor. Both the athwartships after berth and the forward vee berth are queen-sized with 4" mattresses. The two cabins are separated by 30 feet of boat and closed doors. Each has a private head.

There are good hanging lockers, lots of drawers, a few scuttles and assorted nooks and crannies. Yet someone forgot to build in places to store dry, warm food. For cold food there are, now get this, one front opening Norcold refrigerator (standard) and two, yes two, large top-opening iceboxes. In fact, both iceboxes are so sizable that their bottoms are difficult to reach. One of them (under the rudimentary chart table) might be better used for dry food storage except that getting at its contents would be at best inconvenient. The alternative is to use the galley icebox as a dry well and rely on the Norcold despite our longtime prejudice against using front opening boxes which depend on electrical power away from a dock. Perhaps this refrigerator is the best giveaway as to what type of cruising the 37 is best suited for.

Two other points about the interior deserve comment, one favorably and one not so. Engine access and sound insulation are among the best we have seen in a production boat, helped by removable panels on the sides of the walkthrough. To check the dipstick and heat exchanger water there is no need to move the companionway ladder. In short, if the engine of the 37 seizes from lack of oil or overheats for lack of water, the owner has only himself to blame.

On the other side, the bulkhead-mounted fold-up, drop-leaf cabin table will not survive the first fall against it when a powerboat leaves a wake. It might not even withstand the weight of a rib roast. The first thing we would do after buying an Irwin 37 is find ourselves a rugged, attractive fixed cabin table. (The next thing we would do is to make the seats comfortable.)

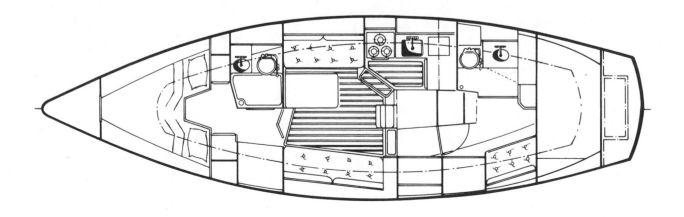

We urge anyone ordering a new 37 to choose his options carefully and plan at least some hassle in taking delivery

Deck Layout

The Irwin 37 is a handy boat to sail. The sidedecks are wide, the rail rises to a low bulwark forward to give a sense of security and the cockpit coaming has an opening to starboard but is low enough to climb out of anywhere. The bowsprit is designed to carry a 30 lb plow anchor housed in a roller chock. Hawseholes (of polished aluminum, replacing the line-chafing fiberglass on older boats) are mounted in the bulwark for docklines. Oddly enough neither the hawseholes nor the roller chock give a fair lead to the pair of deck cleats.

The stanchions are mounted through the deck into blocks drilled to fit, a system that we think gives a rugged support. In early 37s the stanchions went into fiberglass tubes glassed under the deck; now they go into wood blocks (saving cost and complexity). It remains to be seen if the wood rots out in time. In contrast to this sturdy structure, the bow and stern pulpits are screwed on the teak rail cap. We hardly recommend that attachment.

The cockpit is small, accommodating at the most four adults at a time. Yet the seats are long enough to stretch out on and access below is easy. We are not bothered by the absence of a bridgedeck or companionway sill for safety because the cockpit is high and amidships, hence dry. Besides, Irwin's advertising notwithstanding, we doubt if many owners would consider offshore passages, given all the limitations the 37 would have at sea.

We like the number, design, and placement of the "smoked glass" opening hatches/skylights. Like many designs that have tropical cruising and chartering as part of their destiny, the Irwin 37 has a well ventilated interior.

On deck stowage is limited to one gigantic locker, the lazarette. The trouble is that for storing fenders, docklines, sheets, snorkeling gear, etc. as well as an odd sail or two, it would leave everything hard to get at. You cannot reach the bottom from the deck and without some owner-installed shelves, hooks, and bins the contents would be in chaos.

CONCLUSIONS

Having exposed our prejudices we hasten to add that the more than 600 Irwin 37s sold thus far conclusively prove that many sailors do not share those prejudices.

The all-up price of an Irwin 37 is $75,000 with the options we mentioned as desirable, plus a flow-through/holding tank head system, commissioning, and freight. This price includes working sails (made by Johnson Sails), fresh water pressure system, 110vAC system, and basic electronics. We also would add a Bimini top if we expected to sail in a warm climate.

At this price the Irwin 37 is $15,000 less expensive than, say, the Tartan 37 or the Pearson 365. A Hunter 37, by contrast, could be sailed away for about $10,000 less than the Irwin 37.

Ironically, considering the persistent badmouthing of the Irwin 37 around the waterfront, older models have retained their value. A five-year old 37 is still bringing more than $50,000 on the used boat market, having appreciated at about half the inflation rate in the intervening years. The reason seems simple: the Irwin 37 offers many buyers what they are looking for in a boat, new or used.

And for the dollars the Irwin 37 is a lot of boat. Many owners report looking seriously at smaller boats and settling on the 37 when they (and their wives) see the spacious 37 for the same price as the smaller boat. For that price they get what they see as a summer home afloat. Deep water cruising may be a distant dream but the immediate desire is a comfortable and impressive boat for weekending and two weeks in the Bahamas, the Eastern Shore, or out of Long Island Sound.

We urge anyone ordering a new 37 to choose his options carefully and plan at least some hassle in taking delivery. Check the new boat over meticulously and don't be shocked if you have to negotiate with your dealer over what with many other new boats would be routine warranty claims; remember, the dealer is not likely to find settling such claims against the builder an easy matter.

Then, in time we'd plan systematic and regular upgrading. Expect to replace the standard through-hull gate valves with seacocks or ball valves. Divide the homungous lazarette. Run the halyards aft to the cockpit when they need replacing. Build some pitch into the seats of the settees. Rebuild the "navigation station" into handy food storage. Mount a larger diameter steering wheel so you will no longer have to steer standing up or perched on the edge of your seat. Smooth the rough texture of the interior teak trim.

Finally, take a sail on a boat meant to sail effectively to windward, just so you'll see what you are missing.

The Tartan 37: A Banker's Buick

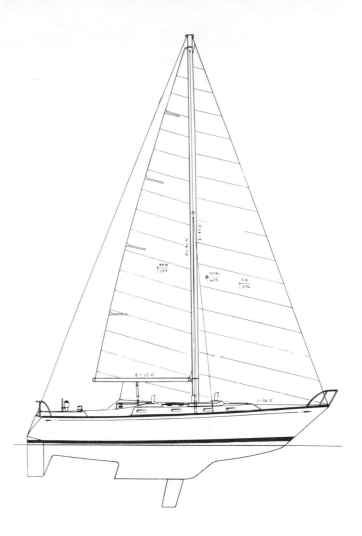

THE BOAT AND THE BUILDER

The Tartan 37 is a moderately high performance, shoal-draft keel-centerboarder, built by Tartan Marine, with headquarters in Grand River, Ohio, and primary construction facilities in Hamlet, North Carolina. High labor costs in the Great Lakes area relative to those in other parts of the country have forced a number of boat-building firms to seek greener pastures with friendlier labor markets.

Over the years, Tartan has specialized in the production of well-finished boats geared toward the upper income cruising sailor. Most of these boats have been Sparkman and Stephens designs, and many have been keel-centerboarders. Tartans were also in the past geared toward "civilized" racing, with boats such as the Tartan 41 and Tartan 46. With their Sparkman and Stephens designs and high quality joinerwork, Tartans have provided a lower priced alternative to lines of boats such as the very expensive Nautor Swans.

About 300 Tartan 37s have been built. Most have been the keel-centerboard version. An optional deep-keel version is also available. A racing version of the 37, called the Tartan 38, was also built in limited numbers.

Tartans are known for good resale value, although there is likely to be a certain amount of depreciation in the first year of ownership. In 1981, base price for the Tartan 37 was $74,900. Typical price, commissioned in New England, with basic sails and electronics, was between $85,000 and $90,000. The average price for a comparably-equipped 1978 Tartan 37 on the used boat market was $72,000.

The Tartan 37 is attractively modern in appearance. She has a gentle sheer and a straight raked stem profile, with moderate overhangs at both bow and stern. Underwater, the boat has a fairly long, low aspect ratio fin keel, and a high aspect ratio rudder faired into the hull with a substantial skeg. Freeboard is moderate. The boat is balanced and pleasant in appearance. She is not a character boat, but is attractive, fairly racy, and functional—a typical modern Sparkman and Stephens design.

CONSTRUCTION

The Tartan 37 is a well-built boat. Tartan makes use of both unidirectional roving and balsa coring in stress areas. This yields a stiff, fairly light hull that is less likely to oilcan than the relatively thin solid layup used in many production boats.

Specifications

LOA	37'3½"
LWL	28'6"
Beam	11'9"
Draft (board up)	4'2"
(board down)	7'9"
(deep keel)	6'7"
Displacement	15,500 lbs
Ballast (standard)	7,500 lbs
(deep keel)	7,200 lbs
Sail Area	625 sq ft

Tartan Marine Company
320 River Street
Grand River, OH 44045

Some roving printthrough is evident. There are also some visible hard spots on the outside of the hull. These may be the result of the heat of secondary bonding of bulkheads and partitions. Gelcoat quality is very good. The rudder is faired into the skeg with fiberglass flaps to minimize turbulence. All through-hull fittings are recessed flush to the hull skin. For a cruising boat, remarkable attention is given to reducing skin friction and improving water flow.

Tartan's hull-to-deck joint is simple and strong. The wide internal hull flange is bedded with butyl and polysulphide, the deck dropped on, and the two bolted together via the stainless steel bolts which hold on the teak toerail. This toerail is not always properly bedded. We were able to easily insert a thick knife blade under the toerail in several areas near the bow, where the rail is subject to the most twist. Water will lie in this joint if it is at all open, making it impossible to keep varnish on the toerail.

Most deck hardware, such as cleats, is backed with thick aluminum plates. Pulpits are through-bolted but lack backing plates. The hull-to-deck joint is through-bolted across the transom—one of few boats so built.

Running lights are mounted in the topsides, about a foot below the sheerline. The wiring for these lights is located in the forepeak locker, where it could be damaged by anchors or rodes stored there. We generally dislike running lights mounted in the hull. They look neat, but they are nearly invisible at sea, often leak, and frequently stain the topsides with long tears of oxidation after periods at sea.

Interior glasswork is some of the best we have seen. Fillet bonding is absolutely neat and clean. There are no raw fiberglass edges visible anywhere in the hull.

One of the reasons that the Tartan 37 costs so much is that there is a lot of expensive engineering and construction in the boat. The starboard main chainplate assembly, for example, is a complex construction of stainless steel weldments and tie rods that probably adds hundreds of dollars to the cost of the boat.

To keep the interior of the boat neat, the centerboard pennant comes up on deck through the center of the mast. This necessitates a complex mast step with transverse floors and a massive hat beam under the mast step to absorb compression. Add a few hundred dollars of engineering and construction.

If price is not a concern, perhaps this is little ground for complaint. However, the more complex a piece of construction is, the more subject it may be to failure, and the more expensive to repair or replace.

Tartan uses bronze ball valves on through hull fittings below the waterline. Exhaust line, cockpit scuppers, and bilge pump outlets are above the waterline, and have no shutoffs. The cockpit scuppers, which would be submerged while the boat is underway, should have provision for shutoff.

PERFORMANCE

Handling under sail

Owners report that the Tartan 37 is a well-mannered boat under sail. The boat will not perform at the Grand Prix level, but she is no sluggard, either. Several Tartan 37's participated in the 1979 Marion-Bermuda race, and performed respectably.

A large percentage of the boats are purchased for family cruising. On these boats, headsail roller furling systems are usually installed. Almost inevitably, there will be some sacrifice in windward performance with roller-furling headsails.

The optional inboard genoa track should be considered essential to those concerned with optimum windward performance. Coupled with the standard outboard track, this will allow versatility in sheeting angles.

Headsail sheets and winches are within reach of the helmsman. This feature is vital for short-handed cruising, and can help make the difference between a boat that is easy for two people to handle, and one that is a pain. However, no real provision has been made for the installation of secondary headsail winches, should you wish to carry staysails. Small winches could be mounted on the cockpit coamings forward, but they could well interfere with the installation of a dodger.

With good sails, performance of the Tartan 37 will not be disappointing on any point of sail. Tartan brochures show the 37 happily romping along on a beam reach in a 15 knot breeze. We suspect that under those conditions her owner is likely to be as happy as any sailor afloat.

Handling under power

The standard 41 horsepower Westerbeke 50 diesel is more than adequate power for the Tartan 37. The tendency in many production boats today is toward smaller, lighter, lower-powered diesels—the opposite of the past American boatbuilding practice, which, like our automobiles, tended toward excessive horsepower.

For a cruising boat, the excess of mechanical power represented by a 40 horsepower engine in a 15,000 lb boat makes sense. The cruising boat needs the ability to punch into a head sea when necessary. Frankly, we prefer a boat to be slightly overpowered, rather than underpowered. We'll take the greater weight and the higher fuel consumption without complaint.

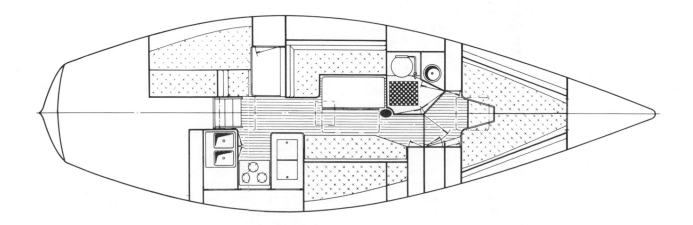

Due to an abundance of teak and teak plywood, the interior is dark and cavelike—a rather elevant cave, with excellent joinerwork throughout

The engine box of the Tartan 37 is only partially sound insulated. Access to the front end of the engine is good, by removing the companionway ladder. Access to the oil dipstick is another matter. To reach the oil dipstick, one must climb into the starboard cockpit locker. This necessitates removing much of what could be stored in that locker every time the oil is checked. If one is conscientious enough to check the oil every time the engine is run, a lot of loading and unloading will be required. In practice, it means that the oil level is unlikely to be checked regularly. Most sailboat owners rather shockingly neglect their engines. Making the oil dipstick inaccessible can only exacerbate that tendency toward neglect.

LIVABILITY

Deck layout
With wide decks, inboard chainplates, and a relatively narrow cabin trunk, fore and aft movement on the deck of the Tartan 37 is relatively easy. It would be easier if the lifeline stanchions had been positioned further outboard, rather than about 3" inboard of the toerail.

There are proper bow chocks, and two well mounted cleats forward. However, a line led through the chocks to the cleats bears against the bow pulpit. Shifting the cleats further inboard would provide a better lead.

Surprisingly, there is no foredeck anchor well. This means that an anchor must be stowed in chocks on deck, if one is to be readily available. Then, you must face the problem of anchor rode storage. Molded foredeck anchor wells are becoming almost universal in modern boats. While the weight of anchor and rode—about 65 lbs in a boat this size—might be objectionable stowed all the way forward, the convenience of such a system generally outweighs the increase in pitching moment that might result. Removing the ground tackle from the deck also reduces clutter and toe stubbers, and simplifies foredeck work.

There are strong, well-mounted teak grabrails on top of the cabin trunk, although the reasoning for using two short rails on each side rather than a single long rail escapes us. The molded breakwater/cockpit coaming is a common Sparkman and Stephens feature, and greatly facilitates the mounting of a dodger—almost standard equipment on a cruising boat.

The T-shaped cockpit of the Tartan 37 is very comfortable for five while sailing. It has several unusual features. Rather than the usual unyielding fiberglass, there are teak duckboards on all cockpit seats. This means that you won't sit in a puddle when it rains, or when heavy spray comes aboard. These duckboards are comfortable, but they are held in place only by wooden cleats, with the exception of the starboard seat. A more secure arrangement should be provided for offshore sailing.

There is a teak-grated cockpit sump under the helmsman's feet. This shifts the cockpit drains inboard from the edge of the cockpit. The result is that a puddle can collect in the leeward corner of the cockpit when the boat is well-heeled in a blow, with heavy spray coming aboard.

Access to the steering gear is via the lazarette hatch. There is good provision for an emergency tiller, but the lazarette hatch must be held open in some way to use the emergency steering. There is a drop-in shelf in the lazarette which allows using the locker with less risk of damage to the steering system, but we would be reluctant to store anything small there that might possibly jam in the steering gear.

With a low cabin trunk, visibility from the helm is excellent. We suspect that many helmsmen would prefer a contoured seat to the flat bench provided, however. The relatively wide flat top of the cockpit coaming provides reasonably comfortable seating for the helmsman who prefers to sit well to leeward or well to windward.

The main companionway is narrow and almost parallel-sided—features we like—but the sill is much lower than we prefer for offshore sailing. The low sill facilitates passage of the crew below. Unfortunately, it also greatly facilitates passage of water below should the cockpit fill. Coupled with the thin plywood dropboards, we feel this is a potential weakness in watertight integrity, compromising the boat as an offshore cruiser. For offshore racing, for example, the Special Regulations require that the companionway be permanently closed up to the main deck level or the height of the lowest cockpit coaming.

Belowdecks
Due to an abundance of teak and teak plywood, the interior of the Tartan 37 is dark and cavelike. This is much the same criticism we have made of other well-finished boats. Mind you, it's a rather elegant cave, with excellent joinerwork throughout. Somehow, boat designers and builders have convinced most of the consuming

public that teak is the only wood to use belowdecks. The fact is that there are many wonderful woods—ash and butternut, for example—that yield interiors that are lighter in both weight and color than teak.

The forward cabin of the Tartan 37 is truly comfortable for a boat of this size, with drawers, hanging lockers, separate access to the head, and enough room to dress in relative comfort. The completely louvered door separating the forward cabin from the main cabin looks nice, and does assist in ventilating the forward cabin. It limits privacy, however, and one good blow from a crew member caught off balance in a seaway would probably reduce it to a pile of teak toothpicks.

The head is quite comfortable, and it is possible to brace adequately for use offshore. The shower drains into a separate sump—not into the bilge.

Layout of the main cabin is conventional, with settee and pilot berth to starboard, dinette to port. Including a pilot berth on the starboard side necessitates the complex chainplate arrangement mentioned earlier, for the berth prevents a simpler and cheaper bulkhead-mounted chainplate.

In what is a rather remarkable lapse in good design for such a boat, there is bulkhead-mounted, fold-down cabin table. Pins in the bottom of the two legs must be inserted in corresponding holes in the cabin sole—no mean feat at anchor, and a ridiculous expectation offshore. The new Tartan 37 we examined already had a pockmarked cabin sole from setting up the cabin table for potential buyers. Metal plates recessed in the cabin sole would at least minimize the potential for damage here. Once set up, the table is disappointingly flimsy.

While there is excellent storage space in the galley, one must reach across the stove to reach much of it—and it's a long reach for a short person. The stove is securely mounted and has a grab bar across its well to protect the cook, but this grab bar also inhibits the stove's gimballing function. There is no on-deck provision for storage for propane bottles, should you wish propane rather than the standard alcohol stove. There is room for CNG bottles to be stowed in the starboard cockpit locker, but CNG has never really impressed us because of its bulkiness compared to propane.

The icebox appears to be well insulated. Why Tartan, like many other builders, fails to insulate and carefully fit the tops of their iceboxes totally escapes us. We have found this shortcoming on every variety of boat, from the cheapest to the most expensive, and it repre-

sents a rather strange disregard of the basic laws of thermodynamics.

The Tartan 37 has a large, well-designed navigation station. The quarterberth above it converts to a double berth.

Ventilation is excellent, with eight opening ports and three hatches. There are also four ventilators for the accommodations areas—two exhaust type and two low plastic cowls in dorade boxes. We think four taller cowls in the dorades would be more effective, or better still, the five tall cowls shown in the original plans for the boat. The vertical aft deckhouse bulkhead also allows a drop board to be left out when it rains, further improving ventilation.

Despite our complaints about the darkness of the interior, joinerwork is of excellent stock boat quality throughout. The degree of enclosure of the interior of the hull can complicate access to deck hardware, and certainly does not facilitate survey of the vessel. In traditional wooden yacht construction, structural members are often left exposed for their intrinsic beauty, as well as for ventilation and preservation. In fiberglass boats, it is rather difficult to find intrinsic beauty in the structural material. Perhaps we are better off with it all hidden—as long as we know what holds the boat together. We certainly have confidence in what holds the Tartan together, even if we do pay a premium for that confidence.

CONCLUSIONS

The Tartan 37 is a well-built, well-mannered fast cruising sailboat. Like many S&S designs, there is a lot of complex engineering in the boat, which helps to boost the price. The boat also shows a generally high degree of finish, and a fair amount of attention to detail—perhaps more than most consumers are willing to pay for.

The Tartan 37 may never appreciate in the manner of some well-finished cruising boats that have practically become cult objects—the Hinckley Bermuda 40, or the Concordia yawls, for example. She is a grey flannel Buick of a boat, the perfect banker's, lawyer's or stockbroker's boat. She's neither ostentatious nor plain. She is neither cheaply designed, nor cheaply built. One pays a lot for good breeding. Whether $90,000 is too much to pay is something only you, and the loan officer at your bank, can decide.

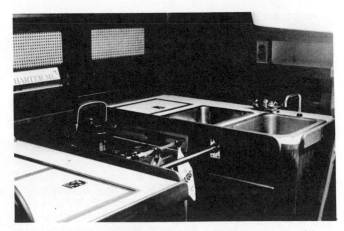

Complex chainplate engineering is necessitated by the presence of the pilot berth

The galley offers plenty of storage space, but much of it requires a long reach to use

The Tayana 37:
For Experienced Cruisers

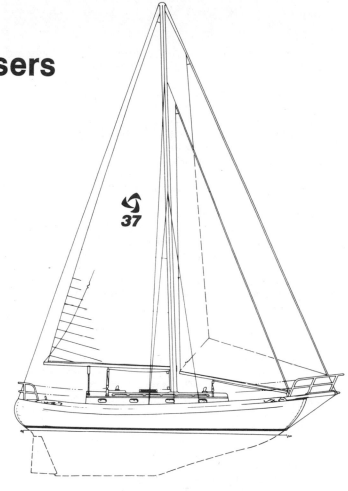

THE BOAT AND THE BUILDER

With over 320 boats sailing the seas of the world, the Tayana 37 has been one of the most successful products of the Taiwan-built boat invasion of the US that began in the early 1970's. Her shapely Baltic stern, scribed plank seams molded into the glass hull, and lavish use of teak above and below decks have come to epitomize the image that immediately comes to mind when Oriental boats are mentioned.

Not all thoughts of Far Eastern boats are pleasant, however. To some, Taiwan-built boats mean poor workmanship, overly heavy hulls, unbedded hardware of dubious heritage, wooden spars that delaminate, and builder-modified boats light years removed from the plans provided by the designer. Add to that a serious language barrier and the inevitable logistical problems of dealing with a boatyard halfway round the world, and you have a situation readymade to generate potential nightmares for the boatbuyer. To the credit of the builder, the designer, the primary importer, and a powerful owners' association, the Tayana 37 has weathered six years of production — a lifetime in the world of boatbuilding — while making steady improvements and maintaining a steady output of over 50 boats per year.

Washington-based designer Bob Perry had just hung out his own shingle when the Tayana 37 was designed in the early 70's. The Sherman tank Westsail 32 had just come lumbering onto the scene, bringing with it a resurgence of interest in the double ended hull form, and more people than ever before were beginning to have the dream of chucking it all and sailing away to a tropical paradise.

In the last eight years, Bob Perry has become an enormously successful designer of cruising boats, from traditional full keel designs such as the Tayana 37, to modern fin keel cruisers such as the Nordic 40, Golden Wave 42, and the Valiant 40. A remarkable number of his designs have been built in the Orient, in both Hong Kong and Taiwan. This year almost 20 different Perry designs are under construction in the Far East.

Perry conceived the Tayana 37 as a cruising boat of traditional appearance above the water, with moderately heavy displacement, a long waterline, and a reasonably efficient cutter rig of modern proportions. Below the water, the forefoot of the long keel has been cut away, and a Constellation-type rudder utilized rather than a more traditional barn door. Perry sought to cash in on the popularity of the double ended hull while keeping displacement moderate and performance reasonable, avoiding the plight of boats such as the Westsail 32 — the inability to go to windward, and sluggish performance in anything short of a moderate gale. The stern design of the Tayana 37 borrows heavily from the well known Aage Neilsen designed ketch Holger Danske, winner of the 1980 Bermuda Race. It is one of the more handsome Baltic-type sterns on any production sailboat.

Specifications

LOA	42'2"
LOD	36'8"
LWL	30'10
Beam	11'6"
Draft	5'8"
Displacement	22,500 lbs
Ballast	7,340 lbs
Sail Area:	
cutter	864 sq ft
ketch	786 sq ft

Ta Yang Yacht Building Co.
Kaohsiung, Taiwan

The Tayana 37 began life as the CT 37. In 1979 the boat became known as the Tayana 37, named for Ta Yang Yacht Building Company. While some snobbishness exists among some owners who own the CT version, Perry insists that this is illusory. According to the designer, the CT 37 and the Tayana 37 are the same boat, built by the same men in the same yard. In much the same way that the early Swans imported by Palmer Johnson were known by the name of the importer — the names Nautor and Swan were unknown here in the late 1960's — early Tayanas were known as CTs because the name CT had already become known in this country.

Perry, who has worked with many yards in the Far East, considers Ta Yang one of the best. The yard has been very responsive to input from both dealers and

The hull-to-deck joint is incredibly labor intensive, but labor intensive is the name of the game in Taiwanese boatbuilding

owners. Over the years the Tayana 37 has been in production, this has resulted in steady improvement in the quality of the boat.

The vast majority of Tayanas now imported into this country are brought in by Southern Offshore Yachts, which has offices in eastern Canada, Rhode Island, Maryland, and both coasts of Florida. By working closely with the builder and maintaining good contact with the owners' association, Southern Offshore has had significant input into improving the quality of the boats. Two years ago, for example, Southern Offshore yachts sent Tayana a new swaging machine to improve quality control in the rigging.

Owners report that Southern Offshore has been very responsive to handling warranty problems. The same cannot be said for all Tayana dealers. One west coast Tayana 37 owner responding to our owner survey reported that "basically, the dealer treated us like second-rate citizens." A similar comment was voiced by a midwestern owner.

CONSTRUCTION

The hull of the Tayana 37 is a fairly heavy solid glass layup. Some roving printthrough is evident in the topsides. The hull-to-deck joint has in the past occasionally been a problem with the boat. There is no doubt it is strong, but there have been numerous reports of leaking.

Part of the problem with the hull-to-deck joint is the fact that the hull and deck moldings form a hollow bulwark extending well above the main deck level. This bulwark is pierced by hawsepipes and several large scuppers at deck level. Careful bedding of all fittings that penetrate the bulwarks is essential to avoid leaks. On new boats, the entire hollow bulwark is glassed over from inside the hull, greatly reducing the possiblity of leaks. This results in an incredibly labor intensive joint, but labor intensive is the name of the game in Taiwanese boatbuilding.

None of the numerous through hull fittings is recessed flush with the exterior of the hull. The argument is frequently made that this is unnecessary on cruising boats. Nothing could be further from the truth. The cruising boat is frequently undercanvassed for her displacement and wetted surface. Add to this the low speed drag associated with projections from the hull, and you have a boat that spends a lot of time motoring in light air, when she should be sailing. While the Tayana 37 is far from undercanvassed, she could benefit from a little more bottom fairing as much as the next boat. An option to recessing the through hull fittings would be to fair them in with large microballoon blisters—not as effective as recessing, but perhaps easier to do after the fact.

The rudder stock is a substantial stainless steel rod, with the rudder held on by welded arms riveted through the rudder blade. The heel fitting is a bronze casting. This is fastened to the hull with stainless steel bolts. Inevitably, there will be galvanic action between the bronze and the stainless, with the fastenings coming out on the short end. There is provision for protection of the rudder straps with zincs.

All hardware, including cleats and stanchions, is through-bolted and backed with stainless steel pads. Most hardware is fairly accessible from belowdecks.

The ballast keel is an iron casting dropped into the hollow fiberglass keel shell. The casting is glassed over on the inside of the boat. We prefer an external lead keel for its shock absorbing qualities in case of grounding.

The glasswork of the Tayana 37 is of good quality. There are no rough edges, the fillet bonding is neat, and there is no glass or resin slopped about. Tayana warrants the hull against defects for ten years.

Until recently, the standard steering system was a Taiwanese worm gear system copied from the Edson worm gear. Recurrent problems with this system, notably extremely sloppy and mushy steering, have resulted in significant changes. The standard system is now a pedestal system Taiwanese-built but remarkably similar to the Edson pedestal steerer.

Seacocks are used on all through hull fittings. The seacocks appear to be copies of US-made Groco valves. Hoses to seacocks are all double clamped.

PERFORMANCE

Handling Under Power
Three different engines have been used in the Tayana 37: the Yanmar 3QM30, the Perkins 4-108, and the Volvo MD17c. The standard engine is now the Yanmar. This makes good economic sense, as Japan is rather closer to Taiwan than either England or Sweden. Both the Volvo and Perkins are still available as options, at an additional cost of $1400 and $2100 respectively. We see no reason to choose either engine over the Yanmar.

There have been some instances of failure of the Yanmar motor mounts. This was the result of a Yanmar defect, rather than an installation problem, and Southern Offshore Yachts reports that the problem has been solved by redesigned mounts. The only problem with the Yanmar is substantial vibration at low rpm, which is typical in most engines in the Yanmar line with which we have had experience. When this vibration is transmitted through the mounts to the hull, the whole boat seems to shake. Once again, Southern Offshore reports that the change in engine mounts has greatly reduced the vibration.

While the engine box removes completely to provide good access for service, there is no provision for easy access to the oil dipstick. This means that this vital task is likely to be ignored. A simple door in the side of the engine box would solve the problem.

The placement of the fuel tank has caused substantial discussion on the part of owners. The standard 90 gallon black iron tank is located under the V-berth in the forward cabin. When full, this tank holds almost 650 pounds of fuel. This is about the same weight as 375 feet of 3/8" chain—a substantial amount to carry around in the bow of a 37-footer. A Tayana 37 with the bow tank full and a heavy load of ground tackle will show noticeable bow down trim. The design was originally drawn with the fuel tanks under the main cabin settees, but the builder put the tank forward to create additional storage in the main cabin.

This is a good example of one of the basic recurring problems with Far East built boats. Frequently the builders have good glass men and good inside joiners, but their inexperience in sailing results in strange inconsistencies which may compromise their boats.

Fortunately, thanks to the pressure from owners and from Southern Offshore Yachts, the builder offers optional tankage amidships, where it belongs. By all means select this tankage option so that the fore and aft trim of the boat will remain unchanged as fuel is consumed.

Although any of the engines is adequate power for the boat, don't expect the Tayana 37 to win any drag races. With her substantial wetted surface and fairly heavy displacement, performance under power is sedate rather than spritely. Owners report handling under power fair to good, although one reported that his boat "backs up like a drunk elephant."

Handling Under Sail

The Tayana 37 comes as a ketch or cutter, with wood spars or aluminum, with mast stepped on deck or on the keel. Few builders offer you so many options.

The standard rig is a masthead cutter with wooden spars, the mast stepped on deck and supported by a substantial compression column. The designer strongly recommends the aluminum cutter rig, and we heartily concur. The wooden mast is poorly proportioned, with a massive section and extremely thick side walls. One new mast we looked at had a large knot on the forward side of the mast just at spreader level. Despite the huge mast section, we feel the knot could weaken the mast significantly.

In contrast to the large section of the mast, the boom is an extremely small spruce box section. With mid-boom sheeting, this spar will probably be about as stiff as a rubber band, complicating mainsail shape. The clew outhaul slide is far too flimsy for a boat of this size, and owners report that the outhaul slide frequently distorts or explodes. Once again, these problems are not atypical in Taiwan boats, where you frequently find excellent craftsmanship but a poor understanding of engineering or the forces involved in ocean sailing.

In contrast, the aluminum rigs, which may come from a variety of sources including France, New Zealand, and the US, are well proportioned and suited to the task.

We see no reason to select the ketch rig. Both performance and balance with the cutter rig will be better. The cutter's mainsail is 342 square feet. Any couple healthy enough to go world cruising should be able to cope with a sail of this size.

The cutter rig is tall and well proportioned. Perry has drawn an unusually high aspect rig for a cruising boat, and the result is a boat with good performance on all points of sail. With the aluminum rig, the optional Nicro Fico ball bearing mainsheet traveler, and a well cut suit of sails, the Tayana 37 will be surprisingly fast. Her working sail area of 864 square feet is generous

Despite a ballast/displacement ratio of 33 percent, the Tayana 37 is not a stiff boat. This is due in part to the tall, heavy rig and the substantial amount of other weight above the boat's vertical center of gravity. Much of the boat's heavy joinerwork and glass work is well above the waterline, raising the center of gravity and reducing initial stability. Perry believes the initial tenderness to be an asset, reducing the snappiness of the boat's roll and making her a more comfortable sea boat. We agree.

Many owners report that the boat carries substantial weather helm. The sail plan is drawn with significant rake to the mast. This creates just enough shift in the center of effort of the sail plan to create a lot of weather helm. Bringing the mast back toward the vertical by tightening the headstay and forestay while loosening the backstay should cure much of the problem, according to reports from other owners. It may be necessary to shorten the headstay to do this.

The weather helm and initial tenderness may also be due in part to the poor cut of the standard sails provided with the boat. For years, the standard sails have been made by Lam of Hong Kong. The sails have the reputation of being stretchy and having very poor shape. Mainsail draft with the stretchy fabric is almost uncontrollable, with the sail becoming baggy and the draft shifting aft as the wind increases. This will create weather helm and increase the angle of heel.

The builder is in the process of switching to sails from Neil Pryde's Hong Kong loft. This may bring real improvement in the sailing qualities of the boat. Better yet, consider ordering the Tayana with no sails at all, and have your local sailmaker cut them for you. Unfortunately, the Lam sails are so inexpensive that you don't get much credit from the builder if the boat is ordered without sails. Your out of pocket cost for a basic suit of good American sails from a major loft would probably be about $3000. It could be worth it if you want to get the best performance from your boat.

LIVABILITY

Deck Layout

With her bulwarks, high double lifelines, and substantial bow and stern pulpits, the Tayana 37 gives the sailor a good sense of security on those cold, windy nights when he's called out for sail changes. A teak platform grating atop the bowsprit coupled with the strong pulpit relieves that appendage of its widow-maker reputation.

The bowsprit platform incorporates double anchor rollers which will house CQR anchors. Unfortunately, there is no good lead from the rollers to any place to secure the anchor rode. Line or chain led to the heavy bowsprit bitts would chafe on the platform. An anchor windlass mounted to port or starboard of the bowsprit would provide a good lead, and is an available option.

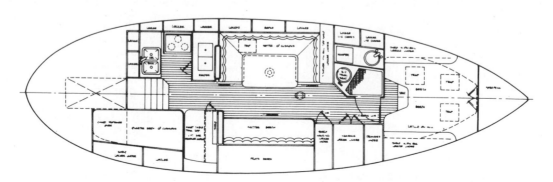

The Tayana 37 would make an excellent retirement cruiser for the experienced sailing couple.

There are hawsepipes through the bulwarks port and starboard well aft of the stem. These will be fine for dock lines, but are too far aft to serve as good leads for anchoring. There is room at deck level outboard of the bowsprit to install a set of heavy chocks for anchoring, although anchor rode led to this point will chafe on the bobstay as the boat swings to her anchor.

This is a classic problem of the boat with bowsprit. The anchor rode must really lead well out the bowsprit to avoid the bobstay, yet the long lead complicates securing the inboard end of the rode.

The long staysail boom makes it difficult to cross from one side of the boat to the other forward. The standard staysail traveler is merely a stainless steel rod on which a block can slide on its shackle. Under load, this can bind when tacking, so that it may be necessary to go forward and kick the block over after every tack. By all means get the optional Nicro Fico travelers with their roller bearing cars. Complaints about the standard travelers are rife.

Standard winches on the boat are Barlow. In their highly desirable Voyager model option package, Southern Offshore Yachts includes a package of larger Barlow winches for all functions. Along with this package, we suggest that you request self-tailing winches for all sheets.

Although the side decks are relatively narrow due to the wide cabin trunk, there is reasonable access fore and aft. A full length hand rail on either side of the cabin trunk provides a good handhold.

The cockpit of the Tayana 37 is small, as befits an oceangoing sailboat. There are cockpit scuppers at each of the four corners of the cockpit well, with seacocks on the through hull outlets.

With the now-standard pedestal steering, the cockpit seems to have shrunk. Only three can be seated in real comfort, although this is no real problem for the cruising couple. It is not a cockpit for heavy entertaining in port. The elimination of the coaming around the stern of the boat has made the cockpit seats long enough for sleeping on deck, but at the expense of exposing the helmsman to a wet seat in a following sea. The coaming can optionally be continued around the rear of the cockpit. Cockpit locker configuration varies with the interior options chosen, but the lockers are large enough to provide reasonable storage, although you should resist the temptation to load them heavily so far aft.

Belowdecks
The interior of the Tayana 37 probably sells more boats than any other feature of the boat. There is not really a standard interior. Every boat that comes through is custom built, and almost every owner takes advantage of the opportunity to create an interior suited to his or her own needs.

The cost of producing these interiors is not prohibitive. Interior joinerwork is labor intensive, and labor in the Orient is still far cheaper than it is in this country.

Like other Taiwanese boats, the interior of the Tayana 37 is all teak. This results in an interior that can be oppressively dark to some people, exquisitely cool to others. To keep it looking good, someone is going to have to do a lot of oiling or a lot of varnishing.

The interior joinerwork is some of the best we have seen on any boat, whether it is built in the US, Taiwan, or Finland. Joints were just about flawless, panelled doors beautifully joined, drawers dovetailed from solid stock. There were no fillers making up for poorly fitted joints, no trim fitted with grinders, no slop anywhere. The men who put the interior in the new boat we examined were real craftsmen. Older boats we have looked at did not boast quite this caliber of workmanship, but their joinerwork was certainly of good quality.

With such an array of interior options it is difficult to really evaluate the boat's interior. This may be a mixed blessing to the buyer. For the couple who have owned other boats, have kept copious notes about what they want and don't want in their next boat, and who are experienced, well read, and knowledgable, the ability to plan their own interior offers an opportunity that is probably unequalled in a boat in this price range.

If you have only vague ideas of what you want in the interior of a cruising boat, one of the real advantages of owning the Tayana 37 may be lost. Do you want a pilot berth or storage? Drawers or bins? Propane or kerosene for cooking? Quarter berth or wet locker? Fold up or drop leaf table? To the inexperienced, the choices may be bewildering. To those who know what they want, the opportunity is a gold mine.

In all fairness, there is a "standard" interior. It is prosaic but good, with V-berth forward, followed by head and lockers just aft. The main cabin has a U-shaped settee to port, straight settee and pilot berth to starboard. Aft is a good U-shaped galley to port, nav station and quarterberth to starboard. For not much more money, you can have pretty much what you want, from a "standard" array of interior options to a fully custom interior. You're missing a good bet if you don't spend some time creating your own dream interior.

CONCLUSIONS

The Tayana 37 is both typical and atypical of Taiwanese boats. She is typical in the problems that existed due to the builder's inexperience with seagoing yachts, typical with communication and language problems, typical in having dealers who varied widely in both ability and their desire to help their customers after the sale.

She is atypical in that many of these problems have been solved over six years of production, in that a good owners' association and the domination of one dealer—Southern Offshore Yachts—have resulted in real improvements in the boat. Anyone considering a Tayana 37 should join the owners' association and read all the back newsletters before buying the boat. If your dealer either fails to mention the owners' association or denigrates it, find another dealer.

Because of the myriad options, we don't really suggest the Tayana 37 as a first boat. Between pilot house and trunk cabin versions, ketch and cutter, and the incredible array of interior options, the first time boat-owner would have a great deal of difficulty coming up with just the right boat.

A well-equipped Tayana 37 with most of the desirable options will cost about $80,000 delivered and commissioned on the east coast. This compares very favorably with other boats of her size, type, and displacement.

The Tayana 37 would make an excellent retirement cruiser for the experienced sailing couple. Properly handled and equipped, she could take you anywhere with confidence and reasonable dispatch. If you want to design your own interior, are willing to wait for your boat to be built, and have a lot of confidence in your dealer, she just may be the right boat for you.

The C&C Landfall 38: A Stylish Cruiser

THE BOAT AND THE BUILDER

The C&C Landfall 38 is the midsize boat in the Canadian company's three-boat Landfall range, which also includes a 35-footer and a 43-footer. Unlike other C&Cs, whose interior and deck layouts are designed for racing as well as cruising, the Landfalls are geared toward cruising, with more comfort amenities, a slightly higher degree of finish detail, and deck layout concessions to the cruising couple.

These are performance cruisers, however. Despite more wetted surface, more displacement, and a slightly smaller rig than the original C&C 38, the Landfall 38 is a fast boat, designed for cruisers who want to get there quickly, as well as in style.

The Landfall 38 is a direct descendant of the old C&C 38, tho older hull design having been modified with slightly fuller sections forward, a slightly raked transom rather than an IOR reversed transom, a longer, shoaler keel, and a longer deckhouse for increased interior volume.

Nevertheless, the hull is more that of a sleek racer rather than a fat cruiser. For the additional performance that makes the boat a true performance cruiser, you trade off a hull volume that is slightly smaller than you would expect in a pure cruiser of the same waterline length. This is most notable in the ends of the boat, where the V-berth forward narrows sharply, and the hull rises so quickly aft that C&C's normal gas bottle stowage at the aft end of the cockpit is eliminated.

The builder has an excellent reputation for warranty service. The company's dealer network also has an excellent reputation.

C&C was a pioneer in composite fiberglass construction. Balsa coring has just about become synonymous with the company name over the years.

In addition to production boat facilities in the US and Canada, C&C maintains a custom division which turns out both high-tech IOR racing boats and custom cruisers such as the huge schooner *Archangel*.

CONSTRUCTION

Construction of the Landfall 38 is typical of the C&C line. Hulls are a one-piece, balsa cored molding. The deck and the top of the cabin trunk are also balsa cored. Hull and deck are through-bolted with stainless steel bolts on 6" centers. The hull-to-deck bolts also serve as fasteners for the teak toerail, which replaces the familiar and business-like slotted aluminum toerail used on other boats in the C&C line.

Specifications

LOA	37'7"
LWL	30'2"
Beam	12'
Draft	4'11½"
Displacement	16,700
Ballast	6,500 lbs
Sail Area	648.5 sq ft

Landfall Yachts
C&C Yachts Inc.
Box C, Oliphant Lane
Middletown, RI 02840

C&C uses butyl tape as a compound in the hull-to-deck joint. Although this is a good, resilient bedding compound, it has no real structural properties. We would rather see an adhesive rubber compound such as 3M 5200 used in the joint to provide a chemical backup to the strong mechanical fastening.

The keel is an external lead casting, bolted to an integral keel sump. The keel is a fairly low aspect ratio fin, keeping the draft of the Landfall 38 to 5'. The keel is flat on the bottom, and the boat will stand on its keel, something that can't be said for a lot of fin keel boats.

All deck hardware is through-bolted, and is equipped with either backup plates or oversize washers. The relatively narrow hull-to-deck flange, however, means that some of the backup plates do not lie flat on the underside of the deck, as they bridge the narrow flange.

The mast step spans two deep floor timbers in the bilge sump, keeping the heel of the mast out of the water and providing stiffness

---

This can result in uneven local stresses which can lead to gelcoat cracks in the vicinity of hardware such as lifeline stanchion bases.

The Landfall 38 uses bronze seacocks on all underwater through hull fittings. These are properly bolted to the hull, and their hoses are double clamped. The skin fittings are neither recessed flush to the hull nor faired in, however. This would be a fairly easy task for the owner.

In contrast to many boats, the mast step does not sit in the depths of the bilge where it can slowly turn to mush, taking the bottom of the mast with it. Rather, the mast step spans two deep floor timbers in the bilge sump, keeping the heel of the mast out of the water and providing stiffness in an area which is frequently too weak in fin keel boats.

Although most construction details are excellent, there are some shortcomings surprising on a boat of this quality. The engine compartment has no sound-proofing, despite the fact that the engine sits a few feet from the owner's berth.

C&C construction is light but strong. The Landfall 38 is heavier than the old C&C 38 because of extra ballast, more interior joinerwork and molding, and a longer deck.

PERFORMANCE

Handling under sail
Although the Landfall 38 is a cruising boat, her performance approaches or exceeds that of many production racer-cruisers. Her hull is basically an undistorted IOR shape, and the rig is a slightly shorter version of the old C&C 38 rig.

The Landfall is a full 2,000 lbs heavier than the original C&C 38. Nevertheless, there is relatively little difference in the performance of the two boats.

In typical C&C fashion, the rig is aerodynamically clean, with airfoil spreaders and Navtec rod rigging. Shroud chainplates—also Navtec—are set inboard for good upwind performance.

The large rig and big headsails of the Landfall may be intimidating to some cruising couples. The 100% foretriangle area of 385 square feet is pretty intimidating, since it means that the 150% genoa has an area of almost 580 square feet.

Because of the large foretriangle, the boat is a natural candidate for a good roller furling headsail system if it is to be cruised by a couple.

Main halyard, reefing, and cunningham lines are all led aft to the cockpit. Headsail halyards, however, lead to winches atop the cabin trunk just aft of the mast. This prevents the helmsman from assisting with headsails when the boat is sailed by a couple. This may or may not be a problem, depending on how agile the foredeck crew is. Since you can get two headsail halyards and two headsail halyard winches, a better solution might be to relocate one of the headsail winches aft, leaving the other near the mast. Then, headsail hoisting and dropping can be tailored to the particular crew's needs.

Surprisingly, self-tailing winches are not standard on the boat, except for the mainsheet winch. On a $100,000 boat which has hot and cold water as standard items, we'd certainly expect to see self-tailing genoa sheet winches, particularly if the boat is to be used for short-handed sailing. Self-tailers make sail handling so much easier when cruising that they are just about the first thing we'd add to any cruising boat. And they'd be the biggest self-tailers we could fit on the winch islands.

The Landfall 38 is stiff and well-balanced under sail. Owners report that she is as fast or faster than similar boats of the same size. The Landfall 38's PHRF rating, for example, is 120, squarely between the 114 of the Cal 39 and the 126 of the Tartan 37—two boats to which the Landfall 38 will inevitably be compared in size, type, and price.

To our way of thinking, performance cruising is what it's all about. It's all well and good to have a heavy, under rigged boat if you're cruising around the world. Most people's cruising, however, is limited to a few weeks a year, with moderate distances between ports, and schedules that have to be met. A boat that will get you there fast, safely, and in comfort is a highly desirable type of boat for this kind of cruising. From a performance viewpoint, the Landfall 38 meets those requirements.

Handling under power
C&C was one of the first boatbuilding firms to introduce Yanmar diesels into the US market, and they have stuck with Yanmar through thick and thin. Yanmar engines have been a paragon of reliability, but they have had the reputation for vibration and noise. Vibration has at times been so bad that engine mounts have broken and shafts have refused to stay in their couplings. It is always difficult to say in an engine installation whether the engine, the design of the installation, or the person

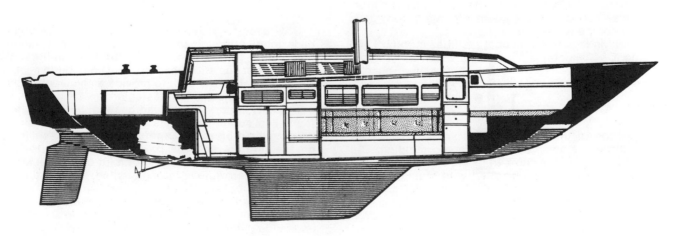

doing the installation is at fault when there are problems. One Landfall 38 owner has had three prop shafts in his boat. Now, after careful matching of the shaft flanges and careful alignment of the engine, he reports satisfaction with the installation. C&C picked up a hefty bill on that one, but they did it without hesitation.

When buying a new boat, be sure to align the engine after the boat is launched, and before you use it. Don't just blithely hook up the coupling. Careful engine and shaft alignment is a key to good engine performance, particularly in a modern boat with a short shaft and a flex-mounted diesel engine.

The 30 hp Yanmar 3HM, which has replaced the 3QM in the Landfall 38, is perfectly adequate power for the boat, easily achieving hull speed. The boat handles well under power in either forward or reverse.

Engine access for service is a mixed bag. The engine is tucked well aft, under the cockpit, and drives the prop through a V-drive. The oil is checked by removing a panel in the quarterberth in the owner's cabin. The companionway ladder and a bureau next to it remove fairly easily for access to the back of the engine, although it will probably be necessary to empty the drawers before the bureau can be lifted out. The oil filter is reached by climbing down into the starboard cockpit locker. Once again, emptying the locker may be necessary.

Since there is no engine drip pan, you must exercise great care when changing oil and oil filters to keep the bilge clean. The engine is wedged so tightly under the cockpit sole that a funnel is required—with a long hose—to add either oil or engine coolant. A partial plywood bulkhead that hangs over the engine complicates this, and could easily be cut away to give slightly better access.

Battery access is poor. A mirror is required to check electrolyte levels, and filling the batteries just about requires removing them from the battery boxes.

The standard prop is a solid two bladed wheel. To reduce the considerable drag of this installation, we'd change to either a folding two bladed prop such as a Martec, or a feathering prop such as the Maxprop.

LIVABILITY

Deck layout
Although the deck layout of the Landfall 38 is similar to that of other boats in the C&C line—performance

oriented—some changes have been made to make the boat more suited to cruising. The stern rail incorporates a fold down swimming ladder, and the bow pulpit is the walk-through European type, suited to tying up bow-to at the dock. The bow pulpit also incorporates international style running lights, rather than the running lights mounted in the topsides that were a C&C trademark for years. Thank God for progress.

Unfortunately, the wiring for the running lights is relatively unprotected inside the anchor locker, and the electrical connections there are simple butt splices with no weathersealing.

The anchor locker has strong hinges, but lacks a positive latch. There is also no means of securing the bitter end of the anchor rode. Prudent owners will install an eyebolt or through-bolted padeye.

A new stainless steel stemhead fitting incorporates bow rollers for both chain and rope. There is no provision for a keeper pin in the bow roller, however, and the cheeks of the fitting do not extend high enough to guarantee that the rode will not jump out of the roller when the boat pitches at anchor.

With the shrouds set well inboard, fore and aft access is excellent. There are handrails along the cabintop, and a stainless steel guardrail over the forward dorade boxes to keep headsail sheets from fouling.

Two Landfall 38's have been built with teak decks. This is a $10,000 option that really makes the boat elegant, and is practical underfoot. However, you could also buy a whole suit of first-class sails with that $10,000, or go cruising for a year. You pays your money, and you takes your choice.

Although this is a cruising boat, there is no molded coaming for the attachment of a cockpit dodger, except a small lip around the companionway hatch. Admittedly, leading all sail controls aft along the cabintop complicates the installation of a dodger, but it can be done. Of course, the dodger can be installed even without a breakwater, but it won't be as effective in keeping water out of the cockpit.

The cockpit is a fairly typical T-shaped C&C design. A large-diameter Edson wheel makes it possible for the helmsman to sit to weather or to leeward, but requires making the cockpit seats too short to lie on. On some C&C models, molded seats in the aft corners of the cockpit serve both to support the helmsman's seat and as storage for propane bottles. On the Landfall 38, the

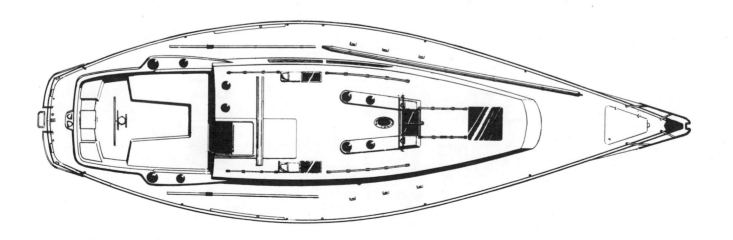

cockpit has been pushed so far aft—because of the longer deckhouse—that the hull is too shallow under the aft end of the cockpit for the traditional gas lockers. A separate molded bottle locker that fits under the helmsman's seat is installed when a gas stove is used. Unfortunately, this eliminates the normal life raft storage position. Owners who want both propane and a life raft are going to have to figure out another place to stow the life raft.

A shallow locker under the port cockpit seat is handy for small items, and there is a deep locker under the starboard seat. Changing oil filters requires climbing down into this locker, as does adjusting the stuffing box.

The forward end of the cockpit is protected by a good bridgedeck. Although the companionway is slightly off center, it is not enough to be concerned about in heavy weather. The companionway has other problems, however. Since the bulkhead slopes forward, the dropboard must be left in place when it rains. Also, since the bottom of the companionway is below the top of the cockpit coamings, ORC requirements demand that it be left in place when racing offshore. Although this isn't a racing boat, the ORC requirements make good guidelines for offshore cruising practices. Because the dropboard is a single teak-faced plyboard, in either situation the companionway must be all the way closed—or left all the way open.

The companionway sill has no lip, so that water can enter the cabin under the dropboard. This is a simple fix for owner or factory. The prudent owner will also install a barrel bolt to secure the dropboard in place when sailing offshore.

Belowdecks

C&C's interior design is usually among the best in the business, and the interior of the Landfall 38 is no exception. The preponderance of teak is a little overwhelming, but it is varnished, rather than oiled, making it slightly lighter than you might expect. Optional light pine hull ceiling will make the interior even lighter.

It takes quite a bit of ingenuity to cram a three-cabin interior and huge head with separate shower stall into a 38' boat. In the Landfall 38, this has been accomplished with a reasonable amount of success.

The forward cabin has the usual V-berth, drawers, several lockers, and a cedar-lined hanging locker. This hanging locker is the only really usable hanging space on the entire boat, despite the existence of a rudimentary hanging locker in the aft cabin.

A large hatch over the forward cabin can be used as an escape hatch; a single step is mounted on the bulkhead to make it possible to climb out the hatch. There is solid 6' headroom in the forward cabin, and enough standing room for comfortable dressing. The V-berth, however, is too pointed at the foot for reasonable comfort for two tall people. There are reading lights over each side of the berth, and a light in the hanging locker—a welcome feature.

The main saloon begins immediately aft of the forward cabin, with no intervening head compartment.

Lighting and ventilation of the Landfall 38 is about the best we've seen in a production boat. Both fluorescent and incandescent fixtures are located throughout the main cabin. Remember that you should not use fluorescent lights when you are operating the Loran, as the RF noise of fluorescent lights may interfere with signal acquisition.

The main cabin, galley, and head are ventilated by four large cowl vents in dorade boxes, plus small opening hatches in head and galley. C&C gets an A+ for ventilation in this boat.

Water tanks are located under the main cabin settees, where they belong. Unfortunately, these tanks vent to the outside of the hull, risking contamination of the water supply. This is a common fault in American production boats, and one with no real justification. We'd rather risk spilling a little water in the inside of the boat by overfilling the tanks than risk salt water in our fresh water supply from water siphoning into the tanks in heavy weather through vents mounted in the topsides.

The Landfall 38 uses molded polyethylene water tanks. Occasionally, these tanks are "overcooked" during manufacture, imparting an unpleasant taste to the water that cannot be removed. We've seen it on more than one boat, including C&C's.

Fresh water plumbing is butyl tubing rather than the more commonly seen clear PVC. Butyl is far less likely to impart any taste to your water, and is highly desirable. It is easily recognized by its battleship grey color and relative rigidity. A manifold under the sink allows switching between the three water tanks, which have a total capacity of 99 gallons. In addition, the 30 gallon holding tank could easily be replumbed as a fresh water tank, giving a very respectable water capaci-

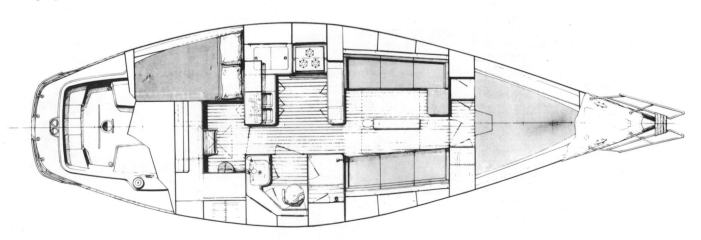

ty properly distributed throughout the boat.

In typical C&C fashion, the galley is well laid out and well executed, with deep centerline sinks, kickspace under the counters, and a large icebox. The icebox lid is insulated (hurray!) but ungasketed (boo!), and the icebox meltwater is pumped overboard (hurray!) rather than draining into the bilge.

Counter space is excellent. In an attempt to get more, a fold-down counter is fitted over the stove. Unfortunately, it must be folded up when the stove is in use, making the locker behind the stove inaccessible. Since the boat already has good counterspace, we'd eliminate the folding nuisance.

The standard stove is a large gimballed alcohol affair. Don't even consider it. Get either the optional propane installation, or the optional CNG stove. Alcohol has no business as a cooking fuel on any boat to be used as a serious cruising boat.

The stove recess is protected by a stainless steel grabrail which gives the cook a handhold and prevents him from being thrown against the stove in a seaway. A counter with built-in bottle storage separates the galley from the main cabin.

Generally, the galley is usable at sea or at anchor, with excellent storage, usable spaces, and functional appliances. Hot and cold pressure water is standard, and a backup fresh water foot pump is provided at the galley sink.

The main cabin table is strongly mounted to both cabin sole and mast, and easily—and honestly—serves six at dinnertime. Port and starboard settees can be used for sleeping, although the backrests at the head and foot of each settee will have to be removed and stored somewhere for anyone over about 5'8" tall.

Storage is provided outboard of each settee. The handy owner will install shelves in these lockers to better utilize the space.

Opposite the galley is a huge head complete with separate shower stall. The sink and counter are a single fiberglass molding with a large sink and a high protective lip, making this part of the head infinitely more usable than the usual tiny oval sink.

Although at first glance there appears to be a great deal of storage in the head, much of the locker space is occupied by plumbing. The only locker really suited for linens is located in the shower stall, and is equipped with a latch which must be reached through a finger hole in the locker door. Water will inevitably find its way into this locker. The locker could easily be fitted with another type of catch, and ventilation holes could be bored through to the head compartment to help prevent mildew. The separate shower stall will make those unused to boat living far more comfortable, although some might prefer the additional storage space the boat had before the separate stall appeared.

Oddly, the water closet is tucked so far under the side deck that it's impossible to sit upright on it. While you may argue that few people sit upright on the toilet, there will be plenty of cracked heads before you get used to the required position.

Another oddity is that the head door is louvered. Admittedly, there is little privacy in the head on any boat. Since the Landfall's head is well-vented by a cowl vent and an opening hatch, we'd eliminate the louvered head door to restore at least a modicum of privacy.

The aft cabin makes a good owner's stateroom, with large double quarterberth to port and chart table to star-

board. Unfortunately, the chart table makes a better dressing table than chart table. There is no provision for the installation of instruments such as radio or Loran in the nav area. A shallow hanging locker occupies the space outboard of the chart table where these instruments would normally be mounted. It is a poor hanging locker, since the garments face thwartships rather than fore and aft. The only thing you can see in the locker is the last item you put in. It is unusable as a wet locker, since you'd have to drag your wet foul weather gear over the chart table.

For serious cruising, we'd eliminate this hanging locker, using the space to mount radios, Loran, repeaters, and provide a bookcase for our navigation books. This has the serendipitous byproduct of allowing the shallow chart table to be made deeper, which it sorely needs.

What about hanging space? Well, here goes. Make the linen locker in the shower stall a hanging locker by eliminating or reducing the size of the holding tank under it. Or (and we can see marketing people putting guns to their heads), eliminate the separate shower stall and create more stoage space. So much for redesign.

In the way of modifications, however, the nice double quarterberth is going to get soaking wet the first time a big one comes over the weather rail and water pours through the companionway when the boat is on starboard tack. In the same situation on port tack, the chart table will get soaked. A set of plexiglass screens on either side of the companionway should solve that one, and should be considered if the boat is to be used offshore. For shorthanded cruising, that quarterberth is the ideal place for the offwatch, provided it can be kept dry. The necessity for keeping the sacrosanct nav station and its fragile electronics—and equally fragile navigator—out of the weather should be obvious.

The basic interior layout of the Landfall 38 is excellent for the cruising couple that likes a private cabin aft, and will sometimes entertain others for extended periods of time. As with most boats, a certain amount of fine tuning of interior spaces will be necessary to get the most out of them. The boat has a fair number of complex systems: hot and cold water, electric pumps, multiple tanks. In fact, the 16 circuits provided for in the electrical panel are almost all used up before you get to things like naviagation and performance electronics. Fortunately, there is space for an additional electrical panel. You're probably going to need it.

CONCLUSIONS

With a base price of just over $97,000 and a typical sailaway price of about $110,000, the Landfall 38 is not a cheap way to go cruising. The price is typical of luxury performance cruisers in its class.

General design and construction are excellent. The hull is a proven design, the rig is efficient and strong. There are a number of design details that should be improved for serious cruising, notably the companionway, cockpit protection, life raft storage, and provision for shorthanded handling under sail.

A serious cruising boat must function as well bashing to windward for days on end as it does at the dock. Above all, it must keep its crew dry and comfortable. We have yet to find the perfect cruising boat, but many of the things we'd look for are found in the Landfall 38. We wish they were all there, but the fact that they aren't is what keeps designers and builders in business.

The Whitby 42 Improving with Age

THE BOAT AND THE BUILDER

The Whitby 42 is one of the small success stories of the boatbuilding industry. Designed by Ted Brewer in 1971, the Whitby 42 has been in production since 1972. Almost 250 boats have been built.

While most boats have been built by Whitby in Canada, hulls numbered between 200 and 300 were built under license by Fort Myers Yacht and Shipbuilding in Florida.

It is safe to say that Whitby is a conservative boatbuilding firm. The 12-year old Whitby 42 is the newest boat in the Whitby line, which also includes the C&C-designed Whitby 45, the Alberg 37, and the Alberg 30. Yes, Virginia, you can still have an Alberg 30 built.

When the Whitby 42 was introduced in 1972, cost of the boat, including such features as diesel auxiliary generator, hot and cold pressure water, and refrigeration, was $42,000, including US duty. In the same year, the Morgan Out Island 41 had a base price of $33,000, and the Coronado 41 was $30,000.

In 1983, the Coronado 41 is a memory, an Out Island 41 will set you back about $130,000, and the Whitby 42 will cost you just shy of $103,000 with the US duty paid. In other words, the Whitby 42 has good staying power, and, if anything, has improved on its value position in the market.

When we first saw the Whitby 42 in 1973, it seemed an ungainly whale of a boat, with high topsides, white decks, white everything. Over the years, through the subtle use of color — dark sheerstrake, two-tone decks — the appearance of the boat has been quietly altered. While the Whitby 42 will never have the sleek grace of an ocean racer, she has acquired a sturdy grace of her own, the product of endless refinement and subtle improvement over the 12 years of her production history.

Much of the credit for the changes in the Whitby 42 goes to Karl Hansen and his wife Doris, who both own Whitby and oversee most of the details of production. A large portion of the rest of the credit goes to the owners of the boats, who exhibit extraordinary interest in improving the breed.

The Whitby 42 is a fully-powered auxiliary, rather than a motorsailer. Although she won't go to windward like a light displacement fin-keeler, the boat is fully capable of performing well as a sailing vessel.

Many owners have put tens of thousands of sea miles on their boats. A fair number of owners are retired couples who purchased the boat as a cruising home. Since the boat has the elbow room, accommodations, storage, and comforts that you would associate with a retirement home, it has proved a remarkable success in that capacity.

The Whitby 42 does not particularly look like an oceangoing boat, with her center cockpit, high topsides, wide beam, and shoal draft. Nevertheless, an astounding percentage of the boats are used for serious passagemaking.

Specifications

LOA	42'
LWL	32'8"
Beam	13'
Draft	5'
Displacement	23,500 lbs
Ballast	8,500 lbs
Sail Area	875 sq ft

Whitby Boat Works Limited
1710 Charles St.
Whitby, Canada L1N1C2
(416) 668-7755

CONSTRUCTION

Construction of the Whitby 42 is sturdy, but without the dramatic overkill frequently seen in cruising boats. The hull is balsa-cored from just below the sheer to just below the waterline.

Hull and deck are joined with an internal flange, which is glassed together and mechanically joined with stainless steel rivets. In the way of the genoa track and some deck fittings, hull and deck are also bolted together. If you prefer, the builder will use bolts throughout to join hull and deck, for a slight additional charge.

On current boats, all through-hull fittings are equipped with through-bolted bronze seacocks. Older boats may have gate valves on underwater fittings.

Deck and deckhouse are also balsa-cored. Solid glass is used in the way of deck hardware. In some older boats, owners report that the area under the mizzen-mast was not solid glass, resulting in compression of the deck in the vicinity of the mast. Owners of older boats also report that the underdeck support for the mizzen was marginal. Boats currently in production appear to have solved these problems.

For those used to looking at the massive construction of some cruising boats, notably those built in the Far East, some of the construction details of the Whitby 42 may look a little light. The success of these boats as cruisers indicates that proper proportioning in design and construction are more important than massive scantlings.

PERFORMANCE

Handling Under Power

With a fuel capacity of 210 gallons, the Whitby 42 has a range under power of about 1500 miles. The Lehman Ford 4-254 diesel produces about 67 hp, enough to drive the moderate displacement hull in almost any conditions.

Fuel tanks are located amidships. This means that the trim and balance of the boat will not change significantly as fuel is consumed.

Although a three-bladed prop in aperture is standard, light air performance would be significantly improved by replacing the prop with a feathering prop such as the Maxprop or the Luke feathering prop. Using this prop there would be little or no sacrifice in performance under power, but there could easily be an increase in speed of a half knot or more under sail in winds under 10 knots. If you're off cruising in the South Pacific, just carry along the standard prop as a spare.

Amazingly, none of the Whitby 42 owners we talked to had added a feathering prop. It would be one of our first major changes if we owned the boat.

Because of her windage and fairly long keel, the boat does not exactly handle like a sports car under power. One owner says that his boat "turns like the Queen Mary," so give yourself plenty of room and take your time when docking.

Like most center cockpit boats, the Whitby 42's engine is located under the cockpit. The result is a huge engine room with stooping headroom. The entire cockpit sole is the engine room hatch cover, and it can be unbolted in an hour or so to allow removal of the engine without tearing the interior of the boat apart. For a cruis-

ing boat that puts a lot of hours on the engine, this is a real plus.

The engine room has enough space for a small auxiliary generator. A generator was standard when the boat was first built, but is now an option. If you intend to do extensive cruising in the boat, a generator of about 3.5 kw would be worth installing. Unfortunately, the weight of the generator, which is mounted on the port side, may give the boat a slight port list.

Access to the stuffing box is good, through hatches in the cabin sole in the aft cabin. General access to the engine is excellent.

Dual Racor fuel filters are now standard.

Handling Under Sail

Owners characterize the Whitby 42 as slightly faster than other boats of the same size and type. When equipped with a mizzen staysail and a spinnaker — a very reasonable combination for offwind sailing offshore in this boat — the boat is quite fast. One West Coast owner has raced his boat with remarkable success, but that is certainly not the boat's forte.

In the past, there have been problems with the mizzenmast. Since the main boom ends fairly close to the mizzen, the mizzen forestays do not have a very good angle for forward support. Until this year, it was also absolutely necessary to use the mizzen running backstays when carrying a mizzen staysail. Earlier boats also reported problems with the under deck support system for the mizzen.

All of the mizzen problems are exacerbated if the boat is equipped with a radar antenna mounted on the mizzen — the natural location on a ketch.

Fortunately, most of these problems have been resolved on boats currently in production. The mizzen spreaders are now swept back enough to provide good after support without the use of running backstays, although we would probably still rig them in heavy weather or sloppy seas. Forward support of the mizzen is improved by the addition of a triatic stay between the main and mizzen mastheads.

The use of a triatic probably constitutes a second-best solution, as loss of one mast could well result in the loss of the other, since the masts are tied together. However, there is no simple way to improve the staying of the mizzen.

The mainsail is now equipped with slab reefing, a

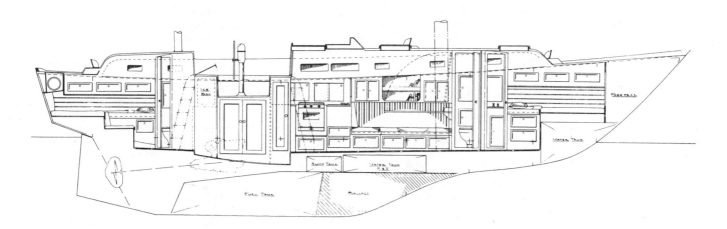

For offshore use, the louvered companionway drop boards should be replaced with solid boards to prohibit water going below in heavy weather

great improvement over the roller reefing found on older models of the Whitby 42. A separate track on the mainmast for a storm trysail is an option we'd go for if the boat is to be used offshore.

Another highly desirable rig option is the doublehead rig, which comes in a package with a platform bowsprit and a removable inner forestay. Owners report that the extra sail area forward improves the balance of the boat as well as giving her more sail area forward.

Despite the great beam of the boat, her midships hull section is almost round. This means that the boat picks up very little form stability as it heels. Coupled with a ballast/displacement ratio of about 35%, this yields a boat that is not particularly stiff under sail, according to owners.

Although the boat comes with hydraulic steering, it is also possible to use an Edson pull-pull system. Since this is a less powerful steering system than the hydraulic steerer, you should go with the maximum size steering wheel that will fit in the cockpit — about a 40" diameter wheel. In addition to providing the extra leverage for the pull-pull system, a larger wheel lets you sit further outboard, an absolute necessity on a center cockpit boat when using a large genoa.

We prefer the pull-pull steerer because it gives the helmsman feedback about the balance of the boat. In the long run, the steering feedback will make you a better sailor. When the boat steers hard, it is out of balance, and is not being sailed to maximum efficiency.

With a high aspect rig and a generous sailplan for her moderate displacement, there is no excuse for the Whitby 42 to be a dog under sail. If you have the boat heavily loaded, you'll just have to add more sail to maintain performance. Fairing in the through hull fittings and adding a feathering prop will also help performance, particularly in light air.

Finally, by all means spring for the bowsprit and the extra sail area it gives you. According to one owner, designer Ted Brewer said the addition of the bowsprit is the single greatest improvement in the boat over the years.

LIVABILITY

Deck Layout

The deck layout of the Whitby 42 is about as simple as the deck on a boat can be. There are sturdy Skene chocks and large cleats forward, and chocks plus big cleats aft. With the platform bowsprit, anchors can be made self-stowing. Large urethane bow rollers would be preferable to the small stainless steel rollers on the bowsprit-equipped boat we examined.

The foredeck has plenty of space for an anchor windlass, an absolute must if the boat is used for extended cruising. The forepeak locker could be used to hold anchor chain, but we'd be reluctant to add another 500 lbs of ground tackle in the front of the boat, since there's already a large water tank under the forward berths.

Despite a wide cabin trunk, access forward along the deck is good. To go from the cockpit aft, however, it is necessary to go over the top of the aft cabin, as the mizzen standing rigging takes up much of the side decks aft.

Stanchions, bow, and stern rails are tall and sturdy.

There are two lockers on the afterdeck, one useful for lines and fenders, the other containing the propane bottles. Although the lids of both lockers are equipped with gaskets, surprisingly flimsy turnbutton latches are used

to secure the lids. For offshore passagemaking, we'd replace these with sturdier latches.

There is also a large locker on the port side of the cockpit. This locker, too, lacks a good set of hatch dogs, and since it opens into the engine room, we'd give high priority to making it secure, despite its location well above the water.

The cockpit is huge. However, it is not particularly vulnerable, since it is fairly high. We've seen few cockpits which would be better in port. There's even a big icebox next to the helmsman, making it unnecessary to truck down to the galley for a cold one.

A sturdy molded breakwater protects the front of the cockpit. We'd add a dodger for offshore use. The original drawings of the boat also show a permanent windshield, which would be a good feature on a boat used primarily in northern latitudes.

One Whitby 42 we've seen has a permanent shelter over the front end of the cockpit, which both improved the looks of the boat — the shelter was designed by someone with a good eye — and gave remarkable protection to the front of the cockpit, allowing the companionway hatch to be left open in all but the worst weather offshore.

For offshore use, the louvered companionway drop boards should be replaced with solid boards, since a remarkable amount of water can get below in heavy weather. This is particularly important in the companionway to the aft cabin, which faces forward.

The companionway to the aft cabin makes it impossible to fit a mainsheet traveler. Therefore, a good boom vang is a must.

We strongly recommend the two-tone deck option. Not only will it break up an otherwise overwhelming amount of deckspace visually, it will be much easier on the helmsman's eyes. Although it's not listed as an option, you could probably also get the deckhouse top in a color other than white. This would visually lower the height of the deckhouse as well as reducing glare.

Belowdecks

Down below, the Whitby 42 really shines. The boat has one of the more livable interiors we've seen.

The owner's cabin aft has two large berths. If they are to be used as sea berths, they must be fitted with lee cloths. Since the berths are not parallel to the centerline of the boat, they do not make particularly good sea berths. The person sleeping in the leeward berth will find his head lower than his feet, while the occupant of the weather berth will be in the opposite situation.

Although there are a fair number of storage bins and a good hanging locker, the aft cabin has few drawers. Although drawers are not a particularly efficient way to use space, they are extremely convenient, particularly for those who have lived their lives in houses.

The aft head is huge. A few handrails would make it more comfortable offshore.

A passageway with stooping headroom joins the aft cabin to the rest of the boat. Getting full headroom in this passage would unnecessarily complicate the cockpit layout.

A workbench which can be converted to a berth is on the starboard side of the passage. The space below the bench is filled by a fuel tank, some storage space, and a big chart storage locker.

Outboard of the workbench is the electrical panel. Despite the stooping headroom, this is just about the

The Whitby 42 is an excellent compromise between the needs of the long term livaboard and the long distance cruiser

ideal location for the electrical panel, since it is completely protected from spray.

On the port side of the passage, just aft of the companionway, there is a large locker for foul weather gear. Little touches like the chart storage area and the wet gear locker make the difference between a floating condominium which is miserable at sea and a true cruising boat.

The main cabin is roomy, light, and well-ventilated. The galley to port has a large refrigerator and deep freeze — Grunert holding-plate refrigeration, driven by an engine-mounted compressor — a three burner propane stove, and, on new boats, deep double sinks.

The only weak point in the galley is the mounting of the stove. On starboard tack, it fetches up against the back of the stove well when the boat heels much over 15°. On port tack, the stove blocks access to the drawers under the sink counter. Although the boat is meant to be sailed at slight angles of heel, the stove should be free to gimbal through at least 90° without inconvenience.

There is a ventilation hatch over the galley, a real boon for the cook in hot weather.

Except for the stove limitation, the galley gets an A+.

To starboard is the navigation table, with adequate room for the mounting of instruments and a good chart table. The chart table slopes toward the navigator, making it easier to work on from a seated position, but it is equipped with a folding support which allows the table to be leveled for use in port, making a handy desk.

Originally, there was no settee on the starboard side of the boat. Rather, the boat had two swivel chairs, a familiar touch to those used to life ashore. However, if the boat is to be used offshore, it should be ordered with the optional starboard settee, since the main cabin settees are the only good sea berths on the boat.

There is plenty of storage space outboard of the settees on both sides, including a rather excellent liquor locker with a folding cocktail table.

The main cabin table folds up against the port forward bulkhead. On a boat of this size, a fixed cabin table makes more sense. If we owned a Whitby 42, we'd build a narrow dropleaf table with deep fiddles, incorporating a pipe to the cabin overhead for a handhold when sailing offshore. While this would intrude into the main cabin space, it would reduce the chance of a bad fall in rough conditions, would free up the bulkhead for other uses, and would create a storage space on the cabin sole

where bulky objects like spare sails could be stowed offshore.

The forward cabin and head are almost as roomy as the aft cabin. In port, the occupants of the forward cabin are not second class citizens. Except for light air sailing downwind, the forward cabin will probably not be used for sleeping offshore.

All in all, the interior of the Whitby 42 is an excellent compromise between the needs of the long term livaboard and the long distance cruiser.

CONCLUSIONS

In these days of astronomical prices, the Whitby 42 represents a good value for living aboard or cruising. While finish detail is not particularly fancy, the boat is solidly built, and should be easy to maintain.

The boat comes with a rather remarkable list of standard equipment included in the base price of just under $100,000, with such items as hot and cold water, refrigeration, huge tankage, two showers, dual voltage electrical systems, and ground tackle.

The options are practical and born of experience. Many of them are highly desirable, such as the double headsail rig option with bowsprit, contrasting deck color, dark sheer indent, autopilot, and windlass.

Fully equipped for cruising — and we mean fully equipped — the boat will cost about $120,000.

You can expect reasonable sailing performance from the Whitby 42. Obviously, her best point of sail will be reaching in moderate to heavy air.

Because of the improvements that have been made in the boat over the years, we would prefer a new boat rather than a used boat. Given the fact that used boats sell for nearly as much as new boats, and given the fact that you can pretty much customize the boat any way you want when you have it built, a new Whitby 42 looks very good indeed.

Part of the reason the boat is relatively inexpensive is the strength of the US dollar. When the boat first went into production, the Canadian dollar was worth about $1.05 US. Today, the Canadian dollar only fetches about $.81 US.

Most owners are very enthusiastic about their boats. For most of them, this is not a first boat. Although most consider the boat a good boat dockside, they also consider it a boat in which to go places. We agree.

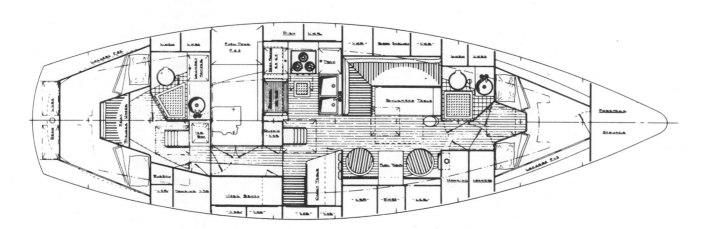

Original Publication Date of Articles